PUT US DOWN IN HELL

PUT US DOWN IN HELL

THE COMBAT HISTORY OF THE 508TH PARACHUTE INFANTRY REGIMENT IN WORLD WAR II

PHIL NORDYKE

PUBLISHED BY
HISTORIC VENTURES LLC

First published in 2012 by Historic Ventures, LLC.
Copyright © 2012 by Phil Nordyke

Library of Congress Cataloging-in-Publication Data

Nordyke, Phil.
Put us down in hell: the combat history of the 508th Parachute Infantry Regiment in World War II / Phil Nordyke.
p.cm.
Includes biographical references and index.
ISBN 978-0-9847151-3-8

1. United States. Army, Parachute Infantry Regiment, 508th. 2. World War, 1939—1945—Regimental histories—United States. 3. World War, 1939—1945—Campaigns—Western Front. I. Title

CONTENTS

ACKNOWLEDGMENTS

I am indebted to so many generous and helpful people for their contributions to the book. First, I want to thank my wife, Nancy, whose proof reading and suggestions to improve the manuscript are always invaluable.

The research materials for the book came from a number of repositories and archives. I am indebted to a number of wonderful people who provided help in obtaining the information from these sources.

The Cornelius Ryan Collection at Ohio University at Athens, Ohio contains a wealth of veterans' accounts and documents relating to the Normandy and Holland campaigns. I want to express my deep appreciation to Doug McCabe, Curator of Manuscripts, Robert E. and Jean R. Mahn Center for Archives and Special Collections, the Alden Library, Ohio University for providing the large volume of materials referenced in this book.

I want to thank Martin K. A. Morgan, the outstanding author and historian for providing copies of veterans' oral history transcripts and written accounts of D-Day from the Eisenhower Center and National World War II Museum at New Orleans, Louisiana.

I want to extend my gratitude to Dr. John Duvall, Museums Chief, and Betty Rucker, Collections Manager, who opened up the Ridgway–Gavin Archives at the 82nd Airborne Division War Memorial Museum at Fort Bragg, North Carolina, a rich source of primary documents for this book.

Ericka L. Loze, Librarian at the Donovan Research Library at Fort Benning, Georgia, provided monographs of 508th Parachute Infantry Regiment veterans from the library's massive collection.

The U.S. Army Heritage and Education Center at Carlisle, Pennsylvania provided a wealth of information, including the papers of the great historian and author Clay Blair, as well as the papers of General Matthew B. Ridgway, General James M. Gavin, and many other officers who served with the 82nd Airborne Division during World War II. I want to thank everyone there who assisted me with these documents.

The dedicated people at the National Archives at College Park, Maryland provided much assistance with locating such primary source documents such as general orders, awards files, hospital interviews, after-action reports, and map overlays and their efforts are very much appreciated.

The archive at the Camp Blanding Museum at Starke, Florida was a wealth of written accounts. I would like to thank George Cressman for his help.

I am deeply indebted to Dick O'Donnell for his unlimited support and for his preservation of the legacy of the 508th Parachute Infantry Regiment through his tireless work with his outstanding website, http://www.508pir.org. His website has been a wealth of information, from documents, written accounts, names of the members of the regiment, etcetera. Dick was also kind enough to proof read and fact check the manscript, and help to correct errors in it.

My sincere appreciation is extended to Father G. Thuring and Frank van den Bergh with the Liberation Museum at Groesbeek, Holland. They provided much information about the campaign in Holland. Their books and expertise helped correct errors in my understanding of the battle for the Nijmegen bridges. Jan Bos, R. G. Poulussen, Frits Janssen, and other very knowledgable and helpful historians from The Netherlands were of tremendous help and I appreciate their great expertise.

Dave Berry is the world's authority regarding the Normandy pathfinders and has been a rich resource for questions relating to pathfinder activities. His valuable help is greatly appreciated.

The veterans of the 508th Parachute Infantry Regiment deserve the greatest credit and appreciation for making this book possible. They unselfishly provided written accounts, participated in oral interviews, gave permission to quote from their published books, and responded to questionnaires. They encouraged and inspired me to write this book. There were individuals with each unit who helped me with contact information, provided entrées to others in their units, and provided information regarding their units. Among the veterans to whom I extend my heartfelt gratitude are Mark Alexander, Merrel Arthur, Walter Barrett, Briand Beaudin, Don Biles, Jim Blue, Dwayne Burns, Mike Cahill, Bill Call, Bob Chisolm, Gordon Cullings, Bill Dean, John Foley, Ralph Gilson, Darrell Glass, John Greene, Oliver Griffin, Brody Hand, O. B. Hill, Don Jakeway, Homer Jones, Bob Kolterman, Francis Lamoureux, Hank Le Febvre Lane Lewis, Frank Longiotti, Frank McKee, Rock Merritt, Gene Metcalfe, George Miles, Worster Morgan, Bob Newhart, Tom Porcella, Zane Schlemmer, Nathan Silverlieb, Alex Sopka, Allan Stein, Norb Studelska, George Stoeckert, Dave Thomas, Bill Traband, Bill Tumlin, Robert White, Bill Windom, and Ed Wodowski. I am sure there are veterans who contributed whom I have failed to mention. To those veterans, you also have my abiding appreciation. This book would not have been possible without the first person accounts of the veterans.

I also want to thank the family and friends of the 508th who have provided support for this book. They include Leland Burns, Aaron Elson, K. C. Horne, William C. Nation, Kristine Nymoen, Brian Pesce, and Normand Thomas

As in my other books, I want the veterans to tell the story. In some cases, I have made minor changes to some of their accounts, correcting grammatical and spelling errors, rearranging sentences to put the action in chronological order, or omitting repetitive or irrelevant information in long quotes, and to maintain consistency in unit designations, equipment, and other items. However, the first person accounts are true to the original words of the veterans.

This book is dedicated to the officers and men who served with the 508th Parachute Infantry Regiment and the attached units of the regimental combat team during World War II.

INTRODUCTION

This is the compelling true story of one of the elite parachute regiments of World War II. The 508th Parachute Infantry was the first parachute regiment to undergo selection and basic training as a unit. All previous parachute regiments had been formed from a cadre of qualified paratroopers and those newly graduated from the Parachute School at Fort Benning, Georgia. The cadre of the 508th subjected all arriving volunteers to a rigorous physical and mental selection process, eliminating many of them. The regiment's basic training was much more intense and physically demanding than normal, which eliminated still others. The result was that only the most physically fit, mentally strong, and highly motivated of those who volunteered, remained with the regiment. The process of officers and men undergoing basic training together fostered bonds of loyalty, friendship, and unit cohesion.

After completion of basic training, the regiment's three battalions were each sent to Fort Benning for parachute training in early 1943. Upon completion, the regiment then went to Camp Mackall, near Fort Bragg, North Carolina, where advanced infantry training was undertaken. The 508th then participated in a number of training exercises, including the U.S. Second Army's huge Tennessee maneuvers during the fall of 1943.

It was a regiment honed razor sharp and highly trained that arrived in Northern Ireland in January 1944. There, it was attached to the already legendary 82nd Airborne Division for the coming invasion of Normandy. The 508th moved to England in March 1944 to begin invasion training.

The 508th Parachute Infantry parachuted into Normandy, France, along with the other parachute regiments of the 82nd and 101st Airborne Divisions during the predawn hours of June 6, 1944—among the first Allied soldiers to land on Hitler's fortress Europe. Those who landed near the drop zone were met with intense enemy fire. The regiment was so badly scattered that it was unable to assemble after the jump. Despite this, groups of troopers attacked enemy forces where they found them. Lieutenant Colonel Thomas J. B. Shanley and a group of mixed troopers from every regiment of the division secured Hill 30 and prevented movement of German forces over the causeway at Chef-du-Pont to attack the amphibious landings at Utah Beach. The decimated regiment was finally able to assemble and reorganize beginning on the fourth day of the invasion. The 508th spent thirty-three days in Normandy, where it made an assault crossing of the Douve River to link up with elements of the 101st Airborne Division west of Carentan and made costly attacks to capture strategic hills north of La Haye-du-Puits.

Just over sixty days later, the regiment made a daytime combat jump fifty-three miles behind German lines to spearhead the Allied invasion of Holland and provide a corridor for the British Second Army's drive to the Rhine River. The 508th captured and held strategic high ground southeast of the city of Nijmegen against strong German attacks, then attacked and seized the ground south of the Waal River to secure the corridor against enemy attack from the nearby German border. It had the distinction of being the first parachute regiment to fight on German soil when it captured the town of Wyler. The regiment spent fifty-four days in Holland before being withdrawn to Camp Sissonne in France to rest and receive replacements.

When the German army launched a powerful offensive in the Ardennes, breaking through the thinly held American line, the 508th Parachute Infantry Regiment along with the rest of the 82nd and 101st Airborne Divisions, rushed to Belgium, where the regiment secured key high ground at Thier-du-Mont and positions along the Salm River to screen the withdrawal of 20,000 troops from the St.-Vith pocket. After the division was ordered by British Field Marshal Bernard L. Montgomery to withdraw to straighten the line, the regiment stopped a strong thrust by elements of the 9th SS Panzer Division, one of best equipped, most powerful armored divisions in the German army. The 508th then made a costly attack in deep snow to recapture the high ground it had previously held. After a brief rest, the division spearheaded a drive to push German forces across eastern Belgium to its start line for the Ardennes offensive. The regiment made attacks in the midst of the worst winter conditions in Europe in fifty years, driving the enemy back to the German border and the Siegfried Line.

The regiment and the division were then sent north to clear German forces from the Hürtgenwald forest. The regiment assaulted and captured the strategically vital Hill 400 and the high ground south of the Kall River. After the division was withdrawn and sent to France for rest, the regiment was detached from the 82nd Airborne Division for possible missions to jump and liberate Allied prisoners from German prisoner of war camps if the enemy started killing them.

At the end of the war in Europe, the 508th was selected to guard General Dwight D. Eisenhower's headquarters at Frankfurt-am-Main, Germany. The regiment remained in Europe in strategic reserve until November 1946, when it returned to the United States and was disbanded.

Supported by Company D, 307th Airborne Engineer Battalion, the 319th Glider Field Artillery Battalion, and Battery B, 80th Airborne Antiaircraft (Antitank) Battalion, the men of this great regimental combat team participated in some of the fiercest combat of World War II.

This is the story of the 508th Regimental Combat Team's great feats of arms on the battlefield, of close combat, incredible devotion to duty, tremendous courage, and sacrifice—told as only frontline combat infantrymen can.

CHAPTER 1

"SEE YOU ON THE GROUND!"

On December 7, 1941, nineteen year old William J. Call heard the news that the United States had been attacked by forces of the Empire of Japan at Pearl Harbor, Hawaii, plunging the country into World War II. "I was working at the General Motors gun plant in Saginaw, Michigan. We were making the machine guns for the U.S. Army. I had just gotten out of work on that Sunday, because we were working seven days a week.

"When I first heard about it, at least my group of guys, who were eighteen, felt that this war wouldn't last long. The longer it went, the more I wanted to be a part of it. I didn't want to get drafted or get an exemption.

"One day, I was riding a bus in Saginaw and I saw this guy get on it—he must have been about twenty or twenty-five—and he had on a beautiful uniform. On the patch on his hat was a parachute. He had a set of wings and I thought, 'That is sharp.'"[1]

MAJOR ROY E. LINDQUIST was a member of the West Point class of 1930 who had served in a number of assignments after graduation, eventually commanding Company B, 29th Infantry Regiment in 1937. He then served at the Infantry School at Fort Benning, Georgia, where he wrote the field manual for the M1 Garand rifle, the primary infantry weapon of the U.S. military during World War II. During 1940, Lindquist was the adjutant of the newly formed 501st Parachute Infantry Battalion, America's first parachute unit, under the command of Major William M. Miley. After the test platoon had completed work to develop the procedures for parachuting, Lindquist was one of a group of thirteen officers to make the first jump by an organizational unit of the U.S. Army. Lindquist left the 501st in the spring of 1941 to become the S-1 (the staff officer responsible for personnel) for the Provisional Parachute Group at Fort Benning. In the spring of 1942, Lindquist was promoted to major and assigned as the G-1 of Airborne Command at Fort Bragg, North Carolina.

Technical Sergeant Woodrow W. Millsaps was the noncommissioned officer in charge of marksmanship training at Fort Benning during the spring of 1942. "I was called to the Parachute School for a meeting with Major Roy Lindquist, my old company commander of B Company, 29th Infantry. He only knew after looking over the records of airborne soldiers that I was a qualified paratrooper and was still at the [parachute] school. He told me he had been put in charge of organizing a headquarters company consisting of approximately 160 enlisted men and 60 officers of different rank. This company was to be formed at Fort Bragg, North Carolina for the purpose of drawing requirements for the strength of a division in personnel and armaments. He was looking for someone to take over the first sergeant duties in the new company when he ran across my name on the roster. He asked me what I thought about going to Bragg as a first sergeant. I told him I would have to talk it over with my wife before I could give him an answer. He asked me how long that would take, and I told him that I lived in Columbus [Georgia] and I would let him know the next day.

"He said he would be expecting an answer as soon as possible, for all the troops he had selected would depart for Fort Bragg Saturday morning. This being Thursday, things began to develop at a rapid pace. I left for home in Columbus at once, talked it over with [my wife] LaVerne, and returned to Benning with the answer Major Lindquist was expecting—I would go with him to Fort Bragg. He said he had counted on my going and had already printed the orders for me to go with the other soldiers as first sergeant.

"LaVerne was left behind until I could find a place to live at Fort Bragg. I found a place in Fayetteville, North Carolina and LaVerne joined me there. We lived in Fayetteville for only a short time before I returned to Fort Benning to go to Officers Candidate School. This was in September 1942."[2]

On September 9, 1942, Major Lindquist returned to Fort Benning to begin planning for the formation of the 508th Parachute Infantry Regiment, which he would command. The cadre would be furnished by the 502nd Parachute Infantry Regiment, the casual company of the Parachute School (mostly short timers about to leave the Army, voluntarily or involuntarily), and the 26th Infantry Division.

On September 22, Lindquist was promoted to lieutenant colonel, and the following day the members of the cadre not yet present at Fort Benning arrived. The planning for activating, processing, and training of the new regiment continued until October 19, when the cadre departed for Camp Blanding, Florida, where the regiment would be formed and basic training conducted.

LYNN C. TOMLINSON had served with the U.S. Army prior to America's entry into the war. "I reenlisted in January of 1942 and volunteered for the parachute troops. The reason for this was that I knew if I was drafted, I would be sent directly to the infantry, and would be walking for the rest of my life. I figured that by joining the paratroops, at least I would be riding to where I was going. I completed jump training in February 1942 at Fort Benning, and was assigned to the 502nd Parachute Battalion. I was promoted to staff sergeant and first sergeant in the 504 at Fort Bragg, when I received orders to OCS [officer candidate school] in July '42. I was commissioned in October of 1942 and was assigned to the 508th Parachute Infantry Regiment. I caught a plane from Fort Benning, Georgia going to Camp Blanding. Aboard was Colonel Lindquist, who was the commanding officer, and Lieutenant Colonel [William E.] Ekman, the assistant commander, as well as several other officers.

"I and a buddy of mine, who was also assigned to the 508th, were late getting to Lawson Field, so they had to radio the airplane and ask them to return to Lawson to pick up two officers. This didn't set with the commanding officer, having to come back, but that's the way it was."[3]

The 508th was officially activated at Camp Blanding on October 20, 1942. The processing of enlisted personnel from reception centers began immediately. The battalions were filled in numerical order and basic training was begun as each battalion reached its allotted strength. Captain Harry J. Harrison became the first commanding officer of the newly forming 1st Battalion.

THAT OCTOBER IN SAGINAW, MICHIGAN, BILL CALL read a notice that the U.S. Army Air Corps would be conducting entrance testing at the city. "They advertised come and take the test for the air corps. There were about forty of us who took the test and two of us passed. I wasn't one of them. Prior to that, I had taken up flying trying to get a license because I wanted to get into the air corps. When I flunked that test I felt so bad.

"I walked across the street to the post office and went down to the basement. There was this sergeant, an ugly looking guy. He asked, 'What the hell do you want, kid?'

"I said, 'Hey, give me something to get into the air.'

"He said, 'Here, take this,' and he threw this pamphlet at me.

"I looked at it. It said, 'Jump into the fight,' and it showed a paratrooper coming down. I said, 'Where do I sign?'

"He said, 'What's the matter? Are you crazy, kid?'

"'No, I want to sign.' So I signed up that day and I left two weeks later."[4]

Call, who had just married in May, delivered the news to his wife, his parents, and his wife's family. "My mother-in-law was the most upset. My mother had so much going on. Six of her sons were in the service at the same time. She asked, 'Are you sure you want to do this, Bill?'

"I said, 'I do, Ma, I really do.'

"She said, "Well, God bless you. I'll pray for you.'"[5]

After arriving at Battle Creek, Michigan for induction into the army, Private Call received a phone call from his wife. "She said, 'Honey, I've got news for you—I'm pregnant.

"I said, 'Oh shit!'"[6]

After his induction, Call boarded a train for Camp Blanding. "When we got there, they had already assigned us to companies. I remember Sergeant [Forrest V.] Brewer and [Staff] Sergeant [Anthony J.] Mrozinski waiting for us when the buses got to the post. I was assigned to Company B, the 2nd Platoon, from the outset."[7]

When Private Adolph F. "Bud" Warnecke arrived at Camp Blanding, he underwent a physical examination followed by a battery of tests to check his mental acuity. "It seemed crazy to me when they tested your mental fitness and fired questions like a machine gun. 'What's your name? Why? Is Mickey Mouse a boy or a girl? Lift your left foot off the ground.' By the time the interview ended, I was not sure exactly what I had gotten into."[8]

Warnecke was subsequently assigned to the 1st Platoon of Company B. "My platoon leader was Lieutenant Homer [H.] Jones. His assistant was Lieutenant [Lionel O.] Lee Frigo, and the platoon sergeant was Forrest 'Lefty' Brewer. Our CO [commanding officer], Lieutenant Royal [R.] Taylor, whom I soon idolized, had been a first sergeant before graduating from OCS. Taylor set an example by not asking anyone to do anything he couldn't do himself. He was always in the lead during our runs and endurance marches. He taught me the first thing is to take care of your men and they will take care of you. If you get that right, you won't have time to worry about yourself. The other lesson was you must prove your loyalty to your men before you can expect theirs."[9]

Sixteen year old Private Robert B. White, from St. Albans, West Virginia, was initially assigned to Headquarters Company, 1st Battalion, but after he demonstrated outstanding proficiency and accuracy with an M1 at the rifle range, it became apparent those skills could be best utilized in a rifle company. "I was sixteen when I joined the service. I had my mother sign for me, but I had to change my age to seventeen. I had been hunting for some time. My brother had started me real young and I could shoot a rifle. They transferred me to A Company."[10]

Once the 1st Battalion reached its allotted strength, it began basic training while the 2nd Battalion was brought up to strength. For new recruits like Private Broughton L. Hand, who was assigned to Company C, the training was more intense than what they would have otherwise undergone during basic training. "We ran all day and night and did all kinds of calisthenics. We took all of our training there: rifle, machine gun, bazooka, and everything the army had at that time. Every weekend was washout day. There were probably two people to one that couldn't make it. They told us to look to your left and look to your right. Those people are going to be gone. And sure enough, they whittled us down."[11]

It was during this tough training in which many recruits quit that Private John Hardie realized that his Company C first sergeant, Leonard A. Funk, Jr., cared deeply for each of the enlisted men entrusted to him. "He readily tolerated the efforts of our group to circumvent the army way, yet insisted upon our conformity to the rules and never took it upon himself to be cruelly unfair. He even respected and loved officers at a time when most of us raw recruits were too naive or too stupid to appreciate the value of officers."[12]

As the 1st Battalion training progressed, the 2nd Battalion was formed under the initial command of Major Wesley H. Armstrong, a member of the cadre.

Private Richard C. "Dick" Reardon was assigned to Company E upon arriving at Camp Blanding. "Some fifty to sixty of us were put in the custody of Sergeant [Leonard J.] Woodruff, the cadre sergeant for the 2nd Platoon, E Company. While awaiting our physical exams for the paratroopers, Sergeant Woodruff decided to keep us busy with a few pushups and accordingly, we all 'did twenty-five' with Sergeant Woodruff counting the cadence. After the first twenty-five, there were some ten to fifteen of us who were not flat on our stomachs. 'OK,' shouted Sergeant Woodruff, 'Let's do twenty-five more.' At the end of the second twenty-five pushups, only Sergeant Woodruff and I were still up. 'Well,' shouted Sergeant Woodruff, 'I see we have a tough guy— twenty-five more.' I was dying when I finished the third set of twenty-five pushups, but so was Sergeant Woodruff.

"During our physicals that day, I was a short distance behind [Private William A.] 'Shorty' Piatt, and when he stepped on the scales and height-measure, the lieutenant called out, 'Fifty-eight and a half inches.' Sixty inches was the minimum, I believe.

"'Shorty' grabbed the height bar and pushed it up to sixty inches and said, 'What the hell's the matter, lieutenant? Can't you read?'

"The lieutenant looked at the bar again, laughed and called out, 'Correction, sixty inches.'

"The final step in the physical exam routine was for the recruit to enter the last small room in the examining hut to face two young officers who were to evaluate him 'psychologically' as a potential paratrooper. Standing before them, stark naked, the potential paratrooper was at a distinct disadvantage. The officers were already wearing parachute wings; they were officers, and we had to stand at attention and speak only when spoken to. They used a variety of ploys to try to discourage potential paratroopers; the most used was to comment that this was a fine young man who would 'be dead in six months.'

"The ploy used with me was to ask, 'What makes you think you can be a paratrooper?

"I looked the questioner in the eye and replied, 'You made it, lieutenant.'

"He laughed and said, 'Passed.'"[13]

The platoon leader of the 2nd Platoon of Company E, Lieutenant Robert M. Mathias, was a member of the cadre and an officer who impressed almost everyone with whom he came in contact. Private Joseph E. Watson, one the recruits assigned to the 2nd Platoon described Mathias as "an exceptional individual in the company of many outstanding men. To be a paratrooper of that era a man had to be adventurous, willing to try the unknown, and dedicated to becoming a paratrooper. All were volunteers and physical and mental demands of training were substantially more stringent than those of the average soldier of World War II.

"Paratrooper officers were a special breed. To be an effective officer, one had to be able to run just a bit longer, be a bit faster on the obstacle course, be able to outshoot—or at least be competitive with any of the various weapons with which the men were armed—and be the first man out of the plane over the drop zone. Lieutenant Robert Mason Mathias was such an officer...

"He mastered every weapon and skill involved in the deployment of a rifle company in combat. He was also highly knowledgeable of the functions, capabilities, and limitations of the supporting arms and services. He was a student of military history and of the order of battle of the German army and its tactics...

"Life in the 2nd Platoon was anything but easy. In all training, Lieutenant Mathias always required more of his platoon than was expected of the men of the other platoons of the regiment. He led, cajoled, and drove us to meet his standards, but he drove himself more. He made allowances, but never compromised his standards. He seemed deeply hurt on the few occasions that the platoon failed to meet his expectations; but he never lost his temper. I also never knew him to utter a profane word...

"I never knew an officer who was more concerned when the physical and emotional well-being of his men was involved. On the other hand, Lieutenant Mathias instilled the will to deal with and destroy the enemy by any and all means available. A deep commitment to God and country is required to resolve these conflicting philosophies within oneself." [14]

Lieutenant Chester E. "Chet" Graham had been in the army since 1940 and transferred to the regiment from the 807th Tank Destroyer Battalion. "After I reported in, I was posted as the acting commander of Company F. There were two other officers in Company F with me—Lieutenants Hoyt T. Goodale and Fred E. Gillespie. The first sergeant was regular army. I remained with Company F through thirteen weeks of basic training at Blanding. When I first reported in to the 508th as a first lieutenant, the 2nd Battalion [executive officer was] Captain Louis Mendez. He was a challenging personality. I remember the first officers' meeting he called when he handed me a pencil and told me to talk for five minutes about the pencil. Another time, when I walked into his tent wearing my cap, he said, 'Lieutenant Graham, is your head cold? You are under cover.' He was a very interesting and beloved man.

"Major Thomas J. B. Shanley, class of 1939, West Point, was the regimental S-3 at Blanding. Colonel Shanley was a small man with a large amount of ability...

"Major Louis G. Mendez, Jr. was assigned as commanding officer of the 3rd Battalion at Blanding. Both Shanley and Mendez were class. Lindquist was pompous—they were not.

"At Camp Blanding in October and November 1942, the regiment was filled entirely with volunteers, all of whom were subjected to tough physical and mental examinations to determine their fitness to be airborne soldiers.

"Our thirteen weeks of basic training was very efficient and designed to weed out those incapable or unable to become paratroopers. The same training was for all personnel—officers and enlisted men."[15]

Upon arrival and screening at Camp Blanding, Private Frank E. McKee was also assigned to Company F. "The outfit was a cross section of America with good men from all segments of the population—farm boys, woodsmen, city boys from the East, rebels from the South, Indians and Mexican transplants from the Southwest. The officers were mainly from colleges and military schools, many of them from the South.

"We were in camp for oh a good eight weeks, maybe more, without going to town. We were on a little field maneuver for a couple of days, and at the end of that we were supposed to get passes to town, which was Jacksonville—a navy town really. While on maneuvers some of us didn't feel too good and the medics checked us out and decided that there was a measles epidemic in the unit, so all of these [passes] were canceled and I think the rest of the regiment could have killed us, the guys who had the measles.

"While we were in the hospital they did get to town and I'm probably glad I didn't make it. They busted up the town and had terrific fights with the navy. I heard we came out on top."[16]

After the 2nd Battalion was brought up to strength and training was underway, the 3rd Battalion formed under the initial command of Major J. G. Turner. Shortly afterward, Captain Mendez was promoted to major and replaced Turner as the battalion's commanding officer.

When Private William G. "Bill" Lord, II, arrived at Camp Blanding, he was interviewed by Mendez as part of the screening process for all newly arrived volunteers. "Mendez interviewed every one of us. He asked me to take my left foot off the ground, which I did, and then to take my right foot off the ground, and finally both feet. I jumped. He asked whether Mickey Mouse was a boy or a girl. I said, 'He's a mouse.'"[17]

Private Lord passed the screening interview and was subsequently assigned to Headquarters Company, 3rd Battalion and was quickly impressed with his battalion commander. "Mendez was an exceptionally fine officer, very strict, absolutely no nonsense, completely devoted to training as well. He took the attitude that because we came from all over, a lot of us didn't know how to take care of each other. Very early on he used an expression 'combat morale,' which he told us had nothing to do with movies at the USO. He said it was a spirit among us where everybody realizes nobody can win a war or battle alone. You're completely interdependent. He taught us the necessity to respect those people we might command and to obey those who led us. He later told me he was much tougher on his officers. Generally, they were very good. Those who weren't stayed only a short time."[18]

By December 2, approximately 4,500 enlisted men had been screened, 2,300 of whom successfully passed all requirements and were retained. Officers who had volunteered for the airborne, but had yet to qualify as parachutists, arrived from various branches of service and replacement centers to bring the regiment up to strength.

Back at Fort Benning, Woodrow Millsaps graduated from Officer Candidate School on December 14, 1942 and was commissioned as a second lieutenant. "On the day of graduation at the OCS, the battalion commander of the school received a telegram from Lieutenant Colonel Roy E. Lindquist, who was now regiment commander of the 508 Parachute Regiment at Camp Blanding, Florida. Lindquist requested that I be assigned to the 508 Parachute Regiment upon graduation from the OCS.

"I reported to the 508 Parachute Regiment just after Christmas and became a platoon leader in Headquarters Company, 3rd Battalion. The regiment was about up to full strength when I arrived, and we were preparing to go to Fort Benning for parachute training (this was the first unit to take parachute training as a regimental unit)."[19]

While at Camp Blanding, Technician Fourth Grade Andrew J. Sklivis, with Headquarters Company, 3rd Battalion designed the "Red Devil" and it was adopted as the regimental insignia. Lieutenant Edward F. King, the regimental special services officer, began bi-monthly publication of the regimental newspaper, *Diablo*.

The 1st Battalion finished basic training at the end of January and departed Camp Blanding for the Parachute School at Fort Benning, Georgia on February 3, 1943. The following week, the 1st Battalion began jump school, while the 2nd Battalion finished basic training and left Camp Blanding for the Parachute School. The 3rd Battalion departed the following week, arriving at Fort Benning on February 20, where the 1st and 2nd Battalions were already well into parachute training.

Parachute training consisted of four stages, each one week in duration. A-stage was designed to separate the paratroopers from the men. It was a grueling physical test to weed out those physically unfit or not ready mentally for the training. Every day was filled with long runs and calisthenics. Instructors ordered trainees to do pushups for any infractions, real or fabricated. Trainees double-timed everywhere.

However, the regiment's trainees like Private Frank McKee, with Company F, had already gone through very rigorous physical training at Camp Blanding.

"We were in such good physical shape that we were permitted to skip A-stage of parachute training, which was designed to physically toughen the men. We went directly into B-stage."[20]

In B-stage, the physical conditioning continued and training to teach the proper parachute landing techniques was added. The trainees would jump from two, three, and four feet high platforms and land in sawdust, where they practiced tumbling techniques known as parachute landing falls (PLFs). The trainee would land with his feet close together and knees bent and execute a right or left front tumble or a right or left backward tumble as he landed. These techniques prepared the trainees to land by parachute and avoid injury from the shock of hitting the ground. In addition, trainees were suspended in a parachute harness attached to a circular pipe five feet in diameter and taught to guide the parachute during descent by pulling down on the risers to release air from the other side of the parachute canopy, which would cause the parachute to drift in the direction of the pulled risers. The trainees were also taught Judo and hand-to-hand combat techniques using knives and bayonets.

The third week of jump school was C-stage, where towers were used to simulate various aspects of a parachute opening and descent. The thirty-four foot tower was a shed made to simulate the inside of a C-47 airplane and doorway and raised to a height of thirty-four feet at the floor. The trainee wore a harness, similar to a parachute harness and it was attached to a twelve feet long canvas "static line" that the trainee would hook up to a steel cable that ran through the inside of the shed. The trainee would then jump from the tower's doorway and execute the proper technique to exit an airplane. He would freefall until the twelve feet long static line caught him. The static line slid diagonally down the steel cable to a trip mechanism, which would release the trainee to drop into a pile of sawdust, where he would perform a PLF. This tower was feared by most trainees and was responsible for some trainees washing out of jump school.

The other towers used in C-stage were the 250-foot high towers. These consisted of an A-tower, which was a chair that two trainees rode to the top, where the chair underwent a sudden drop, and then was slowly lowered to the ground. On the B-tower, trainees wore parachute harnesses and were suspended in an upright position similar to the same position used when actually descending by parachute. The trainees were then raised to the top, released with a sudden drop to simulate the freefall before the parachute opens, and then lowered to the ground.

The C-tower was especially memorable for Private Robert White, with Company A. "You were lying in a prone position and this harness was hooked to you and it suspended you in the center of your back. It pulled you up and you went all the way to the top and you had to pull the [D-ring] ripcord. You had a fifteen foot fall before your harness took hold. They wanted you to pull the ripcord with your right hand and while you were falling, they wanted you to change hands [with the D-ring] to see if you were thinking. Then they just lowered you back down."[21]

On the D-tower an actual parachute with the canopy deployed was hooked up to the trainee's parachute harness and he was raised to the top. The parachute canopy was released and the trainee floated down in a manner much like an actual parachute. An instructor on the ground below used a bullhorn to instruct trainees on using their risers to guide them down to the ground where they executed a PLF.

Also during C-stage, trainees received instruction in how to pack a parachute. On Friday, the last day of C-stage, the trainees packed their own parachutes for their first qualifying jumps the following Monday. At the packing shed, Sergeant Bill Call, with Company B, listened intently to the instructor as he demonstrated the proper technique for packing a parachute. "They showed us how to pack them and fold it just right so the air would rush up through the fold and it would explode and expand the rest of your parachute. Making us do things precisely was part of the training.

"They gave us a guarantee. They said, 'If this chute doesn't open, bring it back, and we'll give you a different one.'"[22]

The school's parachute riggers observed and corrected the trainees as they packed their own chutes. After completing the packing of his parachute, Private Frank McKee, like most trainees, worried about whether he had packed it properly. "I laid in my bunk all that night trying to remember whether or not I made the last tie to the backpack of the chute, which was the static line to pull the back cover off and pull the chute out. I couldn't remember making that tie, so I wound up with some questions in my mind."[23]

The final stage of jump school was D-stage, where each trainee made five qualifying jumps. Sergeant Call was probably typical of most trainees making their first jump. "On the first one you're scared—you're afraid. I was no different. We were all very apprehensive.

"God, we went out the door and heard that bang when the chute opened—and looked up—what a wonderful feeling. You felt superior and you know, 'nothing could happen to me.' You landed and you wanted to go right back up and do it again. You've conquered it and the fear was gone."[24]

There were others whose fear of failure far outweighed the fear of their first jump, such as Private Robert White, with Company A. "We just all wanted to qualify. During all of our training, they taught us so much pride in the regiment that nobody wanted to fail."[25]

During White's first qualifying jump, the violent opening shock of his parachute deploying caused him to bite his tongue. "I was hollering out 'one-thousand, two-thousand, three-thousand,' and it opened on 'three-thousand' when my mouth was still open."[26]

Despite the bleeding, White was immediately ready for the next qualifying jump. "I don't ever recall being nervous, I liked it."[27]

The 1st Battalion completed parachute training on February 26, the 2nd Battalion on March 7, and the 3rd Battalion on March 12. At the 1st Battalion graduation ceremony, Sergeant Bill Call stood at attention in his Class A dress uniform, with his pant legs bloused above his highly polished jump boots. "When they pinned the wings on me, I had a wonderful thought that, 'Oh God, I wish my mom could see me.'"[28]

After graduation, the entire personnel of each battalion were given a furlough. The furlough was particularly memorable for Sergeant Call, who went home in the same Class A type uniform he had seen the paratrooper wearing while riding the bus the previous year in Saginaw, Michigan. "I was king of the block when I got home. It was wonderful. My wife was pregnant and she looked wonderful."[29]

IN EARLY MARCH 1943, THE 508TH RECEIVED ORDERS to move from Fort Benning to Camp MacKall, North Carolina, which was near Fort Bragg for additional training, where it would come under the command of the 2nd Airborne Brigade. The regiment moved by battalion echelons beginning March 17 and completed the movement by April 1.

On March 27, 1943, Lieutenant Colonel Lindquist was promoted to the rank of colonel.

When the regiment moved to Camp Mackall, numerous officers and enlisted men who had been injured during parachute training were left at the Fort Benning hospital. This necessitated a number of changes in assignments of officers and key enlisted men. The battalion and separate unit commanders were Major Harry J. Harrison, 1st Battalion; Major Ernest Sallee, who took command of the 2nd Battalion when Major Wesley Armstrong transferred to the newly forming 13th Airborne Division as inspector general; Major Louis Mendez, 3rd Battalion; Lieutenant Robert Abraham, Headquarters Company; Captain James A. Dowling, Service Company; Captain James C. Klein, medical detachment; and Lieutenant Melvin V. Peterson, regimental band.

Shortly after arriving at Camp Mackall, Captain Chet Graham, the commander of Company F since its formation, received a new assignment. "I was reassigned as the S-3 (operations and training officer) of the 2nd Battalion, and Captain Francis E. Flanders assumed command of Company F."[30]

The regiment began thirteen weeks of unit training to toughen the troopers to the rigors of the battlefield and to develop proficiency at both small unit and battalion level maneuvers and tactics. Additional practice jumps were also conducted.

One thing that Sergeant Bill Call hated at Camp Mackall was the sand, which seemed to be everywhere. "I don't know if they brought that sand in on purpose. We had sand all over the place. Pushups in that sand—you'd put your arms down and they would go in over your wrists, sinking in the sand. Every time you did a pushup you were sucking in sand.

"They started us on our advanced training there. They trained us in platoon and squad tactics, and of course, we would practice in battalion and regimental [maneuvers] as a whole unit."[31]

After the regiment arrived at Camp Mackall, Major David E. Thomas joined the 508th as the new regimental surgeon and commanding officer of the regimental medical detachment. Thomas had broken his ankle during an earlier practice jump with the 505th Parachute Infantry Regiment, where he had served as its first regimental surgeon. Major Thomas described Colonel Lindquist as "a very competent soldier. He was an entirely different fellow from [Colonel James M.] Jimmy Gavin. Lindquist's forte was personnel. He knew how to pick people and was ruthless in getting rid of officers if they didn't measure up to his standards. Unlike Gavin, who always dressed in fatigues, Roy would go out to check the training while wearing his Class A uniform."[32]

From May 21 to 28, the 508th participated in airborne maneuvers conducted near Cheraw, South Carolina, where it operated as ground infantry against the 101st Airborne Division.

The regiment returned to Camp Mackall and completed unit training on July 26, then conducted its first night jump on August 9. Troopers like Sergeant Bill Call, with Company B, quickly realized how much more confusing and potentially dangerous night jumps were than those made during daytime. "When I came out of the door, I looked down—a moonlit night—here was this, it looked like a river. Then right alongside this river was a forest. You think of your family jewels. [Private First Class Alphonse A.] Al Caplik was behind me. We were talking coming down, yelling at one another. I said, 'God Al, those are woods, let's try and hit that river.'

"He said, 'I'm going to try for the woods.'

"What happened was we landed in a cornfield, standing up. It was the easiest landing. It was a cornfield, but it looked just like a woods. What we thought was a river was a road."[33]

At the beginning of September 1943, the 508th Parachute Infantry Regiment began preparations for participation in the Second Army's Tennessee maneuvers which were scheduled from September 13 to November 15. Replacements were scheduled to be received by the regiment during the maneuvers. Lieutenant Colonel Tom Shanley, who had just returned from the hospital after an injury suffered during a practice jump at Camp Mackall was designated as the commanding officer of the regiment's rear detachment, which was to remain at Camp Mackall. The rear detachment would guard the regimental area and train the replacement personnel upon their arrival.

That September, Captain Chet Graham, the 2nd Battalion S-3, was given a new assignment as the commanding officer of Headquarters Company, 2nd Battalion. "They accepted me as their new company commander. I was blessed with some great noncommissioned officers like [Kenneth M.] Ken Schroeder, who was our first sergeant and a great help to me; [Staff Sergeant] George [E.] Christ [Jr.], the communications platoon sergeant; [Staff Sergeant Robert S.] Bob Brand, the machine gun platoon sergeant; and [Staff Sergeant Howard R.] Howie Smith, the mortar platoon sergeant. George Christ was also a member of the cadre when the regiment was first organized. These NCOs were outstanding leaders. The entire company functioned like a well-oiled machine and they were a family of young men who liked each other. We also had two outstanding NCOs in our supply room—[Staff Sergeant] Francis [L.] Benedict and [Technician Fifth Grade] Paul [F.] Gugliotta."[34]

On September 2, 1943, the regiment's advance detail, along with advance details of the 2nd Airborne Brigade and the 501st Parachute Infantry Regiment, left Camp Mackall by motor convoy, arriving at Lebanon, Tennessee on the afternoon of September 3, and bivouacked near Taylorsville, Tennessee.

The main body of the regiment arrived at the area prepared by the advance detail on September 7. Because of a shortage of transport planes, the regiment made preparations to operate as ground infantry, as it had done during the Cheraw maneuvers. Approximately forty additional vehicles were received by the regiment for use during these operations.

On September 12, the regiment moved to the vicinity of LaGuardo, Tennessee and began the first exercise the next day. The 1st Battalion moved by motor convoy twenty-five miles to seize and hold bridges for a coming attack by the 12th Armored Division. The 2nd Battalion and the regiment's Headquarters Company followed on foot. The 3rd Battalion remained in reserve. During this exercise, as in others which followed, the speed with which the regiment moved placed it far out in front of friendly troops, and its successful accomplishment of the assigned mission caused it to be commended for its aggressiveness and mobility.

At noon on September 16, the exercise for the week was completed and that night all units of the regiment moved to the vicinity of Unionville, Tennessee to spend three cold, wet days before beginning the next exercise.

At about 6:00 a.m. on September 20, the 508th moved into a concealed bivouac and two hours later began a twenty-eight mile march to an assembly point. The next day, the regiment moved to another assembly area and waited while engineers brought up equipment to be used for crossing the Cumberland River. Early that evening, the 508th crossed the river and assembled a few miles to the north, bypassing all opposing forces under the cover of darkness. It then moved to Gladesville, Tennessee and captured the town. The regiment was attacked by the opposing forces and by the end of the exercise all three battalions were declared "destroyed" by the umpires, with only the regiment's Headquarters Company holding the town.

On September 29, the regiment moved to Tullahoma, Tennessee and encamped at Northern Field to prepare for a night jump on October 5. It was during this period that Lieutenant Colonel Tom Shanley rejoined the regiment in Tennessee, where he assumed command of the 2nd Battalion.

Two days before the jump, thirty-six planes of the 365th Troop Carrier Group arrived at the airfield. The regiment would be dropped in three serials, the 1st Battalion in the first serial, the 3rd Battalion and the regiment's Headquarters Company in the second serial, and the 2nd Battalion in the third serial. Due to a misinterpretation of signals between the pilots and their commanding officer, the 1st Battalion was dropped over an area of twelve miles, while the second and third serials were dropped over the proper drop zone. The regiment accomplished its mission and on October 7, it moved to a bivouac at Gallatin, Tennessee.

During the next two weeks, the regiment participated in two new exercises as ground troops.

During one of the exercises of the Tennessee maneuvers, Private First Class Frederick J. Infanger and the 2nd Platoon of Company E surprised and captured one of the opposition force's artillery batteries. "We turned their guns around to fire at their own forces. About this time, an officer umpire arrived and congratulated us on our tactics, but also told Lieutenant [Robert] Mathias that we couldn't use the weapons against the other forces since we would not know how to fire the weapons. Lieutenant Mathias contended that this was false since he had schooled his troops for any eventuality and that the 2nd Platoon could operate artillery pieces. The debate developed into a very heated argument, which Lieutenant Mathias ended with a very solid one-punch."[35]

On October 18, the regiment received orders canceling further participation in the maneuvers and ordering it to return to Camp Mackall to prepare for overseas movement. Colonel Lindquist was very proud of the regiment's performance during the various exercises. "During the course of the Tennessee maneuvers, the regiment was highly commended for its aggressiveness and celerity, despite the fact that it operated as a regular infantry unit for the greater part of the time with no change in T/O [table of organization] or T/E [table of equipment], except for additional transportation. The lessons learned during this period and in this type of action, and the success the unit enjoyed on all problems, did much to weld it into a more cohesive, formidable fighting team, anxious to prove its worth in actual rather than simulated combat."[36]

On November 17, the regiment received orders to proceed to Camp Shanks, New York for overseas shipment. The 508th and 507th Parachute Infantry Regiments would move overseas under the command of the 2nd Airborne Brigade, commanded by Brigadier General George P. Howell.

During the period between the regiment's return to Camp Mackall and its departure a number of changes in key officer assignments and promotions were made.

The key regimental staff assignments and separate unit commanders were Lieutenant Colonel Bill Ekman, regimental executive officer; Captain Melvin V. Peterson, adjutant and band commander; Captain William H. Nation, S-1 (personnel); Captain John A. Breen, S-2 (intelligence); Major Otho E. Holmes, S-3 (plans and operations); Major James R. Casteel, S-4 (logistics and supply); Major Dave Thomas, medical detachment; Captain Robert Abraham, Headquarters Company commander; and Captain James Dowling, Service Company commander.

The 1st Battalion commander, Harry Harrison was promoted to lieutenant colonel. Captain Abdallah K. Zakby was the battalion's executive officer. The 1st Battalion staff members were Lieutenant Herbert Hoffman (S-1), Lieutenant James D. Dietrich (S-2), Captain Walter H. Silver (S-3), and Lieutenant John J. Jampetero (S-4). The 1st Battalion company commanders were Lieutenant Gerard A. Ruddy (Headquarters Company), Captain Jonathan E. Adams, Jr. (Company A), Captain Royal R. Taylor (Company B), and Captain Robert L. Milam (Company C).

Lieutenant Colonel Tom Shanley remained as commanding officer of the 2nd Battalion. The executive officer of the 2nd Battalion was Major Shields Warren, Jr. The 2nd Battalion staff consisted of Lieutenant James D. Tibbetts (S-1), Lieutenant Robert N. Havens (S-2), Lieutenant George W. Simonds (S-3), and Lieutenant George E. Miles (S-4). The 2nd Battalion company commanders were Captain Chester Graham (Headquarters Company), Captain Alton L. Bell (Company D), Captain Wayne K. Harvey (Company E), and Lieutenant Francis E. Flanders (Company F).

The 3rd Battalion commander, Louis Mendez, was promoted to lieutenant colonel. Major Jack T. Shannon was the executive officer of the 3rd Battalion. The 3rd Battalion staff members were Lieutenant Paul E. Lehman (S-1), Lieutenant James H. McDuffie (S-2), Lieutenant Hillman C. Dress (S-3), and Lieutenant Joseph I. Shankey, Jr. (S-4). The 3rd Battalion company commanders were Captain James C. Driggers (Headquarters Company), Captain Frank J. Novak (Company G), Captain Hal M. Creary (Company H), and Captain Erle H. Bridgewater, Jr. (Company I).

The overseas movement would be made in strict secrecy so that those left behind would be unaware of the imminent departure of the regiment. Lieutenant Woodrow Millsaps, the platoon leader of the 3rd Platoon of Company B, couldn't tell his wife of the impending movement. "In December 1943, the 508 Parachute Regiment departed by train for parts unknown. We entrained at night and were gone from Camp Mackall when daybreak arrived. It was some time after we had departed before the women of the regiment found out that we had left Mackall. LaVerne told me later when I returned from the war that she would never forget that day when they found out we were gone. Women and children were weeping while they prepared to move out of the area to return to their homes or other places to stay."[37]

Lieutenant Briand N. Beaudin, the 3rd Battalion's assistant surgeon, like almost every other officer and enlisted man, didn't know the destination of the trains transporting the regiment. "Finally, on the evening of 20 December, the 508th closed in on Camp Shanks, New York, just forty-five minutes from Broadway.

"More varied training followed, such as double-timing about the post, 'abandon ship' in case of emergency, and so forth. Without patches or wings, and with boots unbloused, the troops set out for New York fifty percent at a time, trying to take in as much as possible of the town in one night. Few of the men returned to camp 'til reveille, and the long steep walk up the hill from the ferry and train was extremely tiresome.

"The final alert was soon given and the men of the 508 were restricted to the camp on Christmas Day. Just before dark on 27 December, we were loaded on a train to the Weehawken ferry, and set to appear on Staten Island, where at 8.00 a.m. the 28th of December, our ship, the USAT James S. Parker slid away from the pier.

"After more than eleven days at sea, we entered the harbor at Belfast, North Ireland."[38]

The regiment finished debarkation by late afternoon on January 9, 1944 and then marched through Belfast to the train station. Upon arrival at the train station, Sergeant Bill Call waited in formation with the rest of B Company for the company's train assignment. "They gave us a bag lunch and put us on a train and headed to this little town of Portstewart, on the Irish Sea. They put us in Nissen huts."[39]

The trains transporting the regiment pulled into Portstewart late that night. The 508th then made a short march to its new encampment. The following morning, Lieutenant Beaudin was able to get his first look at the estate at Cromore, where the regiment was bivoucked. "It was there that definitive training such as demolitions, mine laying and neutralization, and long overnight marches were entered upon, plus VD prevention and treatment.

"It was miserably cold there, with only peat to warm our quarters. Men of the 505 Parachute Infantry, veterans of the Sicily and Italy jumps, lived with each company of the 508th for about a week and gave many helpful hints about fighting the Germans."[40]

On January 20, 1944, the 507th and 508th Parachute Infantry Regiments were attached to the veteran 82nd Airborne Division, which was also billeted in Northern Ireland.

In early February, secret orders were issued for the 82nd Airborne Division to jump in Normandy, France on the Cotentin Peninsula in support of an amphibious landing on the east side of the peninsula at a beach codenamed Utah. The division would drop by parachute and land by glider well to the west of the landing beach to capture a key crossing over the Douve River to expedite cutting the peninsula off from the rest of Normandy. The division then assigned regimental missions to the commanding officers and members of their respective staffs who had the proper security clearances. The 505th Parachute Infantry Regiment would jump just west of St.-Sauveur-le-Vicomte and capture the town and the bridge over the Douve River, and send patrols to the south of the Prairies Marécageuses marshland. The 507th Parachute Infantry Regiment would land to the north of Hill 110 near Hills 71 and 82, and would defend against a German attack from the north. The 508th Parachute Infantry Regiment would drop astride Hill 110, consolidate its position, and move south and west to intercept German forces attempting to reinforce those on the Cotentin Peninsula.

On February 13, the 82nd Airborne Division began moving from Northern Ireland to pre-invasion bases in England clustered around the cities of Leicester and Nottingham. During the first week of March, as the 508th prepared to move to Nottingham, Lieutenant Ralph E. DeWeese, the assistant platoon leader of the 2nd Platoon of Company H, arranged to have a party for his platoon sergeant. "Just before we left Ireland we had a platoon party for our Staff Sergeant Joe Bundy. It was a birthday party and was mighty nice. I arranged to get some sugar and cocoa and the lady at the hotel made a fine birthday cake for Joe."[41]

By the time orders were issued for the movement to England, Lieutenant Briand Beaudin was very much ready to leave the bitter cold of Northern Ireland. "On the 10th of March, the 508 boarded trains for Belfast, and then loaded on a boat which sailed into the Firth of Clyde and discharged passengers at Greenock [Scotland] before dusk. Then entraining again, the regiment arrived at Nottingham, England, at Wollerton Park about midnight.

"After combat jump training plus specialist training, the men of the regiment had reached the point where they had confidence in their buddies and in each other."[42]

Several days after the regiment arrived in England, Major Shields Warren had an opportunity to meet the commanding officer of the 82nd Airborne Division, Major General Matthew B. Ridgway. "All field grade officers of the regiment were assembled to meet General Ridgway, who gave us a short talk welcoming us to the 82nd Airborne Division. While the entire talk could not have lasted longer than five or ten minutes, I have never been more impressed by any individual's personality as much as that exhibited by General Ridgway. His personality could truly be called magnetic, since I found myself literally hanging on each word he spoke. I said as much to my friend and classmate, Tom Shanley afterwards, who agreed wholeheartedly with my opinion."[43]

The 508th Parachute Infantry settled into its new encampment at Wollaton Park and began intensive training for the upcoming invasion. The training was tailored specifically for each of the regiment's units according to the planned mission, even though the officers and enlisted men of those units didn't know the specific location or date of the operation. Staff Sergeant Worster M. Morgan was a member of the regiment's Headquarters Company. "My own group in the regiment (about sixteen men) was the headquarters intelligence S-2, and we were involved in night scouting and patrolling, map reading, interrogation, photo interpretation. Again our training was specialized—night problems, demolition, communication, live fire with mortars and bazookas."[44]

During their free time, the troopers of the regiment explored Nottingham and began meeting the local citizens, usually at pubs. Staff Sergeant Morgan and his intelligence section usually gathered at their favorite pub, The Cocked Hat. "A pub is the neighborhood social club. Their young men were away in service, so the older people adopted us. The beer was warm, but we learned to like it.

"Just before 10 o'clock the bartender would call out, 'Time please, time please,' meaning the pub was closing. We would buy large pitchers of beer and put them under our tables. This kept the pub open and the neighbors would help us drink it up. That's one reason they liked us so much."[45]

Shortly after arrival in England, a call went out for volunteers for a secret operation. A great many more troopers volunteered than were required. Those troopers selected were sent to an airfield at North Witham, about ten miles south of Grantham, England, where they learned that they had volunteered for pathfinder training. Both the 82nd and 101st Airborne Divisions formed provisional pathfinder companies specifically for the invasion. These units would train with the IX Troop Carrier Command at the Command Pathfinder School located at North Witham.

Captain Neal L. McRoberts, a veteran of the Sicily and Salerno combat jumps with the 505th Parachute Infantry Regiment, was selected to command the 82nd Airborne Provisional Pathfinder Company. McRoberts was in overall command of the division's pathfinder mission and would jump with and command the 508th regimental pathfinder team during the Normandy jump. "The regimental pathfinder teams consisted of three battalion teams [each] composed of two officers, two Eureka operators, one wire man, seven light men, and from four to six security men. The 507th and 508th pathfinder teams had four security men per each battalion assigned from the 504th Parachute Infantry, plus one officer for each regimental team. The 508th regimental team, in addition to the above equipment and personnel, dropped two BUPS [Beacon Ultra Portable S-band] beacons."[46]

The Eureka was one half of a radio transponder system. The other half was a transceiver unit codenamed Rebecca that was mounted in the noses of troop carrier planes. Because of a concern of over saturation of signals from the Rebecca units, the use would be restricted to the lead plane of each serial. A Eureka set on the ground would act as a beacon for the lead plane using its Rebecca. The other planes in the serial would guide off of the lead plane.

In addition, seven colored lights would be set up in the shape of a "T" by each battalion team to act as a visual signal as the serials made final approaches to the drop zone. Over the coming months, the pathfinder teams would hone the execution of this critical mission during night practice jumps in which the equipment was set up and operated to guide planes to the drop zone.

On March 18, the 508th made a daylight practice jump. One incident during this jump served to remind the troopers that no jumps, not even practice jumps, were without substantial risk. Sergeant Paul R. Sands, with Headquarters Company, 2nd Battalion, jumped last and was the "pusher" of his plane's stick of paratroopers. "Everything was going well as I floated toward the ground with a slight forward drift when another jumper came in from the high right side, slipped under me, and I dropped onto his canopy just missing the center vent, and my chute collapsed. My canopy was nowhere to be seen—right or left—it had to be draped over the edge of his canopy. Here I was, deep in nylon and couldn't see where we were headed. I tried to walk on his canopy, but each time I tried to take a step the nylon came up, so I started doing a shuffle and it worked. A jumper falls seventeen to twenty feet per second. When the other man came under me, I thought I was about eight hundred feet from landing. Believe me, you are thinking fast. I figured I had thirty to forty seconds to get off that canopy. I had traveled about half the distance from the vent to the canopy edge, at which point I could see the men who had already landed looking up. It takes about a seventy-foot drop for a chute to open, jumping into the prop blast after exiting the plane. When I looked down and saw the ground, I felt I was out of time—and I was. Luckily, I had both feet planted square, so when the man under me landed (my free fall was about thirty-five feet), I am sure my legs took a lot of the shock, but my lumbar area was my biggest hurt from being pulled backwards by my own canopy, landing largely on my back. I woke up when the medics gave me a pain shot and then I passed out again, not coming to until we arrived at the 30th General Hospital."[47]

On March 21, less than two weeks after arriving in England, Lieutenant Colonel Herbert F. Batcheller, who had replaced Brigadier General James M. Gavin as commanding officer of the veteran 505th Parachute Infantry Regiment the previous October when Gavin was promted to assistant division commander, was relieved and sent to the 508th as commanding officer of its 1st Battalion. Lieutenant Colonel Bill Ekman, the regimental executive officer, was transferred to command the 505th. The 1st Battalion commander, Lieutenant Colonel Harry Harrison replaced Ekman as the 508th executive officer.

Captain Abdallah Zakby, the 1st Battalion executive officer, left the regiment to join the 504th Parachute Infantry Regiment, upon its arrival in England at the beginning of April. Because Lieutenant Colonel Batcheller was new to the regiment, Major Shields Warren transferred to the 1st Battalion as executive officer to provide continuity and knowledge of the personnel of the battalion.

Captain Robert Milam replaced Major Warren as 2nd Battalion executive officer on April 8.

Major Jack T. Shannon, the executive officer of the 3rd Battalion left the 508th to lead a three man inter-Allied Office of Strategic Services (OSS) team, codenamed "Bergamotte", which would later jump behind enemy lines in France in July 1944. Captain Alton Bell, the commanding officer of Company D, replaced Shannon as executive officer of the 3rd Battalion.

During the second half of April, daily aerial reconnaissance photos of Normandy began to reflect ominous signs of enemy activity on Hill 110, the drop zone for the 508th. A quarry located on the western slope of the hill began to show signs of German heavy weapons emplacements. Then on the lower slopes of the hill near some wooded hedgerows, parking areas for vehicles began to appear in photos, indicating a command installation. Subsequent photos showed other areas of the lower slopes being cleared of hedgerows. Then about three weeks before the division was scheduled to move to the airfields, aerial reconnaissance photos showed black specks in a geometric pattern on the lower slopes of the hill. The number of these specks continued to grow, eventually covering much of the hill. These were initially not identified, until photos taken in the early morning failed to show shadows. It was clear; these were holes. Shortly afterward, other photos revealed poles about eight to ten feet tall being planted in the holes. These were anti-landing obstacles, to deny the fields to glider landings. These poles were known as Rommel's Asparagus. The invasion planners and the 82nd Airborne Division officers with top secret BIGOT clearances wondered if the Germans knew of the planned drop zones.

About a week before the move to the airfields, the 82nd Airborne Division's mission was changed and its drop zones were moved east, to areas slightly west of the Merderet River and west of Ste.-Mére-Église. This change was due to the detection of the German 91st Luftlande (Air Landing) Division, a unit specially trained in antiairborne tactics, which had recently arrived on the Cotentin Peninsula. The German 91st Luftlande Division's Bataillon 3, Grenadier Regiment 1057, had moved into the area around Hill 110. The 508th had been just days away from parachuting directly on top of it.

On May 28, the 82nd Airborne Division headquarters issued Field Order Number 6. With this order, the veteran 505th would land west of Ste.-Mère-Église, capture the town, and protect the beach landings against German attacks along the main highway running south from Cherbourg. The 507th would land west of the Merderet River near Amfreville, seize and secure the river crossing at la Fière, and defend against German attacks from the north and west. The three parachaute regiments, plus Company B, 307th Airborne Engineer Battalion, various division headquarters detachments, and air and naval fire support parties were designated as Force A, which would be under the command of General Gavin, the assistant division commander.

As part of this order, the 508th mission was assigned as follows:

The 508th Parachute Infantry Regiment, with Company B (minus one platoon), 307th Airborne Engineer Battalion attached, landing in DZ "N" will:

Seize and destroy the crossings of the Douve River at Beuzeville-la-Bastille and Ètienville.

Seize, organize and defend the general area along the general line of CR (261938) [Ètienville] – Renouf.

Clear and secure the Division area within its sector

Assemble one battalion without delay in area indicated [Hill 30] as Force [A] Reserve.

Patrol aggressively to the line indicated. Be prepared on Division order to advance to the west to the line of the Douve River.

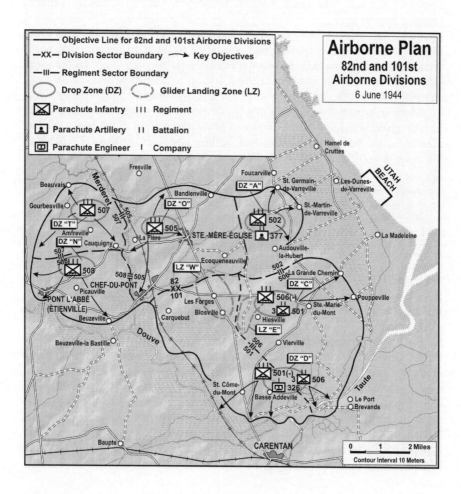

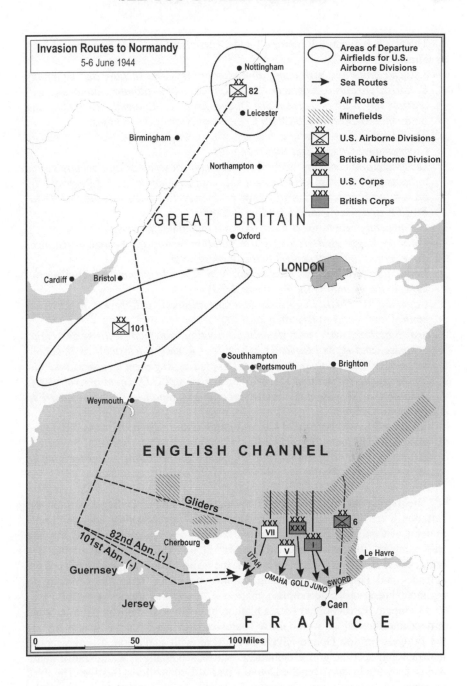

The 508th Parachute Infantry's Field Order Number 1 was therefore revised as follows:

3.a. 2nd Battalion, with demolition platoon, less one section, and Company B, 307th Airborne Engineer Battalion, less one platoon, attached, will destroy the bridges across the Douve River at Ètienville (270934) and Beuzeville-la-Bastille (308910). Upon completion of demolitions:

The 2nd Battalion, less attachments, will revert to Regimental reserve. The Commanding Officer, 2nd Battalion will:

Designate one company under Battalion control to clear and occupy sector indicated on overlay and protect the southern flank of the Regiment by preventing reconstruction of blown bridges at Ètienville and Beuzeville-la-Bastille, and seizing and defending Picauville.

Occupy and prepare for defense the area indicated on overlay.

Clear the Regimental area, less 3rd Battalion sector, of all enemy resistance. Be prepared to counterattack to the north or west.

Demolition platoon, less one section, will revert to Regimental control and move to the vicinity of the Regimental C.P.

Company B, 307th Engineers, less one platoon, will revert to Division control and report to [the division].

3rd Battalion, with one demolition section attached, will seize, clear, organize, and defend the area Ètienville – Renouf (inclusive), as indicated on overlay. One company will be designated as Regimental reserve and will not be committed without authority of Regimental C.O. Upon arrival of 2nd Battalion in Regimental reserve area this company will be released to Battalion C.O.

1st Battalion will constitute Force A reserve and will move without delay to area [Hill 30] indicated on overlay.

Battery B, 80th Airborne Antiaircraft (Antitank) Battalion, will place guns in direct support of Regiment as indicated on overlay.[48]

The regimental orders were then translated into specific orders at the battalion level. Lieutenant Barry E. Albright was the platoon leader of the 1st Platoon of Company E. "The battalion commander, realizing that his mission was complex, divided it into two phases: phase one, destruction of the two bridges over the Douve River to prevent the enemy from reinforcing his coastal defenses and phase two, mopping up the regimental area and reverting to regimental reserve. To accomplish phase one, the plan of attack was as follows:

"Company E, reinforced with a platoon of engineers, a machine gun section, and a demolition squad would move southwest and attack Ètienville and destroy the bridge over the Douve River. Reinforced with a platoon of engineers, a machine gun section, and a demolition squad, Company F would move south and destroy the bridge over the Douve River at Beuzeville-la-Bastille. The third company of the battalion, Company D, would be in support to reinforce the attack of either E or F Companies, with priority to Company E. Headquarters Company mortars would support the attack companies by fire from the vicinity of the drop zone. Upon completion of phase one, the engineer company (-) and the demolition section would revert to regimental control.

"To accomplish phase two, the 2nd Battalion would dispose its forces as follows:

"Company F would pull back and seize Picauville, which had been bypassed and would establish a roadblock south of Ètienville and one north of Beuzeville-la-Bastille. The battalion (-) as regimental reserve would occupy and defend Hill 30 and conduct mopping up in the regimental area."[49]

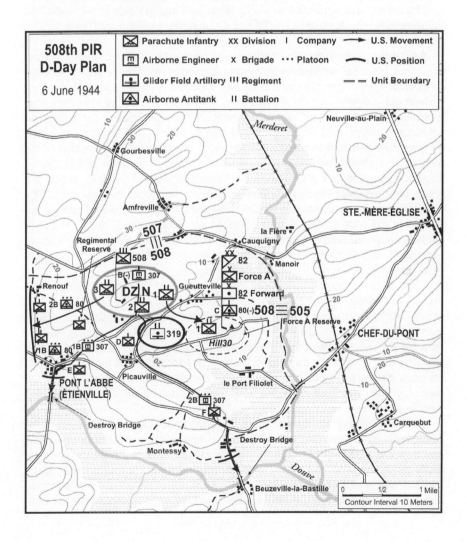

Lieutenant Robert C. Moss, Jr., the assistant platoon leader of the 1st Platoon of Company H, was also assigned as the 3rd Battalion liaison officer with the air corps. "This meant I would handle the detail for jumps to be made by the 3rd Battalion. Toward the end of May, the battalion CO told me to go to a certain airfield (I forget which) and set up a drop. No date was given. Then before I left, the battalion CO said, after swearing me to secrecy, 'This is the big one. We are going.' I remember it was Whitsuntide or Whitsunday [June 1] that the regiment took off from Nottingham in British busses and went to the field and bunked in a hangar that I had arranged for us. It was enclosed with barbed wire. Only special people could go in or out. I could go out but had nowhere to go."[50]

The 1st and 3rd Battalions would fly from Folkingham airfield while the 2nd Battalion and Headquarters and Service Companies would depart from Saltby airfield.

After being sealed in at the airfields, the necessary equipment, ammunition, and other essential supplies were issued and briefings and orientations were conducted. Lieutenant George D. Lamm was the platoon leader of the 2nd Platoon of Company A. "We studied sand tables and aerial photos of European areas, but with no hint of the countryside itself. This information would be withheld to just prior to the jump. We, however, were issued 'escape kits' made up primarily of a small compass which could fit nicely in certain parts of the body, a very strong thin 'file' which could be taped to the inner upper arm or thigh, a thin silk map that could be folded into a small oval and sewn within the seams of a jumpsuit. Included along with these wonderful gadgets were fifty dollars of script invasion currency, this to be printed later as it would include the symbol of the country of our destination. Many 'betting pools' were formed to guess the honored captive country such as France, Belgium, Holland, or Norway as favored target areas. The invasion money was to be used to assist us in foraging for necessary items needed for our mission.

"Just prior to the big day, we woke up and were briefed on destinations. France, an old ally, was it and they were waiting. The sand tables suddenly had names we would never forget—Chef-du-Pont, Ste.-Mère-Église, la Fière, etcetera, etcetera, and suddenly our mission was magnified with reality, and we received our tasks on our initial objectives. The 2nd Platoon was given splendid missions that we thought important, 'Assemble after jump and move to Hill 30, dig in a roadblock (one that would deter enemy forces from [reaching] the beaches). Then take a patrol to the bridge at la Fière and meet up with the 505 Parachute Infantry there.'

"On this evening as I was briefing the troopers on the sand table and aerial maps, I was called to report to the chaplain [Captain Ignatius P. Maternowski]. I told him that I had already made my confession, but he broke the news of my dad's death. My dad had a very serious stroke before I left the States, and I recalled how proud of me he was because I had jump wings and was a second lieutenant. He made 'signs' to my mother that I must go overseas with my unit.

These memories passed through my mind when the chaplain said that I must stay at the airfield until after the invasion when I could then go home. I told him my dad had already made the decision for me."[51]

Inside the hanger at Saltby airfield, Major Dave Thomas, the regimental surgeon and commander of the regiment's medical detachment, and some of the other troopers passed the time by engaging in card games and gambling. "Everybody was getting a big dose of religion and both our chaplains did a sold out business in the hangar. I was in a poker game and was not doing too well (I've been a big poker player all my life and I've made a hell of a lot of money with poker) and I thought, 'Well, gee, I might as well hit a lick for Jesus,' (might as well get everything I can on my side) so I went to the hangar where Chaplain [Lieutenant James L.] Elder was preaching.

"I was just about to sit down in the last seat on an army canvas cot when Chaplain Elder said, 'Now the Lord isn't particularly interested in people who only turn to Him in times of greatest need.'

"I thought, 'To hell with the SOB—he saw me come in.' I got up and left."[52]

Private David M. Jones, with Headquarters Company, 1st Battalion, knew more than most enlisted troopers in his battalion by the time the briefings were conducted. "We in the S-2 section knew by this time exactly what kind of terrain and the general area we were to be faced with, the objectives we were to secure, and so forth; but at this point, we still didn't know exactly where in France we were to land. We had been assigned to build sand tables of our drop zone using three day old aerial photos taken by recon flights over the area, but so high that much of the flooded area failed to show up."[53]

THE 319TH GLIDER FIELD ARTILLERY BATTALION, a veteran unit of the fighting in Italy, was assigned to support the 508th as part of the regimental combat team. The 319th was sealed in at the airfield at Membury in Berkshire, southern England to await flying into Normandy by glider on the evening of June 6. Lieutenant Charles L. Sartain, Jr., was the executive officer of Battery A. "When we finally got to the airfield there was a big Nissen hut and I guess maybe twenty feet by forty feet of a sand table of Normandy, showing where the drop zones were and the landing zones. I forget what scale it was, but it had every tree and farmhouse and road, elevations and everything else on it. It was thought to be exact in every detail. All the officers and NCOs, down to and including corporals, were allowed to study the sand tables at their discretion. Large aerial photos were hanging on the wall, too. The only problem was that the aerial photos were taken at high noon, so they didn't show the height of the hedgerows. You'd look at the aerial photos and those hedgerows looked like those little jumping hedges in England. We thought maybe they were two or three feet high."[54]

AT FOLKINGHAM AIRFIELD, Private First Class Edward C. "Bogie" Boccafogli, with Company B, was becoming frustrated with the seemingly endless preparations. "Studying the sand tables and the photographs, we thought we would pretty well know the area when we got there. We had to wrap up our equipment and go over it, inspect it, make the para-bundles, which were hooked underneath the C-47 airplanes. We had to unwrap them, and wrap them up again, and hook them up. It was very nerve-racking."[55]

Inside the hanger at Folkingham, Lieutenant George Lamm and the rest of the 1st Battalion were addressed by the assistant division commander, Brigadier General Jim Gavin. "General Gavin spoke to us and told us of the combat standards he expected, and that he would be Force 'A' commander for the initial taking of objectives. This placed all three parachute regiments at his command. We had no idea how much we would see him personally as we went about our combat duties. We had the highest respect for him as a combat leader. He was a general of the mold and tradition of the Civil War's young aggressive generals who led their men by personality traits of courage, knowledge of tactics, and outstanding battlefield decisions. He demonstrated the ability of choosing to be in the right place at the right time to influence the tide of battle. Jim Gavin was at this time the youngest combat general in the United States Army and we were the youngest combat troops. He could be seen in midst of battle with his M1 rifle in one hand and a map in the other with a radio man and an aide. He would break 'cover' suddenly and head directly for you to obtain a 'situation' report, and you best know the situation when he arrived!"[56]

The invasion was scheduled for June 5 with the jump on the night of June 4-5, but rain and rough conditions in the English Channel forced a postponement. On the evening of June 4 after the jump was cancelled, Private David Jones, with Headquarters Company, 1st Battalion, sat in the large hangar where the battalion was quartered. "A motion picture was shown by the name of *The Littlest Angel* with the child actress Margaret O'Brian in a very sentimental role. I can remember tears welling in my eyes and at the time thinking it was probably the last picture I would probably ever get to see."[57]

Practically every American parachuting into Normandy or assaulting the beaches was overloaded with weapons, ammunition, equipment, rations, extra clothing, and a myriad of other items. It would cost many their lives. Lieutenant Lynn Tomlinson, the platoon leader of the 3rd Platoon of Company D, carried a combat load typical for an officer. "My weapons consisted of a .45-caliber Thompson submachine gun, a .45-caliber automatic pistol, and a trench knife. We were also equipped with two hand grenades and material for stocking [Gammon] grenades. This consisted of a detonator, the stocking, and C-2 composition, which was the explosive. We also had rations for three days. This was three packs of K-rations, which consisted of three small cans of food. There was also D-rations, which were chocolate bars requiring extremely strong teeth to penetrate. We also had extra ammunition over and above that required for our own weapons, for the platoon weapons. As an officer, I was issued a silk map for escape purposes, if needed, and fifty dollars in French Francs. And last, we were all issued a small noise device, which, when squeezed together with the thumb and forefinger, produced a sound which someone said sounded like a cricket. It reminded me of something out of a Cracker Jack box. The way this cricket was to be used, was that if we heard someone approaching, we would snap the cricket two or three times, and wait to see if we got a cricket response. If there was no response, we avoided that person if possible." [58]

During the seemingly interminable wait for the word to start putting on their parachutes and gear for the jump, one of the very young B Company troopers caught the attention of Private First Class Ed Boccafogli. "I don't think he was seventeen years old—his name was [Private John A.] Johnny Daum, a blond, tow-headed kid. In the morning he was standing there and he was staring into space. I went over to him and I said, 'What's the matter, Johnny?' I get emotional just thinking about it.

"He said, 'I don't think I'll make it.'

"I said, Nah, you'll be all right.' I sort of shook him because he was like in a daze. As it turned out, he was one of the first men killed in Normandy." [59]

Corporal Carlos W. Ross was a member of the regimental demolition platoon. "Until the afternoon of June 5, 1944 I didn't know how I was going on the invasion, as our demolition section had been split up and no one to command [it]. Then the 'Brass' decided they wanted a bridge demolished near Picauville. [Private] Henry [J.] Stutika, [Private First Class Alexander] Al Jacksich, [Private First Class] Cumer Green and myself were assigned to Lieutenant Bruce [E.] Bell [with Company C] and a squad of riflemen from the 1st Battalion to get the job done." [60]

For Private Donald I. Jakeway, with Company H, the wait was excruciating. "Tensions ran high, as the men were wound up, anxious to move along. Every effort was made by the commanding officers and noncoms to keep men at ease; it was not easy. There were accidents from men toying with hand grenades, men cleaning their rifles, and pistols. A live grenade was thrown out of a hanger when a trooper couldn't get the pin back in. A trooper was shot through the mouth when his buddy on the next cot pulled the trigger after cleaning his pistol—the weapon fired." [61]

This accidental shooting involved a couple of Company I troopers who were buddies of Private First Class Robert E. Chisolm. "[Private] John [F.] Henscheid was sitting on his bunk and [Private Joseph L.] Joe Petry was cleaning his .45 and some way a round went into the [chamber] and he shot John Henscheid. John Henscheid was medically evacuated." [62]

In another instance, Jakeway heard the sound of rifle fire in the hanger. "A trooper cleaning his M1 pulled the trigger and put a few rounds through the roof of the hanger. Man, we were ready to get out of there. We were well trained paratroopers, but waiting was enough to make you mad.

"June 5th evening, Red Cross girls were handing out coffee and doughnuts. Most of us were gorging ourselves, for we knew not when we would ever enjoy such treats again."[63]

Finally on the evening of June 5, the troopers received the order to put on their gear and prepare to board their assigned aircraft. Technician Fourth Grade Ralph H. Mann, with the 508th's Headquarters Company, had a typical combat load: "underwear shirt and shorts, long johns, olive-drab shirt and trousers, jump pants, jump jacket, wool socks, jump boots, a trench knife tied below the right knee, a gas mask, a belt and suspenders holding a canteen, shovel, first aid kit. Around our necks were our dog tags, taped together so as not to make any noise. The main parachute was on our backs, over a map case. In front, we had the reserve chute and below that a canvas [musette] bag with a raincoat, extra underwear, socks, towel, soap, toothbrush, and razor. On our heads, a wool cap and a helmet with a liner and a chin strap. You needed the chin strap to keep your helmet on when you were going out of the airplane at ninety miles per hour. I carried a folding-stock .30-caliber carbine with two hundred rounds of ammo in my pockets. We were each issued two grenades, one taped to each suspender. To go over the channel, we put a Mae West life preserver on top of all this equipment. Our pockets were filled. I had a vest-pocket Kodak camera in the left upper pocket and a New Testament in the right upper pocket. We had three K-rations— breakfast, dinner and supper. The food was packed in waxed boxes: coffee, gum, cigarettes, tasteless crackers and cans of cheese, ham and cheese, or hash. We broke the boxes apart and stuffed our pockets. We also got a big Hershey bar, about a half-inch thick and three by four inches.

"And each of us got two condoms. Evidently the Army knew something we didn't. I'm not sure it was war we were headed for.

"My boss, Captain William Nation, [S-1] in our Headquarters Company, asked if I would jump with a typewriter. As his assistant, I occasionally used one. But I said, 'No, I'd rather not,' and carried a Coleman stove instead. I had to have something to heat my coffee.

"We were trucked out to our plane, where we helped each other check equipment. I yelled to my friend [Staff Sergeant John H.] Jack Wills, who was going to another plane, 'See you on the ground!'

"There were sixteen to twenty men in each plane. The C-47 I was assigned to was *Rambling Wreck Number 2*. We wondered what happened to *Rambling Wreck Number 1*.

"We [had] blackened our faces and hands so we wouldn't stand out in the dark. It was hard to walk, at double our normal weight with all the equipment, so climbing on the plane was tough. The door had been removed. As the number two man in the stick, I sat close to the opening. The fresh air kept me from getting airsick."[64]

Lieutenant Malcolm D. Brannen, the commander of Headquarters Company, 3rd Battalion, estimated his total weight including himself, his main and reserve parachutes, weapons, ammunition, uniform, extra clothing, food, and equipment was approximately three hundred pounds. "Our jumpmaster, Captain Alton Bell, battalion executive officer, and our S-3 (plans and training officer), Captain Hillman C. Dress, aided me into the plane.

"I was number sixteen and behind me were our operations sergeant and our draftsman, [Staff] Sergeant Warren [G.] Peak and Sergeant Calvin W. Hall, respectively. We were right up against the cockpit trying to get comfortable in our small seats, regardless of the unusual load attached to our persons."[65]

Like many troopers, Staff Sergeant John D. Boone, with Headquarters Company, 1st Battalion, applied burned cork to blacken his face and hands so as to be less visible at night. "Our company formation was called before our departure to the planes. Our company commander, Captain Gerard A. Ruddy, talked to us and presented a well thought out speech. We were prepared, he said, and it was up to us to use that preparation and ingenuity to take care of the Germans. In his talk, he said among other things, he would rather die than have to bury one of his men."[66]

Lieutenant Colonel Wesley T. Leeper, with the Eighth Air Force's 91st Bombardment Group was at Folkingham airfield that evening to observe the preparations and takeoff. "Never have I seen a finer group of physical specimens than the men who made up the 508th Parachute Infantry. I cannot say that they were 'good looking' from a sense of beauty, for actually they looked almost 'horrible' as we stood there and watched them prepare for takeoff. Their faces were blackened, and their steel helmets were covered with green nets, into which had been fastened bits of green foliage. They looked like some savages I had seen in the films! Most of them were dressed in their fatigue clothing, and they had all kinds of guns and knives. Fastened to their person was more than I thought possible for one man to carry. Loaded with their 'impediments' these men could not stand for long, and most of them, after carefully checking to see that everything was in its proper place, laid down on the ground beside the plane which was to carry them to enemy soil. Each man wore two parachutes, one on his chest and one on his back—just in case. I had an opportunity to talk with some of these men before they took off, and I must say that at that moment, I was indeed proud to call myself an American—to know that I came from a country which produced men like these. Here was a group of young men—the flower of America—many of them, no doubt, about to face a horrible death, yet they laughed and joked about what they were going to do when 'they got home.' Many of them perhaps would never go back to America, for many soldiers prefer to have their bodies rest in the soil where their life-blood was spilled.

"Two men were particularly outstanding in this little group of eighteen men who were to board one particular plane—a 'stick' each little group was called.

Staff Sergeant [Earl D.] Williams, [with Company H] a native of New York City, was the jumpmaster, and I found him to be a very intelligent and charming youth. It was he who would be the last to enter the plane, and the first to leave it—dangling in midair from a parachute.

"The other man was a native of my home state—soldier [Private First Class Thomas A.] Horne, from Oakdale, Louisiana. Underneath his 'war paint' he was a fine looking young man, built like an ox, and possessed a keen sense of humor. He knew my hometown well and even had a few friends in common with me. As he prepared to board the plane, I gave him a slap on the shoulder and shouted to him, 'Happy landing, soldier!'

"I trust I shall never forget his response. With a smile on his face, and a wave of his hand he said, 'Some of us won't come back colonel, but we're going to win! They can't stop us!'"[67]

Captain William Nation, the regimental S-1, was a member of Colonel Lindquist's stick. "I was in the middle of the ship to follow our assembly light out the door so I could be right near to take reports. Across from me was the colonel's driver who had never made a jump before. He weighed about 230 pounds and had quite a bit of guts to go through with it. Nevertheless, he was there. Down from him was another boy with two pigeons--the best that the army had. They had been flown over the channel and released many times and know their way back from the invasion area. Along in other planes we had two photographers with movie cameras and two newspaper writers. You can't imagine how complete and accurate this thing was set up."[68]

Sergeant Bud Warnecke and his Company B squad boarded their assigned plane with Captain Royal Taylor, the company commander and the stick's jumpmaster. Warnecke helped his heavily laden men climb into the plane and then climbed aboard. "A few minutes before takeoff, the battalion commander's runner came to the plane with a bicycle and cargo chute attached. He informed us that Colonel [Herbert] Batcheller wanted us to drop the cycle into Normandy so he would have transportation. We had our plane full of bundles, but Captain Taylor said okay."[69]

The 508th Parachute Infantry Regiment would be guided to the drop zone in Normandy by its three battalion pathfinder teams, which would jump at 1:38 a.m., thirty minutes prior to the arrival of the regiment's first serial. Each battalion pathfinder team would set up a Eureka transponder and automatic direction finder (ADF) equipment and would mark the drop zone with lights in the shape of a "T".

In all practice and combat jumps, each plane and its stick were designated with a "chalk" number, which was used to identify its place in the formation of a serial. A serial is a group of planes typically carrying a battalion, but also were used to designate an element as small as the three regimental pathfinder teams. The three plane 508th pathfinder team serial would be designated as Number 5.

Chalk 16, the 1st Battalion pathfinder team, consisted of 2nd Lieutenants Elmer R. Stull (Company B) and Robert J. Weaver (Company C); Technician Fifth Grade Paul Demciak (Company B medic); Corporal Roy L. Smith (Company A); Privates First Class John T. Barkley (Headquarters Company, 1st Battalion), Theodore F. Bossert (Company C), Cipriano Gamez (Company C), John Sivetz (Headquarters Company, 1st Battalion), Wilburn L. Stutler (Company B), and Nicholas Trevino (Company B); and Privates A. B. Cannon (Company A), Donald E. Krause (Company B), Thomas W. Lindsey, (Company C), Willie E. Smith (Company A), and James H. Weinerth (Company B). In addition, the security assigned to the 1st Battalion pathfinder team from the 504th Parachute Infantry Regiment was composed of Private First Class William J. Hannigan (Company H, 504th); and Privates William F. Lee (Company D, 504th), Joseph H. Manfredi (Company E, 504th) and Cicero J. Parchman (Company G, 504th). Captain Neal McRoberts (Company F, 505th), the commander of the 82nd Provisional Pathfinder Company would jump with and lead this team.

Chalk 17, the 2nd Battalion pathfinder team, was composed of 2nd Lieutenants Elbert F. Hamilton (Company D) and Lloyd L. Polette, Jr. (Company F); Sergeant Robert V. Barbiaux (Company D); Corporal Ernest J. King (Company F); Privates First Class Murray E. Daly (Company D), Carl W. Jones (Company E), Robert L. Seale (Company F); and Privates Robert Andreas (Company E), John G. Gerard (Company F), Frederick J. Infanger (Company E), Howard Jessup (Headquarters Company, 2nd Battalion), Stanton H. Mesenbrink (Company E), Beverly J. Moss (Company D), John P. Perdue (Company D), and Norman C. Willis (Company E). The 2nd Battalion team's security would be provided by 2nd Lieutenant Thomas A. Murphy (Headquarters Company, 3rd Battalion, 504th); and Privates Joseph A. Byrne (Company H, 504th), Nick Forkapa (Company I, 504th), Eddie H. Livingston (Company I, 504th), and John P. Ternosky (Company I, 504th).

The 3rd Battalion pathfinder team, Chalk 18, consisted of 2nd Lieutenants Edward J. Czepinski (Company H) and Gene H. Williams (Headquarters Company, 3rd Battalion); Technician Fifth Grade Francis M. Lamoureux (Company G); Corporal Charles F. Calvert (Company I); Privates First Class Warren C. Jeffers (Company G), Arnold H. Martin (Company H), Fayette O. Richardson (Company H), Charles H. Rogers (Headquarters Company, 3rd Battalion), and John E. Sternesky (Company I); and Privates Walter W. Harrelson (Company H); Ralph W. Nicholson (Company G), Eric Stott (Headquarters Company, 3rd Battalion), and Roscoe H. Walker (Company I). Privates John J. Baldassar (Company H, 504th), Hal A. Murdock (Company I, 504th), Henry S. Pawlings (Company G, 504th), and John Rigapoulos (Company H, 504th) would provide security for the 3rd Battalion team.

The three planes transporting the 508th pathfinder teams departed the airfield at North Witham on time. The serial crossed southern England, flew out over the

English Channel and then turned east to approach the west coast of the Cotentin Peninsula. As they neared the coastline, Private Infanger, a Company E trooper with the 2nd Battalion pathfinder team, heard the order to stand up and hook up. "We had ten more minutes to go. My legs were asleep from sitting with all of that equipment on for two hours. After we checked equipment and sounded off, there was nothing to do but stand and wait. I kept looking out the window to see what France looked like."[70]

BACK IN ENGLAND, LIEUTENANT COLONEL WESLEY LEEPER, with the Eighth Air Force, witnessed the awe inspiring spectacle of the takeoff of just a part of the huge armada bound for Normandy. "Takeoff time was set for 11:15 p.m., but according to my watch the first plane, piloted by the [313th Troop Carrier] Group commanding officer, Colonel [James J.] Roberts, pulled out at 11:13. One by one, each of the giant planes took off, until seventy-two were in the air over our heads. The entire time consumed in takeoff was twenty-five minutes, which I thought was very good. The planes maneuvered over our heads until the last ship had left the ground, and their red and green wing lights made a beautiful picture as they soared over us. Gradually they disappeared in the distance, and we knew the long awaited invasion was on. I said a little prayer for them as they passed from our view."[71]

Shortly after takeoff, Sergeant Bud Warnecke, with Company B, turned his thoughts to the mission that lay ahead. "As our plane joined the formation before crossing the channel, I thought about what guys from the 505th had told us about what it would be like jumping into combat. I thought about where and how we were to assemble. I reminded myself of the sign and countersign, 'Flash' and 'Thunder' and the cricket issued. I reminded Captain Taylor to release the parapack bundles under the C-47 when the green light came on. There wasn't much talking among the troops, but a lot of smoking. I knew all the men prone to airsickness had taken preventative pills before we took off."[72]

Lieutenant Woodrow Millsaps, the platoon leader of the 3rd Platoon of Company B, looked out of the open doorway as his plane rose into the night sky. "We had taken off in a 'Vee of Vees' formation, three planes at a time. The aircraft formed their final formation in the air and as far as you could see, there was nothing but planes moving along. Indeed, it was a beautiful sight."[73]

After his plane was airborne, Lieutenant Malcolm Brannen, commanding Headquarters Company, 3rd Battalion, looked down the aisle at the faces of the troopers in the plane. "The men began to smoke and a few talked. I spoke a few words to [Staff] Sergeant [Warren] Peak and to Corporal King S. Burke, one of the battalion intelligence section noncommissioned officers, who was number fifteen in our stick. Then I tried to settle in and sleep."[74]

Sergeant Bill Call, a squad leader with the 2nd Platoon of Company B, was jumping last and sat near the cockpit of the C-47 carrying his stick. "As it got darker, there was no light in the fuselage where we were all sitting. We all lit up and all you could see were these red [glows made by the burning] cigarettes. Nobody was talking, just the hum of the motors on that C-47.

"I had heard and read that you could smell fear. In that plane, you could smell it. It was a pungent odor—sweat, worry, concern, and fear."[75]

Private First Class Frank McKee, with Company F, was jumping number two in his stick. "I sat near the door next to Lieutenant [Arthur F.] Snee, who sat right in the door[way]. I was the next man in; which let me see a good deal on the way over even though it was night; I could make out the channel. It was very quiet. I don't think, well there might have been some [who were] worried, no doubt about it, but some guys actually fell asleep and other guys just sat waiting for the jump, like we did on many jumps in training."[76]

Sergeant Bud Warnecke, with Company B, stood in the doorway of the plane with his company commander along with a bicycle and a cargo chute put aboard the plane for use by the battalion commander as transportation after landing in Normandy. "We reached the English Channel and Captain Taylor had the troops stand up and hook up. In case we were shot down we would have a chance to get out. In the middle of the channel we looked out the door on a beautiful moonlit night at a sight no one will ever see again. Ships, so many ships it looked as if you could walk from England to France without getting your feet wet.

"About this time, Captain Taylor or I asked, 'What the hell are we going to do with that damn bicycle?' Simultaneously, we kicked it into the channel without hooking up its chute."[77]

As the mighty armada flew the 508 relentlessly toward its rendezvous with combat, Staff Sergeant George Christ, the communications section leader, with Headquarters Company, 2nd Battalion sat alone with his thoughts inside his plane. "It was dark. The plane was crossing the channel, flying toward France. The men in my platoon, with their faces blackened, were trying to doze, get some rest. It had been a long day, and we were about to experience war firsthand. Looking out the window, I could see other planes and was reflecting on my life in the military and all that led up to this point."[78]

Meanwhile, the three planes transporting the regiment's pathfinder teams passed over the west coast of the Cotentin Peninsula. In the plane carrying the 2nd Battalion pathfinder team, Private Fred Infanger and the rest of his stick were hooked and ready to jump as the three planes flew over St.-Sauveur-le-Vicomte. "With about six minutes to go, the flak and tracers started hitting and sounded like hail on a tin roof. Then the ship started to bounce around, and I thought 'this is it.' Then that green light came on and I saw the guy in front going out. When I reached the door and started to go out, the plane felt like it went on its side. As a result, I came in with it and had to reach for the side of the door and pull myself out. When I got out, I saw flak and tracers coming up and the whole plane seemed to be lit up. I forgot about the opening shock and didn't check the canopy—but just slipped [the parachute risers] fast—cause those 'Heinie' bullets sounded too damn close. All I thought of on the way down was that those bastards were just waiting for us, because those machine guns were all over. I finally landed in a small weedy orchard, after coming [down] through a small tree. Half the chute stayed in it and the other half came down over me, which included the suspension lines. After I untangled myself I got out a grenade and assembled my rifle and laid them next to me. I cut one leg strap and started to unbuckle the other when I heard someone coming through a hedgerow. I halted him and he was a trooper. He covered for me while I finished getting out of my harness. We moved out from there and ran into seven other radar men from different battalions. There were three 2nd Battalion men including myself. Our [2nd Battalion] radar section landed between Ètienville and Picauville."[79]

The three 508th pathfinder sticks landed southeast of the drop zone. Tracers crisscrossed the night sky as intense German small arms and machine gun fire raked the descending pathfinders. After landing, many of the pathfinders came under machine gun fire, pinning some of them down. Hedgerows bordering fields and orchards separated members of the sticks from one another.

After landing, Lieutenant Bob Weaver could find only a few of the men of his 1st Battalion pathfinder stick. "The rest were on the other side of the road and couldn't get back across, since the Jerries are firing a FPL [final protective line[80]] down it."[81]

Lieutenant Weaver and Captain Neal McRoberts, the commander of the 82nd Provisional Pathfinder Company, and the few men with them were only able to set up a BUPS beacon and two lights. The 1st and 2nd Battalion Eurekas were not able to be put into action.

Technician Fifth Grade Francis M. Lamoureux, a Eureka operator with the 3rd Battalion pathfinder team, jumped number four in the stick. His parachute only oscillated three times before he landed in soft dirt in an apple orchard about a mile southeast of the drop zone and just east of the village of Picauville. "The Germans were patrolling a dirt road right outside [of the apple orchard] and they were shooting. When we landed, we weren't there even a minute on the ground when we had tracer bullets going right across over our heads."[82]

Lamoureux quickly got out of his parachute harness and checked his Eureka set to make sure it was undamaged. "All of a sudden, Lieutenant Gene Williams [with Headquarters Company, 3rd Battalion and the 3rd Battalion pathfinder team] came over to me. He was right in back of me [in the stick]. He got out of his chute fast.

"He said, 'Lamoureux, are you OK?'

"'Yeah.'

"The next thing you know, [Private First Class Fayette O.] Richardson [the other operator carrying a backup Eureka], who was in front of me [in the stick]—he was there. Then Sergeant [Robert V.] Barbiaux [Company D and the

2nd Battalion pathfinder team] was there. So there were four of us and then finally the others.

"So the first thing that Williams said, 'How's your Eureka set? Is it OK?'

"I said, 'Yes, I don't think there's anything wrong with it. I had a nice soft landing. Everything looks OK. Do you want me to test it?'

"He said, 'No, wait a while. Don't start sending a signal yet. Barbiaux and I are going to reconnoiter and see what kind of DZ we have here—check our position. Hold still here. Just wait until we come back.' Barbiaux and Lieutenant Gene Williams took off and went to see if they could find a little farmhouse or something. Finally, they came back and said, 'We're not going to find any place better than this. We don't have time to move anyway. We've got to send a signal. Start sending the signal.'

"Richardson had crawled over to me and he had his set. The two of us were side by side. I had my Eureka set and he had his Eureka set. So Williams said, 'Lamoureux, you send the signal.'"[83]

Lamoureux immediately got his Eureka working to guide the 3rd Battalion serial. The enemy fire was so intense where the 508th pathfinders landed, that Lamoureux's Eureka was the only one in operation among the three teams.

As the planes carrying the 82nd Airborne Division approached the Cotentin Peninsula, Sergeant Delbert Z. "Zane" Schlemmer, a nineteen year old forward observer with the 81mm Mortar Platoon, Headquarters Company, 2nd Battalion, had a good view of the armada from his position in the plane transporting his stick. "The only lights that I saw were several glows of cigarettes. From where I was, next to the cockpit bulkhead, by standing I could see past the pilot through the cockpit windshield, the blue wing light tips of the formations stacked ahead of us in our serials. After flying over the dark waters of the channel for some time, and then a left turn, I saw two small blacked out islands appearing off our left wing. I later learned that these were the Guernsey Islands, off the coast of France. Soon thereafter, our plane crossed the French sea coast, and though it was dark, we could see the roads, the fields, some small houses, which stood out in a reddish brown color. We then stood and hooked up our parachutes to the static lines and arranged our equipment in order to be prepared to jump, should any problems arise."[84]

Lieutenant Malcolm Brannen, the commander of Headquarters Company, 3rd Battalion, was jumping number sixteen and at the front of the plane when he heard a commotion at the rear of the plane. "Later, I found out that when we had passed between Jersey and Guernsey islands and we had received the twenty minutes to drop warning, one private, [Private First Class John H.] Calhoun said to our jumpmaster, Captain [Alton] Bell, 'My chute has broken open.' So, in the brief space of less than twenty minutes, Calhoun was relieved of his equipment and chute—the rear of which had broken open—and another parachute substituted and all of the equipment replaced."[85]

CHAPTER 2

"NO IDEA WHERE THE HELL I WAS"

In an apple orchard east of Picauville, the 3rd Battalion pathfinder team's lone Eureka transponder triggered about twelve minutes prior to the scheduled drop of the lead serial. The BUPS beacon set up by the 1st Battalion pathfinder team triggered when the first serial was about twenty minutes away. The 1st Battalion pathfinder team also turned on two lights. Some of the hard pressed pathfinders were separated from one another by the hedgerows and being raked by German machine gun and small arms fire, when they began to hear the low sound of aircraft approaching in the distance.

The first serial, Number 20, consisting of thirty-six aircraft transporting the 2nd Battalion, led the 508th Parachute Infantry Regiment into Normandy, with Headquarters and Headquarters Company, 2nd Battalion in Chalks 1-9, followed by Company D in Chalks 10-18, then Company E in Chalks 19-27, and finally Company F in Chalks 28-36. Coming in over the western coast of the Cotentin Peninsula, Sergeant Zane Schlemmer, with his Headquarters Company, 2nd Battalion stick, was already standing and hooked up, ready to jump. "The red light had come on. Then, suddenly, and without any warning at all, our plane was engulfed in the middle of a cloud, or dense white fog. This really concerned us, because all we could see outside the plane was white; we couldn't even see the blue wing lights at the end of our plane's wings. This, of course, caused the pilots of the planes and the formation to disperse in order to avoid any midair collisions with the other planes in the formation.

"The time seemed endless with us standing there, going through the cloud or the white fog, until suddenly the cloud cleared just as rapidly as it had engulfed us. It was at that time that we started to experience the German flak and small arms fire, which, when it hit the plane, sounded very similar to gravel crunching on a metal roof (it was quite an unmistakable sound, and one which once you have heard, you remember it forever). Our equipment check proceeded. We then closed the stick up to exit just as fast as possible, as we awaited the green light during this flak period. During this time, I had time for two personal thoughts. The first was to get the hell out of the plane just as rapidly as possible, since I was the last one in the stick to jump, and secondly, I found myself asking myself what I had done to find myself in such a predicament."[1]

46

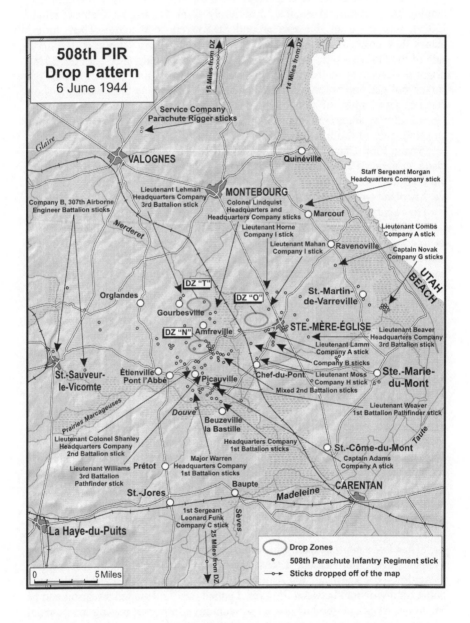

508th PIR
Drop Pattern
6 June 1944

Service Company
Parachute Rigger sticks

15 Miles from DZ

14 Miles from DZ

Glaire

VALOGNES

Quinéville

Staff Sergeant Morgan
Headquarters Company stick

Lieutenant Lehman
Headquarters Company
3rd Battalion stick

MONTEBOURG

Company B, 307th Airborne
Engineer Battalion sticks

Colonel Lindquist
Headquarters and
Headquarters Company sticks

Marcouf

Merderet

Lieutenant Horne
Company I stick

Lieutenant Combs
Company A stick

Lieutenant Mahan
Company I stick

Ravenoville

Captain Novak
Company G sticks

UTAH BEACH

DZ "T"

Orglandes

Gourbesville

DZ "O"

St.-Martin-
de-Varreville

DZ "N" Amfreville

STE.-MÈRE-ÉGLISE

Lieutenant Beaver
Headquarters Company
3rd Battalion stick

Lieutenant Lamm
Company A stick

Company B sticks

St.-Sauveur-
le-Vicomte

Étienville
Pont l'Abbé

Picauville

Chef-du-Pont

Lieutenant Moss
Company H stick

Mixed 2nd Battalion sticks

Ste.-Marie-
du-Mont

Prairies Marcageuses

Douve

Beuzeville
la Bastille

Lieutenant Weaver
1st Battalion Pathfinder stick

Lieutenant Colonel Shanley
Headquarters Company
2nd Battalion stick

Headquarters Company
1st Battalion sticks

St.-Côme-du-Mont

Lieutenant Williams
3rd Battalion
Pathfinder stick

Prétot

Major Warren
Headquarters Company
1st Battalion sticks

Baupte

Captain Adams
Company A stick

CARENTAN

St.-Jores

Madeleine

Taute

1st Sergeant
Leonard Funk
Company C stick

Sèves

25 Miles from DZ

La Haye-du-Puits

Drop Zones

508th Parachute Infantry Regiment stick

Sticks dropped off of the map

0   5 Miles

As the 2nd Battalion serial emerged from the clouds, enemy antiaircraft fire, ranging from 20mm to 88mm, most likely from Gemischte Flak Abteilung 153(v), rose up from the area around St.-Sauveur-le-Vicomte. Then, as the planes flew onward and approached the area around Pont l'Abbé on the north side of the Douve River, Kompanie 3, Panzerjäger Abteilung 352, of the 352nd Infantrie Division, unleashed devastating fire from nine 37mm rapid fire antiaircraft guns mounted on motorized vehicles, known as flakwagons. A short distance later, most of the thirty-seven machine guns of Pioniere Bataillon 191and 20mm antiarcraft guns of Flak Kompanie 191 of the 91st Luftlande Division, opened fire from positions in the vicinity of Picauville.

Private First Class Harold O. I. Kulju was one of the troopers in the lead plane, designated as Chalk 1. "As we approached our DZ we were reminded of the Fourth of July at home. The tracers and white hot shell fragments filled the air. My plane was being hit up front with ack-ack."[2]

The twenty-six year old battalion commander, Lieutenant Colonel Thomas J. B. Shanley, stood in the door of Chalk 1's C-47, searching for landmarks below as tracers from German antiaircraft guns crisscrossed the moonlit sky. "The planes started taking evasive action due to the flak. I threw an A-4 radio bundle out—the chute on it failed, its contents were smashed. My battalion assembly light in it was also smashed."[3]

Shanley followed the equipment bundle, jumping into the night sky lit by tracers and explosions from enemy antiaircraft and machine gun fire. Private First Class Kulju, jumping number six in the stick, pressed against the trooper in front as he shuffled toward the door, and then went out into the maelstrom. "Tracers were coming up everywhere. There were so many tracers going through my chute I was afraid they would set it on fire."[4]

Kulju landed near a German gun emplacement. "I taped my trench knife to my boot and had difficulty getting it. I tore it out and cut all my straps and ran to a hedgerow a short distance away. Immediately, two Germans approached me on the opposite side of the hedgerow. When they reached my position they ducked and one rose up with his rifle. I had unscrewed the cap on my Gammon grenade and when his shoulders appeared I tossed it just as he fired. The bullet went through the crotch of my outer pair of pants and the concussion from the grenade knocked me out. When I came to, I could hear the two Germans moaning as my grenade had done its job. I tasted gunpowder for a long time afterwards.

"Then I was approached by an American trooper. We talked and then noticed someone else approaching. I challenged him with 'Flash' and he replied 'Thunder', so I knew he was American. Next, there was an orange ball and a bullet hit my helmet between the eyes. I rolled over and started swearing and he fired once more and the bullet went through my hip pocket tearing my maps of France. He then quit firing as my swearing registered.

"I then dove into dry brush as two Germans were approaching. My gun wasn't loaded, as we had orders not to load up until we organized. My knife was under me and I dared not move as the Germans were standing over me. I had to go to the bathroom, so I went. I guess the Germans thought they were looking at blood, so they moved on."[5]

Captain Charles S. Cartwright and the crew of aircraft number 42-93002 were transporting Headquarters Company, 2nd Battalion's Chalk 7. "On seeing the stick leave the lead ship we gave the green light, but our stick did not jump. The jumpmaster, Captain [George] Simonds [2nd Battalion S-3], instructed the crew chief to tell the pilot that the plane was too low, and that he would not jump his men at that height. The intercom was damaged, and the crew chief could not reach the pilot through it, so [he] passed the message to the navigator, who relayed it to the pilot. As soon as the message was received, we went up to eight hundred feet indicated, made a right turn, and began a second pass at the DZ."[6]

Meanwhile, the other seven sticks of Headquarters Company, 2nd Battalion, jumped when the green lights were turned on in their respective aircraft. Lieutenant Edward V. Ott was the platoon leader of the Light Machine Gun Platoon and the jumpmaster of his stick. "The drop was doomed to disaster when the C-47 pilot began to take evasive action to avoid heavy flak. He gave us the green light when the plane was in a climbing attitude as the engines roared at top speed. When I jumped, the prop blast was so severe that it tore off my pack and equipment, so when I hit the ground, the only weapon I had was my jump knife."[7]

Sergeant Paul Sands was the pusher or last man in his stick. "The last three of us in the stick were going out the door as the plane was in a tight left bank and heading home. I landed on the east side of a German motor pool. We assembled on Captain Chester Graham, [commanding officer of Headquarters Company, 2nd Battalion] the ranking officer."[8]

Sergeant Zane Schlemmer stepped through the doorway of his plane and began falling through the tracers coming up past him when his parachute opened with a violent shock. "My helmet had been jarred forward over my face and I had to push it back in order to see. The sky seemed alive with pink, orange, and red tracer bullets, which would arc up gracefully, then snap by with little tugs as they went through the parachute canopy. In the distance to the east, I could see a sizeable fire burning on the ground. This must have been Ste.-Mère-Église, although I didn't know it at the time. I hit in a hedgerow, coming up with very sore bruised ribs from the impact of all the equipment that I had strapped onto my body. I quickly cleared my chute harness assembly, assembled my rifle, and tucked my little revolver away. The moon, at that time was behind broken clouds and the reflection of the tracer bullets on these low hanging clouds created a reddish sky glow against which I could see a small lane next to the field and a small building with a tile roof.

"As I went from the field out into the lane, a very large orange ball of fire appeared overhead, coming in a steeply descending easterly line of flight. It looked very much like a meteor or a meteorite. But, it was accompanied by the roaring whine of two runaway, full power plane engines. Obviously, a troop carrier going down, and my immediate thoughts were of the troopers and of the crew who might still be aboard.

"I was alone. I had no idea where the hell I was, other than being in France."[9]

Just behind Headquarters and Headquarters Company in the 2nd Battalion serial were the nine planes transporting Company D. Lieutenant Norman MacVicar, the company commander, was the jumpmaster of Chalk 10. Private First Class Frank L. Staples was jumping third in that stick. "The plane was pitching so that we could scarcely keep our feet when we stood up. They got a direct hit on the left wing just as I left the door. At least that is what the man behind me said when I saw him two days later. The Heinies were waiting for us, and as they say, were throwing the kitchen sink at us. It looked like the Fourth of July multiplied a thousand times. They machine gunned us with tracers all the way to the ground."[10]

Lieutenant Lynn Tomlinson, the platoon leader of the 3rd Platoon, Company D, stood in the doorway of the Chalk 16 plane with his stick pressed up behind him ready to jump. "The antiaircraft fire and small arms fire was still intense. We could see it coming, because of the machine gun fire. About every fifth bullet was a tracer. There were four not-lighted bullets for every one that was lit up. By the number coming up, I knew that the fire had to be terrific. We received the green light to jump, and I led my troops out of the plane, and we coasted toward Normandy soil. Upon hitting the ground and getting out of my parachute, I looked at my watch. The time was 2:10 a.m., June 6th, 1944. I was on French soil, just where was a complete mystery to me."[11]

Private First Class William M. Sawyer, the third man in Tomlinson's stick, wasn't as lucky as he descended onto a field to the east. "I looked down and I saw Germans running around on the ground, shooting my buddies. They ran over to me and I played possum. I hung there like I had already been hit because I landed in a tree. I just laid still. Finally, some of A Company landed right on top of us, and it was too many troopers and those Krauts took off. But they were spraying the chute and I was hanging some fifteen feet below the chute.

"Finally when they left, I got my trench knife loose from my leg—it was strapped to my leg—and I had to cut the risers because I knew I had to get out of there. I cut one riser and I swung out, then I cut the other riser, and I dropped to the ground some five or six feet. I had a landmine on my chest and it knocked the breath out of me and I had to lay there for a couple of minutes from the pain. Then I remember I got the [parachute harness] straps off and I loaded my rifle, because we were not allowed to load our rifles. They said there would be no firing on the drop zone until daylight; that we would have to use cold steel.

"I laid there for a few minutes and looked around, trying to figure out where I was, and I heard something coming through the bushes. I said, 'Flash,' and he came back with 'Th-th-th-th' and I said, 'Oh, come on over here, Sergeant [Charles D.] Bray.' It was Sergeant Charlie Bray, our mortar squad sergeant. He hugged me and I hugged him."[12]

Private First Class Billy B. McClure, was supposed to jump number twelve in his Company D stick, but had traded places with a superstitious trooper who was supposed to jump number thirteen. "The ack-ack was so bad that the plane I was on tried to go under it. As soon as my chute opened, I hit a tree (on the first oscillation) and broke a rib and [was] just about knocked out. I rolled into a ditch and my chute settled on a stump. I was in a small field surrounded by hedgerows. A German machine gunner in a nest in the corner of the field shot the stump to bits. I guess it looked like the chute came down on top of me. I remember how bright it was that night when the clouds moved and the moon shone out, illuminating the field. Every time the moon went behind a cloud, I would inch backwards. It took me about an hour to get off that field. I got out intact, except for a bullet hole in my canteen. I wiped out the machine gun nest with a Gammon grenade and my rifle, and I began picking up people as I went along."[13]

Another Company D trooper, Private Frank Haddy, landed in a field all alone. "Then I heard footsteps; I was scared shitless until I heard him call. It was [Private First Class Paul E.] Webb from our stick. He came over and helped me get untangled from all my gear. When I got up, I saw I had lost my K-rations I jumped with. Such was the opening shock of my chute, my pockets had burst open."[14]

One Company D trooper, Private First Class Frederick J. Carden, cut his hand with his knife while cutting off his parachute harness. "I was so scared I was not aware of it at the time."[15]

The next nine planes in the serial carried Company E, commanded by Lieutenant Eugene C. Hetland, the jumpmaster of Chalk 19. As that stick prepared to jump, Private Trino F. Maldonado's parachute broke open from its pack and spilled onto the plane's floor. "I stuffed the chute back into the pack and hooked up and stood in the door. The chute fell out again."[16]

As his stick exited the plane, the troopers last saw Maldonado on the floor of the plane trying to stuff his parachute back into the pack. "I gathered it up in my arms and jumped out of the plane anyway."[17]

Prior to the jump, Private First Class Louis W. Yourkovich, with Company E, had been on his knees, looking out of the small window behind his seat. "I could see the flak from German guns hitting our wings. I could see holes being made and gasoline spewing over the wings. Our plane was going down quickly, really dropping. Finally, we were nearing our drop zone and ready to go. I shouted out my position and readiness, 'Number nine OK.'

"Suddenly an artillery shell burst right under the plane. The plane dropped two feet, leaving us in midair before the floor came back up to meet us. Some of the remarks were, 'Did you feel that?' Everyone was yelling, 'Let's get the hell out of here!'"[18]

From his position in the doorway of his aircraft, Lieutenant Barry E. Albright, the platoon leader of the 1st Platoon of Company E, could see that the tight formation of the serial was no longer intact as the planes emerged from the clouds. "By the time the area of the drop zone was reached, the aircraft were well scattered and were flying at excessive speeds and altitudes higher and lower than those ideal for jumping."[19]

Private Richard R. Hill was jumping second in Albright's stick. "The plane was bouncing and most of the men couldn't hook up to jump. They were thrown about on the floor of the plane. The sound of gunfire hitting the plane sounded like a hailstorm. My fear level was off the chart. I couldn't even speak. The night was black, with bright spotlights on each plane and on each man. As the moment came to jump, Lieutenant Albright was first. He hooked his chute and told his men to follow. I was second in line. On the way down I could see tracer bullets coming at him. I thought he got shot. Then they were shooting tracers by me. I landed in a big hackberry tree. My chute hung in the tree and only my knees and elbows were touching the ground. My chute had bullet holes in it."[20]

First Sergeant Ralph H. Thomas was the jumpmaster of his Company E stick. "My plane was bouncing around like a bucking bronco. Our pilot turned on the red light short of our destination and my stick (the jumpers in the plane) stood up and hooked up at my command. I ordered them to stand in the door and sound off. Each man called out his number all OK, meaning that he was hooked up and ready to jump.

"We could hardly stay on our feet the plane was bouncing around so much. Then the pilot turned on the green light and my stick followed me out the door into the night and the flak. Once out of the plane the night was very quiet and the flak not so near.

"We were very low when we jumped; about five hundred feet above the ground, just high enough for our chutes to open before we hit the ground. I had only a moment to check my feet and my equipment before landing. I landed in the corner of a cow pasture in tall thistles that made it impossible to see anything at ground level.

"As I lay on the ground getting out of my chute I heard footsteps coming toward me so I rolled over on my stomach, cocked my Tommy gun and waited breathlessly. Whatever was coming toward me was making plenty of noise against the brush and bushes and their pace was very steady. I was ready, tensely waiting and ready to fire.

"Then out of the night came a black and white milk cow that was as glad to see me as I was to see her. She walked right up and licked me in the face as I lay there. She did not want to leave me. Within a moment I was out of my chute; I stood up, arranged my equipment and listened for other sounds. The cow followed me to the fence, which I crawled through.

"I could hear footsteps on my left so I walked toward them and ran into one of my own men. It was strange, we had just separated from the plane, yet I was so glad to see him it was as if we had been apart for years.

"I asked him if he had seen any others from our stick and he said, 'No.' Then another man from the stick walked up and I sent him up a telephone pole to cut the wires. Within the next ten minutes, all eighteen men in my stick reported in and we started down a road in the direction of a firefight and burning buildings we could hear and see in the distance. The burning buildings lit up the sky in a bright orange glow—we were at war."[21]

When another Company E trooper, Sergeant Ralph E. Cook, stood up to hook up his static line he had noticed that the floor was slick with vomit. "The red light turned green, and somehow I managed to stumble out the door. It was almost a relief. Then came the shock of the chute opening. Something hit me in the face—I never did know what it was—some of my equipment pulling off, probably. Everything seemed to get quiet, and I looked around for a split second. The air was full of planes and the ground was pitch-black. I could see the tracers coming up. I tried to tell when I got close to the ground, but it was so dark that you couldn't tell until you hit the ground. And when I hit, I hit hard and rolled around. For a few minutes, I didn't think I would be able to move. But a C-47 came by about that time, low overhead, and its engines were running wild and it was on fire.

"I started struggling about that time to get out of the parachute harness. Then, I heard a burp gun on the other side of the hedgerow that I was behind, and that really got me in action. In the small field I was in, I could hear some scurrying around and people on the other side of the hedgerow moving around. We'd been issued crickets (that kids used to play with) to identify each other in the dark and I started moving and popping my cricket. I found a guy I didn't know. He was on the other side of the hedgerow, and from another company. Together, we started moving around. We found a small group with an officer in charge. Even in the dark, we realized we weren't where we were supposed to be. Later, we found out that our pathfinder groups had been dropped south of our drop zone."[22]

Corporal Robert B. Newhart was a member of one of the Company E 60mm mortar squads. "The plane tilted downward, gaining speed at the green light. [Private First Class Joseph M.] Joe Rendina and I landed in a quiet square field next to a dirt road. We stayed at the road to block any passage until first light."[23]

The troopers of Company F jumped from the last nine planes of the serial. Company F was commanded by Captain Francis Flanders. Private Dwayne T. Burns was the company headquarters assistant radio operator. "Flak was getting heavy as we stood waiting for the green light. Now the ship's being hit from all sides. The noise was awesome. The roar of the engines, the flak hitting the wings and fuselage, and everyone was yelling, 'Let's go!' but still the green light did not come on. The ship was bouncing like something gone wild. I heard a ticking sound as machine gun rounds walked across the wings. It was hard to stand up and troopers were falling down and getting up; some were getting sick. Of all the training we had, there was not anything that prepared us for this. As bad as we wanted out, I knew we must wait for the green light. But if we waited too long, we'd be back over water. I could see tracers sweeping by in a graceful slow motion arc. Flak was knocking holes in the wings, and I prayed that none of them came up through the bottom of the ship where I was standing.

"Then the red light went out and the green snapped on. We shuffled out the door into the dark fresh air. I was amazed at how quiet it was outside. We were to jump at six hundred feet but it seemed to be much higher than that. I heard the sound as the ship faded away. I heard gunfire, but it all sounded far away. I seemed to be far south of our drop zone. It looked like I was on the outer edge of all the action. All was quiet to the south, but to the north, I saw tracers arcing across the sky. And in spite of all of this going on, I thought of how beautiful they appeared. I heard a plane that sounded out of control. Looking back over my shoulder, I could see one of our C-47's far north of me going down, the left hand engine was trailing fire all the way back to the empennage. The engine was revving up to full power and seemed to scream in protest as I watched it dive into the tree. I wondered if the troopers and all the crew got out all right.

"I looked around, I felt as though I was just hanging up there all by myself, just one big target for someone to shoot. I couldn't see my stick, but I knew they were out there somewhere drifting down in the dark. I looked down. It seemed quiet. I could just make out rows of trees. I thought to myself, 'This is France, and now I'm in combat. This is for real.'

"I landed in a long narrow field with two anti-glider poles in it, and I hit hard and rolled over on my back, tangled in my shroud lines. I was all alone. No one else had landed in the field with me. It was very quiet.

"I saw one chute go down behind the trees on the other side of the field, so I knew that I wasn't not completely alone. I'd landed on good solid ground."[24]

Lying in the grass, Burns worked to get out of his parachute harness. "In my mind's eye, I could see Germans running with fixed bayonets to kill me, and I had trouble with the harness buckles. To say I was scared is an understatement. I reached down to my right ankle and pulled out my trench knife and stuck it in the ground beside me. I thought at least a knife is better than no weapon at all. Then, taking my time I unsnapped my harness, untangled myself from the shroud lines, stood up and ran to the hedgerow where I had seen the chute go down. 'Flash' was our code word and countersign was 'Thunder'. We also had been given a child's cricket snapper. One snap was to be answered by two snaps...or was it the other way around. 'Oh hell,' I muttered. Just snap the damn thing a few times.

"In reply, I got, 'Look out, I'm coming over.'

"He sounded good to me, and I said, 'Come on.'

"We went back across the field I had landed in and found some troopers coming up the hedgerow. I didn't know who they were but right now it didn't make any difference as long as I was with somebody."[25]

Pressed up behind the jumpmaster in his aircraft, Private First Class Frank McKee, with Company F, was waiting for the green light. "Lieutenant Arthur Snee was the first man in our stick. I was second. I was an assistant squad leader at this time and [Sergeant] John Dobransky was the squad leader, the last man in the stick. Being the second man in the stick, I could see out the door quite clearly. We flew right into the heavy flak. There was a loud burst and our plane pitched and yawed a bit and began to fly rough. The green light went on at this point, but Lieutenant Snee did not immediately go out. I think he was studying the ground looking for landmarks before jumping. I hollered, 'Let's go lieutenant!' and away we went. We were quite low at this point, probably about six hundred feet. We dove right into the tracers coming up at us. My chute popped open and I was soon on the ground. I had a good landing in spite of about one hundred pounds of chute and equipment.

"I landed in a dry field and quickly shed my chute. There was machine gun fire coming from the field, but it was not on me. I immediately heard someone coming toward me and he identified himself as Lieutenant [Hoyt T.] Goodale—one of our best lieutenants. More guys, including Lieutenant Snee gathered around.

"Lieutenant Goodale spied an equipment bundle light on a nearby hill and had us head for there. We got off that field in the dark and up that hill without losing a man. What a relief. On the hill, Lieutenant Goodale sent some men out in different directions to cover an area, pick up some men, and return to our temporary CP."[26]

Company F trooper, Private Ralph Burrus, Jr., was fortunate to land on the opposite side of a hedgerow from a German machine gun position that was shooting at other troopers who were descending nearby. "I took a hand grenade and lobbed it over the top of the hedgerow, which was maybe ten or twelve feet high, and dropped it on the machine gun position."[27]

Just after the last of the serial jumped, German antiaircraft fire concentrated on the plane carrying Captain George Simonds and his Headquarters Company, 2nd Battalion stick as it made a second pass. The aircrew later stated that "the jumpmaster had come up to the cockpit to confer with the pilot, who said to him, 'Get the hell out, everyone except your stick has jumped.' During this second pass we were hit by explosive flak—probably 40mm—two rounds of which went through the plane; one round narrowly missed crew chief [Staff Sergeant Raymond H.] Farris, who was at that time in the door of the companionway, and the other went through the rear of the fuselage. Paratrooper number seventeen in the stick [Private Legrande T. Mangus] was hit by fragments of this flak, which detonated two of the hand grenades in his pouch, seriously injuring him. We went over the DZ again, and again the troops did not jump, although they received the signal.

"We turned for a third pass, and this time the navigator told the jumpmaster that there was going to be a forced landing. The stick went at once, and as it jumped the aircraft was near the DZ, a short distance south of it, going in a westerly direction at 750 feet altitude and 110-115 miles per hour. The injured paratrooper, number seventeen, did not jump.

"Immediately after the jump, both engines went out, either at once or so closely together that it made no difference. The pilot turned the plane 180 degrees to the right in an effort to reach the ocean; saw that he would be unable to do so, and made a farther 90 degree turn to the right (putting the aircraft on a southwesterly heading) hoping to reach the flooded area to the south of the DZ. The altitude was not sufficient to reach this area, so the crew took crash positions in the plane and it was set down in the available open field. On going in, it clipped a row of trees bordering the field. Both engines were on fire. A comparative smooth belly-landing was made, the plane came to a rest in the middle of the field, and the crew evacuated it with all speed. The wounded paratrooper got out by himself. The pilot, crew chief, and the radio operator carried the paratrooper, who had collapsed close to the plane, farther away, and then the pilot went back into the plane for a first aid kit and supplies. He recovered a kit, but was unable to reach anything else. Upon return to the paratrooper, the pilot found that he [Private Mangus] had his own morphine, and was asking to have it administered; this was done by the copilot and navigator.

"We then began to carry the paratrooper toward the hedge bordering the field, which offered the only cover close by. A short distance was traversed when the aircraft exploded. The paratrooper, now unconscious, was placed in concealment in the hedge, and about 02:45 we began traveling south in a zigzag line, looking for a place to hide out. About three-quarters of a mile from the plane, a dry ditch covered with brambles was found, and became the hideout for all of us."[28]

Six minutes behind Shanley's battalion, the second serial (Number 21) of the 508th, consisting of twenty-four planes carrying Force A Headquarters, the 508th's Headquarters and Headquarters Company, Service Company, and Company B (less the 3rd Platoon), 307th Airborne Engineer Battalion approached the area of the drop zone.

The first nine planes of the serial transported Force A Headquarters personnel in four C-47s, division artillery headquarters personnel in two aircraft, and 82nd Airborne Signal Company personnel in three planes. General James Gavin, the Force A commander, was the jumpmaster of the lead plane, Chalk 43. "We had studied very carefully by the time of flight, and in my case I knew that I was to jump seven and one half minutes after crossing the coastline. More significant however, was that after twelve minutes we went back over the English Channel. So we had to get out between that seven and a half minute period and twelve minutes to be near where we expected to be to do our fighting. While we went through the fog and finally came out at about seven minutes, there was nothing to be seen except a lot of flak and small arms. However, looking ahead, there was a wide river that seemed to turn off to the west. I knew that no river on the map [was] so wide; only the Douve and if it were the Douve it was in the wrong place. So it couldn't quite be it.

"Time was going by very quickly and small arms began to come up. [At] about eight minutes the green light went on. I took one last precious look at the ground, because once you hit the ground you can only see the edge around front of you. I gave the command, 'let's go' and out we went. I landed with a pretty loud thud in an apple orchard. I got out of my equipment, made my way to the hedgerow on the edge of the field, and ran into a Captain [Karl R.] Price of my G-2 office, who was rather slipping along the hedge on the other side."[29]

Most Force A Headquarters sticks dropped north of Drop Zone "N", astride the Merderet River, east of the 507th Parachute Infantry's Drop Zone "T".

The next nine planes in the serial carried the 508th's Headquarters and Headquarters Company and Service Company. Most of those sticks were dropped well north of the 508th drop zone, near the west side of the Merderet River and in the operational sector of the 507th Parachute Infantry Regiment.

Colonel Roy Lindquist jumped east of Amfreville from what he estimated to be an altitude of about 1,200 feet. "It was a good opening and a soft landing in about two feet of water. The light went up within ten minutes after hitting the ground. The area was open and marshy, and the assembly light could be seen for about six hundred yards. The assembly light worked well for about twenty minutes and then went out because of water soaking into the batteries. When the light went out I stayed there thirty minutes before we moved out. There was no light on the embankment; the light was in the center of the drop of regimental headquarters."[30]

Technician Fourth Grade Ralph Mann, with Headquarters Company, jumped number two behind Lindquist and landed alone in a field. "I got out of my chute as fast as I could, then went to a hedgerow and into another orchard in the next field. I saw someone and clicked my cricket, a small toy each of us had—you click once and the other GI responds with a double click. He didn't respond, but then I saw that he was another jumper and rushed over to him.

"It was [Private] William [J.] McKinnon, who was in my company, lying on the ground. He was nervous and trying to get out of his chute. I helped him.

"The two of us walked farther and picked up Captain James Klein, who was a medic, and a guy named [Technician Fourth Grade Clifford J. "Jim"] Campbell, from the intelligence department. In another field, we found a GI with an injured ankle and put him in a hedgerow. No one knew what to do, so I foolishly elected to be the leader. Then a blue flare hit the sky, our signal to reassemble on the light."[31]

Captain Bill Nation, the regimental S-1, was farther back in Lindquist's stick, about midway. "Right after the chute opened and I stopped being jerked about I looked down and saw the reflection of the moon in water. We were out over a river. I began to tug at the risers to try and slip to land, but I was coming down too fast and was too close to maneuver the chute very much. The closer I got I could see that it could be the swampy waters backed up by a river, or the area that could be flooded and which was flooded by the Germans.

"So with a last minute landing position I hit water knee deep and fell backwards into it half shocked, surprised pleasantly, and unable to get up. I could see tracer fire and hear machine gun and machine pistols firing at the men as they descended to the ground. As I lay there, I listened for movement of anybody in my direction and also for fire in my direction, but saw nor heard nothing.

"Grabbing my knife I began to cut myself out of the harness and the life jacket about my neck. I could already feel the harness tightening in the water and I could hear the machine pistols and enemy fire all around us firing steadily at others falling and already landed. I did not notice the cold water at all because everything was too hot. When I managed to get out of the harness I checked my two cases and bag that I brought down and my weapons. We were soaked."[32]

While awaiting assembly of his troopers, Colonel Lindquist dispatched small groups of troopers in a futile attempt to recover equipment bundles. "All of our equipment went into the water and went out of sight. We stumbled upon two bundles, but it was nothing that we could use."[33]

The plane carrying Staff Sergeant Worster Morgan and his regimental S-2 section dropped the stick far to the northeast of the drop zone. "All but two or three of the men in our stick assembled by a road [which led] into the small village of St. Marcouf, close to the channel coast."[34]

Major Dave Thomas was jumping number two behind Lieutenant Colonel Harry Harrison, the regimental executive officer. Major Thomas was the regimental surgeon and commanding officer of the medical detachment. "When we came out of the clouds, we were the only aircraft I could see in the sky! I thought, 'Oh Christ, here we have one bunch of troopers, and we get to fight the whole damn German army by ourselves.'

"I couldn't tell where we were and the pilot didn't know where he was either. So we kept flying around and looking. By this time, it was getting clear and we saw something. It looked like the Merderet River below. I said to Colonel Harrison, who was jumping ahead of me, 'That's the Merderet River. Let's get the hell out of this thing.' So we exited the aircraft. I landed in a field, an uneventful landing."[35] Thomas had landed east of the Merderet River, farther north than Colonel Lindquist.

Technician Fourth Grade Paul Bouchereau, a member of the regiment's medical detachment, landed in the same area as Major Thomas. "When I hit the ground there was not a single soul in sight, but in short order, about fifteen minutes, we had a group of about fifteen troopers. Directing us was a first lieutenant from the 507th Parachute Infantry Regiment."[36]

The parachute riggers of Captain James A. Dowling's Service Company were particularly unlucky as they were dropped far to the northwest, almost on top of the headquarters of Bataillon 1, Grenadier Regiment 1058, 91st Luftlande Division at Le Haut Gelay, just northeast of Valognes.

Sergeant Marcel Bollag was jumping number sixteen in Dowling's stick. "All of a sudden the flak came up real heavy. Our plane bounced up and down and took off from the formation to the left. I knew then that we were alone; no other plane was near us.

"We flew straight through the peninsula and soon hit the east coast. The pilot turned around and headed inland again. Flak came up very heavy and knocked out our jump light. The pilot then ordered us to jump by telephone.

"We got ready to leave the door. I had never been so glad to jump out before than this particular time. Our plane was hit rather heavily by machine gun fire. The bullets bounced off left and right of the door, but I got out. The opening shock was not bad at all. Maybe my thoughts were somewhere else. I looked around to see where I was. Machine guns were shooting at me, but I didn't get hit. I landed two hundred feet away from a house, which I found out later to be a German command post. The landing itself was rather good. I hit an electric wire with my arm, which did not hurt badly. I then came down on the road. I felt a little relieved.

"Immediately I slipped back on the side of the road near a hedgerow. My parachute was across the hedgerow in the next field. I started cutting myself out of the harness. By that time the machine guns were hammering away. One cannot mistake those machine guns as being German. You hear a short burst, 'Brrrrr, brrrrr, brrrrr.'"[37]

Another Service Company trooper, Technician Fifth Grade Carl H. Porter, came down as streams of tracer rounds crisscrossed the sky around him. "I was more concerned with the tracers piercing the chute above my head than I was in checking oscillation and where the chute and I were headed. Crashing through the branches of a large hedgerow tree and winding up dangling among the lower branches reminded me that it's always a good idea to check your landing position! By the time I had extricated myself from the harness and branches, three German soldiers (who had probably been responsible for the tracers through my canopy) materialized. I made a partial turn toward their shadowy figures, and as realization that I held an unloaded rifle electrified my brain; I dropped the Ml as if it were a white hot poker and responded to a harsh, 'Hande Hoche.'

"One of the Germans motioned me into the clearing that was encircled by hedgerows and as the moon brightened their figures I saw that one held a rifle and the other two machine pistols. The two with machine pistols took positions a few yards apart while the rifleman put his weapon down a safe distance away and proceeded to disarm me of my grenades, trench knife, bandoliers (which I had strapped around my thighs above my bulging patch pockets for better balance), a picture of my girlfriend Marly from my breast pocket, and literally everything else that would come off, including my musette bag, my watch, and—oh yes—the pocket knife that was carefully concealed in the 'secret' pocket near the collar of my jump jacket."[38]

The last six planes of the serial carried Company B (less the 3rd Platoon), 307th Airborne Engineer Battalion, which was attached to the 508th for the mission of demolition of the Douve River bridges. These troopers were veterans of the Sicily and Italy combat jumps. The company commander and jumpmaster of Chalk 39, Captain William H. Johnson, landed about a mile west of Gueutteville. "I joined with Lieutenant [Norman] MacVicar of the 2nd Battalion, 508 Infantry, and moved into position southeast of Gueutteville on high ground. I attempted to contact my company the remainder of the day on the SCR 300 radio."[39]

Four of Johnson's six sticks of engineers attached to the 508th were dropped far to the west of the drop zone, in the vicinity of St.-Sauveur-le-Vicomte when evidently the troop carrier pilots mistook the Douve River for the Merderet River. Lieutenant Alfred A. Cappa's Chalk 38 stick bailed out over the town. "I landed near the center of St.-Sauveur-le-Vicomte. Failing to find any of my stick before daylight, I was forced to hide. With the help of the kind French [townspeople] my chute was buried and I hid in the upstairs of a bicycle shop."[40]

Jumping behind Cappa in the stick, Sergeant John J. Gabrielson, Private First Class William Dobson, and Private Joseph F. Clancy also landed in the town and were hidden by French civilians in the town's post office. The remainder of the stick were either killed or captured.

Chalk 37's jumpmaster, Lieutenant James A. Rightley, commanding the 1st Platoon, tried to round up his stick after landing. "We were scattered all over. I only found one engineer after landing, but many from the 508. We were to blow a bridge at Pont l'Abbé, but couldn't get there. For the rest of the night and D-Day, we kept losing men—lost and killed."[41] Rightley was subsequently wounded in the head and taken prisoner.

Technician Fifth Grade Thomas C. Goins, one of the 1st Platoon engineers, jumped with Chalk 40 and landed in St.-Sauveur-le-Vicomte, about 150 feet away from a German command post and in the middle of a nightmare. "My platoon sergeant, Sergeant [Everette H.] Langford's throat was cut while [hanging in his chute] in a tree. We did not have any chance. I moved around and picked up Lieutenant James L. Durham (Chalk 41), who had a broken leg. We were surrounded by Germans—five of us ran into a German officer and we surrendered. The officer kept us from being shot."[42]

Lieutenant Edward P. Whalen was the jumpmaster of Chalk 42. "I landed on the east bank of the Douve River in the southeast edge of St.-Sauveur-le-Vicomte. I swam the Douve River to the west bank and tried to get into town to locate the main body of troops, but was unable to get there due to machine gun emplacements. I retired to high ground south of St.-Sauveur-le-Vicomte and stayed there until 24:00 D-Day."[43]

The third serial (Number 22), consisting of thirty-six planes, transported Lieutenant Colonel Herbert Batcheller's 1st Battalion. Chalks 1-9 were made up of Headquarters and Headquarters Company, 1st Battalion troopers. Captain James Dietrich, the battalion S-2, was the jumpmaster of Chalk 4. Standing in the door with him, Major Shields Warren, the 1st Battalion executive officer, could see the lead "V" of planes that included Batcheller's Chalk 1. "As battalion CO, he flew in the lead plane of the flight column and as battalion XO, I flew in the right lead plane of the 'V-of-V's.

"As we hit the coast we got some flak. I checked and noted that all the planes were back there. But then we hit the clouds and it spread us a little. I could still see the leading 'V' even in the fog. We passed over St.-Sauveur-le-Vicomte and got a lot of flak, which spread the formation. Then we went over Ètienville and got a hell of a lot of flak there. Then I looked around and there were no ships around my plane. I jumped on the green light, and just after coming out of the plane I turned around and looked over my shoulder and saw the Douve River behind me very close. I landed about halfway between Picauville and the Douve. I landed in an orchard. We got a great deal of flak practically all along the entire route between St.-Sauveur-le-Vicomte and Ètienville. After coming down I only saw one plane, which was towing a glider and kept on going, and another C-47 which was shot down in flames. I did have a light, but I didn't put it up because it was obvious it would not be seen. I toured the area in ever widening circles trying to collect as many men as I could."[44]

Private David Jones, a member of the Headquarters Company, 1st Battalion S-2 section, was jumping number thirteen in Chalk 1, the lead plane in the serial. Captain Gerard Ruddy was jumpmaster of the stick, which included the battalion commander, Lieutenant Colonel Batcheller. Jones had earlier decided to leave his Mae West life preserver in the plane. "Our jump was at approximately 350 feet above the ground and to my amazement after receiving the opening shock of the parachute, everywhere I looked there was water. At 350 feet there wasn't much time to think. I know I prepared to drown. I never had learned to swim, not that it would have done any good, for the way we were loaded down with equipment we probably would have gone under and stayed there anyway. I was very fortunate in that there was just enough breeze to cause the chute to billow on the surface of the water, and it aquaplaned me toward a tree-lined causeway or built-up road. The chute wrapped up in the trees along the roadway and I pulled myself the rest of the way to the causeway by pulling on the suspension lines and dragged my bedraggled self to dry land.

"Having taken part in the building of the sand tables now gave me an advantage I hadn't realized before. I knew generally where I had landed in relation to the causeway, and I knew which direction I wanted to go on that causeway to our assembly area. There was a problem, however. The Germans had positioned machine guns at both ends of the causeway, but by staying slightly below the roadway itself, it was possible to stay out of the line of fire.

"During our brief stay in [Northern] Ireland and during one of our night training patrols, and after warming ourselves at a roadside pub, a fellow parachutist and I had gotten into a fairly good fistfight. After the rest of the group had separated us, this trooper had vowed that once we got into combat he was going to get my ass. Naturally, you can guess who the first person was that I met, while crawling along the edge of that causeway. Sure enough, the same trooper had me looking into the barrel of his Thompson submachine gun. Well, after we hugged and slapped each other on the back telling each other how fortunate we were to have made it through this far, we started off together along the causeway toward a group of houses at the far end of the roadway." [45]

Private Otis E. "Gene" Hull jumped number fourteen in Chalk 1, just behind Jones. "I landed in a small fenced area adjacent to a farmhouse that was located fifty feet from the junction of two large fields with a hedgerow between them. I heard a machine gun firing and heard men on the driveway of the farmhouse. I walked through a barn until I came to a door that opened on the driveway. I saw a squad of Germans; one man was pounding at the farmhouse door. A light came on and the soldier and the farmer talked. Then the light went out and the Germans marched out to the main road and turned back toward the way they had come. I decided to move away from the farmhouse and go looking for our men."[46]

The 1st Battalion message center chief, Technician Fourth Grade Owen B. "O. B." Hill, was by a twist of fate, the last man in the Chalk 1 stick. "Normally, I would have jumped behind my company commander, Captain Gerard A. Ruddy. He and my platoon leader, First Lieutenant Charles J. McElligott were very good friends and McElligott wanted to jump behind Ruddy. As a result, I traded places with McElligott and I was then the last man to leave our plane."[47]

From his position near the cockpit, Hill pressed up against the trooper in front of him to close up the stick. "As the green light came on, we were out of the door in a few seconds. We did not know that we were not over our drop zone at the time.

"On the way down, we were shot at with machine guns and rifles, and it looked quite bad. We were not very high for the jump, but it seemed like forever before we reached the ground. My chute opened with a hard jerk. The extra weight made the opening shock quite rough. I looked up to check my chute and saw numerous holes in it from small arms fire. I looked down and saw tracers coming up at me. Instinct caused me to raise my feet, but I put them back down because I would need them down for landing.

"I could see that I was going to land in water and I figured that this must be the Merderet River. That was the river closest to where we were supposed to land."[48]

In fact, Hill was heading for a landing in the floodplain of the Douve River, a good distance south of the drop zone. "I then landed in the water and found it was only waist deep. They were still shooting at me, so I went back down in the water with just enough sticking out for me to breathe. I remained in that position for some time after the shooting stopped. Once again, I stood up and there was no firing at me, so I started walking toward the dry land. After organizing all of my gear, checking my rifle and getting out of the chute harness, I started walking away from the water.

"It was quite dark and I could hear lots of action around me. Lots of firing into the air at the planes and this seemed to be in all directions around me. I kept walking in what I assumed to be the right direction."[49]

Lieutenant Edward A. Napierkowski, the light machine gun platoon leader, was the jumpmaster of Chalk 2. Corporal Kenneth J. "Rock" Merritt was behind him, jumping number two. "When I jumped, I could feel the bullets zinging by me, and when daylight came, I counted thirteen bullets in my chute. As I hit the ground, I landed in a briar patch, and I was receiving machine gun fire on my position. I was having trouble getting out of my parachute with all the equipment. We had the old harness type fasteners on our parachute harness, where the British had the quick release. We adopted the quick release after the Normandy drop. You had to get out of your chute before you could get to your rifle, since it was over your shoulder, muzzle down, and secured by your parachute belly band. After Normandy, in addition to your rifle, you were issued an Army .45 pistol for protection prior to getting out of your parachute.

"As I was lying on my back trying to get out of my chute, I saw a C-47 on fire coming directly at me, I thought. Anyway, it was about fifty to one hundred feet above me, and I could see that the jumpers had already jumped because I could see the backpacks of the parachutes attached to the plane. The plane crashed and burned one thousand yards from my position.

"I got out of my chute and set out to find my machine gun and ammo bundles that we had released during the jump. The procedure we used was the door bundles were kicked out first, and then the number one man followed them out. The bundles in the racks underneath the plane were released by the middle man in the stick throwing the switches in the plane. The last man in the stick would check just before he jumped to be sure that all of the switches had been thrown. All of the equipment bundles were color coded with lights, like green for weapons, red for ammunition, and so on and so forth. This didn't do us any good, since the whole sky was full of tracers, flames, burning planes, and what have you. The plane that had crashed one thousand yards from my position lit up the whole drop area and within ten minutes, I found my two equipment bundles. I couldn't carry all the ammo, so I took the light machine gun and what ammo I could carry and moved out. I had no idea as to where I was.

"Within five minutes, I was challenged. I think the password and countersign was 'Flash' and 'Thunder'. Plus each paratrooper had been issued a toy cricket, the one like you get out of [a box of] Crackerjacks. You would give three clicks and your challenger would click you back. My challenger was one of our chaplains.

"He said, 'Corporal, what are we going to do?'

"I said, 'First, you can help me carry some of this light machine gun ammo, and then we're moving out.' I had figured since I was the number two man in the stick, our direction had to be in the direction that the plane had crashed and lit up the sky.

"Within ten minutes, I heard something on the opposite side of the hedgerow. I challenged with my cricket and password and it was Lieutenant [Edgar R.] Abbott, the platoon leader of the 81mm Mortar Platoon of Headquarters Company, 1st Battalion, 508. He had with him seventeen men."[50]

Corporal Thomas J. Gintjee was a squad leader with the 81mm Mortar Platoon and a member of the Chalk 9 stick. "I was jumping number three, with number four [Private First Class Herbert W.] Hesse, [Jr.], number five [Private First Class Hubert M.] Johnson, and number six [Private First Class James L.] Alexander directly behind me in a stick of about sixteen; preceding me was the jumpmaster, number one, [Sergeant Harry S.] Higgins and number two [Private Marion I.] Pence, a radioman."[51]

When the green light flashed on Corporal Gintjee pushed against the back of the trooper in front of him as he left the aircraft. "The opening shock of my parachute was the hardest that I have ever encountered! I felt every pound of my extra weight. Quickly and automatically checking my canopy overhead, I could see the sky and knew that I had blown out some panels. But I could only see half of my canopy because the American helmet won't allow it—it tips forward when the back of it hits the nape of you neck.

"But that wasn't my immediate problem—things were going zip zip zip through what remained. I had no time to study the terrain to try to pick out any landmarks as my attention was focused on the light show below me—all kinds of tracer bullets arcing up at you…coming up as fireflies, then zapping past. Thankfully, I was coming down like a bat out of hell!

"Two guns did finally isolate on me as I was coming down on a field about fifty by one hundred yards—each straddling a corner of the field and holding me in a shallow crossfire as I headed directly toward them.

"I desperately tried to maneuver my landing position so I could come in frontally, but still had the presence of mind to flip back my holstered carbine and entrenching tool before I hit. I came down between both guns which continued to track me all the way down.

"I landed like a sack of shit, for which I am eternally grateful. Shit will splatter on impact. If I had bounced so much as six inches there would have been a terrible thing done to my head, providing of course, that I still had one. Just then, another paratrooper was coming down (the only other on the field) and the two guns began tracking him. He simply blew up in the air. They must have hit his landmine or Gammon grenade for that explosion—but he just went 'boom!' about seventy-five feet off the ground.

"Mortar fire began to fall in the field—one near enough to scatter some sod on my legs. But none were closer because they would also have taken out the two machine guns.

"The field suddenly lit up with that I thought was a flare—but it was a plane whining overhead on fire. And I saw for the first time the 'Rommel Asparagus' planted in the field—stakes to break up the glider landing, but also to catch an unwary paratrooper as I saw the ends were pointed. Then everything went dark again.

"The two guns again gave me a few bursts which were passing but a few millimeters over my head; the guns were evidently zeroed, like ours, to cut someone a few inches above the knee in the middle of a field.

"One damn thing for sure—those gunners were sure that they had taken me out on the way down. I [played] dead.

"I was lying there facing a gun on my right and left—lying some twelve inches above the ground over a landmine. But more importantly, I was atop my rifle still in its canvas container. I could not, in my position, draw my holstered carbine—and could only reach a knife strapped to my boot. With this knife, I watched (with rising panic) these gunners who now had my full attention: I was afraid they would come out and bayonet me for more practice.

"I continued to play dead. I will never how why, [being] so close to the enemy, [that] my hand movements did not give me away. That fickle helmet kept blocking my view and I had to keep tipping it up to see! Why my movements were not detected is one of the many questions I intend to address my Maker…later. In any event, those Germans would never have believed that they could have missed me.

"I was not conscious of any firefights around me as the two guns sent a few more bursts over my head [during] the next hour—but no one came out—even to search me for valuables. Then it became very quiet. I knew it would be light too soon and that I had to get my ass off that frigging field."[52]

Staff Sergeant John Boone, with Headquarters Company, 1st Battalion, had strapped his Thompson submachine gun, with the muzzle down, under his parachute's belly band. "When my chute opened, the Tommy gun flew up and the butt of the stock hit me hard just under the lip of my helmet in the right temple area. I was completely stunned. I thought, 'My God! I've been hit and I haven't even gotten into combat yet!' I honestly thought the war was over for me.

"Like so many others, I came down in a field more like a meadow, which was partially enclosed by hedgerows. The grass was dry and almost waist high. As I lay there trying to get out of my chute, the slight breeze would cause the grass to rustle and I just knew at any moment I would be attempting to dodge a German bayonet. I allayed this fear with some logic, as they were traversing the area across the meadow with machine gun fire, which would not allow anyone to stand up, whether friend or foe, without being hit.

"Having a much better idea of what was needed for a submachine gun in the way of ammunition, I had tripled the amount called for in this instance, 1,500 rounds rather than 500. I want to tell you, that's heavy ammunition. This was in my field bag, which was hanging below my waist. I squirmed into a kneeling position to avoid the machine gun fire and flipped the bag over my head. The ammo was so heavy it pulled me down to the ground again on my back. I again had to disentangle myself, which seemed to be an endless effort. It took an hour and a half for me to contact another trooper, and it turned out to be the fellow who had followed me out of our plane."[53]

The next nine planes in the 1st Battalion serial transported Captain Jonathan "Jock" Adams and his Company A troopers. Captain Adams, the jumpmaster of Chalk 10, was standing in the doorway looking for landmarks below, trying to ignore the intense fire coming up at the low flying planes. "Immediately behind me was my runner—a young kid about nineteen years old named [Private First Class Virgel] Gainer. I had picked him for my runner because he was so clean cut, well bred, and just a damn nice kid. As we were standing in the door he remarked how beautiful the scenery was. I admit I hadn't noticed until then. It was really one of the most beautiful sights I have ever seen, but which I would not want to ever see again. It was a moonlit night and the small hedgerowed fields contained more different shades of purple and green than I knew existed.

"Gainer said, 'It just doesn't seem right going to war in a country as peaceful as this.' As far as I know, these were the last words he spoke, because three-quarters of an hour later he was the first American I came across. He was dead in his chute and apparently had been shot while still in the air and killed before he hit the ground.

"I landed in a small field all by myself. There was a German in one corner of the field armed with some kind of automatic weapon. There may have been others around the field and at the time I thought there was. However, they or he did not know I had landed or were as scared as I was. Anyway, they stayed in their foxholes and just fired blindly."[54]

The Chalk 14 plane, on which Lieutenant Rex G. Combs was the jumpmaster, was shot down. Lieutenant Combs' stick jumped from the burning plane between Foucarville and St. Germain-de-Varraville, far to the east of the drop zone in the 502nd Parachute Infantry Regiment's area of operations. Staff Sergeant Herman W. Jahnigen jumped number fifteen in the stick. "There were two other fellows, [Sergeant Sherman] Van Enwyck and [Technician Fifth Grade John E.] Brickley, who landed close to me.

"Sergeant Van Enwyck said, 'What are we going to do?'

"I said, 'Well, we don't know where we're at, we don't have a map, let's go across that field and get in a hedgerow until morning.' So we crossed the field and got into a hedgerow."[55]

When his Chalk 16 plane emerged from the cloudbank, First Lieutenant George Lamm, the platoon leader of 2nd Platoon of Company A, looked out the door to check for other planes in the serial. "They were gone and we seemed alone. The pilot reported an expansive section of water ahead. The green light flashed on and then 'all hell broke loose' as the saying goes. Small arms fire from below increased, flak was coming up, and the pilot went to evasive action. The troopers were sprawled over the floor and some penetration through the aircraft floor was reported. As we bobbed around and got our troopers close up on the door, the pilot called and said we had missed the drop zone and were going out to sea over the landing beaches. I requested he turn back and drop us in a quiet area. This he accomplished and we slowed down and jumped.

"As I jumped, my right knee and foot tangled with the [suspension] lines and I was suspended sideways and I had dropped quite a distance from the other chutes. Suddenly, I hit a hedgerow and my rifle stock was broken in the landing. I pulled out my trench knife and cut the chute loose. Taking care, I cut off the harness, pulled my .45 and searched for the troopers and bundles. The only person I ran into came through a hedge opening, saw me, knocked me down, and ran off, leaving his rifle. It was a bolt action. I had met my first 'Jerry' in France."[56]

Lieutenant Lamm and his stick landed east of the Merderet River about 1,500 yards west of Ste.-Mère-Église.

As he waited to jump, Lieutenant Henry E. Le Febvre, the platoon leader of the 3rd Platoon of Company A, watched red tracers crisscrossing the night sky. "The green light came on and I was out some four hundred feet in the air above the Normandy countryside falling into that sea of tracers. My chute opened and suddenly the ground was coming up at me. Fortunately for me, I landed right in the middle of one of those fifty yard square fields. As soon as I hit the ground, I heard this German who must have been in charge of his anti-paratroop group really shouting at his troops. I didn't know what he was saying, but I could tell that he really meant business. I knew I had to get out of my chute and away from it as soon as possible. We were loaded down with extra equipment, plus having a harness that snapped around each leg at the groin and across the chest with a snap fastener. In order to minimize the opening shock, these straps were very tight and under all the other equipment that we carried. Because of this and what I knew would only be a short time to get out of my chute, I used my razor-sharp knife that was attached to my jump boot to cut my way out of my harness. In my haste, I also cut my way through my rifle sling. If I didn't have enough problems already, I was also confronted by a cow right next to me with a bell around its neck. It stood looking down at me, moving her head and ringing the bell.

"I was fortunate to be able to get out of my harness and slither about ten yards away toward the opposite corner of the field from the Germans. Suddenly, I heard the very distinct 'pop' of a Very pistol and I knew that in a few seconds the whole area would be flooded with the white light of a parachute flare. I got as low to the ground as possible and faced the chute. As soon as the flare came on, the area was flooded with light and a hail of bullets came from the German position on the corner of the field. I saw my parachute and equipment being shot to pieces. The firing continued for the whole time the flare was lit (about twenty seconds). It seemed like an eternity to me. The only thing that saved me was the fact that I had gotten a little distance away from my chute, that my hands and face were blackened, and that I was hugging the ground. When the flare went out, they didn't fire another one. For whatever reason, they did not come into the field after me; so as soon as the flare went out, I started to crawl to the far corner of the field. There, I ran into a pathfinder who was lost. We almost shot each other before we realized who was who."[57]

Private First Class Robert White was a member of Lieutenant Le Febvre's stick. "After I got the opening shock and checked my canopy, I saw I had a busted panel. So, automatically I threw the reserve chute out and it was white. The field I landed in, the grass was pretty high; it must have been eighteen inches or higher. The white chute landed on top of the grass. There happened to be a machine gun in the corner that was firing at the reserve. He just kept raking because he could see the white. I couldn't raise up—I had to get out of that harness while lying flat on my back. I thought about taking them out; but our orders were to assemble as the first thing. After I got out of that harness, I crawled out of that field into another field.

"I don't know whether I challenged him or he challenged me, but he turned out to be from my company. He went in with the pathfinders—[Private] A. B. Cannon. He was by himself."[58]

In the lead plane of the nine carrying Company B, Sergeant Bud Warnecke stood in the door behind his company commander, Captain Royal Taylor. As their plane cleared the cloudbank, Warnecke couldn't see any of the company's other eight planes. "We got a green light and I bailed out right behind Captain Taylor. Just as soon as I bailed out, I just knew that was the end of it—that I was not coming back, because I had never seen so many tracers in my life.

"I hardly got the thoughts [of German automatic weapons fire] out of my mind when I went through an apple tree. I went through this apple tree, and luckily went all the way through it; my feet just barely touched the ground. The top of my canopy had caught my fall, and I just hung there real nice. No problem. I took my knife, cut myself out of my harness, and immediately started to roll up the stick.

"The first man I found was my company commander, Captain Taylor. I gave the sign and he gave the countersign, also using the cricket."[59]

Sergeant Warnecke quickly determined that Captain Taylor had been injured on the jump. "He was hurt pretty bad. He could not get up, could not walk. He was lying adjacent to a field along a hedgerow. One of our bundles was in this field. I was going to proceed to get the bundle and Captain Taylor stopped me. He said it wasn't worth it, in that it was covered by machine gun fire, and to just leave it.[60]

"Taylor instructed me to roll up the stick, then find Lieutenant [Homer] Jones and tell him he was now acting company commander. It tells you something about Jones when you realize he was not the senior lieutenant under Taylor."[61]

Lieutenant Homer Jones was the jumpmaster of a stick composed primarily of the 2nd Squad of the 1st Platoon of Company B. Private First Class John R. Taylor was jumping number two in the stick. "I remember looking out the plane and seeing the tops of trees. The trees in Normandy were not very large, and I thought, 'We don't need a parachute for this; all you need is a step ladder.' Anyway, suddenly the plane veered up, which made me feel quite good at that time. We straightened out. Usually, when you're going to jump, you can tell because the plane would slow down and they would raise the tail, so to give you clearance when you jumped out of the plane. This pilot did not slow down, and as I recall, we weren't over two or three hundred feet in the air.

"We jumped. No problem. I remember coming down. I had a recollection of all these people on the ground—looked like a circle—and I think they were all firing up at me. I doubled up, held my jackknife position anyway, before I hit the ground. I was lucky, I hit right at the middle of a big open field, luckier than lots of fellows who landed in trees or water or on top of buildings.

After landing, I lay there. I thought, 'This is a bad dream. This is not real.' Now, all of a sudden I heard Germans talking. It was still a bad dream, but it was real.

"You do funny things, and I thought, 'I've got to get out of this parachute.' We were heavily loaded with equipment. At that time, I was a machine gunner, so we also had a machine gun, which was in a separate bundle. The theory was that if you jumped in a straight line, you get up and you move in one direction, because they were supposed to release the equipment after about the seventh fellow had gone out the door.

"These were the old fashioned chutes with snap harnesses, not the quick release type. I took out my knife, and I said, 'Now, let's not cut an artery here.' And then I thought, 'Well, maybe I'll get in trouble if I cut this parachute up.' Very economy minded. Anyway, I cut myself out and looked up to see this person approaching me. You trained so much with the people in your squad and your platoon that you recognized people in the dark, and this was my best friend. So, we got together, we got the machine gun, and we started moving out.

"We hadn't gone very far; we ran into our company commander [Captain Taylor], and he said, 'Well, let's wait here and try to regroup.' So, we waited there until it was after dawn."[62]

Private James Q. "Jim" Kurz jumped next to last in Lieutenant Jones' stick, just ahead of Corporal William N. Theis. Private Kurz landed in a tree, cut himself out of his harness, dropped to the ground, and assembled his rifle. "I started along the line of flight; planes were still flying overhead and you could see tracers going up to meet them. I heard a sound in front of me and ran into Private [Arthur] Wolfe. He had broken his leg. I told him I would return with a medic. When I reached the edge of the field against a hedgerow, I found Lieutenant Jones and part of the stick. The medic who jumped with us was there. We went back to Wolfe, who told us he had heard others nearby. We discovered

Theis and one other man. All three had broken a leg. We put them together in a hedgerow ditch and left them. I realized that the only reason I wasn't hurt was because I had landed in the tree and been saved the shock of hitting the ground."[63]

Lieutenant Walter J. Ling, the platoon leader of the 2nd Platoon, was the jumpmaster of his Company B stick. Sergeant Bill Call was the last man in that stick. "When I went out the door it looked like fireworks, there were all of these bursts and everything coming. I thought, 'My God, what is this?' I don't think we were in the air that long. I landed evidently in a farmer's field and there was a machine gun maybe fifty or a hundred yards away from me firing up at the paratroopers coming down. I landed and God, I was so afraid. I was shaking so badly. I was lying on the ground and I heard this guy running towards me and I couldn't get the gun out [of the Griswold case].

"He came over and he was from my squad, named [Private First Class Steve J.] Kowalski. He said, 'What are you laying there for sergeant?'

"I said, 'Get me out of this damn harness.' He had to help me get out of my harness. Finally, I got myself together. He wasn't even afraid. I thought, 'God, this guy's stupid.'"[64]

Sergeant Harry L. Reisenleiter, the squad leader of the 2nd Squad of the 2nd Platoon of Company B, landed with several other troopers in a field containing "Rommel's Asparagus" obstacles, designed to destroy gliders during landing. "It was mass confusion, as all of us were under very heavy fire. I had a terrible time getting my rifle assembled. Under normal conditions, I could detail-strip an M1 rifle and take it apart and put it back together in the dark, but I couldn't seem to get the three pieces of the rifle to stay together. I put the barrel and the stock together, and I put the trigger assembly in, and when I snapped it shut, it would come apart in three pieces again. I think it took me about four times before I got it together, and all the time I was thinking, 'Boy, this is great. All this training and everything, and here I am and I'm gonna get shot and killed and I didn't even get one round fired. What a loss!'"[65]

As his Company B stick finished the equipment check, Private First Class Ed Boccafogli heard the command by the jumpmaster to stand in the door. "We closed in very tight, one against the other, and in the meantime, several of the fellows had vomited and the floor was pretty well slimy. We were slipping and sliding to the rear of the plane—the door was opened. We got the green light. The fellows started going out. I went out the door, I slipped, because of vomit on the floor and slammed against the side of the door[way]. My feet and knees hit the back of the door and I thought for sure I was going to get tangled up. I went out upside down. Fortunately, my parachute opened up, and I believe we were between 700-800 feet off the ground, which was fortunate, because we got to the ground very fast. As I started to look down, I could hear firing coming up. I could see some flashes down below, but I was sliding towards it. I climbed the risers and I collapsed half of the chute, so I slid in the opposite direction. The bullets were hitting my canopy and I could hear the crackle. How in the hell I didn't get hit I don't know till today.

"I landed behind a hedgerow. My chute was still up on the tree, but fortunately, I was close to the ground. As I hung halfway on the ground, I took my knife, cut the risers, and fell the rest of the way. I got out of the parachute harness, and the first thing I did was cut loose and threw away the gas mask, the Mae West, and the landmine. I didn't want any of that stuff to hold me back. I started crawling on my hands and knees and heading towards a corner of one of the hedgerows, trying to get as far away from where those bullets were coming. I saw something move. It turned out it was a cow. I passed a cow another hedgerow over, and then I heard some noises. Then I laid flat on the ground and heard a click. I felt all over for my clicker, because we had clickers to make sounds to signal to each other. I couldn't find the damn thing, so I laid flat on the ground. I watched and I saw the silhouette of one of our men going by. It was three of them. So, I hooked up with them. I was very happy to see someone."[66]

The Company B operations sergeant, William F. Knapp, landed alone in a field covered by an enemy machine gun. "I hit the ground in this tall grass and all I could do was pray that God would let me get my rifle out and assembled. If I could just get my rifle out, I had some protection. I was lying there—they were shooting at me—I was trying to take my reserve chute off and get my gun.

"Every time I'd move, I'd move the grass. The moon was out and they just kept shooting at me. On top of that, they were firing flares and I had to freeze every time one went off, because if you moved, they were going to see you."[67]

Lieutenant Woodrow Millsaps, the platoon leader of the 3rd Platoon of Company B, dropped west of the Merderet River, landing on his entrenching tool and injuring a leg. "I landed in the middle of a German antiaircraft battery. I lay on the ground, and from my position I could see and hear Germans as they fired at other planes flying overhead. They were so excited and busy firing at the other planes that they didn't pay any attention to me lying on the ground just a few yards away.

"As I began to quietly crawl away from more Germans, I knew I would have to get moving and work myself out of this mess before daybreak, for it wouldn't do to have daybreak find me in the middle of a German unit. When I had worked out of the immediate range of the antiaircraft battery, I began to make short rushes to a hedgerow that was nearby. The Germans saw me and started chasing me, but I made it to the hedgerow and jumped over, landing on one of my men who was seeking cover there."[68]

The nine sticks of Company C, which was commanded by Captain Walter Silver, were widely scattered, with several dropping south of the Douve River. First Sergeant Leonard Funk's stick was dropped some twenty miles south of the river. Sergeant William H. Traband was the last man in that stick—the pusher. "We had the puke buckets in the plane. You were passing that around. Thank God I never got airsick. Even when we went out of that plane, we were sliding on puke all the way up to the door. We didn't jump out, we slid out. There was plenty of flak. When we did land, I saw which way the plane was going, to know which way to go. I went one way and Funk came in the other and we picked up everyone."[69]

Funk badly sprained his ankle upon landing, but he and Traband succeeded in rounding up all eighteen troopers. Private William R. Tumlin, a member of that stick, was one of the few troopers in the regiment to jump with his rifle assembled. "When I jumped I had my rifle ready instead of in my [Griswold] pack in three pieces."[70]

Lieutenant Bruce E. Bell was the jumpmaster of a composite stick of mostly Company C troopers that also included Corporal Carlos Ross and three other members of the Demolition Platoon of the regiment's Headquarters Company. Corporal Ross was jumping number two "with my demo buddies [jumping numbers] three, four, five, the riflemen next, then a Sergeant [Robert R.] Brewer [with Company A] bringing up the rear. When the red light came on, Lieutenant Bell and I hooked up first and then pushed an equipment chute with eight miles of communication wire out the door. By this time everybody was holding a short static line with both hands because the plane was being bounced around by flak. I thought the green light would never come on. It did though and we all tumbled out about four minutes early (by my calculation). I had my legs drawn up as far into my belly as I could get them because of the tracers coming my way. If I had ever hit the ground in that position I believe I would have broken every bone in my body. Luckily I made the only tree landing I had ever made. I still managed to hit the ground hard enough to sprain my left knee. The tree then jerked me back into the air about two and a half feet. After cutting myself loose and assembling my gear, Lieutenant Bell and I got together. While hunting for the rest of the stick, we got into a little skirmish with a few Jerries and Lieutenant Bell didn't come away from it."[71]

Private First Class Robert E. Nobles was one of the Company C troopers who were members of Lieutenant Bell's composite stick. Nobles, upon "landing in a pasture among a few cows, gave the password to the first trooper I met.

"I received the following response, 'Don't shoot, don't shoot, this is Kokomo, Indiana. I forgot the password.' This helped relieve the tension. [Private First Class Robert F.] Bob Harper was the trooper from Kokomo.

"Some of the stick from our plane landed in the center of a small village. The machine gun team of [Private Vincent J.] Vinny Barry and [Private] John [J.] Middleton was in that group. Barry was hit during the action and later lost his arm. Middleton felt he was not shot because he was caring for Barry." [72]

Another member of that stick, Corporal Brodie Hand, landed without incident and began rolling up the stick. "I picked up three or four other men: [Private First Class] Bob Harper, [Private Cornelius] Neal Connaghan, and [Private First Class] Bob Nobles. We headed out in the direction that the planes were headed—northeast—until we came to a dirt road. About the time we reached the road, we heard a motorcycle coming. We went across the road and went for up to three or four hours—walking, running, hiding."[73]

The regiment's last serial, Number 23, consisted of thirty-six planes transporting the 3rd Battalion into Normandy. The first nine planes carried Company I, commanded by Lieutenant John J. Daly; followed by Headquarters Company, 3rd Battalion; then Company G; and finally, Company H.

Lieutenant Colonel Mendez was the jumpmaster of Chalk 37, composed of mostly Company I troopers and the lead plane of the 3rd Battalion serial. From his position in the doorway, Mendez studied the landmarks below as the serial flew eastward across the Cotentin Peninsula. "We ran into a lot of trouble as soon as we hit land. The flak was terrific. I never saw a T—we jumped on the green light. We jumped from about 2,100 feet, the entire serial, and were going rather fast."[74]

It was a long ride down, with German small arms and antiaircraft fire crisscrossing the moonlit sky. Lieutenant Colonel Mendez landed somewhere in the vicinity of Gourbesville, far to the north and west of the planned drop zone. "I checked my field bag and found three bullet holes in it."[75]

Minutes later, Mendez heard someone challenge him with the word 'Flash'. "I couldn't remember the countersign, 'Thunder' but I recognized [Technician Fifth Grade] Richard [E.] Fritter's voice, so I responded, 'Is that you, Fritter?'

"The voice answered, 'Yes sir, colonel.'"[76]

Private First Class R. B. Lewellen, with Company I, was also a member of Chalk 37 and jumped number five. After his parachute opened, Lewellen checked the canopy and then looked down to see what was below. "There was a pasture, kind of pie-shaped, with one big tree in the middle. I aimed for the pasture. I was able to climb the riser and missed the tree and fell into a low spot. I took off my chute and put my rifle together. I ran up under the tree and saw three men coming towards me. I was afraid to shoot, because they might be Americans, so I challenged them. They muttered something in German.

"Taking cover behind my equipment bag that held an eleven pound mine, I opened fire, swinging right to left. I could see the German on my left had his rifle on his hip. He fired and hit me in the hand and the stock of my rifle shattered. With my left hand wrecked and my right peppered with lead fragments, I ran toward the hedgerow at the far end of the field.

"While I was running, I was shot at probably at least fifteen times and was hit once in the left leg between the hip and the knee. At the time, I thought it was a lot of fire to come from just three men. Although I gobbled down a few [sulfa] pills, I was unable to effectively treat my wounds. My arm was too small for the tourniquet and my right hand was too sore to tighten it on my leg. I was also beginning to become weak from the loss of blood."[77]

Lieutenant Kelso C. Horne, the platoon leader of the 1st Platoon of Company I and jumpmaster of his stick, realized the pilot of his plane was not following the proper procedure for the jump. "He did not slow down and he did not come down to eight hundred feet where he was supposed to, because I saw airplanes flying down under me. I think we must have been about two thousand feet high."[78]

After landing and getting out of his harness, Lieutenant Horne moved toward a nearby wooded area. "I saw somebody else walking at an angle to me. If we had kept walking, we were going to intersect. I had a magazine in my carbine, so I just pulled the bolt back and slipped one into the chamber. We both kept walking and when we got about twenty feet apart, we both stopped and I spoke first. I had my gun on him, but he was just a form. But if he had been a German he would have killed me, because he knew I was an American first, because I said, 'Flash.' Well, the boy immediately came back with 'Thunder', the countersign and I knew he was an American. When I got over there and could see who it was, it was the messenger for my company commander, Lieutenant [John J.] Daly."[79]

Lieutenant Horne had landed just north of Ste.-Mère-Église, northeast of the 505th Parachute Infantry Regiment's drop zone.

Lieutenant Francis L. Mahan was the platoon leader of the 2nd Platoon of Company I and the jumpmaster of his plane. Private First Class Bob Chisolm was his radio operator and was jumping number two behind him in the stick. "When I jumped we were still above the clouds. When I hit the ground I tried to get out of my chute and I was unable to, and I had to take my trench knife and cut my way out. I was in an open field and I didn't recognize any of the landmarks, so I didn't know where I was at. I got my equipment adjusted and got my weapon out [of the Griswold case]. I didn't hear any gunfire and I didn't hear any crickets. I started walking and walked into a road. I decided which way I was going to go, and was going down the road. The first thing I saw was a glider on the side of the road that was cracked in, and I walked over and looked and everybody in the glider was dead, at least no one was moving that I could see. So I continued to walk down the road, no idea of where I was going. I heard a motorcycle and I knew that we didn't have any motorcycles, so I got off the side of the road in a ditch. It was a German motorcycle and I opened up on it and knocked it out. That was my first combat action. I walked on in and I was in Ste.-Mère-Église.

"I [had] landed just north of the town right in the field on the side of the main road. I heard all the firing going on around there. We were in a combat situation. I ran into some 505 people. I was with G Company, 3rd Battalion of the 05. At the time I didn't know who I was with. I didn't see anyone in my stick for three days."[80]

Lieutenant Denver D. Albrecht, with Company I, made a water landing. "It looked like it was a wheat field. I didn't realize it was water until I hit. It was right up to my nose. I could barely keep my head above water. Of course, I had to throw my equipment loose. I felt like throwing my rifle away, but feared I would need it. I tried to walk and swim and finally I got ashore, close to a couple of hedgerows. I had seen a German machine gun—at a distance. It was still dark and apparently I came right to the right of that machine gun when I came out of the water. I threw a Gammon grenade at it and moved out."[81]

Another Company I trooper, Corporal Fred Gladstone, had taken some airsickness pills and had fallen asleep on the trip over. "I did not hear the bursting antiaircraft shells, or the command to stand up and hook up. However, I was awakened in that darkened plane just in time to hear the jumpmaster cry, 'Let's go.' We didn't spill out very rapidly as the plane was rolling about as it flew at around 150 knots to evade enemy gunfire.

"My parachute opened about 2:00 a.m. and the glowing tracer bullets in the air were an unforgettable and frightening sight. I believe the Germans were firing from platforms in nearby Ste.-Mère-Église."[82]

Sergeant Donald M. Biles was the assistant jumpmaster of his Company I stick. "There were so many in our stick, that being the last man, I couldn't reach the static line to hook up when the order was given. It had been a rough flight; guys had gotten sick and threw up on the floor. I slipped and fell getting to the door, and by the time I got up and got out, everybody else was long gone. I came down from much too high an altitude, and was shot at all the way. (I can still hear those bullets 'snapping' past my ears and through my chute.) I landed in an apple tree, cut myself down, and shot a back azimuth on my compass to try and roll up my stick. While walking along a hedgerow, a Gammon grenade was poked in my face, with the challenge 'Flash!' I answered 'Thunder, who the hell is this?' It was our supply sergeant, who lost everything except his musette bag on the opening shock and was afraid to leave the drop zone unarmed. We were together, behind the lines for five days, until picked up by a patrol from the 4th [Infantry] Division."[83]

After his chute opened with a violent jerk, Company I trooper, Sergeant James C. "Buck" Hutto, the 2nd Platoon 60mm mortar squad leader, looked down to see a hedgerow lined field below. Tracers from more than one German machine gun were rising up from a farmhouse and shed in one corner as C-47s flew over. Hutto noticed a white horse running around the field below, just before he landed in the middle of it. After landing, Hutto also identified a black donkey that hadn't been visible as he had descended. "The firing from that house and shed frightened the white horse and black donkey, perhaps even more than it did me. Those animals were running around like crazy, round and round inside the hedgerow[s].

"At first, I was too scared to move. I just laid there, as still and quiet as I could. As long as the Jerries were firing from the corner of the lot, the horse and donkey kept up their full speed gallop—round and round. I didn't even try to get out of my harness. My chute fluttered in the wind and stretched out the suspension lines to their full length away from me.

"With a lull in the shooting, the donkey and horse stopped running. Then the donkey decided he was going back to his shed. He headed straight toward me and passed between the fluttering parachute and me, got himself entangled in the suspension lines, and started dragging me toward the shed.

"I grabbed the suspension lines with my left hand and my trench knife, which was strapped to my leg, with my right hand and started hacking away at those lines. The donkey was making a beeline toward that shed full of Germans, pulling me behind him. When I cut the last line, I was only about fifty feet from the shed, and the donkey was all wrapped in my parachute.

"Carefully, I got out of my harness and pack, keeping only my grenades, weapons, and ammunition, and crawled toward the opposite corner of the field from the house and shed. I made it to the hedgerow and stopped, feeling a little relief, but not much.

"Then I could hear something around the corner of the hedge to my left, but couldn't see anything. I recognized the sound of a machine gun as the gunner pulled back the feed lever. Could that be friend or foe? Most likely foe! I wouldn't snap that little old cricket they gave us for identification, less the enemy found me. So I waited quietly. Every once in a while I would hear a sound from the machine gunner around the corner.

"Looking out of the hedge to my front, I saw an orchard. Over to the right, a patrol quietly moved toward my position, one at a time. I could see the outline of the helmets—definitely German, with that curve down over their ears. I debated in my mind about shooting at the Krauts, but decided it would give away my position and they would get me in the end, so I lay quietly. The lead man in the patrol came within twelve feet of me. He stopped and signaled to those behind him, turned to the right and moved away through the orchard."[84]

When Private John W. Richards and his Company I stick finished the equipment check, "Lieutenant [Majorique G.] Morann yelled out, 'Stand in the door!'

"This was it, and I remember thinking, 'Oh God, oh God.'

"The green light went on and Lieutenant Morann yelled out, 'Let's go!' In a matter of eight to ten seconds, everybody was out the door. That was the last I saw of Lieutenant Morann. After the initial shock of the prop blast, I was floating very softly towards the earth. I looked around me, but I couldn't see any other parachutes. The moon was shining, but it was very hard to see the ground. I was descending very fast because of all the weight I had. I was waiting for the shock of hitting the ground when suddenly I felt a quick jolt on my shoulders. My feet didn't hit the ground as I landed in a tree in a big orchard. Fortunately, I was suspended about three feet off the ground. I fumbled around with my parachute harness for about fifteen minutes before I released myself and fell to the ground. As I lay on the ground, everything seemed very quiet. The planes had vanished; the ack-ack guns had ceased firing. I was alone and scared. I looked around me and nothing looked like the sand tables that we had studied for the past week. What amazed me most was that I didn't hear any fireworks at all. Everything in the area was very quiet. After rolling up my chute, I very quietly made my way to the corner of the orchard. I knew that there had to be some men from my stick in the area, because it didn't seem that windy that all the men would have landed that far apart. Then I heard movement in the hedges and I knew it had to be one of the men from my stick. It happened to be [Private John J.] Jack Fawkes, who jumped two [places] behind me [in the stick]. We tried to get our bearings, and then ran into another man from the stick. His name was [Private] John [J.] Pisula. He jumped in front of me. I could not find anybody else from our stick. We decided to wait until daybreak before moving on. We wondered what happened to the rest of the stick."[85]

Private James A. Campbell jumped number nine in that same stick. "I met up with [Private] Joe Petry, [Private Carrol M.] Carl Zimmerman, and [Private] James [T.] Robinson. The four of us met with some resistance in a farm yard and after shooting back and forth for a few minutes, the Germans that were left took off. We then took off cross country, having no idea where we were."[86]

Prior to the jump, Company I trooper, Private Herbert M. James, asked his jumpmaster "about those little red things that were going by our airplane. He said he thought they were the wing lights of our fighter planes. But just a few minutes later, they said, 'Stand up and hook up,' and we jumped.

"When I got out the door, and my chute opened, I knew what those little red things were. They were tracer bullets from German machine guns. They were so darned thick it looked like you could walk down on them. I slipped my chute hard to get down as fast as I could, and landed hard but safe. I undid my chute and started to undo my backpack, but it was gone. All I had were the buckles and the straps that it hung on. The opening shock was so bad that the weight of the antitank mine tore it away, along with my cigarettes, K-rations, and clean socks."[87]

Following just behind Company I were the nine planes carrying Lieutenant Malcolm Brannen's Headquarters Company, 3rd Battalion. Lieutenant Neal W. Beaver, the platoon leader of the 81mm Mortar Platoon was the jumpmaster of Chalk 52. Corporal William Lord was jumping second in Beaver's stick. When the green light flashed on, Corporal Lord slapped him on the back and shouted, "Go!" as loudly as he could. "He backed out of the door. I thought at the time he said, 'We're not jumping. There's nothing but water down there. I'm going to talk to the pilots and we'll have to go around again.'

"That meant we'd fly out over the bay [east of the Cotentin Peninsula], do a 180-degree turn to the left, and come back east to west, well north of the flight path coming in so as not to run into other planes. While Beaver went up and talked to the pilots, I stood by the door. I saw us head over the beaches, [then] pass out over Saint-Bains-Louche. As we banked, I saw the invasion fleet."[88]

Lieutenant Beaver returned to his position in the door. Corporal Lord then watched as the plane passed over the beach again. "All hell broke loose with small arms fire coming up at us. My impression was that the pilot shoved the stick forward and added throttle while diving for the deck. As an afterthought he hit the green light." [89]

As the green light flashed on, Lieutenant Beaver, who was standing in the doorway of the plane, was hit in the chin. "That plane was going low and fast and was being hit with machine gun fire. All we wanted to do was get out and on the ground—our element so to speak.

"I landed exactly in front of a pillbox. I took a look at that dark opening and froze. I then slowly waved one hand and when nothing happened got up. The hand waving was sort of superfluous."[90]

The opening shock of his parachute broke the chinstrap of Corporal Lord's helmet and the aiming circle for one of the mortars. "But because I had strapped the rifle to my body I didn't lose it. I looked down between my feet to see if I recognized any of the road net. As I looked up, I saw tree tops level with my eyes. I hit the ground; my chute stayed hung up in a small apple tree. I fell forward, but the chute held me at about a forty-five degree angle.

"Then I heard hobnail boots running down the road. I knew we didn't have hobnail boots. The French civilians didn't have hobnail boots. I was so scared when I tried to spit it felt like I had pebbles in my mouth. It took several minutes to get out of the harness. I put a round in the chamber of the M1 and began to pull back in the direction from where I thought we could roll up the rest of the stick. The field I was in had barbed wire. As soon as I saw it, I knew from all the training there would be booby traps that would blow if I touched the wire. A cow came up, licked my hand, and I realized there couldn't be booby traps in this field.

"Just about that time I heard someone say, 'Flash.'

"I replied, 'Thunder.'

"He said, 'Welcome,' and it was Beaver. We hugged each other. He told me he had felt pretty lonely until he saw this big splayfooted hulk that couldn't be anybody but Lord." [91]

Lieutenant Paul Lehman was the 3rd Battalion S-1 and the jumpmaster of his Headquarters Company, 3rd Battalion stick. "As I stood in the door awaiting the signal to jump, three different machine guns sent their streams of tracer bullets up toward me. Fortunately, they were just a little off in taking into account the speed of the plane and the bullets swerved into the tail of the plane and riddled the rudder.

"After my chute opened, I almost floated down into another cone of tracers, but he must have run out of bullets just then, as they ceased in the nick of time. Upon hitting the ground, I cut myself free of the harness and finally got together with three other troopers from my plane."[92]

After Private First Class Lawrence F. Salva, with the Light Machine Gun Platoon, Headquarters Company, 3rd Battalion, checked the canopy of his chute, he looked down to see a large fire. "My first reaction, 'Oh boy, our pathfinders are on the job.' Then, there they were—tracers—bullets below. I naturally raised my legs up toward my stomach, the burning objects still several hundred feet below. And then, there I was—hanging three or four feet above the ground. Hearing ammunition going off all around, I took my bearings and saw the tail section of a plane that had been shot down. I took my trench knife out of my boot and cut my right riser and fell and dropped my knife."[93]

Another Headquarters Company, 3rd Battalion trooper, Private Curtis L. Johnson, came down almost on top of the headquarters of the 91st Luftlande Division at the Chateau Bernaville, north of Picauville. "I saw tracers flying everywhere and some of them started swinging [my] way. There was nothing I could do and my chute was full of holes and five or six [suspension] lines cut before I hit the ground. Upon landing in a ditch, I cut myself free from the parachute. I heard shooting all around, but never saw another live paratrooper. I went over to another trooper and found him dead. Shortly, several bullets struck the ammo I was carrying and glanced away from my heart and one buried itself in my left shoulder. Fortunately for me, I was loaded down [with] .30-caliber machine gun ammo belts that crisscrossed my chest. I landed virtually on top of a German tank park and kept firing at anyone who approached the vehicles. I was wounded again under my right arm and right wrist during the continuing firefight."[94]

Lieutenant Malcolm Brannen, the commanding officer of Headquarters Company, 3rd Battalion, was jumping number sixteen in an eighteen man stick. "As I was descending I was trying with all of my strength to turn myself around so that I wouldn't come into the ground backwards. I just couldn't get turned around—all my efforts did were to make me slip to my back. I saw the planes leaving us amid machine gun bullets galore and I saw many machine gun nests on the ground and streams of tracers pouring through the air and I decided in a twinkling that I would have to steer clear of them when I did land. I was 250 feet above the ground when I jumped…

"Then—SWISH—through about three quarters of an apple tree. I was left hanging in the apple tree—dangling about one foot off the ground. But, I couldn't seem to get myself free of the parachute, struggle as I did. I got my trench knife and started cutting at my risers and at my leg straps. I couldn't seem to make much headway.

"Every other minute somebody would run by me on the ground and it was impossible to for me to see them to distinguish their identity. So when someone was approaching I had to quit struggling to get myself free. After they passed by I started trying to get free again. Finally, my risers slipped enough to drop me the remaining foot or so to terra firma."[95]

After Lieutenant Brannen finished cutting himself out of his parachute harness, he jumped into a nearby ditch to avoid machine gun fire coming from a position about one hundred yards away. "I could hear other men breathing and whispering the password and receiving the countersign. I found out that the men were three other paratroopers—right there in the ditch beside me—all watching that machine gun spit death to anyone in the way."[96]

The nine planes transporting Captain Frank J. Novak's Company G stayed together, but flew far past the regiment's drop zone and continued east, passing over Drop Zone A, designated for the 101st Airborne Division's 502nd Parachute Infantry, and approached the flooded area behind the northern end of Utah Beach. Technician Fourth Grade Robert J. Kolterman was the company's communications NCO. "We got the green light and began jumping. Company commander [Captain Frank J.] Novak was first, Sergeant [Lloyd L.] Henning second, I was third, and so on. Henning's rifle, carried under his reserve chute across his chest, had shifted diagonally and got hooked on the frame of the door. I saw the problem, twisted his rifle free, and we went out the door together. The pilots were to throttle back and feather the left engine as we were jumping—which we did in training. But not this time! Instead of 90 miles per hour and little prop blast, it was 120 miles per hour and when my chute opened, it was a helluva jerk!

"The area where we dropped was flooded—apparently by the Germans just to deter any landings. Most fields had a foot or so of water; ditches, canals, etc. up to several feet. Well, I splashed down with my usual three-point landing—heels, ass, and head! I was totally wet, sat on my musette bag, took out my jump knife (a four-inch switchblade) to cut off my parachute harness."[97]

Sergeant Joseph M. Kissane was the last man in his Company G stick. "I ran half the length of the plane, which was accelerating and bucking as it lost weight. Looking down, flares and tracers were spouting in all directions. Close by, a machine gun was firing at us. An alarming thought; he's going to be looking for me and not for my well being. I splashed down in about two feet of water in darkness and total disarray. With my jump knife, I feverishly hacked at the suspension lines, anticipating an imminent visit by a hostile German. Finally freeing myself, I headed in the direction of the planes' flight. Groping in the swamp I had to swim through the deeply flooded paths. I dispensed with the landmine. My rifle, of course, was soaked. I came across a few 101st troopers, one idly smoking a cigarette. I didn't need them. Walking along a road, I saw a flashlight beam—Lieutenant [Woodrow C.] Plunkett studying a map. Nearby were several G Company men. Evidently many had landed in a group on the extreme northern edge of Utah Beach."[98]

Company H, commanded by Captain Hal M. Creary, was the last nine plane formation in the serial. Lieutenant Ralph DeWeese, the assistant platoon leader of the 2nd Platoon, was the jumpmaster of one of the Company H sticks. "I was standing in the door and it seemed as if the flak was coming right up to us. It looked as if we were going through one immense Fourth of July celebration. At times I ducked away from the door because it came so close. [Private First Class Arthur W.] Puffer was right behind me and he kept his hand over the red light to keep it from showing. Lieutenant [John A.] Quaid's [three] planes were in a hot spot due to the fact the tabs had blown off the bundle lights and they had come on. That left the plane a target in the sky and everything was zeroing in on him. I thought surely they were going to get hit.

"We circled over Étienville three times and I knew the planes were lost. You can imagine how anxious we were to jump, because I knew we couldn't fly around much longer without getting hit. The flak and machine gun fire was worse and it is hard to realize how these planes can fly through it. I was watching Quaid's plane and saw some men jump. At that time, I drew my head back in and saw the green light was on. At that moment I hollered, 'Let's go' and hit the silk! The plane was going a little too fast, but I had a nice easy opening. The flak and machine gun fire was so heavy I believe I could have walked down on it. It was too bad some men were hit and never had a chance to get out of their chutes. Others had their canopies on fire due to the fire of tracer bullets. I looked around to see if all the men had jumped and they had. Much to my surprise, I looked down and all I could see was water. There was no place to slip to and I thought to myself, 'this is it.' It would have been impossible to get off all that equipment before drowning.

"I hit and much to my surprise the water was only about three feet deep. I sank in the mud a good foot. Before I could get out of my chute, the wind inflated the canopy and started to drag me. I was helpless at the moment and couldn't collapse the chute. I landed on my back and all of the heavy equipment on my stomach. It included my reserve and also my field bag and rifle. The risers came up in front of my helmet and my helmet was fastened by the chin strap, so I couldn't get it off. All that time my head was under water and the chute dragged me for about three hundred yards. Several times I thought it was no use and decided to open my mouth and drown. Each time though, the wind would slack up and I'd get a chance to put my head up out of the water and catch a breath.

"With the last bit of energy I had, I reached down and pulled out my trench knife and cut the risers. What a relief it was to get away from that chute. Bullets were singing over my head from machine guns and rifles, but it didn't bother me because at that point I didn't care. I laid in the water for awhile and just panted, I was so exhausted."[99]

Private First Class John P. Delury was one of the troopers with Lieutenant Quaid's stick. "The ride was very bumpy with flak concussions bouncing the plane up and down and our pilot must have had a heavy date back in England, because we didn't slow down for the jump. I had to climb up the plane's aisle to the door, fighting the Gs holding me back and when I tumbled out of the door, I had the sensation of being on the end of a cracking bullwhip. The opening shock ripped my helmet off. It spun with such force it smashed my nose and then went whistling earthward. As I was descending with a face full of blood, I heard it hit the ground and in my mind I had Germans waiting by my helmet for me to come down. Tracer machine gun bullets were spewing from the surrounding shadows and it looked like a fireworks display. The higher the tracers went, the slower they appeared, going into an illuminated slow arc during their descent.

"I hit the ground hard and lay in the middle of a grassy field with hedgerows bordering it. The moon was very bright, so I tried to get out from my illuminated position quickly. The only weapon I had was in a carrying case under my reserve chute and musette bag, which was loaded down with an antitank spider mine, grenades, etcetera. I tried cutting through my harness with my trench knife that was strapped to my leg. Somehow I dropped the knife in the grass and for the life of me (literally) I couldn't find it, so I finished cutting myself out with my bayonet. I crawled toward the shadows with what felt like a mouth full of cotton. I assembled and loaded my M1 and started to move out very slowly. I had a feeling that all the ground was planted with antipersonnel mines. I walked very warily, then saw a silhouette coming towards me in the shadows. I lay down and aimed my M1 at him and gave the challenge, 'Flash,' and waited for the password, 'Thunder,' which didn't come. Once again, I said, 'Flash,' and no reply. I was very close to pulling the trigger when I heard a faint, guarded, 'Thunder.' It was Sergeant [Technician Fourth Grade Desmond A.] Matthews from my company. He was part of a group that included my company executive officer, Lieutenant John Quaid, who during the next few days would be responsible for my not getting killed on more than one occasion.

"We were bordering a hedgerow in the dark when this trooper came up to me and said, 'You've made me the happiest fellow in the world.' I was the first contact he made. He was from I Company and named [Private] Glenn A. "Red" Fateley. We moved out in single file, about six of us, and came to a moonlit farmhouse that looked very dark, with no sign of life showing from the windows. Lieutenant Quaid knocked on the door and we were let in. With the help of a candle, his map, and a French-English dictionary, the lady of the house managed to show us approximately where we were—which was not where we supposed to be by miles."[100]

Private First Class Tomaso W. "Tom" Porcella, with Company H, felt the violent opening shock of his parachute, which caused his head to snap forward and his feet to come up. "My helmet was pushed over my face. The jolt of the opening of the chute soon made everything a reality. I looked up at my chute to make sure it was OK. Then I looked down and I couldn't see anything but blackness. I unfastened the main belt, unsnapped my reserve and let it drop to the ground. I opened the chest strap. Now, all I had to do on the ground was to remove the leg straps and I would be free of the parachute. For a few seconds on the way down I looked around and saw the red and green flares. The brightness of the tracers flying into the sky and the sound of the machine guns firing seemed to be all around me. Looking up at the chute and then down at my feet, I had the shock of my life. I plunged into water. My heart was pounding and my thoughts were running a mile a minute. 'How deep is this water? Can I get free of my chute? Am I too heavy? Will the weight keep me on the bottom?' All this in a split second.

"I hit the water in a standing position and when my feet touched the bottom, I was leaning forward. I managed to straighten myself up and realized that the water was over my head and I had to jump up for air. The water was not as deep as I expected, so I held my breath and tried to stand. The water was just above my nose. Quickly, I stood on my toes and I was gasping for another breath of air. My heart was beating so rapidly that I thought it would burst. I pleaded, 'Oh God. Please don't let me drown in this damn water in the middle of nowhere.'

"Below the water I went and I tried to remove the leg straps. They were just too tight and wouldn't unsnap. I needed some more air, so I jumped up and as soon as my head was above water I began splashing around. I started to pray, standing on my toes with my head barely above water. My heart was beating faster.

"After a few seconds I calmed down and decided to cut the straps. 'God, my only chance is the knife. Please let it be there.' Going down into the water again, I felt for my right boot. Yes, the knife was still there. 'I'm lucky.' I slipped my hand through the loop and I tightly gripped the handle. With a fast upward motion, I removed the knife from the sheath. Quickly, I jumped up for more air and stood still for awhile, thinking, 'Now, I have a chance.' Holding the knife tighter, I went below the water. I slipped it in between the leg and the strap, working the knife back and forth in an upward motion.

"Nothing happened. I was in a panic.

"I came up for another breath of air and I thought my heart was going to burst with fright. I wanted to scream for help, but I knew that would make matters worse. I told myself, 'I must think. Think! Why can't I cut the strap? My knife is razor sharp.'

"As I was gasping for air, I kept on saying Hail Marys. It seemed an eternity before I realized I had the blade upside down. 'That's it! I'm using the back of the blade.' I touched the sharp edge and made sure it was in the upright position. Taking another gulp of air, I went down again to cut the leg straps. With a few pulls of the knife on each strap I was finally free of the chute. 'Thank God!'

"Getting rid of the chute calmed me down a little. But the weight of the musette bag and the land mine were still holding me down. With a few rapid strokes of the knife, I cut loose the landmine. Then, I unfastened the strap of the musette bag and let it fall. I adjusted the rifle and the bandoleers of ammunition to a more comfortable position. I cut away the gas mask, and removed the hand grenades from my leg pockets and put them into the lower pockets of my jacket. Reaching up, I unfastened the chinstrap of the helmet and let it fall into the water. I bent down to retrieve the musette bag. Except for the wool cap, the entire contents of the bag were disposed of, and the bag was then thrown over my head to hang behind me. I became conscious of the rifle and machine gun firing in the distance, and I was gripped with fear. All the training had not prepared me for such a landing."[101]

Another Company H trooper, Sergeant Daniel T. Furlong, was the assistant jumpmaster on his C-47 carrying eighteen troopers and was the last to jump from his plane. "I was probably no more than two hundred feet from the ground, if I was that far. When the chute opened, it popped and my feet hit the trees. I went through the trees and I got a limb that went underneath my leg strap, came up on the side of my ear underneath my reserve chute. The limb broke and I came on through the tree and landed in a field flat on my back in a cement cow trough. It was full of water.

"The Germans were walking up the road. They could see my chute up in the tree, so they were looking for me. I could hear them running up and down the road. They had hobnail boots. They didn't see me because I was behind the hedgerow, while they were in the road. I cut my chute loose and took off."[102]

When his plane emerged from the clouds, Lieutenant Robert Moss, a platoon leader with Company H, knew something was wrong. "I could no longer see the formation lights of other planes. The guys were getting edgy and the line was surging and pushing. And there was some profanity, I believe.

"Then the crew chief came up to me and said, 'Lieutenant, we can't find the drop zone. We are lost. Do you want to go back to England?'

"Gawd amighty! Go back to England? Those guys would have thrown me out and jumped anyway or killed me when we got back to England.

"I said, 'Are we over France?'

"He said, 'Yes.'

"I said, 'Give us the green light. We're going.'

"I had a large, sharp, GI knife in a boot holster with a lanyard to my belt, a carbine (.30-caliber) and a .45 pistol which was cocked and ready in a shoulder holster. Thus, I departed the good old C-47.

"I knew there was something bad on the ground, but it didn't worry me particularly. I was happy to get out of that plane. This feeling was shared by all troopers.

"My chute opened as usual, I checked the swing somewhat. A strong breeze was blowing and I knew I was moving fairly fast in some direction. I was not going straight down. What looked [like a] large pasture below me was really a flooded section of the Merderet River. I removed my reserve chute and dropped it to have no interference when removing the backpack on the ground. I knew we had jumped about 700 to 800 feet, which is not bad. Then I realized I was moving backwards. I could have turned my body to come in forward but said, 'To hell with it, I'll go in as the Good Lord permits.'

"The 'pasture' was gone now and I could see houses below. I realized I was coming in fast, mostly horizontal—more so than vertical. Then WHAMMMM.

"I hadn't trained for this with that thatched roof. I was swinging in the corner of a room. Bang—right wall, bang—left wall. Then I knew—nobody told me—I had come through the roof of a stone barn. I saw the joists, about two feet apart and up to a peak like any house roof.

"I pulled the knife from my boot and slashed through the nylon suspension lines that go from the shoulder to the parachute. I was now swinging by my left shoulder and still banging the wall. Left—right—left—right.

"Then I heard voices and I recognized the tongue. They were not French. A Schmeisser (German machine pistol, smaller rounds than our submachine gun) started firing through the door and through the window of the barn, but I was swinging behind the window and not close to the door and they missed me.

"I could make out two persons outside the barn and they were coming close. I pulled my .45 out of the shoulder holster—it had a hair trigger and it went off as I pulled it out. Remarkably, I didn't shoot my arm off—and I kept firing, nervous reaction, and just as I reached the door with my rapid fire this German came in still firing and the .45 slug caught him somewhere and knocked him up in the corner. A .45 is a rough damn gun. I did not see this man move again. I grabbed the lanyard on my knife and pulled it up and slashed the suspension lines on the left side and dropped a foot or so to the floor. I went down flat and crawled to the door. I saw the other one standing about five or six feet away and shot him. He spun around and went backwards and fell and lay there. Still on my hands and knees, I crawled through the doorway (there was no door) around the side of the barn into a driveway to a road behind the barn. There was gunfire but not right there. I dashed across the road into what was an orchard and stopped to survey the situation in the dark. I could not see more than thirty yards, if that.

"Reconnaissance—that is a military positive and it comes up front—reconnoiter—patrol—and that's what I did. There were seventeen or nineteen men on my plane and we would have come down in a generally straight line. I did not know about the river then. I was in the village of Chef-du-Pont, but did not know where I was.

"I spent about one hour going from end to end of that place which was spread out with several fields and many open places along a main drag. No lights, no sign of habitation. The natives were lying low. I found none of my boys. How much time went by I can't recall and I was ready to leave the village and make my way toward some firing that had started up. I don't know just how far away. I could tell from the sound that our rifles were firing.

"Actually, I was heading for cover behind fences, posts, bushes—just like a good soldier doing it by the book. That was the easy part. I was back at the orchard and I heard someone moving. The weeds were about knee high. A normal pace through [the weeds] could make noise and I was tuned for a pin drop. I went down in a prone position, brought my carbine up on this figure. I could make him out as he came toward me and why I didn't take that perfect shot, only God knows. Something held my finger and I snapped, 'Halt!'

"Right back, came the words, 'Lieutenant Moss?'

"I said, 'Damn it, [Corporal Theodore Q.] Svendsen, what the hell are you doing walking through here like that? That's the way to get killed!' The training officer—still training my men."[103]

The 508th was dropped over a large area of the Cotentin Peninsula from St.-Sauver-le-Vicomte on the west side to the flooded area behind Utah Beach on the east, and from Valognes area in the north to some twenty miles south of the drop zone. This would make assembly of the regiment and accomplishment of its objectives on D-Day an impossibility.

CHAPTER 3

"MOVE TO HILL 30"

After landing, Lieutenant Colonel Tom Shanley attempted to assemble his 2nd Battalion troopers, but the assembly light had been destroyed during the jump. "The S-3 [Captain George Simonds] was supposed to have a light, but I did not see it. I used flashlights up in the trees when I landed. On the ground there was considerable fire, which was all around us. A lot of the men who came into the assembly area had already killed a German or two. We landed just north of Picauville and there were quite a few Germans around there. I sent several patrols out in different directions to get more men."[1]

When Private Ralph Burrus, with Company F, arrived at Shanley's position, he was assigned to one of the patrols. "He sent [Lieutenant Barry] Albright, myself, and [Technician Fifth Grade Thomas K.] Tom Clevenger (a guy we called 'Dink') to see if we could locate any other guys."[2]

As the patrol moved eastward along a narrow dirt lane that ran through an apple orchard, Private Burrus heard a noise. "Dink heard it at the same time and we all hit the deck. We could see a farm gate at the end of the road, which was maybe one hundred feet in front of us. There was a German machine gun over there. I don't know if anyone saw us or not, but he just started firing, right over the top of our heads. I rolled over into the ditch. I had the bayonet attached to my rifle. I was in the lead, Dink was behind, and the lieutenant behind him. I whispered, 'Dink, go on, get back over that ridge.'

"I heard him move ahead and he in turn passed it to Albright."[3]

Burrus turned and crawled down the ditch away from the German machine gun. "I was slinging that rifle ahead of me and I jabbed him [Clevenger] right in the ass. He sat straight up and called me everything he could think of. I had to get on top of him to get him down on the ground. We crawled on out of there and he was bleeding like a stuck ox. We finally got back to the assembly area. The medics patched him up. He never did forgive me for that."[4]

Before leaving on one of the patrols Shanley dispatched, Lieutenant Ed Ott, with Headquarters Company, 2nd Battalion, placed the group's only light machine in what he thought would be the most effective position. "We returned an hour later and noticed the machine gunner advancing the gun to another position. We heard a shot and saw the gunner had been hit, dropping the machine gun where he lay. The officer in charge was Lieutenant [James] Tibbetts [the 2nd Battalion S-1] and I remember saying to him, 'Stay here, you have a wife and a couple of kids and I'm single.

"Tibbetts replied, 'I ordered the gun moved, so I am going after it.' Before I could reply, Tibbetts started across the field. As he neared the gunner, Tibbetts was hit in the left leg. He threw himself forward, apparently out of the sniper's view, and was not shot at again.

"I started for the gun and was abreast of the machine gunner when I was hit in the helmet. I could feel the bullet buzzing around between my helmet and my head cover and then exiting the rear of my helmet. I passed out. I have no way of knowing how long I was out, but when I came to, I picked up the machine gun and dove into the ditch and ran about twenty-five yards west of where I had been shot, crossed the field, and handed the gun to one of our men. I then went back and retrieved the gunner, clearing the way for Lieutenant Tibbetts to get back safely."[5] Lieutenant Ott would later be awarded the Bronze Star for his actions in saving the machine gun and its gunner.

By the early morning, Shanley had assembled only about thirty-five troopers. "At that time I sent more patrols out and started encountering fairly heavy resistance."[6]

Shanley's position began to receive fire from a large enemy force advancing from the south. Since little in the way of equipment bundles had been found, the ammunition supply was largely limited by what each trooper had carried with them on the jump. Therefore, Shanley ordered his troopers to withhold their fire unless they could identify targets. Throughout the morning, enemy fire increased as the Germans slowly advanced toward Shanley's position.

THE PLATOON LEADER OF THE 3RD PLATOON OF COMPANY D, Lieutenant Lynn Tomlinson, moved silently through the predawn darkness, looking for his men. "I located several troopers even without using the cricket at all, but these troopers were not in my unit. They were from other units that had made the jump at the same time, or just prior or after my planeload of people jumped. I did locate one of my troopers, a fellow by the name of [Private] Frank Haddy. Frank was from Iowa, and he went by the nickname of 'The Stick'. Frank was certainly a welcome sight to me.

"With this small group, we set out in what I thought was the direction of the bridge, which was our objective. As a part of my briefing, I learned that if we didn't have this bridge by daylight, June 6th, the Army Air Corps, with fighter planes, was to knock it out by skip bombing. As daylight approached, which we called in the military BMNT, which means Beginning of Morning Nautical Twilight, we came up on a clearing with a French farmhouse in the middle.

"As I approached the house, a man dressed in farm clothes came out. Upon seeing me, he made some motions which I interpreted to mean Germans were nearby, and I should leave.

"Not looking for any trouble not connected with our objective, we withdrew and continued toward what I thought was our objective again. At daylight, we were in sight of a bridge. To this day, I don't know if this was our objective. At any rate, two planes, either fighters or dive bombers, I'm not sure which, came in at treetop level, flying down the river, skip bombed the center span of the bridge out of existence.

"Our primary objective, now destroyed (we thought), we started in the direction of what I thought was our battalion assembly point. By now, I suppose there were twenty troopers from several units in our group. We decided against using the roads and started going across country, hedgerow to hedgerow. They worried about the roads in Normandy. These were mainly one way trails about ten or fifteen feet wide, which served their purpose for carts, wagons, motorcycles, and bicycles, but it would be very difficult for modern day vehicle transportation to pass on these trails.

"During this journey, I looked across a hedgerow, and on the other side, which was the road side, a group of soldiers wearing German uniforms were going in the opposite direction. The group consisted of four of what I consider kids. I was within five feet of them. One of these kids saw me and smiled. As we were going in opposite directions, I decided that if they would stay out of our way, we would stay out of theirs. So we kept an eye on them until they were out of sight and continued on our way.

"I knew that the bombardment of the Normandy beaches was supposed to start before 6 a.m. on June 6th. And it was going to be heavy fire from our battleships, cruisers, and bombers and so forth. When this fire started, we could barely hear it from where we were located. I knew by this that we were ten to fifteen, maybe twenty miles from the beaches.

"Around 10 o'clock in the morning on June 6th, we came upon a road junction [on the western edge of the village of Gueutteville], which looked like it was fairly well traveled. Having not found our battalion assembly point, or any of my own unit, it was decided that we should set up roadblocks on this road junction, and prevent any movement from going there, Germans troops and whatever.

"By this time, there were probably fifty or sixty troopers in my group, including several officers, none of whom I knew. We divided up the responsibility for coverage of the roadblock, and I was given the section facing towards what we thought was the beach.

"Within minutes, it seemed, two tanks that we assumed to be German, approached our position. Now these were not Tiger tanks, but small post WWI armored vehicles that had a full tank tread. The first of these was quickly knocked out with a stocking [Gammon] grenade. The other tank reversed course and got out of there. The next to appear was a column of troops of platoon size. These troops were engaged, and several killed and others wounded."[7]

Soon, enemy strength built as Bataillon 3, Grenadier Regiment 1057 of the 91st Luftlande Division, supported by light tanks of the attached Panzer Ersatz und Ausbildungs Abteilung 100, closed in on the troopers occupying the village.

Lieutenant Tomlinson later reported to Lieutenant Norman MacVicar, the Company D commander, regarding the subsequent attack. Lieutenant MacVicar used this report for the following award recommendations: "A battalion of German infantry, reinforced by five tanks, arriving from the direction of Ètienville attacked Gueutteville from the west. Corporal [Ernest T.] Roberts, together with Private [John A.] Lockwood and Private [Otto K.] Zwingman had been set as an outpost in a building on the west side of the town. They were the first to see the approaching enemy force and immediately opened fire. First Lieutenant Tomlinson, upon hearing the firing, went to the building and ordered the men to withdraw from their position and proceed to the causeway. He saw that the attacking force had set up machine guns and mortars and had two tanks in position, all of which were firing at the building. They called back that they could hold the attack while the other outposts and the remainder of the out guard withdrew. Lieutenant Tomlinson counted fifteen dead Germans in front of the building and determined to hold the position.

"Lieutenant Tomlinson returned to his own position and directed the defense in other portions of the town. Corporal Roberts, together with Private Lockwood and Private Zwingman, held the enemy at bay for two hours, at the end of which time, Lieutenant Tomlinson saw and heard the tanks fire four shots into the building they occupied. When he observed the enemy beginning to advance, he decided to pull in the outpost, returned to the building, and ordered the men to withdraw. There was no reply. Another soldier near the building reported that the three men had been killed. Due to the severity of the attack, there was no time to verify the statement, and the group under Lieutenant Tomlinson was gradually driven back to the northeast where they joined a group from the 2nd Battalion of the 507 Parachute Infantry defending a position east of Amfreville."[8] Corporal Roberts and Privates Lockwood and Zwingman covered the group's withdrawal and were all captured during the final German assault. All three were later awarded the Distinguished Service Cross for their heroism.

MAJOR SHIELDS WARREN, THE 1ST BATTALION EXECUTIVE OFFICER, had spent the predawn hours of June 6, searching the area around where he had landed for other troopers. "I collected some twenty odd men and ran into Captain [Neal] McRoberts [82nd Provisional Pathfinder Company commander] who had the entire 508 radar outfit. They put up no lights because their lights were lost. The hedges were high and the orchards were practically all over the place near Picauville. I collected between forty and fifty men and headed for Gueutteville, just north of Hill 30."[9]

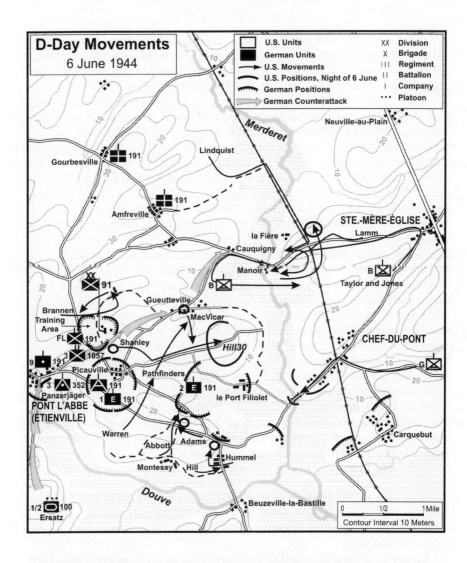

D-Day Movements
6 June 1944

U.S. Units
German Units
U.S. Movements
U.S. Positions, Night of 6 June
German Positions
German Counterattack

XX   Division
X   Brigade
III   Regiment
II   Battalion
I   Company
•••   Platoon

Contour Interval 10 Meters

Lieutenant Woodrow Millsaps, with Company B, had landed west of the Merderet River and by daybreak had found only four other troopers. "It was about 09:00 hours before my small group ran into any more troopers. When we did, they came in and joined my unit in small groups of five or six at a time. With this small group, I decided to move to one of the regimental objectives—Hill 30.

"By now, I realized that the regiment was scattered all over France and the best I could do was to move to Hill 30 and try to make contact with other units of the regiment. Up until now there was little firing from the paratroopers, for we were still trying to assemble our units and move to our objectives without a firefight. But now, rifle fire seemed to be all over France. American troops were returning the fire and there seemed to be Germans everywhere."[10]

Major Warren's group moved north to join Lieutenant MacVicar's group near Gueutteville, picking up troopers as it advanced. Sometime before noon, Lieutenant Millsaps made contact with this group. "With Warren was a group of about 150 paratroopers. We both had the same idea—to move to Hill 30 and join forces with the rest of the regiment or take the position if it was occupied by the enemy troops. Major Warren and I were the only officers in the bunch at this time. While we were talking on the side of the road, a German scout car came barreling down the road. It got right up in front of us when one of our soldiers tossed a hand grenade. It landed right in the middle of the scout car and blew it to pieces.

"While Major Warren and I were talking, we could hear a good firefight going on in the distance from where we were. There was American rifle fire mixed in with it. We knew that it was one of our units, so Warren told me to take a small patrol and go over and see if we could make contact and bring the unit over to join us. I took six soldiers from the group and headed in that direction. On our way over, I ran into a small German unit and we became engaged in a firefight. This went on for sometime and finally we were able to escape and move toward the position where American rifle fire was coming from. The unit we were trying to make contact with saw us retreating from the Germans and recognized us as American soldiers. They opened fire on the Germans so that we could better escape, but my unit thought we were running into another German unit in the rear of us. We started firing at them when American flags began to appear and we recognized that they were friendly troops. This fire from our friendly forces stopped the Germans one hedgerow to the rear of us, and we were able to reach the line group that had been there all day."[11]

When Lieutenant Millsaps and his six troopers arrived, he found a small group led by Lieutenant Colonel Shanley. "I told him that I was from Major Warren's unit and that I would lead him to Warren if we could find a way to evade the Germans."[12]

During the morning, Shanley had been able to make radio contact with Lieutenant MacVicar, who had a group of approximately sixty troopers near Gueutteville, about a mile to the northeast of his position. Shanley and his small force were now confronting at least one company of Grenadier Regiment 1057 of the 91st Luftlande Division. "At approximately noon we were very heavily engaged on three sides, and I pulled out after I found that another group [Warren's], larger than mine, was east of us."[13]

Lieutenant Millsaps then led Shanley's group east to find Warren's group. "When we reached the area where I had left Major Warren, he was not there."[14]

Lieutenant Millsaps then informed Shanley that he and Warren had planned to move to Hill 30. With this information, Lieutenant Colonel Shanley decided to continue moving east in hope of finding Warren's group.

When the patrol led by Lieutenant Millsaps didn't return during the timeframe he had expected, Major Warren had decided to move north with his group to join MacVicar's group near Gueutteville. "I got up to Gueutteville and found part of D and E Company and a platoon of the 505 under Lieutenant [William] Meddaugh. We were on the verge of attacking Gueutteville with one hundred men, but we had no supporting weapons—just rifles and carbines. Since there was an estimated German battalion in Gueutteville, we just stayed on the hill and shot at them. About fifteen truckloads of Germans went by, going in the direction of la Fière."[15]

AFTER ALMOST DROWNING UPON LANDING, Lieutenant Ralph DeWeese, the assistant platoon leader of the 2nd Platoon of Company H, was lying near the edge of a flooded area. "There were two men that were just about twenty yards from me and the grass was so high they couldn't see me. They were talking back and forth, but I didn't know whether they were Germans or French. I finally cut the rest of my harness off and stood up. I was so weak I couldn't carry all of my equipment, so I left my field bag. That was a mistake I found out later, because most of my rations were in it. I didn't know where I was, but started walking away from the heaviest fire. I must have stayed in the water for a good two hours. I finally reached a road, but as I was walking to it, some Jerries kept firing at me, but I just kept going. When I hit the road, I laid down and rested for awhile. I was still panting like a dog that had run for about ten miles. It was pretty cold and I was wet and shivering and shaking. I looked around and couldn't see anyone. I walked up the road and found it was flooded and didn't go any farther. About that time, I heard someone in the water and I walked over and challenged them when they came close to the road. At first they didn't reply, and I didn't know whether I should fire or not. I challenged again and they came back with the reply. It was [Privates First Class Robert L.] Smith and [Thomas E.] Wogan [Jr.].

"We stayed on the road for awhile and soon I saw a dark figure coming toward us. I walked up and challenged and he came back with the reply. It was [Private First Class Edward] Polasky and he had been up to the road junction and had run into a German patrol and had killed two of them. There were four of us now, and of course it was our duty to try to assemble with the rest of the men. I knew we had missed the DZ and estimated we had missed it about five miles. There were still planes flying around trying to get their men in the right spot. Off to the west we saw what might have been a flare. It kept coming closer and soon you could see it was a plane on fire. It had been hit by flak. Just before the plane crashed, I heard the pilot gun both motors. I knew then that the crew was still in the plane. It crashed about fifty yards from where I landed and lit up the whole countryside. The Jerries fired their machine guns into the burning plane. How many were killed I don't know, but I know that no one came out alive.

"The four of us started up the road towards the road junction. About twenty-five yards from the junction, the Jerries challenged us and we hit the ground. They opened up and we fired back. I was lying between the two Germans Polasky had killed. They had a machine pistol and a few rifles. All we had were two rifles and two carbines. We had to withdraw, so I told the men to move back. At that time, I heard Wogan cuss and he had been hit in the shoulder. He was the first casualty and that was our first firefight with the enemy. Smith and Polasky helped him back and Polasky gave him first aid treatment. We laid on the ground for awhile and it was almost daylight. We could hear the firing over the beach now, where the first troops were coming in.

"We came up to a road junction and there I saw my first Frenchmen. There were two men there and we tried to ask if they had seen any Americans. I pointed to the flag on my sleeve and pointed up and down the road. One of the Frenchmen pulled out a package of Lucky Strike cigarettes and pointed down the road. We also met Lieutenant [Victor] Grabbe and Captain [Chester] Graham at the road junction.

"We started working down the road where the Frenchmen said the Americans had gone. We ran into about seventy of them [near] the little town of Picauville. We inquired about the 3rd Battalion and one officer said he had seen Captain [Hal] Creary. We also contacted the machine gun platoon of the 3rd Battalion and that made about forty-five men. In all, we had about two hundred men. We started marching toward Étienville and couldn't go all the way because it was still in enemy hands."[16]

Sergeant Zane Schlemmer with Headquarters Company, 2nd Battalion, joined this same group during that morning. "We came across additional troopers in the various fields waiting to ambush any German activities on the roads and lanes. Each of these fields seemed to be a separate battleground. Before entering, we would examine it through the hedgerows. If there were any cows, we were pleased because we could be reasonably certain that these fields were not mined. Also, by watching the cows, who were by nature quite curious animals, we could tell whether there was anyone else in that field. The cows seemed to associate people with milking and they would stand, waiting, facing anyone in anticipation of being milked. Over all these years, I've had a place in my heart for those lovely Norman cows with the big eyes and the big udders.

"We too, became accustomed to the sound of German hobnail boots on the Norman back roads, whereas paratrooper jump boots were rubber soled and made a much different sound. In this way, we were able to ambush many patrols, merely by the sound on the other side of the respective hedgerows, which were too tall and too thick to see through.

"Also, we were able to distinguish between different rates of fire of the automatic weapons and machine pistols that identified Germans or friendlies, even without seeing them."[17]

BY THE MORNING OF JUNE 6, Private First Class Thomas A. "Tommy" Horne, with Company H, had joined a group led by his company commander. "[Private First Class] Kenneth [E.] High and I got together and came upon a bunch of fellows—about thirty—but one of them was our company commander and another was a lieutenant. Our company commander's name was [Captain Hal] Creary and the lieutenant's name was [Michael C.] Bodak. He was from Headquarters [Company], 3rd Battalion [and the platoon leader of the Light Machine Gun Platoon].

"Well, they had an idea where we were supposed to go. I joined them and we hadn't been with them long, and this German machine gun started firing at us, really close. Well, Bodak, this lieutenant, came back and said, 'Thomas, you all go get that machine gun. We need a machine gun.' Well, I took it that a bunch of us would get up and go get the damn thing, but there were only four of us who went over to get it. They shot one of the fellows as we were going over there, so that meant that only three of us. But going over there, I fired two or three rounds out of my [M1] rifle at where these guys were shooting at us. We got into this area that we figured the machine gun was [positioned], and it was an overgrown road. There were three of us left, and one of them was [Private First Class Richard W.] Canterbury, from Headquarters [Company,] 3rd, and we called him, 'Cannonball'. He had a rifle. The other fellow with us was a guy who had been a German. He claimed he had been in the German glider troops before the war. He was in our unit, but he spoke good German. Anyway, he had a broken foot and was walking around with a foot that was all swollen.

"We got in there where this German machine gun was, or thereabouts, and we couldn't find it. So we started walking down this little road that was all pretty close together [narrow]. Now, I had already fired say, four rounds out of my rifle. I've only got four rounds in my rifle and I looked down to the left and I almost stepped on them. There were five Germans down there. One of them had a grenade in his hand, one of those little potato-masher grenades, but they had a machine gun there. So I just opened up with my rifle until I emptied it. Well, that M1, when you fire that last round, that clip went BLING! It threw the clip out. The other guy had a rifle and the other one had a Thompson submachine gun to finish them off. But in doing so, we damaged their machine gun—the gun we wanted. We [had] hit it with some armor [piercing] ammunition and it shot a hole through the receiver.

"Then, while we were there, some Germans started talking to us, down this little road a piece, and this boy who spoke good German said, 'They want to give up, but they're afraid we're going to shoot them.

"I told him, 'No, tell them to come on in,' but the talking went back and forth and they quit talking.

"In the meantime, Captain Creary and Bodak sent Kenneth High over to tell us to hurry up, get that gun, and come on, because we've got to get out of there. I said, 'No, we've damaged this gun. We're going to try to get another one.' So anyway, we went down there to where this other [German machine] gun was supposed to have been, but they were gone.

"Then we went back to where the company was and they were gone. We never did find out where they went. We found out a month or so later that they had been captured while we were over there getting this German gun."[18]

Horne and the other two paratroopers with him soon found the Company H operations sergeant hidden in the bushes. "His name was [Sergeant William A.] Medford [Jr.].

"I said, 'Medford, do you have any idea of where we've got to go?'

"He said, 'I know where we've got to go.' We took off and started down this road with Medford. He had the maps and he knew where we were going. He was kind of at the front of us. He came to a blacktop hard surface road and saw somebody down the road a piece, and he hollered at them. He thought it was one of our guys, but it was a German MP directing traffic. We finally got away from those guys and we got across the road."[19]

Private First Class Tom Porcella, another Company H trooper, joined the group led by Sergeant Medford and Private First Class Horne. This small band soon joined the large group of around two hundred troopers, of which Sergeant Zane Schlemmer and Lieutenant Ralph DeWeese were members. However, Private First Class Porcella wasn't sure who was in command of the group. "This group of paratroopers got the order to move single file along the hedgerow, which at that time paralleled the road. While we were proceeding alongside this hedgerow, the column stopped when we received word that someone heard a vehicle coming down the road toward us. So we wanted to know whose vehicle it was. Was it ours or was it the Germans'?

"They believed it was a German motorcyclist. The man in front of me, his name was [Private First Class Richard] Canterbury said, 'I'll shoot the son of a bitch.' He raised his rifle and was waiting for the motorcyclist to come down the road. He took careful aim and waited until the cyclist was about fifty feet away and he fired a single shot. The German was suspended in midair, while the motorcycle continued to go on and crashed into the side of the road. The German soldier just laid there in the middle of the road on his back; his arms were outstretched. He looked very young. This was the first dead German I had seen since I parachuted into Normandy. We stayed in our position for awhile and we waited to see if there were anymore Germans on the way. A few minutes seemed to pass and then they gave the all clear. 'Move on.' We ran in leaps and bounds, keeping our eye on the road and on the field towards our right.

"An amazing thing was somebody was always shouting an order at us, but we never knew who the hell it was. We never knew if it was an officer or noncom, but we just followed the man in front of us and just did what we were told. After running a short distance, the column stopped again. I asked, 'Why are we stopping?'

"Someone said, 'Well, there is a road up ahead and we have to cross this road and we've got to be careful. As soon as the first man crosses, we'll get the OK to keep going.'

"So I guess one trooper decided to make his run and be the first one to cross the road. He reached the middle of the road and all we could hear was a shot that was fired and the trooper fell, face down.

"I'll never forget; his arms were outstretched as if he was reaching for the other side. Immediately there was an exchange of machine gun fire and rifle fire. A hand signal was given to keep going. We were all moving very rapidly. Still, we didn't know where we were going and we had to leave this trooper there, right where he fell   right in the middle of the road, all alone. It was very sad. With all of this uncertainty of not knowing where we were going, fear began to grip us. I know I was scared as hell."[20]

After finding Ètienville too strongly defended, Lieutenant DeWeese and this group of approximately two hundred troopers withdrew to the northeast. "We kept bypassing the enemy and finally set up in a field [east of Picauville]. We heard some of our weapons fire and thought it was some of our men in an attack. After sending out a patrol, we found Germans who had gotten some of our equipment and were firing our weapons."[21]

After arriving in that field, Lieutenant DeWeese decided to eat something. He had left his musette bag in the water where he had landed by parachute, which contained most of his rations. "I had some rations in my pocket and took them out and much to my disappointment they were soaking wet. I had to throw them away and that left me with no food. Everything I had was ruined."[22]

While moving eastward in search of Major Warren's group, Lieutenant Colonel Shanley's group found Lieutenant DeWeese's group in the field east of Picauville. Lieutenant Colonel Shanley took command of the combined group. "I collected approximately two hundred men and officers, lost members of the 508th and from all battalions who had gotten together there, and I set up in that location, which was one thousand yards east of Picauville. With two hundred men, I had two machine guns, no mortars and no other automatic weapons."[23]

Lieutenant Colonel Shanley organized the combined group into three platoons and moved the force to more favorable defensive terrain a couple of fields away. Shanley then sent out patrols to look for equipment bundles, cut telephone lines, and bring French civilians back for the purpose of obtaining information about German dispositions. "We didn't have much success in getting the bundles on the ground. I did have SCR 300 radios, however. By radio, I got in touch with another group which was commanded by [Major Shields] Warren.

"Several different groups of Frenchmen informed me that there were about five hundred Germans in Picauville [two companies of engineers of Pioniere Bataillon 191 and Batterie 9, Artillerie Regiment 191, both units of the 91st Luftlande Division] and more than that in Étienville [Kompanie 3, Panzerjäger Abteilung 352, of the 352nd Infantrie Division].

"Having almost no heavy weapons and with so many Germans between my group and the objective I selected the one mission that the regiment had that I felt I could accomplish—seizing a crossing of the Merderet River."[24]

NEAR GRAINVILLE, SEVERAL MILES NORTH OF THE DROP ZONE, Technician Fourth Grade Paul Bouchereau, with the regiment's medical detachment, was with a group of about fifteen paratroopers, led by a lieutenant from the 507th Parachute Infantry. "We attacked a railroad station that was guarded by no less than twenty-five Germans. We suspected that the fact that it was guarded at all meant that something there should be destroyed. The Germans were taken completely by surprise and all were killed or wounded. We set fire to a few boxcars and blew up a locomotive but didn't find out the reason for it being guarded. Perhaps something of greater value was expected to come through. At any rate, we didn't wait to find out. We moved out and were joined by other groups and by dawn had a group of about three hundred headed by a very nervous captain.

"It was about 9:00 in the morning of our first day on the continent that I witnessed an unusual event. Our group was joined by a group of some twenty-five or so troopers mostly from the 508th. Among them was a Colonel [Harry] Harrison. Our captain greeted Colonel Harrison with enthusiasm, saying that he was happy to turn over his command to a higher ranking officer. Colonel Harrison refused. The captain was beside himself with anger. He cited his inexperience, rank, rules, regulations, and so forth, but the colonel was quietly adamant, even after the captain promised that he would make a full report of the incident. Unfortunately, I cannot recall the name of our captain. But be that as it may, I believed then as I do now that he did a masterful job of leading our [group]. I do not know if he was a regular or a civilian soldier, but I am certain that if he lived through the war and chose to make the army his career, he served with distinction and rose to a high rank."[25]

Major Dave Thomas, the regimental surgeon, had jumped behind Harrison and was with the same group of troopers. Thomas also observed the actions of this West Pointer. "He abrogated command to a red headed major [Benjamin F. Pearson, executive officer of the 2nd Battalion] out of the 507th. He, Colonel Harrison, refused to take charge."[26]

AFTER LANDING ON THE WESTERN EDGE OF FLOODPLAIN of the Merderet River a mile or so north of the la Fière causeway, Colonel Lindquist assembled around seventy-five mostly Headquarters Company, 508th troopers and another twenty-five or so artillerymen serving as an advance party for the divisional artillery, which was due to arrive by glider that evening. Enemy fire began to build in the area to the extent that it was deemed impractical to attempt to advance south along the area west of the river. Instead, Lindquist decided to take his group across the flooded area to a raised railroad embankment and follow it south and cross the Merderet River at either the la Fière causeway or the causeway farther south at Chef-du-Pont. A submerged road across the floodplain was discovered and Lindquist and his group used it to get to the railroad embankment. There, a French family at a house located at the intersection of the submerged road and the embankment, oriented Lindquist as to his location. While there, another group of about fifty troopers, mostly with Company G, 507th Parachute Infantry joined his group. Lindquist formed his group into three companies: the 507th troopers under the command of Captain Floyd V. "Ben" Schwartzwalder, the commanding officer of Company G, 507th; the artillerymen under the command of its senior officer; and his 508th troopers under the command of his headquarters company commander, Lieutenant Robert Abraham. Since seizure and control of the western end of the la Fière causeway was a mission of the 1st Battalion, 507th, Lindquist put the 507th troopers at the front of the column. He placed the artillerymen behind his Headquarters Company troopers at the rear of the column.

The group proceeded south along the embankment, which gradually dropped below ground level to a cut and underpass below the road running west from Ste.-Mère-Église to the la Fière causeway.

Just east of the causeway and bridge over the Merderet River, on the south side of the east-west road, a large farmhouse known as the Manoir and a number of outbuildings dominated the approach to the eastern end of the causeway and the ground to the east. Lindquist's group left the railroad tracks and moved in columns west along the road leading to the causeway. Lieutenant John H. Wisner, the S-2 of the 2nd Battalion, 507th, was leading a small group ahead of the column when an enemy machine gun opened up on them about three hundred yards east of the Manoir. "A dozen or so men in my party all hit the ditch. I sent a message back to Lindquist that I was getting fire from my front, and that I would like a patrol to knock it out. Time passed while the men rested in the ditch. Since nothing was happening as a result of the message, I decided to see if I could work up toward the machine gun. In the field on my right, to my surprise, I found a platoon of the 508th, and in the field on the left I found a company of the 505th. Some minutes passed and a message came up from Lindquist that he wanted me to join him for the move south."[27]

Lindquist withdrew the lead element of Company G, 507th troopers about a thousand yards and decided to execute a flanking maneuver to the south and then west toward the river, just as Company A, 505th had done earlier when it ran into German machine gun fire. Meanwhile, the division commander, General Matthew Ridgway found Colonel Lindquist at about 10:00 a.m. and released the artillerymen to proceed to the division command post, located just east of the railroad and north of the Ste.-Mère-Église to la Fière causeway road.

LANDING EAST OF THE MERDERET RIVER, about 1,500 yards west of Ste.-Mère-Église, Lieutenant George Lamm, the platoon leader of the 2nd Platoon of Company A, followed a herd of cattle along a lane until he found another trooper. "He told me that the 505th Parachute Infantry Regiment pathfinders were just up the hedgerow, and gliders were now coming in on the night lights and radar. The officer in charge I knew. He was [Lieutenant Michael C.] Mike Chester, commander of the [1st Battalion] 505 PIR pathfinders. He directed me to the assembly area and I was sent to division headquarters where the 508 men were coming in. An officer came by and asked me if I was from the 508 PIR and he took me to a trooper leaning against a tree. I had been told that it was General Ridgway, the division commander and ranking general officer now in 'Fortress Europe.' The general came forward, grabbed my shoulder and asked if I was a 508 officer. When this was confirmed, he laughed and said, 'I have forty men for you from the 508 PIR. Take them to the la Fière bridge and help Colonel Lindquist take it.' He directed me to a big, burly sergeant with a red beard and lo, I had a combat command!

"When I asked directions to the bridge I was told straight down the road and to follow the sound of the guns. The general laughed again. We formed two columns and hit the road toward the bridge. Dawn was breaking as we lit out.

"Ahead of us we soon saw a platoon of troops marching in the direction we were headed. Our scouts reported that they were Germans. We halted and decided to ambush them farther down the road. As we swung out to flank them, we discovered they were engaged by a force to their front. They had been ambushed by another column of ours. Bypassing the fight, we were continuing toward the bridge."[28]

TECHNICIAN FIFTH GRADE WILLIAM A. DEAN, a radio operator with Company B, had landed in the flooded area on the east side of the Merderet River just north of Chef-du-Pont. "Others had landed nearby, and soon we had a small group of about six or seven and we headed north, guiding on the Paris-Cherbourg railroad right-of-way. It was past 3:00 a.m. when we got to the [road leading to the] la Fière causeway. Here, the rigors of the preceding day and night made us first sit down, and not long after, lie down in a ditch and go to sleep."[29]

Southwest of Ste.-Mère-Église, Sergeant Bud Warnecke, with Company B, checked the time on his watch. It was about 5:00 a.m. "We had assembled one group of about eighty men and two officers. One of the officers was Lieutenant [Homer] Jones, who was my platoon leader. We had instructions to go to our objective area regardless; though we did not have a company per se. Lieutenant Jones became the company commander of this particular group. He broke it down into two platoons. He designated me as a platoon leader of the 1st Platoon. Another sergeant by the name of [Bill] Call was designated as a platoon leader of the 2nd Platoon.

"We got oriented, so we moved out towards our objective area. We went through Ste.-Mère-Église at about 6:00 in the morning. The town had been secured, but we could see all the damage that was done the night before. We were headed for a causeway that could get us to our objective."[30]

As Lieutenant Jones and his group moved along the road running west from Ste.-Mère-Église, they found and joined Colonel Lindquist's group, just as Lindquist was executing the flanking movement to the south. With his newly arrived troopers, Lindquist now decided to attack the Manoir from the east with Lieutenant Jones' group of about eighty mostly Company B troopers, advancing in the fields adjacent to the south side of the road running to the causeway. Company G, 507th troopers would attack west through fields to the south to flank the German positions, then turn north to assault the Manoir from the south. Lindquist kept the Headquarters Company troopers in reserve.

Lieutenant John W. Marr, a platoon leader with Company G, 507th, led the flanking movement. "Schwartzwalder sent me around to the south of the Manoir to near the water's edge to see if we couldn't get around there. We had five people in my group and we were going down this hedgerow which was exposed to the water on one side, and the Germans opened up with a machine gun at the southeast corner of the cattle feed lot. They had a machine gun emplacement there; manned by two Germans. They opened fire, luckily high. We were within grenade distance of that machine gun when they opened up. We hit the ground and lobbed grenades, probably at least one apiece. The two Germans that were manning that gun jumped up and surrendered. But they did hit two of our people. We had to haul one out and the other was walking wounded. We went back to Schwartzwalder and told him what had happened."[31]

As this was occurring, Lieutenant Lamm's group of around forty troopers came upon Lieutenant Jones and his group of about eighty troopers. They joined forces and moved forward to attack the Manoir. As they approached an old Roman burial mound a short distance east of the Manoir, they came upon Lieutenant Ernest J. Hager, with Company C, along with Technician Fifth Grade Bill Dean and a small group who were firing at the Manoir. This small group joined Lieutenant Jones and his group and together they moved forward. Lieutenant Jones took the point just behind a scout, along with "Bill Dean, George Lamm, and George's runner. Between us and the buildings was an earthen Roman wall on the side we were on. The house was built on a slope that led down from that Roman wall. We were going down in a combat formation—

spread out, but we were pretty naked on the slope going down toward the building. We came under fire—automatic weapons fire as well as rifles. They were largely in a tower of the main building, the residence of the area. Bill Dean was my radio operator, and he and I headed for a tree that must have been about five inches in diameter."[32]

The group returned fire from their exposed position, but the Germans were firing from small windows, protected by the thick stone walled building. Despite this, Technician Fifth Grade Dean kept up a steady fire with his carbine. "One hell of a firefight erupted, during which point scout [Private] John [J.] McGuire, who was just at my right elbow, was shot through the head and killed. I just stared down at him, not wanting to believe what I saw. But my shock was short lived when several more volleys from the Manoir whizzed by my head."[33]

Caught on the open slope, the group was in trouble. Lieutenant Jones acted quickly, using a white phosphorous grenade. "When I threw [it], that created tremendous smoke. We went back up the slope and when I went back, I discovered a little sunken lane that led into the courtyard of the buildings. I started down that lane, which gave cover right up to the courtyard. I ran across the courtyard and got up to a door [on the second level] that went into the house itself. They heard me knocking on the door—there was a machine gun mounted inside the house, and they fired out right through the wood of the door, but didn't hit me. It just cut the knee of my trousers a bit. There was a lieutenant from Charlie Company named Ernie Hager and he was in the building across the lane from me, and that same burst hit his earlobe. The door had a small window about eye level, six by eight inches or so, with bars across it. There was no glass in it. I threw a hand grenade in through the window in the door, so the firing stopped.

"The house was built on a slope like a three level house, the top floor was the main floor, and on the uphill side the house would just be one story. On the downhill side there was a basement. I went down the steps on the same side of the building, into the basement of the house, [in order to go] up the stairs to get into the room where I first threw the grenade. Up above, I realized there were people. So I started firing through the floor. About this time, [Lieutenant Lee] Lee Frigo came in. Lee was my assistant platoon leader. We started shooting up through the floor together, and then they started shooting back down through the floor. Either Lee or I had thrown a grenade through the door in the back of this cellar. A first sergeant [Ralph Thomas, with Company E] came bursting in all fired up."[34]

First Sergeant Thomas had a Thompson submachine gun, a devastating weapon at close range. "I ran through the basement door into a very dark room. It took a few seconds for my eyes to get used to the darkness and then I saw the two lieutenants standing next to the wall on the left side of the door.

"I could hear the Germans running across the floor above me, so I started firing through the ceiling of the cellar, the floor of the room above, and the

Germans ran faster and fired down at me, but their firing was way off target. I fired in front of them and pulled the gun back into them as they walked and ran across the floor. I could hear some of them talk in a loud voice.

"I carried ten twenty-bullet clips for my Tommy gun in a canvas bag, and as soon as I fired them all I ran back out to the barn [to get more ammunition]."[35]

Shortly after Thomas left for more ammunition, Lieutenant Jones decided to enter the main house from the cellar. "There was a flight of stairs that went up to the floor that was the level of the ceiling of this garage. As we were going up the stairs, somebody yelled, 'There's a white flag out.'"[36]

When Lieutenant Lamm and other troopers entered the house to clean out any Germans who might be hiding, he saw the effects of Thomas' submachine gun. "The room seemed full of bleeding and moaning soldiers, some on benches and tables. Some were pulling off trousers to attend to leg wounds. Several were on the floor with heads covered with blankets. Those not engaged in assisting a buddy, held their weapons at the ready—watching us. Troopers from Company B herded those apart and took their arms.

"An NCO found an attic or hidden room. I followed, and suddenly there was loud shouting and a muffled roar. When I arrived, a bloody encounter was in progress. Apparently the cease fire and surrender order had not been passed on, or had been ignored. Troopers prodded POWs along with bayonets and pulled several Germans out of hiding places."[37]

By approximately 2:30 p.m., the Manoir and eastern end of the causeway were secure. For his bravery and leadership during the capture of the Manoir, Lieutenant Jones would later be awarded the Silver Star. Lieutenant Jones ordered his troopers to turn over the German prisoners to the 505th. "I got my people together and we went across the causeway."[38]

When he received the order to move out, Technician Fifth Grade Bill Dean was getting ready to eat his first meal since the previous evening. "After hastily eating a distasteful K-ration in the presence of eight or ten dead Germans, we proceeded to cross the bridge."[39]

Earlier, around the church at the hamlet of Cauquigny near the west end of the la Fière causeway, Lieutenant Joseph Kormylo, with Company D, 507th Parachute Infantry, established a small defensive position to hold that end of the causeway. "Just about the time [Lieutenant Louis] Levy and I had finished setting up our position around the church, two 508 officers came up the west bank of the river with about forty men. There was a conference, and we told them that we considered this position very important, and so the 508 party joined us and set up a defensive position covering generally from the fork in the road and the ground southward from it. They had a bazooka, and so a roadblock was established near the church."[40]

Meanwhile, Lieutenant Jones led fifty to sixty or so mostly Company B troopers across the causeway. When the group reached the western end of the causeway, Lieutenant Jones deployed them for the move south. "[Lieutenant] George Lamm had one of the platoons and went down to the village [of Cauquigny] where a little group of shacks were. And [Lieutenant] Kelso Horne [with Company I] had another platoon that went toward the riverbank. There was a group from the 3rd Battalion of the 508 set up right at the end of the causeway."[41]

Lieutenant Jones and his two composite platoons advanced south in the fields east of the road leading to Gueutteville. "We heard tanks and there was a lot of automatic weapons and small arms fire coming toward us. Then, the leader of the group that was at the end of the causeway came over and said, 'We're withdrawing.' By the time we were able to move, they had already withdrawn and we were cut off from the end of the causeway. We had to make it back as best we could across the river."[42]

Lieutenant Jones' group was now forced to withdraw eastward across the flooded Merderet River. Company B trooper, Technician Fifth Grade Bill Dean, was near the front of the column. "We came under heavy fire from tanks, mortars, and machine guns from our right rear. They had us in a pocket. We could not go back across the bridge! Straight ahead, or to the right put us in their gun sights, and to the left was the flooded river.

"When the tank machine guns opened fire, [Private Forrest V.] Lefty Brewer and I broke for the water. An instant later, Brewer, my old Camp Blanding platoon sergeant lay face down in the water, dead! I swam the river back to the east shore, swimming like a porpoise, down and up, down and up, because I was being fired at the whole way over and beyond, since I had a ten foot bank to get over after leaving the river!"[43]

Sergeant Bud Warnecke led one of the groups of Company B troopers down to the river. "I took my platoon through a marsh. We had concealment with the tall reeds, but very little cover. I moved, took my platoon, and got to the river. At this point, a tank pulled up on the causeway approximately one thousand yards away from us. I took my men into the river, which had steep banks. We could crawl along the banks with everything covered but our heads. We were still in machine gun range. The bullets were dancing off the water and you just don't know how you could live through something like this, but we did.

"I got my platoon and got them around a bend in the river where we had cover and [were] well concealed. At this point, we saw some of our own troops on a small piece of higher ground in the area. We made our way over to this area where they were. They were from another battalion. At this time I took a headcount and found that I had at least two men missing, one was [Private First Class Ralph] Tooley from Tennessee, and the other was [Private] Forrest Brewer from Florida. I became very fond of these two men over the past twenty months. Forrest Brewer was a professional baseball pitcher."[44]

Company B trooper, Private First Class John Taylor, and two others crossed the floodplain and approached the deeper river channel. The two troopers with

Taylor were afraid to try to swim across. "One was a Mexican kid who couldn't swim and the other fellow was from Iowa and he was no great swimmer. So I said, 'Well, I'll go first.' So I had the rifle and my helmet, and I started to swim, and I could see this tank [on the causeway] swinging the gun around down in our general direction. You kind of stick out like a sore thumb when you're trying to swim a river with thirty pounds of equipment in your pocket. So I thought, 'Well, I'll outsmart them. I'll duck under the water and swim under the water.' Well unfortunately, I was under the water and I tried to come up and I couldn't come up. I was waterlogged, had all this equipment—hand grenades, Gammon grenades, K-rations, first aid kit—you name it, in our heavy pockets. I just went down. I said, 'This is it. I'm never going to get out of here.' For some reason then, I started crawling on the bottom and all of the sudden, I could feel the bank of the river going up and I was able to crawl out and lay on the bank just utterly exhausted. I told the other fellows, 'Don't try to swim underwater.' Luckily for the Mexican boy, there was a Mae West laying there and he inflated that and was able to float across."[45]

Upon reaching the east side of the river, Technician Fifth Grade Bill Dean, a radio operator with Company B, was exhausted. "I lost my rifle, ammunition, and all my gear during the frightful swim. After my breathing returned to normal, I headed north along the river until I came upon a makeshift aid station where twenty or more troopers were being attended to by several medics. The weapons and other gear of the wounded had been stacked in a corner of the room, so I went to the pile and reequipped myself."[46]

Lieutenant Jones, who helped cover the withdrawal, was one of the last to cross the river. "Close behind me were the Germans. The flooded area was maybe three feet deep and the bull rushes were maybe three feet higher than the water. I discovered that every time I moved, the bull rushes would move. The [Germans] on the bank would see that and fortunately they underestimated the height of the bull rushes and so they fired at me. So I stopped moving and just sat there in the water for a long time. I waited for most of the afternoon and into the evening."[47] Lieutenant Jones then finished crossing the river under the cover of darkness.

During the time Lieutenant Jones and his group had crossed the causeway, Colonel Lindquist and his Headquarters Company troopers had remained on the east side of the Merderet River and had dug in along the river south of the Manoir. The 1st Battalion of the 505th subsequently relieved Lindquist's group and General Gavin ordered him to withdraw to the intersection of the railroad and the road from Ste.-Mère-Église to the la Fière causeway to form a division reserve. There, a defensive line was established along the hedgerow just east of the railroad in order to cover a withdrawal from the river, should it occur. It was while at this position that Colonel Lindquist's group became a collecting point for stray 508th troopers who had landed east of the Merderet River.

ON THE MORNING OF JUNE 6, CORPORAL THEODORE SVENDSEN, with Company H, concealed himself along the east bank of the Merderet River, south of the causeway at Chef-du-Pont and acting as a sniper, inflicted numerous casualties on German troops defending the causeway.

Also that morning, after following Lindquist's group south along the railroad tracks to the intersection with the road running west from Ste.-Mère-Église, Brigadier General Gavin ordered Lieutenant Colonel Arthur A. Maloney, the 507th executive officer, to take seventy-five troopers and execute a wide flanking movement to capture the causeway at Chef-du-Pont with an approach from the east. A short time later, Gavin received word that the Chef-du-Pont causeway was undefended, and he took another seventy-five men under the command of Lieutenant Colonel Edwin J. Ostberg, the commanding officer of the 1st Battalion, 507th, directly south to Chef-du-Pont via the railroad tracks.

After landing east of the Merderet River and assembling his Company D platoon, Lieutenant Francis J. Bolger, led it toward Chef-du-Pont with the expectation of crossing the causeway to join the regiment. Upon arriving, Bolger found the town under attack by Lieutenant Colonel Ostberg's mostly 507th troopers. Lieutenant Bolger and his platoon joined the attack and after clearing the town, the combined force, now reinforced by the seventy-five mostly 507th paratroopers led by Lieutenant Colonel Maloney, destroyed a German strongpoint defending the causeway, then neutralized Germans dug in along both shoulders of the causeway. From his position south of the causeway, Corporal Svendsen inflicted many more casualties on enemy troops attempting to reinforce the defenders of the causeway.

Despite being wounded in the leg, Lieutenant Bolger continued to lead his platoon in the capture and defense of the causeway that afternoon and evening against repeated German counterattacks to recapture it. Lieutenant Bolger was later awarded the Silver Star for his valor during the seizure and retention of the Chef-du-Pont causeway. Corporal Svendsen would be killed in action on July 4, and never knew of the award of the Silver Star posthumously for his actions, which contributed greatly to the capture of the causeway at Chef-du-Pont.

AFTER LANDING IN THE FLOODED AREA BEHIND UTAH BEACH, Technician Fourth Grade Bob Kolterman, the Company G communications NCO, had been unable to find the equipment bundle containing his radio. "By daybreak, three-quarters of G Company was assembled and ready. About this time, a French farmer with a shovel and rubber boots came warily along. He would know where we were, so the call went out, 'Frenchy, front and center!' Frenchy was a Cajun from Louisiana and naturally spoke some version of French.

"So Frenchy shows up and in his soft, slow voice says, 'Parlez vous Francais?' This, of course, was quite obvious, but we did get an idea of where we were. So G Company bypassed Ste.-Mère-Église and headed for Chef-du-

Pont. A sniper in a tree held up the whole company for many minutes until one of our mortars got him. Our first engagement!

"Of course, I had no radio—didn't know if it was dropped, or if dropped, where to look. Besides, it would be water-soaked and useless. With no contact with the outside world, we began to wonder if the invasion was called off and we were just plain left out in the cold. Anyway, by nightfall we did get to the east end of the causeway to the bridge over the Merderet. We encountered live and dead German soldiers—also dead American troopers, and even worse— dead civilians—including two 3-4 year old kids."[48]

During the march to Chef-du-Pont, Captain Frank Novak and Company G picked up another group of approximately twenty-five troopers, led by Captain George Simonds, the 2nd Battalion S-3.

BY SUNRISE ON JUNE 6, 1944, TECHNICIAN FOURTH GRADE O. B. HILL, with Headquarters Company, 1st Battalion, was very fortunate to be alive. He had landed in the floodplain on the north side of the Douve River, west of the confluence with the Merderet River, and had almost drowned. "I was making my way in what I felt was the right direction, I heard a noise coming from my left side. It was men walking and I did not know if they were enemy or friendly. I stopped and laid flat on the ground. I then realized that I was at the edge of a trench that was about four or five feet deep. The men were walking in my direction in this trench. I remained quiet and they passed me. There were about twenty-five of them and at the end of the column, one of the men spoke to another and I knew that they were German. I could have reached out and touched their helmets as they passed me. I was sure that they could hear my heart pounding, but they did not.

"When they had passed, I jumped the ditch and continued until I heard someone say, 'Flash'. My reply was not the proper codeword, I said, 'Oh shit!' I had completely forgotten the proper password for the moment. I was lucky, because the person challenging me was one of my corporals, [Technician Fifth Grade] William P. Brown from Detroit. We compared notes and decided that we were going in the right direction and continued on the path that was there.

"Along the way, we picked up more jumpers and soon discovered that we were not the only troopers who were dropped in the wrong place. We found men from the 505, the 507, and even two from the 101st Division.

"At our first crossroad, we met our first resistance and we engaged in a fierce firefight. My guess is that this lasted about twenty minutes. We eliminated this problem and continued on in the chosen direction.

"We were challenged again before we reached one of the main roads. This time we were seriously outnumbered and the only explanation for our coming out ahead is that we were more determined and perhaps better trained. We lost some of our men along the way. That was our first experience and it was not a good one. We had been trained for this, but nothing can prepare you for seeing friends and comrades falling around you. The memory of that experience will stay with me forever. We had some wounded men also, but they were able to keep up. We had no medics, so each of us took turns treating the wounds. Each man had a first aid kit.

"At about 10:00 a.m., we arrived at a village which we later learned was Beuzeville. Across the river from Beuzeville was the village of Beuzeville-la-Bastille. We were on one side of the road and we found Staff Sergeant [Raymond J.] Ray Hummel on the other side of the road. There were some houses on his side of the road and on our side there were two buildings. Both of these buildings had troops in them and we went to the one on our right to secure it. There were only a few Germans in it and we now thought that the other building was occupied with our troops. I made an attempt to cross the bridge [and causeway over the Douve River to Beuzeville-la-Bastille] and immediately was met with artillery fire from the other side of the river. The explosion blew me off the road and into the ditch. It also discouraged me from making another attempt. I returned to the group and we crossed the road to join forces with Staff Sergeant Hummel. At this point [Private] Melvin [H.] Beets said that he would go over and get the rest of the troops from the other building. It resulted in Mel being captured, because the building was filled with Germans.

"Staff Sergeant Hummel and I compared notes and decided that together, we had about fifty-two men and that we had lost about twenty-five of them up to this point. Our best guess is that we had twenty-six still able to fight. We had secured ammunition from all of the men that we had lost, and at this time we were in fair condition. We had no heavy weapons, no officers, no medics, no radios, and we were not sure where we were. We could see where the two rivers came together and decided that this village must be Beuzeville. We knew that there were numerous Germans at the crossroad just ahead of where we were. In order to make a better decision on what we should do, we decided that we should get to a higher spot and try to see what was around us.

"I knocked on the door of the house we were behind and got no response. I then shot the lock off the door and found that people were in the house. The mother was just about to open the door when I shot the lock off. These people were badly scared, but they did not interfere and seemed glad to see us. Hummel and I went up the stairs and we were followed by [Corporal James J.] Jim McMahon, who waited at the top of the stairs to notify us of any action from below. Hummel and I went to two large windows at the front of the house and we were looking in all directions to see if there were any signs or other items that might help us along.

"At this point, we heard [three French Renault] tanks approaching from the bridge that I had tried to cross earlier…One passed the building and the second one stopped immediately under the window where Ray was standing. The turret opened and the German stood up so he could see around also. I handed Ray a

Gammon grenade and he dropped it in front of the man standing in the turret. This knocked the tank out of action and the other two were trying to figure what had hit it. They did not see either of us in the window.

"We left that building and once again joined the men in the fields behind the houses. If the two tanks had pursued us, we could not have stopped them, because we had no heavy weapons and an M1 rifle will not stop a tank." [49]

While waiting in the field behind the houses, Private David Jones, with Headquarters Company, 1st Battalion, had field stripped his M1 rifle and was cleaning it after landing in a flooded area the previous night. "Up to this time I had not fired a shot. No sooner did I get the M1 all laid out and drying nicely, someone yells, 'Tanks!' I finally got my weapon reassembled and watching those tanks rattling up that causeway towards the farmhouse that we were hiding behind gave no cause for celebration.

"Now these were French Renault tanks, probably the smallest tanks used during the entire war. But to me, they were larger than life. I remember the lead tank had its hatch open and the black-capped tank commander was exposed from the waist up, hands resting outside the turret. I can't explain why in the world I said it, but to my nearest companion I said, 'I think it time to get our war started.' There was immediately a lot of discussion as to what the results would be if we fired on them, and the comments were not encouraging. I did fire at that tank commander with an armor piercing round that I had loaded as a number one round. It hit the turret. The black uniform disappeared, the hatch clanged shut, the tank backed off a few feet, and our group scattered to the four winds. Not only had I missed my first shot of World War II, but was now confronted with where and how to hide. All I could think of were those tank tracks running up my back as I'm lying there in the vegetable garden behind this farmhouse. The tank fired a round into the side of that farmhouse. We in our small group offered no more resistance and took off through an adjacent hedgerow." [50]

After assessing the situation from their position on the second floor, Technician Fourth Grade Hill left the house with the other two troopers to rejoin their men. "While in the upstairs of the house, we had not seen anything that would help us to escape from this area. In the area behind the houses, we soon learned that we could not cross the river to our west [where the floodplain of the Douve River extended north, between Beuzeville and Montessy] and could not cross the floodwaters south of us. There were machine guns in both of these directions, plus the 88 across the river that had knocked me into the ditch. Our only hope at this time was to move in [a northerly] direction across the hedgerows.

"We had a 101st man who had been shot through the stomach and we did not think he could do any hedgerow jumping. We gave him a supply of morphine and some sulfa powder and promised that if it were possible we would send help for him. We placed him in one of the outbuildings and started making our way across the fields and crossroads.

"We were plainly visible from the road as we were jumping the hedgerows. Hedgerows are not easy to cross. We crossed two at a time and the others kept watch for resistance from the road at each field. Everything went fairly well and we made it to the next road, which we found was the causeway going to Chef-du-Pont. That was one of our objectives, and we were now sure that we had gone in the right direction after landing in the water. There was firing in all directions around us. It sounded as if the battles were quite fierce. At the present moment it was quiet in our area and we were thankful for that. We quickly learned the difference in the sound of the Germans guns when compared with ours."[51]

As Hill and Hummel's group moved north, Private David Jones glimpsed a small group of farm buildings in the distance. "To our direct front was a farmhouse sitting on a T-intersection and shortly we learned it to be occupied by about a squad of Germans. When they showed themselves, we fired on them."[52]

When the firefight erupted with the Germans in the farmhouse and barn, Technician Fourth Grade Hill took immediate action to deploy the group. "[Staff Sergeant] Hummel and I had the men spread out along the two hedgerows—one row facing each direction, so that we were protected regardless of where they hit us. During the periods of no firing, they dug foxholes along the edge of the hedgerows. I remember Dave Jones was dug in immediately to our rear. Hummel and I were at the north side, closest to the road. There was a barn and a barn lot in front of us and a two story house on the corner. It was occupied by the Germans and we started firing at it in force. We could not go farther as long as they occupied that house. In the middle of this firefight, we heard an American voice yelling for us to stop shooting or the Germans would kill them. Some of our men were being held prisoner in the house. We stopped firing at the house, but we were still being fired at from the road. [Private First Class Augustus D.] August Labate was killed at this time by a burst from a machine pistol.

"Our ammunition supply was rapidly disappearing. If we had not taken an extra supply at the airfield and had not taken the ammunition from those who were killed, we would have been out by now.

"Hummel and I discussed this problem and wondered about the opinion of the men with us. We decided to ask them if they wanted to surrender or stay till the end. Every man said the same thing, 'We have come this far and we do not intend to give up now.' There would be no surrendering from this group.

"In the beginning of our ordeal on June 6, we ended up with a total of about fifty-two men. We had lost half of them along the way and we had some wounded. We were pinned down in that final field."[53]

Private Jones felt the group had a pretty defensible position. "We had the flooded area to our backs, hedgerows on each side, a rock wall next to the adjacent row. It was a fairly secure position."[54]

LANDING NORTH OF THE DOUVE RIVER, Corporal Kenneth "Rock" Merritt with Headquarters Company, 1st Battalion's light machine gun platoon had found two equipment bundles shortly after landing, illuminated by the flames from a C-47 that crashed a thousand yards away. Being alone and not knowing where he was, Merritt had taken one of the machine guns and all of the ammunition cans he could carry and had set off to find his unit. Later, Merritt had heard some noise on the other side of a hedgerow and challenged with his cricket, and had given the password. "It was Lieutenant [Edgar] Abbott, the platoon leader of the 81mm Mortar Platoon of Headquarters Company, 1st Battalion, 508. He had with him seventeen men. By daybreak, we had assembled thirty-five men.

"Prior to moving out towards Hill 30, I received my first combat order. We were receiving fire from one machine gun to our right flank, and Lieutenant Abbott turned to me and said, 'Corporal, take two men with you and knock out that machine gun.' I guess it was a calm way that Lieutenant Abbott ordered me to knock out the machine gun nest, like, 'Take two men and go fill up the water cans.'

"Anyway, I picked a man by the name of Private [Wilbur E.] James and a former sergeant reduced to private by the name of [Delbert E.] Fairbanks to go with me. Private James knocked out the machine gun, and Fairbanks and I kept the Jerries pinned down. This was the first time we learned the little trick that the Jerries had—firing tracers three feet above the ground and then firing regular ammunition eighteen inches off the ground."[55]

In the moonlit early morning of June 6, Staff Sergeant John Boone, the platoon sergeant of the Light Machine Gun Platoon, Headquarters Company, 1st Battalion, found Private First Class Lawrence G. Fitzpatrick, the trooper who jumped behind him in his stick. In the course of looking for other troopers they came upon a house. Staff Sergeant Boone decided to ask the people living there where the Germans were located. "Having had high school French, I thought I could handle this query. I rapped, the door opened, and I said, 'Où' and the door slammed in my face. So much for that—we wearily wandered trying to locate our equipment bundle. We had no success in this. I had seen it when I jumped out of the plane, but when my Tommy gun cracked me in the head, I lost track of it.

"It was getting on towards daybreak and the firing of weapons was rather sporadic. We then heard some sustained firing quite close and moved in on it. We found several other members of our platoon. They had knocked out a German observation post. Several of the Germans had been killed and our boys were using their bodies (the Krauts) for bayonet practice. This really shook me up; it was really appalling to see what was happening. It was though these men had been loosed, and they had actually gone bezerk. They looked it. When I hollered at them to knock it off, they immediately stopped. I just felt for a few brief moments, their minds had slipped. They were not themselves. Not a bit. They appeared to me to have just gone mad for a short time, but they immediately snapped out of it.

"Before we left this spot, daylight had definitely established. From the observation post action, others were attracted and we soon had thirty or forty men, all in good shape, and we started to travel north to the highway connecting Chef-du-Pont and Ètienville. While crossing this road, as I recall, a couple of German weapons carriers came down the road."[56]

Private First Class Robert White, with Company A, was acting as the scout for the group. "There was a gap [in the hedgerow] that opened up to the roadway and just as I stepped out in the road, here came two truckloads of Germans. They saw me and swerved into one of the fields and they all unloaded, and a firefight started. I went ahead and crossed the road and was lying in a prone position on the other side of the road with my little folding stock carbine. Not being that used to it [the carbine], I hadn't really had it too long. I went around one of the hedgerows and peeked out and when [this German] saw me he drew back. Well, I started to take the safety off of the gun. It still had the safety on and I hit the release for the clip. One was in front of the trigger guard and one was behind. I hit the wrong one and it fell out. I put it back in and I put the thing right where he had put his head before, lying there in the prone position. Sure enough, he peeked back again and I squeezed the trigger. He fell out in the road lying on his back and was wiping his forehead. I don't know whether it went through his helmet or what, but I lost all faith in that carbine. I shot him two or three more times in the rib cage."[57]

Meanwhile on the other side of the road, Staff Sergeant John Boone and the rest of the group engaged in a deadly and fierce firefight at close range. "I was the last man in the column and was able to fire on the two vehicles with good effect. From the screaming and hollering, I know some of the Germans were hit, and the second vehicle crashed into the ditch."[58]

The firefight ended when the Germans withdrew down the road and the group of troopers pulled back one field to the south. When Private First Class White crossed back over the road he didn't find the group—just two dead troopers. "One of them had a Thompson and I traded him right there. He had an ammunition bag. I started crawling up through the field and they hit my backpack. My pack was above the grass—that was all they could see. I rolled up on my shoulder and that's when I got a bullet hole through the sleeve. I made it back to the field where they had pulled back and set up a circular defense."[59]

Staff Sergeant Boone and his group were soon joined by another group of troopers. "Apparently this noise brought us to the attention of another group of troopers headed by Captain Jonathan Adams of A Company. We joined this group, resuming our push to Hill 30. We were soon hit by some heavy resistance. One of my closest buddies was at the head of our column and was one of the first casualties in our group. I later learned by a burst of machine gun fire."[60]

Corporal Rock Merritt and the others in the group were quickly pinned down by fire from their front, right, and left flanks. "Our lead scouts were killed. We tried to counterattack, but got repulsed. Keep in mind that we had no artillery support and only two machine guns. We pulled back to the line of the departure area, and dug in and set up a roadblock to our rear. We finally reestablished radio contact with Lieutenant Colonel Shanley on Hill 30. We tried several times to break out of our twenty acres of real estate that we were holding, but each time we got pushed back. The decision was made to hold our position and the roadblock. Our location was in the vicinity of the Montessy area." [61]

Throughout the fighting that day, Captain Jonathan Adams, the commanding officer of Company A and leader of this group, showed great personal bravery and skill in leading the troopers, many of whom didn't know him.

Staff Sergeant Boone helped to get the group organized into a perimeter defense. "We dug in and prepared to defend ourselves. It turned into a rather quiet time, as we waited, and apparently the Germans did the same, no one knowing what was there and what we were faced with on either side. We were all aware of their presence as their armor and trucks could be heard very clearly from the nearby road.

"Towards dusk, I decided I was not going to leave my buddy's body out there in no man's land. I decided to go out and bring him back, so we could at least give him somewhat of a decent burial. I went over the hedgerow into the next field of the same nature, and I made my way along the hedgerow towards the spot where he was reported killed.

"After a couple of hundred yards, I noticed a farm shed across the field from me. I suppose this was a shelter for cattle. I noticed someone in this shed waving at me, sitting inside, leaning against one of the walls. It turned out to be one of our troopers who had been wounded, and he was unable to move.

"In view of this, or this bit of change in my plans, after all, I couldn't help my buddy, but I might be able to help this fellow. So, I went over to the shed, I got the trooper up over my shoulders and I carried him back to our area, where he could be given medical attention. By this time, darkness was coming on and necessary security measures had to be taken. We all looked forward, hopefully, to a little sleep, and the food that would be dropped to us the next day, neither of which happened. It had truly been a long day." [62]

That night, Private First Class Robert White heard an explosion at the group's roadblock. "A German vehicle came down the road, one of those I'll call a jeep [Kübelwagen], with three guys in it. [Private First Class Joseph E.] Chuck Atkins, from Headquarters 1st, threw a Gammon grenade out there and it hit right on the hood and that's where the gas tank was and the thing burned up with the three Germans in it." [63]

ON THE AFTERNOON OF JUNE 6, LIEUTENANT COLONEL SHANLEY received an order by radio from Colonel Lindquist to move his men to Hill 30. Shanley then relayed the order via radio to Major Warren, whose group broke contact with the enemy at Gueutteville and moved south to join Lieutenant Colonel Shanley's group. Private First Class Joseph C. Bressler, with Headquarters Company, 1st

Battalion's 81mm mortar platoon, was with Major Warren's group. Bressler had been wounded badly in the ankle shortly after landing. "As the combat capable men prepared to move, all the ammunition was collected from the wounded and injured. Warren told the injured and wounded men, 'We do not have the capability to take you with us. You will either have to surrender to the Germans or hide until friendly troops get here.'

"When the group left, [Private] Oscar [S.] Prasse, carrying me piggyback, tried to keep up with them. Then the troopers deployed as a firefight started. When the fight finished the group assembled and continued toward Hill 30, I was left behind."[64]

Major Warren's group joined Shanley's east of Picauville about 7:00 p.m. As the double column moved toward Hill 30, the 2nd Battalion S-4, Lieutenant George Miles, near the rear of the column, heard another officer shout to exhort the troopers onward. "I suspect that the noise frightened another paratrooper on the other side of the famous hedges. In his fright, he sprayed bullets through the hedges and one of them hit me in the left thigh and knocked me down and into a ditch which ran along the line of the hedges.

"I am diminutive, about 5'7" and in those days, I weighed about 130 pounds. As I lay in the ditch, face up, another good friend of mine, an officer from F Company, [Lieutenant] Hoyt Goodale, a gangly fellow seeking to escape the flying bullets, dove down over me and we found ourselves face to face in the ditch. I can recall still to this day saying to him in a calm voice, 'Oh Goody, would you mind getting off of me—I have been hit. And I remember this giant of a man barely lifting up his helmet where the edges of his met mine and repeating three or four times, 'Am I off you now, George?' Of course, the 6'4" which remained of his body still covered me as I lay in the ditch.

"I felt no great pain, as I recall, and received almost immediate medical attention after the confusion of the scared soldier was sorted out. The medics covered my wounds with sulfur and gave me a shot of morphine and then—and I find this surprising, I suppose even today—the column marched off and left me in the ditch."[65]

As darkness fell, Private First Class Joe Bressler, the Headquarters Company, 1st Battalion trooper with the badly wounded ankle, had not been discovered by the Germans. "That night [Private Oscar] Prasse came back for me. He carried me about a quarter of a mile to an unoccupied house alongside a road. We moved into the third floor of that house and had a view of the road in both directions.

"During the night, we heard an approaching motorcycle. Prasse was at the window and killed the rider with his rifle. He went out, dragged the cycle and rider out of sight, and returned with the German's Schmeisser (machine pistol).

"Still later that night, we heard another motorcycle on the road. Prasse killed the second cyclist with his newly acquired Schmeisser. He hid the dead rider and his cycle and brought the German's Schmeisser for my use."[66]

During the night on Hill 30, paratroopers were busy digging defensive positions and establishing outposts and roadblocks. Many of the enlisted men were taking orders from NCOs and officers they hadn't previously served with and didn't know. Staff Sergeant George Christ was the communications section leader with Headquarters Company, 2nd Battalion. "Colonel Shanley had his hands full trying to organize us, as we were from all different regiments. It was Lieutenant [Lloyd] Polette [with Company F] who activated combat patrols and set up roadblocks at various points leading to Hill 30."[67]

Late that night on Hill 30, Private First Class Tom Porcella, with Company H, dug a two man foxhole with a buddy. "We were told that one man sleeps and the other man stays awake. We were also told not to smoke and keep in close contact with each other during the night. We were going to move at the crack of dawn. I remember shivering from the cold night air. My thoughts were of GI blankets and a hot cup of coffee; and thinking, how the hell did I get into this predicament? My teeth would not stop chattering and I continued thinking of England, the mess hall, the food, the hot coffee, and the warm stove. It was not possible to sleep at all. The night became colder and colder."[68]

Midnight on June 6, found Sergeant Zane Schlemmer with Headquarters Company, 2nd Battalion, on an outpost at the bottom of Hill 30. "Six June, 1944, 11:59 hour found my body bone weary, but mentally alert, dug in with a parachute; which was very, very warm, and very luxurious in my foxhole."[69]

Private First Class Walter H. Barrett, with Company B, had been wounded in the thigh during the movement to Hill 30. The medic had refused to give him morphine, because he was concerned about Barrett being able to keep up with the group. Barrett was one of the last to arrive, at around 2:00 a.m. with the help of his best friend. "Ed [Private First Class Joseph E. Suits] assisted me by putting my right arm around his neck and his arm around my waist. With this arrangement, we were able to maneuver."[70]

By 2:00 a.m., Lieutenant Colonel Shanley had collected about four hundred troopers from every parachute regiment of the 82nd and 101st Airborne Division, some of them wounded. Shanley's men were desperately short of automatic and antitank weapons, as well as mortars. They had only one 60mm mortar, three .30-caliber machine guns, one Browning Automatic Rifle (BAR), and one bazooka. Private First Class Frank Staples was a bazooka gunner with Company D. "I was the only one on Hill 30 with a bazooka. Someone found one and gave it to me. I wasn't all that eager to get it. I don't know why they picked on me."[71]

Making matters even worse, Staples didn't have his assistant gunner—he would have to load the bazooka. "[Private First Class Joseph] Joe Lizut was supposed to be my loader when we jumped in Normandy. He came out of the plane right behind me. It was a real lonely feeling when I'd draw fire."[72]

Coming into the perimeter on Hill 30 late that night, Private First Class Ed "Bogie" Boccafogli, with Company B, was shocked by what he found there. "It was a mess there. There were so many wounded along the ditches. They had them head to toe. I believe it was Major [Shields] Warren who took command of our battalion, because [Lieutenant] Colonel Batcheller had been killed. I found some of the men from my company—[First] Sergeant James [W.] Smith [from Elizabethton, Tennessee], and [Private] Jim Kurz, [Private First Class] Albert [J.] Patchell, [Private John E.] Payet, and a few others who were there. That made me feel better, because we had a confused mess. We had men from the 505 PIR; we had men from the 101st Division mixed in with us."[73]

AT 6:40 P.M. ON JUNE 6, 176 GLIDERS BEGAN THE JOURNEY from airfields in England to Normandy in the largest glider mission of the war thus far. The plan was for the gliders to land at Landing Zone "W" southeast of Ste.-Mère-Église near Fauville. The gliders carried Battery C, 80th Airborne Antiaircraft (Antitank) Battalion, with thirteen 57mm antitank guns; the 319th Glider Field Artillery Battalion, with twelve 75mm pack howitzers; the 320th Glider Field Artillery Battalion, with its twelve short barreled 105mm howitzers; and medical personnel of the 307th Airborne Medical Company. In addition, the gliders carried ninety-two vehicles (mostly jeeps), and 107 tons of ammunition, medical supplies, water, food, mines, grenades, and other ordnance. The mission was divided into two echelons, each consisting of two serials. The landings would commence at 9:00 p.m. The 319th Glider Field Artillery Battalion, which would be in direct support of the 508th after landing, would be transported in the first serial of the second echelon.

Major James C. Todd, the commander of the 319th Glider Field Artillery Battalion, and the battalion's advance party had come in by glider at 4:00 a.m. on June 6. "The remainder of the battalion, consisting of 16 officers and 321 enlisted men, under the command of Major James T. Wilcoxson, battalion executive, departed Membury airdrome at 21:37 hours in forty Horsa gliders."[74]

As the gliders carrying the 319th came in over the east coast of the Cotentin Peninsula, Corporal Salvatore J. "Ted" Covais, with Battery A, was standing behind the pilot and copilot to get a good view through the cockpit windshield. "All of a sudden, as we crossed the beach, we went into a whole barrage of antiaircraft and machine gun tracer bullets."[75]

Technician Fourth Grade Edward R. Ryan, with Battery C, was riding in one of the huge British Horsa gliders. "We experienced ack-ack fire and saw a lot of fires on the ground; then they cut us loose. We crashed at over one hundred miles per hour in a lot less than two acres; the wings were torn off, it rolled on its side, and stopped. The pilot and copilot were killed instantly. There were about thirteen killed and ten escaped. The Horsa should never have been used."[76]

The wings of the Horsa glider carrying Captain John R. Manning, the Battery A commander, were torn off and the glider fuselage crashed through a row of trees and came to rest in a hedgerow. The pilot was badly injured and the copilot killed. The passengers and cargo were all thrown forward into front of the glider. Captain Manning was knocked unconscious. "I came to on a pile of rubble still holding the watch [he used to count off the seconds after release of the towrope for the pilot]. I found my right hand to be cradling my partially disconnected thumb. Naturally, I bypassed my medical packet and wrapped my thumb in a dirty handkerchief. I found that I could hardly move my back, dragged out my .45 Colt and tried to take charge."[77]

The Horsa glider in which Corporal Covais was riding also broke apart during the landing. "We smacked right into the trees at least a hundred feet up and we splattered right down. We had both of our wings sheared off, and when that happened—man, the whole top of the glider came off with it. We pancaked right down...

"I could hear the machine guns firing all around us—bup, bup, bup, bup, bup, bup. My knee was banged up and I had a bad cut across my forehead and left eye. I was bleeding like a pig, but I was lucky."[78]

Lieutenant Laurence F. Cook, a replacement officer who had joined the battalion in March, landed with his glider more or less intact. "I counted eight [gliders] that crashed in the same field I was in, but we were the only one that landed at least halfway right."[79]

Private First Class Silas Hogg, with Battery A, was nearly killed during the landing. "The glider I came in on, it hit, and it hit with such force that it drove the pilot through the top [of the glider]. The pilot was crushed, you couldn't even recognize him. We hit the ground so hard that we ricocheted across a road. The left wing hit a tree, pulled us to the left. We're still in the air. Now get this, we got shoved to the left, we hit another tree on the right and that swung us back to the right. Another glider came in right at exactly that second and it crammed straight into us.

"When I came to, well, I heard, 'Get off of me you son of a bitch! Get off of me you son of a bitch!' I was knocked out and laying on top of [Corporal Robert] Bob Carte."[80]

The collision of the two gliders killed Sergeant Ralph W. Wade, who was a passenger in Hogg's glider.

Major Todd learned that the air corps had badly missed the landing zone, southeast of Ste.-Mère-Église. "This part of the battalion landed at 22:55 hours about two miles north and east of Ste.-Mère-Église, approximately 5,200 yards from the designated landing zone. The gliders landed in the German front lines and the outpost lines of the 4th Infantry Division. As a result of the landings, two officers and fifteen enlisted men were killed, four officers and sixty-eight enlisted men were wounded and evacuated, and two officers and eighteen enlisted men were wounded but not evacuated.

"The elements of the battalion that assembled in this area moved to an area which was in the rear of the 4th Infantry Division front lines. This move was completed at 05:00 hours on 7 June 1944; and the balance of the day was spent salvaging equipment, evacuating wounded, reorganizing the battalion and contacting division. Upon checking with the 4th Infantry Division, it was learned that the battalion was cut off from the [82nd Airborne] division."[81]

The total of 109 killed, wounded, and injured suffered during the landings represented a thirty-two percent casualty rate and this was incurred before the 319th could even get its guns into action.

AT AROUND MIDNIGHT ON JUNE 6, PRIVATE HARRY REISENLEITER, with Company B, reflected on what he had seen on D-Day. It had been an experience he would never forget. "The first dead paratrooper that I saw was apparently killed by a mortar round, because the fins were in the near area and it looked like a piece of the shrapnel had hit him in the back of the head. He was laid out with his hands folded and flowers between them, just like he had been laid out in a mortuary. I thought this was a very nice gesture from whoever did it for him. I'm sure it must have been one of the civilians. I also saw other troopers that were in trees that had been hung up there by their parachutes. And as they hung there, they had been shot and had their throats cut. One of the troopers had landed on the roof of a building, and his parachute was wrapped around a chimney, and he was hanging there when someone had reached out the window where he was hanging and cut his throat. Another was tied to a tree with suspension lines from his chute, and apparently he had been shot."[82]

"It was a time of mixed emotions: there was fear—fear of being injured yourself, fear of having to inflict injury on other people to survive, fear of being afraid. It was a time of even prayer, which a lot of the troopers were not all that familiar with, and I guess I made some rash promises. Then, as the day wound down and began to settle down a bit, the dawning of the next day seemed to be a little brighter."[83]

CHAPTER 4

"THE GERMANS HUNTED US"

During the predawn hours of June 6, 1944, individuals and small groups of paratroopers fought desperately for survival. Widely scattered during the jump, they moved through the Norman countryside, trying to find organized units, fighting their own small wars against German troops, who were hunting them. It was a deadly game, where one mistake could be fatal.

In the moonlit darkness of that morning, Lieutenant Paul E. Lehman, the 3rd Battalion S-1, and a few other paratroopers moved down one of the hedgerow lined Norman lane. "We came across a group of five men from another battalion who were standing up in a close group talking. Immediately I went to them and strongly ordered them to scatter out into a patrol formation as to have some security and to move out at once toward their objective. No sooner had I finished my order than firing burst out nearby and we all ducked for the ground. In the darkness my chin came down on one of their bayonets, entering my throat between the chin and windpipe. The blood gushed out as if a spigot had been turned on, and Lieutenant [Briand] Beaudin could not stop the flow because of the type and location of the wound. Luckily he was with me, as he was the battalion surgeon, and jumped number two in the stick I jumpmastered. A facial artery directly off the jugular had been severed and each time I swallowed, it moved the artery and thus prevented the formation of a clot there."[1]

Upon seeing Lehman's wound, Lieutenant Beaudin, the 3rd Battalion's assistant surgeon, took immediate action. "I was able to apply a hemostat, but with subsequent movement in the brush, the two-piece hemostat flew off, never to be found. So I applied a Carlisle dressing which was too bulky and soft to stop the flow of blood. Then, two medics, Corporal [Technician Fifth Grade] Frank Kwasnik and Private First Class Frank Ruppe, and I fanned out in different directions to locate a medical bundle, which Kwasnik did find in about thirty minutes and brought me some plasma."[2]

By the time they returned with the plasma, Lehman was barely clinging to life. "By then I was terribly weak from loss of blood and the plasma probably saved my life."[3]

Beaudin administered the plasma while the group was still under sporadic German fire. "Unfortunately, I had no way to hook the plasma bottle up, so I had to hold it up myself with my arm extended while German snipers kept peppering me and the bottle with shots. Fortunately, they missed, and were soon routed out and killed. We then brought Lehman out with a few other wounded to a farmhouse barn. After being there an hour or so, I noticed some German soldiers coming down a nearby field towards us. I could not leave my wounded, so I waited. Soon, the open barn was raked with rifle and Schmeisser fire. I stuck my Red Cross helmet on a long pole and pushed it out the door. They stopped firing and came in to capture us."[4]

Lehman was lying on a stretcher found in the medical equipment bundle. "They searched us and then knocked on the door of the next room. When the French women didn't answer quickly enough to suit them, they threw a potato-masher grenade through the window and probably killed them instantly."[5]

Lieutenant Lehman, very weak from the loss of blood, became concerned as the German patrol prepared to move out, that they might shoot him rather than be burdened with moving him. "Instead we were put out in front of them—with the doc and one of his medical aid men carrying my litter—and we were taken to their company aid station [near Gourbesville]. Shortly afterwards we were evacuated by truck to a German field hospital several miles away, where we were placed in a framed barracks. The German hospital was located in what had once been a large chateau [near Orglandes]. The main building was of stone and concrete and at one time it must have been a magnificent home. Around it were many large stone barns and outbuildings to which the Germans had added five [wooden] frame barracks as additional housing for the wounded. We were well treated by the enemy medical personnel.

"The Doc [Lieutenant Beaudin], of course, supervised all the medical attention that was possible with the limited facilities at hand. Through his efforts, a few of the most critical cases were operated on by the German surgeons. They were overwhelmed with cases to the point of exhaustion, day and night. One operated on me the next night [June 7] and tied off the severed artery and sewed up the wound on the inside only. Every day, additional wounded were brought to our building, and when I was strong enough to get up and move about, I interviewed each one for information of our troops.

"When some of my strength had been regained, I took over administration of our barracks—the serving of the meals, sterilization of water, cleaning up the building, fixing of the beds, carrying some of wounded outside during the hours of sunlight, salvage of equipment and collecting of personal effects of those who died, etc."[6]

Lieutenant Beaudin saved as many patients as possible with the limited means available. "All we had were our first aid kits. A Catholic priest who was a sergeant in the German army and in charge of scheduling in the surgical suite in the chateau proved to be a godsend in enabling us to rush a few Americans in for definitive surgery. Private First Class [and medic Frank] Ruppe spoke fluent German, which was very helpful in many respects, not the least of which was getting us all some rations, including some ersatz tea from the German mess sergeant."[7]

AFTER GETTING INTO A FIREFIGHT WITH SEVERAL GERMANS and being badly wounded in the left hand and leg shortly after landing near Gourbesville, Private First Class R. B. Lewellen, with Company I, hid out hoping to contact other Americans. "Burrowing under the hedgerow, I spotted some Americans in a firefight with German troops in a nearby farmhouse. I decided if I could get through the hedgerow and get to the road and reach those GIs, I might find a doctor or a medic. I wiggled halfway through, but was caught on my equipment and couldn't go either way. Hearing a German vehicle approach, I forced my way back into the pie-shaped pasture. Taking only my knife, this time I decided to try the other side of the field, where I promptly ran into two German soldiers who took me prisoner. By this time I was real thirsty, and I asked for a drink. The Germans told me the water was no good, but one of them offered me a drink from his canteen. It was milk. I spit it out and lay back down, convinced I was going to die. Feeling something falling into my face, I wiped and discovered it was blood, my blood. An artery in my shattered hand had severed and was spraying into the air. I showed my captors, and they took me to a trench just on the other side of the tree where my night in France began. I had almost landed on top of a trench full of German troops. The Germans I had shot at must have been going to the trench when they saw me. I assume they were part of a German roadblock at a nearby crossroad.

"The soldiers in the trench took me to a farmhouse which the Germans had converted into an aid station. A German doctor there told me in English that the hand needed to be amputated. They put me on the floor and eventually gave me a shot to knock me out. When I awoke, my left hand had been amputated and a rough bandage had been wrapped around my leg. I was given a quart of weak wine to slake my thirst. I also drank the quart of wine they had given to a U.S. major who had been wounded, although I would regret it during the long ambulance ride to come.

"They placed the major and me into a converted school bus, along with two wounded Germans, one I assumed I had shot. We traveled about fifteen hours to a German hospital and were strafed a couple of times along the way. Once at the hospital, the major and I were separated and I never saw him again."[8]

Also that day at Gourbesville, there was a heroic stand by Private James R. Hattrick, with Company I. Staff Sergeant Michael Rainer, with MII Team Number 412, which was attached to the 82nd Airborne Division, filed an investigative report on July 7, 1944, about the actions of Private Hattrick. "The mayor of Gourbesville, Mr. Michel Delaune, who seems to know all the details of the story, was contacted.

"Several paratroopers of this division dropped northeast of Gourbesville, about 1/2 to 3/4 mile from the village during 5-6 June and obviously worked their way toward the village during the night.

"Mr. Delaune's home is the chateau of Gourbesville, destroyed by fire by the enemy on 13 or 14 June. Up to 23:00 6 June it was being used by a German medical company as a CP and first aid station. More than one hundred German medics armed with rifles, machine pistols, and light machine guns were stationed there; the remainder of that medical unit, probably a battalion, was stationed at Amfreville. From 07:00 7 June to 14 June the castle served as a CP for a German regiment.

"Mr. Delaune became aware of the presence of American soldiers in the vicinity of the castle at about 06:00 6 June, because the guards had been replaced by a cordon of outposts surrounding the castle, some of them dug in and others in ditches and hedgerows. These enemy soldiers were being fired upon throughout the day, but Mr. Delaune could not see the soldiers doing the firing. However, he believes that there were five or six in the vicinity of the castle and some others in another part of the village. That morning Mr. Delaune went to a farmhouse, about four hundred yards north of the castle and there found two wounded paratroopers and another taking care of them.

"The Germans lost men from the fire all day long and were returning it fiercely. They sent out several patrols to locate the paratroopers and probably found one or two of them hiding near the castle. In the afternoon at about 17:00, Mr. Delaune, under the pretext of bringing his horse out of the firing zone, tried to locate one of the paratroopers from the direction the heavy firing had been coming from and in which the Germans were firing all day. That soldier was hiding in a hedgerow in a large field, adjoining the garden of the castle. Mr. Delaune wanted to tell him to go to the farmhouse where the wounded were, to get some food from the farmers and to hide there. However, the soldier was so well camouflaged that he could not discover him. Shortly afterwards both sides were again firing heavily. The Germans sent out another strong patrol and apparently killed that trooper at about 18:00 and captured or chased away the others. At about 19:00 the Germans brought in the body of this American paratrooper. At the same time, they collected the bodies of nine German soldiers, at least six of them fell in direct line of fire of the paratrooper and credited to him by the mayor. The medical soldiers buried him in the cemetery of Gourbesville, also the nine dead Germans, and four or five other dead Germans who had been brought to the cemetery earlier. Later that evening, they brought to the cemetery at least eighteen other dead German soldiers and they were preparing to bury them there. However, when they suddenly started to move westward they took those bodies along. The mayor also claims to have seen them taking along a large number of wounded, including some American paratroopers and several [unwounded] American prisoners. The two wounded in the farmhouse were never discovered by the Germans and were being cared for by the farmers until the arrival of our troops in Gourbesville. On 1 or 2 July they came back to Gourbesville to thank the farmers for hiding and caring for them.

"When the American Graves Registration personnel removed the body of the paratrooper on 30 June (they were going to bury him in an American cemetery) the identity of this soldier became known: James R. Hattrick, ASN 34591767. The people of Gourbesville, who had taken fresh flowers to the soldier's grave every day, requested that a memorial stone be erected on the site of the soldier's grave. It has been decided that a memorial plaque to the heroic soldier's memory will be placed on the memorial stone in the cemetery for the French dead of the Wars 1914-1918 and 1939-1940."[9]

Another Company I trooper, Private John Richards, was able to join a small group of troopers during the predawn hours of June 6. "Looking around the area told us that we were not near the designated drop zone. At daybreak, we had breakfast from our K-rations and decided to travel by way of the hedgerows. I can't remember in what direction we decided to travel.

"We traveled several miles, staying close to the hedgerows. We came to a brick wall along the roadway, and on the other side of the road, there was a white farmhouse, so we decided to check it out. One by one we climbed the wall. I was last to get over the wall. While [Private] Jack Fawkes was about in the middle of the road, there was a squad of German soldiers just at the bend in the road. Let's just say we got caught with our pants down. Right there and then, the war was over for us. They took our weapons and marched us back up the road. Much to our surprise, we were in a German bivouac area. The Germans were washing clothes and cooking in a wooded area, and there was a large building in this area. After we were stripped of our gear, we were taken one by one into a room for interrogation. All they got from us was name, rank, and serial number. That evening, we were turned over to some SS guards and started our move towards Paris."[10]

PRIVATE FRANK M. RAMIREZ, A MEDIC ASSIGNED TO COMPANY B, was captured on June 6, while giving aid to a trooper who had broken his leg. "All of my possessions were taken from me, and after I had been taken up into the line to be questioned by an officer who seemed to know more about me than I did myself, I was marched to a collecting point ten miles in the rear. The next day, while we were being moved from here in trucks we were strafed by Allied planes. I was hit in the arm, but I made a break from the column and ran about two miles. Then my arm was bleeding so badly that I entered the first house that I saw.

"The woman there bandaged my arm; but while they were doing so, the man went out and returned with a German sergeant who was guarding an American lieutenant. The sergeant took us to an enclosure, from which on 12 June, we were moved to the hospital in Rennes."[11]

Private First Class Roland E. Archambault was also one of the Company B medics. "About thirty of us got together as soon as we landed and defended a hedgerow until the afternoon of 6 June. Our party then retreated, leaving me to look after seven men who were too badly wounded to move. We were surrounded and taken to a barn near the German [91st Luftlande] divisional headquarters.

"The next day, 160 of us were taken by truck to St. Lo. On the way, we were strafed by Allied planes and 19 of our 160 were killed and 48 wounded. About fifteen kilometers out of St. Lo, I was left with twenty wounded men for two days. On the second day when I was sent down the road to get a cart, I made off into the woods and hid, but two days later I was recaptured by some Germans who did not know that I was an escapee and who sent me to another regimental aid station. I tended wounded soldiers there for four days, did the same for a week at an evacuation hospital near St. Lo, and was then marched to Villedieu where for ten days I assisted Captain Koleman, whom I found working in an operating room there. We were then sent to Mortain overnight and from there to the hospital in Rennes, where I was put to work with a French POW in the X-ray room."[12]

Private Ramirez and Private First Class Archambault eventually escaped while still in France and made their way back to Allied lines.

MOVING THROUGH THE BOCAGE AND STAYING CLOSE TO THE HEDGEROWS on the morning of June 6, Corporal Thomas Gintjee, with Headquarters Company, 1st Battalion, had seen only Germans and a couple of French citizens since he had landed. "Sometime in the late afternoon, I spotted two paratroopers coming toward me, whom I recognized as riflemen from A Company. I could have kissed them! Since we had come from opposite directions and had not seen any of our group—which direction now?

"I had cut across a narrow paved road some time earlier—and now emboldened by company and more firepower—led the way back. My reasoning was that the 'briefing' said we could expect to meet our own armor coming up from the beaches about noon. It was well past that, but they would have to come up a road such as this and not through the bocage. There was a semi-covered hollow in a corner of a field by the road—high embankments around us but open to the front with a clear field of vision and fire. (It had, alas, no 'backdoor' or escape.)

"So I made my stupid decision! We would hold there and observe the traffic— and if the beach armor didn't get there—to cut across that road at night moving east. There was a lot of traffic—all German. Armor and men started down that road about an hour later and continuously; some even supped with us (five feet of hedgerow separating us) as we could hear their mess gear. I kept waiting for the column to pass. I was certain that we should get the hell away from there. But they kept coming. This impasse continued for some time. Then about six Germans—two officers with non-coms—came onto the field *with their backs* to us. They were pointing to the other end of the field. Turning, they saw us trying to huddle into invisibility. But we had those six cold. They also had us cold.

"My instinct was still to open fire when one of the riflemen grabbed my barrel and said, 'It's useless. They'll kill us!' He was right without question. But the tussle was academic as a horde of Germans flooded onto that field and we stared into, by my frenzied count, about umpteen-and-three barrels!

"The Germans were very slick; they went immediately to a hidden pocket on the chest which held a switchblade knife—not a weapon as much as something to cut parachute shroud lines if you were hung up in a tree. I was amazed at how many Germans were there. They moved us down the road about five thousand yards, [which was] lined with them, to some sort of command post.

"Here I found their 'bag' of paratroopers, among them [Privates First Class Herbert] Hesse, [Hubert] Johnson, and [James] Alexander, who had been 'rolled up' immediately upon landing. Hesse had been shot in the back, but was upright and stable, Johnson was intact, Alexander had been shot through the wrist, but most important he landed waist deep in the flooded fields. Anything deeper and you drowned!

"Coming dusk, we were ordered to stand. I was sure that they were going to gun us down. We faced them with stoicism. But, the Germans turned us around and put us on a truck. I was one of the best map readers in the battalion, even giving classes on it, but I still to this day do not know precisely where we landed or probed. I do know that we were about twenty minutes away by truck to St.-Sauveur-le-Vicomte, where we were taken for possible interrogation."[13]

PRIVATE FIRST CLASS WILLIAM SAWYER, WITH COMPANY D, was captured north of the Douve River on June 6, after his small group had been hunted by the Germans for most of the day. "After we were captured, they carried us to this building and put us in this room and I met one of my buddies, and he told me my platoon sergeant was there. So I went over to see him. That was [Private] Walter [V.] Turner, who was [previously] the platoon sergeant for 3rd Platoon, D Company. When I knelt down beside him, he said, 'Watch it, my leg's broken.' I went around to the other side of him, and he said, 'Watch it, that one's broken, too.' He had broken both legs on the jump. Also, Captain [Francis] Flanders was there, company commander of F Company."[14]

FAR TO THE NORTHWEST OF THE 508TH DROP ZONE, near Le Haut Gelay, northeast of Valognes, the parachute riggers of Service Company had dropped almost on top of the headquarters of Bataillon 1, Grenadier Regiment 1058 of the 91st Luftlande Division. Technician Fifth Grade Carl Porter was captured almost immediately upon landing. "Apprehensively, I followed the command to march across the field. I admit to a somewhat theatrical conscious thought that if they were going to shoot me I would die like a man, so I squared my shoulders and marched, wondering as I did so if I would hear the sound of the shots that killed me. Crazy thing to think about at a time like that but the mind has to do SOMETHING all the time.

"Through the field, across the road, and into what this midwestern boy would call a barnyard, I walked ahead of my captors. There, I was deposited with what I took to be a dozen or so American paratroopers and glidermen who had preceded me in becoming prisoners of war. They took one boot from each of us so we couldn't run off and left us with two guards for the rest of the night.

"In the early morning we were marched, with fingers laced and hands locked behind our heads, a mile or two down a dusty road to a formidable headquarters area. Let me tell you, marching for a long distance in that posture becomes excruciating. Even so, not one American allowed his discomfort to show and we made the distance in orderly marching style. Even as prisoners, we were of a single mind to give the best account of ourselves that circumstances allowed.

"Our new home was within a stonewalled courtyard and we were imprisoned in a room about twenty by twenty-five feet. The stone walls were perhaps two to two and one-half feet thick, with two small windows about head high from the floor. I believe we numbered seventeen, thirteen of whom were paratroopers and four were glidermen."[15]

Technical Sergeant John D. Kersh, another Service Company trooper who landed near Le Haut Gelay, was able to evade capture during the predawn hours of June 6. "I had a carbine, a .45-caliber pistol, and six grenades. Before long, I had used up all my grenades. By then, it was nearing daybreak, so I crawled up in a thick hedgerow and was going to hide out, if I could, during the day. About 10:00 o'clock, I saw two German patrols coming toward me—one on each side of the hedgerow. When they got close, I stepped out and surrendered."[16]

Other parachute riggers, like Sergeant Marcel Bollag, also managed to initially evade capture after landing. "I crept along the hedgerow in the opposite direction of the house. Every time I moved, the Jerries opened up on me with machine guns and machine pistols. I also heard a few rifle shots, which didn't bother me much. What I was most interested in was to find some troopers from my plane and try to assemble somehow. So I advanced very slowly. I came to a corner of a field when machine gun bullets began flying too close for comfort. I also heard two Germans shout at each other back there. I reached for one of my hand grenades and threw it over the bush into the machine gun nest. Also, we had been told to fire only if necessary. I realized I was on my own and had better make sure the way was clear. This gun kept silent from then on. I never went to check, but continued on my way.

"So far I had not met a single American—a rather disgusting situation.

"The Germans moved in closer on me from all sides. I tried to find a real good hideout, but it was beginning to be daylight. I could not cross the road to my left as that side was full of Germans. I could not climb over the hedgerow for the fields were covered with machine gun fire and nests. It was almost daylight and I believe the Germans must have spotted me right then. From my right a machine gun opened up. From behind I heard rifle fire, and about three Heinies appeared in front of me on the road and sprayed their Schmeisser machine pistol.

"I was lying on the ground, having my carbine ready. I fired three shots, then had a stoppage. I was still pulling my bolt back when [suddenly] two Germans were in front of me pulling me out of the ditch. The third Nazi covered me with his pistol from the rear.

"The fight was over at that moment. They took my gun away and took me back on the road. I posed as though I was wounded and they believed it. In fact, they let me put my arm on their shoulder as I pointed out to them that my knee was hurt. Anyhow, we got along on the road and came to the house which was actually a German command post. We entered the room and there I saw about forty-four fellows from our formation sitting with their hands up. I knew right away what had happened—in fact, I was aware all the time that we had jumped into a German strongpoint.

"Well, from then on things were not too good. I was stripped completely and they actually did not miss much. My jump suit was taken off, my shirt was ripped open, and my boots and pants were removed. The Germans were amazed at our equipment, and we really had plenty. The K-rations (candy, razor blades, soap, etc.) were rather welcomed in that house."[17]

Staff Sergeant Elmer E. Martell, a member of the same stick as Bollag, found another Service Company trooper shortly after he landed. "We were somewhat confused because of our mis-location. Our assigned task was to set up a command post for the colonel. [Lindale] Keating was a master sergeant and I was a staff sergeant. The Germans were shooting at us and we were in a tough way. Our instructions were, 'Do not load your guns until daylight' for fear of shooting our own people. Now, I loaded my rifle; but it didn't do any good. Anyway, we decided to try to locate the other fellows who we knew were close to us. We started going in one direction; but we ran into a lot of small arms fire. We weren't hit, so we turned to another direction and ran into a railroad. This was supposed to be there according to our preflight briefing and this should run the whole length of the Cherbourg Peninsula.

"It started getting light so we hid in a hedgerow. After daybreak we moved over about sixty yards and we saw Germans riding by in the back of trucks. They didn't seem too concerned. Keating wanted to start shooting at them. I said, 'No, there's something wrong. We can't be in the right place. There shouldn't be that many peaceful Germans here.' They were just sitting there in the back of those trucks. I think they were actually going towards the front as reinforcements.

"So we hid in the hedgerow until dark. Then, we walked into the nearby town. We had this language book so we could talk to the people there. We waited in the dark in a church cemetery. There was a church there and we thought we'd go in and talk to the padre. Well, we didn't realize it, but some Germans actually saw us go into the cemetery. We were sitting with our backs to the tombstones and Keating was looking the other way. You know, it isn't very glorious to be captured. A couple of Germans came out of the church. I don't know what they said, but obviously they meant for us to raise our hands. I was sitting down and made some movement and one of them got real nervous. He fired four rounds and the dirt was flying around me! The shots didn't hit me. I'm not sure that he actually intended to. They took us over to the church and we found out that they were using that as a German headquarters. The Germans weren't stupid. There was no priest there, of course."[18]

By the end of June 6, the Germans had killed or captured most of the 508 parachute riggers who were dropped in the vicinity of the headquarters.

OTHER TROOPERS BARELY ESCAPED CAPTURE DURING THE EARLY HOURS of June 6, 1944. Private Fred Infanger, a Company E trooper and member of the 2nd Battalion pathfinder team, had been dropped east of the Merderet River and had hooked up several other pathfinder team members. "I hid the [holophane] light in some weeds, as I didn't want to be slowed down by unnecessary weight. (It should have been destroyed.)

"We kept on the move until it got light and we came upon an equipment bundle, which we opened and got a machine gun and some ammunition. After this, we moved out again and ran into our first German opposition. It was a machine gun position and there were more Jerries than we figured on. We attacked and this was when I got my first Jerry. After fighting for about an hour, they started to flank us and throw in a few mortars. So we withdrew. (This was when [Private] Nick [Forkapa] of the 504 security got wounded.) We left the medic with him as we left and [Corporal Ernest] King also stayed.

"As luck was with us—we ran into part of the 3rd Battalion (about forty men, which included medics)."[19]

Private Gene Hull, with the S-2 section of Headquarters Company, 1st Battalion, had landed near the north edge of the Douve River floodplain and then set out to find other troopers. "I moved along the hedgerow until I found a clear spot with less growth on the top and rested for about a half an hour. I heard plenty of gunfire (machine guns and rifles).

"At daybreak, I moved around the field to see where I was and what was around me. As I walked along the hedgerow, I came to a clear spot and saw two Germans walking up to my field. They were about two hundred yards away. I think we saw each other at the same time because we fired our rifles. A bullet nicked my elbow. I fired two more shots and the Germans hit the ground and did not return fire.

"I saw eight to ten Germans moving out of a stone barn about two hundred yards away. So I scrambled over the hedgerow and looked out into the water. There were several dead paratroopers floating fifty to seventy-five feet from the shore. I thought the water looked very shallow with no place to hide. I got into the water and was standing up to my neck. I moved to a large tree at the water's edge, put my rifle in shallow water and hunched down. About ten minutes later some Germans came and stood on each side of the tree.

"At one point, I slowly moved my head to see one of the German soldiers dressed in a gray-green uniform. He had a machine gun slung over his chest. The Germans stood there for ten to twelve minutes and then moved back over the hedgerow. I waited about an hour or more before I got out of the water and into the hedgerow. I stayed hidden in the hedgerow until that afternoon, when I saw paratroopers coming into the field."[20]

AS DAWN BROKE ON JUNE 6, LIEUTENANT HENRY LE FEBVRE, the platoon leader of the 3rd Platoon of Company A, along with a pathfinder he had met during the night, was hiding in a drainage ditch next to a hedgerow from German soldiers who were nearby. "Just on the other side of the hedgerow from us I heard the unmistakable sound of a machine gun being set up. The snap of the trails being extended and the sound of the bolt going back and forth as the belt was fed through. It appeared that we were in the middle of a German platoon position. We could hear them talking quite clearly just on the other side of the berm of earth. What to do? There was no way to throw a grenade through that hedgerow. We had to whisper very quietly.

"I thought we could sneak out of our position, but the dry brambles and weeds would crackle loudly and we would hear, 'Vas ist los?' and we would freeze. My pathfinder friend almost got his hand stepped on by a German who was apparently going out to the platoon outpost on our side of the berm. My friend's hand was on the edge of the ditch in which we were hiding and suddenly we saw these two legs go by us."[21]

PRIVATE TRINO MALDONALDO, WITH THE 2ND PLATOON OF COMPANY E, was moving through the bocage country early that morning and found his platoon leader, Lieutenant Bob Mathias, dead. "It hurts when I remember him hanging on that tree that morning in Normandy."[22] Mathias had been seriously wounded in the chest while standing in the door just prior to the jump, but had courageously led his men out of the plane. For Lieutenant Mathias, one of the regiment's most beloved and respected officers, that decision had sealed his fate—to die leading his men, rather than returning to England with the plane and receiving possible life saving medical care.

TWENTY MILES SOUTH OF THE 508TH DROP ZONE, First Sergeant Leonard Funk moved out with his eighteen Company C troopers. Funk needed to know where he was and get directions to the 508th drop zone. "Not knowing where we were, I took French speaking Sergeant Andrew [W.] Loewi to a nearby house to ask directions. After we came to the first road sign, we realized we had been misled. I told Sergeant Loewi, at the second French house, 'Tell them, if you give us wrong information, we will come back after you!'

"This time the Normans showed us correctly where we were on our map."[23]

First Sergeant Funk acted as the scout for his group. Sergeant Bill Traband was a Company C squad leader and a member of Funk's stick. "He was always out front. It was his squad and he wanted to know what was out there. He didn't want to take any second hand information."[24]

Funk's group traveled at night cross country and hid in the foliage of the hedgerows during the days. Sergeant Traband could see groups of German soldiers hunting them while they remained hidden during daylight hours. "We were in those hedgerows and they were so thick. We had Germans walking twelve inches from our heads and never knew we were in there."[25]

Even though they traveled at night, they still encountered German units searching for them. But Sergeant Traband always had confidence that Funk would get them back to the regiment. "We had firefights every night, but then Funk would get us out of there."[26]

SHORTLY AFTER HE LANDED ON JUNE 6, Private Lee Roy Wood, with Company D, began looking for a fellow paratrooper—any paratrooper. Another Company D trooper, Sergeant Francis E. Williamson, had landed close by. "I was trying to get out of my chute and Wood came up on me. I told him, 'Wood, now don't you shoot me. I forgot the password.'"[27]

Private Wood was just glad to have found a friend. "The next guy we picked up was Lieutenant [Temple W.] Tutwiler [also with Company D]. And then we picked up another officer—a little small guy. They called him 'Tex', but I never did know his name. Then we picked up a 505er [Private First Class John F. Quigg]."[28]

Lieutenant Malcolm Brannen was the officer nicknamed "Tex" and being the senior officer, took command of the small group. Lieutenant Brannen, the commander of Headquarters Company, 3rd Battalion, had landed near the headquarters of the 91st Luftlande Division, which was the Chateau Bernaville, north of Picauville. "A corporal from the 508th acted as my scout and a private from the same company followed me. Then, two 307th Engineers brought up our rear. We came to a main road running north and south, but didn't dare stay on it, so we crossed. We found some wires running along the road—the 307th Engineers said they were communication wires, so we cut them in many pieces, covered the pieces in ditches so that the German linemen would have some work to do to restore normal communication. After following hedges north and east for a time we started due north again.

"We ran into Lieutenant Harold [V.] Richard, A Company, 508th Parachute Infantry and his communications sergeant, Sergeant [Homer E.] Hall. It was nice being with two more of our regiment and we were glad to have met at this time.

"After a conference, we decided to ask directions at a large stone farmhouse, which was about fifty yards away. We had about twelve enlisted men and two officers in our party now. We split up and surrounded the house. Lieutenant Richard, one enlisted man, and I pounded on the door of the house.

"In a few seconds a very excited Frenchman came rushing out of the door. Several other occupants of the house were looking out of windows on the ground floor, as well as from windows on the upper stories of the house. In the house, the upstairs windows were alive with little kiddos, wild eyed at seeing the American uniforms instead of the usual German ones.

"By using our French guide book and maps we found out that we were between Picauville and Ètienville. Good! We were about midway between the two places and now had a definite location from which we could plan on future moves to get with our own troops.

"I said, 'Here comes a car—stop it.' Lieutenant Richard moved out of the doorway towards the side of the house and some of the men went to the stone wall at the end of the house. The house doors shut and I went to the road and put my hand up and yelled, 'Stop.'

"But the car came on faster. When the car went by me I ran to the other side of the road. I guess that all of us fired at the car at the same time, as a dozen or more shots rang out and I, on the far side of the road, found myself in the line of fire from the others in our group. I fell to the road and watched the car as it was hit by many shots, and saw the car crash into the stone wall and possibly the side of the house. The driver lost control of the car as he slouched in the front seat, trying to avoid being hit by the bullets that filled the air around the car. The car was full of bullet holes and the windshield was shattered. I climbed upon a hedgerow six or more feet above the roadbed, and had a perfect view of the immediate situation, including the road, the house, the car, and the personnel—German, French, and American.

"The chauffeur, a German corporal, was thrown from the front seat of the car. I saw [him] trying to escape by crawling into the cellar of the house and I fired my .45 Colt pistol at him—grazing his shoulder and saw him sit down beside the house. An officer sitting on the front seat of the car was slumped onto the floor with his head and shoulders hanging out the open front door, dead.

"The other occupant of the car, who had been riding in the back seat of the Dusenberg or Mercedes Phaeton, was in the middle of the road, crawling towards a Luger pistol that had been knocked from his grasp when the car hit the stone wall and house.

"He looked at me as I stood on the hedge above him, and fifteen feet to his right, and as he inched closer and closer to his weapon he pleaded to me in German and also in English, 'Don't kill, don't kill.'

"I thought, 'I'm not a cold hearted killer, I'm human—but, if he gets that Luger—it is either him or me or one or more of my men.' So I shot! He was hit in the forehead and never knew it. He suffered none. The blood spurted from his forehead about six feet high, and like water in a fountain when it is shut off, it gradually subsided.

"Upon examining the personnel that we had encountered we found that we had killed a major and a major general (later learned that he was a lieutenant general) and had as a captive, a corporal [Gefreiter Baumann], whom we made carry two brief cases that were full of official papers that we found in the car. Our intention was to turn the papers in to our headquarters when we rejoined the 508th Parachute Infantry Regiment. As we left the scene, I tore the general's hat apart, looking for further identification of name or unit to which he was assigned. I found only a name printed in it—the name was 'Falley.'"[29]

Generalleutnant Wilhelm Falley was the commanding general of the German 91st Luftlande Division, which was specially trained in antiairborne warfare. His loss no doubt delayed a coordinated reaction by the division to the parachute and glider landings. Although a chance encounter, it was one of the pivotal actions during the first crucial hours of the invasion.

Lieutenant Brannen conferred with the other officers regarding what to do next. "We thought the sooner we left this spot, the better it would be. So we headed southwest, toward Étienville, the town in which our 2nd Battalion was to engage the Germans.

"We headed that way with the same 508th corporal as scout that I had when I met Lieutenant Richard. I followed the scout, then came Lieutenant Richard, Sergeant Hall and the German corporal prisoner, Sergeant Johnson and the rest of our men. Our rear guard was a good man from the 307th engineers.

"We kept close to the hedgerows and avoided several houses before coming to a secondary road and then a small settlement. We went right through the group of houses and turned west into a yard with a large barn. A driveway went past the rear of the barn and passed through a hedge and stone wall, showing a large expanse of field several hundred yards long and wide. My scout and I went south of the barn toward the opening in the hedgerow. The others went to the north of the barn and house toward the solid hedgerow. I saw no one moving in the large field and hesitated while trying to decide what our next move should be, when I looked back and saw most of the men just passing the barn.

"I yelled at the rear guard engineer, 'Watch our rear – don't let anyone creep up on us – don't violate our rear security.'

"No sooner had I said that than BANG—that same engineer shot and killed a German who was aiming his weapon directly at my scout and me. Whew—close.

"What to do now? We thought that anyone in the vicinity surely heard that shot, and of course, would be more alert for anyone moving in the area. Before us was a draw, an open field two or three hundred yards long and wide and completely visible for possible enemy emplaced on the other side of the field.

"My scout and I were standing beside the hedge, next to the opening looking over the situation when I heard a SNAP—SNAP—and heard the scout say, 'Who shot me?'

"My scout turned toward me, looked at me with the most pitiful look on his face that I had ever seen. When he said that to me I realized that I also was out from cover and dove to my right, behind the hedge. As I jumped, and before I could answer him, I heard two more 'PINGS', saw my corporal's bewildered face, saw a stream of blood actually gush from his mouth, and saw him fall straight down on his face, arms outstretched and his heels wide apart—pointing to the heavens!

"Reaction! Realization! There was the first American that I had actually seen killed—a paratrooper—a corporal from our own 508th. Could it be? More rifle fire snapped me back to the reality of the situation that I was facing and I pulled the corporal out of the opening and to the hedge.

"We decided to get out of the area in which we had spent the last few hectic minutes. So we ran around the house and barn, past a couple more houses, and really ran down the road that we had just passed over, actually running for our lives now. Rifle fire had ceased, but voices were following, so we knew we had to keep going as fast as we could and put as much distance between the voices and ourselves. We went north and west to see if we could get into the 3rd Battalion, 508th sector. At a crossroad we met a young Frenchman who told us that the main part of Picauville was to our right a little farther up the road. While at the crossroads we decided that our equipment was too bulky and was a hindrance to fast travel, which was imperative now due to the nearness of the voices that were pursuing us.

"Much lighter, we took off, but kept being pushed north and east, rather than north and west by the large number of German machine gun positions we encountered. The sun was just pouring down us, making us very hot, dusty, and thirsty. Also, since it had been a long time since we had eaten anything, we were hungry. Being in such a physical state of discomfort, and being winded from our rapid flight, we thought that a few minutes' break was in order.

"The voices were getting closer, so we took off to the only patch of woods available that we figured would give us some cover and perhaps throw our pursuers off our track.

"A guard was established and the men not on duty napped. Two or three men did not nap, but stayed awake, talked in low tones, and kept very still, lest our movement be spotted by some German who was just roaming around. I sat facing our prisoner and the two briefcases. I tried to catnap, but my eyes just wouldn't leave the German. I didn't trust him. One quick move and he could have had either an M1 or could try to get away. Neither would have done him any good, because he would have been shot in quick order. But that would have brought the Germans on us or at least given our position away, and we didn't want those complications.

"But to give the prisoner his due—he was exemplary. He just followed along in line, walked, ran, covered up when necessary, and never once made a move that made us suspicious of his intentions. When we moved, he moved; when we stopped, he stopped. He kept the proper interval between the men next to him and never made a noise. I knew that his shoulder was in pain from the wound that he had received, but he was just like one of us. The only difference was that we were carrying weapons and he was carrying two briefcases full of official papers.

"About the time we were really enjoying the break, we heard more voices and some shots right near us—right up the trail we had used to come into these woods. We got up, and with our line of march in the same order, except for the scout, who was now one Private [First Class] Jack Quigg, Company I, 505th Parachute Infantry, from Pennsylvania.

"Into a ditch on the south side of the area we went. We moved upright when we could, lower when we had to, and crept when it was necessary to keep below the top of the ditch. The field was about two feet higher than the bottom of the ditch. When the voices got louder we had to stay still. At times we just laid still, hardly daring to breathe for fear one of our enemy might see or hear us. We could hear the bullets snapping as they went over our heads.

"The Germans hunted us systematically, taking routes a few yards apart and going from one boundary to the other, and then doubling back a few yards from their original route. The moment that we heard a voice get a bit faint, we moved forward—inch by inch; under long thorns, under fallen trees, between trees and the sides of the ditch—scratched, bleeding, sweating, aching—but never giving up. At last, our pursuers seemed to have gone and we continued to creep and crawl away from the last possible enemy. We kept going east. That ditch seemed eight hundred yards long. Perhaps it was three hundred to four hundred more or less. But it was eight hundred yards hard, though. Quigg was tired and showed it. Breaking that kind of trail was a real man's job and it was well done.

"We all now felt completely justified of having discarded the items that we did several hours ago, before we were hunted and pursued so intensely.

"With Quigg leading, we moved from the field north and east through the very same woods that we had just been chased through, to the field that we had avoided while being chased. Quigg stopped suddenly, hit the ground, and I waved the rest of our group to get down as quickly as possible. On the field in front of us, about 100-150 yards wide, we saw a scene familiar in training exercises, but not looked for in actual combat—a chow line."[30]

"We stayed low and watched the German soldiers line up for their noonday meal. They were in varied states of dress—some had their coats open, some had them buttoned and some had none at all. Some had steel helmets and some didn't. Some had their helmets on and some carried theirs. Some had weapons in their hands, across their backs and some were dragging theirs. One or two were yelling, maybe orders for the others; others were laughing and at least one was singing at the top of his voice. All were jovial to say the least. And not a one of them were aware that about a dozen American paratroopers were about 150 yards from them, watching them frolic in the warm noonday sun! Wow! It was a sight to behold—one to see and not be seen.

"While we were watching the progress of the chow line, we began to think of getting away from it before the participants finished and started strolling across the field and into the woods that we were hiding in, watching their every move and wishing that we could partake in their food.

"We decided that we would go east and try to get around the field where the chow line was set up and was, I'm sure, greatly enjoyed by the Germans. We moved in an easterly direction and saw where the two fields that we had been concerned with during the last couple of hours, converged. There was a stream between them and a small footbridge over the stream. We arrived at this point just in time to see a German cross the bridge and move towards the chow line. He disappeared behind us and then two officers came along the same path, then went up on the bridge and stood there, looking into the stream. They appeared to be discussing a problem, because every few sentences one or the other would raise his hand and arm and gesture as though emphasizing a point.

"After minutes that seemed like hours, the two German officers moved across the bridge and disappeared in the direction of the chow line site. We waited for them to get out of sight and hearing and to make sure that there was not anybody else coming to the place at which we were making our plans to get out of the area and get to our respective units.

"We surveyed the situation and the area from a point near the bridge. To the right there was a large open field just beyond a road; to the left was a path leading to a road and a field beyond—all just a few yards away. We seemed to be at the junction of several fields, a couple of roads or trails, and a few yards away was a stream flowing south.

"Quigg, Lieutenant Richard, Sergeant Hall, and myself moved to the stream bed. We wanted to go north and since the stream was partially covered and concealed by trees and brush along its banks, we thought it might be a good covered route to move to where we wanted to go. I stepped into the stream and sank up to my waist at once—and immediately backed out. It would be too hard and slow to use such a route.

"We then decided to go by path or road in a southerly direction and then turn east and resume our parade north. We could see and hear gun crews to our immediate northwest across the open field, which aided us in making our decision.

"Just as we started to move in the direction decided upon, we had to take cover because a German soldier was crossing the field directly in our route. After a few minutes' wait, we resumed our forward progress. More ditches, more walking, stooping, crawling, and creeping. We crossed the path on which the German had been on and then we took to a ditch bearing east. In this ditch, we only had to crawl at intervals when the left bank got so low that we could be seen from the open field.

"After crossing a small open space, we once more were safely in a small wooded area and decided that another short break was in order. It was a beautiful grove of pine trees—all tall and majestic. The trees produced a wonderful pine odor, were tall enough to keep the sun out and let the cool air circulate. It was as someone said, 'a beautiful place to have a picnic.'

"We thought that it was so nice that we could plan our immediate future while resting on a blanket of pine needles that the beautiful trees had supplied. We put out guards, kept our prisoner in good view, and decided we would go in an easterly direction to see if we could get to our own troops before dark.

"All was serene for about thirty seconds and all of a sudden German voices, right close, nearly took us out of our minds, and along with the voices were about twenty-five to thirty Germans either relieving a gun crew in that vicinity, or on a patrol—possibly looking for us! We got up silently and very quickly, and moved north for a few yards and came to the edge of the woods and looked out upon what ordinarily would have been a nice wide field, but now it was a real hazard. We tried to cross it by crawling. I started, but only made ten yards in what seemed to be several minutes, so I had to turn back, and as I returned to the edge of the woods, I looked to the southeast corner approximately two hundred yards distant and saw a sight that we hadn't been able to understand. It was a German standing on a fence and waving to us, beckoning us to come his way. At first a faint hope entered our minds that at last we had reached one of our units.

"In sign language, I asked our prisoner if that was a German. He said, 'Ja.' I then asked him if the man was a soldat. Again he said, 'Ja.' I then asked him if the soldier knew that we were Americans—by using sign language and pointing to the American flag on our shoulders. Again, 'Ja.'

"Then I asked, 'Are there many soldats and were they coming after us?' He once again said, 'Ja.'

"This 'Ja' was the automatic signal to take off from that lone figure and the fast approaching voices.

"Once again, Quigg led off, in an easterly direction. I was behind him and Lieutenant [Harold] Richard was near the end of the column with the prisoner ahead of him. Quigg and I got so far ahead of the others that we had gone one field east and were on the next field before we waited for the rest to catch up. I then told Lieutenant Richard to go north one field and then go east to the next field and we would meet him at the road because we had seen motorcycles passing along it while we were approaching it. Looking back, we saw about twenty-five or thirty German soldiers following us. Full speed ahead was now the order.

"Quigg and I reached and crossed the road and hid in the hedge and stone wall on the other side. We waited for five minutes, looked back to where we had last seen Lieutenant Richard, saw no movement, and then we went north along a hedge for about two hundred yards and hid in an opening in the hedge, right behind a cow shed and one hundred yards or less in front of a large set of buildings. Here, we covered the entrance and camouflaged ourselves and waited for what was going to happen next. We were hoping that the rest of the group that we had spent the last several hours fleeing the Germans with would rush across the road as we had done, and then climb through the hedge and head for us.

"Out of the clear came shots—five minutes of shooting in the very area in which our friends were—and then silence.

"We discussed it, Quigg and I. Had they been killed? Or captured? Or had they gotten away and reached safety? Who knows? Would we ever find out?[31]

"It meant now that Quigg and I were on our own. We came to a decision— we would wait right where we were and at midnight we would take off, going north and west and see what happened between midnight and light of day.

"It was 19:00—7:00 p.m. at this time, so a five hour wait was in store for us. I got up to look around a bit from our hiding place. Through an opening in the rear I could plainly see a large house and barn, and to my horror, Germans rushing around as though getting ready to chase some small group of Americans. I was watching an opening in the hedge across the field towards the big house when three Germans, fully dressed and camouflaged, stopped in the opening. I froze, leaning on a mud bank with my elbows in a small opening in the hedge, with my field glasses up to my eyes. Two Germans stooped below their hedge line and one stayed up looking directly at me. I just knew that he was. I was still frozen. Then, that one German raised his rifle and aimed it directly at my head. It was just as though we were aiming at one another. We were too, but his weapon was much more devastating than mine. I was still frozen. He ducked behind the hedge, but I held my position, very luckily, for almost at once he raised and again took aim at me. I still froze and he repeated his action a couple more times and I was still frozen—in fact I was nearly paralyzed. Then the three Germans got up and moved off south. PHEW—I sat down—my back was wet. I was unfrozen, but plenty nervous. If I had moved before the Germans went away we probably would have been ferreted from our hiding place.

"About this time, two Germans walked a few yards in front of us, left the cow pen gate open, and proceeded one hundred yards to our front and got into foxholes and immediately began firing—just firing. No particular targets, but just to make noise and harass the Americans in the area.

"The yard gate being open, the cows took a holiday and one very nosey bovine began to eat our camouflage and was making it nervous for us. But that was nothing! Suddenly, she spotted us—jumped—mooed—and then looked, shifting her head and body to get the best possible view. We were so afraid that anyone who might be watching would notice this gal's queer actions; but again it seems we were on the right side and being guided from above. However, after she left us for half an hour, she returned and went through the same routine once more."[32]

LIEUTENANT COLONEL LOUIS MENDEZ, the commanding officer of the 3rd Battalion, had found only a few other troopers since landing near Gourbesville, northwest of the 508th drop zone. Mendez led this small group cross country trying to find other elements of the regiment. "We seemed to run into anti-paratroop groups of about sixty men and we shot back and forth. We drew the conclusion that these groups called other groups who were waiting for us. Altogether I had three men, one officer and my messenger. The most outstanding thing I learned was the accurate intelligence of the Germans. They used full name, even nicknames to confuse my company commanders. My company commanders stated that they received messages in my full name and even my nickname."[33]

Sometime during the day on June 6, Private First Class John Delury and Lieutenant John Quaid, both with Company H, joined Lieutenant Colonel Mendez and his small group. Delury, acting as the scout for the group, came to a road that night choked with units of Grenadier Regiment 1057, moving up to attack Hill 30 and defend the area west of the Merderet River. Delury hid in a hedgerow bordering the road, observing the enemy force. "We came across a whole column of Germans; there must have been hundreds of them. There were trucks and tanks and column after column of soldiers with their personal equipment rattling and their hobnailed boots hitting the road."[34]

CHAPTER 5

"THE BEST SOLDIER IN THE 508TH"

Just after midnight on June 6-7, Lieutenant Malcolm Brannen, the commanding officer of Headquarters Company, 3rd Battalion, and the lone trooper from the 505th who was still with him, left the hideout they had occupied since about 7:00 p.m. "We stole through the cow yard to the road we had previously crossed, and went along the side in a southwesterly direction, trying to get around a big German strongpoint to the immediate north of us. Moving west five fields led us to a crossroad where a German roadblock was established. An 88 was in position on the southwest corner and belched forth every few minutes. [Private First Class Jack] Quigg and I crossed the road on all fours and headed south just off [the road] so that our footsteps would not echo in the stillness of the night (except when the 88 belched). A sentry, walking his post was sighted as he came towards us—but before he reached us he halted, about-faced, and returned from whence he came. We saw him do this several times, thus realizing that he was pulling sentry duty for the 88 crew at the crossroads that we had been so fortunate to pass by unnoticed just a few minutes before. We climbed into a field so as to give the sentry his part of the road—and ours, too. Just as soon as we got into the field we thought all hell had broken loose—a barrage of 88s—lasting ten minutes whizzed over our heads—how close I'll never know, but we crouched there, hugging the ground and wondering if they knew we were there or was the barrage for some other reason. Later, we decided it was a half hourly occurrence, with a lesser barrage between regular ones. We crawled towards the hedge to our south and as we approached the thick part of the hedge, as it branched off along the side of the road that we had just crossed, we heard someone cough and clear his throat. Then later, we could hear the hobnails on the road from the German sentry. Minute after minute went by—the coughing continued, the hobnails kept coming, and the 88s kept going off. Occasionally, a rifle shot rang out. Quigg and I were still there in the corner of the field, behind the hedge as daybreak came. It was time, I decided, to find out who, or what was on the other side of the hedge. I told Quigg to crawl and watch the corner while I crawled over (through) the hedge and, pistol in hand, cocked and ready to fire, approached the spot where the adversary was.

139

"Closer and closer and closer I wiggled, slowly and noiselessly—and there he was—a half asleep U.S. paratrooper, one Private Russell Nocera, who belonged to Headquarters Company, 1st Battalion of the 507th Regiment. What a relief! I quietly called Quigg and he came quickly and we settled down for the day—and half the night, too. We camouflaged our hideout and we watched Germans all day long—watched them walk up the sloping road singly, in pairs, in groups, and even in platoon formation. We saw truckloads of troops and busloads of them pass our hiding place going to their new defensive positions, I guessed. We saw a group of officers, partly dressed, with their bags stuffed with clothing, partly dragging on the road, hurriedly follow a large van up the slope and when it reached the top they climbed aboard and drove off in a northeasterly direction, towards the way we had come from last night. We saw the Germans set up 88s and mortars while load after load of shells were piled near their weapons. We saw horse drawn vehicles, so heavily loaded that both officers and enlisted men had to put their shoulders to the horse drawn wagons to be sure that they got to their destination. They used two horse teams, four horse teams, and at least once, they used a team with six horses and four men pulling and pushing to get the wagon and its load in the field beside the weapons. And while we watched all 'the goings on' during the day, we dared not breathe out loud, let alone cough, and we moved in slow, slow, slow motion, so as not to attract an eye that might happen to be looking in our direction. The day was long—not because of lack of German movement and activity, but because we were waiting for time to pass and for darkness to set in so that we could move on and continue to try to meet up with our units. While we were waiting, we ate all of our food, which wasn't much, and drank most of our water—regrets later."[1]

PRIVATE FIRST CLASS JOE BRESSLER and Private Oscar Prasse, both with Headquarters Company, 1st Battalion were hiding on the third floor of an empty French farmhouse. Bressler had been unable to move to Hill 30 due to a badly wounded ankle. "I suffered terribly from my broken ankle and frequently used morphine to kill the pain, which caused me to have severe dysentery. Oscar left to get medical help for me. He returned alone and told me Germans were all around the house. The Germans even searched the house, but failed to find us. About three days later, the Germans left the area. However, each night the German activity on the road increased. One night Prasse went out, shot another German, and from his body obtained cheese, bread and ammunition."[2]

ANOTHER TROOPER, PRIVATE TRINO MALDONADO, with Company E, had landed alone among German troops and used a rather ingenious method to avoid capture. "I stayed in trees [during daylight hours] and walked at night, sometimes in the early morning, too."[3]

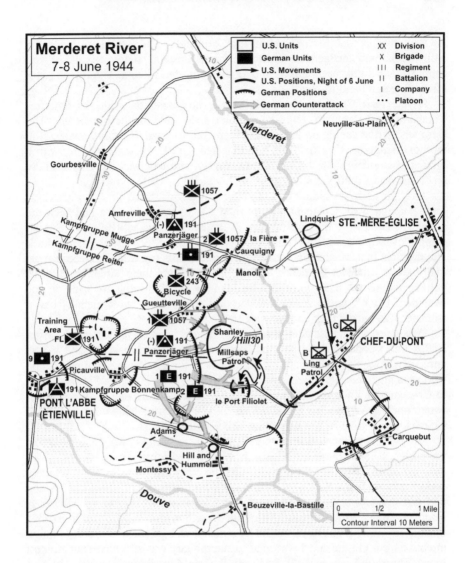

Merderet River
7-8 June 1944

U.S. Units	XX	Division
German Units	X	Brigade
U.S. Movements	III	Regiment
U.S. Positions, Night of 6 June	II	Battalion
German Positions	I	Company
German Counterattack	···	Platoon

AT DAWN ON JUNE 7, THE 91ST LUFTLANDE DIVISION attacked the Hill 30 area with two kampfgruppen, or combat teams. Kampfgruppe Reiter,[4] consisting of Bataillon 1, Grenadier Regiment 1057; supported by one heavy 105mm mountain howitzer platoon, using GebH 40s; one light infantry howitzer platoon, armed with captured Russian 76.2mm Infanterie Kanone Haubitze (IKH 290); one platoon of 75mm antitank guns; and two tank destroyer squads, attacked Hill 30 from the west and north, while Kampfgruppe Bonnenkamp, consisting of two companies of engineers from Pioniere Bataillon 191, assaulted positions of those troopers on the southern sides of the hill who were defending the western approach to the Chef-du-Pont causeway. The fighting was vicious, with fields and hedgerows changing hands several times as attack and counterattack swept back and forth over the contested ground. The fighting was often close and hand-to-hand.

Private First Class Harold Kulju was a radio operator with Headquarters Company, 2nd Battalion, but was manning a foxhole on the perimeter. "The Germans started setting up French 75s [captured Russian 76.2mm howitzers] in the next hedgerow. We had one guy that had a 1903 Springfield rifle, with a [grenade] launching attachment on the muzzle, and that was our only artillery piece. He delayed the Germans somewhat, which was quite fortunate."[5]

After the German assault that morning was thrown back, Private First Class Tom Porcella, with Company H, revisited one of the fields that had been the scene of some of the fiercest fighting. "I remember Sergeant [Ralph J.] Busson coming over to me and a few other troopers and asking for volunteers to go back into the field that we just left and see if we could find any wounded, because we didn't know whatever happened to those troopers over there. About eight of us volunteered to go back into this field and we volunteered to bring in the wounded. I don't know where the stretcher came from, but somebody had a stretcher. We picked it up and we went to the next field.

"We entered this field and we saw two troopers lying on the ground. I looked at this one trooper and he had his head completely blown apart, and it was unrecognizable. So I fished around and I looked for his dog tag, and on his dog tag I read the name, [Private First Class Robert W.] R. W. Benson. He was from H Company. I knew R. W. Benson very well. He was one of the original paratroopers from the 3rd Battalion, and it was a terrible shock for me to see what happened to him. The only thing I hope—he died fast.

"A few feet away from him, there was a trooper lying down. He looked like something a bomb blew up; he was just butchered meat. There was blood all over the place. One leg was mangled and the other leg was sort of grotesquely underneath his body. So I tried to find out who it was, and I pulled out his dog tag, and it was a guy named [Private First Class Harry B.] Deem, another H Company man. While I was moving him around a little bit, I heard a groan. I thought for sure he was dead, but he let out an awful groan, and he sort of threw me back for a minute and I was glad to see the guy was still alive, but I didn't know if he would ever make it. So I [got] the stretcher and we carefully, the best we could, put this poor trooper on the stretcher. So we had to take him back to the position where we were.[6] Somewhere around the line, we found a place to put all these wounded troopers.

"All the troopers were laid in this field right alongside the hedgerows for as far as your eye could see. Exactly how many troopers were there, I don't know. We grabbed the stretcher and back we went to the field to see if we could find anymore wounded troopers. While we were searching for troopers, I happened to notice, in the corner of the field there was a German, evidently trying to escape between the hedgerow. Some trooper shot him and he never got through the hedgerow. He was half on one side and half on the other.

"Alongside this German, there was another German; you could see that he took his boot off. Evidently, he was shot in the foot and he was attempting to put a bandage around the wound. And I'm sure that some other trooper came along and shot him while he was trying to bandage himself.

"Then we proceeded to jump over this hedgerow, down onto the road, still searching for more American paratroopers. All we saw were dead Germans all over the place. There were two [dead] Germans in the hedgerow. They were lying on their backs. There was this one German, he had both hands together like he was praying and he was begging for his life; his eyes were wide open and I could visualize judging by the look on his face that he was terrified. I could imagine him saying something in German and was begging this trooper not to shoot him. His expression seemed to be frozen right on his face. It looked like fear. It looked like he was pleading for his life. A few feet away from him, there was another German lying on his back. He had a different look on his face. He looked like he had a sneer on his face. Who knows, he could have been cursing this trooper out. Maybe he knew the trooper killed the other German, and he figured he was going to die, but he had a sneer on his face. He also died with his eyes wide open.

"We proceeded down the road. We weren't able to find anymore troopers. So we decided to go back to our positions and report to the sergeant that we hadn't seen anymore.

"While walking along the hedgerow with another trooper, where the wounded were lying, a voice called out to me, 'Hey, trooper, come over here.' As I walked toward him, I asked him how he felt. He wanted to know how badly he was hit. Looking down at him, I saw all the flesh was blown away from the right side of his face. He started to cry and he was reaching for his face with a hand that was black as dirt. Quickly, I grabbed his wrist and told him not to touch his face and that he would be all right. He asked me for a cigarette and a drink of water. I didn't have any cigarettes because I had lost everything I had [when I landed] in the water. He said he had some in his pocket. I removed one of the cigarettes, lit it for him, and I gave him the cigarette."[7]

West of Hill 30, Lieutenant George Miles, the 2nd Battalion S-4, was lying in a ditch where he had been wounded in the left thigh the previous evening. "I beheld the figure of an officer from the 1st Battalion, [Lieutenant] Bob Weaver, a friend of mine from training days, in the company of an enlisted man medic [Private Donald R. Adams], whose name to my great shame I have forgotten. These two men had come from Hill 30. Weaver carried me piggyback until we reached Hill 30, where I was cleaned up, treated, and put into another ditch for safekeeping."[8]

That day, word spread among the 508th troopers of the death the previous day of one of the favorite men in the regiment, Captain Ignatius P. Maternowski. Most troopers like Sergeant Zane Schlemmer, with Headquarters Company, 2nd Battalion, were livid when they heard the news. "We learned of the death of our Catholic chaplain, who had jumped with us, when the Germans grenaded a gully where he was attending our wounded. So we vowed then and there, to avenge his death with little regard for any proprieties of warfare thereafter."[9]

ON THE MORNING OF D+1 NORTH OF AMFREVILLE, Technician Fourth Grade Paul Bouchereau, with the regiment's medical detachment, found himself with a large group of approximately two hundred troopers, mostly from the 507th Parachute Infantry. Among them was the 508th regimental executive officer, Lieutenant Colonel Harry Harrison, a graduate of West Point. Bouchereau was thoroughly disgusted with Harrison's failure to lead. "On the second day of our trek, the scouts reported that they had come across a very large motor pool, the garrison was undoubtedly much larger than our force, but with just a little luck, we could hit them hard by surprise and do a bit of damage and get out before they could counterattack.

"It was after 10:00, and our captain and other officers agreed that the best time for our attack would be shortly after noon when hopefully most of the Germans would be at lunch. Colonel Harrison was not privy to the formation of these plans; in fact, even when we were told, Colonel Harrison was pretty much ignored. We were deployed in a semicircle around the motor pool, and the attack went off to perfection. The Germans withdrew in complete confusion leaving behind many casualties. We used their fuel to start numerous fires, and had the largest bonfire I have ever seen. I must admit that during the melee, I was very apprehensive that haste would breed carelessness that would produce casualties, but we were very fortunate. We went in, did what we wanted to do with fantastic speed, and we got out with only a few minor burns before the Germans knew what hit them. We were somewhat surprised that the Germans made only feeble attempts to follow and counterattack. We had had our baptism of fire in two direct confrontations with the enemy and without question were the victors. It was a very good feeling.

"We were moving towards the coast, and I was about in the middle of a column when a soldier just a few yards ahead of me was curious about what was on the other side of the hedgerow. Unfortunately, to get a better view, he used his bazooka to push aside the vegetation, and even more unfortunately, his bazooka was ready to be fired and a twig must have touched his trigger and fired the weapon. He caught the full blast in his face. I stopped to do what I could to help, but it wasn't much.

"[Private First Class] Leo [M.] Jenson, [Technician Fifth Grade Richard G.] Ed McCurdy, and myself stayed as long as we could, then fell in and traveled at the end of the column. It was stop and go travel on a forced march. The length of both the stop and go was erratic. We were almost exhausted and tried to get a few moments of sleep at each stop. It was more or less the duty of the man ahead to let the guy behind him know when to stop and when to go."[10]

ON JUNE 7, A LARGE GERMAN TRUCK CONVOY transporting captured American paratroopers was moving south toward the city of St. Lo when American P-47 fighter-bombers appeared overhead. Private First Class William Sawyer, with Company D, was standing in the back of one of those trucks. "The convoy of trucks stopped. I was up near the cab. Of course, the old truck had canvas over the top, but you could see out through the front, and I told the guys, I said, 'Let's get out of here!' I said, 'They're going to work this thing over!' And they said they couldn't because the Germans had gotten in the ditches, they were holding rifles on them and wouldn't let them out of the tailgate. And we had to stay in that truck until our own planes opened up on us. I remember when I was trying to get out of the truck I could see arms and legs shearing off all around me, from our own .50-caliber bullets, from our own P-47 planes. But I was just like a kangaroo; I bounced out of that truck and hit the ground and up the hedgerow and over in the field."[11]

Private First Class Jack W. Schlegel, with Headquarters Company, 3rd Battalion was among the survivors of the strafing. "Approximately thirty to forty of our men were killed and over eighty wounded. All of us pitched in to help with the dead and wounded. I remember removing three from my own company with the dead and placing Lieutenant [Michael] Bodak with the wounded. He was hit by three .50-caliber shells in the spine and never walked again, but survived the war."[12]

Among those killed were Captains Hal Creary (commander of Company H) and Francis Flanders (commander of Company F); Lieutenants Joseph Shankey (the 3rd Battalion S-4), and Talbert A. Smith (with Headquarters Company, 2nd Battalion); Privates First Class Raymond H. Bolin (Company H), John P. Evert (Headquarters Company, 2nd Battalion), and Donald R. Scholz (Company B); and Privates Raymond Carriere (Headquarters Company, 2nd Battalion), Albert L. Heinz (Headquarters Company, 2nd Battalion), John E. Lane (Company C), Francis J. Slane (Company B), Walter V. Turner, (Company D), and Donald J. Wood (Headquarters Company, 3rd Battalion).

WEST OF HILL 30, LIEUTENANT COLONEL LOUIS MENDEZ, the 3rd Battalion commander, and his group of about fifteen troopers made their way south from the Gourbesville area to the vicinity of la Bonneville, destroying communication lines they found on the way. Private First Class John Delury and his Company H executive officer, Lieutenant John Quaid, had joined the group on June 6.

Delury had acted as the scout for the group since joining it. "Most of us were strangers to each other, so it wasn't conducive to a well-oiled machine. One would find oneself continually in the forefront if you were known to the officers. So that was the situation where I became first scout.

"We were trying to cross a road one midday, so I went first and lay inside the hedgerow on my side of the road when two German soldiers walked by chatting and smoking cigarettes. I literally could have reached and grabbed their boots. I started to crawl back into the field and met Lieutenant Quaid. We were both in this kneeling position when a German tank came up the road and was opposite the opening that afforded access to the field. I could have sworn they saw us. We lay down flat on the ground and waited for the tank to turn into the field. I could feel my heart pounding against the ground and terror swept through me. There's something about a tank coming up against an infantryman on a one to one basis that puts the fear of God in you, especially when you're not dug in. But the tank continued straight down the road. The Germans on foot had apparently walked on, continuing their conversation and cigarette smoking.

"On our left was a dirt road that led out to the road we were trying to cross, but it was nine feet below our field and it was completely enveloped in vegetation as the hedgerows on both sides had grown together at the top to form a dark green tunnel. Quaid lowered me by holding onto the top of my rifle while I climbed down holding the butt. I had to let go of the gun and drop about two feet to a soft dirt path. About twenty yards in front of me where the dirt road hit the one we were trying to cross was a German sentry, his Mauser [rifle] slung over his right shoulder. There I stood without a weapon, not even a trench knife, and the tube like shape of the road afforded me no concealment. God only knows why he didn't turn when I dropped. The only reason I can think of, was the German helmet with its low wrap around the back obviated hearing light sounds coming from the rear. I signaled back to Quaid what I saw and he lowered my rifle and pulled me back up. After I climbed back up, we tried a different route. We tried to be invisible by day and do most of our moving by night. I remember one night coming to a farmhouse, trying to get water for our canteens. There was a horse trough filled by a hand pump that squeaked. Every time the arm of the pump was lowered, it sounded like someone stepping on a cat's tail. There were Germans all around the place, and to top it off, some big watchdog started barking his head off. We were grateful to get the slimy water and not get our heads blown off. I remember going down a sloping field in the moonlight, close to the ground, and we could hear German soldiers talking and working the bolt on what sounded like a machine gun a few yards away from us.

"One of our worst enemies was sleep. At night, when we stopped for a five minute break and lay back, the danger was falling asleep and being left behind. So it was with [Private John Z.] Posadas,[13] a member of my company, who after a break, was left behind when we moved out and no one realized it until daylight."[14]

As a scout, Delury had been extremely lucky not to have already been killed. "Then it happened: I walked across this field, about two-thirds of the way, on a beautiful sunny early afternoon, and without any warning, someone right in front of me, behind the next hedgerow, opened up with a Schmeisser submachine gun right at me. I started to run a broken field that in my mind would have made Tommy Harmon or Red Grange in their prime look like old men: five yards right, two yards left, three right, six left, etcetera. All the while, the machine gun bullets were snapping all around me. There was a wide white plank swing-gate at the right rear corner of the field. In full stride, with my rifle held stiff over my head, I made one leap head first and went sailing through the air, just skimming the top plank, and landed in a heap on the other side. After that, we tried an alternate route."[15]

ON THE EAST SIDE OF THE MERDERET RIVER, the 508th group led by Colonel Lindquist moved from its reserve position at the intersection of railroad tracks and the road running west from Ste.-Mère-Église to the river on the morning of June 7. It cleared the area to the north on the left flank of the 2nd Battalion, 505th Parachute Infantry. Upon receiving an order from the division, Colonel Lindquist then took his group south to Chef-du-Pont to mop up that area. He then established the regimental command post in the town.

NORTHEAST OF STE.-MÈRE-ÉGLISE, the 319th Glider Field Artillery Battalion spent much of the day salvaging equipment and their 75mm pack howitzers from wrecked gliders. As a result of the casualties suffered during the landings, Corporal Robert G. Rappi was now acting sergeant of his Battery A gun section. Corporal Rappi and several of his men used axes to cut a hole in one of the crashed gliders in order to remove a howitzer. "The gun we got out, but the elevating arcs were bent. We weren't much good without our artillery piece, so the gun mechanic [Private First Class Flavious B. Carney] and I went around looking for parts and we found them. The paratroopers dropped theirs in pieces. A lot of those bundles went into the water. There were water holes around there, kind of swampy, but we found a pile of gun parts. We found the elevating arcs and took them and made a usable gun out of it."[16]

Major James Todd, the commander of the 319th Glider Field Artillery Battalion, arrived at the assembly area of his unit at about 6:20 p.m. and set about reorganizing command of the battalion due to casualties suffered by the officers during the landing the previous night. "Lieutenant Frank B. Poole was placed in command of Headquarters Battery and Lieutenant Charles L. Sartain, Jr. was placed in command of A Battery."[17]

ON HILL 30 ON THE NIGHT OF JUNE 7, Lieutenant Colonel Shanley sent patrols out to find equipment bundles. Private First Class Ed Boccafogli, with Company B, was a member of one such patrol. "We went down through the farmhouses, behind the farmhouses, through the brush, until we got to the swamps by the Merderet River. There were twelve of us. We waded out into the water. The parachutes with the colors we knew were supply chutes. So we waded out and we started to drag them in, and the water in some places was three feet deep; some places it was just almost over your head. One of the chutes we dragged in had a body on it. The next thing you know, we're dragging the chute in, and were getting fired on from the other side of the swamp, quite a distance (four hundred to five hundred yards). Bullets were striking the banks all around us and in the water, and as I went underwater with my head to keep myself from getting hit, I lost my helmet. One of the fellows on the bank got a direct hit. He was killed. We had to leave his body there. We got the chute out. The bundle, when we got it back, it turned out it had anything but what we needed. It was a lot of spare parts. There was a machine gun, but there was no ammunition. Another bundle had mortar rounds, nothing but mortar rounds and landmines."[18] Unfortunately, of the ten bundles recovered, none contained rations, medical supplies, or 60mm or 81mm mortars. Only one machine gun was recovered from the bundles.

That evening, Sergeant Robert D. Shields, with Company A, left Hill 30 and courageously crossed the causeway to Chef-du-Pont, where he scrounged critical spare parts to fix the only two SCR 300 radios with Shanley's force on Hill 30, and returned before daybreak.

By the night of June 7, the suffering of the wounded on Hill 30 was terrible. Sergeant Zane Schlemmer, with Headquarters Company, 2nd Battalion, was glad he was assigned to outpost duty. "I preferred the outpost, even though we would sometimes receive fire from both sides; for back in the perimeter, we had many wounded and dying. There was no way to evacuate them. It was difficult to listen to their cries and the moans, because we had no medical supplies. We had not received a resupply of ammunition, equipment, food, or water. We could do without these items, but the lack of medical supplies and blood plasma was really felt by everyone."[19]

A buddy of Private First Class Billy McClure, with Company D, was among those suffering, after being wounded during a German artillery barrage. "When the Germans shelled us with airbursts, [Private First Class] Paul [E.] Webb, next to me was hit in the face, and I was hit in the hand and under the arm. The shrapnel went into the side of Paul's face and came out of his mouth. It took a lot of his teeth and part of his lips. His mutilated gums made him look like his brains were hanging off his chin. He could hear and understand me, but couldn't talk.

"A trench was dug in the center of the encircled hill for the wounded. I started carrying Webb to the trench, about 150 yards away and behind a fence.

We had to hit the ground several times during airbursts. When we got to the fence, I needed help getting Webb over. An officer had his foxhole nearby. I asked him to help, but he wouldn't get out of his hole. I laid my wounded buddy down, unslung my rifle from my shoulder, pointed it at the officer and said, 'I will count to three. If you don't get out of that hole and help, you'll get a bullet right between the eyes.' The officer was out at the count of one."[20]

While on Hill 30, Private Donald Adams, a Company C medic, repeatedly made very dangerous trips into enemy territory to find, treat, and evacuate wounded troopers. Private Adams would later be awarded the Silver Star while listed as missing in action in Holland. Tragically, Adams was killed in action on September 20, but his body had not been recovered at the time the Silver Star was awarded.

During the evening of June 7-8, Lieutenant Lester W. Pollom, the executive officer of Headquarters Company, 2nd Battalion, and two enlisted men volunteered to cross the flooded Merderet River to obtain blood plasma at Chef-du-Pont and bring it back to Hill 30. Despite being under fire, Pollom and the other troopers made the eight hundred yard trip each way and brought the vitally needed plasma to Hill 30, which saved the lives of a number of the wounded. For his heroism, Lieutenant Pollom was later awarded the Silver Star medal.

At 8:00 p.m. on June 7, a combat patrol of three officers and sixty-seven men moved out from Hill 30 with the mission of establishing a roadblock at the western end of the causeway that extended across the Merderet River to Chef-du-Pont. Maintaining this roadblock would deny the causeway and a direct route to Utah Beach to German armor. Lieutenant Ralph DeWeese, the assistant platoon leader of the 2nd Platoon of Company H, was one of the three officers who led the combat patrol. "We moved down Hill 30 and set up a defense to hold until we could contact the rest of the outfit. We hit no opposition and set up a roadblock at the road junction."[21]

Near midnight that evening, Lieutenant Walter Ling, the platoon leader of the 2nd Platoon of Company B, was ordered to take a patrol from Chef-du-Pont across the causeway to contact Lieutenant Colonel Shanley on Hill 30. Sergeant Bill Call was one of the platoon's squad leaders. "Lieutenant Ling told me to gather up four or five guys, and I did. There were six of us in the patrol with Ling. On this route, there were Germans who had dug in on the side [of the causeway] that were dead. One in particular had been hit with a phosphorous grenade. He was half out of his hole; he was probably about six foot seven, a big guy. He was burned like a hot dog that had been left on the fire too long. He was split open, and he stunk to beat hell.

"When we got to the hill, they challenged us and I forgot the countersign. After we got to the top of the hill, Ling had us stay right there and he went to wherever Shanley had his headquarters."[22]

While Sergeant Call was waiting for Ling's return, he heard a German truck approaching a farmhouse below the hill, where a French farmer and his family had been treating a few wounded 508th troopers.

Lieutenant Ralph DeWeese knew that two of the wounded in that house were Company H troopers. "The French people were very good to us and were taking excellent care of them. That night we heard some noise over around the house and a truckload of Jerries had come down to set up a roadblock at the junction. They went into the house and found Lieutenant [Donald J.] Johnson [with the regimental demolition platoon] and a medic. They took them outside and shot them. They also burned the house, but the French got [Technician Fifth Grade Melvin H.] Pommerening and [Private First Class Thomas] Wogan out OK. They also killed one of our men and we got about four or five of them. They loaded in a truck and took off, leaving mines and all kinds of equipment behind." [23]

A short time after the Germans left the farmhouse, Lieutenant Ling returned. Sergeant Call and the rest of the Company B patrol moved out to cross the causeway once again. "Ling wanted to get out of there before morning. It was scary as hell. But Ling got us there and he got us back." [24]

ON THE EVENING OF JUNE 7, NORTH OF AMFREVILLE, Major Dave Thomas, the regimental surgeon, administered aid to several wounded men with his group of mostly 507th troopers. "This one kid got hit with a big artillery shell fragment, just at his knee, and his lower leg was detached except for the patella tendon. All I had was my medical aid kit. I had a scalpel and a few things like that. I had nothing to put him asleep with, so I said, 'Son, this is just like the days in the wild west, you're going to have to bite the bullet.' So he did, and I amputated his leg. He never whimpered. He was a real man.

"Well, by this time, we were in radio contact with a bigger group that was commanded by [the commanding officer of the 507th Parachute Infantry, Colonel George V.] Zip Millett [Jr.]. Later that day, at night time, we made a night march and joined up with Zip Millett. We carried our wounded with us. We used barn doors, blankets on poles, anything like that from which we could make a litter, and we carried all of our non-walking wounded.

"We put six Krauts to a litter and one rifleman with an M1 rifle, to make sure that the Krauts stayed strictly to their duty. We made it to the bigger group, which had something like three hundred troops and some more medics." [25]

AROUND MIDNIGHT ON D+1, CAPTAIN MALCOLM BRANNEN, the commander of Headquarters Company, 3rd Battalion, and his two companions left their hiding place in a hedgerow to try to find friendly forces. "The moon was not up very high, was quite bright, but the skies were a bit cloudy. The latter fact interested us, because we couldn't be seen nearly as well [due to the clouds] if the moon was real bright.

"Again, [Private First Class Jack] Quigg led off as we left our hideaway of the past twenty hours. I followed and [Private Russell] Nocera brought up the rear. We started out traveling northwest, but as on previous moves, we had to bear towards other directions to avoid enemy gun positions, so our first deviation was to the northeast. We headed for what we thought was our own mortars firing, but each time we got fairly close to where we thought that the firing was coming from, they seemed to have moved. So we just continued moving on. We traveled quite fast this night—we were anxious to get as near to our own troops as we possibly could in as little time as we could.

"At one time we came to a junction of roads and trails and we took a break to get a rest and to think the situation out. In the quiet, we could hear Germans all around us—we heard their voices, and we could hear wagons [being] loaded and [moving] out, hearing the Germans give commands to the horses that were pulling the wagons. Some passed just a few feet from us as we hid in the grass beside the road—real tall grass, about three or more feet high."[26]

ON THE MORNING OF D+2, CORPORAL KENNETH "ROCK" MERRITT, with Headquarters Company, 1st Battalion, was dug in with a group of about forty troopers around a hedgerow lined field north of Montessy, a small village on the Douve River, south of Picauville. "We received a call from Lieutenant Colonel Shanley on Hill 30 that they needed blood plasma real bad. We had plenty of it. It just happened to land in the area our equipment bundles did. Captain [Jonathan] Adams asked for volunteers—three men volunteered. They strapped blood plasma to their bodies and when night fell, they took off. The blood plasma patrol did not get through. Lieutenant [Roy W.] Murray [Headquarters Company, 3rd Battalion] got killed, Corporal [James E.] Green [Headquarters Company, 3rd Battalion] was found in a hedgerow one week later, completely dazed due to a concussion hand grenade. Private First Class [Frank J.] Circelli [Headquarters Company, 1st Battalion] made it back to our position, his lip and chin almost shot off. He was also shot in the neck and [had] several shots in his right arm."[27]

AT DAWN ON JUNE 8, KAMPFGRUPPE REITER, consisting of a reinforced battalion of Grenadier Regiment 1057, resumed its attacks against the troopers defending Hill 30, while two companies of German engineers with Kampfgruppe Bonnenkamp, supported by French tanks and Sturmgeschütz III assault guns, moved up to attack the roadblock at the western end of the Chef-du-Pont causeway. From his position south of Hill 30, Lieutenant Ralph DeWeese, with Company H, could see movement in front of the paratroopers' positions. "We saw some men coming up in the woods. I was looking at them through my field glasses and gave the order to fire because I could see they were Jerries. Some of the men were not sure and it took a little time to get fire on them. As soon as the Jerries started firing back, all the men knew. We thought they were enemy paratroopers because of the camouflage smocks they wore. We later found out they were engineers that had been sent down to mine the road junction.

"We had a terrific battle with them and were firing pointblank at about two hundred yards. They had a company of about one hundred men; we only had sixty-seven men and ten of these were on the roadblock. We battled back and forth for about two hours. Colonel Shanley came up and said he'd send a platoon around the right flank. I remember we were up on a hedgerow and I was looking over and a mortar shell hit just in front of the position and I felt pieces of dirt hit my lips. Lieutenant Polette had his rifle resting on the hedgerow and an [enemy] automatic pistol zeroed in and filled his rifle with dust, so he had to take it all apart and clean it. They kept working down the road and placed a lot of mortar fire on the roadblock we had. They [the troopers manning the roadblock] held up a little too long before withdrawing and we lost five men killed. A little later, two tanks came up and one of our .30-caliber machine guns knocked one of them out. We thought they were getting ready to attack, so we sent back and had antitank rifles [that fired armor piercing rifle grenades] brought up. We were all set for an attack when they started firing mortars. I have never seen such accurate [mortar fire]. They started at one end of the hedgerow and came right on up. We lost another man killed and several wounded. Many men were hit by shrapnel. I had a piece in a pack of cigarettes and also one through my gas mask. We withdrew back up to Hill 30 and set up a defense."[28]

COLONEL LINDQUIST SENT PATROLS SOUTH FROM CHEF-DU-PONT on the morning of June 8, to contact the 101st Airborne Division, which was supposed to be holding Carquebut and le Port. Instead they found both towns held by strong enemy forces. When the patrols reported back, Captain Royal Taylor, the commanding officer of Company B, was ordered to take his force of less than one hundred men and eliminate the German forces in both towns. As Taylor's paratroopers approached Carquebut, they received fire that passed overhead. As they closed in, a short firefight ensued and the German force surrendered. Taylor's men killed about fifteen Germans and captured two officers, seven NCOs, and 102 privates. Captain Taylor sent about half of his force to le Port, where the Germans there also surrendered after a short fight. Lindquist's group now held positions east of the Merderet River running from le Port on the left to a position about two-thirds of a mile north of Chef-du-Pont on the right.

AROUND 4:00 P.M. ON HILL 30, the troopers were able to get one of the two SCR 300 radios working. Private First Class Harold Kulju, a radio operator with Headquarters Company, 2nd Battalion, tried to make contact with friendly forces. "I got an answer back from three guys who were holding a bridge. They stated that they had contact with regiment, and that they thought that regiment would be able to contact division, and division was in contact with division artillery. So, Colonel Shanley gave me coordinates, which I forwarded to them, and we asked for artillery fire as soon as possible on these coordinates. They agreed to relay the message. We had no idea whether we were going to get any artillery support or not; whether the artillery unit would even get the message or not."[29]

By the afternoon of June 8, Major James Todd, the commanding officer of the 319th Glider Field Artillery had his battalion in position southwest of Ste.-Mère-Église to support the 508th. "The battalion started firing at 17:15 hours with one battery of seven howitzers, one of which was attached from the 456th Parachute Field Artillery Battalion. The other howitzers had been damaged and left at the glider landing area."[30]

Back on Hill 30, Private First Class Kulju heard the sound of artillery shells coming from the eastern side of the Merderet River. "I was lying in a slit trench facing the hedgerow where the [German] artillery was being set up, and then in front of me, in another slit trench, was a glider pilot. Suddenly, I heard this weird noise and the shells started exploding where the Germans were. The message we had sent got through, and the division artillery hit the target dead center the very first volley. It caught the Germans out in the open, completely by surprise. Some of them had shells in their hands ready to throw into the open breeches of the French 75s. There were dead Germans all over the place when we got over there."[31]

After the initial barrage at 5:15 p.m., the 319th fired an additional thirteen rounds at 6:32 p.m., targeting two German Renault tanks preparing to attack Hill 30, knocking out one and forcing the other to withdraw. Then, the battalion fired another eighteen rounds at 8:00 p.m., breaking up German forces massing for another attack on the hill.

Sergeant Zane Schlemmer, manning an outpost at the foot of Hill 30, was thankful for the artillery fire, because he was running very low on ammunition. "This [artillery] fire broke up several German attacks at very critical times for us in the outpost. After one firing to break up a German attack coming up a sunken lane very near our outpost, we captured and retrieved two small German artillery cannons and some shells. These, we hauled back up to Hill 30 to turn around and use for the next attack."[32]

After dark on D+2, Lieutenant Woodrow Millsaps, with Company B, was told to report to Major Warren. "Warren called me off the line and told me the story about the contact he and Shanley had with the regimental commander...

"He told Shanley to continue to hold Hill 30. It was easier said than done. Ammunition was running low; food was nearly gone. As for medical supplies, the unit had only first aid kits. Casualties were mounting rapidly. The Germans had closed in and we were getting intense mortar fire.

"Colonel Lindquist told [Lieutenant] Colonel Shandley that he would try to send a patrol over to Hill 30 and if the patrol arrived safely, he would then send a convoy to assist Colonel Shandley in holding the hill. Colonel Shandley told Lindquist that the enemy had a roadblock on his side of the causeway [which] ran about one thousand yards across the river to Colonel Lindquist's position. This had to be eliminated before the convoy could reach him, so the convoy was held up.

"Warren told me the only way to get relief on Hill 30 was to destroy the enemy's roadblock on our side of the causeway so the convoy could get through. He wanted me to form a patrol from the front line and slip through the enemy's line and go down and destroy the roadblock. I tried to find men from Company B (my company) to form the patrol, but was only able to find one or two men. I had to pick soldiers who were strangers to me and who were willing to go on a patrol of this nature, but I finally got a small group of twenty-three men. We prepared to move out after dark."[33]

Lieutenant Lloyd Polette, with Company F, would be the only other officer leading the patrol. Lieutenant Millsaps now waited for nightfall before moving out with the combat patrol. "I had a chance to study my map and formulated a plan to attack the roadblock.

"After dark, we moved out toward the village and were able to slip through the enemy's lines without a firefight. Guiding on the dirt road leading into the village, we were able to get within three hundred yards before we were fired on from the roadblock. The enemy's machine gun and rifle fire were directed down the road toward the river and along the hedgerows running parallel to the road (just as I would have done if I were setting up a defense for the roadblock against a daylight attack).

"There was an open field on my right that offered no cover if I were to attack in daylight. But the enemy hadn't thought about a night attack and hadn't deployed his troops to defend this open field. Most of his weapons were concentrated on the river and hedgerows that would offer cover and concealment if I were to approach the positions from that direction. I took a chance on this plan and moved the patrol around to my right so I could attack through the open field and apple orchard. I told the patrol we would wait and see if the enemy would quiet down before we attacked. I wanted him to think we were a small patrol that would return to Hill 30 and leave him nothing to worry about until the next day.

"About 2:30 in the morning, enemy quieted down and then I was ready for the assault on the position. The moon was out and I could see my men as we moved out in a skirmish line toward the roadblock. I was out in front of the patrol and had given orders that no one was to fire until I gave the order to fire. We moved through the orchard until we were about fifty yards from a row of buildings to my front when I heard a command in German to halt. I pointed my M1 in that direction and fired, at the same time ordering my patrol to fire. I must have hit the German, for he let out a cry and jumped over a hedgerow and ran down a row of buildings, still yelling. That brought the Germans out of the buildings on the run. My unit was separated from the enemy by a hedgerow and a row of buildings which lined the road. We were stopped momentarily by these, thus giving the enemy time to bring fire on us.

"We found a gap in the corner of the hedgerow where the German was standing and we charged through, moving to the left and to the right of the row of buildings. I was with a couple of my men standing at a street running away from our position. Because of the moonlight, we could see the Germans as they ran from the buildings and hit the street. That was the end for most of them. Some of the Germans were still in the buildings, and they began to throw hand grenades at us as we charged from building to building. One of the hand grenades hit one of my soldiers in the head and blew his head off."[34]

The combat patrol cleared the buildings and the roadblock, some of it in vicious hand-to-hand combat. No prisoners were taken. After the assault ended, Lieutenant Millsaps reorganized his small force to defend the area. "My second in command, 2nd Lieutenant Polette, and I began to collect our men and outpost the position. We found that we only had eleven men out of the twenty-three we started out with. We needed all the men we could get to set up a defensive position, for we knew the enemy would attempt to take the village back as soon as they recovered from the shock. But I needed someone to go with me across the causeway to join Colonel Lindquist on the east side. I recognized Sergeant [Phillip] Klinefelter, one of my [B Company] men, and told him we would go across.

"He said, 'Ok, let's go.'

"We headed across the causeway as fast as we could go and shortly ran into one German soldier coming back toward the village. We jumped to the side of the causeway and got [bayoneted] him before he saw us. Then another German appeared on the causeway, and he was taken care of in the same manner.

"Sergeant Klinefelter kept lingering behind and was delaying our crossing. I stopped to see what was the matter, and when he came up to me I could see that his [jumpsuit jacket] coat was black on the right side of his chest. I ran my hand inside his coat and my hand came away with a handful of clammy blood. That frightened me and I said, 'My God, man, you're shot!' When I said that, he began to slump over and stagger. I told him he couldn't stop now, for I could not carry him and there was no one to help him. He would have to go on. He staggered on and finally we heard the word, 'Halt!' in English. We reached Colonel Lindquist's troops on the other side of the causeway. That was the last time I ever saw Sergeant Klinefelter, but he was given first aid and moved out of the area later, so I understand.

"It was now daylight and the patrol Colonel Lindquist had promised to send Colonel Shandley on Hill 30 was ready to go across the causeway, but the enemy was now shelling the causeway with artillery, and the patrol was held up. I was now with Colonel Lindquist giving him all the information. I knew about the troops on Hill 30, the strength, number of casualties, etc., and fell asleep while talking to him. I had not had any sleep since the 5th of June and it was now the [night of the] 8th of June. He had me lie down on some hay in a barn loft and try to get some sleep, but I was so upset that I didn't sleep much."[35]

Lieutenant Millsaps later found out the casualties his patrol had inflicted at the roadblock. "Some of the men who helped evacuate the wounded men from my patrol told me they counted forty-three dead Germans. Judging from the amount of kitchen equipment the enemy had left behind, they estimated that at least a company of German troops was in the village when we struck. My patrol suffered nine wounded and one dead—the soldier whose head was blown off from a hand grenade."[36]

Lieutenants Millsaps and Polette were awarded the Silver Star for their courageous leadership. Private Frank Haddy, with Company D, was a member of the patrol and felt that after seeing Lieutenant Polette in action during the patrol, that Lieutenant Polette was "the best soldier in the 508th."[37]

AS DAWN APPROACHED ON THE MORNING OF JUNE 8, Lieutenant Malcolm Brannen, the commanding officer of Headquarters Company, 3rd Battalion, and two other troopers had been moving through the night in enemy territory. "Daylight was fast becoming a reality and we all knew that we just had to find a good place to hide, and to get some type of food and water. We had shared our food and water for the last day and a half and had eaten and drank more than we should have. Some of the rations we ate so as not to have the bulk in our pockets to carry around, especially if we had to run away from prospective captors. So, into the daylight we went looking, listening, and hurrying.

"At one place we came to a ready made trail and on it we found a jump rope carried by paratroopers. This encouraged us and we kept on—finally coming to a road that led into a small village. It was decided that we needed water—but not at the risk of being captured. We also needed food and directions as to where we were at the time. Before we knew it, we were in the village—it just popped up as we went up a slope and turned a bend in the small, dusty road.

"All the time, voices of a patrol were closing on us and we were now in a maze of little streets and could hear the Germans very well. At this point, [Private First Class Jack] Quigg stepped into a manure shed. He looked out of the window at me and pointed towards three German soldiers setting up a machine gun. I saw them and when they moved behind a house, I stepped into the shed beside Quigg.

"The Germans had not seen anyone of us yet, because Quigg and I were in the shed and [Private Russell] Nocera was outside and behind the shed. Our hearts were in our throats, because as Nocera moved into the shed with us, the Germans chose that time to come from behind the house and saw Nocera make his move. We knew it, because we could see the three Germans pointing to the shed door. They didn't know how many of us were in there, but they knew someone was there.

"Nocera said, 'Let's hide under the manure.' I said that we could not because they knew we were in here and would shortly come after us. We'll have to make a break for it. It was agreed that they would follow me. I yelled, 'Follow me,' and I dashed out of the door, turned left, ran ten feet down a narrow alley, came to a narrow street running right and left. I turned left and as I turned the corner, I saw four or five Germans setting up a machine gun. I ran close to the building, so close that I was whirling like a football player as he frees himself from an opponent's grasp. I looked right into the machine gun muzzle and I saw tracer bullets coming right towards me. I felt the entrenching tool that I had on my belt—a shovel, shot completely off the pistol belt—and I got completely turned around and just picked up my feet and kept laying them down. If those buildings, the one that the machine gun was beside, and the one that I ran along side of had not been of a rounding shape, I know the bullets would have hit me. As it was, they were shooting a bit to my right and I was bearing a bit to my left with every stride. I knew that I wasn't safe yet. I ran into an orchard, headed down the right side for about twenty yards or so and then turned a ninety degree angle to the left and crossed a forty yard field in nothing flat, dove into a ditch in front of a hedgerow and started to crawl in the ditch, going right, and away from the manure shed where I had left; or should I say, when and where Quigg and Nocera didn't follow me.

"After crawling about ten yards, I stopped and crawled backwards, covering my trail as I moved slowly, camouflaged myself and my trail as much as I could. After about five minutes of this I stopped moving, and really I guess that I nearly stopped breathing, too. I put my knit [cap] on at this time to hide my face so it wouldn't be seen, because I was certain that it was ghostly white, because I felt for certain like an empty sheet!

"Once in a spot where I thought I could rest and hide from anyone chasing me, I covered my legs with leaves and dead briars, put my left hand in my steel helmet, to help cover some of my face that was not covered by my knit [cap], and grasped my carbine, that I had managed to hold on to during all the time and action I had been through since I first put it into the violin case and strapped it to my body way back in good old England. I was lying right out straight, thanking God that I was small and short and that I had made it safely to the ditch that was now protecting me from being seen. Before finally settling where I was now located, I checked my pistol and my trench knife to be sure that they were readily available and ready to use in a hurry if needed.

"I very nearly had climbed over the dirt hedge beside which I was now snuggled, in order to get as much distance between me and the Germans soldiers that I knew would come looking for me. I would have had to cross another field, a road, climb through a hedgerow and settle in the field beyond, which I discovered later was thick with German foxholes, using machine guns and mortars in addition to riflemen. I was happy when I found out that I had not been too greedy and tried to get more safety than I had. This fact was one of several happenings that made me later realize that I was not alone in my travels and troubles—that God was really looking out for me.

"As I lay there, I started to worry and wonder what happened to Quigg and Nocera—but not for long! It was just a short time until I heard voices, yelling excitedly, high pitched, nervous voices—German and American. The German voices were half in the German language and half in the American English language. The voices were saying, 'Come oudt—hans oop—hans oop—we kill—we kill. Then I heard one of my companions of the last few hours, one of my paratroopers yell, 'No, no, I don't want to die—I don't want to die!' Then Brrrrrrr—Brrrrrrr—the fast shooting of machine gun pistols that the Germans carried had done their work—no more American voices—no more English words![38]

"I knew what would happen next—I scarcely breathed—I knew—yes—the voices, like a pack of hounds, came into the field and orchard in which I was hidden. I prayed and I knew that every word I said I meant, and I meant every word I said. I prayed—asked forgiveness—asked blessings for my folks and dearest friends—human and canine. Yes, I prayed and really felt like I had seen the last of life on this earth.

"They came! The Germans first went down the field on the side that I started down before I made my dash across the field and orchard. For two hours and more, they shot in every nook and corner, in every house on the border of the orchard. They shot that high velocity machine pistol which sounded like a burp—Brrrrrrrpt, rather than like our Tommy gun, with its slow, nearly single shot sound, or our machine gun with its ack-ack-ack-ack.

"Then the inevitable—they came to the side of the field on which I was hiding. My carbine was rusty already, from the perspiration that had dropped onto the receiver from the end of my nose and chin. I was so still that I think several times that my heart did stop—but I thought surely that the thud-thud-thud that came from it would cause me to be discovered.

"One German soldier walked through the briars about five feet in front of me and jumped over the dirt hedgerow. PHEW! He yelled something to his companions—'Nobody here,' I guessed and hoped! Then he kept going on across the field. I could hear him running away from my position.

"Then those Germans with the shooting irons came along, and because the grass was a couple of feet high, eight or ten feet in front of me and the briars were so thick around me, they stayed that distance from me. But they shot and shot and shot right over my body. I could feel the breeze of the flying lead and I could feel and see the dirt as it fell on me as the lead burrowed into the mud bank behind me. Later on, I could see the holes where the lead was buried in the hedgerow.

"Twelve times I counted the German soldiers as they walked up and back in front of my hideout, firing with every other step or so. I was wondering about the thirteenth time, but it never came.

"This was Thursday morning, D+2. I had entered my hideout about 08:00 hours and knew that I had to stay there until darkness anyway—that would be twelve hours, more or less.

"All afternoon our artillery fell around me—then our planes, the P-47s and P-51s did a beautiful job on bombing—but I was too close—right in the middle of it all. Then, the German artillery would go off. Also, the German 88s and mortars were being shot continuously. I thought that they would never cease. It was a very poor place to be—I knew it, but I just couldn't get out, and right at the moment, I couldn't do anything about it. I was waiting for darkness to come and was praying that it would come soon.

"However, before dark arrived, more cows did. They started to eat the hay in front of me—and I remembered about the other times when a cow came and gave me quite a bit of concern. It wasn't long before some French men and women came and drove the cows home for the night. But the French men and women nearly stepped on me when they tried to get behind the cows to shoo them home.

"Dinner and supper time came and went, but I hadn't eaten. I had nothing. I was patiently waiting for darkness. I thought I would crawl out of my position and cross the hedgerow to my right, cross the field, the road on the other side of the field, and be on my way across more fields to the northeast, hoping to run into the Allied troops advancing from the beachhead.

"About this time, the Germans started moving into the fields around me. They brought mortars and 88s, machine guns, machine pistols, and rifles. By dark, the fields were alive with Germans and firepower. I would have to plan another route of escape.

"A new day was dawning—it began to get light. I had not slept because I wanted to get out of my place and out of my predicament. I could not sleep in the daylight for fear that someone would see me. I couldn't sleep during the hours of darkness because I was afraid I might snore and bring attention to my hiding place. I just lay there—my binoculars, inside my shirt were cutting into my chest; my carbine had numbed my right hand, especially my fourth and little fingers. I had to move and change my position. I was hungry, I was thirsty. Daylight was here. I had no food, no water. I'd have to wait until night. I tried to relax. I thought of home, of my friends, of my dogs, my travels, my friends who I had met while assigned to various camps and stations in the U.S.A. I swore I'd drink anything anybody offered me, be it buttermilk or vinegar. I shuddered—I hated buttermilk—but I would drink it now if it was in front of me—or behind me! I was hard up, but I still had my head, my senses, and my heart. I still had my belief in God—but I was alone, so all alone. It was getting to look like I would be alone for a long time to come. 'But who knows,' I said to myself.

"Not for long, because about then—this being Friday, D+3—the P-47s began dropping eggs and the artillery of our troops started popping at the German positions. This continued with the Germans answering nearly round for round all morning. All afternoon and in the evening the Germans moved more 88s and mortars into the area. A German with a machine gun and one with a machine pistol moved right beside me on the other side of the hedgerow. I could hear them talk, cough, spit, and nearly hear them breathe. But most of all, I could hear their weapons keep up the most consistent clatter that I had ever heard. All night long—only our artillery silenced them and I had it doped out that I'd just as soon have the Germans fire, because they were just making noises, whereas our artillery was landing here and there and all around me! If it hit some of the Germans, it was OK, but it just didn't seem to. Every time that I thought one of the German guns had been hit, it seemed as if two weapons started shooting where there had been just one.

"I made up my mind on Friday morning to wait for the Allies to come along. I knew that anytime after D+3 that they should make their appearance, so I waited with renewed hope.

"It rained Friday at supper time—just a few drops hit my cup when I tried to catch some water to moisten my lips, but the drops were not large enough to do any good. The leaves were wet a little, so I lapped them, but it didn't help much either. I decided to wait and not get careless while I was looking for water that wasn't there. I felt certain that help would come before long."[39]

ON JUNE 8, FAR TO THE SOUTH OF THE DOUVE RIVER, Private First Class Bill Tumlin and other members of First Sergeant Leonard Funk's stick of Company C troopers moved north, led by Funk. Tumlin and the other members of the group avoided contact with enemy troops where possible and only "fired on any who fired on us."[40]

With Funk acting as the scout, the group traveled at night and had several engagements with enemy groups. Sergeant Bill Traband noticed that a couple of troopers from the 507th Parachute Infantry, who had been picked up by the group during the journey, began to lose hope that they would get back to friendly lines. "At the end of Thursday we were out of food. We could get water where cows were. They had a pill then that you could just drop in the dirty water and you could drink it. Nobody got sick. One of these two other guys, not from our unit, went up to Funk and said, 'You know, we ought to give up.' There were so many paratroopers who just gave up.

"Then Funk got us all together and said, 'The next guy who mentions that, I'm going to cut him in half with this Tommy gun.' That was when I was so proud to in the airborne."[41]

ON THE NIGHT OF JUNE 8, GENERAL RIDGWAY ordered Colonel George Millett, the commander of the 507th Parachute Infantry Regiment, to move his group of approximately 425 mostly 507th troopers from west of Amfreville to join Lieutenant Colonel Charles J. Timmes and his force of mostly 507th dug in at an orchard east of Amfreville just north of the la Fière causeway. Lieutenant Colonel Harry Harrison, the 508th executive officer, and Major Dave Thomas, the 508th's regimental surgeon, were among those with Millett's group. As the group prepared to move out, Major Thomas was forced to make a very difficult decision. "By this time, I had quite a few wounded and I also had a couple of wounded medics. We couldn't possibly carry them all along with us. So I left the wounded medics with the wounded troops to surrender to the Germans. By this time, nobody had had any sleep for a couple of days. As we marched in column, we would stop for some reason, and somebody in the column would fall asleep. We ended up with the outfit all broken up into smaller elements.

"This one kid was walking with this armed [Gammon] grenade in his hand—and he dropped it. It blew off his left leg at the hip, and his left arm at the shoulder. I just put a KIA medical tag on him and moved on."[42]

Technician Fourth Grade Paul Bouchereau, also with the 508th's medical detachment, was moving near the rear of the same column. "It was about 2:00 a.m. that I thought the stop was unusually long. I walked up the column to see why we had stalled. I found two soldiers at the top of the column sound asleep. I realized that the main body had departed and was probably a march of possibly an hour, perhaps a mile and a half away.

"In a quick consultation with a captain who had joined our group the previous day, we decided to continue in the direction we thought the main body was headed. We traveled thus for several hours and it was just about dawn when we met a small German patrol of about six men. We attempted to continue our march, firing as we moved, but reinforcements arrived for the Germans and blocked our advance. In fact, we were soon completely surrounded and hopelessly pinned down. The small arms fire was intense and the Germans were closing in and would soon be within grenade range.

"The captain called me over to him and said he was going to attempt to surrender the group. He told me that if he was shot down to try and find the weakest point in the German ring and for all of us to head for that point, firing rapidly as we ran like hell in that direction. Hopefully some of us would get through.

"Just before the captain stood up frantically waving his white handkerchief, I am sure he was thinking the same as I: by accident due to the intensity of the small arms fire or by design he would be shot and killed. I was fully prepared to carry out his final order. A miracle took place and the German firing stopped. He emerged unscathed. We fell in behind him and walked towards the German lines. The enemy came from the areas of concealment and completed the procedure of taking us as their prisoners.

"We were taken to a small command post where an attempt was made to question us about the size and the immediate objective of our invading force. In answer to the question of how many Americans jumped into this area, one soldier replied, 'Millions and millions.' In answer to the same question, another soldier replied, 'Just me.' The Germans interrogator seemed to realize the futility of it all and abruptly cut off the questions.

"We were formed into a rather ragged column and with hands clasped to the top of our heads, were herded north. It could not have been more than fifteen or twenty minutes when we came under mortar attack—it had to be airborne troops, perhaps from our previous contingent. A mortar barrage is always scary, because unlike artillery, you do not hear the shell until it explodes. Such an attack from your own troops is much worse. The German guards took to walking in the deep ditches on either side of the road while we walked pretty much in the center of the road. The bombardment was quite intense and it seemed quite possible that we would be killed by our own troops. Morale was understandably low, but was given a boost when the captain started making cracks about the brave Germans hiding in the ditch. It was contagious and soon everyone was joining in. I don't know how much English the Germans understood, but they soon got the gist of it, and became increasingly furious.

"When the shelling stopped, we waited for the attack and liberation to come as we continued to walk in the road with the Germans following alongside in the ditch. In due time, it became apparent that the group that had shelled us had withdrawn and had no immediate intention of pressing for our liberation. When the Germans were certain of this, they took up their more orthodox guard positions on each side of our column.

"[Private First Class Leo] Jenson, [Technician Fifth Grade Ed] McCurdy and I were walking together, with McCurdy between Jenson and me. After a few minutes, McCurdy called our attention to the fact that the guard on the right side had dropped back. Our curiosity was aroused. The German NCO in charge of the guard detail moved from the head of the column to our left at about midpoint, and almost immediately opened fire with his submachine gun. I had had more than a passing glance at this character. When he was placed in charge of the detail, he was only a few feet from me, and I can still recall his appearance. He was short and stocky and mean looking. His most striking feature was a scar on the right side of his face that ran from the corner of his eye to the midpoint on his jaw.

"It felt like a severe bee sting in the area of my left knee, and I realized that I had been wounded. I fell to the ground and lay there for a short time, until I was roughly jerked to my feet by a guard. Two non-wounded fellow prisoners whom I did not know stepped in on either side of me and attempted to give me support.

"With the butt of the rifle to their heads, they were informed that this was 'verboten', and I was told to walk. I soon realized that it was their intention to see how far or how long we individually and collectively could walk before pain and fatigue took their toll. Considering the sadistic aspect of the shooting and subsequent treatment, I believe that at that point, I or we would meet with a sudden demise.

"Details of the walk, time, distance and scenery were meaningless, but the pain is still vivid in my memory. The wound, when inflicted felt like a bee sting, but each step afterwards was much worse. I have no idea how long or how far I walked, but one other detail I can recall—that was the squish of the blood in my boot as I took one step after the other.

"Eventually the inevitable happened, and I dropped to the ground unable to rise. A Kraut came over and rolled me over on my back. He cocked his rifle and put the business end to my head. I probably set a speed record for saying the rosary, but instead of pulling the trigger, the German laughed, then bent over me and offered me an American cigarette. I suppose I should have been grateful that my life had been spared, but instead I was furious at the physical and mental torture to which I had been subjected. My mind and head were filled with hate. I took the cigarette and enjoyed each inhalation while waiting to be transported to a German hospital. I dreamed of the day when I would repay them in full measure for my suffering."[43]

Major Thomas was also among those captured and put to work at a German aid station, until he escaped and made his way back to friendly lines. He made a report of his activities on June 15, when he was returned to the 82nd Airborne Division command post.

BY THE MORNING OF JUNE 8, the small group led by Lieutenant Colonel Louis Mendez, the commanding officer of the 3rd Battalion, was moving into the rear area of Bataillon 1, Grenadier Regiment 1057, which was attacking Hill 30. The group had previously commandeered two camouflaged German trucks, which were being driven along the roads adjacent to the direction of travel by the group. Private First Class James T. Wynne and several other troopers with Headquarters Company, 1st Battalion had joined the group earlier. "I was told to get a detail and gather all the canteens and fill them at a stream that we could see in the next field about five hundred feet away. I chose two men to help carry the canteens and just before we started through the hedgerow into the next field, one of the men spotted a company of Krauts in the woods about five hundred feet away. Talk about luck—we would have been right out in the open with no protection.

"Mendez immediately organized a defensive position with me all the way up the field to his right. It was not long before about a company of Krauts came out of the woods. As they came across the field toward us, [Private First Class] James B. Howard, [with Headquarters Company, 1st Battalion] who was next to Mendez, shot a German with a Red Cross armband charging with a rifle. Howard knocked the German down with his little carbine, but he got up and continued to advance. Howard asked Mendez, 'What do I do now?'

"Mendez replied, 'Shoot the S.O.B. again!' which he did.

"By this time Mendez decided it was best for us to abandon the field for a better place, because there were too many for us. I was still up to their right, guarding the right flank and rear. I heard the firing, but I did not see the action. James Howard called for me to come on, they were pulling out. We left in a spread formation into a field to our rear. The field was full of weeds and stubble about twenty-four inches high. We came under intense fire, so I hit the ground. I could hear bullets hitting the weeds and stubble. I thought the bullets were as thick as fleas on a dog's back. A tank was spraying the field and the road next to the field with machine gun fire.

"I heard Mendez holler, 'Everyone to the left!' Mendez was standing in a gate directing his men across the road. One man was hit in the fleshy part of his thigh. Mendez started toward the wounded man. The wounded man hollered for Mendez to stay back and he made it across the road on his own. I had not yet crossed the road. It was the inspiration of Mendez that gave me the power to move. All of us got across the road. We stopped to dress the thigh wound of the injured man, gave him a full canteen of water, but we had to leave him. It was a hard thing to do. While others were taking care of the wounded man, Mendez and his officers were studying maps to see how to get to Hill 30."[44]

During the fighting and withdrawal, the two captured German trucks had been abandoned by the two troopers driving them just before a German armored vehicle destroyed both trucks.

Private First Class John Delury, with Company H, had acted as a scout for the group since June 6, while Lieutenant John Quaid, the Company H executive officer, had been up front with the point throughout that same time. As a result of being out in front of the group almost continuously, Delury had very nearly been killed several times. "Lieutenant Quaid asked if someone else wanted to take a turn at the first scout position. There were a lot of troopers who weren't with their own officers, and were just content to stay in the middle of the group and follow the crowd. His looking for a first scout was directed towards them, but one of our own stood up and said he'd take the point. He was [Technician Fifth Grade Daniel F.] Dan Koziel from I Company. He was older than most of us and we called him 'Pappy'. A few minutes before, somehow he salvaged a bottle of German wine from one of the [German] camouflaged trucks. It had a very long neck and no shoulders. He pulled the cork and gave me a swig. It really tasted good, more for sustenance than pleasure.

"We started out with Pappy as first scout, and could not have walked more than two or three hedgerows when three Germans came out of the woods surrendering. One had a rifle in his up stretched hands, and brought it down and killed Pappy instantly. We immediately dispatched the three to Valhalla. We laid trooper Koziel with his arms crossed on a sort of berm—a mound between two fields. I took his trench knife to replace the one I lost on the jump, and we said a prayer; then we moved on.

"We regrouped and Lieutenant Quaid took some of the aforementioned troopers who were strangers to us, as his point. I said to Sergeant [Philip] Gantz [with Company I] that I was going to ask Quaid for he (Gantz) and I to take the point. I felt somehow if I had the point instead of Koziel, I wouldn't have been killed as was Koziel. It was a gut feeling and in reality I would probably have been just as dead as Dan Koziel. Lieutenant Quaid told me he wanted to use some of the people who were not up front yet, and said for me and Gantz to take the rear guard with Lieutenant [Arthur R.] Stevens [the assistant platoon leader of the Light Machine Gun Platoon, Headquarters Company, 1st Battalion].

"Well, we couldn't have traveled more than a few hundred yards and our luck ran out. They probably had our movements pretty much for certain after we ran from the trucks, because they were waiting for us behind an innocent looking hedgerow that the point approached. The first salvo of machine gun fire killed everyone up front. It is difficult to tell just how many were killed, but Quaid and the entire point went down instantly. There was a small opening in the left rear of the field in which we were being slaughtered. We were funneling ourselves through this tight space, and the kid next to me got hit in the head. When we finally got out of the field of fire and assembled, we had one trooper with a bullet wound through his thigh. We administered first aid giving him a morphine syrette and put some sulfa powder on his leg. Then we had to leave him and move out. He just sat there and understood our predicament. He certainly was a cool piece of work.

"We traveled about four or five hundred yards through hedgerows until we came to an area that appeared safe for the moment. We hid there for over an hour. The colonel [Mendez] then told me to take someone with me and see if I could locate the trooper we left, and bring him back. I took a staff sergeant from the 507th Parachute Regiment and we went to the area where a few hours earlier the Krauts had slaughtered us. It was very eerie—late afternoon—the sun filtering down through the leaves on the giant hedgerows and birds fluttering around and chirping, and any second waiting for a German machine gun to open up. We were crawling around on our hands and knees whispering for our wounded comrade, but he was nowhere to be found. Whether the Germans captured him or he crawled away from the area and hid, we didn't know, so we returned to our group and reported it.

"We kept traveling at night and it was very tiring. We were going almost continually since the night of the jump without a square meal or a night's sleep. With three or four days of no real sleep, you start to get bug-eyed. So it was, when we made contact, about four o'clock in the morning with our forces holding Hill 30. Before we entered into the perimeter of our own lines we had to lay almost in single file for what seemed over an hour to insure that our own troops didn't open fire on us. There was not a sound to be heard—just the stillness that was compounded by the morning dew and blackness.

"Then a terrific explosion broke the silence and it was all still again. Soon an agonizing voice started screaming out, 'My legs, my legs, help anybody, help me.' His voice was almost undistinguishable. At first I thought he was a German, but in retrospect he would have been yelling in German; but the pain must have distorted his diction. Whether he stepped on a landmine or a grenade rolled in his foxhole God only knows, but it was one of the most pathetic sounds I've ever heard. When we finally entered our lines there was about a battalion of paratroopers, and they were surrounded by [elements of] a German division. But to us, after being on our own since D-Day, it felt as secure as a baby in its mother's arms."[45]

Lieutenant Colonel Mendez had skillfully led his small group through the Norman bocage country that was thick with enemy troops hunting for paratroopers, to reach friendly forces on Hill 30 after three harrowing days and four nights.

CHAPTER 6

"THE FINEST MAN I HAD EVER MET"

On the morning of June 9, the 2nd Battalion of the 401st Glider Infantry (attached to the 325th Glider Infantry Regiment), together with three composite companies from the 507th Parachute Infantry Regiment, captured the la Fière causeway and established a bridgehead on the west side the Merderet River. At 11:30 a.m., Colonel Lindquist's group of 508th paratroopers crossed that causeway and began fighting their way south with the objective of linking up with Lieutenant Colonel Shanley's troopers on Hill 30.

Meanwhile, Lieutenant Barry Albright, the platoon leader of the 1st Platoon of Company E, arrived at one of the observation posts he had established on Hill 30. "I found enemy infantry milling around a few hedgerows away, apparently preparing for an impending attack. Upon reporting this information to the battalion commander, it was learned that radio contact had been established with the 319th Glider Field Artillery Battalion. Securing the only SCR 300 on the hill, I was able to direct effective fire, breaking up all semblance of organization among the enemy in the area. Throughout the day, as these small probing attacks developed, the availability of artillery fire greatly offset the acute shortage of crew served weapons. In the latter part of the afternoon, reports were received that enemy troops in considerable strength were in the vicinity of a road junction west of Hill 30. I again directed artillery fire, this time knocking out a complete battery of German 75mm howitzers that were moving into position to fire on Hill 30. Shortly after this action, Colonel Lindquist, commanding officer, 508th Parachute Infantry Regiment, with approximately two hundred men and officers joined the position on Hill 30."[1]

Colonel Lindquist recommended Lieutenant Colonel Tom Shanley for the Distinguished Service Cross for his courageous leadership during the fighting on Hill 30, but the division awards board approved the award of the Silver Star instead. Major Shields Warren was also awarded the Silver Star for his heroism during the same action.

After Lindquist's group of troopers joined those on Hill 30, the assistant platoon leader of the 2nd Platoon of Company H, Lieutenant Ralph DeWeese, learned from them that his platoon sergeant, Staff Sergeant Joe Bundy had been killed. "He was found in the water with two bullet holes in his head, so he was

167

probably killed coming down [during the jump]. I also learned that Corporal [Lewis W.] Latimer had come through the roof of a house and had been bayoneted by the Germans. Also, Private [Donald] Cornbread, the little Indian boy, and Private [Elwood] Morris and [Private First Class Thomas P.] Saccone had drowned. Sergeant [John J.] Judefind, another one of my best noncoms was missing. Also, Private First Class [Ward S.] Hutcheson, Private [John] Posadas, and Private [First Class Donald R.] Scholz were missing. Captain [Hal] Creary and Lieutenant [John] Quaid were also missing."[2]

The following day, June 10, 1944, Lieutenant Albright and the other officers and NCOs began reorganizing the regiment. "On D+4, the 90th Infantry Division pushed west toward Étienville. This secured the area around Hill 30 and allowed the entire 508th Parachute Infantry Regiment a badly needed period for reorganization. For the next forty-eight hours, men were shuffled from unit to unit until tactical integrity was finally regained. With the arrival of seaborne forces, the much needed crew served weapons, ammunition, and other equipment became available. In the process of reorganization it became apparent time after time that men, who had not previously carried an MOS [military occupational specialty] of machine gunner, mortar man, BAR man, etcetera, had to move in and fill these vacancies. The effective personnel strength of the 2nd Battalion at this time was approximately seventy percent."[3]

Also on D+4, Major Shields Warren, the 1st Battalion executive officer who had been the acting battalion commander over the last four days, finally received information regrading the fate of Lieutenant Colonel Herbert Batcheller, the battalion commander. "I heard by word of mouth that his body and that of his radio operator had been found together next to a hedgerow. Apparently he had absorbed a 30-40 round burst in the chest, which would have resulted in instantaneous death."[4]

IN THE PREDAWN HOURS OF JUNE 10, LIEUTENANT MALCOLM BRANNEN, the commanding officer of Headquarters Company, 3rd Battalion, lay hidden in tall weeds, grass, and briars in a field that had been occupied by Germans during the previous two days and nights, and was suffering greatly from thirst and hunger. "Finally, dawn—it was Saturday, D+4, and I was still in a hot bed of fire—ours and now their shells and mortar rounds were landing in the area, also. They had been landing there all day, but it was more severe now, it seemed as they really meant it now. This meant one thing to me—the Germans were pulling out and back, because the Allies were pushing forward and claiming the area. I prayed some more. I waited for what I thought was an eternity and then I heard voices. I couldn't make out if they were German or American voices.

"Then I heard someone say, 'Now hear that gun? That's for y'all.' Then I heard a German burp gun—Brrrrrrrpt, and the voice said, 'Now that gun's AGIN y'all.'

"Then I yelled, 'Hey American—hey soldier.' I knew no German ever said, 'That gun's AGIN y'all.' I knew it was an American.

"In a moment, two privates came over to see me. I asked what division that they were with and they answered the 90th. They pushed through the briars and picked me up, gave me a drink of water and after I brushed myself off, they let go of me. I started to move and my legs were just like rubber—they just wouldn't stand stiff. The soldiers helped me and as soon as I got my strength and could control my legs, which was just a few seconds, I was off under my own control.

"I reported to Lieutenant Lovell, Company I, 357th Infantry, 90th Division. Then I went to the manure shed to see what happened there if I could. I found one M1 rifle, which I took with me. That was all the evidence of Americans having been in the vicinity. I decided to go forward with the 90th Division as they advanced to where I thought my unit was, but was told that there were some airborne units just a little way back in the direction from which they came.

"So I moved in the direction mentioned and sure enough, I found airborne troops of the 82nd Division and they informed me where the 3rd Battalion of the 508th Parachute Regiment was located and gave me a jeep ride to a position just a few hundred yards from where I had been hiding for the last few days and nights. I reported into my battalion headquarters, to my battalion commander, Lieutenant Colonel Louis G. Mendez, Jr.

"I was happy and thankful and I thanked God for His guidance and help."[5]

Also by June 10, the situation had grown dire for Technician Fourth Grade O. B. Hill and a group of about twenty-five troopers who had been defending a field north of Beuzeville since the morning of the invasion. They had run out of food and the number of wounded had grown substantially. "The 101st man who had been shot through the stomach and left behind came to our field. We continued to give him sulfa powder and morphine.

"[Technician Fifth Grade Charles P.] C. P. Reynolds was shot in the head and did know that he had been hit until he took off his helmet and wool knit cap. We treated him also.

"[Staff Sergeant] George [M.] DeCarvalho was hit in the ankle by a German rifle grenade. The grenade did not go off, but it did severe damage to his ankle. [Staff Sergeant Ray] Hummel buried [Private First Class August] Labate where he had been killed.

"We had been visited one night by a French gentleman who brought us some cheese, bread, and wine. He also told us how many Germans were around us and where they were located. He risked his life doing this and he was nearly [accidentally] killed by us.

"In the late afternoon of the fifth day we were practically out of ammunition. We were hearing a lot of firing coming from the causeway which led into Chef-du-Pont. It was getting closer all the time and that promised to be help for us. The firing got very close and we knew that someone from our army was close to us. The first words that we heard were said by a master sergeant from the 90th Division who yelled, 'Bring up that damned bazooka.' At this, all of us stood up and cheered. The master sergeant yelled for us to get back down and we did. Remarkably, none of us were shot during that brief ordeal. The good part was that the Germans were now running from that corner and we had been found by friendly forces. The master sergeant took our wounded and got them on their way back to an aid station. He took our one prisoner and sent him back to a POW compound. He then gave us a guide to get us through the minefields and we were on our way back to the unit.

"We proved to be a stubborn group because we held our ground against every attempt to get us out. [Staff Sergeant] Ray Hummel and I agree that we did quite well with what we had. Our crew was from a variety of units; we had little equipment; we had no medics, officers, or heavy weapons; and we had no chance of being supplied with ammunition for our small arms weapons.

"When we arrived back with the unit, we learned that Captain [Gerard] Ruddy was killed, Lieutenant [Charles] McElligott shot through the stomach and captured, 1st Sergeant Earl [J.] Smith was killed, 1st Lieutenant [Edgar] Abbott was killed, and many others from my platoon. That was a severe shock to me and others. We had seen many killed along the way, but these men were very close friends. I cannot explain the feeling that day, but I had lost some extra good friends. Captain Ruddy was the finest man that I had ever met. McElligott was a very good man and a good friend, and others from my platoon were top notch, also. I felt quite sorry for all of them and for their families."[6]

That same day in a field north of Montessy, another group of 508th troopers being led by Captain Jonathan Adams, the commanding officer of Company A, awaited a linkup with friendly forces. Corporal Kenneth "Rock" Merritt, with Headquarters Company, 1st Battalion, was having doubts about the success of the invasion. "I was giving Private First Class [Frank] Circelli water through a blood plasma tube. He was one of the blood plasma patrol members who got back to our position all shot up. He asked me when did I think the seaborne troops would arrive. According to the big plan, they were supposed to reach us in the first twenty-four hours of operation, and here it was, four days later and they haven't reached us yet. I was thinking how to answer Private First Class Circelli. I looked up and saw a 2½-ton truck, American truck, coming towards us. At that moment, I knew that the seaborne troops had arrived inland, because the largest vehicle we had in Normandy was a jeep that came in by our gliders. The troops and the equipment that followed it were with the Oklahoma/Texas division. I believe it was the 90th Division. They picked up all of our wounded and med-evaced them to the rear.

"Captain Adams moved up to Hill 30, where the 508 Regiment was now being assembled. We got our first hot meal in five days. The next three days were spent regrouping the units, issuing new weapons, and getting ready for our next mission. I was promoted to sergeant since my section chief, Sergeant John Pavlich, got killed on the first day."[7]

Merritt had certainly grown into a combat veteran over the first days of the invasion. "I think most of my fear left me after daylight on the 6th of June. My only regret was that we could not break the siege of the twenty acres of real estate, but I do not fault Captain Adams. He probably saved our lives."[8]

Captain Jonathan Adams had shown tremendous courage and leadership in keeping the group from being overrun and was later awarded the Silver Star for his actions over those five days.

PRIVATE FIRST CLASS HAROLD L. PARRIS, WITH COMPANY C, was with a small group of troopers west of Gueutteville, behind German lines on June 10. "We woke up and everybody was hungry. No food. We had been getting our water from the creek. Everyone was lying around napping. I was lying in a ditch with my machine gun pointing toward the road. [Private Carmen J. "Peg"] Pagnotta [with Company B] was lying in the ditch above me. A German officer broke through the hedge below us, walked right past me; he got even with Pagnotta and saw him. He reached for his pistol, but Peg swung up and shot him. He headed back towards me, and I shot him, also. He fell five feet in front of me and raised his pistol to shoot me. Peg and I both shot him again. Shortly after this, a [German] soldier came rushing out in the field, shouting a man's name. We stayed down out of sight and he went back down the hill. I told the sergeant, 'We've got to move now.' We rolled the dead officer into the ditch and we headed out in the direction we had been the day before. Halfway to the [German] artillery, we turned left and found a deep ditch along a hedgerow among a group of trees. We stayed there the rest of the day."[9]

That same afternoon, Parris saw a large group of Germans in the direction from which his group had just come. "We could see they were setting up an artillery battery. The sergeant passed the word by the line: 'Tomorrow we might as well surrender, because we are completely surrounded now.'

"I was the end man in the ditch and when word got to me, I said, 'Bullshit. I didn't come over here to surrender just because the Germans are all around us. They don't know where we are. There is a chance to get out. I'm leaving the cowardly bastard in the morning. Anyone who wants to go—be ready.'"[10]

Early the following morning, Parris moved out with his small group. "I said, 'Let's go.' Seven men volunteered. We single filed along a hedge in the direction of the front. We could hear it real plain now. We hadn't gone over a thousand feet when two German soldiers stepped out in a break in the hedgerow and spotted us right there. I was the only one in a position to fire. They both went down. We went on at a faster clip, but no one else showed up. When we came to a road, a convoy was passing, apparently headed for the front; but we were shielded by the hedgerow. After the convoy passed, one by one, we ran across the road. We found a deep drainage ditch and hid out the rest of the day. I said, 'No more traveling by daylight.'

"We went on that night. We moved inland, away from the road and turned parallel to the road. We turned right and traveled toward the front. All of us were quiet and we moved real slow. I led them out to the center of a pasture, away from the hedgerow. As we approached the [next] hedgerow, I would go up to the hedgerow and listen—if I didn't hear anything, I would go back to the men and touch the first man. He would touch the next man and on down the line. Absolutely no talking. The nights were so black and overcast that you couldn't see your hand in front of your nose. We would proceed up to the hedgerow—put our hands in front of our faces like we were diving and proceed through the hedgerow very quietly! As slow as we were going, we couldn't make more than one quarter to one half mile a night. We found a ditch and holed up for the day. We listened to the machine guns and could hear German artillery all day—lots of activity."[11]

ON THE MORNING OF JUNE 11, CORPORAL CARLOS ROSS, a member of the regimental demolition platoon, was with a mixed group of approximately fifty troopers, led by Lieutenant Leon E. Lavender, with Company C. Corporal Ross and the others had been dropped south of the Douve River. "When we started back to the beachhead we were strung out in single file zig-zagging back and forth going around German patrols and placements. Finally, we arrived at a farmhouse and in the distance (five hundred yards) was the Douve River. From the farmhouse to the river there wasn't a sprig of grass over six inches tall and we knew we couldn't ever cross that in the daylight. The French in the farmhouse agreed to find boats for us.

"Defenses were set up, as the Germans were within three hundred yards of us. They were shooting with their rifles at the P-47s circling overhead. There were some men in the barn, some in the house, some men were put in the hedgerow that was an extension of the house and in another hedgerow two hundred yards away toward the river as the last line of defense. Everything was quiet and I was picking strawberries near my position (I'll never forget that the green strawberries were as sweet as the ripe ones, but the flavor wasn't there) and the only noise was when a P-47 would circle overhead, then there would be about twenty shots from the Germans trying to down it.

"About 3:30 p.m., all hell broke loose, a lot of firing up the road from the house and barn. Soon it was all along the hedgerow I was in. Then all at once bullets started plowing in the ground by my left knee—talk about cold chills.

"I knew that the Jerries couldn't shoot from that direction as there were paratroopers backing me up. Sergeant [Robert] Brewer [with Company A] started swearing, then ordered me back to the hedgerow behind us to give them a few choice words and identify ourselves.

"The battle went on until about 10:00 p.m. (it was still daylight) when they brought up an armored piece with an 88 mounted on it. They threw five rounds into the house and then five rounds into the barn.

"Lieutenant Lavender put the white flag out the window of the barn, but they shot it off. The German paratrooper who had been our prisoner ran out of the barn in all that fire and stopped them. We were ordered to put all of our personal belongings in our helmets.

"A paratrooper by the name of [Sergeant Edward V.] Dugan spoke fluent German and told us that the German commander had said, 'We're not Russkies, we're not going to shoot you,' which relieved my mind somewhat."[12]

Another Company C trooper, Corporal Brodie Hand, was positioned with some of the other troopers behind hedgerows around the farm buildings. "Lieutenant Lavender called us all in. We all stacked our rifles, guns, everything we had, in a pile. We lined up in front of the barn. We were marched down this road in a northerly direction to a sharp bend, *L* shaped, where the artillery piece was stationed. Then we turned due west, paralleling the Douve and marched possibly thirty minutes or an hour, in a westerly direction until we came to the road that crossed the causeway."[13]

WEST OF GUEUTTEVILLE ON THE NIGHT OF JUNE 12, Private First Class Harold Parris, with Company C, moved out leading a group of seven troopers to find friendly lines. "We could hear more activity in the German rear ranks. We moved more cautiously than ever. We came up to a hedgerow and listened—we heard a man cough—smelled cigarette smoke—a canteen rattled and Germans were talking. I found a break between [the hedges] and we stood upright and walked through and headed for the next hedgerow. We kept to the center and out in the open fields and orchards. After traveling all night, we found a deep ditch behind a hedgerow—on the front side of an orchard.

"When it got light enough, we could see a break in the hedge to our right. We could see a house with a rhubarb patch growing along the side of the house. One other man and I crawled out into the rhubarb patch and each of us cut a bundle. I looked at the house and there sat an old man and old woman, just looking at us. I put my fingers to my mouth, signaling them to be quiet. They just stared. We crawled back to the ditch and distributed the rhubarb. We had breakfast. We sat back and ate the rhubarb—getting ready to take a nap.

"From the corner of the orchard, [two Germans] an officer and an enlisted man headed across the orchard, back in the direction we came from. Shortly after that, we could hear voices in the hedgerow behind us. I crawled up to the hedgerow and took a look. Not far down the slope, about three hundred feet, sat five 88s, facing the front lines. Shortly after that, down the road past this house came two horse drawn covered wagons. They turned into the field and the first wagon passed us, just beyond the hedgerow. When the second wagon passed, the driver made eye contact with me, but didn't do or say anything. They went to the far end, unloaded the shells. The first wagon passed and the second wagon got just beyond us and stopped. He came back to the back of the wagon, opened canvas flaps and looked right down the muzzles of eight rifles. I had previously advised these men not to shoot unless they absolutely had to. The driver hurriedly put the flaps back, got back to his horses and went to the road and said, 'Americans.' Right then and there, I thought we [had] had it. We sat tight.

"A little bit later, one German soldier came by, walking up past the house to the break in the hedgerow, with his rifle at port arms. He turned his head to the right, scanned the orchard to the left and finally, looked at us—eight rifles. His eyes popped up and then went from right to left. When his eyes hit the rifles again, his eyes went to the tree tops and [he] slowly backed away. Out of sight, he turned and ran. I said, 'Let's get out of here!'

"We headed down to the far corner of the hedgerow, back in the direction we had come, down a slope. I stepped through a hedgerow and there was a drop off of about six feet. When I stood up, there to my right—twenty feet from me— stood a German officer, pistol in hand. I swung my rifle around right at his head. He raised his pistol, but not at me, pointing at different objects. Although he never looked in my direction, I knew he had heard me and saw me. He knew that I knew if he looked at me I'd have to shoot. A rifle came through the hedgerow right in the back of his head. When I saw this, I held my rifle up to one of our soldiers and he pulled me up and back through the hedgerow.

"We continued on to the corner, another thirty feet. We went through the hedgerow into a drainage ditch that went out to the center of the pasture and turned left and went down the hill, where it emptied into a creek. We followed it, crossed the creek, turned left again, and went into the woods about five hundred yards ahead. This put us down the slope in front of the 88s.

"We sat there awhile, trying to figure out what to do. Then I noticed that back in the direction from which we had come, coming across the field were two young girls, about eighteen or nineteen years old. Each was carrying a bucket. 'I'm going to see where they are going and what they know,' I said.

"Two other fellows, [Private Carmen] Pagnotta and [Corporal Roy J.] Henderson [with Company C], said they would go along. We intercepted the girls where we had crossed the ditch. They said they were going to milk two cows across the field. So we waited there for them and when they returned, I asked them for some milk because we were hungry. They poured part of the milk in the other bucket and left five inches in the bucket and gave it to me. I handed them a handful of invasion money and asked where the Germans were. She pointed to the next hedgerow—toward the front.

"By this time, machine guns began to rattle, but no artillery. After we drank the milk, the sun was coming up, so we stayed in the area where the cattle had been loafing. I was sitting down, looking across the creek; Henderson was stretched out on his back. Pagnotta was lying on his stomach, looking back up the hill where we had come from. We had been in this position about two minutes, when around the hedgerow came three Germans, tracking us. They were looking at the ground at our footprints.

"We froze in the positions we were in, and I said, 'Germans.' They didn't see us right away because our khaki jumpsuits blended perfectly with the bare ground. Finally, one German, about thirty feet away, looked across the creek and saw us. As he went down to one knee, raised his rifle and pointed it at Henderson, I swung my rifle around, hitting Henderson in the side of the head with my rifle. I fired, hitting the German in the midsection. He went down, hollering. It rattled the other two and they jumped into the hedgerow.

"A cartridge ruptured in my rifle and it jammed. Pagnotta could not get the safety off his Tommy gun, because it was too cruddy. All of our guns had been in the mud and rain and had not been cleaned.

"Henderson had his back to them and said, 'Let's go.'

"We ran at least two hundred yards, across the field in the direction of the front lines, to the next hedgerow, with the other two Germans shooting at us all the way. I could hear bullets going past us, but none of us got hit. I was in the lead, nearing another hedgerow, when I spotted a tail light in the woods ahead. So I turned left [and went] over a wooden gate, ran about sixty feet and jumped in a drainage ditch. The other two were right behind me. The other five men were coming up the hill because they heard the shooting. I related to them what had happened and every man there started cleaning and oiling their guns. It took me the rest of the day to get the other half cartridge from the chamber. Not one of us had an extractor. I finally finished by taking my gun apart, and whittling a stick down and then ramming it into the chamber until it loosened the shell.

"We stayed in this position the rest of the day and observed two Germans who crossed the gate and went down through the woods to the creek to get some water. From where we were, I knew the front line was a short distance away. I could hear the American and German machine guns, but very few artillery shells. The five 88s behind us never fired a shot. We decided to go through [the German front line] that night.

"We waited until about midnight. No moon, slight overcast, jet black; we started out, I was in the lead. We crossed the wooden gate and went straight out and down to what I thought was the middle of the pasture. Then we circled back up to the hedgerow and listened. I could hear talking to my left, and quite a way down to my right, a man was snoring. When I found a thin spot in the hedgerow, I went back and got the men. As quietly as we could, we went through standing up. We traveled on through three hedgerows just like that—one quarter to one half mile. I could see it was starting to break day.

"I crawled through the hedgerow with my rifle ahead of me and looked to my right. There stood a German, about twenty feet away, looking at me. I left my rifle laying there, got up on my knees and grabbed the knife strapped to my ankle. I walked right up to him and said, 'Achtung!'—it was all I could think of and it meant 'attention' in German. When I said that, he stiffened and I plunged my knife below his breastbone as hard as I could. He bent forward and I grabbed his head and slit his throat. In a shell hole behind him, several other Germans were either asleep or dead—they never made a sound.

"I went back, picked up my rifle, got the other men through the hedgerow and hurried to the next hedgerow because it was getting light. We never stopped at the next hedgerow. About halfway through the next field, someone hollered, 'Halt! Password.' I told him I didn't know the password because we were just paratroopers trying to get back to our outfits. 'If you are Americans, what outfit are you in?

"'Company C—508.'

"'Put your rifles over your heads and walk toward me—you have two machine guns looking at you.' When we got a little closer, he said, 'Come on in, you are OK.'

"We went back to [that unit's] headquarters and got debriefed, then ate Spam and [drank] coffee. The rest of the day, they put us to hunting snipers left in the trees. We managed to find two snipers. We scanned the trees with field glasses.

"The next day, we hitched a ride back to the beach and found out where our unit was. Then we bummed a ride to the 508 area."[14]

Private First Class Parris was later awarded the Distinguished Service Cross for his extraordinary heroism and leadership during the journey to reach American lines.

AFTER THE REGIMENT REORGANIZED, THE 508TH PARACHUTE INFANTRY received orders to conduct an assault crossing of the Douve River from Beuzeville to establish a bridgehead on the south side of the river at the town Beuzeville-la-Bastille, then drive south to link up with the 101st Airborne Division. The 508th Regimental Combat Team was formed to provide the combined arms needed for the mission. The combat team would consist of the 319th Glider Field Artillery Battalion; Batteries A and B, 80th Airborne Antiaircraft (Antitank) Battalion; Company A, 307th Airborne Engineer Battalion; and one platoon of Troop B, 4th Cavalry Reconnaissance Squadron. The planned assault was scheduled for one minute after midnight on the night of June 12-13. Company A, 307th Airborne Engineer Battalion engineers would row Company F across the river west of the causeway in assault boats, while other engineers would repair the bridge over the river channel. The remainder of the 508th would begin crossing the river over the causeway on foot beginning at 4:00 a.m. after the repairs were completed.

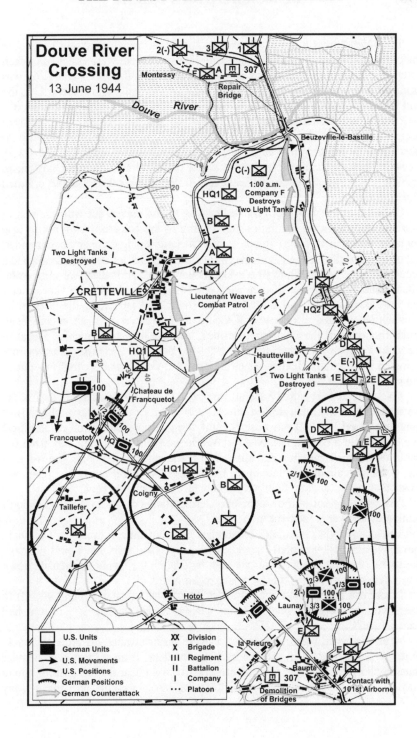

Douve River Crossing
13 June 1944

Montessy

Repair Bridge

Douve River

Beuzeville-le-Bastille

C(-)

HQ1

1:00 a.m.
Company F
Destroys
Two Light Tanks

B

A

Two Light Tanks
Destroyed

3C

CRETTEVILLE

Lieutenant Weaver
Combat Patrol

F

HQ2

B

C

D

HQ1

Hautteville

E(-)

A

1E 2E

Two Light Tanks
Destroyed

100

Chateau de
Francquetot

HQ2

1/2

D

100

F

Francquetot

HQ

100

HQ1

2/1

Coigny

B

100

Taillefer

A

3/1

100

3

C

1/3

2(-)

100

100

1/3

100

100

Hotot

Launay 3/3

100

1/1

100

E

la Prieure

E

	U.S. Units	XX	Division
	German Units	X	Brigade
	U.S. Movements	III	Regiment
	U.S. Positions	II	Battalion
	German Positions	I	Company
	German Counterattack	···	Platoon

F

Baupte

Contact with
101st Airborne

A 307

Demolition
of Bridges

The 319th Glider Field Artillery Battalion would provide supporting fire for the crossing. Forward observer teams and liaison officers were assigned to each battalion of the regiment. Lieutenant Marvin Ragland, with Battery A, was assigned to the 1st Battalion; Lieutenant John D. Gutshall, with Battery A, to the 2nd Battalion; and Lieutenant Irving Gelb, with Battery A, to the 3rd Battalion.

German commanders were expecting a crossing of the Douve River from somewhere west of Carentan, not from the north in the area of Beuzeville-la-Bastille. They had therefore used Panzer Ersatz und Ausbildungs Abteilung 100, a reserve panzer training battalion attached to the 91st Luftlande Division, to provide a security screen from Beuzeville-la-Bastille south to Baupte oriented toward the east.

On the night of June 12, Private Dwayne Burns moved out with the rest of Company F, following the man ahead of him in the column, trying not to lose contact. "Lieutenant [Hoyt] Goodale, who was our acting company commander, led us down to the Douve River. We waited on the bank for two hours. We had a reporter from *Life* magazine who asked us our names and where we were from. That would be something if they used our story! At midnight, we very quietly got into assault boats and started for the south bank at Beuzeville-la-Bastille. This action worried me because F Company had never seen an assault boat, much less crossed a river in one. Besides, it didn't look like much of a boat to me! I was a poor swimmer and being loaded down with combat gear was not going to enhance my chance of getting across if the Germans caught us out in the middle of the river.

"We paddled very quietly and all went well. I was surprised at how warm the water felt when my hand dipped into it. 'Just right for a Saturday night bath,' I thought. 'Good Lord! If the wind is right, the Germans will smell us coming!' We hadn't had a bath in twelve days! While we still were a long way from the bank, we stopped paddling and slipped over the sides of the boat. The water at this point was about four feet deep, but I was glad to get out of the boat. We sloshed along for another hundred yards before reaching the bank.

"As we came out of the water, two German tanks drove up the road. I don't think they knew that we were in the area."[15]

The company's radioman, Technician Fourth Grade Edward B. Chatoian, saw Lieutenant Lloyd Polette quickly grab a bazooka, then move out to engage the tanks. "Polette knocked out one tank by dropping a Gammon grenade down a vent. He destroyed the other with a bazooka rocket."[16]

Lieutenant Polette was later awarded an oak leaf cluster (second award) to the Silver Star he would receive for his actions during the Hill 30 patrol he had led on June 8.

After the tanks were knocked out, Private Burns awaited the order to attack. "Lieutenant Goodale then radioed back for artillery. It must have been heavier than anything we had ever used before, for we could hear it coming from a long way back. It sounded like they were throwing boxcars at the Germans. We lay there, hugging the river bank as the town exploded, thanking the good Lord that it was ours coming in."[17]

The barrage by the 75mm pack howitzers of the 319th Glider Field Artillery Battalion, the 320th Glider Field Artillery Battalion's 105mm pack howitzers, and the 155mm guns of the 188th Field Artillery Battalion shook the earth as almost continuous explosions impacted the small village of Beuzeville-la-Bastille.

During the fifteen-minute barrage, engineers with Company A, 307th Airborne Engineer Battalion worked to repair the bridge that spanned the channel of the Douve River, which was destroyed by U.S. aircraft on June 6. Burns felt the ground shake as the artillery barrage struck the town. "After the artillery lifted, we attacked the town."[18] Company F moved into Beuzeville-la-Bastille against almost no opposition.

The engineers completed repairs on the bridge across the river channel and the 1st Battalion crossed the causeway at 4:00 a.m., turned southwest and moved toward the villages of Cretteville and Francquetot. A combat patrol led by Lieutenant Bob Weaver, with Company C, advanced ahead of the main body of the 1st Battalion. As the patrol approached Cretteville, the paratroopers heard the sound of tank engines. Company A was advancing just behind the combat patrol and two of its bazooka teams were brought forward to deal with the threat. Private First Class Robert White was the gunner of one of those teams. "There was a two story, long, house at a crossroads, the only thing there. We moved up behind it and got the bazooka loaded.

"Lieutenant [Rex G.] Combs said, 'I'll cover you.' We stepped out from the corner of that house and blasted this tank and 'Hack' [Private First Class Paul A. Haskett] had a bazooka and he went around the other side and blasted the other tank. We found out they were sitting there with the engines running and the radios on, and there was nobody in them. So we threw a white phosphorous grenade in [each of] them."[19]

The 1st Battalion moved through Cretteville about 7:45 a.m. and by 9:00 a.m., continued toward Coigny. Private First Class Ed "Bogie" Boccafogli and another Company B trooper were out front of the company as scouts. "We were moving along this dirt road, and they said they spotted a large body of Germans from the air. Another company, a quarter of a mile away, was moving forward, trying to see if we could contact and flank them. I was going along this dirt road. All of a sudden the road dropped off on the side of the hill and went down, then leveled off, and there were farmhouses. And they opened fire on us.

"Well, my job was done. I drew fire. I hit the ground. And the next squad deployed immediately and opened fire. I couldn't fire back. If I stood there, the second shot was gonna get me for sure. So I hit the ground and let the squad take care of it. Now, two soldiers come out with their hands up: 'Me Polski! Me Polski!' That was bad, because up ahead was the main body of Germans, or enemy. The enemy had everything there. They had Poles, they even had

Russians that were taken prisoner and were put up in the front as soldiers. Now they heard the shooting, so they knew that there was a movement coming towards them. We took the two prisoners.

"The old man, [Lieutenant Woodrow] Millsaps said, 'Okay, move ahead.' So I went ahead. We were two hundred yards ahead of the main body, one on each side of the road. We were going along, and we came to thicker brush, and then thicker woods. On the side was low ground and fields up above. So as we were coming in I heard a high pitched screech. I stopped, put my hand up, and moved over to a wall. I looked and saw a farmhouse inside the walls, like a chalet, and another building. So I stopped. The old man came running up and said, 'What's up?'

"I told him what I heard. I said, 'It sounds either like a woman screaming or a high-pitched voice yelling.'

"He said, 'You and [Private First Class Frank R.] Hernandez take off on the right flank.' He called up [Private Lawrence V.] Thomas and another kid and said, 'Skirt those buildings and keep going.' That scream was the angel on my shoulder. The old man must have thought I was starting to get jittery. So we went off about a hundred yards to the right flank of the column, as side riders. We were going along, going along, maybe another six hundred yards. The two scouts ran right smack into the German positions, and instead of waiting to let the main body come forward, one of the Germans opened up and killed both of them. Then the company deployed and the firing started. We had some battles that were brutal, but this one was unbelievable. There must have been thirty or forty machine guns going at any one time. Bullets were cutting everything apart. Mortars were coming in. We were out on a flank, and I was trying to work my way back in. I worked over to a hedgerow. I got to this dirt bank, and I climbed up, trying to see ahead, and I looked out and I saw something shine, and I opened up. Next thing I knew, 'Poom!' The dirt flew up against me. I got down and crawled away from there. I climbed up on the bank again, and looked, looked, looked. I was next to a tree. I was looking, looking, and saw something out there like brush moving. I opened up. Then, 'Pow!' The bark and everything flew off the tree. I figured this guy could see me. I didn't know where it was coming from. I went down the third time. I got up again. I got down in the brush. I fired two or three rounds. The next thing I knew, 'Pwwaaangg!' That was it—I got nailed. The bullet came from the right. The bullet went through the stock [of my gun], through my first aid packet, and tore my arm. I was lying on my back with my arm under me. I'd rolled off the bank and passed out. Then I started to come to and I figured I was dead. All I saw were clouds, like a mist, and I figured I was going to heaven. Then I started to feel pain, and in the tree above me I could see the leaves start to form. I said, 'Holy Christ, I'm still here.' Then I heard machine guns going. Everything came back and I thought I must have been hit in the face. I was numb from [the top of my head] down. I had one pain all through my body. I didn't know where I was hit. Finally, I looked and I saw the blood squirting out. My arm was under me. And I thought, 'Jesus, they blew my arm off.' I rolled over, finally got my arm out, stuck my hand in and squeezed the blood into the hole.

"Hernandez came over. In the meantime, I went into shock because of all this blood I was losing. 'Ahh,' he said, 'You're okay.' He took my canteen and he gave me a drink. I'd milked a cow just before, and I got some milk. The milk was sour. I spit it out. So he gave me some of his water. Then he took off and he got hit in the shoulder. Then I got a handkerchief and put a tourniquet as tight as I could get it around there. I worked my way over to where the kid from Peoria [Private Paul B. Atwood was positioned]. He had the machine gun. The machine gun was firing so much that it was squealing. The bullets were squealing trying to get out. That's how hot the barrel was. And then I went crazy. I had a Luger, and I started firing, going from hedgerow to hedgerow. The old man was yelling at me to get the hell out of there, and I refused. I went berserk. I started going after the Germans through the hedgerows.

"Finally, they got me and they calmed me down and made me go back. I got the Bronze Star, because when I went back I told Captain [Royal] Taylor, he was back where the mortars were, I said, 'You've got to come in closer. You're firing way the hell beyond.' So they brought the mortars in and started pounding them. And then eventually, after about twenty more minutes, the fighting broke off. The Germans pulled out and we pulled out."[20]

At 11:00 a.m. the 1st Battalion knocked out five French Renault tanks at Francquetot, but a sixth tank continued to fire, holding up the advance. Lieutenant Rex Combs was the assistant platoon leader of the 1st Platoon of Company A. "The remaining tank [a Mark III] used the others for added armor protection and was exposing only part of the turret and cannon barrel as a target. [First] Sergeant [Frank C.] Taylor, with another man to give covering fire, worked his way around to the rear of the remaining tank and hurled a white phosphorous grenade into the motor vents, setting the motor and fuel afire. On jumping on the side of the tank to hurl a grenade inside, the tank blew up, hurling Sergeant Taylor across the road."[21] First Sergeant Taylor was awarded the Silver Star for his courage while knocking out the tank.

Major Shields Warren and the 1st Battalion continued south and approached the village of Coigny. "We came to the edge of the largest clearing I had seen in Normandy at that stage. Two hundred yards into the clearing, between us and our objective were five Renault light tanks armed with one low power 37mm gun and one MG-42 machine gun. While these tanks were not too significant a threat, we had no antitank weapons other than our 2.36 inch bazookas, which were ineffective at that range. I tried moving them [the tanks] out with heavy 81mm mortar rounds, without success. In the meantime, the tanks were getting air bursts in the trees with their 37mm's and dusting the hedgerows with their MG-42s.

"I was becoming quite frustrated when my artillery liaison officer suggested he might be able to get something to bear that could move the tanks out. He suggested 155mm howitzers. The 155s ranged in with one [artillery] piece, then fired one battery—four rounds. One of the rounds destroyed one tank with a near miss, and the rest of the tanks fled the area.

"I had been watching all of this from one of the hedgerows nearest the tanks, and was observing them through my field glasses as they disappeared down the road, when a voice at my elbow said, 'Well, Shields, how are things going?' The voice sounded familiar, so I dropped the glasses from my eyes and turned to the speaker, who turned out to be General [Matthew] Ridgway.

"I told him that I'd been held up by the tanks, but now that they were gone, we'd be on our objective in one hour.

"General Ridgway expressed satisfaction with that schedule, and then asked what I'd been shooting at the tanks. I recounted my experience with the 2.36 inch bazookas and the 81mm mortars, and then told him we moved them out with 155mm howitzers. The general said, 'Well that's fine, but be careful how you use that heavy stuff, there's a storm in the Channel and we're having problems getting supplies ashore.' And then, as he turned to go, he said with a smile, 'Besides, isn't that sort of like swatting a fly with a sledgehammer?' I had no rejoinder to the comment, since I had been quite aghast at the appearance of the division commander at my elbow, where he could have been hit by some of the hot lead and steel flying around. No one had to tell General Ridgway what his assault troops were doing—he knew from personal observation."[22]

At about 4:15 p.m., the 1st Battalion entered Coigny, its final objective, forming a perimeter defense. About 7:00 p.m., Companies A and B moved to clear the area around the town. Accompanying the battalion were two 57mm antitank guns of Battery A, 80th Airborne Antiaircraft (Antitank) Battalion. The German tanks driven off by the 155mm artillery prior to entering Coigny were encountered once again. Staff Sergeant Richard E. Rider deployed one of his 57mm antitank guns to stop the threat. He directed the fire while exposing himself to enemy fire. When the gun was attacked by four Renault tanks and a Sturmgeschütz assault gun mounting a 75mm high-velocity gun, Rider took over for the gunner. While under heavy fire from the German armor, Rider quickly knocked out the first vehicle, then calmly destroyed the next two, causing the remaining tanks to pull back. Ryder moved the gun to another location and when the tanks attempted to move, he ambushed both, destroying them. Staff Sergeant Rider was awarded the Distinguished Service Cross for his outstanding courage and leadership.

The 3rd Battalion and regimental headquarters crossed the Douve River at 4:30 a.m., behind the 1st Battalion and moved south then southwest toward Taillerfer. While moving across a field during the advance, Private First Class Bob Chisolm, the radio operator for the 2nd Platoon of Company I, heard enemy

Renault tanks approaching. "The armored column of those light tanks was coming down [the road toward us]. [Sergeant James C.] Jim Hutto, our [60mm] mortar squad leader in the 2nd Platoon, was with us and saw the tanks coming. He took a mortar tube without a base plate and set that tube up and dropped 60mm rounds in it. He was hitting the road and hitting those damn tanks and they had some troops [with them] and they turned around and went back.

"At one point it was fighting from hedgerow to hedgerow. The opposition was there, but it wasn't strong enough to hold us up on the advance. As the advance continued, there was rather sporadic incoming fire."[23]

The 3rd Battalion reached Taillerfer by 7:00 a.m., where it established a perimeter defense and blocked the road between Pont Auny and Hotot. The regimental command post was established at Taillerfer.

The 2nd Battalion, less Company F, crossed the causeway at 5:00 a.m., and then pushed south on the eastern side of the regimental sector toward Baupte. Company E led the advance. Lieutenant Barry Albright was the platoon leader of the 1st Platoon of Company E. "The formation utilized, placed 2nd Platoon of E Company in the fields on the left of the road, with the 1st Platoon in the fields on the right. The remainder of E Company, D Company, battalion headquarters, and F Company [were] following on the road. After moving south about a mile, two Renault tanks were encountered."[24]

It was shortly before 8:00 a.m. when Corporal Bob Newhart, with one of the Company E mortar squads, heard the approaching tanks. "A very little tank came down a narrow wagon track between two hedgerows. We used our Gammon grenades."[25]

Sergeant Herbert S. Sellers, with Company E, was the second man in the column, behind the lead scout. "When the two lead tanks reached us, they were buttoned up for combat. At least three Gammon grenades, a bazooka rocket, and a rifle grenade were launched at the same time. Some of our people were firing M1's and Tommy guns also. It was a staccato of noise loud enough to hurt your ears at fifty yards. I had to scream at the top of my voice for ceasefire, because every time I raised my head a volley from the other side of the road came my way. I needed a prisoner to find out what to expect at Baupte. As soon as the firing stopped, I was on top of the lead tank to get the occupants out. I had the first man out when someone shot him. Then, as soon as I got the second man to the top of the hatch, someone shot him."[26]

As the 2nd Battalion approached to within a mile and a half of Baupte, it was hit by heavy machine gun and small arms fire. The battalion formed a perimeter defense and sent out patrols to try to determine the strength of the enemy. The patrols reported that the opposition consisted of an enemy battalion, supported by tanks and artillery. At 4:15 p.m., the 2nd Battalion attacked with Company F on the left, Company D on the right, and Company E following in reserve.

When Company F was stopped by intense 20mm antiaircraft fire, Private Dwayne Burns received the word to take cover. Just moments later, the 319th and 320th Glider Field Artillery Battalions pounded the German positions, as Burns and his buddies watched. "After an artillery barrage, good old F Company was on its way again."[27]

The 2nd Battalion eventually prevailed in the fight, which lasted for more than an hour. Four 20mm antiaircraft guns and a number of machine guns were destroyed, and several large groups of Germans were lying dead among the hedgerows and ditches they defended. Private First Class Robert Broderick was one of the troopers out front, leading the Company F attack on one of the 20mm antiaircraft guns and its crew. "I shot the first [crewman] and all the rest of them started running. Our guys then started firing at everything, like a turkey shoot. I got up by this sparse hedgerow and a guy named [Private] Glenn [H.] Ward jumped up on a stump. He was firing away at these Germans who were running. I told him to get his ass down. I had a pair of binoculars on me and a German sergeant, who was one of the wounded or playing wounded, must have seen the glasses and thought I was an officer. He heard me yelling at Glenn, I guess. You could see through the hedgerow, a bit.

"The next thing I knew I thought my head had exploded. It nicked my ear, went in [my neck], and came out by my spine.

"A guy named [Private Leo R.] Coletti, a great soldier, darted through the opening in the hedgerow, followed by [Lieutenant Lloyd] Polette. The German shot [and wounded] Coletti. Polette killed the guy—first he rolled him over and then shot him."[28]

The 2nd Battalion attack drove the surviving enemy back into Baupte. As Company F approached the town, Private Ralph Burrus and some of the other troopers made the mistake of bunching up while standing behind a hedgerow. "A grenade landed right here and there were eight or nine of us standing in that area. I got hit in the face."[29]

As Company F moved into the southern outskirts of Baupte, Private Burns found himself in a cemetery. "At first I thought that this was great luck as I made my way forward, slipping from tombstone to tombstone, until the firing got heavy and a machine gun opened up around me and I had them ricocheting off the tombstones all around me, and I had them coming at me from all directions.

"'Damn! I have to get out of here,' I muttered. 'This is a hell of a place to die!' Using what cover I could find, I started working my way over to the edge until I came to a fence. I lay there waiting for things to quiet down. When the firing eased off, I came up and over the fence in one motion, making a dash across the street and into the doorway of a building. We worked all the way through the southern part of town. Heavy fighting lasted more than an hour as we went from building to building."[30]

Company D ran into a company of German infantry and a number of tanks defending a vehicle park north of the town. Company E was brought around the left flank and through the Company F sector in the southern part of the town. Company E then attacked and cleared the northern part of Baupte, then moved north to assist Company D in capturing the vehicle park. Bazooka teams from the two companies knocked out another ten Renault tanks, and the few surviving Germans fled, leaving about fifty vehicles behind. As Corporal Bob Newhart, with Company E, entered the park, he noticed a large amount of food left behind by the fleeing enemy. "We finished their food. Someone discovered a locked box. They blew it open to discover a box full of money. Pictures were taken of guys lighting cigars with money. Most of the money was burned, but most everyone kept a souvenir."[31]

About four hours after the capture of the vehicle park, German infantry and one of the French built light tanks counterattacked in an attempt to recapture it. Private Charles B. Wilkins, with Company E, organized a group of leaderless troopers and attacked the enemy force. The enemy tank concentrated heavy fire on them, but through his aggressive leadership, Wilkins and his group forced the Germans to withdraw. Private Wilkins was later awarded the Silver Star for his courage and leadership.

Company D reorganized and established a defensive position just east of Baupte. Private Frank Haddy and several other Company D troopers took with them to Baupte three Germans who had been captured during the fighting at the vehicle park. "When we got into town, Colonel Shanley told me to get rid of them. I refused and Lieutenant [Francis] Bolger took my Tommy gun and did the job—so help me God."[32]

After securing Baupte, Private Dwayne Burns and other Company F troopers were taking it easy. "We had been fighting all day and were getting some well deserved rest behind some of the houses in town when we heard the sound of a tank coming down the main street. Sergeant [Vernon] Thomas and I reacted at the same time. We both grabbed our M1s and a Gammon grenade. I went around the left side of the house, but Sergeant Thomas went through the house and got there first.

"Just as I reached the corner of the house, I saw Sergeant Thomas throw his grenade. I watched it spinning through the air. I saw the lanyard unwind and pull the pin. It seemed to be happening in slow motion. Then, boom! The tank stopped going forward and slid sideways, right into the side of a building. The top hatch was open and we both stood there waiting with our weapons ready. It was so quiet that I could hear my heart beating. Nobody moved inside the tank.

"Sergeant Thomas yelled, 'Cover me!' and moved toward the tank, climbed up and looked down inside. 'Come here,' he said, motioning for me. I climbed up and looked in. It was a small French tank with German markings. Inside, I saw the crew. Both of them had died from broken necks. We closed the hatch and went back behind the house to finish resting. Scratch one more tank. We dug in for the night after the fiercest action the regiment had seen. We could use a good night's rest."[33]

A patrol from the 508th made contact with elements of the 101st Airborne Division on the causeway south of Baupte. Engineers with Company A, 307th Airborne Engineer Battalion blew the railroad bridge west of Baupte, the bridge on the causeway south of Baupte, and the culvert west of Hotot.

To plug the breakthrough created by the 508th, the 91st Luftlande Division was given a newly arriving kampfgruppe (or combat team) of the 265th Infantrie Division and a battalion of the 77th Jäger Division, which were moved into the line to the south and west of the regiment's positions.

At about 10:30 a.m. the following morning, June 14, the 1st Battalion moved to clear the area in front of the 3rd Battalion near Pont Auny. The operation went well until about 12:30 p.m., when the battalion ran into heavy resistance, which was later confirmed to be a German battalion. An intense firefight developed and lasted most of the afternoon.

"During this fighting, Sergeant Sherman Van Enwyck, a squad leader with Company A, attacked a machine gun nest single-handedly and destroyed it, killing five enemy soldiers. When the company's advance was held up by another machine gun, Van Enwyck crawled forward and knocked it out with hand grenades. As the advance resumed, yet another machine gun opened fire from the flank. Van Enwyck rushed the position and shot and killed two of the crew, before he was himself wounded. And finally, as he was being evacuated, he shot and killed an enemy sniper. Sergeant Van Enwyck was awarded the Silver Star for his tremendous courage during the attack.

When Company C moved out to clear the area, Lieutenant Bob Weaver, the assistant platoon leader of the 3rd Platoon, was unsure where the enemy was located. "So, we went into a skirmish [line] as you would go through tall grass to beat out jackrabbits, and waiting for him to fire so you could put a line up. Our left flank company was fired on first and from the flank and our company being [the] right flank, we swung around until we came under fire and it was here our men really first received their real taste of war. The Jerries kept shifting their automatic weapon, you were unable to see him move and no target was to be seen. We sprayed a hedgerow and moved forward and our life would be saved by a man on the left or right or up to the front calling to you.

"In my case a soldier called out, 'Look out lieutenant, there is one in front of you, crawling toward you.' I looked up and there he was drawing a bead on me, but due to his slowness he never got it off. Our left flank company got pinned down in an open field and [it] was some time before they were able to get to a hedgerow to cover. In front of them, the enemy was very strong and couldn't be moved, but in front of our company, due to daring, skill and determination, the Jerry was routed and was forced to move very disorderly.

"Being second in command, I was free to move forward with several men, and in doing so I placed myself on the flank of the enemy between his two units. This not only placed us in danger from the enemy fire, but until we could place ourselves and notify our lines where we were, we needed their fire to enable us to move freely. After getting set on the enemy's flank, our company opened up and the Jerries withdrew back to be very surprised to find a TSMG [Thompson submachine gun] on their flank covering them. They had one desire and that was get out of there to fight another day and this only a few did. They rushed across the open field in groups of three or four and very few ever reached the other side. We had narrowed their route of escape down to one field since the road was covered by our two MGs [machine guns] and we were one field in. Commands were being shouted by a German officer and we tried to find him, but he proved to be one jump ahead of us all the time. They sent two men out to clear us off their flank, but these men had more guts than brains and our men are now wearing their P-38s [pistols]. They got within three feet from us, but again they were too slow on the draw and never got the shot off. After the one died, the other still without a chance in the world to succeed tried to remove us, but also proved he was no match for our men. Our small mortar knocked out their MG position with a direct hit at the corner of the road and a sunken trail. This trail was eight feet lower than the field and it was over this route the two men moved to try and knock us out. After throwing a grenade in this sunken trail, we jumped down and moved up it toward the road. This had been their main line of defense and there were at least thirty-five bicycles, undamaged with blanket rolls on [them], which was their means of transportation. Clearing the sunken trail and arriving at the corner we saw the results of our mortar, which was two dead Jerries and signs of more wounded who managed to escape. Checking the road, we saw two Germans covering the road and it was our mistake this time by not firing first, but instead we withdrew to cover and found we were unable at that time to get a shot at them. A machine pistol had worked its way around to our right flank and had our MG and mortar pinned down, along with a Jerry rifleman firing rifle grenades, our men were very held down at this time. They were happy to see us pull back and knock this position out. Checking ammo, we found several of us had run out of ammo and very glad we weren't in a tight spot at that time.

"We redistributed ammo and checked the hedgerows closely for any Jerries we may have passed and found a lot to our surprise. After we cleaned our front up, we received orders to withdraw, as our left flank company was still pinned down on some parts and unable to advance. Mortar and artillery were to be dropped in as soon as we moved clear. After moving back, we received orders from our CO that we had completed our mission and would return to our position.

"Our company pulled out at 16:00 hours after five hours of battle with every man we went in with and two of them were wounded, but only slightly. We accounted for thirty-five dead Jerries, two MG-34s captured, and one MG-42 destroyed; thirty-five bicycles and lots of equipment and German ammo."[34]

At 4:00 p.m., the 1st Battalion broke contact with the German force and withdrew to Baupte after receiving a regimental order to do so. At 6:30 p.m., the regimental command post was moved from Taillerfer to Chateau Francquetot. At 10:30 p.m., the 1st Battalion moved from Baupte to a reserve position at Francquetot.

Around dawn on June 15, Sergeant Joseph E. Bullard, with Company D, received word of a German attack on one of the company's roadblocks near Baupte. "About day[break] forty Germans came up the road on bicycles. They opened fire and [our troopers] sent back for help. I wasn't on the roadblock with [Sergeant Charles K.] Baldwin, but they notified us and I was there within thirty minutes after the attack. When I got there, Baldwin was already killed and his men were driven back and scattered about. We found five live Germans and killed them. The rest turned around and went back. I was talking with a boy that was with Baldwin when he was shot. They said they were attacked and it scattered Baldwin's squad out and he lost control. No one knew where the other was. Some of his men [with]drew back to a better position. Baldwin kept a boy with him and after the Germans turned around, he tried to locate his boys.

"He was walking down the road and a boy from another company [mis]took him for a German and shot him. It was still not day[light] good, and all were excited. It was an accident that happens in combat."[35]

At 11:00 a.m., the regiment received orders to prepare to move north of the Douve River. The 2nd Battalion relieved the 3rd Battalion at 3:00 p.m. at Pont Auny. The 3rd Battalion assembled and moved by truck north of the Douve to a position a half mile west of la Bonneville and was placed in division reserve at 5:00 p.m. The 507th Parachute Infantry relieved the remainder of the regiment by midnight.

BY JUNE 12, LIEUTENANT PAUL LEHMAN, THE 3RD BATTALION S-1, who had been a POW since D-Day, had recovered somewhat from a punctured artery in his neck. At a German field hospital at a chateau near Orglandes, Lehman was put to work as the administrator in one of five wood frame barracks housing German and American patients. "From day to day some of our wounded were evacuated by ambulance to another German hospital to the north. From D-Day plus six, the artillery of our own forces moving in from the beaches fired on the roads just to the rear of the hospital. Many [explosions] were very close and large hunks of shrapnel fell around our building. One short round actually hit the road outside the main chateau, killing a German doctor and wounding three other men. It was a most trying ordeal and for about three consecutive nights we lay trembling in the [wooden] building or in the lean-tos we had built outside, as the shells whistled overhead or crashed into the adjacent fields. Another frame building constructed while we were there and not a good thirty yards away, was torn in half by a direct hit. Luckily, no one had moved into it.

"We ripped sheets in half lengthwise and laid out a big panel outside our building in the letters 'USA' so that our planes would know that American troops were in the building. All of the buildings had large red crosses painted on the roofs, and we knew that they were not the targets of the artillery, but were merely close to road networks over which the Heinies were moving supplies, men, and equipment.

"When our forces had gotten to within a mile or so, evacuation was stepped up and with only German wounded left in the chateau, we moved into the building too, so as to have better protection. The night before our forces captured the surrounding territory we had 108 men there. They tried to evacuate as many as possible before the roads were cut off.

"We stalled in every conceivable way, so as to slow the process down. They would ask for, say, walking wounded and two litter cases. So we made all the wounded get into cots and act as if they were litter cases. It turned out that they moved forty-eight that last night, when it is possible they could have taken close to a hundred.

"All the next morning [of June 16] we could see American troops passing on a road not too far away. With recapture in sight, Dr. [Briand] Beaudin and I took over the hospital. The pistols of the two remaining German doctors were handed over to us, as well as the keys to various supply rooms.

"Early in the afternoon, after considerable skirmishing and firing on the other side of the chateau, our troops surrounded the hospital. [They] passed out cigarettes and rations to our [wounded] and it was really a happy occasion.

"Soon they moved on after making arrangements for the evacuation of the wounded on the following morning. The following day they were evacuated, the most serious cases first. Then the doctor, myself, and a number of aid men got transportation back to our unit.

"First we reported in to higher headquarters. While there, newspapermen took our pictures and notes on our experiences, and said that this outfit serviced the *Washington Star* and *Post*. Personally, I received the most touching welcome by both the men and officers. Stories had circulated of how I had bled to death or died any number of ways (according to the imagination of the teller) and it had become an accepted fact. Everywhere I went, men got up to shake my hand and express their happiness at my being alive. I'll never forget it. The colonel [Lieutenant Colonel Mendez] then assigned me as battalion S-2."[36]

ON JUNE 16, THE 508TH, LESS THE 3RD BATTALION, moved by truck to division reserve at La Rue, just northwest of Ètienville. Meanwhile, the 3rd Battalion moved to a position approximately two miles northeast of St.-Sauveur-le-

Vicomte, astride the road to Valognes to protect the division's right flank. The 3rd Battalion's position also covered the U.S. 9th Infantry Division's approach, which was advancing west until it could come up alongside the right flank of the 82nd Airborne Division.

That afternoon, the remainder of the regiment moved to an assembly area approximately a mile and a half northeast of St.-Sauveur-le-Vicomte, astride the road from Ètienville. At 10:00 p.m., the 2nd Battalion passed through the 505th Parachute Infantry southwest of St.-Sauveur-le-Vicomte and extended the bridgehead to a line running from les Hameaux on the left to the railroad on the right, while mopping up small pockets of German troops. At 10:30 p.m., the 1st Battalion relieved the 3rd Battalion, 505th occupying a line south of the town from the highway to La Haye-du-Puits extending east to the Douve River. The regimental command post was set up in a bakery in St.-Sauveur-le-Vicomte.

That same day, Major Dave Thomas, the regimental surgeon, arrived at the 508th command post after having escaped from German captivity. "Enroute to report to Colonel Lindquist, I saw Lieutenant Colonel [Harry] Harrison, who [had] abrogated command to a major early on. Lieutenant Colonel Harrison, regimental executive officer, was sitting in the CP with an M1 between his legs, just staring at the floor—a sorry sight. I reported to Colonel Lindquist and told him I was surprised to see Lieutenant Colonel Harrison still around. He asked me why, and I told him of what had happened. In fifteen minutes, Lieutenant Colonel Harrison was headed to the rear, never to be seen again in the airborne world. Lieutenant Colonel Harrison got busted to major and was killed as the XO of an infantry battalion in the Hürtgen Forest."[37]

Lieutenant Colonel Harrison, a West Pointer, was relieved and transferred to division headquarters after an investigation of his actions during the first three days of the invasion concluded that he had disobeyed orders from General Ridgway to remain on the west side of the Merderet River.

Lieutenant Colonel Mark J. Alexander, the executive officer of the 505th Parachute Infantry, was transferred the same day, June 16, to replace Harrison. Alexander had proven to be one of the most effective combat leaders of the 505th in Sicily and Italy, when he commanded that regiment's 2nd Battalion. General Gavin found Alexander to be "a superior troop leader in combat. He is possessed with exceptional courage and performs brilliantly on the battlefield."[38]

General Ridgway also thought very highly of Alexander who had "been under my close observation for eighteen months, including participation in the campaigns in Sicily, Italy, and Normandy. This officer is one of the finest battle leaders I know."[39]

Nevertheless, Alexander received a cold reception when he arrived at the 508th regimental command post. In a conversation much later with General Ridgway, Alexander was told of the reason for the move. "Ridgway said the senior command of the 508 was not aggressive enough. They wanted me over there to try and fire them up a bit. That's all I was ever told."[40]

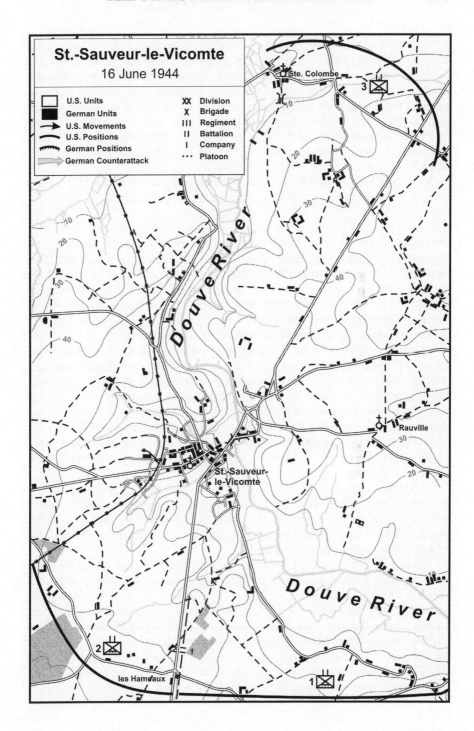

St.-Sauveur-le-Vicomte
16 June 1944

U.S. Units
German Units
U.S. Movements
U.S. Positions
German Positions
German Counterattack

XX Division
X Brigade
III Regiment
II Battalion
I Company
··· Platoon

AT ABOUT 5:00 A.M. ON JUNE 17, FIRST SERGEANT LEONARD FUNK, leading his stick of Company C troopers, along with others the group had picked up during the twenty miles over which it had traveled the past ten days, slipped through the German main line of resistance. First Sergeant Funk, despite a badly sprained ankle had acted as the scout throughout the harrowing journey. "We made it with about thirty-five men to the U.S. 90th Infantry Division. Those troops didn't know anything about any paratroopers. I demanded to talk to their commanding officer. They phoned their CO and he sent a truck to take us to the 508th."[41]

First Sergeant Leonard Funk would later be awarded the Silver Star for his courage, determination, and leadership during the ten day journey.

ON JUNE 17, THE 1ST AND 2ND BATTALIONS mopped up the area south of St.-Sauveur-le-Vicomte to the edge of the Prairies Marecagueses marshland. The road bridge on the St.-Sauveur-le-Vicomte to La Haye-du-Puits highway across the Prairies Marecagueses was mined for demolition. Company C established a combat outpost and roadblock at the bridge, which was subsequently blown that evening. Company A was also sent to reinforce the Company C roadblock. Aggressive patrolling was conducted within the regimental area.

The following day, the 3rd Battalion moved through St.-Sauveur-le-Vicomte on the way to an assembly area west of Ètienville. When the battalion marched through the town, it was witness to the effects of a massive artillery barrage and subsequent attack by the 505th Parachute Infantry to capture the town. Private First Class Tom Porcella, with Company H, was shocked by the sight of the destruction. "We could see that houses were damaged, destroyed, and blown up. It was a horrible sight to see. As the troopers were marching through this village, no one spoke. Everybody was looking around because it was one of the biggest villages we went through.

"I thought to myself, 'What the hell have we done to these people over here in their houses? My God...Thank God we're fighting the war over here. I wouldn't want this to happen to our folks back home. I wonder what these people think of us. We destroyed everything they owned. Don't forget, the French were supposed to be our friends.'

"Then I thought to myself, 'This is the price that they have to pay for their freedom. They have to sacrifice their lives, their homes, their cows, dogs, and sheep. It's a horrible thing.'

"While we were still marching through this town, a lady came running up to us and she was crying. She was saying a lot of things in French to us and shaking her fists at us. I could imagine what the hell it was all about. So, one of the GIs who spoke French interpreted to us what the lady was saying. She said the Germans came over and took their land. We didn't like the sons of bitches and they took over our homes. But they didn't blow them up.

"We were still marching through the village when we noticed a lot of dead horses, cows, and dogs. It was like a nightmare. It was really horrible. There were dead Germans lying all over the place. They were lying in the streets, some of them next to their vehicles; some were in the vehicles, some alongside their cars. They just never made it to where they wanted to go. Somebody did a hell of a job on them. It was something you'll never forget. It scars your mind forever."[42]

The 3rd Battalion arrived at its assembly area near Ètienville shortly after midnight of June 18-19.

CHAPTER 7

"A TIME TO BE BOLD"

At 5:00 a.m. on June 19, the 3rd Battalion crossed the Douve River in assault boats and established a bridgehead on the south side of the river and was then attached to the 325th Glider Infantry Regiment. Lieutenant Ralph DeWeese and the 2nd Platoon of Company H set up a roadblock as part of the bridgehead. "We had just gotten into position when word came up that we were going to move out and attack a little town by the name of Prétot. We moved out and were told it was about a five mile march. We moved very slow and were held up at a little town of Vindefontaine. Here the Jerries poured in a lot of artillery fire and mortar fire. In the little town [of Prétot] was a very high church steeple, and it was believed an enemy observer was in that steeple, because the mortar and artillery was so accurate. We lost several men at that town. We were all scattered along a road and finally Captain [Hillman C.] Dress [the Company H commander] told us to move into a little field and dig in. We did move in and faster digging I had never seen before. When we moved out, H Company led the battalion and the 3rd Platoon was out as the point. They ran into some machine gun fire and we were held up for quite some time."[1]

It was about 2:00 p.m., when the 3rd Platoon of Company H encountered an enemy strongpoint about nine hundred yards south of Vindefontaine. The enemy machine guns and snipers were difficult to locate as Private First Class Tom Porcella and the 3rd Platoon advanced across an open field toward a small group of farm buildings in the distance. "Sergeant [Kenneth O.] K. O. Benson was to my left a few feet in front of me. We tried to keep a distance between ourselves as we were running and firing our weapons. We were cursing and shouting at the Germans, who were firing at us with bursts of machine gun fire and rifle fire. From the corner of the field, I noticed a burst of machine gun fire with tracers— that's the only reason you could see it. They must have been firing at Sergeant Benson. All of a sudden, I saw Benson spin around and he hit the ground. I thought he was dead for sure. I crawled over to him and I asked him if he was hit and he had a dumb look on his face. He didn't know what to say for a moment. He was dazed. I examined him. I spoke to him. He was alive. That was the only thing I was interested in. I said, 'You're all right? You're OK?' He finally said he was OK.

"We checked him out and asked, 'You didn't get hit anywhere?' But what I noticed was that the burst of machine gun fire must have hit his canteen and the shovel and that's what spun him around. The only thing he said was he had a pain in his backside. We examined that and he had just a little nick. A little blood was coming out of his backside. So he wasn't hurt too badly and I was glad of that.

"This machine gun had the entire company pinned down and you could hear shots from all over. The men said, 'Anyone see where that damn machine gun fire's coming from?'

"Well, I happened to see where it was coming from and I remember shouting back at the top of my lungs, 'I'm going to put a clip of tracer ammunition in my rifle and just watch where the tracers are going and it'll give you a good idea where the machine gun is located.' I put the clip of tracers in my rifle and I fired the entire clip of ammo and you could see the tracers from my rifle shooting in that direction. It gave everybody a good idea where the Germans were [located], and everybody that saw it, opened fire. They fired all the weapons and machine guns in that direction. We waited awhile and all of a sudden everything got real quiet.

"So I guess we felt it was safe to stand up and start walking again in the high weeds. The machine gun never did fire again and we continued advancing."[2]

While the 3rd Platoon of Company H was pinned down, Lieutenant Ralph DeWeese received word to take the lead. "Contact couldn't be made with Lieutenant [Russell C.] Wilde, so the 2nd Platoon again had to put out the point. Lieutenant [Paul] Lehman came with us to act more or less as a guide. I had [Privates First Class William E.] Pollock and [Edward] Polasky act as scouts and we started to bypass the enemy. The column kept closing up on us so that we didn't have time to scout out the hedgerows as we went. We came upon a group of houses and had to send some men forward to search them out. Here we took two prisoners and they said their company had moved out. We kept moving and finally came to a position just about where we were to set up a defensive position. Pollock and Polasky were out in front and I was close behind. We were on the road now and just rounding a curve when I heard Polasky yell something in German and then fire a couple of rounds. It wasn't long until the Jerries started opening up with automatic weapons. They fired right up the road and the bullets threw gravel in our faces. I sent some men around the right flank to see if they could run them out, but no luck. So, I called for mortar fire and the mortar squad leader laid in about three rounds.

"Right after the mortar rounds fell, I heard an awful racket coming up the road. I couldn't imagine what on earth it was. Soon a horse came into view pulling two ammunition carts. My first thought was the Jerries had mined the carts with a time bomb. I got up and waved my hands and just as the horse got opposite me it seemed to slow up. I kept waving my hands and the horse kept going. It was a big black fine looking animal. After it had passed I could see it had been hit with one of the mortar rounds and had part of its harness torn off. We set up in position here and stayed the rest of the day."[3]

The 3rd Battalion halted about six hundred yards northeast of Prétot and formed a perimeter defense for the night. Two Polish prisoners captured that afternoon were identified as members of Kompanie 5, Grenadier Regiment 1049 of the 77th Jäger Division. During an interrogation, the two prisoners revealed that the company strength was less than sixty men, with only one officer, and had four machine guns and two mortars. Kompanie 6 of the same regiment was about the same strength and had been on the right flank, but they believed it to have been withdrawn. The 3rd Battalion also observed three enemy armored vehicles north of Prétot. The German infantry in this sector was under the command of the 91st Luftlande Division and supported by that division's Artillerie Regiment 191.

Lieutenant DeWeese checked on his men that night to make sure that half of the platoon stayed awake and on guard while the other half slept, then returned to his slit trench and tried to get a little sleep. "At about one o'clock that night I was called over to the CP and given information we were going to attack the town the next morning. We were to be ready to pull out at 4:30 and I didn't wake up until then, so we were about half an hour late. We moved into position in a large field just at the bottom of the hill. At that point we stretched out in a long skirmish line and waited for the attack. Artillery was to fall on the town ten minutes before we attacked. Six o'clock was H-hour."[4]

As the 3rd Battalion prepared to move out for the assault on Prétot, Corporal William W. Farris, with Company G, felt tired. "Yet, when the attack got under way I did not feel tired. In fact, it was quite the opposite.

"Our battalion was about a mile away when we were ordered to go into the attack. It was early morning; not yet daylight. We were to move up under cover of darkness, deploy around the [northeast] side of town and attack at the first crack of dawn. There was to be ten minutes of artillery before our jump off. We checked our crew served weapons, drew hand grenades, the necessary ammunition and rations. All NCOs were called in by platoon leaders for briefing; the NCOs had just returned from a briefing by the company commanding officer who had just been briefed by the battalion commander. I was told to orient my squad and make last minute checks on things like water, ammo, etc. Everything was now ready. Everyone was keyed up and having that last smoke before the jump off, under cover of course. We were making feeble attempts at stale jokes to show everyone we weren't scared—actually, we were scared to death. The fear of death is a fear I don't believe anyone ever masters. Our battalion commander used to say, 'It takes a brave man to be scared—and admit it.' By his ruler I can say I was feeling extremely brave that morning. Cigarettes were put out, a last warning for silence was given, squads were lined up and we moved out.

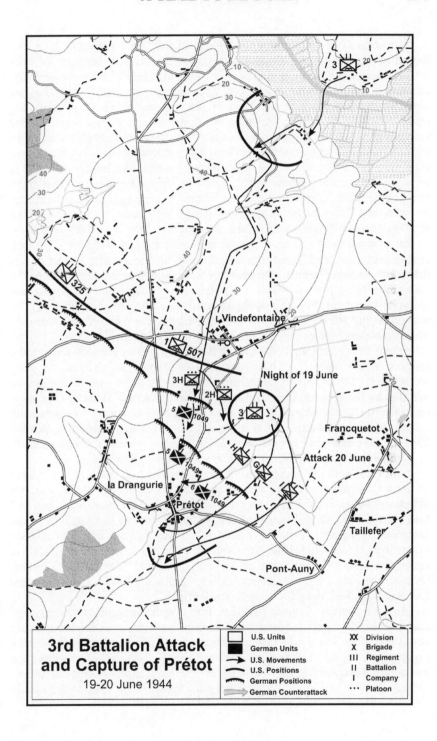

3rd Battalion Attack and Capture of Prétot

19-20 June 1944

☐ U.S. Units	XX Division
■ German Units	X Brigade
→ U.S. Movements	III Regiment
⌒ U.S. Positions	II Battalion
German Positions	I Company
German Counterattack	··· Platoon

"We arrived at our destination (the jump off point) in less than an hour. We moved into position and prepared to wait for our artillery barrage. When it lifted, that was our signal to attack. Here is the big picture: We were deployed companies abreast, squads in line, one battalion strong. Roughly speaking, we were six hundred yards from Prétot on the forward slope of a hill to the [northeast] side of town. We were attacking from the [northeast] to the [southwest]. The 1st Platoon of G Company was to swing through the southern edge of Prétot and set up machine guns on the road leading out of town, catching the Krauts as they started to pull back. We waited about ten minutes before our artillery went out and I believe it was one of the longest ten minutes I ever spent in my life. Finally, after what seemed a lifetime of waiting, I heard a dull boom far to our rear. Then the funny whirring sound a shell makes tracking across the sky. They usually fire one lone shell in to see if the range is correct—then lay it on. Such was true in this case, for seconds after the first shell hit—just long enough for the observer to radio back to the guns to 'fire for effect'—the air was filled with whirring sounds, like angry bees. I could hear the dull boom of the 105s firing far to the rear. Then the ground would shake with the impact and everyone would hit the dirt praying there wouldn't be any short rounds. Ten minutes of that and the countryside was as quiet as before, except now we could hear the soldiers in town cussing and running to their stations."[5]

As the barrage lifted, Technician Fifth Grade Francis Lamoureux, a radio operator with Company G headquarters, looked over at his new company commander. "I stood beside Lieutenant Woodrow Plunkett. The day before, he was told by [Lieutenant] Colonel Mendez to take over as CO for G Company. He replaced Captain [Frank] Novak, who had been G Company's commanding officer since the activation of the 508th at Camp Blanding, Florida, in October 1942. I had been his radio operator since joining the regiment at Camp Mackall, in April 1943. This would be my first day working with Plunkett.

"All eyes were on Lieutenant Plunkett, waiting for his signal to move forward. He swung his right arm in an arc over his head and pointed toward our objective. We were off. I was in a crouched position. I measured each step as I kept abreast of Plunkett. Straight ahead, we looked for any signs of movement. Occasionally, I glanced left, then right, to see if our line was intact. I could see [Technician Fourth Grade Bob] Kolterman and [Private John L. 'Red'] Hargrave and [Private Ralph] Campagna on my left. [Corporal Walter E.] Vanmeter, [Private First Class Olen W.] Oley Majers, Sergeant [Lloyd L.] Henning, and Lieutenant [James] McDuffie were on my far right."[6]

From his position, Corporal William Farris, with Company G, "heard some Joe yell, 'Let's go get the bastards!' And with that every man seemed to move out as one man. The gentle slopes leading into town were alive with charging paratroopers yelling like drunken Indians. The air was full of snarling lead looking for a body to stop in. The attack on Prétot was in full motion. Before we had run the first half of the six hundred yards separating us from town, I could hear the slugs ripping through the foliage as gunners fought to get our range. It seemed so thick that I thought it impossible to advance through it and not get hit. The Jerry guns were reaping their toll but we were too near; nothing could stop these hell-for-leather troopers now."[7]

As assault began, Lieutenant Ralph DeWeese was out in front leading the troopers of the 2nd Platoon of Company H forward. "The Jerries opened up with machine guns and caused quite a few casualties. One of my men was hit in the head, but not bad. His name was [Private Robert A.] Feliz and he had been in the platoon a short time. We advanced across an open field and finally I could see one of the machine guns that was causing all the trouble. Luck was with us again, because if it had been covering the field we were coming across, it would have gotten each and every one of us."[8]

As Private First Class Tom Porcella and Company H approached from the northeast, the fire suddenly increased in intensity. "We were advancing towards the village when about halfway across the field the Germans began firing their rifles and mortar shells at us. They caused us to be pinned down for awhile."[9]

German artillery and mortar fire, togther with the fire from the German machine guns, succeeded in pinning down the battalion and inflicting a number of casualties. Lieutenant Colonel Louis Mendez rallied his men and personally led them forward under the withering fire and inspiring the battalion to resume its charge into the town. Lieutenant Colonel Mendez would later be awarded the Distinguished Service Cross for his courageous leadership throughout the Normandy campaign.

As the 3rd Battalion charged forward, Private First Class Porcella spotted an approach route that might provide some cover and concealment. "When we entered this field, I remember seeing that there was a sort of a small river to my left. So I decided that I was going towards the riverbank. And if the river wasn't too deep, I was going to jump right in it. I reached the river and I jumped into it. It turned out to be waist high. It was a very small river but it afforded us excellent protection. We could still advance towards the village, meanwhile firing at the houses and at the windows. So this is what I did, and I was advancing up the river and before you knew it, the other troopers spotted what I did [and joined me]. As we were advancing up this river, we were shooting into the village. We didn't see any Germans in our sights, but we were receiving a lot of mortar fire and artillery fire."[10]

Porcella and others suspected that the accurate mortar and artillery fire was a result of a German forward observer team calling in adjustments to the artillery regiment supporting the infantry defending the town. "The Germans must be up in the attics of these buildings there looking through the windows giving our position away. So we got the order to shoot up at all the windows. As I neared the village, I saw a full pane window on a slant of the roof. I aimed my rifle, one shot and the full pane window went tumbling in. It surprised me. It was the first time I saw anything happen when I fired my rifle. As I was advancing up this river towards the village, there was a trooper named [Private First Class] Walter W. Harrelson. He was sort of staying very close to me. As he was firing his rifle, it was only two feet away from me. He was firing it [near] my right ear. I gave him hell. I said, 'Red, (that was his nickname) your firing that rifle is making my ears ring. I can hardly hear. I can hardly hear anything anymore. Stay a least fifteen feet behind.'

"He said, 'Oh.' Harrelson listened to what I had to say and he let me advance a little farther and he stayed behind.

"We finally got to a section in this river where it was time for us to leave the river and they were advancing to the town. When I stopped, I noticed a bunch of troopers climbing a wall and at the bottom of this wall was a big shell hole. The troopers got out of the river, ran towards the shell hole that was alongside the wall, and after one or two of them were there one helped the other over the wall. Then they gave the signal for the next trooper to come over and this is what we were doing. I got to that position and I waited for the come along. The trooper waved me on and I got out of the river, got to the side of the wall inside that shell hole and I looked behind me and I waited for Harrelson to get up [to] that spot. I waved for Red to come on over because he had to help me to get over the wall. As soon as I waved him over, Red climbed out of the river and took one step and a German shell came by right alongside of him. It exploded. I saw Red throw his rifle and fall backwards back into the river.

"The GI on the other side of the wall was hollering, 'Come on! Come on! Let's keep moving!' I didn't know what to do. So I remembered there was [Private First Class John P.] Johnny Downes in that river and I hollered to him. He asked me what I wanted. I said, 'Harrelson fell back into the river, see if you can help him. I've got to keep going.'

"He said, 'OK.' So I kept advancing into the village and eventually I got to the village. By that time there was no more firing; all the Germans took off." [11]

As he advanced, Private First Class John Delury, another Company H trooper, could see a number of enemy troops in the distance. "All the while we were advancing into the town the enemy was retreating out the other side. We were on high ground going in and had a panoramic view. You could see them running away in their camouflage ponchos.

"We got into a wooded section on the right side of the town and overran a machine gun nest and the supporting troops surrendered. Because I had a Thompson submachine gun, my lieutenant, Victor Grabbe, yelled for me to take the prisoners and the rest ran forward. One other trooper, [Private Lewis] Milkovics, stayed with me. We had the prisoners lying on the ground on their stomachs with their arms and legs extended, with their bodies under their ponchos. There were probably twelve or fifteen of them. They were a mixed bag, mostly Asiatic Russians, who looked very sinister. There were some German noncoms and some Poles." [12]

Corporal William Farris and the other Company G troopers charging across the fields closed rapidly on the village. "Things were moving fast now; no time to think, just act automatically and move. The Jerries were surprised and didn't have much chance to organize. As we approached the first street in town we came to I could hear the 'blam' of hand grenades and the nasty whine of flying shrapnel above the sputter of Tommy guns and the crack of rifle shots. I knew the main weight of the attack had started to fight through town and was systematically cleaning out house after house with hand grenades and bazookas."[13]

When he reached Prétot, Sergeant Marvin L. Risnes, with Company G, came to a house that lined the main road through the village. "I started to go around by the right side, but changed my mind, and went around the left side. That was a good move. When I got behind that house, I saw a German machine gun pointing down the right side. The Jerry swung his machine gun around in my direction, but I shot him before he could aim at me."[14]

Meanwhile, Corporal Farris and his Company G squad moved through another part of the village. "Nothing too exciting happened to my squad going through town. That is, nothing that didn't happen to squads in combat every day. There was one squad ahead of mine and they caught most of the dirty work. They were on one side of the street and we were on the other, followed by the mortar squad. I could hear all hell busting loose farther to my left; I knew the boys were having it hot. As we neared the edge of town the first squad was held up by a machine gun in a front yard. The platoon leader sent a runner back to tell me to take my squad and swing around to the right and come in from the flank. I took seven men and myself and started swinging to the right down a little alley between the houses. I left my machine gun crew and assistant squad leader behind because it is hard to climb fences and move fast with a machine gun.

"We started down behind the row of houses, climbing the fences, and zig-zagging through the flower beds, keeping as close to the buildings as possible. As I stepped through the last hedgerow before the corner house I nearly bumped into a Kraut who was standing with his back to me, facing the street. I will never forget his look of surprise as he turned and saw me. I pressed the trigger on my Tommy gun and he went down like an unseen hand had just smacked him with a sledgehammer. I had no sooner let up on the trigger when two more jumped to their feet and began to run. They had been hiding in the hedgerow. I had twenty-five slugs left in my clip, so I just split it up between them. It always amazes me how much power there is in a bullet. If a man is hit solid it is like a house was dropped on him. Needless to say, these two were surely hit solid; they weren't over fifteen yards away from me.

"A scout and myself moved on around the house. The two of us crawled up towards the street to try and spot the machine gun that was holding our two squads up. We saw it. I sent the scout back for the man with the grenade launcher on his rifle and he proceeded to polish it off. It took two rounds. We then moved on through the town with no more than the occasional sniping to hold us up. Arriving on the [far side] of town we set up our two machine guns covering the road leading out of town. We put out local security and waited.

"All of this time I could hear the boys raising hell in the main section of town. Later, I learned we had attacked so fast that two tanks were bottled up in town and they were rushing around like bulls in China shops; up one street, down another. Everywhere they went there were troopers laying it on. They finally knocked them out. We hadn't done much more than set up when the Krauts started pulling back down the road leading out of town. They were very disorganized and needless to say we had a field day. Dead and dying German soldiers were lying along that road for a quarter of a mile. Later we learned we had chalked up about 150 Krauts.

"While one of our machine gun's gunners was zeroing in, I was standing behind him. As he fired, I would slap him on the shoulder which meant he needed to raise his sights by two mils. I noticed there was no rifleman protecting the left flank of the gun. I turned sideways and yelled to one of the boys, 'Hey [Corporal Walter E.] Vanmeter, come here.'

"We were standing behind a hedgerow, out of sight, except for the hole in the hedge I had been looking through at the road to correct the firing of the gun.

"Vanmeter came over and yelled, 'What do you want?' I turned sideways and reached back to pull him close so he could hear above the noise of the gun. I had just grabbed his arm when a sniper got in a lucky shot and plugged Vanmeter right through the chest—clean through. He fell at my feet and I drug him in close to the hedgerow and yelled for the medic. I pause here a minute to explain exactly what happened. The sniper that shot Vanmeter was actually zeroed on me. I just happened to turn sideways leaving Vanmeter facing the hole in the hedge. I never had a closer miss. I felt the wind from that slug across the back of my hand. Vanmeter was hit bad and he knew it. He died later on. He told me to take his pistol, that he wouldn't be needing it. He refused to let the medic bandage up his wounds; he said it would be a waste of time. He was bleeding awfully badly and he had a feeling he was cashing in. Funny how a guy knows, for I believe they do in most cases. We got our orders to move on. We were to set up and dig in on the high ground beyond the town. I went over to Vanmeter where I had dragged him. I couldn't think of any pretty speech, so I just said, 'Take it easy.'

"He answered, 'Yeah, yeah.' As I left, his face was gray as ashes and he was bleeding like a stuck pig. I knew he had had it. I learned later from the medic who stayed with him that he died in about twenty minutes. He was a nice guy; a good friend of mine. Well, Prétot was ours. It had taken just a little more than two hours. It was one of the most organized attacks I ever took part in."[15]

The troopers mopped up the town and rounded up prisoners, who were taken to a collection point set up in a barn where they were held under guard. Private First Class Tom Porcella, with Company H, was ordered to search another barn in the village. "The other GIs said they would take the house on that side of the street. I was hugging up against the wall, walking against the wall and I got to the door and I lifted the latch of the door with my rifle and I pushed the door open. As soon as I pushed that door, two Germans came flying out of that barn. It scared the hell out of me so bad [that] I dropped my rifle. I quickly retrieved my rifle and the Germans were giving up. They had their hands up and were running around in circles because they didn't know what to expect. They kept saying, 'Kamerad, kamerad.'

"I'm saying, 'Comrade, my ass. You probably are the guys who were shooting at us a few minutes ago.' So I took the two prisoners and I brought them to another section [of the town] and I gave them to some sergeant and I said, 'Here, get rid of these. I've got to finish flushing out this barn.' I went back to the barn. I cautiously went into it. I figured I could get blown to bits any minute now. As luck would have it, there were no more Germans in there, but as I searched the barn, there was a machine gun and lots of ammunition. So I said, 'These were the characters who were probably shooting at us in the field for all I know.' So I went back outside on the road again."[16]

Porcella was then ordered to clear a nearby house. "I cautiously opened this door and I listened and didn't hear any noise, so quietly I walked into this building. I went to my right. There was sort of a living room with a fireplace in there. When I opened the front door, I noticed that there were stairs going up. I thought, 'I have to go up there.' The French are notorious for their homes—everything squeaks. Maybe that's a form of protection. But this was a form of inviting yourself to be killed, because if you had to walk up these steps and they squeaked, you would alert the Germans if they were up there. So I started to go and as luck would have it, these sets of stairs didn't squeak at all. So I managed to get up there without making any noise. Again, I went to the right. I had my back up against the wall, because I was coming to a door. It had another latch on it. So I stood there and listened and heard some commotion in there. I thought, 'What am I going to do? Here I am all alone. I don't know what's behind that door.' I started to get very panicky. I thought, 'Should I just empty a clip of ammunition into the door and run like hell?' Then I remembered the orders. We had to be careful because there were French civilians hiding in these houses sometimes. I thought, 'Yeah, they could be hiding in there and there could be Germans behind them.' All of these things went through my mind real fast, so you have to make decisions. So I thought, 'If I fire in there, I may kill the civilians. If I throw a grenade, I may kill a lot more. What am I going to do?' So my judgment said, 'OK, open the door and step back and let's hope for the best.' I was as scared as hell in doing all of this. I reached over with my rifle and I undid the latch and the door opened inward. I quickly looked and pulled back and the next thing you know, I heard this screaming and hollering. There were a bunch of men, women, and children in there. Most of them were old men and ladies and young women with babies.

"I must have looked like an awful sight with my wool cap on and I hadn't shaved since June the 5th. I probably stunk to high heaven. I hadn't taken a bath.

"I went in there with my rifle pointing at them and saying, 'Boche! Boche!' (Germans! Germans!) They were screaming and hollering and talking; they didn't know who I was. I had no identification except the American flag on my shoulder. I showed them and I was saying, 'American. American.' I don't know if they understood me or not. So I had to try to calm them down a bit...

"I reached in my musette bag and I took out these candies. In the K-rations we had these charms candy and I usually saved them. I saw the kids and I was giving it to them. I remembered the old man. I pulled out a pack of cigarettes and I started to give cigarettes. He was the only one who would take them, so I gave him five or six cigarettes. They said something to me. Then I said, 'Well, I'm going,' and down the steps I started to go. I started to shake like hell, when I realized what I had just done. I know we were taught that [we were to] either shoot into the door or throw a hand grenade. But I thought if I would have done that, I would have killed all these people. I became very emotional when I thought of this and then I thanked God I didn't do it. But, then also I thought the next time I might not get away with this. Being kind to people may cost me my own life. So I got out to the road and I reported to the sergeant that there were no Germans. There was just a bunch of frightened French people up there in the attic."[17]

Lieutenant Ralph DeWeese and the 2nd Platoon of Company H cleared other buildings in the village. "The men had a lot of fun cleaning [out] the houses, throwing grenades and shooting down doors. One of my men robbed the post office and came out with a handful of Francs. Sergeant [Lyle K.] Kumler and I were going through one house that had three stories. We were up on the third story and admiring the house and more or less taking it easy. I happened to walk over to a little door that led to an attic and casually opened it. There sat a German officer, just as calm as you please. I didn't have my gun [in a position] so I could shoot, but did step back because I thought he might be covered from the top. I motioned for him to come out and he came out with his hands up. He was a typical looking Nazi officer. I kept him covered and Kumler searched him and took his pistol. He evidently had given up hope and was waiting for someone to come and get him. We took him outside to the colonel [Lieutenant Colonel Mendez] and he stepped back and saluted the colonel. He was surely a good looking soldier. They talked back and forth in French. He was a first lieutenant and I felt kind of proud to think I had captured him."[18]

Private First Class John Delury, with Company H, who had been guarding some prisoners captured outside of town during the initial attack, brought them into the village. "There were animal sheds, or sheds to store vegetables built into the side of a hill where I thought I could confine them. I had finally acquired a Luger [pistol]. A German officer was already in an open-doored, smaller shed on my left, but the shed in front of me was locked with a padlock. I aimed the Luger at the padlock and fired several times to shoot it off.

"The German officer in the open shed to the left could not see what I was firing at; he thought I was executing other prisoners. He got on his knees with his hands over his head in prayerful supplication. When he realized I wasn't shooting the other prisoners, he quickly got off his knees and immediately returned to the carriage of an officer of the Third Reich.

"We put a German noncom in with the German officer. We tried to separate the brains from the brawn. All the Mongolian type Russians and their fellow travelers were put in a larger shed, from which I had just shot off the lock. They were being interrogated by a trooper named [Private First Class Robert G.] Mangers, who was with our battalion S-2 [section]."[19]

A short time after the town was cleared, a German tank sitting outside of the town shot up Lieutenant Robert M. Mitchell's 3rd Platoon of Company I. The full weight of the 91st Luftlande's Artillerie Regiment 191 rained down on the town. This artillery fire along with enemy mortar fire from the high ground to the east and south was particularly accurate and inflicted additional casualties. Private First Class Fayette "Rich" Richardson and several other Company H troopers moved out to deal with the German mortar fire. "[Sergeant William] Medford led the way to a German mortar position up the hill. He and I were a little ahead of the rest. When we came to a hedgerow bank, he jumped up on the bank and shouted for the Germans to surrender. Then we jumped over the hedgerow and a German noncom came out of hiding and turned his machine pistol over to me.

"I told Medford, 'It seemed foolish standing on top of that bank exposing yourself that way, you could have been killed.'

"'Listen Rich,' he said, 'There is a time to be cautious and there is a time to be bold. This was time to be bold.'

"I had to smile, but I didn't forget his comments."[20]

After the 3rd Battalion cleaned out the town, Lieutenant Woody Plunkett, the new commanding officer of Company G, made preparations to defend it against a counterattack by getting his company dug in on the edge of the village. "Two platoons dug in on line, with one platoon in reserve, and I set up the CP."[21]

Technician Fifth Grade Francis Lamoureux, despite being weighed down by a heavy SCR 300 radio, had managed to stay close to his new company commander throughout the assault. "Lieutenant Plunkett pointed to a two-story stone house. He decided to set up his CP there. I followed him into the building. He wanted to survey the terrain from the second story. As we started to climb the stairs, the entire building shook; it had been hit by a German 88. Chunks of ceiling showered down on us. We all made a hasty retreat. The building was being shelled, one round after another. We ran along the road away from the building and crossed into an open field, where we took cover along what looked like a denuded hedgerow. The earthen wall resembled a New England stone wall, but there were no trees growing from it. Plunkett gave us orders to dig in. It was hard digging. In minutes the shells were exploding along the wall. The Jerries had zeroed in on us. The shells came in succession, one—blast—two—blast—three—blast! I was really scared. I prayed to God to help us. Lieutenant Plunkett knew that we had to move to a new position."[22]

Despite taking out one of the enemy mortar positions earlier, Private First Class John Delury, with Company H, could feel the tide of battle shifting. "The artillery fire was devastating; it was decimating our battalion. Our casualties were becoming unacceptable, so we were ordered to withdraw a few hundred yards and dig in until our artillery could be brought into play to silence some of the German 88s. I remember looking at my friend [Private First Class John P.] Jack Downes walking back badly wounded, looking gray-green, and ranting about [Private First Class Walter W.] Bud Harrelson being hit by mortar fire during our assault and drowning in the stream. He seemed in a state of shock.

"When evacuating the wounded from Prétot we utilized German prisoners to help as stretcher bearers. Two Krauts were running by me with a blanket covered stretcher and I heard a voice call my name. I told them to lower the stretcher and it was a trooper I knew who appeared to be seriously wounded. He begged me to give him a drink of water which I couldn't refuse; he looked so forlorn. We were instructed never to give water to anyone with a stomach wound and I couldn't tell where he was wounded. So I tried to wet his lips while still restricting his intake. I then sent him on his way to the aid station. I never did find out if he survived his wounds or not.

"The entire battalion had to withdraw under the punishing mortar and artillery fire. You had to run in a type of duck waddle, staying close to the ground, but trying to gain distance to get away from the enemy fire. When you came to a defilade you'd catch your breath and then start again. All the time I had the two Germans with me—the sergeant and the lieutenant—running for survival, just like the rest of us. It was about midway during this withdrawal and when some troopers I didn't know saw my Kraut prisoners running with me. They had just pulled back after having many of their company killed—probably good friends, too. They yelled over to me, 'Shoot the bastards!' But I brought both back to the rear unscathed."[23]

The 3rd Battalion withdrawal from Prétot took place around 4:00 p.m. As they withdrew, Private First Class Rich Richardson and other Company H troopers found one their buddies who had been wounded earlier. "[Technician Fifth Grade Orville K.] O. K. Harris, his legs riddled with machine gun bullets calmly waited for us in the field; he talked on happily as we carried him toward the aid station until the makeshift stretcher of dry sticks broke and dropped him on the ground and then he cursed us in fierce pain."[24]

Technician Fifth Grade Francis Lamoureux and the rest of Company G headquarters personnel headed for what appeared to be a good location for their command post. "We headed through a rich green pasture which sloped down toward a wooded ravine. What a place for a picnic—we were sheltering from incoming freight and we were getting hungry. This was to be our new CP. We dropped down to catch our breath. Everyone felt secure. Time to eat. I stretched out on the ground, opened a K-ration, and munched on some crackers.

"[Private John] Hargrave hollered at me, 'Lamoureux, do you have a stick of gum?' I was preoccupied with looking for the gum in my Cracker Jack-like box of K-rations. I found a stick of gum, and as I threw it over to him I rolled over face down and heard the familiar screaming sound of a mortar shell. I pressed my tensed body into the soil and waited. A loud boom—it hit between Lieutenant Plunkett and Lieutenant [James] McDuffie. Another scream, another more deafening boom—it hit between Oley Majers and Sergeant [Lloyd] Henning. A third shell hit about ten yards farther down the ravine. When the air cleared, I pushed up slowly on my elbows to look around. To my left I saw Plunkett and McDuffie both bloodied and writhing in pain. To the right were Majers and Henning.

"Closest to me was Majers, who was moaning, his face buried in the ground. I was struck with horror as I watched Sergeant Henning pull himself up to a position kneeling on his haunches. His left hand covered the left side of his face. Bright red blood was dripping from his face and his hand. He tried to talk, but at first made only gurgling sounds. He made a sign as he looked over at the two stricken lieutenants and as he extended his hand, I could see that his face was severely disfigured. He had only half a face. His left eyeball was suspended on a white cord to below his chin—I cringed. What was he feeling and thinking?

"When I looked again at Majers, I did a double take. There was something strange and furry-looking on the back of his jump pants. A closer look revealed that the bristles from a shaving brush in his back pocket had been sheared off by shrapnel. More amazing still, was the way in which the bristles were fanned out surrounding a gaping wound in his left buttock. It was as though someone had carefully laid each bristle side by side into the wound to form a perfect circle. I finally spoke to him. 'Oley, you're going to be OK,' I told him.

"I looked back at Henning. His tongue and his lips were severed. He tried desperately to speak. 'Kill me,' he said.

"Lieutenant Plunkett heard him and with great effort, he said, 'Henning, don't you think about it. They'll fix you up.'

"Mercifully, medics arrived. With the help of G Company men, the wounded were evacuated to a holding area and given immediate aid by [the assistant] battalion surgeon [Lieutenant] Briand Beaudin.

"The news soon reached Colonel Mendez. He quickly assessed the situation and ordered Lieutenant Russell Wilde of H Company to take command of G Company. In less than twenty-four hours, G Company had gone through three company commanders.

"I was dazed and numbed and did not know to whom to turn. I did not have a scratch on me, but the concussion of the shell bursts made it all seem dreamlike.

I felt as though I had lost my anchor, but seeing Sergeant [Marvin] Risnes and Sergeant [Frank L.] Sirovica taking charge reassured me."[25]

The 3rd Battalion was relieved that night at 11:30 p.m. by the 1st Battalion, 507th and moved north to prepare for an attack on Hill 131. Lamoureux collected his gear and moved out that night with what remained of Company G. "We started our march toward evening. The companies were staggered. We filtered through battalion headquarters CP. I learned that Oley Majers was killed by a shell burst an hour after he had been taken to the temporary field hospital. This was another blow to me.

"We were marching silently up a dirt road in single file—one file on either side of the road. The men ahead of me turned their heads down to look at something. As I got closer I saw the body of a paratrooper lying in the middle of the road. He was stretched out on his back, wearing his helmet. I looked back at his face. What I saw seared into my memory as though by a branding iron. It was Lieutenant Gene Williams—not a mark on his body. He looked as though he had fallen asleep there. His face still had the color of life. To me it seemed as though he had been looking up to the sky and had fallen asleep. His lips were gently pursed into what I can only describe as an angelic smile.

"My surprise at finding him there quickly turned into shock and indignation. Someone had removed his paratrooper boots and had stripped him of his jump pants. He lay there wearing his long johns and still had on his jump jacket. To me it was a desecration!"[26]

Lieutenant Ralph DeWeese also saw the body of Lieutenant Williams as he marched north. "He was the youngest officer in the battalion and one of the best liked fellows."[27]

It was one more shock to Technician Fifth Grade Lamoureux, who reflected on how he and Lieutenant Williams had worked so closely together over the last few months while training for the invasion. "He had been the officer in charge of the 3rd Battalion pathfinder team. I was one of his radar operators, and I had jumped with him into Normandy on D-Day. We had trained for nearly three months in England to prepare for our pathfinder mission...All of us on the pathfinder team had worked closely with Lieutenant Williams and had learned to admire him. As dusk set in that evening, Colonel Mendez received a communication for Lieutenant Williams to inform him that his wife, Mary, had given birth to twin boys in Mobile, Alabama, on June 8, 1944.

"Word spread quickly throughout the battalion, and there were many heavy hearts among the officers and enlisted men who had known him.

"We were getting ready to settle in for the night. There was a chill in the air. I was in no mood to talk to anyone. Someone came toward me. I motioned him away. I huddled on the ground in a fetal position to keep warm. As events of the day reeled through my mind I started to cry, quietly at first, then I sobbed uncontrollably and I was close to hyperventilating. After a while I dropped off to sleep."[28]

Like others, Lieutenant Paul Lehman, the 3rd Battalion S-2, was shocked when he received the news about Lieutenant Williams. "Sure was a pitiful case, which affected all of us on the staff very deeply. One thing is certain, that the difference between life and death is almost one hundred percent a matter of luck, as far as being in the combat zone is concerned."[29]

On June 20, the remainder of the regiment was relieved by elements of the 90th Infantry Division and trucked across the Douve River to an assembly area near la Quenauderie to join the 3rd Battalion for a planned attack on Hill 131 to the west. The following day, the operation was postponed for twenty-four hours. On June 22, the 1st Battalion moved from the regimental area to prepare and occupy a defensive position on the regimental reserve line in the vicinity of Vindefontaine. Also that day, the attack on Hill 131 was postponed indefinitely.

At 10:15 a.m. on June 23, an order was issued to conduct a reconnaissance of enemy defensive positions. Lieutenant John P. Foley, the platoon leader of the 1st Platoon of Company A; his assistant platoon leader, Lieutenant Rex Combs; and three Company A enlisted volunteers conducted one of the reconnaissance patrols to determine enemy strength and dispositions. After penetrating through the German front line, Lieutenant Combs suddenly heard the sharp crack of bullets from several automatic weapons concealed in nearby hedges. "This patrol was ambushed by the enemy and was receiving this fire at very short range from many automatic weapons and rifles. Though completely surrounded, Private [Charles E.] Schmalz voluntarily crawled through the ring of enemy...[while] being fired on by at least three enemy automatic weapons at almost pointblank range, broke through and organized and directed a group of men in successfully rescuing his platoon leader, assistant platoon leader, and two men from the enemy ambush."[30] Private Schmalz was awarded the Bronze Star for his valor.

The 2nd and 3rd Battalions movement to the new defensive positions began after dark, with 3rd Battalion digging in on the new main line of resistance, with the 2nd Battalion on the regimental reserve line, and the 1st Battalion on the division switch line.

Late that night, the 3rd Battalion dispatched combat patrols to determine the enemy strength and locations to its front. The 23rd of June happened to be Company I trooper Private First Class Bob Chisolm's nineteenth birthday. "We were sending out a combat patrol to feel it out for the attacks that were coming up. Lieutenant Kelso Horne was the patrol leader. [Sergeant] Delbert [A.] Helton, my good friend, had been out on a patrol the night before. He was one of the squad leaders and they were going to wake him up and send him on a patrol again. I said, 'No, don't wake him up. I'll go in his place.'

"It was a pretty good sized combat patrol. [Private William J.] Bill Hughes, who was a good friend of mine in I Company and [who later] moved up to the battalion S-2 section, and I were the point men. We were going up and penetrate to the area around the base of the hill [Hill 131] to find where the Germans were [positioned]. We were going down the road, a stupid thing, and as we were coming to a bend in the road, a machine gun opened up. We walked right into it. It was an MG-42. I caught a burst in my right shoulder and I caught the second burst in the back of my head and knocked me in the ditch. It split open the back of my head. There was an [enemy] armored car there and it was firing. Bill was over on the other side [of the road] and I was lying in the ditch. I didn't know how seriously wounded I was. I knew that I had been hit and I had the pain.

"Bill said, 'Bob, Bob, how are you?' And every time he said that, the damn machine gun opened up and was clipping me in the back of the head.

"I thought to myself, 'I wish he would shut up.' I was carrying a BAR at this time. The armored car pulled out, because they didn't know what was coming at them. The machine gun was still there.

"Bill said, 'Bob, I'm going to jump up and unload on that machine gun nest and then let's get out of here' He was carrying a Thompson submachine gun. So he jumped up and opened up with his Thompson and I jumped up and opened up with the BAR. He knocked out the machine gun. We came back and joined the patrol."[31]

Chisolm was incredibly fortunate to survive the head wound and to do so without impairment. Perhaps what was just as amazing was that he could even lift a BAR and fire it with his badly wounded right shoulder. After returning from the patrol, Chisolm was patched up and taken to the regimental aid station. "[Major] Dave Thomas was the first medical officer to treat me and he gave me some morphine."[32] A plate was later inserted into the back of Private First Class Chisolm's head to cover the hole in his skull.

At 6:35 a.m. the following day, June 24, the 1st Battalion was relieved by elements of the 507th Parachute Infantry and moved to the division switch line near le Bost. A new regimental command post was established just northwest of Vindefontaine.

After the regiment dug in, awaiting orders to attack Hill 131, Lieutenant Colonel Mark Alexander, the new 508th executive officer, began inspections of the new positions. "I had little to do and had Colonel Lindquist's approval to frequently check out the regiment's defensive positions."[33]

Alexander also personally conducted night patrols behind German lines to gain information about enemy dispositions and the best possible avenues for attack. "On one of these patrols, I was with my new runner, [Private First Class] Virgil [M.] McGuire. We were scouting ahead of our lines and went into a fairly substantial stone farmhouse through the back door. We entered that way from the woods, because I knew we were getting close to the German lines. So we went in and peeked out the front window. There was a line of Germans coming, moving along the road and crossing in front of us. I counted them and then, as soon as they went by, we got the hell out of there."[34]

One night, Alexander went out alone and upon his return found two troopers asleep at their post, while they were supposed to be manning a 508 roadblock. "I kicked one of them real hard to wake him up. Scared the hell out of him. But I didn't turn them in or anything like that. Sometimes guys get overly tired and overconfident when they're in a defensive position. You have got to stay alert, which they were not doing."[35]

On June 25, the regiment continued to occupy positions east of Hill 131, with the 3rd Battalion on the main line of resistance, with the 505th Parachute Infantry on its right flank and the 325th Glider Infantry on its left flank. The following day, Company H trooper, Private First Class Tom Porcella, was in front of the main line of resistance at an outpost, dug in alone in a small field. "The Germans kept us pinned down by machine gun fire. I could feel the tension slowly mounting inside of me. Suddenly, the machine guns fell silent and I began listening for movement. The nearest troopers to my position were about fifty feet on either side of this hedgerow. I became bewildered when I heard movement in front of my position, for there were suppose to be troopers in the next hedgerow. Then I began to wonder if they were all killed when the Germans opened fire with their machine guns. I remember gripping my rifle very tightly and I started to say a little prayer and I started to get ready for action. The noise came closer and closer and my heart was beating very fast. I began to crouch very, very low and I kept my rifle pointed in the direction of the noise that was coming over the hedgerow. I remember my mouth seemed very dry and I was perspiring like heck. I could hear someone slowly climbing over the top of the hedgerow in front of me and I became all the more nervous and excited. Then all at once I saw two arms coming over the top of the hedgerow and I was about to shoot and I said to myself, 'No, let me just wait a little bit longer. Let me see who it is.' Then next thing you know, I saw a head and it was Lieutenant [Victor] Grabbe. I became very excited and I said, 'What the hell are you doing here? You're supposed to be in the next field.'

"He said, 'Help me, Porcella. Help me. I'm shot.'

"Quickly, I helped him over the hedgerow and I laid him down. The front of his combat jacket was stained with blood. I ran for the medics and I returned to Lieutenant Grabbe. He was very calm as we put him on the stretcher. He looked at me with his big blue eyes and never said a word and then they carried him away to the aid station. I know he died, but exactly when he died I don't know. I know he died from his wounds.

"The death of Lieutenant Grabbe was a tragic loss for the men of his platoon and to any trooper who knew him. He was one of the original 3rd Battalion officers and as far as I know, he was always with our company—Company H. I could truthfully say that Lieutenant Grabbe was an outstanding officer and his leadership in combat would surely be missed because, he was just one great lieutenant.

"Lieutenant [James P.] Richardson was transferred to take command. His transfer to this platoon was of the utmost concern to the troopers. For very little was known about him, and his ability to lead was in question.

"After a light morning rain, the day turned into a bright, warm, sunny afternoon and the sunshine was welcomed relief after all the rains that we had. Company G replaced Company H on the main line of resistance. The company assembled on the road and the order was given to march in single file on either side of the road. For about fifteen minutes after we began to march, the Germans directed their fire at us while we were on this road. At the sound of the first explosion, the troopers ran for protection in the ditches on each side of the road. The artillery shells were exploding all around us and some exploding on the road. Most of them landed on the field. When the shelling stopped, I raised my head to look at the road and I suddenly heard a report of artillery. Then there was a shell sliding down the road. I shouted at the troopers in front of me, 'Look out! There's a shell going down the road. It may have a delayed action fuse in it.' A few of the troopers left their ditches and they climbed over the hedgerows and the shell finally stopped. It never did explode and we were all happy because it was pretty close to a bunch of troopers."[36]

Beginning at midnight on June 26-27, Lieutenant Elbert F. Hamilton, one of the pathfinder officers, led four of his Company D enlisted men on a patrol to snatch a prisoner for use in gathering intelligence. "The patrol left Bois de Limors at approximately 24:00 hour and went southeast approximately two hundred yards to a point where we encountered the enemy line, consisting of approximately ten riflemen, running north and south. This was at 01:00 hour. Meanwhile, a harassing patrol had been delivering diversionary fire from a point 250-300 yards in front of the 508th lines, with the object of drawing enemy fire and thus causing him to disclose his position, so that we could accomplish our mission of capturing a prisoner. We did not return the fire from the [enemy] riflemen, but moved around their left flank to where we drew machine gun fire from a position 100-200 yards to the west. We could see no flashes, but could hear the fire chopping the weeds about thirty yards to our front and also to our rear. After several attempts to get closer to their positions, [which] on two or three [attempts] of which the enemy nearly caught us with parachute flares, we decided to give up the mission as a bad job. The combination of rain, impenetrable darkness, and the fact that the enemy could hear and follow all our movements, made conditions unfavorable for accomplishment of our purpose."[37]

Intelligence gathered from other patrols conducted during this period revealed that elements of the 353rd Infantrie and 91st Luftlande Divisions, a kampfgruppe of the 265th Infantrie Division, and remnants of the 77th Jäger Division defended the area of Hill 131 and a defensive line extending southeast.

ON JUNE 28, THE 319TH GLIDER FIELD ARTILLERY BATTALION was struck with one of the heaviest German artillery barrages it experienced during the Normandy campaign, killing Lieutenant Frank B. Poole and 1st Sergeant Keith F. Cormany, both with Headquarters Battery. Technician Fourth Grade Ed Ryan, with Battery C, saw both lying in a ditch after the shelling ceased. "Lieutenant Poole was a runner, you know. He ran against Glenn Cunningham for the championship of the world. He didn't know anything about smoking and drinking, but he was a nice guy. Keith Cormany, he was a professional wrestler in civilian life and he could lick any man in the battery. He was our first sergeant when we had C Battery with Captain [John] Manning—a great guy. His wife at home had just had a baby. We took up a collection in the battery and sent her five hundred dollars. She said she couldn't accept it and sent it back, so we bought a savings bond in the kid's name instead."[38]

Near the end of June, Lieutenant Malcolm Brannen, the commanding officer of Headquarters Company, 3rd Battalion, knew that the depleted regiment would soon be making an attack on Hill 131. "At this time, the battalion received three officer replacements—Captain [Frank R.] Schofield went to G Company to take command after the push forward, Lieutenant Southall was to be a platoon leader in G Company, and Lieutenant [Thomas] Fogg was to join H Company."[39]

ON JULY 2, THE 82ND AIRBORNE DIVISION issued orders for an attack the following day as part of a larger offensive to capture the town of La Haye-du-Puits. The 508th was ordered to attack from the Bois de Limors in the center of the division sector to seize the southern slope of Hill 131.

Some of the commanders in the 507th and 508th felt that the casualties suffered thus far had crippled their units and another attack might destroy them. General Gavin recalled that Colonel Lindquist spoke with General Ridgway about the matter. "His rifle companies got down to about 50 men from about 190, and he wanted to get his outfit pulled out, because he said if he had to go to an airborne operation next, he wouldn't be able to do it. Well, Ridgway grew up in the World War I tradition of an infantryman can always take another step and fire another shot. That isn't so, but he wanted to believe it. The last thing they ever did in World War I was to relieve the commander in the trenches—it was so awful. So poor old Lindquist made the mistake of asking Ridgway if he couldn't be pulled out to save his troops, and so on. And to Ridgway, that was the end of him."[40]

That same day, Lieutenant Ed Ott, now the platoon leader of the 81mm Mortar Platoon, Headquarters Company, 2nd Battalion, received orders to zero in on a German mortar position in preparation for the attack on Hill 131. "We did not have a radio, but did have a roll of telephone wire and a field phone. A volunteer and I proceeded to lay the wire, only to find it did not reach the line of departure, which was located at the beginning of the woods. I noticed a couple of troopers behind a barricade and crawled up to them and asked what was going on. When I looked down, I saw a mortar fin sticking out of my leg. I reached down, pulled the fin out, applied sulfa and tied up my wound, saying to the men, 'This is how an officer takes a wound.' I took two steps and passed out.

"When I came to, I found myself in a field hospital and my wound cleaned. A surgeon asked me if I wanted the wound repaired or just closed, as is. I asked him what the difference would be, and he explained that there was powdery shrapnel under a muscle and if I left it in, the shrapnel would gradually work itself out into my body. If I chose to have it repaired, they would have to cut a muscle in order to get the shrapnel out and I would walk with a limp for about two years until the muscle was to 'reshape' itself. I chose to have him close the wound."[41]

That day, Lieutenant Colonel Mark Alexander, the new regimental executive officer, received the orders for the upcoming assault the following morning. "Colonel Lindquist gave me the attack order: the 505th on the right, the 325th on our left. Our 508 regimental alignment had the 2nd Battalion on the right and the 3rd Battalion on the left, with 1st Battalion following in close reserve."[42]

At the 3rd Battalion command post that night, Lieutenant Malcolm Brannen was very worried about his battalion commander. "Colonel Mendez was sick with high fever and diarrhea and after checking all companies, [he] came back to the battalion CP. As I had dug a trench for protection, since we were getting a lot of artillery and mortar fire, I prevailed upon Colonel Mendez to use my hole in the ground, so that he could rest for a few minutes before he made his rounds again. I covered the colonel with a blanket and kept his face and head cool by pouring water on them and sort of bathed him with a bandage that I got from the first aid man there. In less than an hour he felt a bit better and was up and out to check the positions."[43]

The 1st Battalion was holding the line of departure along the edge of the Bois de Limors forest. Before dawn on July 3, Sergeant Howard H. Gouge, with and his squad of six Company A troopers, who were using a captured German machine gun, were suddenly attacked by a large German patrol using automatic weapons to cover their advance. The Germans quickly closed in and used hand grenades to knock out the captured machine gun and wound the two troopers manning it. Gouge rallied his men and despite being wounded himself, Gouge crawled forward under the covering fire of his remaining troopers and threw hand grenades into the midst of the Germans now manning the machine gun, destroying the gun and killing them. Sergeant Gouge was later awarded the Silver Star for his heroism and leadership.

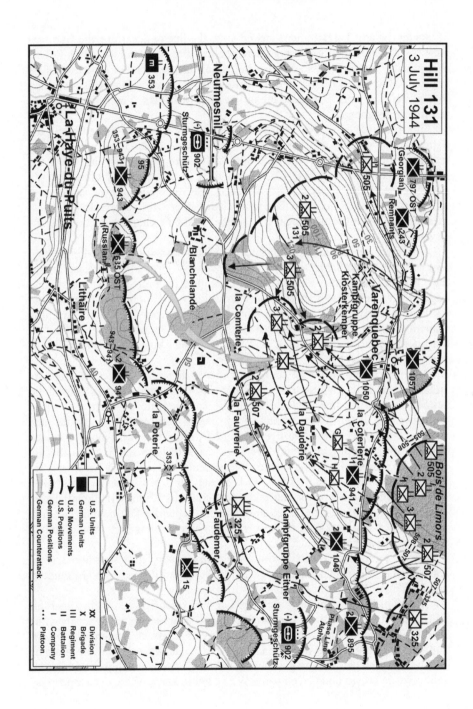

As the 1st and 3rd Battalions moved up to the line of departure, the Germans saturated the area with long range machine gun fire. Private First Class Robert White, with Company A, stayed low in his hole as the sound of German bullets cracked as they passed over head. "I remember thinking, 'This is like jumping into a swarm of bees.' I figured the air was full of bullets. You'd hear so many machine guns going."[44]

Shortly before dawn, Sergeant Zane Schlemmer, a forward observer with the 81mm Mortar Platoon of Headquarters Company, 2nd Battalion, moved up to the line of departure with the battalion's rifle companies. "We all knew the importance of capturing Hill 131—the highest in that part of Normandy. We could not see Hill 131, because of low hanging rain clouds. These clouds also meant that we would not have the promised air support for our attack; but it also meant that if we could not see the hill, neither could the Germans up there see us down below!

"At dawn our supporting artillery and mortars started pounding the German line and rear areas. Since we had to start the attack through the defense line of the 1st Battalion, there were not enough foxholes for protection at the starting edge of Bois de Limors; and the German artillery and mortars started shelling us. Private [First Class] Paul [H.] Winger, of E Company, was from my little hometown and his wife worked with my father. The German barrage killed him that morning (not far from me), so I was troubled about how I was going to address his death, for she was a very nice girl."[45]

As the 3rd Battalion rifle companies moved forward, Lieutenant Malcolm Brannen and his Headquarters Company, 3rd Battalion troopers moved up behind them to the line of departure. "The battalion moved from the line of departure by 05:00 hours under heavy enemy fire—artillery, mortar and automatic weapons. While we were at the LD, many troopers who had moved forward and were hit by enemy fire came back through our lines to the aid station...About 06:15 hours, a friendly concentration of heavy weapons fire helped us as we pushed forward. G Company and H Company captured la Dauderie, after G Company had taken la Cotellerie. Captain [Hillman] Dress [3rd Battalion S-3] was shot through the thigh, Lieutenant [William S.] Scudder was wounded and later died of these wounds, and the new Lieutenant Southall was wounded and evacuated."[46]

Private First Class Tommy Horne was with Captain Dress shortly before he was wounded. "Dress had called me over and he asked if I had seen G Company and I told him, No, I hadn't seen them.'

"He said, 'Well, they've drifted off. Go find G Company.' Well, I had this machine gun then, and there was another fellow with me, his name was [Private First Class Clyde E.] Nestor, and he was carrying a box of ammunition for me, and he had a rifle. While we were talking to [Captain Dress], we were standing in the farm yard gate and he got hit and fell down. I was going to help him. He said, 'No, go on, go find G Company. We've got to know where G Company is.'

"I'd cut those [ammunition] belts in fifty-round strips, or thereabout fifty rounds. That way, I could carry the gun loaded and fire it from the hip. I had a heavy asbestos glove I had taken off a German prisoner, so I kept from burning my left hand."[47]

They set out looking for Company G, just as it pushed some Germans across a hedgerow lined road near where Horne and his assistant gunner happened to be walking. "There must have been a hundred of them coming across that way. The Germans were coming across and they were coming across within fifteen or twenty feet of me. I had this machine gun just standing in the middle of the road, like I had good sense, and I guess I worked them over pretty good. I just used the belts up and then put another in, and as far as I knew, they didn't ever shoot at me. The company [G Company] was moving and they were trying to get away from us."[48]

Sergeant Donald Biles, with Company I, was near la Dauderie when he was wounded in the left leg by three machine gun bullets. "Staff Sergeant [Francis J.] Frank Yost absolutely saved my life. When I was hit, Frank ran across the road, slung me over his shoulder and took me back to a ditch on the other side of the road, all the while being fired at by the machine gun that got me. I never got to thank Frank, for he was killed the next day."[49]

Private Dwayne Burns, with Company F, had made it through the Normandy campaign thus far without a scratch and wondered how long his luck would hold. "Elements of the 2nd and 3rd Battalions were to form the assault wave and as always, it seemed F Company was up front. As we moved toward the hill a halt was called. While we were waiting for word to move up, we started getting hit with artillery fire. The area we were in had trees cut down and logs were lying in rows. We dove in between the logs as the first round came in. The two troopers on my right were both killed by a tree burst. And there I lay, just twelve inches away. Lady luck was sure looking after me!"[50]

During the assault, the 508th ran into stiff German opposition. As a forward observer, Sergeant Zane Schlemmer, with Headquarters Company, 2nd Battalion, had a critical job—that of coordinating the fire of the battalion's 81mm mortar platoon to support the attack. "I was up front with the attacking company commanders, so that if close mortar fire was needed, we could radio to the mortar positions to request it, then adjust it. We NCOs and officers each had a white sheet of paper map showing the hedgerows, orchards, fields, roads, the few farms and houses (obviously reproduced from aerial photographs) so that we could plan our advance; but it did not contain any elevations.

"As we advanced the paper got wetter, dirtier, and more unreadable. It was very important to have this map however, because our supporting artillery had a similar map and would tell us via radio the number of shells that they would fire into the hedgerow in front of us. We could then count the shells landing and immediately rush that hedgerow before the Germans could recover, and the artillery would lift their fire to the next hedgerow. It was the only way that an attack could be successful in that bocage country."[51]

As Sergeant Schlemmer continued to advance with the rifle companies, his peripheral vision glimpsed movement to his left rear. "I turned and saw two young Germans running and jumping into a foxhole. I fired two shots in their direction and called in German three times to 'come out with your hands up,' but [received] no response from them. So I took out one of my thermite grenades, which burns very hot, and bowled it into their foxhole and continued my advance. I am certain that they could not have survived the thermite grenade. We then came to a country road crossing a small stream. There, the Germans had downed and mined several trees across the road, as a roadblock. We radioed this information back so that an armored bulldozer could clear it for follow up armor to advance up the hill behind us."[52]

By 9:00 a.m., the 2nd Battalion was on the first phase line just southeast of Varenquebec on the right and the 3rd Battalion was at la Dauderie on the left. The 1st Battalion was mopping up behind them at la Cotellerie.

As the 2nd Battalion attack continued, Sergeant Schlemmer found himself navigating through a quagmire in the fields. "The rain lessened, but it was very wet and muddy in the fields. I do not recall seeing any houses during our attack, though the map showed several—such was the hedgerow country.

"In one field I was flattened, under intense German machine gun fire, which kept hitting some cow manure several inches from my face. I was pleased that the bullets were not hitting me. The cow manure kept splattering all over me and there was nothing I could do to move, but just lie there and take it with hope against hope the gunner would not adjust his fire."[53]

The assault continued to drive forward and by 11:00 a.m., the 2nd Battalion had fought its way to the base of Hill 131. As the 2nd Battalion commander, Lieutenant Colonel Tom Shandley moved forward, his attention was focused on a German machine gun firing at his men. "I tripped over a red telephone wire. Too late, I realized it was a booby trap. It blew and I flew through the air. I had several pieces of shrapnel in me—one in the neck. I was pretty badly crippled, but I bandaged myself and kept going."[54]

Private First Class Frank Staples, with Company D, was within a few feet of Shanley when he tripped the mine. "I was following him. It didn't kill him, but it banged him up considerably.

"He said, 'It is big enough and it is in the wrong place.'"[55]

Lieutenant Colonel Mark Alexander, the regimental executive officer, was out with the troops monitoring the progress of the assault. "I heard over my radio that Lieutenant Colonel Shanley, leading the 2nd Battalion, had tripped a 'Bouncing Betty' [mine] and caught a ball in the back of his neck. The loss of Shanley was critical, leaving only inexperienced Captain [George] Simonds to lead the battalion. I requested and received permission from Colonel Lindquist to go forward and lead the battalion. I immediately went forward to the 2nd

Battalion, which was involved in cleaning up a German defensive position. The battalion was unorganized and doing some looting of the captured Germans and their position.

"I sent Lieutenant Colonel Shanley back to the medics and proceeded to get the battalion reorganized and moving toward our objective for the day."[56]

On the left, the 3rd Battalion fought to a point three hundred yards west of la Dauderie by 11:45 a.m. and the 1st Battalion, which had been advancing behind the leading battalions and mopping up bypassed pockets of Germans, passed through the first phase line.

When Lieutenant Colonel Alexander and the 2nd Battalion "had proceeded about one thousand yards short of our objective, I heard a hell of a firefight break out to our rear. I took one man with me to backtrack and see what was going on."[57]

The 1st Battalion was struck on the left flank by about sixty to seventy-five enemy troops, who unleashed heavy automatic weapons fire that pinned down most of Company A. Lieutenant Rex Combs, the assistant platoon leader of the 1st Platoon, was near Private Wayne F. Campbell when the Germans opened fire. "Private Campbell and his machine gun was the initial target of the enemy. Though the ground and surrounding vegetation were literally cut to pieces by enemy fire, he returned all enemy fire after lifting the machine gun off the tripod and with a belt of ammunition over his arm, immediately advanced toward the enemy, pinning a large portion of them down with deadly accurate fire."[58]

As Campbell was doing this, Combs saw his platoon leader, Lieutenant John Foley, grab a BAR. "[As] Lieutenant Foley advanced down the center of the road, the object of intense enemy fire, he was able to direct the fire of his men upon the enemy, and personally account for several of the enemy."[59]

Meanwhile, coming back down the hill, Lieutenant Colonel Alexander and his runner, Private First Class Virgil McGuire, arrived at the scene. As they came to a bend in a dirt road, Alexander spotted the enemy troops firing on Company A. "We could see Germans in a deep drainage ditch firing at our oncoming 1st Battalion. My runner and I moved into a good position above them and poured it on from their rear, knocking off a couple of them. I know I got one, because he slumped down when he was hit, and I think I hit a second. The others started crawling along the ditch to try and get away."[60]

As this was occurring, Lieutenant Rex Combs took six of his Company A troopers and crawled forward to a point where he could observe the German force. Combs told his men to open fire, then single-handedly rushed forward and climbed atop the hedgerow behind which the enemy was firing. He opened fire with his Thompson submachine gun at close range, killing fifteen and forcing forty-five of the enemy to immediately surrender. Lieutenants Foley and Combs and Private Campbell were later awarded the Silver Star for valor in saving an already badly depleted Company A from annihilation.

Meanwhile, Sergeant Zane Schlemmer and four other 2nd Battalion troopers moved methodically up the lower slope of Hill 131. "We waited for the artillery to pound the next hedgerow with six rounds; then the five of us rushed it. It was then that the timing went wrong—for instead of raising the artillery fire to the next hedgerow our artillery repeated and pounded us. One shell tore the front of the sole of my jump boot off and blew me into the hedgerow. The second shell then wounded me in the left arm and knocked me down again. All five of us were wounded in this barrage and the calls for 'medic!' rang out. My wound bled a great deal, but did not hurt as much as it was a numbing, aching feeling. It came as a shock and a surprise, for I never thought it would happen to me, but rather to the others. The medics finally got to me after the more seriously wounded were cared for. I then had to find a radioman to get a forward observer up to take my place in the advance."[61]

Late that afternoon, the 505th Parachute Infantry Regiment, which had captured the northern slope and top of Hill 131, was ordered to drive down the southern and eastern slopes to link up with the 508th. The 3rd Battalion, 505th carried out the attack and linked up with the 508th at the base of Hill 131.

At 6:00 p.m., with Hill 131 secure, the regiment was ordered to move east from the vicinity of Blanchelande to a wooded area west of la Comterie to prepare to assault Hill 95 and the la Poterie ridge the following morning. The order of march was the 2nd Battalion, 3rd Battalion, 1st Battalion, and the regimental Headquarters and Headquarters Company.

Lieutenant Malcolm Brannen, the commanding officer of Headquarters Company, 3rd Battalion, was leading his troopers toward the location of the new command post when a sniper opened fire on them. "I heard a 'SNAP' and immediately heard one of my communication men, [Private] Eric Stott, yell, and as he was right behind me, saw him nearly fall and grasp his right shoulder. At the time we were going downhill, and if I had been taller and had not been going downhill I probably would have caught that bullet."[62]

Upon reaching the wooded area, the 2nd Battalion moved into its assembly area within the western part of the woods, while the 3rd Battalion assembled in the eastern portion of the woods. The 1st Battalion moved into an assembly area north of the woods and the regimental command post was established a mile and a half northeast of Blanchelande.

That evening, Private First Class Fayette "Rich" Richardson, with Company H, had a feeling he was going to die in the coming attack the following morning. "The odds were against me. I had jumped with an advanced pathfinder group and three men from our company. I was the only one still alive [of the four]. My foxhole partner had just been killed; the second had lost an eye. I knew it was my turn next. I went to [Sergeant William] Medford and he told me, 'Just look at it like I do. I plan on going home and I'll stick my feet under the kitchen table and eat a good chicken dinner.' It brought another smile to my face and I felt somehow better."[63]

After getting the 2nd Battalion into position for the night, Lieutenant Colonel Mark Alexander decided to conduct a personal reconnaissance in advance of the attack set for the following morning. "I found that there was an open valley about one quarter mile across and between us and the Germans. I moved to the left forward edge of a wooded area, crawled behind a stone wall, pulled a rock out of the wall and with my field glasses spotted two German gun positions on Hill 95.

"About that time, one of our men came walking up to my position. I called for him to get down as the Germans could see him. He kept coming and then ran like hell when the Germans put an 88 round into the wall just ahead of him. I never learned who the soldier was. I don't think he wanted me to know.

"As soon as darkness closed in, I left my observation post and returned to the battalion which was located on the back slope of a small rise in the land."[64]

After telling Captain Chet Graham, the acting battalion executive officer, about his plan to take the 2nd Battalion through a wooded area to avoid the open ground in front of Hill 95, Alexander sent him to the regimental command post to receive the attack order.

After Graham left for the regimental command post, Lieutenant Colonel Alexander contacted Lindquist to give him his plan of attack for the following day. "I talked on a field telephone with Colonel Lindquist and told him that for the attack next morning I was going to move the battalion into a tree covered ridge leading to Hill 95 and not have to cross the open valley and be subject to direct fire from the German guns on Hill 95.

"I had no more than hung the phone back on the tree than the Germans lucked out. They put a round of 80mm mortar into the top of the tree. I think I heard it coming, but took a dive too late. I was hit in the back by two shell fragments. It felt like someone stuck a fence post in my back and all I could do was lie there and cuss and think, 'Of all the times they were shooting at me and missed. They finally lobbed one over the hill in the dark and got me.'

"Doctor [Captain George E.] Montgomery and the medics got to me right away—taped my chest tight, closing the wound so that I would not have a blow hole and collapsed lung. They called regiment for a jeep and put me in the front seat with the driver. On the way to the hospital, we stopped briefly at regimental CP and I had a few words with Colonel Lindquist, but I could not talk very well.

"When we arrived at the field hospital, it was in a ground fog. I put my foot down the dismount from the jeep, saw two orderlies coming with a stretcher and I can only remember falling to the ground.

"The next thing I remember, two doctors were trying to take an X-ray of my chest. I was bare from my waist up, but still wearing my pants. I had the shakes and could not hold still for the X-ray.

"When I came to after surgery, Major General Ridgway was sitting on a stool by my cot holding my hand. He was talking to me, but I do not remember what he said, as I was only semiconscious.

"The next time I awakened, Father [Captain Matthew J.] Connelly [505th Catholic chaplain] was bending over me praying. I remember telling him that I was not Catholic. He told me to just be quiet, that he was taking care of things. When I came to again, the nurse came to me, looked at my dog tags and said your dog tags only say you are a Christian, but you are a Catholic now, for Father Connelly just gave you the last rites."[65]

Private First Class Virgil M. "Mickey" McGuire, a scout with the regiment's Headquarters Company, had been Alexander's runner. "He was absolutely fearless and didn't realize that senior officers could get killed. He went on reconnaissance patrols far in front of our lines. He packed a lot of living, and almost died, in the [eighteen] days he was with the 508th."[66]

CHAPTER 8

"WE PRACTICALLY GOT ANNIHILATED"

By midnight on July 3-4, the 508th reported to division headquarters an effective strength of the regiment of 1,052, having lost five killed and ninety wounded during the fighting that day. An attack order was issued at 12:30 a.m. on July 4 to capture Hill 95, which was defended by Bataillon 1, Grenadier Regiment 943, and the la Poterie ridgeline, which was defended by Bataillon 2, Grenadier Regiment 941; both were units of the 353rd Infantrie Division. The 508th's three understrength battalions would all move from their assembly areas at 6:30 a.m., provided the division gave a positive order to attack. A simultaneous assault would be executed with the 2nd Battalion on the right attacking southwest to capture Hill 95, the 3rd Battalion in the center attacking southwest to seize the center high point of the la Poterie ridgeline, and the 1st Battalion on the left attacking south to take the la Poterie ridge. When Captain Chet Graham, the commanding officer of Headquarters Company, 2nd Battalion and the acting battalion executive officer, received the attack order he was stunned. "The orders were to cross open ground and take Hill 95, with no information given of enemy strength, nor possible help from our artillery. When I received the orders, I said, 'With WHAT?' (2nd Battalion strength had gone from 640 to 225, with 8 officers.) Anyway that was our job.[1]

"I asked Colonel Lindquist, 'What about Colonel Alexander's plan to advance through the cover of the trees?'

"He said, 'You have your orders.'"[2]

When Captain Graham returned to the 2nd Battalion command post, he found out "that Colonel Alexander had been hit in the lungs by a tree burst and evacuated. So I was it (battalion CO)."[3]

Early on July 4, before the assault began, Lieutenant Kelso Horne went to the Company I command post. "I was standing up beside my company first sergeant [Raymond L. Conrad] giving him the morning report on how many men I had in my platoon. I was making the morning report to him when he was killed. He got shot through the chest from side to side, right by me.

"And shortly after that, my messenger and I were walking down by the hedgerow and a German machine gun opened up and got him in both legs. Shells started falling in and one of my mortar men got a chunk knocked out of his right buttocks about the size of both fists and he was moaning and groaning and my platoon sergeant had gotten hit and half his head knocked off. He was moaning and groaning and my medic had already used up all the morphine that we had and I sent him back to battalion to try to get some more and he came back without any."[4]

At 6:30 a.m., the regiment moved up to the line of departure and awaited the order to attack from the division. The order arrived from division headquarters at 7:20 a.m. for the assault to commence at 8:00 a.m.

On the right flank, Captain Chet Graham and 2nd Battalion jumped off, attacking southwest toward Hill 95. "We moved at 08:00 across the area with no cover and were shelled by 88s for most of the two miles...

"We attacked with D Company on the left, less one platoon for reserve, E Company up the hill in the middle, and F Company on the right. That flank was secured by the 3rd Battalion, 505. D Company received mortar fire and lost six men, one officer, and our S-3, Captain George Simonds. D Company, now under [Lieutenant Norman] MacVicar, held the left front of the hill, and E Company had trouble but got where they were supposed to be. F Company was hugging the hill with open ground on its right and being cut up. I pulled them back and planned to move E Company to the right. (Hill 95 had been a Roman outpost. It had a sheltered moat inside the perimeter circling the hill, about ten feet wide. So, we were able to move under cover from side to side.)

"During this time I was being called back to our big radio to converse with Colonel Lindquist. He told me not to move F Company back. ('We don't give up ground we have taken—get them back.') I explained my troubles and my plan, and told him he should come and see for himself, instead of second-guessing from a mile away. I was relieved of command on the spot. Royal Taylor came down and followed the plan."[5]

Private Albert W. "Bill" Giegold, was a machine gunner with Company F. However, his machine gun had been struck by a German bullet during the attack toward Hill 131 and rendered inoperable, so he was now fighting as a rifleman. "We made our attack on Hill 95 with about forty-four men. I was with Sergeant [Technician Fourth Grade Edward] Chatoian and Lieutenant [Hoyt] Goodale. Sergeant Chatoian was our radioman. On the way to Hill 95 he called regimental headquarters. This was fatal as the Germans triangulated our position during the radio contact with regimental headquarters. Heavy artillery came at us, hitting the trees, exploding into shrapnel, and seriously wounding both Sergeant Chatoian and Lieutenant Goodale. I was but three or four meters from them. They both appeared to be dying from multiple wounds, however they both survived."[6]

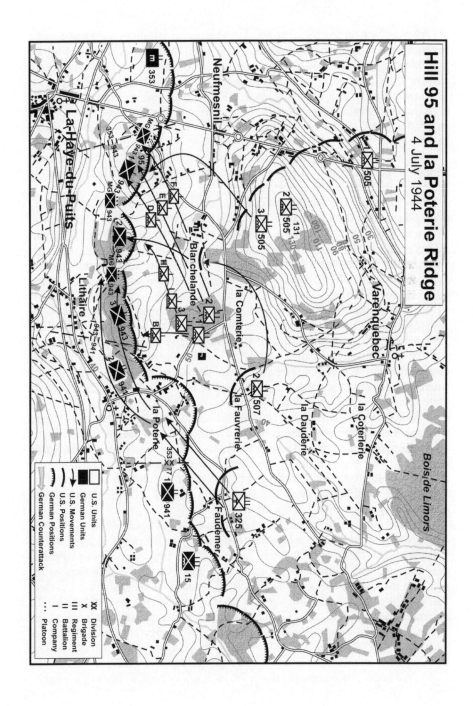

Hill 95 and la Poterie Ridge
4 July 1944

Neufmesnil

La-Haye-du-Puits

Varenquebec

Blarchelande

la Comterie

la Fauverie

la Poterie

Faudemer

la Daydèrie

la Coterie

Bois de Limors

Lithaire

Legend:

U.S. Units
German Units
U.S. Movements
German Positions
German Counterattack

XX   Division
X   Brigade
III   Regiment
II   Battalion
I   Company
...   Platoon

Private Dwayne Burns, now became the communications NCO and radio operator for Company F. "I sure was sorry that [Technician Fourth Grade] Ed [Chatoian] got hit, but that would put a stop to carrying a spare battery. From now on, I would carry the radio and we would do without the spare!

"Lieutenant Polette now was leading F Company, which now consisted of thirty-two soldiers. The men would follow him anywhere! Polette had been hit and had a chunk of steel in one hip, but he would not go back to the hospital, because it would leave us without an officer.

"We worked our way around the base of the hill while D Company went around on the other side. We were picking up lots of artillery fire. We dug in and hung on, sending out patrols to the top." [7]

The 3rd Battalion, 505th was ordered to assist the 2nd Battalion, and by noon had driven the Germans from the northern slope of Hill 95. The 2nd Battalion attacked through the 505th and captured the crest of Hill 95 about twenty minutes later. The 3rd Battalion, 505th then withdrew from the northern slope of the hill. After reaching the crest, Private First Class Frank McKee, together with the other survivors of Company F started to advance down the southern reverse slope. "The firing became too intense to go farther. The 88s were firing pointblank. Men were being killed and wounded all around me." [8]

McKee then received the order to withdraw back up to the crest of the hill. "When I got up, I was suddenly hit by something and was flat on the ground. It felt like a horse kicked me in the back and knocked me down. I put my fist back there, expecting to find a big hole, but only felt numbness. I tried to get up, but couldn't move my legs. I felt no pain. Looking up, I saw [Private] Bill Giegold at the top of the hill. I waved my arms and hollered, 'Bill, I'm hit!'

"He disappeared over the crest. No one around me was moving, but there were many men down. I figured I had had it. But Bill soon came back, dragged me back, and saved my life. A medic joined us, and we went down the back side of the hill. They placed me on a stretcher in a ditch beside the road. There were ambulances lined up on the road, while German artillery tried to zero in. Fortunately, the shells overshot and landed in a field. Bill Gielgold got me into an ambulance and I was off to a field hospital." [9]

Without riflemen to spare to take prisoners to the rear, Private Dwayne Burns, now the company headquarters radioman, was given the assignment. "F Company had captured a machine gun emplacement, and Woody [Private Woodrow W. Phelps] and I were given the job of taking the prisoners to the rear. We marched the four of them down the road until we found the regiment that was in reserve [the 505th] and they said they would take them off our hands. We were glad to get rid of the Germans and get back to our own company.

"As we came back into our company area we jumped into a trench about waist deep and sat down to rest. We were completely worn out. I took one end that had some tree limbs over it and was sound asleep in minutes. Later, I awoke when cold water started running down the back of my neck. It was raining again.

"I looked at Woody at the other end of the ditch. He was sitting there soaking wet. His head was back and his mouth was wide open, but he was sound asleep. 'You son of a gun,' I thought, 'If you're lucky, you will drown and get out of all this mess.'

"Later that afternoon, I had to go back to the rear area and took the same road. There in the ditch were the same four Germans that we had turned over that morning. They were dead. I thought I was going to be sick. Someone had used a machete on their heads. Why! Why like this? Why them? These poor slobs were just pawns in the game of war, the low man on the totem pole. Just like me they had dreams, desires, ambitions, and maybe a wife or a sweetheart back home. Now they lay in the ditch with their brains oozing out into the mud. I wondered how long it would be before it was my turn to be lying in some dirty weed-choked ditch as my life slipped away. 'Oh Lord,' I thought, 'I'm going to be sick! How do you get used to looking at things like that? What is this war doing to us when we can do this to another human being?'

"I asked some of the men why they had killed the prisoners. They explained that it was the same machine gun crew who shot down their medic while he was trying to help our wounded. They demanded an eye for an eye."[10]

At 2:00 p.m., the Germans counterattacked and forced the 2nd Battalion off of the crest of Hill 95. During the daylong fighting, Private Harry J. Smith, Easy Company's last medic, braved enemy fire to reach wounded troopers in exposed positions and evacuate them under direct enemy fire to the relative safety of a ditch. One of those wounded he saved was Corporal Bob Newhart. "I was hit across the back—several of us laid in a ditch for about thirty-six hours."[11] Private Smith was awarded the Silver Star for his courage in saving numerous wounded troopers on July 4.

Late that afternoon, Private Dwayne Burns and the survivors of Company F made a third attack to take Hill 95. "As darkness fell we were able to assault the top of the hill, killing more than 150 Germans in some of the hardest fighting we had ever seen. We also took eighty prisoners, while we had four troopers killed and three wounded." [12]

In the 3rd Battalion sector in the center, the 319th Glider Field Artillery Battalion began firing a planned barrage on the la Poterie ridge at 8:00 a.m., just as the battalion jumped off. However, just as the barrage began, the Germans fired an artillery barrage that hit the 3rd Battalion. Lieutenant Malcolm Brannen, the commanding officer of Headquarters Company, 3rd Battalion, was at the battalion command post just as the attack got underway. "About 08:00 hours a ten to fifteen minute [German] artillery barrage directly hit the CP and the I Company area. Exploding shells sent ragged steel fragments throughout the area. One shell hit the radio of [the liaison officer] Lieutenant [Raymond T.] Carey [Jr.], [and Lieutenant Irving Gelb, the] forward observer for the 319th

Glider Field Artillery Battalion. The radio was demolished and Lieutenant Carey was killed instantly. One of his assistants [Corporal Eugene L. Smith] was also killed instantly, while the other two enlisted men [Private George N. Binnix, with Battery A, 320th Glider Field Artillery Battalion, and Private Theodore S. Ratlief, Battery A, 319th Glider Field Artillery Battalion] were torn apart and died shortly. [Lieutenant Gelb was wounded, but survived.]

"The battery in the radio was knocked into the air and came down on me, hitting my chest, which was protected by a pair of field glasses hanging from my neck, this causing no harm, except my being pushed over onto the ground. While I was on the ground, another shell burst in the vicinity and a piece of steel hit my left inside thigh, causing a wound which gushed blood all over my right foot, just like a hose with water coming out of it. Instinctively, I grabbed my leg and stopped the spurting blood as Captain [Alton] Bell, 3rd Battalion executive officer, rushed to help me. Captain Bell looked at my bloody right foot and said to the others around the immediate vicinity, 'Brannen's foot has been cut off.' I told Captain Bell that it wasn't my foot that was hurt, and to prove it I released the pressure from the wound and right away, the blood gushed out again. I then placed my fingers on the wound and shut off the spray of blood. Then Captain Bell realized where I was wounded.

"The battalion medics came as soon as they had taken care of Lieutenant Carey and his team of forward observers, and bandaged my leg and got some of our mess personnel to help me walk about one hundred yards to a collecting point that had been established because of the many casualties in the area at this time. It was difficult to walk, but it was not necessary to be carried, so I was furnished with a stick and used it to aid my movement to the collecting point, mentioned above, that the 82nd Division had set up. Just before I left the CP for the collecting point I heard someone say, 'Brannen has been wounded.'

"I then heard Lieutenant John Daly remark that it was 'too bad.' I yelled at John and he came over to the place I was preparing to evacuate and said, 'Mal, I'm sorry.'

"I said, "It's OK, John, now be careful.' He went his way, and I never saw him again—he was killed just a few moments after we talked."[13]

The destruction of the 319th Glider Field Artillery Battalion liaison and forward observer party supporting the 3rd Battalion would have tragic and far reaching consequences that day. The preplanned barrage at 8:00 a.m. was fired by the 319th, but subsequent fire missions would depend upon observers being able to adjust the fire on the enemy positions and avoid hitting the 3rd Battalion troopers as they moved forward to assault the high ground. A second liaison and forward observer party was assembled under the command of Lieutenant Marvin Ragland, but would not arrive until the 3rd Battalion was well into the assault.

Lieutenant Ralph DeWeese was told early that morning that he and his 2nd Platoon of Company H would lead the assault. "We knew there would be plenty of fireworks when we attacked the hill. I was given the mission to form three points and lead the attack for the company: one on the right, one on the left, and one in the center. I stayed with the one in the center. "Word came around that they were going to lay artillery fire on the enemy position and we would advance under it. Man! What a terrific barrage that turned out to be. We started to advance and had to go across an open field."[14]

As he waited for the signal to attack, Private First Class Don Jakeway, with Company H, felt a chill in the air. "The day started with a slight fog and mist. It was always cold in the early morning hours of those days in Normandy. For some reason it was even colder, or we imagined it so this particular morning, as H Company and our 508 Regiment prepared for an offensive against a strong fortified hillside. The approach to the hill was fronted by a field. It seemed much bigger than most fields, which were always surrounded by hedgerows. H Company led the frontal attack and began moving out into the field."[15]

Lieutenant Ralph DeWeese and the point elements of the 3rd Battalion attack were advancing ahead of the rest of Company H. "The Germans opened up with machine guns and mowed the men down like flies. I heard someone yell from the rear to keep going, because if the artillery lifted, they would get us all. We kept going and finally halted when word was passed up that no one was following us.

"Sergeant [William A.] Medford, our operations sergeant, had been killed. Two of my men dragged Sergeant [Duane W.] Morris out of the field under fire and brought him to cover along a hedgerow. They were Private [James H.] Daugherty and Corporal [Henning] Olson.

"At this time we had taken cover along a little hedgerow and were holding up. There were thirty-three of us in all, and I was the only officer. I sent two men back a little way to see if they could contact anyone. They came back and said there was no one in the rear. Couldn't imagine what had happened to the battalion. Thought maybe they had all been killed.

"I looked around at the men and they had that look on their faces as if to say, 'You're in command, what are you going to do to get us out of here?' We were isolated and couldn't go forward, because the Germans had machine guns set up there. We couldn't go to the rear or the left because that was also covered by machine guns. Later, we found out the Jerries had the whole area covered by thirty machine guns, so you can imagine the tough spot we were in."[16]

Advancing behind the point with the main body of Company H, Private First Class John Delury felt confident about the assault succeeding. "It was to begin with an exhilarating experience. As we were running we were watching the hill where the Germans were being pounded by artillery and smoke and we were on a kind of 'high'. We were in the midst of this battle watching it almost as spectators because no one was shooting at us. Then, when the whole battalion was strewn out across this open area, our artillery ceased firing. The smoke lifted from the German positions and it suddenly turned into a Kraut turkey shoot. They had machine guns well dug in and fortified in tiers across the side of the hill overlooking the field. Once the machine gun firing started, there was no protection for us..."[17]

As Private First Class Don Jakeway crossed the open field that was about to become a killing ground, he also observed the American artillery barrage cease. "Almost immediately, mortar and machine gun fire began to pour into our ranks. Also, we realized we were in a German minefield. Explosions, screams of, 'I'm hit,' echoed across the field. I began to run to the right, straight down the field, but not toward the hill. I have my jump jacket from that day, and a bullet hole is still visible through the collar of it, near my jump knife pocket.

"I was in shock. There were no officers to guide us. I learned later that the order to withdraw from the field had failed to get passed along to we of the front group. The officers were taking cover in the hedgerow in the approach to the field. With such wicked fire raining down upon us, I can understand their feeling of survival instinct.

"I continued to run and was frustrated by the slowness of my feet. How I managed to survive the crossing of this field, I will never know, but I am not ashamed to admit I was praying to God on every step I took. Afraid? You can bet on it. I finally reached the hedgerow at the end of the field. I was out of breath and it took a few minutes to realize that I was all alone. Peering beyond the hedgerow, I could see [Corporal] Bryant [C.] DeLoach, [Raymond C.] Ray Belair, and [Richard G.] Dick Tanner lying in a crumpled heap, their bodies torn apart by machine gun bullets. I later learned that over thirty men of H Company were either killed or wounded in the attack across this field. Of our immediate platoon of about twenty-four men, I was to find out only eight were able to get back to the company position where we had started from. I was one of those.

"As I lay hidden in the hedgerow, I could see the German weapons firing still. I zeroed in on a machine gun nest and emptied my clip in my M1. I am not sure how effective it was. Suddenly it became deathly still."[18]

Caught in the open field about 350 yards from the line of departure, Private First Class Delury and the other Company H troopers looked for a way to escape the rain of enemy machine gun fire directed at them. "We couldn't outrun the bullets and there was no cover to get behind. I hit the ground and made the smallest target I possibly could by putting my head toward the path of the enemy fire. My exposure in so doing was the width of my shoulders. I had no helmet since leaving it on the ground with [Private John] Posadas. My only headwear was a little wool knit cap, which afforded no protection. Even a spent bullet bouncing along the ground could have entered my skull. I was in weeds about three feet high and I could hear the bullets cutting them and making thudding sounds entering the ground around me. Every instinct told me to get my ass out of there, but my months of combat training overruled my instinct and said to stay put. If I stood up, I was a dead man."[19]

Company I followed Company H into the attack. Lieutenant Kelso Horne, the platoon leader of the 1st Platoon, moved out from a wooded area into the open field in front of the ridge. "I wasn't ten feet away from the edge of the woods when I went down. I never heard that shell coming, and it was a shell because I got the shell fragments. I didn't really know I was hit. It just felt like somebody hit me in the chest with a baseball bat. It knocked me down and when I got up, my pistol had fallen out of the holster.

"[Private First Class Daniel P.] Pat Collins, one of the men in my platoon who was with me also got a cut over his eye, apparently from the same shell. He was standing right there and he said, 'Lieutenant, you got hit too.'

"I said, 'It's just in my arm.'

"He was looking at my arm like that and he saw the hole in my jump jacket and he said, 'It's in your chest, too. You got a hole in your jump jacket under your arm. You got hit bad,' because it started bleeding then. I don't remember how far it was, but I was able to walk the whole way back to the tent hospital."[20]

Private First Class Fred Gladstone was one of five Company I troopers forming the point element advancing ahead of the company. "We quickly got into the grain and slid along on our stomachs. The German machine gun kept raking the area from side to side, cutting the grain over our heads. Our radio operator, Corporal George Petros, decided to run for it. He was hit as soon as he went past me. I can still remember the sickening sound of bullets hitting his body. I was about thirty feet from the safety of a hedgerow, and as I braced myself to make a run for it—'Wham!' A bullet made a huge hole in my entrenching tool and then tore through my thigh. It felt like a red-hot poker was thrust through me.

"By this time, all five of us had been hit and George Petros was dead. I couldn't move and was bleeding badly, but managed to get a compress bandage over one of the holes in my thigh. One of my buddies, [Private] Rene [A.] Croteau, crawled out to me and asked if he could help. I wanted a cigarette. Rene didn't smoke, but got one out of my pocket and helped me light it. The enemy spotted the smoke. The bullets started again and one smashed into my elbow."[21]

Pinned down in the open field, Private First Class Tom Porcella, tried to locate his Company H buddies. "I began to yell for Delury and he answered me. I asked him if he had contact with anybody in front of him. He answered no and he thought they all had been killed from the machine gun fire and the mortar fire. He asked where I was and I told him I was in this hedgerow. The grass was high and Delury started to crawl towards me. I kept talking so he could follow the direction of my voice. Finally, he arrived and I was darn glad to see him. He complained about all the crawling he had to do to reach me. The hedgerow [embankment] was about five feet high and here we had excellent protection. We could not understand why we were in an open field making this attack. The last few minutes left us very exhausted and we rested for a few minutes."[22]

Private Oliver W. Griffin was on the left side of the Company H skirmish line when he entered that deadly field below the ridge. "A German machine gun opened up with grazing fire. I dropped and just by luck I was lying in a low spot, just low enough he couldn't reach me. He must have known exactly where I was, because at the least movement he would open up. I couldn't turn my head without him firing. I must have stayed there for over an hour with him firing at me. Finally, he must have thought he got me as the firing slacked off. I decided to crawl over to the edge of the field where there was a drainage ditch. There, I met a medic who was crawling out into the field looking for wounded. I told him that I didn't know of anyone in front of me, but he wanted to stay and look. He told me to go down the ditch to the woods which led up the hill. There, he said I would find Sergeant [Duane] Morris wounded badly and on a stretcher. Even though Sergeant Morris was shot all the way through the side, he questioned me about what happened as if he was going to stay there and continue the action. I guess the morphine had dulled the pain to where he thought he could go on. I helped the medic carry Sergeant Morris out. Sergeant Morris later received [the Silver Star for heroism and] a battlefield commission."[23]

Pinned down with much of Company H in the field, Private First Class Fayette Richardson recalled his earlier premonition that he was going to die in this attack. "The Germans held a strong position on a hill. The officers in charge sent us across an open field toward the hill in a maneuver I still believe was a stupid blunder—much like the attack of Tennyson's light brigade. Wicked machine gun fire cut our men down like a scythe cutting grass. In a few minutes, thirty of our company of eighty lay dead or wounded in the field. The rest of us hugged the ground behind whatever we could find, and didn't know what to do next. I had followed [Sergeant William] Medford, and as usual, he was one of the first in the field. There were no officers that far in front nor any command noncoms I was aware of. Medford stood up, shouting to the balance of the company, and when he did, a bullet cut him down. He was killed instantly as the bullet had gone straight through the heart."[24]

As Lieutenant Colonel Mendez stood in the open observing the 3rd Battalion attack, his S-2, Lieutenant Paul Lehman, approached with a message. Lehman had survived a severed artery in his throat on D-Day, was captured, and then freed on June 16. As he spoke to Mendez, Lehman was wounded by German machine gun fire.

Mendez immediately put Lehman over his shoulder and began carrying him to safety. "I was trying to weave back and forth so the machine gun would miss us. I was carrying him over my shoulders—he was a 195-pounder.

"I can still hear the thud and I thought I had been hit. It didn't hurt me though—it was Paul being hit again. So I was taking a dead man off of combat, and that was the biggest cry I'd ever had."[25] After the fighting that day, when news spread of Lehman's death, the entire battalion was saddened by the loss.

The 3rd Battalion was pinned down and being raked by German machine guns by the time the 319th Glider Field Artillery Battalion's second liaison and forward observer party arrived. As Lieutenant Marvin Ragland and his party started across the open area to get close enough to adjust the artillery fire on the German positions, they were hit by a mortar barrage. "A couple of more guys got hit. There was a blast and I hit the ditch. I did get skinned up on the arm—a flesh wound on the arm—but mostly I got a concussion out of it. The first thing I knew, the rest of them were gone."[26]

Lieutenant Ragland, suffering from the effects of the concussion, got up and made his way to the rear where at a road, he saw a jeep pulling up. "For some reason this driver—I don't know who he was—decided he better do something, so he took me back to our battalion aid station. Colonel [James] Todd got a hold of the doctor and said, 'Get him patched up.'"[27]

The 3rd Battalion remained without the critical artillery fire support from the 319th. Pinned down by enemy fire, Lieutenant Ralph DeWeese knew he had to take quick action to keep the troopers of his 2nd Platoon of Company H from all being killed. "I thought about going to the right, and just then the Germans started pouring in timed artillery fire. It was a terrific barrage and pulverized the ground. I knew we had to do something quick, because the Jerries would soon start firing mortars and would have gotten us all. Finally, I told the men to follow and I started going down a [ditch next to a] hedgerow that was full of water. We didn't mind getting in the water because we knew we had to get out and do it quickly. All along the hedgerow was a solid line of dead and wounded of the 2nd Battalion that had gone through there. As I went along, the wounded kept cautioning me to stay down, because most of the men were in the same position when they were hit. We started crawling on our stomachs then. I stopped to talk to one wounded man, and he asked me if I would cut some weeds that were preventing him from stretching his legs. I cut them and helped him to straighten out his leg. Word was passed up to hurry, because they were laying mortar fire. Guess we got out just in time. We kept going a good distance, about two miles I would say, and came out on a road where there were some of our tank destroyers. I knew we were safe then. Checked up on the men and found we had only lost one man. His name was [Corporal Theodore] Svendsen, and he was hit in the neck when he turned around to follow me out. He died instantly, the men told me."[28]

During the withdrawal by Company H, Private First Class Don Jakeway came upon a wounded trooper with his back against a hedgerow embankment. "As I approached, he kept waving for me to stay low. I was doing this already, but pressed even lower as I got to him. He had been wounded and could not walk. He was lying where he had been first struck by a bullet, and warned me that fire was still occasionally coming his way. I waited for a few minutes and told him I was going to move along and he was coming with me. I was amazed when he absolutely refused to let me help him or carry him. He complained of so much pain. I swear that I insisted that we both go on, but he was adamant and refused to budge. I did put as much sulfa powder on the wounds that I could see, and promising that if I found fellow troopers, would return for him. To this day, it haunts me that I had to leave this comrade behind. I have often wondered how he made out, because even though I did eventually find my way back to the lines and told the medics about this man, I never saw him again."[29]

When the word was passed to withdraw, Private First Class Tom Porcella and one of his buddies who were not near any other Company H troopers did not receive the order. "Delury and I believed that we were the only ones alive from Company H. We started this attack with about eighty men. Both of us began to holler as loud as we could—trying to contact some of the troopers, but we received no answer. We decided to go up the hedgerow in the direction of the attack. While we were advancing, we heard someone call for H Company men. Delury and I stopped and we pointed our rifles in the direction of the voice. The voice was of Sergeant [Vance V.] Jenkins. When he reached us, he told us we had the order to pull back to the rear. He asked if anyone else was with us. We replied no. Then we asked him, 'Where the hell are all the men?'

"He told us that we were almost wiped out and he was trying to assemble as many as he could to prepare for a counterattack. Delury and I looked at each other when he said counterattack. So far we had only seen three men. We began to run down the hedgerow as fast as we could, following Sergeant Jenkins. We reached the corner of a field and the sergeant said to halt at this field. And when we got there he told us to go straight. Delury for some reason said, 'No, no, no, let's go to the right. Don't go left.' Just as we arrived at the far corner of the field, a shell landed just about where we would have been if we would have gone straight like Sergeant Jenkins suggested. John Delury's premonition saved our lives."[30]

When Privates First Class Tom Porcella and John Delury reached safety they were unable to find any other Company H troopers. Porcella eventually found a Company H officer. "We contacted Lieutenant [William J.] Garry and with him he had a trooper named [Private] Charles [E.] Muffley. We kept asking him about the rest of the men. The lieutenant just looked at us and he wouldn't answer us. So, Delury and I just looked at each other as though we could read each other's thoughts. All of a sudden, I felt a numbness come over us when I saw all that was left was one lieutenant, one sergeant, and three privates. And that was all that remained of our company so far. Lieutenant Garry immediately gave us orders to take our positions and be prepared for a counterattack on the far side of the road. I kept wondering, 'How are five men going to stand off a counterattack if they come down in force?' This was ridiculous. Fear gripped us all. As ridiculous as the orders were, we obeyed the lieutenant. But, we were well aware of the consequences if there was a counterattack.

"All at once there was dropping of German artillery. It started to fall on the road that we were near. We scattered to the hedgerows again. Muffley and I were together in this hedgerow. The lieutenant, Sergeant Jenkins, and Delury took off for cover some other direction. It seemed to be a concentrated artillery barrage, but it seemed to be falling a long way from where we were. The Germans were known to quickly change their range and drop the shells short in order to catch us without protection.

"While Muffley and I were hugging the ground when the shells seemed to be getting closer, Muffley asked me, 'Tom, what are we going to do?'

"I looked at him, 'Muffley, I'm going to start praying.'

"He said to me in sort of a frightened voice, 'Tom, I don't know how to pray.'

"So I told him, 'Don't worry, Muffley, I'll pray for the both of us.'

"After about an hour the shells stopped falling. Muffley and I went across the road and we joined what was left of our company. It was well in the late afternoon and after awhile a few more troopers came down from the top of the hill. Up to this time, I only counted thirty men. All those troopers seemed to have blank stares on their faces. The best way to describe their expression is that they seemed lost in their world. Those of us who never made it up that hill tried to get the information as to what happened. They didn't tell us too much. They were in no mood to speak. But they all agreed that our artillery stopped firing too soon and the troopers were caught out in the open field with no protection to advance the attack. We heard remarks such as, 'We were wiped out. We got caught in the crossfire. We were chopped to pieces by the mortar fire.'"[31]

After the counterattack failed to materialize, Private First Class John Delury and the other surviving Company H troopers started taking a count of the casualties. Delury learned that one of his closest friends, Corporal Bryant C. DeLoach, had been one of those killed. "Someone told me he got hit in the kneecap and when he involuntarily sat up to hold his knee, the machine gun riddled him. They said you could see the sun on his red beard pointing skyward as he lay in the field of dead."[32] DeLoach had left behind a young wife and small son.

When Lieutenant Ralph DeWeese and the survivors of Company H reached a safe area, he told the troopers to stay there while he checked out the situation. "As yet, I didn't have any idea what had happened to the rest of the battalion. I found out where the regiment CP was and inquired there. They told me the battalion had to withdraw and were back in the position we had left from.

"That was really news to me. I got the troops and took them back to the area. The company was surely glad to see us, because before we got there, they only had fourteen in the company. Lieutenant [William] Garry explained they had lost contact and he couldn't give us the order to withdraw. I must say that is one Fourth of July I'll never forget. We were certainly lucky to get out of that mess.

"Just after getting back, I was going into the CP and a couple of 88s cracked right over my head. They hit about ten yards ahead of me and just happened to hit the top of a hedgerow, so all the shrapnel went the other way.

"I had several wounded that day—lost Sergeant [Ward T.] Ecoff, Private [First Class Gerrit] Van Vels, and Private [First Class Theodore H.] Lucht. Later, we lost Private [First Class William E.] Pollock, who was wounded going out after wounded men."[33]

While waiting for Lieutenant DeWeese to return with information about the battalion, Private First Class Fayette "Rich" Richardson witnessed something that caused him to barely contain his rage. "There on the hillside, safely back from the front, I heard two colonels in clean uniforms, watching through field glasses and coolly criticizing the technique in crossing the field. I later had daydreams of demonstrating a technique for them, like leveling my Thompson at them and squeezing off a couple of magazines at waist level.

"But through the years, my memory has been of [Sergeant William] Medford and what he stood for. One of my sons is named after him. I can't equal his courage, but I like to think I have carried on some of his legacy—standing up for things worth fighting for."[34]

With the 2nd Battalion on Hill 95 and the 3rd Battalion withdrawn to the line of departure, a gap existed between the two battalions. Division headquarters ordered the badly depleted 2nd Battalion, 507th Parachute Infantry to cover the gap and it moved into position east of Blanchelande. By 3:00 p.m. this battalion established an outpost line covering the gap.

Division headquarters issued an order late that afternoon for securing the 3rd Battalion objective. The 2nd Battalion, 507th sent a strong combat patrol to the high point center of the ridge, followed by the remainder of the battalion that night, and was in position on the ridge by 4:37 a.m. on July 5.

East of the 3rd Battalion attack, the 1st Battalion prepared to take the ridge at the town of la Poterie by moving around the left flank and avoiding an open draw to its south. Company B would lead the battalion's assault. At dawn that morning, Sergeant Bill Call, a squad leader with the 2nd Platoon of Company B, was dug in with his men awaiting orders. "Lieutenant [Walter] Ling was called back to get the order of attack and he came back and gave it to [Staff Sergeant Harold J.] Brogan and the squad leaders. The attack was to take this hill. We had maybe 1,500 yards to go and every thirty or forty yards you had a hedgerow to go over or go through. One of the platoons was to be on our left flank and one on our right flank."[35]

When the 1st Battalion reached the line of departure, information arrived that the 325th Glider Infantry was advancing along the ridge perpendicular to the battalion's planned axis of advance and was shelling the battalion's objective. As a result the 1st Battalion couldn't make the attack as planned. A new attack plan was devised to attack south across the open draw to assault the ridge.

While awaiting further orders, Lieutenant Homer Jones and Sergeant Bud Warnecke, both with Company B, were conferring when a German machine gun opened fire on them. Sergeant Warnecke was wounded in the left shoulder. "It seemed as if it was going to tear my shoulder off. It knocked me down, spun me around, and apparently as I was going down, put a couple of holes through my canteen. At this time, Lieutenant Jones was hit through the neck and blood was squirting out from both sides. He was in horrible pain. We hollered for a medic, and also at the same time, there was a sergeant nearby by the name of [Roland W.] Fecteau.

"Jones was saying, 'Let me die, let me die, let me die.'

"Fecteau took two fingers and plugged up the holes where the bullet went in and out."[36]

Sergeant Sherman Van Enwyck, with Company A, was nearby when the two Company B troopers were cut down. "We were under fierce 88, mortar, machine gun, and sniper fire. We were pinned to the ground unable to progress or change our route. Many men were hit, among them, Lieutenant Jones. Calling to the rear for aid, we were soon surprised to see Captain [David] Axelrod [the assistant surgeon of the 1st Battalion] double time boldly to the scene of action followed by four litter bearers. Captain Axelrod, with utter disregard for his own safety, proceeded to administer first aid to Lieutenant Jones. Lieutenant Jones, being shot through the throat, was in very critical condition. A delay in aid to Lieutenant Jones would have been fatal had not Captain Axelrod given him blood plasma there at the scene."[37]

Lieutenant Jones somehow remained conscious. "I was seriously wounded and bleeding heavily when Captain Axelrod came forward to give me treatment. Although my position was with the advance element, in spite of the fact that the artillery fire was intense and close range direct fire, the danger from snipers and automatic weapons being great, Captain Axelrod stopped the bleeding and gave me plasma with complete disregard for his own personal safety. When the shells would fall close by, he shielded me with his own body."[38]

Lieutenant Rex Combs, with Company A, was also a witness to the heroism of Captain Axelrod. "After placing Lieutenant Jones on the stretcher, Captain Axelrod walked on the side that the enemy was firing from, to prevent any fire from hitting Lieutenant Jones.

"On moving out, Captain Axelrod heard that there were other wounded lying directly in front of enemy positions. After making sure that Lieutenant Jones was all right, he placed him in a covered position, and asking someone to show him where the wounded were, he proceeded through the hedgerows and across the fields to render aid and carry the wounded men out to safety. During the numerous trips, Captain Axelrod was being continually fired upon, though his Red Cross arm band was in plain view. After rendering medical aid and seeing that the men were evacuated, Captain Axelrod started to the rear again with Lieutenant Jones. They had covered only a short distance when enemy artillery began to fall around them. Setting the stretcher down, Captain Axelrod ordered those assisting him in carrying the stretcher to take cover, while he covered Lieutenant Jones with his own body to prevent him from being hit by the shrapnel.

"After personally supervising and helping to carry the injured to the rear, Captain Axelrod returned to our front line and continued his work. Though there was one wounded man it was impossible to get to, as the enemy had killed and wounded other aid men who attempted to reach him, Captain Axelrod made several attempts, and finally just as it got dark succeeded in evacuating him."[39] Captain David Axelrod was later awarded the Silver Star for his heroism on that terrible day.

When the delayed attack began, Company B crossed the line of departure and attacked toward the ridge. Sergeant Bill Call and his 2nd Platoon squad were deployed in a skirmish line. "We headed out and [Staff] Sergeant Brogan, who was a hell of a good leader and a great soldier, had us cutting holes through the hedgerows instead of going over the hedgerows. We were firing and receiving no fire. We were using walking fire. We started going through and over these hedgerows. Brogan would climb on top of them and would wave us through and we kept going.

"[Corporal Robert L.] Bobby Stutt had hurt his knee on the jump and kind of walked with a great limp. So, I was chopping the holes and going through, and [then] he would crawl through the holes.

"We got to this hedgerow and I was chopping the hole, and he pushed me and said, 'I'm going through this one.'

"He pushed me on my tail and I said, 'You son of a gun!' I crawled through the hole after him. I just got on my feet on the other side of the hedgerow and that's when I saw the rifle fire on our left flank. I saw this tracer hit him in the shoulder. When I got to him, I rolled him over and I didn't recognize him. His face was black...I am sure the heart exploded, because he was dead when I turned him over. His mouth was gaping back and forth. He died instantly, he went down like a...

"We were all out in this open field. Then Brogan got shot through the gut. This German rifle fire and the sniper were taking us one by one. This sniper was taking his time and picking one off at a time. We were all in the open, the whole platoon. When we got to the next hedgerow facing towards the hill, we discovered the fire was only coming from the left flank.

"[Lieutenant Walter Ling] came up to me and said, 'Sergeant, I'm going back to the company and see what's going on.' The other platoon should have been on our left flank, and one on our right. You know, I didn't know what in the hell to do. Brogan was shot through the gut in the middle of the field. [The sniper] was picking us off. So, [Lieutenant Ling] took off running to the rear."[40]

What was unknown to Sergeant Call was that shortly after the attack began and Company B crossed the line of departure, the 325th Glider Infantry, which was fighting astride the spine of the ridge, was approaching German positions that would be the new 1st Battalion objective. The 325th advised the 1st Battalion that it planned to advance through the area selected as the new objective for the attack. The objective was once more shifted to a point on the ridge west of the 325th sector. An order was issued for Company B to return to the line of departure and await a new attack plan. The other two platoons of

Company B received the word and withdrew, but Lieutenant Ling's 2nd Platoon didn't get the order and remained in the field it had reached earlier.

The situation was desperate when Sergeant Call decided to take charge of the 2nd Platoon. "I got the guys and I said, 'Over to the other hedgerow on the right flank,' so we would be facing that left flank and we would have that hedgerow as protection. Then they started zeroing in with the 88.

"We were at the base of the hill. It was no big hill. We were starting to dig slit trenches to get some cover. Every so often the 88 would zero in. [Private Paul E.] Owens was up on a tree that had been knocked down. He was extended up in the air there...I don't know what the hell good he was doing there.

"I said, 'Come on, get over here and start digging.' They got Owens with the 88...picked the top of his head off...killed right away.

"[Private First Class Alphonse "Al"] Caplik was near him. Al had a grenade in his pocket of his jump pants. One of the pieces of the shrapnel hit his leg and set the powder on fire in the grenade. And God, he was screaming and hollering. I pulled him down off the little pine where he was at and ripped his pocket open with my jump knife. And God, the thing is fuming and the blisters started to come up on his leg. We got rid of the grenade. I said, 'Can you make it back?'

"He said, 'Yeah.' So he started crawling back towards the rear.

"[Private First Class Michael S. Niklauski] Mickey Nichols was hit in the forehead with the shrapnel from that 88 and was bleeding like a stuck hog.

"Brogan was the last one lying out there. It's July 4th, and it's about one hundred degrees in the sun. He was out there in the middle of that field for maybe an hour and a half.

"[Private First Class] Clyde [W.] Moline and [Corporal] Jack Gunter came up to me and said, 'Sergeant, we want to go out and get Brogan,' who was lying in the middle of this field. When I picked my head up and looked over the hedgerow, our medic, [Private John A.] Detwiler was out there and he's trying to wrap a bandage around his gut. That damned sniper shot him in the wrist where he was bandaging him and he came crawling back. I sent him to the rear. The hand was paralyzed and I never saw him after that.

"I said to the guys, 'You just saw what happened to Detwiler.'

"Well, they wanted to do it. I said, 'OK, we'll try to give you some covering fire.' But there was nothing to fire at.

"So they went out, they brought him back, and they got him to the hedgerow on the other side of right where I was digging. That damned 88 landed right in that area and it killed Jack immediately. Clyde hopped over on top of me and he said, 'Oh God, Jack is dead. Gunter is dead.'

"I said, What about Brogan?"

"He said, 'I guess he's all right.' So I went back over [the hedgerow] with Clyde and we lifted Brogan over and Jack Gunter, he was dead...he was gone. I was waiting for [Lieutenant] Ling to get back, to give me some sort of direction.

You know you're never supposed to retreat. I don't know what the hell good we were doing up there getting shot at.

"This Lieutenant [Carl A.] Smith [the Company B executive officer] crawled up and wanted to survey the situation. I said, 'God, look at it here. We're defenseless here and all we've got are M1s.'

"He said, 'Just hold your position, and I'm going to send a medic back up with some plasma for Brogan.' Well, he did. The medic came up and put the bottle up. And that damned sniper shot that bottle as soon as it was exposed. We had to take the needle out of Brogan. God, the guy was suffering, but he was very brave, he didn't say much.

"First Sergeant [James W.] Jim Smith came up to report that they were going to shell this hill."[41]

The VII Corps and 82nd Airborne Division artillery planned a twenty minute concentration on the 1st and 3rd Battalion objectives on the ridge at 12:15 p.m., in coordination with an assault by both battalions commencing at the same time.

Up at the base of the ridge, when told of the impending barrage, Sergeant Call knew they needed better cover, but there was not time to dig proper positions. "We had these slit trenches dug, but not enough of them, however. Jimmy Smith took one, and we had a few minutes before they were going to start the barrage.

"Jim and I exchanged prayers...there is a Catholic prayer to the Blessed Virgin called 'The Memorare.' Jim had in his helmet, a prayer, 'The Lord Is My Shepherd.' I said, 'Why don't we trade and read each other's.'

"They started the barrage and it only lasted maybe five or ten minutes. They bombarded the hill in front of us. They traversed up the hill, then back down the hill, back up the hill, and down the hill. I have never experienced anything like that. I can see why the Germans when the artillery barrage hit them would be shaking and give up in a hurry.

"I laid on top of Brogan to give him a little protection. The impact would lift me right off of the top of Brogan...and Sergeant Smith, the same way in his hole. We were bouncing from the concussion.

"The problem was on our left flank. I couldn't figure out what the hell they were doing? There was nobody on that hill. I don't know how it got screwed up, with the wounded going back and explaining where the fire was coming from.

"Brogan asked for a drink of water. He had a hole in his gut like [the size of] a volleyball. You could see his guts. We were advised in our training to never give anybody who had a stomach wound a drink of water, because it was an avenue for an infection. It would travel through their whole system. I gave him a drink of water. I didn't give him much. It was running right out through the hole. He begged for more. And I didn't give him more...I wish I would have.

"It didn't get dark there until about 10:30 at night. We've been there in that situation since about 7:00 that morning. I had no authority to pull back, but we did. About 8:30 that night, Smitty and I got Brogan on a half-shelter and started dragging him and lifting him over these hedgerows. And when we got back to the company area, which was about four hundred yards or so, my first question to Lieutenant [Carl] Smith was, 'Where's Lieutenant Ling?'

"He said, 'He's not here.'

"I said, 'Where is he, lieutenant?'

"'I don't know.'

"They had sent him back to the rear—he had some sort of nervous breakdown. I could have killed the son of a bitch. I found out after getting the instructions he was supposed to have, that he took us four hundred yards farther than we were supposed to go. There's nothing as bad as someone sitting on your flank picking you off one by one, especially when you can't see where the fire is coming from.

"When we got back, Brogan was taken to a medical tent. They put him in it. That was the last I saw of Brogan. [Technician Fifth Grade] Bill Dean told me that he saw Brogan on the hood of a jeep that night, and he was dead. Brogan and I were both Catholic. He was a Canuck."[42]

Extremely heavy German automatic weapons, mortar, and artillery fire had stopped both the 1st and 3rd Battalion attempts to assault the la Poterie ridge during daylight. The 1st Battalion objective was captured by the 325th Glider Infantry advancing west along the spine of the ridgeline. The 1st Battalion was placed in division reserve at 4:52 a.m. on July 5, occupying the positions held earlier by the 2nd Battalion, 507th Parachute Infantry.

Private First Class Tom Porcella, with Company H, probably felt like the soldiers of his father's generation who had made courageous, yet senseless frontal assaults against entrenched enemy positions during World War I. "The losses were heavy throughout the entire regiment we were told. July 4, 1944 is a day that will long be remembered by the survivors of the men of the 508 and the 82nd Airborne Division, because we practically got annihilated.

"After the battle of July 4th, we were told that an overlay map that was taken from a German prisoner and the map showed that the position had about twenty-eight machine guns and mortars zeroed in on that big open field that we ran across. We lost many lives and had many wounded. We were in no position to carry on. Then we were told that we were going to be held in reserve.

"When the battle of the 4th of July was over and the troopers were left with their memories of what happened to all those who were wounded and dead on that hill, we began to huddle in small groups with our heads bowed. No one spoke—just blank looks on our faces. It was a pitiful sight to see troopers in such a saddened condition and it was also hard for us to accept the loss of so many men in such a short time.

"The shock settled on us and we realized that we were through as a fighting unit at this time. There were not enough of us to continue, so we knew what was left of the regiment would be returning to England. The attack had lasted about forty-five minutes and each company had almost fifty casualties. It was the last organized attack that was made by the 508 and I believe of the 82nd Airborne Division. Our losses were many and we experienced a terrible emotional shock, which showed on the faces of the survivors. It isn't possible for me to describe the feelings of the others during the last battle, speaking for myself."[43]

When Lieutenant Colonel Mark Alexander learned of the costly fight for Hill 95, he was angered by the unnecessary loss of life. "They went right across the open space and straight up the hill instead of taking advantage of the woods. There was no reason why they should go across that open valley. I knew if they did they would get their butts blown off. It shouldn't have been that way. They really got nailed and a lot of guys got killed.

"After the war, I asked Captain [Chet] Graham, who took command after I was hit, 'Why did you guys go across the open valley?'

"He said, 'We had our orders to go straight ahead, so we did.'

"Lindquist stayed back in his CP and never did even come up before giving those orders, I found out afterwards. I know he didn't do reconnaissance. It's foolish, in fact. But he was more of a guy that commanded from back a-ways. He always laid back and relied on information from others, and you generally can't do it that way and be successful. Can't do it.

"That operation always bothered me, because I know if I'd been there, a lot of these guys wouldn't have lost their lives."[44]

The 508th reported its effective strength to division headquarters near midnight as 58 officers and 780 men. The attacks of July 4 had cost the regiment 214 casualties. Five officers had been killed that 4th of July, Captains John Breen, the regimental S-2; and George Simonds, the 2nd Battalion S-3; Lieutenants Mack G. Cook, an assistant platoon leader with Company F; John Daly, the commanding officer of Company I; and Paul Lehman, the 3rd Battalion S-2.

BY THE NIGHT OF JULY 4, SERGEANT ZANE SCHLEMMER, with Headquarters Company, 2nd Battalion, who had been wounded by American artillery shrapnel the day before and evacuated from Hill 131 to Utah Beach, was aboard a hospital ship on his way to a hospital in England. "They had to cut off my dirty, bloody, stinking jumpsuit, which I had worn continuously for the past twenty-nine days without a bath. I insisted that they let me keep my jump boots on when they operated on my wounds, for they were my most prized possession.

"I marveled at the incredible luxuries of the navy. Clean blankets, a white sheet, canned peaches, white bread, fruit juice, and real coffee—all of which were foreign and forgotten by us in those Norman hedgerows in which we had endured."[45]

ON JULY 5, THE REGIMENT MAINTAINED ITS POSITIONS and conducted aggressive patrolling to its front. At 6:00 p.m. the following day, a group of enemy troops were encountered by a patrol of the 2nd Battalion south of Hill 95, along the east-west highway running toward La Haye-du-Puits. At 9:45 p.m., Company F, supported by three tanks attacked the enemy positions and met heavy resistance, but cleared the area.

At 10:00 a.m. on July 7, the regiment was ordered to assemble in the vicinity of Blanchelande as division reserve, which was completed by 11:45 a.m. The 508th remained in division reserve until July 11.

Lieutenant Ralph DeWeese's birthday was July 10. "The only celebration I had was a field shower and the news we were going to move to the beach the next day. The 507th was close by so I went over to see if by any chance Lieutenant [James F.] Clarke was there. He and I went through CC [the Civilian Conservation Corps] together and were the best of friends. Much to my disappointment I found he had been killed.

"On the 11th, we got new uniforms and got all set to move to the beach. I must say that was a grand and glorious feeling after being in the front lines thirty-three days and wearing the same clothes all that time.

"We moved up close to the beach and the first night about eleven o'clock the Jerries flew over. All the antiaircraft opened up and it was quite a sight to see all the tracers. The next morning we moved down to the beach and it was quite a sight to see, with all the boats, etcetera. To see all the wreckage made me feel that maybe we were lucky at that to come in by air. A lot of men must have lost their lives on that beach. When the tide went out we loaded an LST.

The loading table for the 82nd Airborne Division reflected a badly depleted division. The individual units of the 508th loaded into just over two LSTs for the return trip to England. The first LST contained Headquarters and Headquarters Company with 148; Headquarters Company, 1st Battalion with 90, Company A with 49; Company B with 47; Company C with 34; and Company D with 58; for a total of 426 officers and men. The second LST loaded Headquarters Company, 2nd Battalion with 129; Company E with 70; Company F with 32; Company G with 72; and Headquarters Company, 3rd Battalion with 103; for a total of 406 officers and men. The third LST contained Company H with 56, and Company I with 51, for a total of 107.

For Lieutenant DeWeese and others, the food served aboard the ship and the beds with clean sheets were something akin to heaven compared to what they had experienced over the last month. "We had an awfully nice trip across the channel, and the food and quarters were great. Maybe you think it wasn't a grand sight when we saw England again. We landed at Southampton and took a train back to Nottingham. When we got back to camp, hot chow was awaiting us, and our bedrolls."[46]

On August 22, 1944, the 508th received a distinguished unit award for its performance during the first four days of the Normandy campaign. The citation read:

The 508th Parachute Infantry is cited for outstanding performance of duty in action against the enemy between 6 and 9 June 1944, during the invasion of France. The Regiment landed by parachute shortly after 0200 hours, 6 June 1944. Intense antiaircraft and machine gun fire was directed against the approaching planes and parachutist drops. Enemy mobile antiairborne landing groups immediately engaged assembled elements of the Regiment and reinforced their opposition with heavily supported reserve units. Elements of the Regiment seized Hill 30, in the wedge between the Merderet and Douve Rivers, and fought vastly superior enemy forces for three days. From this position, they continually threatened German units moving in from the west, as well as the enemy forces opposing the crossing of our troops over the Merderet near La Fière and Chef-du-Pont. They likewise denied the enemy opportunity to throw reinforcements to the east where they could oppose the beach landings. The troops on Hill 30 finally broke through to join the airborne troops at the bridgehead west of La Fière on 9 June 1944. They had repelled continuous attacks from infantry, tanks, mortars, and artillery for more than 60 hours without resupply. Other elements of the 508th Parachute Infantry fought courageously in the bitter fighting west of the Merderet River and in winning the bridgeheads across that river at La Fière and Chef-du-Pont. The Regiment secured its objectives through heroic determination and initiative. Every member performed his duties with exemplary aggressiveness and superior skill. The courage and devotion to duty shown by members of the 508th Parachute Infantry are worthy of emulation and reflect the highest traditions of the Army of the United States.

PHOTO GALLERY

At Saltby airfield, paratroopers with the 508th Parachute Infantry receive V-mail blanks to write last letters home, June 5, 1944. *U.S. Army Signal Corps photograph, courtesy of the 82nd Airborne Division War Memorial Museum.*

The regiment's troopers check equipment at Saltby airfield on the evening of June 5, 1944. *U.S. Army Signal Corps photograph, courtesy of the 82nd Airborne Division War Memorial Museum.*

One of the thirty-six 82nd Airborne Division paratroopers who drowned in the waters of the flooded Merderet and Douve Rivers. *U.S. Army Signal Corps photograph, courtesy of the 82nd Airborne Division War Memorial Museum.*

Troopers with Headquarters Company's S-2 section move through St. Marcouf, France, June 6, 1944. *U.S. Army Signal Corps photograph, courtesy of www.histomil.com.*

PHOTO GALLERY

Captain Kenneth L. Johnson (assistant regimental S-4 and munitions officer), Captain Robert Abraham (commanding officer of Headquarters Company), Staff Sergeant Worster M. Morgan, Technician Fifth Grade Donald J. MacLeod, Private First Class Luther M. Tillery, Private First Class Joel R. Lander, Private First Class James R. Kumler, and Private John G. McCall, take a break in the village of St. Marcouf, France, June 6, 1944. *U.S. Army Signal Corps photograph, courtesy of www.histomil.com.*

Staff Sergeant Worster M. Morgan, with the regimental S-2 section, speaks with a citizen of St. Marcouf, France, June 6, 1944. *U.S. Army Signal Corps photograph, courtesy of www.histomil.com.*

Captain Kenneth L. Johnson, assistant S-4 and regimental munitions officer, and S-2 section troopers speak with citizens of St. Marcouf, France, June 6, 1944. *U.S. Army Signal Corps photograph, courtesy of www.histomil.com.*

Private Robert B. White, with Company A, has just taken the pay book from a dead German soldier. Note the two holes in the right sleeve of his jumpsuit, caused by a bullet's near miss. *Photograph courtesy of Henry E. Le Febvre.*

One of French Renault tanks of Panzer Ersatz und Ausbildungs Abteilung 100 destroyed by the 80th Airborne Antiaircraft (Antitank) Battalion. *Photograph courtesy of Mrs. James Baugh.*

A German vehicle park north of Baupte, France, captured by the 2nd Battalion, June 13, 1944. *U.S. Army Signal Corps photograph courtesy of www.histomil.com.*

Lieutenant Briand N. Beaudin (left), assistant surgeon of the 3rd Battalion, and Lieutenant Paul E. Lehman (right), 3rd Battalion S-1, celebrate liberation from a German hospital at Orglandes, June 16, 1944. *Dispatch Photo News Service photograph, courtesy of the 82nd Airborne Division War Memorial Museum.*

PUT US DOWN IN HELL

Flying in nine plane V-of-Vs formations, C-47 aircraft transport elements of the 508th Parachute Infantry Regiment to Holland, September 17, 1944. *U.S. Army Air Corps photograph, courtesy of the 82nd Airborne Division War Memorial Museum.*

Parachutes of the 508th Parachute Infantry Regiment descend over DZ "T" on the afternoon of September 17, 1944. Smoke rises on the left and right sides of the photo from two C-47s shot down by enemy antiaircraft fire. *Photograph courtesy of the Cornelius Ryan Collection, Alden Library, Ohio University.*

PHOTO GALLERY

Aerial photograph of Nijmegen, Holland, taken by 541 Squadron, British Royal Air Force, September 19, 1944. The Waal River railroad and highway bridges are at the upper left and right respectively, with the Keizer Lodewijkplein traffic circle just below the highway bridge in the photo. The Keizer Karelplein traffic circle where the 1st Battalion was stopped on the night of September 17, 1944 is at the lower left center of the photograph. *Photograph courtesy of Frits Janssen.*

The bodies of Private Walter Dikoon and Private First Class Ray M. Johnson, both with Company A, in the traffic circle at the Keizer Karelplein in Nijmegen, where they were killed during the night of September 17, 1944. *Photograph from author's collection.*

Brigadier General James M. Gavin visits the 508th command post during the morning of September 18, 1944 to obtain a situation report from Colonel Roy E. Lindquist (without helmet talking on the radio). *U.S. Army photograph, courtesy of the Cornelius Ryan Collection, Alden Library, Ohio University.*

PHOTO GALLERY

An aerial photograph of Thorensche Molen, Holland taken by 541 Squadron, British Royal Air Force, September 19, 1944. The Wyler Meer is at the lower left corner of the photo, with the Quer-Damm extending diagonally from the bottom left of the photo to the dike road slightly southeast of Thorensche Molen. On September 23, Company G attacked astride the dike road (from the top left of the photo) southeast to Thorensche Molen. *Photograph courtesy of Frits Janssen.*

Major General James M. Gavin in front of the 3rd Battalion command post at Erria, Belgium, December 29, 1944. *U.S. Army photograph, courtesy of the 82nd Airborne Division War Memorial Museum.*

PHOTO GALLERY

Captain Joseph P. Kenny, the Catholic chaplain, holds Mass for 3rd Battalion troopers, January 6, 1945, the day before the battalion led the assault on the Thier-du-Mont ridge. *U.S. Army Signal Corps photograph, National Archives.*

Troopers of the 508th Parachute Infantry Regiment at the assembly area at Les Avenanterres, Belgium, January 6, 1945, in preparation for the assault on the Thier-du-Mont ridge the following day. *U.S. Army Signal Corps photograph, National Archives.*

One of the German Mark VI Tiger II tank at Goronne, Belgium, which fired on the 508th Parachute Infantry and its supporting armor during the assault on the Thier-du-Mont ridge, January 7, 1945. The tank was knocked out and the crew killed. *U.S. Army photograph, courtesy of the 82nd Airborne Division War Memorial Museum.*

Lieutenant John P. Foley, executive officer of Company A, is awarded the Distinguished Service Cross by Lieutenant General Lewis Brereton, commander of the First Allied Airborne Army, for extraordinary heroism during the capture and defense of Hill 75.9 (Devil's Hill) in Holland. The award ceremony was held January 20, 1945 at Remouchamps, Belgium. *U.S. Army Signal Corps photograph, National Archives.*

PHOTO GALLERY

Troopers ride a tank into Deidenberg, Belgium north of St.-Vith, January 22, 1945. *U.S. Army photograph, courtesy of the 82nd Airborne Division War Memorial Museum.*

Weasels were used to evacuate wounded and bring up supplies in the deep snow of eastern Belgium during the drive to the German border. *U.S. Army Signal Corps photograph, National Archives.*

Major General James M. Gavin awards the Distinguished Service Cross to First Sergeant Leonard A. Funk, Jr., with Company C, for extraordinary heroism during the assault to clear LZ "T" in Holland. The awards ceremony was at Camp Sissonne, France on March 19, 1945. *U.S. Army Signal Corps photograph, National Archives.*

Major General James M. Gavin awards the Distinguished Service Cross to Sergeant Lyle K. Kumler, with Company H, for extraordinary heroism during fighting at Beek, Holland. The awards ceremony was at Camp Sissonne, France on March 19, 1945. *U.S. Army Signal Corps photograph, National Archives.*

CHAPTER 9

"PUT US DOWN IN HELL"

Returning from Normandy, many of the officers and men found the cots of their best buddies empty. Many had been wounded and some of them would return. Others, too severely wounded, would carry painful scars, limps, disfigurements, and paralysis with them as constant reminders of their sacrifice and service with the regiment. Still others were buried in Normandy, never to return to their loved ones and buddies. From an initial strength of 2,055, only 939 returned from Normandy with the regiment. At the end of the Normandy campaign the 508th reported 307 killed in action, 26 died of wounds, 3 died of injuries, 487 wounded in action, 173 injured in action, and 165 missing in action. Many of those missing in action were later reported as prisoners, a few of which escaped and returned to the regiment.

The 508th had inflicted even more casualties on the Wehrmacht, however. The regiment officially captured 554 enemy soldiers, seventy-five vehicles, and eight field pieces. It was credited with destroying twenty enemy tanks. A count of enemy killed and wounded was not kept.

Corporal George D. "Darrell" Glass, a replacement assigned to Company C, had arrived at Wollaton Park just before the Normandy invasion, when the regiment was at the airfields. While the regiment was still fighting in Normandy, Corporal Glass had been called upon to perform a heartbreaking task. "I got a call up to regimental headquarters because I could type. I joined about six or seven other guys and we were assigned to type the letters [of condolence] to relatives—mothers and fathers. We cried every damn day. It really brought the war to our hearts."[1]

Thirty-four Company C officers and men made the trip back to Nottingham with the regiment. Corporal Glass and the other C Company replacements were present when they arrived. "I was standing out in the company area, ready to salute the guys when they came marching into the C Company area. When they started into the company area, we could hear them coming. [First] Sergeant Funk shouted to them and brought them to attention and made them march in. They held their heads high and their chests out and just as proud as hell. There were a lot of tears, to see such a few guys and realize how many must have died or been wounded or captured. It made me very proud to be a part of it.

245

"We kind of milled around—we didn't know how to treat the guys and they didn't know how to treat us. The next morning, we started getting acquainted. That's where I met [Sergeant] John Hardie. He was the squad leader who took care of the squad I was in. I was a corporal, so I was made assistant squad leader. I started getting to know John Hardie just about as well as anybody in the whole world. I got to know everybody in our platoon quite well."[2]

Private Eugene C. Metcalfe, another Company C replacement, was also at Wollaton Park when the company returned from Normandy and recalled a very different picture of the returning veterans. "There were a lot of empty bunks, because the casualties were pretty high. So we got to meet these old guys and these were *old men*. Where was the swagger and all of that? They were just dragging their butts. They'd got the hell kicked out of them. They were haggard. We got stories from some of these old guys that scared the crap out of us."[3]

Upon his arrival at the 508th base camp at Wollaton Park near Nottingham, Lieutenant Ralph DeWeese, with Company H, ate a hot meal, then walked to the four man officer's tent where he had lived before the invasion. "It was much the same, except I was the only one out of the four of us who came back. We lost sixty-three percent of our men in France."[4]

Lieutenant DeWeese couldn't help but recall a birthday party that he had held with his 2nd Platoon of Company H just before the regiment left Northern Ireland to celebrate Staff Sergeant Joe Bundy's birthday. "I wish we could have had a picture taken that night, because it would have been nice to have had. It is hard to realize that so many of those men are now gone."[5] Staff Sergeant Bundy had been killed in action on June 9.

Several weeks later, Private First Class Bob Chisolm returned to Company I from the hospital. Chisolm had been seriously wounded in Normandy on June 23, after taking Sergeant Delbert Helton's place on a patrol. "I remember walking into the orderly room and the CQ [officer in charge of quarters] on duty—I didn't know him.

"I said, 'I'm Bob Chisolm, 2nd Platoon, coming in from the hospital.' I started to ask him about the first sergeant.

"He said, 'The first sergeant is George [H.] Fields.'

"I said, 'What happened to [Raymond L.] Conrad?'

"He said, 'He was killed.'

"I said, 'How about Delbert Helton?'

"He said, 'Delbert Helton got killed.' And that really hit me."[6]

Chisolm couldn't help thinking that if he had not replaced him, Helton might have been the one wounded on the patrol instead and avoided being killed during the attack on Hill 131. "We were just such close friends. I would not let them wake him up. I really felt responsible."[7]

Upon his return, Staff Sergeant Worster Morgan, with Headquarters Company's regimental intelligence section, had a much greater appreciation of England than during the regiment's first stay. "We enjoyed our second stay in

Nottingham. The people were friendly and treated us nicely, the weather was good, the replacements folded in nicely, and our training was mostly physical hardening and small combat maneuvers. While reforming after our five weeks in Normandy the 82nd held a review and parade for General [Dwight D.] Eisenhower [the Supreme Allied Expeditionary Force (SHAEF) commander]. After thanking us for our combat record, he shocked us by referring to larger airborne operations to come. It was announced that all airborne and troop carrier outfits had been placed under one command—the First Allied Airborne Army."[8]

Through the remainder of July and all of August, the 508th reorganized and trained replacements to integrate them. The regiment had learned many hard and costly lessons from the fighting in Normandy, which would be applied during the upcoming campaigns, resulting in fewer casualties suffered and additional casualties inflicted on the enemy.

Robert White, who had been a private first class and later acting squad leader in Normandy, was promoted to sergeant and became a squad leader with the 3rd Platoon of Company A upon his return from the hospital. "I had a squad of almost all replacements. When I got back to the company, they had brought some German rifles and stuff back over. We got on a little hill there and we had our replacements try to take the hill and we were shooting down [the hill over them]. This was with live ammunition for them to learn the sounds of the guns, and that was a big help."[9]

There were a great many changes in personnel throughout the regiment. Among those at the regimental level, Lieutenant Colonel Tom Shanley became the regimental executive officer. Major Otho Holmes, the regimental S-3, replaced Shanley as commanding officer of the 2nd Battalion. Major John W. Medusky became the new regimental S-3.

The 1st Battalion changes included the promotion of Major Shields Warren, the commanding officer of the 1st Battalion, to lieutenant colonel. Captain Benjamin F. Delamater, III, became the executive officer. Captain Jonathan Adams remained in command of Company A, Lieutenant Woodrow Millsaps became the commanding officer of Company B, and Captain Frank R. Schofield became the Company C commander.

The key changes in the 2nd Battalion included Captain Royal Taylor moving over from Company B to become the 2nd Battalion executive officer. Lieutenant Norman MacVicar remained as commanding officer of Company D, Eugene Hetland was promoted to captain and remained the Company E commander, and Captain Harold M. Martin became the new Company F commanding officer.

The 3rd Battalion changes included Lieutenant Russell Wilde becoming the Company G commander, Lieutenant Louis L. Toth became the commanding officer of Company H, and Lieutenant Robert Mitchell became the Company I commander.

IN EARLY AUGUST, GENERAL EISENHOWER designated General Ridgway to command the newly formed XVIII Airborne Corps, consisting of the 82nd, 101st, and 17th Airborne Divisions. The XVIII Airborne Corps, the British I Airborne Corps, the IX Troop Carrier Command, and two British Royal Air Force troop transport groups formed the new First Allied Airborne Army. Brigadier General James Gavin was promoted to commanding officer of the 82nd Airborne Division and assumed command on August 16.

By mid-August, the Allied armies on the continent had broken out of the Normandy lodgment, encircled and destroyed most of the German forces west of the Seine River, and were driving rapidly across France and Belgium toward the German border. The major problem was a shortage of gasoline. General Omar N. Bradley, now commanding the U.S. 12th Army Group, was utilizing troop carrier aircraft to ferry gasoline to keep the tanks rolling toward Germany.

On Tuesday, August 29, 1944, General Gavin attended a conference at the headquarters of British General Frederick A. M. "Boy" Browning, commander of the British I Airborne Corps. There, Gavin was briefed on a planned airborne operation. "We were given a mission of participating in a proposed landing north of Tournai [Belgium] to seize and hold the crossings of the Escaut River to prevent German withdrawal. The drop was to take place Sunday morning [September 3] about 8:30. Participating were the Poles, British, and 101st Airborne Division. Plans were pushed, orders prepared, ammo and chutes issued, troops dispersed at the proper airdromes, all by dark Friday evening. It was raining and continued to rain more. The U.S. armor continued to drive the Germans back, actually threatening to get to our DZ's before Sunday."[10]

Meanwhile, preparations at the airfields continued for the planned jump. Lieutenant Kenneth L. Johnson, the regimental munitions officer and assistant S-4, was responsible for getting the equipment, weapons, and supplies loaded for upcoming combat jumps. "The aerial delivery containers, commonly called bundles, were loaded into parapacks located on the belly of each ship or carried inside, conforming to the tactical loading of the aircraft. In other words, if a squad was loaded on one ship, the bundles containing its crew served weapons and ammunition would also be carried in that aircraft. A platoon consisted of three rifle squads and one 60mm mortar squad. Each rifle squad contained one light machine gun team, one BAR team, and five riflemen. This platoon required three aircraft to transport it, and eighteen bundles for its equipment. These bundles were loaded as follows: three bundles, each containing one light machine gun and four boxes of ammunition; three bundles, each containing seven boxes of machine gun ammunition; five bundles, each containing twenty rounds of 60mm mortar ammunition; one bundle containing one 60mm mortar complete; three bundles containing antitank mines; one bundle containing rifle grenades; one bundle containing one rocket launcher and ammunition; one bundle containing medical supplies.

"The loading plan for other units was basically the same, modified only to fit the different types and quantity of equipment. The basic load of ammunition, medical supplies, signal supplies, spare parts for weapons, CP equipment, maps, and everything else that a unit needs to fight were dropped in these containers. In effect, these bundles constituted the combat trains of the unit. The number of bundles was of course limited by the number of aircraft. No aircraft was allowed to go partially loaded. After all T/O&E [table of organization and equipment] equipment and basic loads were rolled into bundles, there was space left for approximately twenty bundles. These were loaded with mortar ammunition, batteries, mines, and demolition material in excess of the authorized amount.

"For the purpose of identification, each bundle was marked with a symbol of the unit to which it belonged and the color of the parachute attached to the bundle indicated the type of supplies it contained. Blue for weapons, (rations on resupply drops); green for Class III [gasoline]; red for Class V [ammunition and demolitions]; and white for medical and signal."[11]

At the Fulbeck airfield on September 2, the 3rd Battalion loaded its allotted equipment bundles on the planes for the planned jump the next morning. Lieutenant Francis L. Mahan, the Company I executive officer, was responsible for getting his company's bundles loaded. "I sent a detail out to drop equipment bundles off under the wings of our assigned aircraft, to be loaded in the racks later on that day."[12]

Private Eugene G. "Don" Walton, III, with Service Company was assigned to distribute the equipment bundles under those aircraft. Walton had previously served with Company F and was a pathfinder volunteer who had broken his ankle on a practice jump and had missed Normandy. Walton had been transferred to Service Company because of the injury. "There was a detail of four enlisted men under Staff Sergeant Robert W. Shearer [with Company I] to make the distribution of the equipment bundles to the assigned aircraft. I had a two and a half ton truck with a combat cab. The sergeant rode in front with me, and the four men rode atop the bundles. At each plane, the sergeant got out and told the men which bundles were assigned to that particular plane. Two men would get down, the other two would toss them off, and the two on the ground would pull them under the wings. At every stop, I got out and boarded the plane. I am embarrassed to admit it, but honestly, since I was not authorized a sidearm, I went into each pilot compartment hoping one had been careless and left his .45 automatic pistol behind, which I planned to appropriate.

"We had dropped off more than half of our bundles, although the way they were loaded, there were many stacked against the back of the cab and for some reason I did not get out of the cab at the next plane. I suppose I had given up on finding a sidearm. The next thing I knew, two men had me by each arm helping me toward a hanger. I remember seeing parts of bodies smoldering around me. The bundles behind the cab were loaded with shrapnel and fortunately it did not cause additional explosions. I was evidently blown out of the cab and suffered a concussion, and perforated eardrums, but was otherwise all right.

"The way the accident was reconstructed, someone failed to install the safety fork on one or more of the landmines. It was also found that a bundle of 250 pounds of C-2 also blew up, so either the mine was set off when the bundle was pushed off the truck, or the bundle of C-2 was pushed off on top of it, causing the mine to detonate. Either way it proved deadly.

"Staff Sergeant Robert W. Shearer was killed, as was Private First Class William R. Mitchell and Private Louis N. Spera [all with Company I]. I have no way of knowing who the other men were or the extent of their injuries, but they were so close to the explosion, I am sure their injuries were severe. I spent two days in the regimental dispensary before I could hear and then was returned to duty."[13]

Private Robert F. Howcroft, with Company I, and Sergeant Roland P. E. Dahlberg, with the 96th Squadron, 440th Troop Carrier Group were also injured.

While the 82nd Airborne Division waited at the airfields, General Gavin received word that U.S. armor was approaching the planned drop zones for the operation. "Knowing the armor was going to beat us to it, General Browning changed our missions to seize and take over Lille, Roubaix, Tournai, etc. so as to assist the armor in its passage—a hell of a mission for airborne troops. But General Browning was not to be denied and for some unexplainable reason, the high command was hell bent on getting the First Allied Airborne Army into the fight, whether or not the commitment was decisive or even sound.

"Well, Sunday morning [September 3], I was called to Moor Park, General Browning's headquarters and given a new mission. We were to jump on the west bank of the Meuse, opposite Liège [Belgium] to again block the retreating Germans—the historic Liège gap. By now the troops were aware of the apparent lack of necessity of our participation in this type or role, or so it seemed. Again, weather intervened and was conveniently and also typically lousy. The British ground troops were overrunning our DZ and LZ areas in addition. Consequently, by Sunday night the mission was called off, we reverted to the U.S. XVIII Corps, and back home we came, a bit wetter, but hardly the wiser."[14]

BY EARLY SEPTEMBER, SUPPLY PROBLEMS WERE THE PRIMARY OBSTACLE to Allied forces driving into Germany and ending the war. Supplies for the four American, one British, and one Canadian army were still being brought in over the beaches in Normandy and driven by truck convoys to the armies. Until a major port could be captured, supplies would continue to constrain the Allied armies. British Field Marshal Bernard Montgomery, commander of the 21st Army Group, lobbied General Eisenhower to make a single thrust into Germany instead of an advance on a broad front.

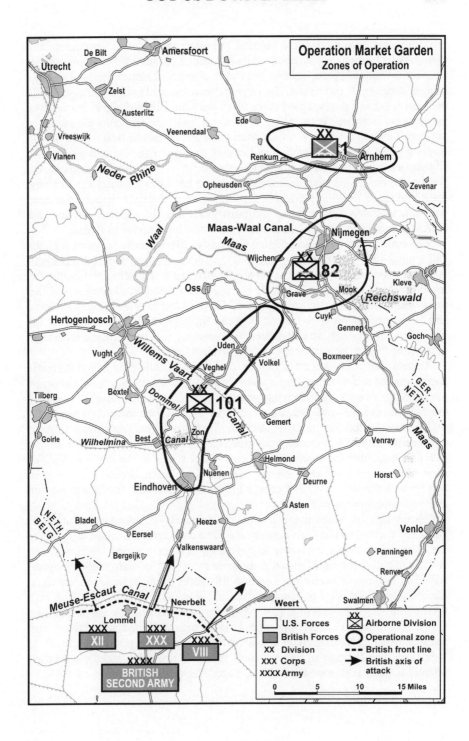

Operation Market Garden
Zones of Operation

The normally cautious Field Marshal Montgomery devised a very daring and high risk operation, codenamed Market Garden. It entailed dropping three airborne divisions behind German lines in southern and eastern Holland to seize bridges over canals and rivers. The airborne forces would hold the bridges while the British Second Army would drive north from the Dutch–Belgian border over the bridges, cross the Rhine River at Arnhem and turn east onto the plains of northern Germany, where it would then seize the industrial heart of Germany, shutting down its war production and ending the war. The plan had a couple of advantages, primarily that it outflanked the Siegfried Line fortifications on the western border of Germany and crossing of the last natural barrier to Germany, the Rhine River, would be made at the lower part of the river where the ground was flat. It also got the elite airborne divisions into the fight, something that SHAEF headquarters had wanted to do ever since the breakout in France.

General Gavin was in London on September 10, when he received a phone call around 4:00 p.m., notifying him of a meeting two hours later at the British I Airborne Corps headquarters. "I took off, arriving a few minutes late for the meeting. It was conducted generally by [General Frederick] Browning and had to do with a new plan envisioning a drop for the 82nd to seize bridges at Grave and Nijmegen and the high ground between Nijmegen and Groesbeek. That the plan would go through was all agreed to, Browning was to command it and had it all set up. The troop carrier lift was not set, however."[15]

General Lewis H. Brereton, the U.S. commander of the First Allied Airborne Army, wanted to make the jump on September 14, just four days later. However, troop carrier aircraft were ferrying gasoline to Bradley's 12th Army Group, so the date was delayed until Sunday, September 17, less than seven days away.

The plan called for the 101st Airborne Division Screaming Eagles to jump north of the city of Eindhoven and seize bridges over the Wilhelmina Canal at Zon and Best, the Aa River and Willems Vaart Canal to the north at Veghel, over the Dommel River at St. Oedenrode, and drive south through Eindhoven to link up with the British XXX Corps, which would spearhead the British Second Army ground force assault.

The British 1st Airborne Division, with the Polish 1st Independent Parachute Brigade attached, would drop north of the 82nd and capture a single bridge over the Rhine River at Arnhem, some sixty-four miles deep in enemy territory.

The 82nd Airborne Division's assignment would be extremely complex, requiring aggressive execution. Landing fifty-three miles behind German lines, the division would seize four major river and five canal bridges, including both the longest single-span bridge (the Nijmegen highway bridge) and the longest bridge (Grave bridge) in all of Europe. In order to protect the route of the British Second Army, the division would seize and hold high ground southeast of Nijmegen. The frontage of the division's area was enormous and the objectives ambitious. Only a veteran division could accomplish the mission.

The 504th Parachute Infantry Regiment, veterans of Sicily and Italy, with more days in combat than any U.S. parachute regiment during the war, would jump north of the Maas River and west of the Maas-Waal Canal and capture the huge bridge at Grave and at least one of the four bridges across the canal.

The 505th, making its fourth combat jump, would jump south of Groesbeek, capture the town and the high ground overlooking the Maas-Waal Canal, then defend it and the southern approaches to Nijmegen against attacks from the Reichswald forest to the east. It would also seize the railroad bridge over the Maas River at Mook and assist the 504th in capturing two of the canal bridges.

The now veteran 508th Parachute Infantry Regiment was assigned to land southeast of Nijmegen, seize the high ground overlooking the approaches to the city from the German frontier a short distance to the east, establish roadblocks south and east of the city to prevent enemy movement south from Nijmegen, and upon the completion of these objectives, seize the highway and railroad bridges across the Waal River at Nijmegen.

Captain Chet Graham was assigned as the regimental liaison officer with division headquarters. "I sat in on a high level briefing at division headquarters. Colonel Lindquist was told by General Gavin to move to the Nijmegen bridge as soon as Lindquist thought practical after the jump. Gavin stressed that speed was important. He was also told to stay out of the city and to avoid city streets. He told Lindquist to use the west farm area to get to the bridge as quickly as possible as the bridge was the key to the division's contribution to the success of the operation."[16]

On September 13, the 508th headquarters issued Field Order Number 1:

The 508 Parachute Infantry Regiment will land during daylight, D-Day, on DZ "T", seize, organize, and hold key terrain features in sector of responsibility, be prepared to seize Waal River crossing at Nijmegen on Division order and prevent all hostile movement south of line Hatert–Klooster.

1st Battalion, less demolition section, will, in priority listed:

1) Seize, clear, organize and defend high ground indicated on Operations overlay [at De Ploeg, two and a half miles south of Nijmegen].

2) Establish and maintain roadblock outposts as indicated on Operations overlay.

3) Mop up area within its sector of responsibility.

4) Establish and maintain contact with 505 Parachute Infantry at 725557 [at the Maldenschebaan and the railroad tracks south of Nijmegen].

2nd Battalion, less D Company, one demolition section attached, will, in priority listed:

1) Seize, clear, organize and defend the area in the vicinity road junction 703591 [at De Hut] and block enemy movement along road "M" main [highway south of Nijmegen].

2) Prevent all hostile movement south of line Hatert–Klooster (712589) by:

a) Establishing and maintaining roadblock outposts as indicated on Operations overlay.

b) Driving out, by counterattack, any enemy penetrations south of line.

3) Mop up the area within its sector of responsibility.

4) Establish and maintain contact with 504 Parachute Infantry at Maas-Waal Canal crossing (677583) [at Hatert].

3rd Battalion, one demolition section attached, in priority listed, will:

1) Seize, clear, organize and defend high ground indicated on Operations overlay [area around Berg-en-Da and Beekl, east of Nijmegen].

2) Mop up the area within its sector of responsibility.

3) Establish roadblocks as indicated on Operations overlay.

4) Establish and maintain contact with 505 Parachute Infantry at 762560 [at Kamp].

D Company, under Regimental control will:

1) Seize and secure LZ "T" for glider landings.

2) Establish and maintain contact with 505 Parachute Infantry at 762560 [at Kamp].

3) Revert to regimental reserve in area indicated upon Regimental order.

319 Glider Field Artillery Battalion, in direct support of regiment, upon landing will:

1) Go into position [750563 west of Kamp and north of Groesbeek] as indicated on Operations overlay, prepared to displace forward to projected position [742580 south of Berg-en-Dal].

2) Be prepared to mass its fire on crossroads 721598 [on Groesbeekscheweg just northwest of De Ploeg], road junction 744602[northwest of Berge-n-Dal at Stollenberg], and other targets within range upon call.[17]

The 508th would be transported in three serials and jump at DZ "T" north of Groesbeek. The 1st Battalion and pathfinders for the 325th Glider Infantry Regiment would lead, followed by the 2nd Battalion, and then the 3rd Battalion. Elements of Headquarters, Headquarters Company, and Service Company would accompany all three battalion serials. The 1st and 2nd Battalion serials would depart from Langer airfield and the 3rd Battalion serial from Fulbeck.

On September 14, the three airborne divisions moved to their respective airfields and were sealed in by military police security. While fighting in Normandy, Private First Class Tommy Horne, with Company H, had lost much of his hearing. "While waiting to board trucks to take us to the airfield for the Holland jump, my commander came up to me and said I did not have to go. Now, don't think I am trying to tell you I am a brave man. Compared to most of the troopers, I am not. After looking in the faces of the other men, I asked him to let me go and he said he was hoping I would say that. I would have gone, knowing I was going to die, rather than turn and walk away from those men. I know anyone of them would have done the same."[18]

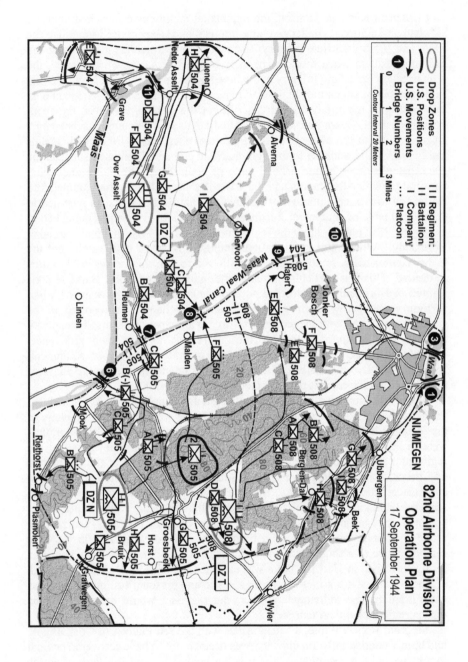

Lieutenant Kenneth Johnson, the regimental munitions officer and assistant S-4, had an additional challenge going into Holland. Experienced units like the 504th and 505th Parachute Infantry Regiments had learned lessons in Sicily and had applied them when they fought in Italy and Normandy. For example, the veteran 505th Parachute Infantry had jumped in Normandy with a load plan that had no carbines, which they had found to be unreliable in combat. The load plan had substituted the highly reliable M1 rifle for the carbine. However, the 505th troopers in many cases had also substituted BARs and Thompson submachine guns for some of the M1s specified in the load plan. Most of the 505th squads had two BARs, in addition to the light machine gun and Thompson submachine guns that were part of the official table of equipment. The 507th and 508th Parachute Infantry Regiments and the 101st Airborne Division had jumped into Normandy with a large number of carbines and almost no BARs, as specified in the official table of equipment. Lieutenant Johnson and his S-4 personnel had to modify the load plan to equip the regiment based on the lessons it had learned in Normandy. "Within certain limitations imposed by space and weight and the higher commanders, smaller units were allowed to arm themselves pretty much as desired. This was particularly true of the individual weapons. Battle lessons learned in Normandy had decreed an abundance of automatic weapons when fighting in hedgerow country. The terrain in Holland was reported to be generally open, and with longer fields of fire. In anticipation of this, the majority of men were equipped with M1 rifles in respect to their own preference. Incorporating other minor variations in the quantity and type of equipment, brought about by experiences of the various commanders, the supply phase of the preparation for combat proceeded according to plan."[19]

Lieutenant Johnson also readied equipment and supplies that were scheduled for delivery subsequent to the initial jump. "There were two more echelons of the regiment in this attack on Nijmegen. Four one-quarter ton trucks and trailers were to be brought in on D+1 by glider. These gliders were not a part of the regimental serials, but were under division control. The rest of the regiment's transportation, amounting to twenty 2½-ton trucks, eleven 1-ton trailers, two ambulances, nine ¼-ton trucks, and five ¼-ton trailers was to constitute the seaborne echelon. The vehicles contained the kitchens, kitchen personnel, bedrolls, maintenance personnel and equipment, and other organizational property normally carried in field trains. This echelon remained in the base camp to move to a staging area on order of XVIII Corps. No definite date was set for its arrival in Holland, but it was expected to arrive by D+15. Until it did, no one would eat a hot meal or have access to any personal equipment that was not carried by the individual. Further, the regiment would have no organic transportation other than four jeeps."[20]

Sergeant Robert White, a squad leader with the 3rd Platoon of Company A, had been wounded in Normandy and was deemed not to have recovered enough to take part in the operation. White was left behind at Wollaton Park when the regiment moved by truck to the airfields. "I thought I was in good enough shape. Sergeant [Anthony] Cianfrani had been wounded in Normandy and they left him behind, also. So Sergeant Cianfrani and I got together and gathered up all of our gear. They were sending some chow out to the airfield and we got on the truck and went out. We looked up Captain [Jonathan] Adams [the commanding officer of Company A] and told him that the doctor released us.

"Captain Adams said, 'I can't approve this,' and took us down to Colonel Lindquist.

"The colonel said, 'If they want to go that bad, let them go.' So we went."[21]

At Langer airfield on September 15 and 16, Corporal James R. "Jim" Blue, an assistant squad leader with the 1st Platoon of Company A, attended briefings regarding the operation. "The war tent was opened and we received word that the jump would be in Holland; this we had never dreamed of. The platoon was first briefed by Lieutenant [John] Foley [the Company A executive officer]. Later, we had the opportunity to use the war tent on a squad level. Inside the war tent was a sand table; this sand table was a miniature mock area of the combat mission in and around Nijmegen. We were issued maps and aerial photographs of the said area. Lieutenant Foley pointed out the assembly area marked by a large haystack in the field. An assigned man in the company was to drape an orange piece of cloth on the haystack. The survivors of the Normandy campaign took this briefing at heart. We remembered how fouled up the drop pattern was in Normandy. We studied those maps and I remember not a pencil mark could be put on them—the reason being that if a soldier was captured during the drop the enemy could gain information by this.

"[Staff] Sergeant [Sherman] Van Enwyck, the platoon sergeant, was looking forward to this operation, his ancestors having come from this country."[22]

It was during the first briefing that Corporal Blue found out that the jump would be made in daylight. "We had jumped into the darkness in Normandy and had one hell of a time assembling. Most of us were at the wrong place—in mixed up units and small groups. We liked the idea of a daylight operation and knew if we landed together as a team we would be hard to handle."[23]

Load manifests assigning troopers and equipment to specific aircraft were issued on September 16. Corporal Blue and his squad were assigned to Staff Sergeant Van Enwyck's stick. "We were assigned an aircraft by tail number and were lined up in stick-jump formation. Lieutenant Foley's plane consisted of one rifle squad and part of his headquarters. Van Enwyck's plane consisted of our squad and part of the weapons squad.

"We moved to the aircraft, drew and fitted parachutes, and secured the A-5 containers (bundles with machine guns, ammo, mortars, rocket launchers, etc.). These we placed in the pararacks (these were racks under the wings of the C-47). An assigned man in the stick would release these by pulling a lever down as he made the turn to depart the aircraft, usually the machine gunner in a rifle squad. This would put him descending close to the bundles. Everyone satisfied with his parachute, we moved to the tents. The rest of the day we checked individual weapons and ammo to see that every round in the clips were even and taped two magazines (reversed) together for our sub-Thompson machine guns. This could save a split second and we knew that a split second could determine between life and death. All of this taken care of, we hit the sack. We knew we had a hard day's work ahead for us."[24]

Captain Jonathan Adams had been wounded in Normandy and had returned a short time earlier to resume command of Company A. "There was plenty of time allotted so that there was no last minute rush. I do remember that after my jumpmasters reported to me that all planes were OK. I checked and found that about half of the parapacks were cocked.

"The briefing was the best I have attended, particularly so because of the attitude of the pilots. When we left the briefing room I believe the jumpmasters had great confidence in the job the air corps would do. This is in contrast to Normandy where the pilots seemed to take the briefing as a big joke."[25]

Like many others who had been armed with a carbine in Normandy, Captain Bill Nation, the regimental S-1, had no faith in the reliability of the weapon. "Instead of a carbine, I was carrying a Tommy gun and three hundred rounds of ammunition, which added about thirty-five or forty additional pounds to my already overloaded frame on which I had two parachutes, a gas mask, life belt, musette bag, dispatch case, full field equipment, which is a load within itself, and other incidentals such as toilet articles, rations for three days, pistol and a score of other items."[26]

It was during the briefings that First Sergeant Wilbur J. Scanlon, with Company F, realized the potential impact of the operation. "We were told if successful, it would enable the Allies to get beyond the Siegfried Line and afford the Allies to break through on all fronts heading into Germany. Definitely, it would have shortened the war on the western front. We were told we would be facing a tougher enemy than we did in Normandy."[27]

At Fulbeck airfield, where the 3rd Battalion would depart, Lieutenant Kenneth Johnson, the regimental munitions officer and S-4 with Service Company, attended the final briefing for pilots and jumpmasters. "The foremost question in everyone's mind was the flak and enemy aircraft that we expected to encounter. The 508th, flying the northern route, was expected to pass over a considerable number of flak guns. It was hoped that some of them would be neutralized by combat aircraft prior to the time we passed over the area. The air support plan included the use of British and American bombers and fighters to attack airfields and flak installations throughout the general area of operations. Fighter cover for the 1,544 troop carrier planes and 478 gliders in the initial D-Day lift consisted of 371 British and 548 American fighters. These aircraft were to fly cover below, around, and above the troop carrier aircraft. The provisions for air-sea rescue were discussed, checkpoints gone over and last minute weather reports checked."[28]

Lieutenant Neal Beaver, with Headquarters Company, 3rd Battalion, also attended the same briefing. "[Lieutenant] Colonel [Frank X.] Krebs of the air corps gave his briefing; then the weatherman (with a much more formal discipline than the air corps). We were very attentive—our lives depended on some of the information.

"Next came our battalion commander, Lieutenant Colonel Louis G. Mendez, Jr. The room was noisy and stuffy and hot. Colonel Mendez stood before that group of his own officers and the pilots and said not a word for at least two or three minutes. Then in the dead hush he had created, he said, 'Gentlemen, my officers know this map by heart—and we are ready to go. When I brought my battalion to the briefing prior to Normandy, I had the finest combat ready force of its size that will ever be known! Gentlemen, by the time I had gathered them together in Normandy—one half of them were gone!' (Tears were rolling down his cheeks at this point.)

"'I charge you all—put us down in Holland, or put us down in Hell, but put us down *All In One Place* or I will hound you to your graves!'

"He turned and walked out."[29]

IN THE PREDAWN HOURS OF SUNDAY, SEPTEMBER 17, civilians in southeastern England awoke to the deafening low roar of bomber engines as American and British heavy and medium bombers took off to bomb German flak positions, airfields, and barracks in Holland in preparation for the airborne landings. The U.S. Eighth Air Force sent 872 B-17 Flying Fortress bombers, escorted by 147 P-51 Mustangs to hit 117 German targets that lay along the troop carrier routes. The British Royal Air Force dispatched 85 Lancaster, 65 Mosquito, 48 B-25, and 24 A-20 bombers, accompanied by 53 Spitfire fighters to attack German defenses on the coast of Holland and German barracks at Nijmegen, Arnhem, and Ede. These planes were the first of over four thousand aircraft that would conduct the largest airborne operation in history.

The sky train of 2,024 troop carrying planes and gliders would takeoff from twenty-four airfields beginning at 9:45 a.m. and continue for over two hours. Almost a thousand Allied fighter and fighter-bomber aircraft would escort the troop carrier planes transporting elements of the three airborne divisions.

The day dawned bright and clear at all of the airfields from which the 82nd Airborne Division would takeoff, except for Langer airfield, where the 1st Battalion and 2nd Battalions would depart, where it was overcast.

The 1st Battalion's executive officer, Captain Ben Delamater, was awake before dawn. "After an early breakfast, the officers attended a final flight briefing on weather, the route, checkpoints, sea rescue measures, expected flak areas, and fighter protection.

"The heavy bundles were then trucked out to the chalk marked C-47s and swung into the belly racks or placed in the open doorways in the case of the most important items. Until the clouds lifted enough for the 10:00 takeoff, the troopers lolled on the grass, joking and bragging about themselves, their favorite Pubs, or their English girls. Only the unusual number of latrine visits betrayed any nervousness."[30]

Corporal Jim Blue and the division's other paratroopers were treated to a combination breakfast and chicken dinner that morning. "We knew this would be the last meal for some, but we didn't know which ones."[31]

After breakfast, Private Eugene Metcalfe, a replacement assigned to the 3rd Platoon of Company C, finished writing a letter to his father that morning, not mentioning anything about the upcoming operation. "I looked around at different corners of the hanger and they were having church services. The guys were sitting on the floor. They had the Protestants, the Catholics, and the Jewish. What was so unique about it was everybody was sharpening their trench knives, checking ammo. I thought I would never see this again.

"Everybody had sick jokes. Everybody was nervous.

"You never saw the Red Cross people around. The Red Cross people were out there and had some doughnuts and coffee. So we knew the invasion was on."[32]

Later that morning, Corporal Blue and the rest of Company A attended a final briefing prior to takeoff. "Lieutenant Foley [the Company A executive officer] put it to us bluntly; it went something like this, 'I have just attended a briefing and this is the word: A reconnaissance plane flew over our drop zones early this morning and photographed the area. There is said to be sixty-four antiaircraft weapons on and around our drop zones. In the wooded area near Groesbeek tanks have been spotted. The division has no alternate drop zones, so we go ahead as planned. I figure the fight will not last over three minutes after we hit the ground, so let's be a winner. Be ready to fight and good luck.'

"Individual weapons were taken out from under the parachute safety belt as they were normally jumped. We used quite a bit of air corps masking tape securing these weapons to our arms as where we could maintain them during the jump. I remember [Private] Walter Dikoon who was armed with a Browning Automatic Rifle (BAR) preparing for the jump. He adjusted the sling on his arm and had me tape it firmly to his arm. Dikoon assured me he could jump this weapon at port arms and he would be ready to contest the enemy as soon as his chute opened.

"From here we went to the planes and began getting into the parachutes and securing our equipment. Lieutenant Foley also told us the planes over the drop zone would not be flying over five hundred feet. So at the planes we decided we would not use the reserve parachute.

"About this time, Lieutenant Foley came over to make his SOP (standard operating procedure) inspection and said, 'What gives on the reserves?' We told him we decided not to use them.

"Lieutenant Foley said, 'Regulation is that you will board the plane with a reserve on.' He smiled and returned to his aircraft. We loaded our plane and immediately off came over two-thirds of the reserves on that planeload. All the combat veterans took theirs off and half the replacements."[33]

Private Gene Metcalfe lined up with his Company C stick to board the plane. "I was about the seventeenth guy in the stick. As we got on the planes, I looked on ahead and there was a lieutenant and a couple of his aides standing down there and they had a clipboard. They had to lift us into the plane because we had so much equipment on, we couldn't get in it ourselves. There was an aircrew and you'd reach your arms up and they'd lift you up into the plane."[34]

Technician Fifth Grade Joseph Kissane, with Company G, had recently returned from pathfinder school and was a spare communications NCO. Kissane would jump with Chalk 1 in the 3rd Battalion serial. "In the communications section with no assigned function, my place was fifth or sixth man in the lead plane. This was an improvement over Normandy as the last man out. Weight conscious, I grabbed a carbine, lighter and easier to carry than the M1 rifle. Our C-47 air corps personnel—the pilot was a lieutenant colonel [Frank X. Krebs] and the copilot a major [Howard W. Cannon], also a captain and two enlisted men. The hapless passengers included [Lieutenant Russell] Wilde, as jumpmaster, followed by [Lieutenant Colonel Louis] Mendez, his dog-robber, and the rest of us. SOP [standard operting procedure] as usual—rush to the runway, then wait alongside the C-47 for hours. Cannon kidded with us. The pilot sat in the cockpit sweating it out. The weather was perfect. The copilot subsequently became a senator from Nevada."[35]

Technician Fourth Grade Francis Lamoureux was the last man and pusher of that same Chalk 1 stick. "I was in the same plane with the company commander, [Lieutenant] Wilde. I respected him very much after fighting with him in Normandy. We were the lead plane in our [serial]. Headquarters people were aboard, including Colonel Louis G. Mendez, our battalion commander. He was one of the very few Mexican Americans to have graduated from West Point before the war—a helluva man, very well respected and loved by the men. [Lieutenant] Wilde was in the same class."[36]

At 10:19 a.m., C-47s carrying the three parachute infantry regiments and other elements of the 82nd Airborne Division began lifting off from the runways of six airfields at five-second intervals, climbing to altitude, and vectoring to form up into nine plane V-of-V formations and then into thirty-six and forty-five plane serials.

After being helped into the plane because of his heavy load, Private First Class James R. Allardyce with Company B, managed to turn slightly in his seat in order to get a look out of one of the windows. "Roaring down the runway we saw what were hundreds of planes either airborne or waiting the signal to take off."[37]

Lieutenant John Foley, the Company A executive officer, was sitting near the door of his plane as it rolled down the runway and lifted off. "Takeoff was into overhanging clouds and fog. However, at 1,200 feet we broke through and seemed to be riding above a continuous cover of clouds. After rendezvous and heading for the coast, one could see nothing but C-47 aircraft in all directions."[38]

Captain Bill Nation, the regimental S-1, was a member of Colonel Lindquist's Chalk 46 stick in the 2nd Battalion serial. "I was in the lead plane. Jumping before me was a Dutch commando who left the continent at Dunkirk. He was going back home for the first time in about four years and was making his first parachute jump and probably his first plane ride. His face was tense and firm, and as he chewed a stick of gum he had outward appearance of nervousness—and weren't we all. I asked him if he was nervous, in my own quivering voice and he admitted it, but assured us he would be all right as soon as he got out that door. We all knew well what he meant, for to get out the door above all gives reassurance of a longer life and a crack at the enemy, even though it might be a few hours. In leaving England and flying over her fields, shocked and stacked with grain—her historic castles, cities, and hedgerows—only then did everyone realize what a nice place it was to be in.

"Then we came to the channel—the famous waters over which so many battles had been fought on shore and in the air. It was dirty black, even against an open sky and in the sunlight. Beneath us were the PT boats patrolling and ready to pick up survivors of any plane or glider forced down. There were two gliders still afloat in the distance and a PT boat was making the rescue. We were promised an air cover and about halfway across we saw fighter planes circling beneath, over and around us."[39]

Lieutenant Wayne H. Smith was a new replacement and the platoon leader of the 2nd Platoon of Company F. "During the trip across, the men talked little and when they did talk, it was about home and their plans for after the war. The replacements, green men as they were, took the operation as a lark, but the old men, who knew what they were in for, were pretty scared. They did not at any time indicate panic or cowardice, but were cautious in their outlook and took the whole operation very seriously."[40]

The troop carrying aircraft serials flew in three columns, together about ten miles wide and over a hundred miles long. It was a spectacular sight to those on the ground who witnessed it and to those involved in the operation.

The 508th serials trailed those of the 504th over the coast of Holland. The German air defenses were now fully alerted and had already had a lot of target practice firing at the earlier serials. Lieutenant Woodrow Millsaps was the new commanding officer of Company B. "I was standing in the door of my plane as we approached the Dutch coast and as far as the eye could see, there were formations of planes—C-47 planes, some of which were towing gliders, and fighter and light bombers from the Eighth Air Force.

"We immediately came under heavy antiaircraft flak from the coast. I could see the fighter planes dive-bombing the gun emplacements, and they were quite effective with their bombs."[41]

Corporal Jim Blue, with Company A, noticed that as the 1st Battalion serial approached the coast of Holland the troop carrier planes descended as planned from 1,500 feet down to 500 feet. "As we passed some small islands we received antiaircraft fire; we knew our jump time was drawing near. We passed a very close island and received fire from it. At this time we were flying no higher than six hundred feet. Standing at the door you could see the [antiaircraft] gun at work. From somewhere came a British Typhoon. It passed very close to our plane and dived straight for the gun position. Halfway to the gun position smoke flew from the Typhoon—we thought it had been hit. The plane was loaded with rockets and I think the pilot fired all rockets, because the gun position went up in smoke. The pilot very gracefully took the plane out of the dive and was on his merry way.

"Shortly, we passed over the lowland and antiaircraft fire increased. We kept checking our watches and the jump time was drawing near. Shells began bursting very close to our plane."[42]

Captain Jonathan Adams, the commanding officer of Company A, stood in the doorway of the lead plane of his company's nine plane V-of-V formation as the 1st Battalion serial crossed Holland. "The flight in [to the DZ] was uneventful until we reached Hertogenbosch. As we were told in the briefing we got some heavy flak. 'A' Company, being second in the column seemed to catch most of it. Two planes were hit so badly they had to fall out of the convoy."[43]

Staff Sergeant Roland C. Ziegler, with Company D of the 307th Airborne Engineer Battalion, was jumping number ten just behind Lieutenant Charles W. Chaplinski, the company commander, in Chalk 21 of the serial transporting the 307th Airborne Engineer Battalion to the 505th Parachute Infantry's drop zone south of Groesbeek. Company D was a provisional company formed to support the 508th as part of the regimental combat team, but along with most of the engineer battalion was initially under division control, assigned to provide security for the division command post. Staff Sergeant Ziegler vividly recalled that bright Sunday afternoon. "We were at about 1,500 feet and Lieutenant Chaplinski and I stood in the door watching as the people ran out of churches along the way and were waving very enthusiastically anything they could lay hold of. At one point we passed over a small garrison of German soldiers, and in the fleeting minutes we could see it reminded me of a Max Sennett comedy. The officer in charge was trying to form them in ranks, three or four were trying to hitch a horse to a cart (the horse had other ideas), while others were still loading it. Some had tied belongings to bicycles and were frantically leaving the area, post haste. I think panic prevailed. The air force covered us with all available fighters. At one point, we were fired on by a flak barge, hitting our plane several times. Those P-51 pilots were magnificent, diving through our formation and putting the barge out of action."[44]

Private Gene Metcalfe was a replacement with Company C and making his first combat jump. "I was so scared I couldn't even swallow. I tried to say something and I couldn't talk. You've got to control your fear. I had control over it. You react to your training."[45]

As the 1st Battalion serial approached the drop zone the Germans unleashed intense antiaircraft and small arms fire, severely damaging several planes.

When the red light flashed on, Lieutenant Woodrow Millsaps, the commanding officer of Company B, started through the procedure to have his stick stand up and hook up, check equipment, and stand in the door, ready to jump. "By now we were dropping down to four hundred to six hundred feet above ground and we had about six minutes before the drop. At this point all hell seemed to break loose, for the air was full of flak and three of my nine planes were on fire.

"I was still standing in the door of my plane getting ready for the jump. I knew for certain we were on course, for I had identified several objects on the ground that I had been briefed to look for. By now I could see other planes on fire and one or two planes had crashed and were burning. I noticed that the three planes in my formation that were on fire were still in formation and we were coming over the drop zone. I was worried plenty about the drop and getting my company assembled in the assigned area. So I figured if the men had to jump from the burning planes before they reached the drop zone, they would at least be in the area and would be able to join the company later. But the planes held formation and put the boys out with the main jump.

"About two minutes before the jump, the plane I was in started bucking like a young bronco from concussion of bursting antiaircraft shells. I thought it would crash for sure, or at least make it difficult for the men to jump, since by now we were standing up ready to jump, but found ourselves holding on to the plane for dear life. I knew if we didn't get out of the planes on time, we would land across the canals over in Germany, since we were jumping just a thousand yards or so from the Holland and Germany border. The plane righted itself just as we came over target and I gave the command to go and we bailed out into the fray."[46]

Lieutenant Colonel Shields Warren, the battalion commander, was in the lead plane of 1st Battalion serial and of the 132 planes carrying the 508th to DZ "T". Warren jumped when the green light flashed on and seconds later, his parachute deployed with the usual opening shock. "When I checked my parachute canopy, I became aware of ground resistance, for a long burst of machine gun fire came disconcertingly close to my right ear. However, the platoon of German antiaircraft guns was soon smothered by the weight of the almost six hundred jumpers, even before the next serial in the regimental air column began dropping four minutes later."[47]

Sergeant Jim Kurz was a member of Lieutenant James L. Keen's Company B stick. Sergeant Kurz was jumping last and was near the cockpit as the plane approached the drop zone. "I was talking to the pilots when flak hit the plane. I turned around and there was a hole between me and the paratrooper ahead of me. I yelled to the pilots that we had been hit. Right then, the green light came on (our signal to jump). As I started toward the exit door, flames started shooting out of the hole in the plane. I told the crew chief to follow me as I went out the door and he jumped right behind me. The plane crashed at the edge of the field.

"As I was floating down, another paratrooper slipped under me. I fell the last seventy feet with very little air in my chute, because the chute below had taken most of the air out of my chute. I really hit the ground hard; but since the field had been plowed, I did not break a leg. I either sprained my foot; or like the medic said, I broke a small bone in my foot. I told him to tape up my foot tight and I would keep up with the company.

"It was the best jump we had ever made, including practice jumps. A good jump is getting organized after the jump, collecting equipment bundles, and having a large number of paratroopers present in each company."[48]

Corporal Jesse J. Womble, also a member of Lieutenant Keen's Company B stick, watched the crippled plane as he descended by parachute. "The plane was burning when it crashed. It crashed on the far end of our DZ. One severely burned airman and an unhurt crew chief were left in a house on the DZ."[49]

Private First Class Jim Allardyce was aboard one of the Company B planes hit by enemy fire. "We started to see some flak and the next thing I knew we were standing up, hooking up, checking equipment, and standing in the door. Well, this was what we volunteered for! By now the plane was being buffeted by flak and we could hear pieces [of shrapnel] tearing through the wings now and then. I wished now that we could get out of this sitting duck target. Then the green light went on and we went out sliding through the puke of the bazooka man who had become airsick. When the chute popped open and the canopy checked OK, I suddenly realized how quiet it had become with the roar of the planes farther away and only occasional flak sounds. I spotted our battalion's orange smoke grenades while still dropping, made all the fancy preparations for a textbook landing, and plopped to the ground feet first and then over onto my belly, borne over by the weight of the equipment.

"I yelled to [Private William V.] Askren, the farm boy from Illinois who was our machine gunner, and together we opened the equipment bundle, he getting the gun while [Private First Class John M.] Aronis, who had come up, and I got the ammo boxes. Then, we headed to our company's rendezvous point one hundred or two hundred yards north of the orange smoke grenades."[50]

After his parachute opened and he checked his canopy, Lieutenant Woodrow Millsaps looked down to see what was below. "Immediately, I could see that I was landing in the midst of farmhouses and barns. I knew if any enemy were in the vicinity, they would most likely be in and around the buildings. I landed in an orchard tree with my feet approximately four or five feet above ground. I jumped up and down as best I could, trying to lower my feet to the ground, but that was too slow. So, I took my jump knife and cut the shroud lines from the parachute and dropped to the ground and made a flying leap for the nearest hedge, drawing my pistol and looking in all directions at the same time."[51]

Corporal Jim Blue and his Company A stick were hooked up and standing in the door ready to jump when the plane began to shudder. "It was bouncing and holes began to appear overhead; the flak was breaking through. I looked around and saw Private [Billie G.] Beaver fall. A piece of shrapnel had hit and actually bent his helmet. He was knocked unconscious and was unhooked and rolled over on his seat.[52] Less than a minute to go another trooper went down. A piece of shrapnel had torn the private's jump boot and gave him a nasty wound. He was also unhooked and put aside."[53]

Corporal Blue was near the door, jumping number three in his stick. "[Staff Sergeant Sherman] Van Enwyck had assigned me duty to keep a sharp lookout from the port side window and give him a sharp slap on the leg when I saw the first trooper make an exit from the plane on our left wing. I took a glance at my watch and the time was 13:28; at the same time I saw the first man make his exit from the plane on our left. I slapped Van Enwyck on the leg; as I did, the green light came on and we were on our way out the door. This was a relief, because I was expecting at any moment for our plane to be hit so severely that it would be knocked down. I went out the door, my chute opened, and I looked around and saw that we had jumped in a very close pattern. This was what we were shooting for. We encountered some small arms fire during the descent. Only one man in the company was hit, Sergeant Anthony Cianfrani. On the way down I observed a small house, and I had to slip like everything to miss landing on it. I did land in the yard and as I did, I saw one of our replacements come straight for the house. As his boots struck the slate shingles, several of them tore loose; his chute collapsed and he came sliding off. He hit the ground very hard. This was very dangerous as he had jumped with full combat equipment (approximately seventy pounds). He was a Spanish boy and spoke broken English. His only comment was, 'damned if a man couldn't get hurt if he did this many times.'"[54]

Prior to reaching the drop zone, Captain Jonathan Adams had observed two of the nine planes carrying his Company A hit by flak and trailing the formation at a lower altitude. "By the time they regained jumping altitude they were past the DZ and just inside Germany."[55]

Lieutenant Nolan R. Schlesinger, the assistant platoon leader of the 2nd Platoon of Company A, was the jumpmaster of one of those crippled planes. Corporal Walter Firestine and Private Edward J. "Woody" Wodowski were members of the stick and later reported that "the plane was hit several times before we hit the DZ, both motors were afire, flames coming through the floor."[56]

Private Wodowski, a new replacement near the end of the stick, could only watch as the inside of the plane filled with smoke. "We had a young lieutenant [Schlesinger] who had had just three jumps at the jump school in England. He froze in the door, but the guy behind him, Sergeant [Vince G.] Pierce, [Jr.], helped him out of the door. When I got out, I guess we were down to [an altitude of] about three hundred feet."[57]

Sergeant Pierce stayed in the burning plane and made sure all of the troopers jumped before he jumped. Corporal Firestine and Private Wodowski both passed him as they approached the doorway of the plane rapidly filling with smoke to jump. "Sergeant Pierce was the last man to jump...The equipment bundles were burning as they came down, and they exploded on the ground. We were unable to save any weapons [from the bundles]."[58]

Lieutenant Rex Combs, the platoon leader of the 3rd Platoon of Company A, was the jumpmaster of the other stricken plane. Flak struck an equipment bundle underneath the plane carrying his stick, wounding Lieutenant Combs in the leg and setting all of the bundles on fire. By the time the plane could be brought under control, it had passed over the drop zone. Lieutenant Combs' stick jumped about 2,500 yards east of the drop zone near Wyler, Germany.

Several nearby enemy flak positions opened fire as the troopers attempted to assemble. A member of the stick, Private A. B. Cannon, gathered three troopers who gave him covering fire and then single-handedly attacked several of the positions, killing two and forcing another five to surrender. Cannon's one man assault successfully diverted fire away from the stick, allowing it to assemble.

Meanwhile, Lieutenant Combs and Corporal Marion E. Kinman organized the troopers into a defensive position, which delayed an enemy attack and allowed the salvage of equipment from the burning bundles. Corporal Kinman approached one of the enemy antiaircraft positions and used a Gammon grenade to kill two Germans and take the remainder prisoner.

A third badly damaged plane was jumpmastered by the Company A executive officer, Lieutenant John Foley. "We received the red light about four minutes off the DZ, but never got the green. The plane encountered heavy flak and small arms fire just as it approached the DZ. The plane crossed the DZ and retained its original position within the formation. Just before we jumped, the number two man [Technician Fifth Grade Charles E. Schmalz] tapped me and said the emergency bell was ringing. Everyone parachuted from the plane with the exception of Private Ralph P. Bellesfield [who had been wounded]."[59]

Sergeant Joseph B. McCann was the last man in the stick to jump. "When I left the plane, Private Ralph P. Bellesfield and the crew were the only ones left in the plane."[60] The plane was able to turn around, but crashed in the 504th Parachute Infantry Regiment's sector, just west of the Maas-Waal Canal, killing Private Bellesfield. The bravery of the airplane's pilots and crewmen allowed Lieutenant Foley's stick to hit the drop zone and assemble with Company A.

First Sergeant Frank C. Taylor was the jumpmaster of another of the planes carrying Company A. Sergeant Robert White was jumping number two behind him. "When the green light came on, he didn't go. So, I poked him and he pointed down with a finger. I stuck my head alongside of him and looked out the door and we've got a C-47 right under our door with a left engine on fire. He didn't get us out over the drop zone. I found a week later that we had landed in Germany. First Sergeant Taylor and I rounded up the squad and headed back toward the drop zone. It wasn't that far away in Germany—we could still see the drop zone."[61]

Private First Class Gordon H. Cullings was a medic assigned to the 3rd Platoon of Company C. "When we got to the drop zone everything was OK—a lot of flak—everyone was glad to get out of the plane. I remember hitting the ground pretty hard. I got up and out of my chute. The first thing I saw was a C-47 that had bellied in. The pilot and copilot were in a clump of bushes. The pilot had a broken leg. I did my best to put a splint on it and said for them to stay put until we [the 1st Battalion] got together."[62]

Following about five minutes behind the 1st Battalion, the troopers of the 2nd Battalion approached the drop zone. Technician Fourth Grade Dwayne Burns, the Company F communications NCO, and his stick of mostly replacements were in the lead plane of the 2nd Battalion serial. "Most of them were green and this was their first combat jump. I was in the front plane in our V-pattern of three ships and would be the fourth man to jump. In line ahead of me were the battalion commander [Major Otho Holmes], his radio operator, and my company commander, Captain [Harold] Martin.

"As we neared the drop zone, we started picking up flak again. But the fighter planes flying with us peeled off and went for the gun emplacements. We saw people below on the roads and they waved and danced around. Although the last few minutes had been through flak, we had taken only one or two hits and had had no casualties. We had been standing for some time and now were ready for them to give us the green light.

"The battalion commander yelled, 'Let's go!' and the stick moved forward as one man. Then, I was all alone. The tail of the ship passed by overhead and I heard the crack of the canopy as I got my opening shock. I was floating in bright sunlight and no sound of gunfire, just the steady drone of the ships passing overhead. The time was 13:30. I landed standing up and with our new quick open harness, I just turned, pushed the knob and the harness fell away.

"I was in the middle of a large field and it looked like all of F Company had landed together. I watched the C-47s as they made their turn and headed back for England. I could see ships still far out coming in for the drop zone. The sky was covered with parachutes.

"We started opening up the bundles and getting out our equipment. I found my radio and turned it on to see if it made the drop all right. We met no resistance during our assembly. We heard gunfire, but it was very far away. We joked and laughed as we moved out. It was just like a practice jump in England. It was hard to believe that we were in German territory, miles from our own front lines. I kept waiting for something to happen."[63]

Two Company F sticks were forced to jump early—one from a crippled plane and the other because the green light was turned on early. Lieutenant Donald J. Burke, the assistant platoon leader of the 2nd Platoon, and his stick were forced to jump early when their plane was hit by antiaircraft fire. Everyone in the stick landed safely except Private Ross Dennison, who was killed by flak while descending by parachute.

Lieutenant Edward M. King's 3rd Platoon stick was the other Company F stick to jump early. It landed between Malden and the Maas-Waal Canal. The stick assembled and started out to retrieve its equipment bundles, which had landed in Malden, one of which contained mines that exploded when the bundle hit the roof of a house. As the troopers approached this house, they were fired on by Germans using weapons they had picked up in the equipment bundles. The troopers took cover in the houses and worked their way to the north, staying in a house for the night, with guards posted at each window.

Lieutenant Robert L. Sickler, the platoon leader of the 3rd Platoon of Dog Company, was the jumpmaster on his plane. "Enemy antiaircraft fire was light and spotty over the route in, but increased as the drop zone was approached. A plane containing elements of the 1st Platoon, Company D, and members of the company headquarters group, had its right motor blown completely from its mounting, and crashed about two minutes out from the drop zone. Paratroopers and crew were seen to parachute safely to earth."[64]

Lieutenant Loyle O. McReynolds, the Company D executive officer, was the jumpmaster of the plane that lost its right engine. Corporal Frank Haddy was jumping number two in the stick. "We got the [emergency] bell, which means get the hell out, we're hit. We were then five hundred feet when we all bailed out into this small grove of pine trees.

"There were only four of us who had seen combat before—[Private First Class Nelson S.] Bryant, the lieutenant [McReynolds], [Corporal John P.] Perdue, and myself. The rest of the stick was replacements. We were about four miles short of our drop zone. Bryant and I led off the squad in the direction of the drop zone."[65]

A second plane, carrying Staff Sergeant Jacob M. Kluttz's Company D stick, had problems with its right engine and lost altitude rapidly. The stick was dropped short of the drop zone, but the plane continued on and dropped the equipment bundles on the drop zone.

Just seconds before the green light was turned on in his plane, the trooper behind Private First Class Frank Staples, with Company D, was wounded. "[Private John G.] Starcevich was standing right beside me. He got his two fingers and thumb shot off in the plane. He didn't jump."[66]

Staples, the company headquarters runner, twisted his ankle upon landing, but moved out with the rest of Company D that landed on the drop zone. "I went to the aid station to get my ankle taped up. One of my buddies, [Private First Class] Carl [W.] Bergstrom, came by without his helmet. 'Better get yourself a helmet,' I told him. 'A sniper is going to get you right between the eyes.'

"'Aw,' he said, 'I broke my chinstrap during the jump.'

"A few minutes later, somebody came up and said Bergstrom bought it.

"'Nah, I was just talking to him.'

"'Yup, a sniper got him right between the eyes.'

"It just gave me the shivers. I carried him off the line. He was a good man, just nineteen years old."[67]

Company E had a successful jump, with all sticks jumping over the DZ. Lieutenant Adolf "Bud" Warnecke, the jumpmaster of his Company E stick, had been a noncommissioned officer with Company B during Normandy and had been awarded a battlefield commission. "It was a nice Sunday afternoon, no problem seeing all the landmarks. The whole company jumped right on our objective."[68]

Lieutenant James Tibbetts, with Headquarters Company, 2nd Battalion, felt the combat jump and subsequent assembly proceeded in an almost textbook fashion. "In an hour and a half our battalion was assembled and moved out. That was better than we had done in any practice jump."[69]

As the 3rd Battalion serial approached the DZ, the Chalk 1 stick, consisting of Lieutenant Russell Wilde, the Company G commander and jumpmaster; Lieutenant Colonel Louis Mendez, the battalion commander; a couple of battalion headquarters personnel; and Company G headquarters troopers, got the green light and jumped over the drop zone.

Technician Fourth Grade Francis Lamoureux was the last man in the stick. "I was pushing the guys ahead of me. As soon as I got out the door, something hit me. I hit the ground. I had a soft landing. Blood was running down my face. I'd been hit by a piece of the flak which hit the plane. But I didn't feel anything. I just let it clot."[70]

The C-47 carrying Sergeant Lyle K. Kumler's stick of 2nd Platoon Company H troopers was in trouble as it approached the drop zone. "Our plane was hit— one motor out, gas pouring from the wing on the side of the fuselage. Seven men were wounded in the plane. We abandoned ship about a mile from the drop zone. A fighter plane saved our lives."[71]

Sergeant Don Jakeway was a member of that stick. "Our jumpmaster calmly gave us the order to stand up and hook up, and stand in the door. Our plane was in a slow descent, and without waiting for a green light, this gave us all time to clear the plane before it crashed. I recall Father [Captain Joseph P.] Kenny was the last man in the stick, and we were all happy to see he made it out all right."[72]

As his plane neared the drop zone, Private First Class George T. Sheppard, with Company H, suddenly felt flak hit the plane. "Several pieces of shrapnel came through the plane and hit some of us. We were already standing and hooked up. I was not injured because the piece [of shrapnel] hit a hand grenade in my pocket, knocked a hole in it and burned the powder out. However, I didn't know it hit the grenade. I just knew my pocket was on fire and a buddy put it out with his hand. We went ahead and jumped. Then I reached in my pocket, took out the grenade, and saw the hole in it. In the other pocket was a white phosphorous grenade. If that had been hit, the whole plane would have been gone!"[73]

Another plane carrying Lieutenant Arthur E. Lange's fifteen man Company H stick was hit by flak, which wounded three of the troopers. The plane caught fire and Lange's stick, except for the three wounded troopers, jumped near the town of Grave, in the 504th Parachute Infantry Regiment's sector. Lieutenant Lange and the remaining eleven Company H troopers would later join Company H at Berg en Dal on D+2.

The plane which carried Lieutenant Robert J. Wickes, the platoon leader of the 2nd Platoon of Company I, was hit by flak near the open doorway just before the jump. Corporal Bob Chisolm, an assistant squad leader, was standing just behind him, jumping number two in the stick. "I was hit in the face, my neck, and the body. Wickes got hit and was medically evacuated."[74]

Corporal Okey A. Mills, with Headquarters Company, 3rd Battalion, landed near Lieutenant Robert M. Mitchell's stick of Company I troopers, who missed the drop zone. Mills and the others landed close to a group of German marines, who opened fire on them. "Lieutenant Mitchell was shot through the groin. The bullet went through a phosphorous grenade attached to his rifle belt, which set Mitchell's clothes on fire. Someone behind me asked me to pass my canteen to put out the fire. I turned to hand my canteen over, and when I turned back to face the road, one of those marines, every bit six feet and nine inches tall, was standing up and looking up and down the road. I was close enough to spit on him. My Tommy gun jammed this time, but someone behind me shot at him, nipping him a little. Talking about fast—that giant man ran with Olympic speed. As other bullets zipped by him, the marine threw his rifle in the air and raised his hands to surrender. Since my Thompson had jammed, I took over Lieutenant Mitchell's Tommy gun and altogether fired about sixteen magazines of ammo in the firefight. Toward the end, two Germans at a time would jump up and fire in our direction, and two others would run back toward the rear. That was repeated several times, as they tried to withdraw. However, some paratroopers from the 505th approached from the flank and circled in behind the German marines. Then those big tall Krauts came out of their foxholes with hands up. They laid down their weapons, took off their steel helmets and put on their bib caps. The paratroopers really looked short among those tall Germans—every one of them was head and shoulders above their captors."[75]

Private First Class Richard G. Wolch, with Service Company, was a veteran of the Normandy jump and aware of the danger associated with a combat jump. "As the planes neared the DZ, the jumpmaster yelled to stand and hook up. My legs felt like rubber as I leaped to my feet. I was scared and scared stiff. With one hand clung to a hand grip above my head and with the other I hooked the static line to the anchor line which runs parallel with the fuselage. A 'butterfly' was slowly creeping into my stomach. Beads of sweat rolled down my cheeks, drenching the collar of my jumpsuit. I kept telling myself everything will be OK, but the butterfly did not leave. I thought of an antiaircraft shell hitting the plane before the word 'Go' was given. Someone behind me was cursing and sobbing.

"'Is everybody ready?' yelled the jumpmaster.

"Twenty-one voices answered as one, 'Hell yes, let's go.'

"Again the jumpmaster yelled, 'OK, pile out.' I saw him disappear through the door, then the second, the third, fourth and I began the speedy shuffle toward the door. As I moved near the door, the 'butterfly' suddenly disappeared. I felt light on my feet. I swore and I threw my right foot out of the door. Swearing always did seem to help. The prop blast caught my body and pulled me into nothingness. The parachute opened with a terrific jerk, shaking every bone in my body. I opened my eyes, but could only see blackness. My helmet had slid over my face at the opening shock, completely obscuring my view. Finally, I arranged the helmet then checked the chute for possible rips or broken suspension lines. I turned my attention to the ground when I heard the sharp barks of M1 rifles. Hundreds of men and parachutes covered the drop zone. The different colored parachutes resembled a large flower with insects crawling over it. Overhead more planes roared over, spewing paratroopers and equipment bundles. The sky blackened with men and parachutes. Running toward the west side of the DZ were seven enemy ack-ack gunners trying to reach the shelter of trees and brush which bordered the drop zone. A few seconds ago, they were shooting 20mm and 40mm shells at us, causing planes and men to crash to death. A score of paratroopers took aim and fired; the enemy fell to the ground and lay still. The swinging of the earth made me realize my own predicament.

"I was oscillating at a terrific rate. Pulling slowly on the risers to halt the oscillation, I clamped my feet together and waited for the ground to rush up. A paratrooper looked up then jumped aside. I relaxed for the landing and said a short prayer. I hit the ground backwards, but not gently. Rolling over on my back caused my Tommy gun to act as a prop and I ended the roll with my face deep in the sand. Half blinded, I shook the sand out of the barrel and tried to pull back the bolt. Jammed! I dropped the Tommy gun and pulled an automatic pistol from my boot and snapped back the hammer. None of the enemy were in sight, except two badly riddled bodies. I had landed near a 20mm gun emplacement. Both barrels were shattered by grenades and the crew killed. I wanted the [gun] sight for a souvenir, but found that a paratrooper had already taken it."[76]

CHAPTER 10

"USE TRENCH KNIVES AND BAYONETS"

The 508th assembled quickly upon landing. Captain Ben Delamater, the 1st Battalion's executive officer, helped to get the battalion organized and ready to move out to its objective. "The SOP [standard operating procedure] assembly assisted by red smoke grenade markers and red cloth streamers was rapid, except for a slight delay caused by the necessity of changing the center of the assembly area. This point was to have been the corner of woods which we soon realized existed only on our maps. To facilitate assembly, each company had subsectors in prearranged compass directions from the center marker, plus a sound locator, such as a whistle blast, klaxon ratchet, bugle note, and (for B Company) the facetious tenor of a French taxi horn, liberated in Normandy.

"Recovery of the equipment bundles was good and soon we realized the air corps had, for a change, done a superior job. Within an hour, the souvenir hunters had cut a piece of parachute nylon, the jump casualties had been gathered, equipment secured, and we were ready to go.

"During the 15-20 minute delay for the 3rd Battalion to join us, we watched from Voxhil the wild entrucking and detrucking antics of several groups of Germans 1,200-1,500 yards to the southwest. They evidently had a preplanned antiairborne scheme of action, but lacked the courage and numbers to put their plans into effect at the most favorable time.

"The strength reports indicated that about ninety-five percent of the 508 were accounted for. Earlier, the three rifle companies had averaged 145 men and Headquarters Company with its CP group, communications platoon, supply section, light machine gun platoon, and 81mm mortar platoon had jumped 153 men. All four 81mm mortars, but only four of the eight light machine guns were found. The battalion supply section had long since been busy gathering bundles and attempting to borrow farm carts for transportation. The jump casualties also were left at Voxhil with the 2nd Battalion's D Company, as the 1st Battalion moved toward its first objective."[1]

Captain Jonathan Adams, despite having three of his company's nine planes go down, assembled Company A and moved out at the front of the 1st Battalion column inside of an hour. "Within a half hour after the jump, A Company had

273

two patrols on their way to the objective as planned. Contact through 536s [hand held radios known as walkie-talkies] however lasted only about ten minutes."[2]

The information radioed by the Company A patrols was then relayed to Lieutenant Colonel Shields Warren, the commander of the 1st Battalion. "The objective was unoccupied by any German troops and [the patrol] was organizing a roadblock on the main road from Nijmegen leading south to Groesbeek. The battalion S-2 [Lieutenant Lee Frigo], who had accompanied the platoon, stated that Dutch civilians asserted that no German troops were in the area, except for a few labor troops."[3]

Receiving information from the patrols that no enemy was between them and the objective at De Ploeg, Captain Adams and Company A increased the pace of the advance. "The march to the objective was (almost) uneventful...Everyone started digging in. I soon found out that the company was not in the best training shape...I found that I was one of the few who still had a (AT) mine in his possession on the first objective. Everyone had the idea that the rest of the job would be as easy as it had been up to that point. That was somewhat my own impression and I still believe if we had marched straight to the [highway] bridge [in Nijmegen] we would have had it without a fight."[4]

Lieutenant Colonel Warren's 1st Battalion arrived at De Ploeg at around 6:30 p.m., about five hours after landing, without encountering any significant resistance. Warren ordered his troopers to dig in and strengthen the roadblock on the Nijmegen–Groesbeek highway to prevent German movement south from Nijmegen. Meanwhile, Captain Ben Delamater, the battalion's executive officer, got the command post organized. "The regimental commanding officer [Colonel Roy Lindquist], with his radio operator and two Dutch interpreters from the British Army soon followed us onto our first objective. The planned defenses were being set up when several civilians wearing arm bands and carrying Underground credentials of some sort told the colonel that the Germans had deserted Nijmegen, that the town and the highway bridge were lightly held.

"The regimental CO had been instructed that if the initial mission were accomplished to 'go ahead and take the highway bridge if you can.' This division order was perfectly understood in relation to the primary missions and was not a weak, conditional order as might be supposed offhand.

"The regimental and battalion COs then planned to send one platoon of C Company [led by Lieutenant Bob Weaver], plus the S-2 section, plus two light machine gun squads on a reconnaissance patrol to approach the bridge from the south, while A and B Companies, with the remaining two light machine gun squads, and two 81mm mortar squads attacked it from the southeast. Before these forces could even get started, another C Company platoon had to be dispatched to our rear to investigate insistent Dutch reports of a large enemy force hiding in our rear. Guided by a civilian, this force approached the dangerous area, only to find the hiding place now in the hands of our own forces, minus Germans. This force returned to the first objective where the regimental CO, myself, about one-third of battalion headquarters, and C Company less one platoon spent an anxious but inactive night."[5]

Lieutenant Colonel Warren remembered the circumstances surrounding the dispatch of the patrol differently. "C Company was in reserve, and A and B Companies occupied the MLR [main line of resistance]. As the battalion was organizing the MLR, a combat patrol consisting of Lieutenant Weaver's platoon of C Company was told to move into Nijmegen, investigate resistance in and around the bridge, and radio back on the strength of the bridge defenses. Lieutenant Weaver was given an SCR 300 [radio] from battalion headquarters for this purpose. Lieutenant Weaver was further instructed that if the bridge was undefended or lightly defended, to secure it, and immediately radio battalion. (It is believed that this patrol was directed by regimental headquarters, and Lieutenant Weaver was selected because he had fought through the Normandy campaign very ably and gallantly.)"[6]

The patrol consisted of Lieutenant Bob Weaver's 3rd Platoon of Company C; Lieutenant Lee Frigo, the 1st Battalion S-2, and his intelligence section; and two light machine gun squads from Headquarters Company, 1st Battalion. Lieutenant Arthur R. Stevens was Weaver's assistant platoon leader.

At 6:30 p.m., the patrol moved along the Groesbeek-Nijmegen highway to the edge of Nijmegen, where it knocked out a German machine gun position using Tommy guns. Upon entering Nijmegen, the patrol made a wrong turn and lost its bearings. The patrol, trying to stay off of the streets, cut through backyards for a half an hour, but wound up lost. Lieutenants Weaver, Stevens, and Frigo decided to approach a home and see if a local Dutch guide could be found to lead the patrol to the traffic circle just south of the bridge. A guide was brought to the house and the patrol moved out, but before it had gone a block, saw two Germans standing behind a tree. Both were taken prisoner without resistance. At the end of the block, a German sentry challenged the patrol and was killed by a burst from one of the patrol's automatic weapons.

As the patrol waited to move forward again, Private First Class Gordon Cullings, the medic with the 3rd Platoon of Company C, heard the sound of an approaching vehicle. "We were lined up on both sides of the street and being as quiet as possible. A truckload of Germans came up behind us. When they got about to the center of the platoon, all hell broke loose. I was behind a tree; my knee was [extended] out from the tree. One of the guys threw a Gammon grenade against the truck and a piece of metal hit my knee."[7]

Private Gene Metcalfe, one of the Company C troopers, was wounded in the back and leg during the melee. "I got hit with something, a grenade or whatever. [Private First Class Ray E.] Mead and a couple of the other buddies rolled me over. They propped me against a tree. There was all of this blood and they figured I was dead. So they had to get out of there and they took off. I was there until the Germans came by and picked me up and took me to an aid station."[8]

The firing alerted a German machine gun position down the street, which opened fire, pinning down the patrol. Fifteen members of the patrol were slightly wounded by ricocheting machine gun bullets. Private First Class Cullings knew the patrol had to get away the enemy machine gun fire. "We started to withdraw. One of the guys was shot in the arm. I asked the lieutenant to get into a house so I could fix him up. We got in a house and I got him taken care of and we proceeded [on the mission]."[9]

Led by their courageous Dutch guide, the patrol took side streets and reached the Keizer Lodewijkplein traffic circle, just south of the highway bridge. While there, Lieutenant Weaver received a message over the SCR 300 radio that Companies A and B were moving to capture the bridge. Weaver decided to take the patrol back and rejoin Company C, which was accomplished without further incident by dawn the following morning.

Back at the drop zone, Company D began to secure Landing Zone "T" for the gliders due to arrive the next day. After landing, Lieutenant Robert Sickler, the platoon leader of the 3rd Platoon, assembled his platoon and awaited orders. "Company D reverted to regimental control upon landing and, less one squad of the 1st Platoon, the company executive officer, the communications sergeant, and the company supply sergeant, who were forced to jump prior to reaching the drop zone, proceeded to the vicinity of Hooge Hof. Here, the company command post was established in a wooded draw. The company commander [Lieutenant Norman MacVicar] ordered the platoon leaders to prepare defensive positions on the ridge east of the command post, platoons abreast, with the 2nd Platoon [led by Lieutenant Temple Tutwiler] on the left in the edge of the woods north of the road [that ran east from Hooge Hof], the 1st Platoon [led by Lieutenant Joseph Hall] south of the road, and the 3rd Platoon on the right. The company observation post was established in an upstairs bedroom of the farmhouse on top of the ridge.

"The regimental ammunition officer and four men from the regimental supply section had remained on the drop zone to recover the additional bundles of supplies which had been dropped with the regiment. This supply section attached themselves to company headquarters and established a regimental supply dump at the company command post. After commandeering a team of horses and a farm wagon from Hooge Hof, they began the immense task of gathering the scattered supplies.

"The company commander ordered a patrol be sent from the 2nd Platoon to determine if there was any enemy in the vicinity of Voxhil. A similar patrol was dispatched from the 1st Platoon to search Lerkendaal, and one from the 3rd Platoon to search the village of Kamp. The patrol which visited Lerkendaal met no opposition and returned with a negative report. The patrols which visited Voxhil and Kamp each killed three Germans, who were apparently attempting to hide after having abandoned their 20mm antiaircraft guns on the drop zone. No prisoners were taken and no casualties were suffered by the patrols.

"It was growing dark by the time the last of the patrols was in, and the company settled down for the night, maintaining a [two] man outpost about 250 yards in front of each platoon, and one man awake in each two man foxhole. The night passed quietly without event, and it was beginning to appear as though the enemy was not going to contest our occupation of this particular area."[10]

Meanwhile, Private First Class Dick Wolch and the Service Company S-4 supply section collected the equipment bundles on and around the drop zone. "Staff Sergeant [William W.] Bill Howe, Corporal Harold Kasper, and I were assigned to haul the supplies and ammunition from the drop zone to the regimental ammunition dump, which was being set up a short distance from the drop zone. The three of us walked towards a farmhouse hoping to find a horse and cart to help us with the job. We knew from experience in Normandy that the enemy would waste no time and would launch a counterattack ASAP, so it was essential to bring the supplies to the right places quickly.

"As we neared the house a boy of fifteen approached. I lifted my gun as a signal for him to halt. He waited with a wide grin until we approached. He spoke fairly good English and began telling us how many enemy troops were in the area and where they were located. I interrupted by asking for a horse and cart. He led us into a big courtyard where other members of the family were waiting to welcome us. I told Bill and Harold to look for the horse and cart, and in the meantime I would stand guard near the courtyard gate."[11]

Meanwhile, the 2nd Battalion, less Company D, was moving to its initial objectives of establishing roadblocks to stop German movement into and out of Nijmegen to the north and assisting the 504th Parachute Infantry Regiment with capturing Bridge Number 9 at Hatert along the Maas-Waal Canal to the west.

The 2nd Battalion's order of march was the 3rd Platoon of Company E; followed by Company F; Headquarters Company, 2nd Battalion; and finally Company E, less the 3rd Platoon.

The 3rd Platoon of Company E, led by Lieutenant Adolph "Bud" Warnecke, moved out from the drop zone at the head of the battalion column at 2:15 p.m. Two scouts, Private First Class Theodore L. "Ted" Quade and Corporal Louis W. Yourkovich were in the lead and two other troopers were deployed on each flank as security. The battalion advanced northwest on the Groesbeek-Nijmegen highway and then turned left on Sionsweg and proceeded west toward its objectives. No opposition was encountered until it reached the railroad tracks running south from Nijmegen, where the scouts found several Germans, some armed and others not, playing games on bicycles, apparently unaware of the airborne landings. When Corporal Yourkovich called to them to surrender, they ran into a nearby house. Private First Class Quade killed one and they captured two others, while the remainder escaped out of the house into the woods.

The advance continued west along the same road, where the name changed to Scheidingsweg west of the railroad. As it did, the 3rd Platoon of Company E was fired upon from the woods, wounding Corporal Walter C. Woods in the knee. The Company E troopers returned fire and drove off the Germans, who left weapons, ammunition, grenades, and ten bicycles behind, which the 3rd Platoon collected and took with them.

While the 3rd Platoon of Company E cleared the Germans from the woods, Company F took the lead as the battalion continued toward its objectives. Company F was short two sticks, which had been dropped early, one in the 504th Parachute Infantry Regiment's sector, west of the Maas-Waal Canal and the other east of the canal near Malden. The company's objective was to establish roadblocks on the main highway running south from Nijmegen at the intersection with Oude Molen. Technician Fourth Grade Dwayne Burns was the company's communications NCO. "Darkness overtook us as we reached the outskirts of town. We put scouts out and moved into the edge of town, but we still had not run into enemy resistance. It was a very dark night. The scouts had stopped the company and we were standing there, waiting for them to give us the word to move up, when a German machine gun opened up right in front of us. The scouts had walked right past it in the dark. Captain [Harold] Martin and I were almost standing in front of it. I saw the muzzle blast right in front of us and off to our left the tracers were going right down the middle of the street where the company was standing. It looked like a long finger of light that you could reach out and touch.

"We scattered and hit the ground trying to find some kind of cover, but there was none. A rifle fired and a grenade exploded, then all was deadly quiet. No one made a sound and I could hear my heart pounding as I laid there. Down the line, someone yelled, 'Medic!' and I knew someone had been hit. We lost one man [Sergeant Richard P. Colaw] who was standing in the line of fire. We were lucky—if they had aimed a little more to the left, we could have lost half of the company. We called a halt for the night, dug in, and set up roadblocks."[12]

Lieutenant Wayne Smith was the platoon leader of the 2nd Platoon of Company F. "Using demolitions, the 3rd Platoon felled some trees across the road and set up a defense of this roadblock. The 2nd Platoon erected another roadblock behind that of the 3rd Platoon and set up a defense according to plan. The 1st Platoon moved to the right flank of the company and set up two roadblocks, six or eight blocks away, to protect the right flank of the company."[13]

The assistant platoon leader of the 2nd Platoon, Lieutenant Donald Burke, and his stick joined the remainder of the 2nd Platoon of Company F at its roadblock around 5:00 p.m. the next day, September 18. The other Company F stick, led byLieutenant Edward M. King, that had been dropped short of the drop zone joined the rest of the 3rd Platoon at its roadblock at about 10:00 a.m. the next morning.

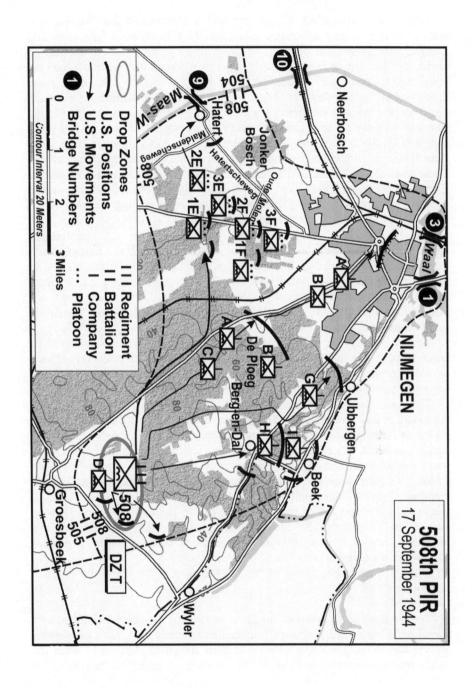

Company E, consisting of 132 men and 8 officers, reached its objective without further enemy opposition after the 3rd Platoon's firefight. The 2nd Platoon, with thirty-eight men, led by Lieutenant Lynn Tomlinson, the platoon leader, and Lieutenant David D. Liebmann, the assistant platoon leader, had the mission of assisting the 1st Battalion, 504th Parachute Infantry Regiment in the capture of Bridge Number 9 at Hatert. However, when the platoon arrived at the objective, the bridge had already been blown. The 2nd Platoon returned to the company area and set up a roadblock on Hatertscheweg about seventy-five yards northeast of the intersection with Maldenscheweg, blocking movement south from Nijmegen to Hatert. The platoon was well armed to stop an enemy attack. It had two bazookas, three BARs, three .30-caliber machine guns, at least twenty Gammon grenades, sixty-four fragmentation grenades, around ten white phosphorous grenades, four Thompson submachine guns, eighteen M1 rifles, and a 60mm mortar with forty rounds of ammunition.

The 1st Platoon of Company E, led by Lieutenant Roy A. Schermerhorn, established two roadblocks. The first was on the main highway running south from Nimegen to Mook near the intersection with Grootstalschelaan, consisting of the 2nd Squad, the 3rd Squad, and the platoon's mortar squad. The troopers defending this roadblock were armed with two .30-caliber machine guns, one bazooka, two BARs, a grenade launcher, twelve M1s, three Thompson submachine guns, and a 60mm mortar.

The 1st Squad, with only nine troopers, set up a second roadblock about five hundred yards to the east, near the intersection of a secondary road and Scheidingsweg. It was armed with one bazooka, a .30-caliber light machine gun, a grenade launcher, four M1s, and a Thompson submachine gun.

The 2nd and 3rd Squads of the 3rd Platoon remained with battalion headquarters and together with Headquarters Company, 2nd Battalion, set up a perimeter defense around the battalion command post. The two 3rd Platoon squads manned a sector about a hundred yards west of the command post. They were armed with two light machine guns, two BARs, three Thompson submachine guns, twelve M1 rifles, numerous hand grenades, and one grenade launcher. The 1st Squad and mortar squad of the 3rd Platoon established a roadblock at the intersection of a side street east of Hatertscheweg and Heiweg, west of the Sanatorium. Its armament included one light machine gun, two bazookas, one BAR, two Thompson submachine guns, six M1s, a grenade launcher, and a 60mm mortar.

There was no enemy action in the 2nd Battalion sector during the night of September 17-18.

The 3rd Battalion assembled quickly after landing. Company H jumped with a total of 132 men and 9 officers, but Lieutenant Louis Toth, the commanding officer, was short two sticks which had been forced to jump early when the planes transporting them were hit by flak while approaching the drop zone. "It took only about one hour to assemble the company and took two hours to assemble the battalion."[14]

After assembly, Lieutenant Colonel Louis Mendez moved out with his battalion to capture the high ground southeast of Nijmegen around Ubbergen, Beek, and Berg-en-Dal and establish roadblocks on the two highways running between Nijmegen and Wyler, Germany. "Initially, from the DZ proper, I Company was to dispatch and did dispatch, a combat patrol to the battalion objective; and then the patrol leader was to dispatch a reconnaissance patrol to the Nijmegen bridge. The I Company combat patrol, commanded by Lieutenant [William D.] Bush, left immediately after the drop. The battalion moved rapidly to its objective, Berg-en-Dal, and the surrounding high ground, being held up only once when the 1st Battalion passed in front of it."[15]

Corporal Bob Chisolm was a member of the Company I combat patrol. Upon arriving at Berg-en-Dal, Corporal Chisolm was treated for shrapnel wounds that he had received just prior to the jump. "I went to the Dutch hospital in Berg-en-Dal and they put stitches in my forehead, a patch on my throat, and nothing on my body. I returned right to duty."[16]

Then, Chisolm left Berg-en-Dal on the preplanned reconnaissance patrol. "Lieutenant Bush was our assistant platoon leader. He had the mission of taking a patrol to penetrate as far up into Nijmegen to the bridge as he could. There was Lieutenant Bush, myself, [Privates First Class] Joe Petry, and Bill Hughes—my buddy from Normandy who had saved my bacon—we were on the patrol. All we were told to do was you don't get in a fight, you get as far up to the bridge as you can."[17]

Lieutenant Toth and Company H were assigned to seize Berg-en-Dal and establish a roadblock on the highway which ran from Nijmegen through Berg-en-Dal to Wyler, Germany. "We marched right in. It was the Gestapo division headquarters [of SS Obergruppenführer Hans Kammler, Special Commissioner for V-2 Operations]. When they heard we were dropping, they had burned all papers, but we still found useful documents for future operations. We took some prisoners (officers)."[18]

After landing, Sergeant Don Jakeway, whose Company H stick had been forced to jump early from their damaged C-47 about a mile short of the drop zone, moved out to join the rest of the company at Berg-en-Dal. "On the way into Berg-en-Dal, I will never forget an act of kindness made by a Dutch family. My squad had dug in on our approach to Berg-en-Dal and the Groot Hotel. As we waited for word to move out, a man and a woman came from one of the houses and indicated that they had some hot food ready and to come in to eat. I willingly agreed and sent my men in by twos. I was the last one to go, and I will never forget the fried potatoes and pieces of meat—a meal fit for a king. Later, as I waited in my foxhole, I became depressed for having my men and I eating what surely must have been their complete supply of food. At the time, we were very hungry, but we should have known how hard it was for these people to find food for themselves. I hadn't taken the time to think how we must have deprived those gracious people. However, we attacked the village [of Berg-en-Dal] and the Groot Hotel located at the top of the hill, and during our search found that this had been a division headquarters [of Obergruppenführer SS General Hans Kammler, Special Commissioner for V-2 Operations] for the Germans stationed in the area. The coffee was still warm in the cups, and the tables were set with silver settings with food on the tables. In the cellar of the hotel we found a hoard of food; meats in lockers, eggs, fruits, vegetables, butter and cheeses and plenty of milk. It was a special delight that I helped distribute this food to the people in the village, including the couple who had fed us.

"We dug in around the Groot Hotel, which overlooked Beek and the flats below. We could look out into Germany."[19]

Upon arriving at Berg-en-Dal, Private Henry McLean's Company H squad were reinforced with two bazooka teams and assigned to establish a roadblock on the highway from Wyler, Germany. "I was told that the bazooka men with me would set up roadblocks on the highway [from Wyler] to Berg-en-Dal. While the bazooka men were busily setting up their position, I walked over to the Hotel de Groot and went inside. In the dining room, I discovered that the German officers had been ready to sit down and eat their Sunday dinner when they were surprised by the parachute drop. Hunger and the sight of food overcame me, so I ate not one, but two plates full of the delicious dinners.

"Back in the village square, I noticed a small café across the street. I decided to investigate the café to see if anything was going on there. Much to my amazement, several people were sitting around talking, apparently oblivious to what was happening. A young girl at the bar asked me, 'Beer?' Never one to refuse the hand of friendship holding a beer, I accepted. To my surprise, the beer was COLD. To most people that would not be momentous, but I had had only warm beer for two years. I will never forget how good that cold beer tasted."[20]

Meanwhile, Private First Class Dick Wolch, with Service Company, was collecting equipment bundles on and around the drop zone. "The companies had already cleared the drop zone and were attacking the city of Berg-en-Dal, a mile away. I could hear the clatter of machine guns and rifle fire. Now and then the dull explosion of a mortar shell could be heard.

"A movement in the brush four hundred yards away caught my attention. Standing on tiptoe, I saw a file of men leap over a fence and squat down in the brush. Friend or enemy? More men were leaping the fence. One man stood up and I saw the blue-gray uniform of a German soldier. He lifted his arm, then crouched down. A moment later the group moved in the direction of the gate.

"With a low whistle, I warned [Staff Sergeant] Bill [Howe] and [Corporal] Harold [Kasper], then crouched down and worked my way into a cluster of brush growing against the courtyard wall. The enemy moved forward almost a hundred yards before they stopped. Their eyes were riveted upon the drop zone where now gliders [which missed the LZ in the 505th sector and landed on the 508th drop zone] threw up great clouds of dust as they skidded to a stop. The front of the gliders lifted, antitank guns and jeeps loaded with men rode out and headed in the direction of Berg-en-Dal. Many of the glider troopers did not wait for the front of the glider to lift; they simply kicked the flimsy partitions of the fuselage out and jumped out. We decided to make a dash for the drop zone, hoping that the arrival of the glider troops would keep the enemy down and out of sight. Bill held the reins and made the horse run at a fast trot. The three of us ran on the off side of the cart for protection. Looking back I saw six or seven of the enemy rise and take aim. Harold stopped and fired a burst. He turned and ran after the cart while I stopped and fired a burst. We kept that up until our clips were empty. Our guns drew the attention of glidermen. They opened up with machine guns mounted on jeeps and kept the enemy pinned down until we reached the safety of the small hill [where the regimental supply dump was located]. A mortar crew had had the time to set a mortar in position and lobbed a half dozen shells at the enemy group. That ended all the plans of that group to advance on us, all were a direct hit.

"We worked for three hours, hauling cart after cart load of ammunition from the drop zone to the regimental ammunition dump. The dump was located on a hill overlooking the DZ. We sorted the different types of ammo into separate piles and loaded our cart to supply the 3rd Battalion. We were about ready to drive off when the enemy began shelling us with 20mm shells. The first shell burst on a rock between Bill and me, showering bits of steel and rock in all directions. Someone cried out and then swore. I made a dive for a deep hole as the next shell burst. I will never know how Bill got into the hole before I did, but he was there. The shelling stopped as suddenly as it began. We crawled out of the hole and administered first aid to the wounded. None of the men were seriously wounded though. A tall fellow slipped off his jump pants, turned them upside down and shook the remainder of a good bottle of whiskey out of his pocket. We all agreed he had had a good reason to curse.

"Bill, Harold, Staff Sergeant Sherman G. Boyd, 2nd Lieutenant Bill Lowder, and I were ordered to take the first load of ammunition to the 3rd Battalion. We threw most of our equipment on our cart and spread out on both sides of the cart in a skirmish line. Bill did the driving. We passed a smoldering C-47 troop carrier and as we walked closer, I saw that the pilot was still sitting in the pilot seat, burned to a cinder. Not far from the C-47 we came upon a wagon trail. Lieutenant Lowder looked at the map and decided that the wagon trail would lead us into Berg-en-Dal and to the 3rd Battalion headquarters. The trail twisted and turned in the thick woods. Harold and Sherman walked in front of the cart, while Lowder and I covered the rear. As the trail dipped into a deep gully, Lieutenant Lowder pointed out a motorcycle to me, half hidden in the brush. He told the others to keep going with the cart while he and I would try to start the cycle and ride it to headquarters. We checked the motorcycle for booby traps and we found out that the motor was still warm. Evidently, the rider was running through the woods with the dispatch papers at that same moment. We found an empty dispatch case on the motorcycle to support that theory. While I was busy checking the cycle, a rifle cracked and a bullet plunked into a tree near the cycle. I rolled off of the bike and lay still, hardly daring to breathe. The rifle cracked again and the bullet passed over my head and plowed into the ditch bank.

"Hearing a commotion behind me, I turned in time to see Lieutenant Lowder run through the ditch bank and disappear across the road. Another bullet chipped a pile of bark from the tree over my head. I looked around for means of escape and decided to take the same route Lieutenant Lowder took a moment before. Another bullet hit the tree and then I rose to my knees and jumped into the ditch. The rifle cracked again, but I didn't hear it passing. I cussed all second lieutenants when I raced up the bank and over the road and dove in the ditch on the opposite side of the road. I groaned in midair. The ditch was over nine feet deep. I landed on my stomach and almost knocked myself out.

"I rose to my feet and ran in the direction of which the cart had disappeared. Judging by the length of the footsteps I saw in the soft sand, I knew Lieutenant Lowder had wasted no time in leaving the area. A half hour later I found him sitting in a ditch with his hands cupped to his head. He was extremely happy to see me. He then told me why he left me lying near the cycle. When the first shot was fired he thought he saw a hole in my chest, over the heart and believed I had been instantly killed. The blood that he saw was evidently a leaf that had been stuck to my jumpsuit. At a time like that, a man is likely to imagine anything.

"When we reached the battalion CP, Bill, Harold, and Sherman had the cart unloaded and were digging foxholes. Lieutenant Lowder and I grabbed shovels and dug our foxholes close together. We had hardly finished when we heard the old familiar whistle, followed by a long drawn out howl which passed over us and exploded near the CP. In a flash we were in our holes, hugging the cool moist earth. More shells passed over, but exploded farther away. We crawled out of our foxholes, picked up our shovels, and dug the holes a foot deeper.

"We established an ammunition dump for the 3rd Battalion five hundred meters below the city of Berg-en-Dal. Due to the active enemy air force it was necessary that the ammunition and cart be camouflaged. Twice enemy planes roared over the treetops. One was recognized as a photography plane. Our equipment was well covered, for the enemy did not come back to bomb or strafe. That night, I fell asleep listening to the screaming of shells and an occasional German plane passing overhead. It was the end of a busy day."[21]

For Lieutenant Colonel Louis Mendez, everything was going according to plan as his 3rd Battalion seized its objectives against almost no opposition. "Berg-en-Dal was taken with only token resistance. By 19:15 the battalion was fairly well established on the objective, and the preparation of defensive positions began.

"The enemy was slow to react in the battalion sector, and the night was very quiet. Roadblocks were established according to plan with the exception of the one in Beek. Here, the selection of officers seems to have been unfortunate, for they lacked the aggressiveness to make the strongpoint stick.

"Initially, the I Company platoon which manned the roadblock did not move to the national highway in Beek, but set up on the Berg-en-Dal–Nijmegen road. Since I was unable to check all the positions of the battalion before dark, I accepted the report of the officer in charge of the roadblock that it was in its proper place.

"I, as commanding officer of the 3rd Battalion received no orders to seize the highway bridge over the Waal. The battalion was, however, to be prepared to do so on division order. In order to reconnoiter for a possible move north, I sent G Company under Lieutenant Wilde into the city on his own initiative with orders to advance as far as possible towards the bridge."[22]

Upon reaching the initial Company G objective at around 5:00 p.m., Lieutenant Howard A. Greenawalt, the platoon leader of the 3rd Platoon, ordered his troopers to dig in. "The company was in position for but one hour when Lieutenant Wilde, the CO, called his platoon leaders to the CP and told us that we were to move to Nijmegen that evening. At 18:30 hour we moved out and upon reaching the high ground southeast of the city and near the outskirts, set up a bivouac for the night. It was getting dark and our knowledge of the town was skimpy. While marching to this position, we met a patrol led by Lieutenant [William] Bush of Company I, who reported that he had encountered no enemy as yet. He was continuing his patrol to Nijmegen and the bridge if possible."[23]

Corporal Bob Chisolm was a member of Lieutenant Bush's Company I reconnaissance patrol. "We went right down the road through town. We didn't have any opposition at all. We penetrated all the way to the bridge. We saw the 88[mm antiaircraft gun] sitting out there in the center of the [traffic] circle just before the bridge. We saw the Germans on it—just the gun crew—that's all we saw. We could have knocked the damn 88 out, right then."[24]

After observing that the highway bridge was apparently lightly defended, Corporal Bob Chisolm and the Company I reconnaissance patrol withdrew from Nijmegen to Berg-en-Dal. "We pulled back and we ran into G Company. They were making the advance up [toward Nijmegen]. We told [Lieutenant] Wilde what we had seen. That was our mission and we made the report. We went back to the company, because that mission was completed."[25]

AFTER LANDING EAST OF WYLER, GERMANY, LIEUTENANT REX COMBS, the platoon leader of the 3rd Platoon of Company A, assembled his stick of seventeen troopers along with several prisoners they had captured from antiarcraft gun positions shortly after landing, and moved into the town. There, they found chaos as German troops and vehicles scrambled to get away from the sudden threat of enemy paratroopers. Lieutenant Combs and his stick opened fire on the German troops and took a number of additional prisoners. As they approached one building in the town, a U.S. Army Air Corps officer unclothed above the waist and badly burned on the upper body and face, came running out of it toward them. A couple of the troopers applied salve on his severe burns and bandaged them with parachute cloth, while the rest of the stick cleaned out the building, capturing a number of enemy troops. A short time later, Lieutenant Combs and his stick picked up two Company A troopers who were members of Lieutenant Nolan Schlesinger's 2nd Platoon stick. They reported that Lieutenant Schlesinger had been killed. Lieutenant Combs ordered the two troopers retrieve Schlesinger's body. When they returned with Schlesinger, Combs could see part of his brain exposed and assumed he was dead. He didn't want to leave Schlesinger behind, so he ordered German prisoners to carry him. They found a barn ladder and with German coats draped over it, fashioned a stretcher on which to carry Schlesinger. Lieutenant Combs with twenty troopers and the injured air corps officer moved out from Wyler toward the drop zone, marching their prisoners in front. The troopers were engaged several times by German troops, but managed to reach the border with Holland safely.

Shortly after crossing into Holland, they came upon a CG-4 Waco glider with its occupants trapped inside. Lieutenant Combs and his men helped them get the nose of the glider up and the jeep removed from it. Lieutenant Combs put the injured air corps officer in the jeep and instructed the glider occupants to drive him to an aid station.

Lieutenant Combs and his troopers moved through Den Heuvel, where they found two other troopers, one of whom was Sergeant Anthony Cianfrani, a member of Combs' 3rd Platoon who had been wounded during the jump. They also found four German soldiers, who they added to their collection of prisoners. Lieutenant Combs and his troopers and their prisoners moved out for Voxhil and the drop zone, where they found an aid station and left their wounded, including Lieutenant Schlesinger. Lieutenant Schlesinger received medical treatment for his wounds and miraculously survived, but did not return to the regiment.

Lieutenant Combs and the other troopers continued toward Berg-en-Dal, stopping along the way at the house of the Vissar family, where Combs' leg wound was bandaged and the troopers were fed by the kind family. The group continued on to the 3rd Battalion command post at Berg-en-Dal, where they turned over fifty-nine prisoners and Lieutenant Combs checked in to the aid station there. Lieutenant Combs and his group had killed an additional twenty-one German troops.

Corporal Marion Kinman and Private A. B. Cannon were later awarded the Silver Star for their valor during the fighting to reach the drop zone. For his herosim and leadership during the action on September 17, Lieutenant Combs was awarded an oak leaf cluster (signifying a second award) for the Silver Star he was awarded for Normandy.

The regimental command post was established at 6:30 p.m. at Nebo, between and to the south of the 1st and 2nd Battalion sectors. That afternoon, Captain Chet Graham, the regimental liaison officer with division headquarters, decided to obtain a status of the progress toward the capture of the Nijmegen highway bridge. "I went to the 508th regimental CP and asked Colonel Lindquist when he planned to send the 3rd Battalion to the bridge. His answer was, 'As soon as the DZ is cleared and secured. Tell General Gavin that.'

"So I went through Indian country to the division CP and relayed Lindquist's message to Gavin. I never saw Gavin so mad. As he climbed into his jeep, he told me, 'Come with me—let's get him moving.' On arriving at the 508th regimental CP, Gavin told Lindquist, 'I told you to move with speed.'"[26]

A COUPLE OF HOURS AFTER THE ALLIED AIRBORNE LANDINGS, SS Gruppenführer Wilhelm Bittrich, commander of the II SS Panzer Korps, correctly assessed the goal of Operation Market Garden: getting across the Rhine River at Arnhem. Bittrich believed that the key to defeating the operation lay at Nijmegen. If he could stop the Americans and British from crossing the Waal River, he could destroy the British 1st Airborne Division at his leisure. The II SS Panzer Korps consisted of the 9th and 10th SS Panzer Divisions, both of which had been almost destroyed during the fighting in Normandy and the retreat across France. Both divisions had only about one-third of the allotted manpower and were without most of the authorized armored vehicles. Bittrich assigned the Nijmegen area to the 10th SS and the Arnhem area to the 9th SS. He ordered his most ready and mobile unit, SS Panzer Aufklärungs Abteilung 9, the 9th SS Panzer Division's reconnaissance battalion, commanded by SS Hauptsturmführer (Captain) Viktor Gräbner, to immediately move from its barracks north of Arnhem to Nijmegen. He also attached Gräbner's battalion to the 10th SS.

Gräbner's forty vehicles raced through almost deserted Arnhem streets, crossing the bridge over the Rhine River at around 6:00 p.m., about an hour before British Lieutenant Colonel John D. Frost's paratroopers seized the north end of the bridge. Upon his arrival at Nijmegen, Gräbner reported by radio that he had not seen any enemy paratroopers during the journey. At Nijmegen, he found troops of Kampfgruppe Henke, under the command of Oberst (Colonel) Henke, the commander of Fallschirmjäger Ersatz und Ausbildungs Regiment Hermann Göring (reserve parachute training regiment), in control of the city and the two bridges across the Waal River. Kampfgruppe Henke consisted of three understrength companies of Ersatz (Reserve) Bataillon 6 (under the command of the 406th Landesschützen Division), a company of the training regiment, the staff of an NCO training school, some miscellaneous military police units who normally guarded bridges and railroads, and twenty-nine 88mm flak guns and a number of 20mm antiaircraft guns of Schwere Flak Abteilung 572, along with their crews who provided air defense around the bridges.[27]

When Gräbner's force arrived, Oberst Henke was organizing a defensive perimeter around the highway and railroad bridges and had dispatched a number of squad sized units to establish outposts in order to provide an early warning of any movement by paratroopers into Nijmegen.

Finding no imminent threat to the Nijmegen bridges and receiving a radio report that British paratroopers had captured the north end of the Arnhem bridge, Gräbner left several halftracks and the SS troops transported in them to bolster the defense of Nijmegen and took the bulk of his force to Elst, about halfway between Arnhem and Nijmegen, where he could be in radio contact with German forces in both Arnhem and Nijmegen and move his force quickly to either sector.

AT ABOUT 8:00 P.M., COLONEL LINDQUIST ordered Lieutenant Colonel Warren, the commander of the 1st Battalion, to seize the Nijmegen highway bridge. It was an order that Warren wasn't expecting. "This was the first time the battalion was told it was to secure this bridge. By the time the battalion minus [Company C, one section of 81mm mortars, and one section of machine guns] was assembled from its rather wide defensive positions, it was well after dark.

"A Dutch Underground worker [Geert van Hees] who had contacted regimental headquarters had stated that the highway bridge over the Waal River was defended by a noncommissioned officer and seventeen men. This Dutch patriot also volunteered to guide the battalion into the town.

"The route into the bridge area was selected in consultation with the Dutch civilian. When I suggested the most direct route to the bridge, on the concept that speed was most important, the Dutch civilian pointed out that that route was covered by an 88mm gun, and that the street was very narrow. He suggested a route nearly as short, which followed a broad boulevard into town, and then swung east into the bridge area from the flank. He also pointed out that this route went by the Underground headquarters in the city, who could give us the last minute information on the bridge defenses. Working on the theory that if the Dutch civilian was loyal we could gain much, since no member of the unit had been in this large city before and [we would] lose only a few minutes of time, if he wasn't. Another contributing factor was the knowledge that the combat patrol under Lieutenant [Bob] Weaver was using the other route. If it was open, and the one the battalion used was blocked, the two were not so far apart that the movement could not be changed in route."[28]

Warren decided to use the route suggested by the young Dutchman and gave orders to his company commanders to begin moving into Nijmegen.

Corporal Jim Blue, a Normandy veteran, was an assistant squad leader with the 1st Platoon of Company A. "We received the order and it was something like this: Company A will lead the way, the 3rd Platoon leading, followed by the 1st Platoon, followed by the 2nd Platoon."[29]

However, Captain Jonathan Adams, commanding Company A, still did not have all of his company assembled from the drop. "At this time we were still short two sticks [those of Lieutenants Rex Combs and Nolan Schlesinger, which had been misdropped], but had the machine gun section of battalion headquarters company attached to us, plus battalion staff. It was beginning to get dark. We moved out to the IP [initial point] and waited for B Company.

"It was about ten o'clock I believe, when I was told to go ahead anyway. By this time it was pitch-black. We checked several houses along the way where the Dutchman said German soldiers might be, but found nothing."[30]

After searching the houses, Company A resumed the march into Nijmegen. Suddenly, Corporal Blue heard German machine gun fire shatter the still night air. "We had not traveled very far when the lead platoon (3rd) was brought under enemy machine gun fire. This platoon had one casualty, Corporal Roy B. Lewis. Under fire, Corporal Lewis jumped into a foxhole [dug earlier by the Germans] that another trooper had already occupied. This trooper had fixed bayonet and Corporal Lewis struck his leg, cutting the artery. Corporal Lewis died before he could receive proper medical aid.

"From this action we, the 1st Platoon moved through the 3rd Platoon and took the lead, my squad taking up the point. As we neared the town of Nijmegen a Dutch Underground agent was dispatched to us (the point). He worked with Private Walter Dikoon (the squad scout) who was preceding the squad [by] twenty-five to fifty yards. The Dutchman was using a bicycle and would ride forward to the next block, report back to Dikoon that all was clear; in turn Dikoon would inform the point and we moved forward. This Dutchman was very helpful and instrumental in the movement of our battalion through Nijmegen that 17th of September night.

"As we entered Nijmegen on the Groesbeek road one block from the Mook intersection [Groesbeekseweg at Fransestraat], the Dutchman reported to Dikoon that a German machine gun was set up [at the "Y" intersection of Groesbeekweg and Sint Annastraat] facing in our direction. This was where the Dutchman was moved aside. We told him to take cover and we moved forward."[31]

Corporal Blue's 1st Platoon squad moved along both sides of the tree lined Groesbeekseweg staying close to the houses and wrought iron fences fronting them. Lieutenant Colonel Warren and his radio operator moved just behind the point squad. "The time was a little after 22:00 hours. A sharp 'Halt,' unmistakably in German, came through the dark."[32]

Just seconds later, Captain Adams saw tracers from the German machine gun as it opened fire on the point. "The first shots fired wounded Lieutenant [Fred H.] Layman, platoon leader of the leading [1st] platoon and killed Lieutenant [Boyd A.] Alexander [the assistant platoon leader of the 3rd Platoon]."[33]

Corporal Blue immediately recognized the 1,200 round per minute rate of fire from the enemy machine gun. "A German MG-42 opened up; you could see the tracers ricocheting off the cobblestone street. The first burst got the lieutenant in the leg. We ran and pulled him along the iron picket fence.

"My first thought was they got Dikoon. But now a BAR opened up, up front and Dikoon came running back and reported that he had knocked out the machine gun crew. At this time and place here came Lieutenant Colonel Shields Warren (the battalion CO), Captain Jonathan E. Adams, CO of A Company, and Lieutenant [John] Foley up to the point to see what the situation was. Colonel Warren said, 'Good work men, keep the ball rolling.'

"Dikoon moved up to the intersection, moved right, and we were one block from the Keizer Karelplein square [and traffic circle]. As Dikoon moved forward he was killed outright by machine gun fire from the square. Captain Adams had the 2nd Platoon attack through the 1st Platoon and for the square. In the meantime, we heard motors warming up at the square."[34]

Lieutenant George Lamm was farther back in the column with his 2nd Platoon. "Captain Adams ordered the 2nd Platoon to pass through the 1st and 3rd Platoons to clear and occupy an area about the center of the circle, and to be prepared to assemble at a rallying point on order."[35]

Halftracks and trucks transporting grenadiers from SS Panzer Aufklärungs Abteilung 9 left earlier that evening by SS Hauptsturmführer Gräbner to bolster the defense of the Nijmegen bridges, arrived at the Kaiser Karelplein traffic circle just as the point element of Company A approached. As he waited along the curb, Corporal Blue heard the ominous sounds of a tracked vehicle up ahead. "Lieutenant Lamm of the 2nd Platoon called for two rocket launchers. These two teams came up immediately and were placed along the curb. All troops were ordered off the curb alongside the picket fence.

"At this time a halftrack moved forward loaded with German SS troops and came abreast of the rocket launcher teams; both opened fire at the same time. This disabled the halftrack, and all the SS troops jumped off the vehicle and ran in all different directions. Our orders were not to fire if we came to close combat. We were to use trench knives and bayonets. Most of the 1st Platoon had been moved inside the fence and between the houses. Here is where Company A, 508th, did some hand-to-hand combat. These SS troops were jumping the fence and trying to get away.

"Private First Class Ray M. Johnson from Munsford, Alabama and myself were between two houses which were very close together. Private First Class Johnson was armed with an M1 rifle with fixed bayonet and was ready for business. It happened that the CO of the SS unit jumped the fence and was trying to make his getaway by the way of our two buildings. We saw him coming.

"I said to Johnson, 'Get him with your bayonet.' As he came between us, Johnson gave him a thrust and completely missed him. The M1 dislodged from Johnson's hands. I was armed with a Tommy gun and trench knife. I had my trench knife out and I had to get this German. At the rear of these two houses was an interlocking tall wooden fence. I came up to his rear trying to make a decision as to contest him with my short trench knife or let him have a short burst from the Tommy gun. I chose the latter, because that trench knife seemed mighty short at that time.

"I knew I couldn't let this German get on the other side of the fence. He could have destroyed us with grenades. When I fired a short burst (three rounds), Lieutenant Foley sounded off, 'Who in the hell's firing the Tommy gun?'

"I sounded off, 'It's me.' He knew who it was and that closed that chapter.

"In the meantime, a self-propelled gun [most likely a Schützenpanzerwagen 251/9 halftrack, armed with a short barreled 75mm gun, belonging to Kompanie 5, SS Panzer Aufklärungs Abteilung 9] fired two rounds in our direction and moved from the circle."[36]

After the melee died down, Lieutenant Colonel Warren ordered Company A to "attack, secure the traffic circle, and block all entrances to it from the west. A Company immediately attacked as ordered."[37]

Lieutenant George Lamm and the 2nd Platoon, pushed forward into the traffic circle. "This move was a ticklish business. Friendly and enemy soldiers were mixed and there was no definite line. However, the darkness, which contributed to the confusion, also assisted us in reorganizing. Instructions were passed along to units: 'Fire only on orders or eyeball to eyeball defense! Use trench knife or bayonet when possible!'

"[Staff] Sergeant [George W.] Clement [III] had the major portion of the 2nd Platoon under control and organized with task equipment. Sergeant [Charles A.] Gushue, [Staff] Sergeant [Alvin H.] Henderson, and myself made a 'recon' of sorts to the curb of the circle. Peering up to the skyline, we made out the outline of a tall AA weapon in the park center. We decided to guide on it. We advanced with Gushue's unit elbow-to-elbow, without fire, and occupied the area. Others followed in column belt-to-belt buckle. (It was so dark, contact was maintained by touch.) As we moved out, there was a pause in the firing and a hush over the area—except for the calls from the lost and the wounded. Rifleman [Private Jean B.] LeBoeuf slipped into a Kraut foxhole, still occupied, and used his trench knife on the unlucky German. Sergeant Henderson's men checked out the foxholes we passed over and collected a couple of AA gun crews, who were rather on the elderly side. Rifleman [Private First Class Vernon F.] Stork took the POWs to the rear and returned promptly.

"As the platoon advanced beyond the AA guns into the center of the circle, BAR man [Private] Ed Wodowski and [Private First Class] James [R.] Benton were wounded. Both, along with [Private First Class] George Lapso, were picked up later by brave Dutch volunteers and medical people. They hid the wounded paratroopers from the Germans and treated their wounds."[38]

Private Wodowski, armed with a BAR, was crouching under a tree in the center of the traffic circle when he was wounded. "The Germans threw a hand grenade at me and I caught it in the left shoulder. It was one of those little 'egg' grenades. It picked me up and threw me over about five or six feet away. I got back up and picked up my weapon. I got back with a couple of other guys."[39]

During the attack on the Keizer Karelplein traffic circle, Sergeant Charles Gushue threw grenades at one machine gun position, then charged it, and bayoneted the three man crew.

Meanwhile Corporal Jim Blue and the rest of Company A moved up behind the 2nd Platoon. "The 2nd Platoon moved to the square and occupied the southeast side; the 3rd Platoon followed up and tied on with them. We, the 1st [Platoon] moved up and tied in with them [the 3rd Platoon]. This left the north side open."[40]

From his position, Corporal Blue noticed a good deal of movement to his front on the other side of the roundabout. "I reported this to platoon sergeant [Staff Sergeant Sherman] Van Enwyck. He told me to take two men and feel out the situation and see what was coming off. I took Ray Johnson and [Private First Class Eugene A.] McMillan and moved across the square facing the street that led to the train station.

"It was here that we stopped and listened to see if we could detect any sound or movement. We were standing by a large foxhole dug by Germans. While standing there listening, we heard the cocking action of a German MG from across the street and we knew what was to follow. McMillan dove for the hole with me following closely. As I landed in the hole and looked up, I saw Ray Johnson falling toward the hole. The tracers from the German MG provided enough light for me to know they were striking him. Johnson fell on me, mortally wounded. Here within two hours, two of my basic training comrades had been killed. 'Mac' and myself were in a hell of a position in this hole and something had to be done. The Germans had spotted us and were throwing grenades trying to hit the hole and they were coming close.

"Mac said, 'Blue, do something.' At this time I was on top of the hole. I pushed Johnson's body aside, reached for a phosphorous grenade, pulled the pin, and threw it in the direction of the MG position. It went off and lit up the area as usual. I could hear the MG crew breaking down the gun and going out of action. I called back for our machine guns to open up and they did. They fired bursts over us in the direction of the Germans' previous position. At this time I called back to cease fire. We returned to our line and shortly another MG opened up to the front of 3rd Platoon. There were several casualties, one being Private First Class James R. Benton. Benton received approximately seventeen MG bullet wounds in the right arm, side, and leg."[41] Benton miraculously survived.

As Company A cleared the traffic circle, Lieutenant Colonel Warren could sense that the attack was "bogging down in the fierce fire and hail of grenades just beyond the traffic circle. The company took a number of casualties and became somewhat confused in the darkness, so it was ordered to hold what it had gained, while B Company was ordered to take up the attack on the right of

A Company. B Company promptly complied with the order and ran into severe resistance, and was stopped by the intensity of the fire. In the meantime, the Dutch civilian had disappeared.

"At this stage, the Germans counterattacked, partially overrunning A Company, which was not completely reorganized from its initial attack. The German attack was stopped, B Company's reserve platoon [the 3rd Platoon] committed to cover the sector occupied by A Company, and A Company was pulled back and reorganized."[42]

As the 3rd Platoon of Company B approached the traffic circle, Technician Fifth Grade Walter Barrett heard the approach of a truck, which he knew had to be a German vehicle. "Our bazooka man crept to the monument in the center of the roundabout and waited patiently until the lorry came within range of his bazooka. His aim was perfect; the bazooka blew the German driver and his companion completely out of the lorry and onto the cobblestone street."[43]

As this occurred, Private Nathan Silverlieb, with the 3rd Platoon, Company B, was standing in the yard of a building facing the traffic circle with his 60mm mortar squad. "The door [of the building] opened up and there was a light and they could see us. The door closed right away. Then there was a hell of an explosion. The explosion spun me around and threw me against a fence. It shook me up a little bit. One of our guys threw a Gammon grenade and it didn't go off. Then one of our guys stepped on it. I heard that he had his foot blown off. I heard it was [Private First Class George F.] May."[44]

Sergeant Jim Kurz was also nearby when the Gammon grenade exploded. "I was knocked off my feet and thrown over a hedge. As I regained my senses, I could hear someone yelling. When I finally got back to the street, a medic was putting a tourniquet on the man's leg. He had lost a foot.

"Just then, we drew a lot of fire, but [Private] Chester [A.] Standley, our BAR man, cut loose with his BAR and we advanced until shortly it seemed the whole world caved in. Machine guns, rifles, and 88s [likely the 75mm gun of a Schützenpanzerwagen 251/9 halftrack] cut loose. This ended our advance for the night. Lieutenant Millsaps said to hold our position, but we could take to the buildings. We were beside a house, so we went in and had a good view from the second story window."[45]

In the almost total darkness of the moonless night, troopers like Private First Class Jim Allardyce, with Company B, couldn't easily distinguish enemy from friendly troops. "Finally it came through that the Jerries had stopped us and we thought we were surrounded, so we set up a perimeter defense around the modern brick school building. I found [Private William] Askren with the machine gun and he found me with the ammo and we got it out in front of the school where Jerries had holes dug and we set up the machine gun. Then we heard German voices out in front and moaning and cries of the wounded. Somewhere, a German was crying in pain for God and his mother. When it got real bad, [one of the officers] said, 'Someone shut that SOB up' and we heard the sound of a submachine gun and then quiet. After a while, Askren and I heard more confusion out front and finally the sound of people running right at us. I made sure that Askren was all set with my ammo loaded. I fixed my bayonet, took off my American style helmet to make a neutral silhouette, and then we waited. We were there all alone defending the front and we waited as the running got closer.

"'Shall I fire now or let them get closer,' says Askren and just as I was about to agree, I realized the charging mass was not shouting and the feet were not making hobnailed sounds on the pavement. It must be our men! In an instant we agreed not to fire and both slunk to the bottom of a hole to hide. The bodies chased by us—still unidentified—but not shouting either. They mixed with our men in the darkness, so they are ours."[46]

After reorganizing Company A, Captain Adams received an order to send a patrol to contact the Dutch Underground. "Lieutenant Lamm went out and reported back shortly. He stated that they weren't at the location given.[47]

"Unable to locate the Underground headquarters and after two visits to the battalion CP, I was told to send the patrol to capture the control station [for demolition of the Nijmegen bridge, reported by the Underground to be inside the post office] and have the patrol proceed to the bridge. If there was no opposition to follow it up with the rest of my company...As time was getting precious (and Lamm could not seem to follow my verbal directions on a small map), I undertook to guide the patrol to the control station. However, I failed to notify [Lieutenant] Foley that he was to assume command of the company...Lamm's patrol proceeded almost to the theoretical control station without any trouble. We had almost reached it when the Krauts opened up on us. It certainly looked as though this was a German strongpoint. We had our first contact here with a Panzerfaust, but we did not know what it was. There was grazing fire coming down the street between us and the building. However, Lamm and six other men managed to cross, got into the building, killed a mess of Krauts and got back with the loss of only one man. As they left, they set the building on fire. Lamm reported to me that there were some switches in the building, but that they could very well have been just ordinary light switches. I personally believe this was a German headquarters of some sort."[48]

The assault killed approximately twenty-five Germans. Lieutenant Lamm personally covered the withdrawal of his six troopers from the building while under machine gun and 20mm antiaircraft gun fire emanating from the Keizer Lodewijkplein traffic circle area south of the highway bridge. Lieutenant Lamm was later awarded the Silver Star for his courageous actions during the assault.

During the patrol, Staff Sergeant Alvin Henderson and Sergeant Charles Gushue exhibited extraordinary courage. When the patrol was hit with machine gun fire while moving toward the bridge, Staff Sergeant Henderson moved forward alone and destroyed two German machine gun positions. Then, as the patrol entered the Keizer Lodewijkplein traffic circle area south of the bridge,

Henderson destroyed two other machine gun nests and forced the withdrawal of the crew of a third machine gun in the traffic circle. Staff Sergeant Henderson was killed moments later as he courageously ran through a storm of automatic weapons fire to throw a phosphorous grenade into a German strongpoint located in a building fronting the traffic circle. Henderson had killed two Germans in hand-to-hand combat, bayoneted four more, destroyed four machine gun nests, and captured six prisoners. Staff Sergeant Alvin H. Henderson would later be posthumously awarded the Distinguished Service Cross. During the fighting at the Keizer Lodewijkplein, Sergeant Gushue single-handedly assaulted a machine gun nest and bayoneted four Germans. Sergeant Gushue was also awarded the Distinguished Service Cross for his extraordinary heroism during the earlier attack on the Keizer Karelplein traffic circle and the combat patrol to destroy the highway bridge demolition controls and at the Keizer Lodewijkplein area.

After the assault, Captain Adams attempted to send a situation report to the battalion. "As usual, the 536 [hand held radio] wasn't any good when we needed it the most, so we started back to the park. We had two badly wounded men, so our progress was slow. We had gotten almost to the park when the Germans opened up on us and we found that we were cut off. We then started to circle around thinking we could pass the Germans. However, every street we entered had Germans in it. As it was beginning to get light, it was apparent we couldn't wander around much longer, so we started to look for an appropriate place to hole up."[49] Captain Adams, Lieutenant Lamm, and the 2nd Platoon found a warehouse and hid out before dawn the next morning.

AFTER RECOVERING SOMEWHAT FROM THE SHOCK OF THE AIRBORNE LANDINGS, German commanders in the area knew that the paratroopers would have to receive reinforcements and supplies by air until British ground forces could arrive. Therefore, they ordered all available infantry and flak units in the area to move to cover likely landing and drop zones to oppose the resupply and reinforcements expected the next day. Infiltrating from the Reichswald and the Wyler area during the night, the Germans positioned 20mm antiaircraft guns and machine guns on the edge of these fields sited to cover the division's glider landing zones. It was imperative that the German troops were forced from the landing zones before the gliders arrived.

CHAPTER 11

"EXTREMELY CAPABLE TROOPS"

Prior to dawn on September 18, Lieutenant Lloyd Polette, the platoon leader of the 1st Platoon of Company F, received an order to capture the Honinghutie bridge and adjacent railroad bridge across the Maas-Waal Canal (together code named Bridge 10), located on the main highway from Eindhoven to Arnhem. Lieutenant Polette's platoon was not at full strength because one of the two Company F sticks dropped short of the drop zone in the 504th Parachute Infantry Regiment's sector were Polette's men, leaving him some eighteen troopers short of full strength. "I received instructions from the battalion commander [Major Otho Holmes] to remove my roadblock south of Nijmegen and move to Bridge Number 10, take the bridge, and organize a defense. My platoon moved out about 03:30. I had twenty-five men."[1]

A section of Headquarters Company, 2nd Battalion's light machine gun platoon was attached to Polette's platoon for the mission. Lieutenant Jean H. Trahin, the assistant platoon leader of the light machine gun platoon, led this section during the attack. "The unit moved out at 04:15. The unit contacted Lieutenant [Lynn] Tomlinson's platoon [the 2nd Platoon of Company E] on the roadblock at Hatert at the break of day, and moved on to carry their mission."[2]

Lieutenant Polette and his platoon arrived south of the bridge just after dawn. "We proceeded without opposition to within three hundred yards of the bridge. It was just breaking day and the light was in our favor. Germans started firing on us with machine guns, rifles, and light mortars. This was inaccurate due to the light. We continued to advance as fast as the situation permitted. My lead scouts advanced within 150 yards of the enemy's positions. By this time, the light was clear enough for the Germans to increase the effectiveness of their fire. My platoon was pinned down within 150 yards of the bridge."[3]

Bridge 10 was well defended by elements of Kampfgruppe Runge, which was made up of Unterführer Lehrkommando 21, Fallschirmjäger Ersatz und Ausbildungs Regiment Hermann Göring (NCO training staff of a reserve parachute training regiment), under the command of Oberleutnant Böhme; Kompanies 4 and 5 of Schiffstamm Abteilung 14 (two companies of a naval training battalion); Kompanie 4 of Ersatz Bataillon 6 (a company of a reserve battalion), commanded by Hauptmann Sieger; and a Pioniere Kompanie of Bau-

Pioniere Bataillon 434 (a construction engineer company), under the command of Hauptmann Zyrus.

Eight troopers were killed and several wounded as the Germans poured intense fire from the area around the bridge and from across the canal into the flank of the troopers as they advanced north along the east bank of the canal. Polette's platoon, now down to half strength, took out a number of Germans inside a house along the canal bank with bazooka and machine gun fire.

Lieutenant Redmond L. Daggett, the 1st Platoon's assistant platoon leader, wasn't optimistic that the few remaining men could capture the bridge. "The situation looked entirely hopeless to me. No one but a guy like Polette would even consider trying to take the bridge with such a small force."[4]

As courageous as Lieutenant Polette was, he knew he didn't have enough men left to break the German defenses around the bridge. "I immediately sent a runner back to contact Lieutenant Tomlinson. Lieutenant Tomlinson was in contact with battalion with a [SCR] 300 radio. He was on a roadblock about one quarter mile to my rear, which was south. The message was for mortar fire, so some of the pressure could be taken off the platoon. Ten minutes later, I sent another runner with the same message.

"I had set up all my machine guns and BARs to return the fire, but after firing only a few rounds the machine guns were knocked out by mortar [fire].

"From time to time we could observe Germans walking, or attempting to get on the bridge. We kept them at disadvantage with rifle fire. It was apparent that the enemy was attempting to destroy the bridge. About 10:30 the enemy blew their charges, destroying the railroad bridge and tracks, but failed to destroy the highway bridge."[5]

Meanwhile, Lieutenant Tomlinson's 2nd Platoon of Company E was relieved from its roadblock and moved to join the attack on the bridge.

Lieutenant Edward V. Ott, a Normandy veteran, was the platoon leader of the 81mm Mortar Platoon, Headquarters Company, 2nd Battalion. "About 11:00 hours on September 18, Lieutenant Lloyd Polette called the battalion's commanding officer on the radio and reported that he was pinned down by 20mm and 40mm fire, plus two mobile 88s on halftracks.

"I loaded one section (two guns) of my mortar platoon on a horse drawn wagon. I also loaded 120 rounds of ammunition, including 12 rounds of smoke. Under the guidance of Lieutenant [David] Liebmann [the assistant platoon leader of the 2nd Platoon of Company E], we double timed to help Polette. As we approached the road leading along the canal, Lieutenant Trahin met us and explained the situation. He was the leader of the machine gun platoon attached to Lieutenant Polette's platoon, but his machine guns were knocked out. So he crawled back along the trenches and met us.

"I went into an orchard and Lieutenant Trahin showed me a blockhouse where the Germans had two machine guns. Corporal John [T.] Barry and Corporal John [A.] Menighan of my platoon manned our guns while exposed to fire. Sergeant George [D.] Fairman [Jr.] and I moved forward. I went to a point where I could observe the effect of our fire, and Sergeant Fairman took a position between us and the guns, so he could pass my information to the gunners. I fired on the blockhouse and then on the gas tower nearby. My smoke ammunition set the gas tower on fire. Then I put a round of smoke ammunition on the bridge.

"Our two [mortars] had a duel with one 40mm and one 20mm gun. We knocked out both of the enemy guns, and then the two mobile 88s withdrew."[6]

Sergeant George Fairman, an 81mm mortar section leader, estimated that "the mortars fired some seventy-five rounds of ammunition on targets; bridge, pillbox, buildings, and small woods."[7]

As accurate mortar fire rained down on the German positions, Lieutenant Polette saw German soldiers retreating from their defensive positions around the bridge. "We fired on enemy soldiers that were withdrawing. I had lost control of my platoon, so I withdrew about three hundred yards to the rear, along a road with a few trees. I reorganized and with twelve men of my platoon and Lieutenant Tomlinson's platoon, also Lieutenant Ott's mortars, moved back to the bridge.

"There was no one from the 504th assisting me in the attack. On returning to the bridge, we found a group of civilians, also several men of the 504th who told us there were more 504 men on the west bank of the canal. We set up a defensive position, remaining in position until recalled by battalion around 17:30 that afternoon."[8]

Elements of the 504th Parachute Infantry Regiment relieved Lieutenant Polette's platoon that evening at Bridge 10, which then moved to establish roadblocks on two roads which ran south from Nijmegen east of the main north-south highway, at Heiendaelscheweg and Driehuizerweg at the intersections with D'Almarasweg.

The capture of Bridge Number 10 had been a costly affair for the small force assigned to seize it. Over half of Lieutenant Polette's twenty-five man Company F platoon and all of the machine gun crews from Headquarters Company, 2nd Battalion were killed or wounded. For his extraordinary courage under fire and outstanding leadership in the capture of Bridge Number 10, Lieutenant Polette was later awarded the Distinguished Service Cross.

With the 1st Battalion in Nijmegen blocking German movement on the main highway south of the Keizer Karelplein traffic circle, the remainder of the 2nd Battalion moved that morning from its blocking positions south of Nijmgen to the area around De Ploeg and Heilig Land southeast of Nijmegen to protect the left flank of the 3rd Battalion.

Early on the morning of September 18, the 3rd Battalion commander, Lieutenant Colonel Mendez, wanted to make sure that the roadblock at Beek had been established by the Company I platoon assigned to do so, but had instead established a roadblock on the Wyler to Berg-en-Dal highway. "I dispatched the S-2 and S-3 [Captain Frank Novak] of the battalion to discover the true location of the I Company platoon. While preparing to push on down to the proper place, the [Company I] roadblock and the platoon of H Company to its immediate right were hit by the enemy. This attack was speedily repulsed and I immediately ordered the roadblock to be properly established in Beek. This was attempted, but the platoon only got halfway to its objective."[9]

Corporal Walter Bednarz, a squad leader with the Light Machine Gun Platoon, Headquarters Company, 3rd Battalion, and his eight troopers manned one of the battalion's roadblocks near Berg-en-Dal, using the section's four machine guns. That day, a patrol of eighteen German parachutists armed with machine guns and machine pistols approached the roadblock behind a group of Dutch civilians moving along the highway. Corporal Bednarz quickly determined that he could not fire on the enemy patrol without endangering the lives of those civilians. Without hesitation, Corporal Bednarz left his dug in position and rushed past the civilians to meet the oncoming enemy force. At pointblank range, he sprayed the enemy with his Thompson submachine gun, killing and wounding most of them, but was himself killed in the exchange of automatic weapons fire. For his extraordinary heroism, Corporal Bednarz was posthumously awarded the Distinguished Service Cross.

At sunrise on September 18, Companies A and B were holding positions in Nijmegen near the Keizer Karelplein traffic circle on the boulevard leading to the highway bridge. Captain Jonathan Adams, commanding Company A, was with the 2nd Platoon in a warehouse to the north, after the platoon became cutoff during a patrol to destroy the demolition controls for the bridge the previous night. Captain Adams was out of contact with the remainder of his company and had spent a frustrating night attempting to extricate the platoon. As dawn broke, Adams had to make a difficult decision of whether to attempt to break through to his company in broad daylight. "I decided to hole up in the day time and make a break the next night."[10]

OVERNIGHT, GENERAL JAMES GAVIN learned that Company G was bivouacked just outside Nijmegen and would move to capture the highway bridge on the morning of September 18. "In order to take advantage of what we believed was a tactical opportunity, G Company was directed to move by the right, advancing from the high ground along the [Berg-en-Dalseweg] road towards the bridge, and grab the southern end of it. From intelligence reports we had just received, this appeared practicable, and although it would normally be well beyond the capabilities of a company, the battalion commander of the 3rd Battalion, 508 Parachute Infantry, Colonel Mendez, was an especially fine combat leader and

G Company was an unusually good parachute company. If the coup could succeed, they could do the job."[11]

Before dawn on September 18, Lieutenant Russell Wilde, the Company G commander, sent a reconnaissance patrol along the Berg-en-Dalseweg to check the route to Nijmegen. A young twenty year old Dutchman, Agardus M. "Gas" Leegsma, lived along the patrol's route. "My brother John and I were at the right place at the right time when the 82nd dropped south of Nijmegen, 17 September 1944. During the night, the Germans had been blowing up gas and ammunition dumps near our abode; we had not slept much and had put ready our orange armbands (meant as 'uniform' for resistance people when they came out in the open to fight the Germans at the same time and preferably with the Allied soldiers) and helmets. We joined the patrol and handed a map of the town to their commandant. At [St. Canisius College] about 150 yards from our home, a firefight caused the death of several Germans and after[ward] a German armored halftrack with about twelve soldiers in it was evaded by the Yanks, taking cover with us behind a garden wall. The patrol returned to their commander, who sent them out, Lieutenant Russell C. Wilde of G Company, 508th, whose company was then at the outskirts of town in the woods near Berg-en-Dal.

"Wilde, who was a first lieutenant, then received us and our map with open arms and after an interrogation for more details about German troops, pillboxes, and gun emplacements, he asked us to guide him and G Company to the bridge across the Waal River. This was what we had been waiting for, for over four years and we gladly accepted the invitation."[12]

Company G moved into Nijmegen advancing along the Berg-en-Dalseweg, with 3rd Platoon, under the command of Lieutenant Howard A. Greenawalt, in the lead. "On the outskirts we found a German hospital and after clearing it of all weapons and leaving a guard, continued into the town. My platoon was the advance guard and after moving about five blocks into the city we were stopped by intense sniper fire. Lieutenant Wilde decided to move to the right with two platoons, using my platoon as a base of fire for the maneuver.

"After the lieutenant left, Sergeant [Stanley E.] Stevens and I, with three men moved behind the buildings and managed to dislodge the snipers."[13]

Sergeant Stevens cleared snipers from several houses; then single-handedly attacked one building, killing two Germans manning a machine gun. As the 3rd Platoon resumed the advance into Nijmegen, at least two German machine guns opened fire on it pinning down the platoon. Sergeant Stevens maneuvered the platoon's point away from the line of fire. He then established a base of fire on the German positions and single-handedly assaulted and destroyed one machine gun position using his Thompson submachine gun and grenades. Sergeant Stevens would later be posthumously promoted to staff sergeant and awarded the Distinguished Service Cross for his courageous actions during the fighting to reach the Nijmegen highway bridge on September 18.

Lieutenant Greenawalt and the 3rd Platoon "then moved forward and upon approaching the circle just forward of the southern approach to the bridge destroyed a roadblock being constructed and killed about seven Germans working on it."[14]

During the assault on the roadblock, an 88mm antiaircraft gun positioned at the roadblock pinned down the 3rd Platoon. Despite intense small arms and machine gun fire directed at him, Private First Class Albert M. Ruttinger worked his way to within twenty yards of the gun. He fired a rifle grenade, killing four of the crew; then fired another to destroy the gun. Still under heavy fire, Ruttinger remained at his position and fired two more rifle grenades, destroying two nearby piles of 88mm ammunition. For his courageous actions, Private First Class Ruttinger was later awarded the Silver Star.

Meanwhile, the remainder of Company G moved around the right and advanced along Ubbergseveldweg. At the intersection with Museum Kamstraat, the company attacked and overran a German outpost consisting of two machine guns. Past that intersection, the street name changed from Ubbergseveldweg to Barbarossastraat. Sergeant Glen W. Vantrease and his 2nd Platoon squad, acting as flank protection for the company, advanced along the houses fronting the south side of the Waal River. "We traveled through backyards, through houses, over high fences that separated the backyards. The homes were representative of high income families—most of whom were very concerned over our trespass.

"Upon exiting from the front of one of the houses, we found ourselves in a medium size yard that appeared to front on the riverbank. The bank was landscaped as a park. I only got a short look, for Germans were dug in on the bank on our side [of the river]. We engaged in several minutes of small arms fire, during which time several of the Germans were at least wounded. However, they were dug in on the opposite side of the river with heavy equipment and began to surround us with artillery shells."[15]

Private First Class Angel Romero was a member of Vantrease's squad. "It didn't take us long to realize we were greatly outnumbered and the shape of the terrain left us sitting ducks. The Germans had all kinds of guns on the opposite bank and were having a field day firing pointblank at us. We were ordered out of there, because it was certain death if we stayed. Vantrease had gone a little farther down the embankment from me. When we were ordered out, he was hit as he turned to leave. He said it was shrapnel. I thought it was a direct hit from a 40mm. He flew about ten feet and it was obvious he was seriously wounded. After he and I got out, [Privates First Class Thomas S.] Beno, [Joseph] Metar, [George F. "Mick"] McGrath, and a medic carried Vantrease a good distance. Some of the residents came to offer help. He was given first aid. One of the residents told us to carry him to a basement where he was hidden a few days until he was evacuated. The fighting within two blocks of the bridge was fierce. I don't think there was a house in the area that wasn't hit by artillery, rifle, and machine gun fire."[16]

After destroying the roadblock, Lieutenant Greenawalt and the 3rd Platoon approached the Keizer Lodewijkplein traffic circle just south of the highway bridge. "Upon reaching the traffic circle [the 3rd Platoon was] met with heavy mortar and 88mm artillery fire."[17]

Lieutenant John P. Dube was the assistant platoon leader of the 3rd Platoon of Company G. "We encountered heavy automatic weapons fire and direct fire from two German 88s. Our small unit directed fire with a bazooka, 60mm mortar, and rifles at visible targets. We were soon pinned down and fragmented as an effective combat unit. I was kneeling behind shrubs in the yard of a structure thought to be a dental or medical building. My location provided some concealment as I observed movement on foot and vehicles of German troops moving toward the bridge about two hundred yards away. Several shell bursts near my location restricted my movement. A shell hit the building behind me, and shrapnel from that explosion hit me in the back of the head, left shoulder, and left forearm. The shrapnel had penetrated through my helmet and helmet liner, leaving a jagged three inch hole. A medic observed my wound and applied sulfa powder to a gaping and profusely bleeding head wound."[18]

Lieutenant Greenawalt knew that his platoon could not take the highway bridge by itself. "Having already lost five men in the advance and being but one platoon in strength, I decided to stand fast and await contact with Lieutenant Wilde. Contact was made with the remainder of the company at 15:30 and the approach to the bridge was assaulted immediately. Direct artillery fire from the opposite bank held up the assault."[19]

Since he had no radio contact with Company G, Lieutenant Colonel Mendez, the 3rd Battalion commander, decided to obtain a firsthand assessment of the situation at Nijmegen. "While the company was reorganizing for another attack, I visited G Company by commandeering a jeep from Lieutenant [Richard O.] Pendergast, Division Reconnaissance Platoon.

"I requested from Colonel Lindquist permission to use the entire battalion to follow up G Company to assault the bridge. I felt fairly confident of success, based on G Company's progress. My request was refused, and rightly so, because had we relinquished the high ground at Berg-en-Dal, as events turned out later, one of the enemy's main thrusts would have sliced right through our center, thus jeopardizing our domination of the division objective. The other reason was the dwindling ammunition supply. When I visited G Company on the afternoon of the 18th, Lieutenant Wilde's first comment was, 'Give me some more ammunition!' We just didn't have it, but the battalion S-4 was busily at work at the DZ with commandeered horses and wagons trying to get the ammunition forward; and then they were subjected to an enemy assault."[20]

Without the opportunity to reinforce the Company G assault, Lieutenant Colonel Mendez had no alternative but to withdraw it, and ordered the company to return to the Berg-en-Dal area. Company G began the difficult task of disengaging and withdrawing from close quarter urban combat with the enemy.

Private First Class Angel Romero and his 2nd Platoon squad were on the right flank of Company G and "the closest to the bridge and thus the last to leave. We had gone about a half a mile when complete exhaustion hit me. I sat to one side of the street and in a moment Gas Leegsma was again at my side. He said I could rest later, but for now we had to move out or chance the Germans catching up with us. He offered his hand and helped me get up. He walked with me awhile until he was sure I could make it.

"Leegsma calls me his liberator, because I was the first American he met. I have the highest respect and esteem for him. This man was super in what he did for G Company. He stayed with us throughout the Netherlands and most of the Bulge. His ability to speak so many languages still amazes me."[21]

As he walked with the Company G troopers, Gas Leegsma observed the reaction of the civilians along the way. "The Nijmegen people who had cheered the Americans coming in were very disappointed now and hastily removed their flags from the houses, for fear of a return of the Germans and reprisals. When we passed our home, my brother stayed there and I saw my father, who was very proud of us. Since early that morning I had been equipped with the carbine of a wounded American, whose weapon was handed to me by the Yanks. So I was able to take a very active part in the fighting. I then and later on was very glad my father had taught us to fire a rifle."[22]

Back in Nijmegen, Sergeant Glen Vantrease, who had been badly wounded in the back earlier, was left behind in the care of a family who lived in one of the houses near the Waal River when Company G withdrew. "I had been there only a short while when they became very excited and took me to the small basement cellar just a few feet from inside of the front door. They finally made me understand that my unit had been forced to withdraw and the Germans had moved back in. At almost the same moment, German soldiers were pounding on the door with their rifle butts. I later learned that they were checking the homes for American soldiers. When my hosts told them there were none, they accepted their word without a search.

"I fell asleep from exhaustion and was awakened during the night by the heavy artillery fire dropping in the immediate area. The house across the street was on fire. I tried to get up the steps just as the house seemed to explode. When I regained consciousness, my right arm was doubled backwards at the elbow and I was matted with blood. There was no sound. I stumbled to the front walk, through a gate and turned to the right. After a succession of blackouts and what seemed like hours, I found myself sitting up against a fence on the sidewalk at an outpost. The two paratroopers were on the walkie-talkie trying to get help."[23]

Shortly after sunrise on September 18, Lieutenant Norman MacVicar, the commander of Company D, called his platoon leaders to his command post at Hooge Hof, west of Landing Zone "T", where much of the 82nd Airborne Division's glider-borne artillery would land later that day, including the 319th

Glider Field Artillery Battalion, which was part of the regimental combat team. Lieutenant Robert Sickler, the platoon leader of the 3rd Platoon, was informed that the gliders were due to begin landing at 2:00 p.m. Company D was to move to positions to protect the eastern and southern edges of the landing zone, so that they could engage at long range and pin down as far from the landing zone as possible, any Germans who attempted to attack it. Lieutenant Sickler then received orders for the new dispositions of the company. "The 2nd Platoon was to occupy positions at Voxhil facing north and east. The 1st Platoon was to dig in east of Lerkendaal along the Kamp–Wyler road. The 3rd Platoon was to protect the right flank from the nose of the ridge directly west of and overlooking Kamp. The command post was to remain in its present location. This placed each of the platoons over a thousand yards from the company command post and extended the company front to over a mile."[24]

Lieutenant Sickler and the 3rd Platoon reached its assigned sector and began digging in. He sent a two man patrol to Groesbeek to contact the 505th. Sickler then "called the company commander on the SCR 536 [radio], and reported that we were on position, digging in, there were no signs of enemy activity, and that a contact patrol had been sent to Groesbeek. The company commander replied with an order for the 3rd Platoon to reinforce the 2nd Platoon at Voxhil with two rifle squads, immediately. He told me to stop at the command post enroute, and he would orient me further. Leaving the platoon headquarters, one rifle squad, and the mortar squad on position, I moved back up the draw with the two rifle squads as ordered, taking the platoon SCR 536 radio with me. Reporting in at the command post, I found the situation to be extremely vague.

"The company commander had received a radio message from the 2nd Platoon stating that it was in trouble and needed some help. That was all. The company commander had been unable to raise a response since that time. The 2nd Platoon had not stated whether it was under attack, or whether it had merely sighted the enemy and anticipated an attack. Neither the number of enemy or the direction of attack had been stated." [25]

Three companies of a Landesschützen Ausbildungs Bataillon (training battalion) of the 406th Landesschützen Division, which had moved from Nijmegen on September 17, and had dug defensive positions in the woods on Hill 62.9, just north of the highway from Berg-en-Dal to Wyler, along with approximately sixty newly arrived paratroopers from Fallschirmjäger Regiment 5, under the command of Oberstleutnant Karl-Heinz Becker, attacked the 2nd Platoon positions from the north. Four 20mm antiaircraft guns provided direct ground fire support for the attack.

Private John M. Greene was a new replacement who was positioned on the left flank of Lieutenant Temple W. Tutwiler's 2nd Platoon. "Our platoon was attacked by a parachute unit supported by at least one light artillery piece. A splinter from one of its shells hit my right hand, as well as putting out the right eye of my foxhole mate. After he left for medical [treatment], I found that the light machine gun squad, supposedly holding our left flank had also departed. It occurred to me that I was alone and with only a rifle, not able to hold the line. So, perhaps ingloriously, I also left, stopping only to get the wounded out of the burning house where the aid station had been set up, and to warn our doughty BAR man that his rear was uncovered."[26]

Private First Class Cornelius M. "Mike" Cahill was also a new replacement with the 2nd Platoon. "My sergeant, James [J.] Potter, positioned me near two big logs with [Private First Class Carroll C.] Hack Wilson. Hack stood up and the Germans opened fire on him. He told me he was hit twice and had to go back to the farmhouse and I was left alone. I was then told to move back to the farmhouse."[27]

Sergeant Joseph Bullard was wounded badly in the leg by shrapnel while in his foxhole and was unable to withdraw to the farmhouse. "After a while we had four or five dead and three wounded. I couldn't move because of my leg, and the rest couldn't move because of German fire."[28]

After withdrawing to the 2nd Platoon command post located in a farmhouse, Private Greene watched German paratroopers close in on them. "Finally, after the remnants of our platoon were attacked in our pitiful little Alamo, our platoon leader surrendered us.

"When the young German trooper, with a burp gun at the ready, ordered me to empty my pockets, I dropped my grenades, ammunition, bayonet, chocolate bar, and cigarettes on the ground. He picked up and tossed aside the grenades, knife and ammunition, and gestured for me to pick up the rest, indicating that I should keep them. Gratefully (if not wisely), I picked up two of the three packs of cigarettes and gestured to him to take the other and the chocolate [D-bar] (a tooth-breaking bar of emergency ration). He did, looked at me, and with a half smile said, 'Danke.'"[29]

Just before the 2nd Platoon surrendered, Private First Class Cahill and the other troopers in the farmhouse attempted to disable their weapons so the Germans could not use them. "We put our rifles in a bucket of water. Prior to the surrendering I [had] shot one of the German soldiers in the stomach as he tried to throw a grenade in the house. As we were leaving the house, the soldier I had shot grabbed my first aid kit off of my leg and another soldier started to bandage him. He wasn't aware that I was the one who had shot him. They lined us up in front of a brick wall and put a machine gun in front of us. Then they took us down to a little tavern to hold us. Many of us were wounded. The ones who were able to walk, walked toward a column of German soldiers."[30]

Sergeant Bullard, a veteran of Normandy, was badly wounded in the leg and still lying in his foxhole when the platoon surrendered. "They took the ones who weren't wounded as prisoners and marched them off. They spent the war in POW camps. They didn't bother us [the wounded who unable to walk] at all. They just took our weapons and left us there. About dark, some Germans came and took us to a nearby house—one they used as a command post. We didn't get any medical attention. They stripped off everything I was wearing except my shorts. They even took my dog tags. They didn't even question me that much. There was another guy wounded in there with me."[31]

Meanwhile, Lieutenant Sickler and the others at the company command post were unable to determine the status of the 2nd Platoon. "The company commander had also attempted to contact the 1st Platoon with no success. He decided to send me, with my two squads to Voxhil to report back by radio immediately on the existing situation. He decided to accompany us about halfway down the Hooge Hof road, taking with him his SCR 536 radio and a messenger. From that point, he dispatched his runner to contact the 1st Platoon.

"As we left the road within about 250 yards of the 2nd Platoon position, we were fired on suddenly by two machine guns from the group of buildings at Voxhil. The fire caught us completely by surprise, and two men were killed instantly. The remainder was pinned rather helplessly in the open field. The fire was not returned immediately because the guns were obviously American LMGs [light machine guns], and it was believed by all that the 'nervous' 2nd Platoon had opened fire, mistaking us for the enemy.

"This hope was short lived however, as a third gun opened up, and its high cyclic rate identified it unmistakably as German. Fortunately, we were well dispersed, and the field in which we were pinned was planted with sugar beets ready for harvest, with the rows running perpendicular to the line of fire.

"I called to my two LMG teams to crawl down the rows to the road on which we had left the company commander while the riflemen covered their withdrawal. This road offered twelve to eighteen inches of defilade. From that point, they could fire on the enemy while the remainder of the two squads withdrew in the same manner. This was accomplished with the loss of two riflemen.

"As the last of the riflemen and I reached the road, the company commander crawled up with more bad news. His runner had been unable to locate the 1st Platoon, and they still did not reply on the SCR 536.

"It was obvious that the 2nd Platoon had been surprised and quickly overrun. The whereabouts of the 1st Platoon was entirely unknown. The remainder of the 3rd Platoon, with the badly needed mortar, was a mile away, entirely unaware of the situation, and with no means by which I might communicate with them.

"At this time a force of Germans estimated at two platoons was observed approaching from the north in attack formation, swinging wide around Voxhil from the direction of Wyler. They had apparently been committed as a maneuver element to flank the 3rd Platoon, in our original position in the sugar beet field west of Voxhil.

"Due to the change in position of the 3rd Platoon, they found themselves making a frontal attack. As we took them under fire, they commenced firing, and continued to advance by fire and movement. The fire of the 3rd Platoon was shifted entirely to the advancing force in an effort to pin them before they could assault. At this time, a tremendous volume of 20mm fire was received from Voxhil, and the number of casualties began to rise; one of which was the company commander. The advancing element [of the German force] was finally pinned about 250 yards out after taking terrific punishment.

"The situation of the 3rd Platoon had become extremely critical, as our position was becoming rapidly untenable. The fire from Voxhil was terrible in its intensity, but could not be returned, because to lessen the fire on the attacking element would be to invite them to assault.

"The SCR 300 [radio] with which regiment could be contacted for assistance was at the command post, but there was no way the company commander could contact the command post as he had the company SCR 536 with him, and it would have been sheer murder to dispatch his runner. Ammunition was running low and there was no route of withdrawal."[32]

As this was occurring, Lieutenant Kenneth Johnson, the regimental munitions officer and assistant S-4, and his troopers were working to collect the equipment bundles not retrieved the prior day. Lieutenant Johnson had set up the regimental supply dump on the edge of the woods west of the drop zone near Hooge Hof. "Supply personnel hurried to complete recovery operations, but were unable to recover a number of bundles that were now under fire from 20mm antiaircraft guns. These guns had been abandoned or captured when the regiment landed, but they had not been rendered ineffective. These guns were now teaching us a not to be forgotten lesson. Recovery efforts were abandoned when one of the supply personnel was killed by this increasing heavy volume of fire. Efforts were now concentrated on moving as many of the recovered supplies as possible out of the danger area. A horse and wagon was taken from a farmhouse in the vicinity of the drop zone and as many supplies as possible were loaded onto it. Enemy fire suddenly increased in intensity, making it impossible to move the wagon out of defilade."[33]

BACK IN ENGLAND, a huge force of 454 gliders and their tow planes which were transporting three of the division's four artillery battalions and two of the three antitank batteries was taking off for Holland, about an hour late, due to fog and low clouds. The gliders flew to Holland in eleven serials, where they would land at LZ "N" and LZ "T" beginning at about 2:30 p.m., with the last serial arriving shortly after 4:00 p.m. The 319th Glider Field Artillery Battalion; the 320th Glider Field Artillery Battalion (less Headquarters Battery); two extra 75mm howitzers; jeeps for the 504th; Battery C and elements of Battery B, 456th Parachute Field Artillery Battalion; elements of Division and Division Artillery Headquarters; the 407th Quartermaster Company; and the 782nd Ordnance Company were scheduled to land at LZ "T".

Lieutenant John Eskoff, with Headquarters Battery, 319th Glider Field Artillery Battalion, was acting as copilot for Chalk 6 of the battalion's serial.

"Our takeoff and flight to the English Channel was uneventful. The load was well balanced and the air was smooth. Shortly after leaving the shores of England, several British bombers towing gliders passed under our glider a few hundred feet below. The prop wash from the bombers rocked our glider and gave me as uneasy feeling.

"Suddenly, our glider swooped upward and to the right. I heard a sharp crack and saw the tow rope 'going away.' The pilot dived out of formation to clear the way for those following. I had the men remove their equipment and kick off their emergency doors and the regular doors. I called off air speed and altitude for the pilot. We braced ourselves and landed head on into a wave at seventy-five miles per hour. Water filled the compartment immediately. I swam and pulled myself to the emergency door. When I came up on the outside I saw five heads, so I knew all of us were out of the glider. A Royal Air Force Sea Rescue launch was pulling up beside us. We crashed at 13:18 hours, eighteen miles from the coast of England. By 13:30 hours, we were all aboard the rescue launch. Dry clothes, medical attention, hot soup, sandwiches, and cigarettes were furnished. We landed at Yarmouth, England, at 21:15 hours. One man had been injured slightly."[34]

AS THE VAST ARMADA FLEW RELENTLESSLY TOWARD HOLLAND, the landing zones were now partially ringed with German rapid fire 20mm antiaircraft guns positioned in dug in gun pits. Lieutenant Robert Sickler and his two D Company rifle squads faced the almost hopeless task of holding off a company sized German force, which threatened to totally overrun LZ "T". However, Lieutenant Sickler began to hear friendly fire coming from the area of the Company D command post on the edge of the woods to the west. "Back at the company observation post at Hooge Hof, the regimental ammunition officer [Lieutenant Kenneth Johnson] had observed the predicament of the company commander and the 3rd Platoon."[35]

Lieutenant Johnson immediately organized the supply personnel and the D Company headquarters personnel into a defensive position. "This force was able to bring heavy fire upon the attackers, utilizing the weapons and ammunition available in the supply dump."[36]

Staff Sergeant Odell E. Cannon, with Company E, happened to be at the regimental supply dump with a detail to assist in the collection of equipment, ammunition, and supplies. Staff Sergeant Cannon quickly organized his men and when a German platoon sized force attempted to overrun his position, Staff Sergeant Cannon grabbed a mortar tube and completely exposed himself to enemy fire while placing approximately fifty rounds on the attacking force. As the German force approached to a point inside of range of the mortar, Cannon picked up a carbine and engaged the Germans at close range until the enemy withdrew. Staff Sergeant Cannon was later awarded the Silver Star for his valor.

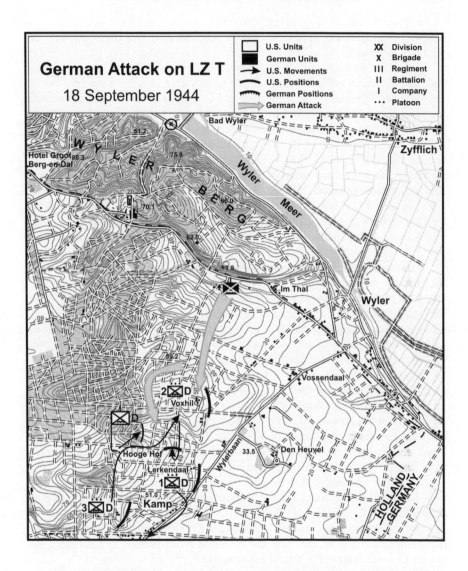

After organizing the defensive position, Lieutenant Johnson used the Dog Company SCR 300 radio to contact Colonel Lindquist to report that D Company was likely surrounded, the landing zone was overrun and the regimental supply dump was in danger of being overrun. "The CO said to hold at all costs, to save the vital supplies, and that he would order the 1st Battalion to counterattack at once. He also stated that he would try to get a forward observer [from the 376th Parachute Field Artillery Battalion, which was already in position after having jumped on September 17] to come forward immediately and adjust artillery fire on the drop zone."[37]

Lieutenant Johnson then "located the friendly forces on the ground by map and the CO caused some [artillery] fire to be delivered shortly thereafter."[38]

The added firepower of the supply and Company D headquarters personnel greatly assisted Lieutenant Sickler. "Having the regimental supply dump at their right elbow, they were naturally not suffering for want of ammunition, and the high and continued rate of their fire eased considerably the pressure of enemy fire on the 3rd Platoon. They sounded like an entire company and their fire apparently dispelled any notion the Germans might have entertained about continuing their advance. Neither the company commander or the 3rd Platoon were aware of the regimental ammunition officer's actions, except that we realized that company headquarters had taken up the fight from the edge of the woods about four hundred yards on our left flank."[39]

While fighting was raging on the landing zone, Lieutenant Colonel Shields Warren, the commanding officer of the 1st Battalion, was preparing another attack to capture the Nijmegen highway bridge. "The remainder of the 81mm Mortar Platoon had been released to battalion control. C Company and the section of machine guns were still retained by regiment. Word also came back that the combat patrol under Lieutenant [Bob] Weaver of C Company had been unable to reach the bridge, and [he] estimated resistance south of the bridge to be about company size. While A Company was being reorganized, preparatory to continuing the attack, the division commander, General James Gavin drove up in one of the division's reconnaissance jeeps and wanted to know the particulars of the action. When he was told that we did not yet have the bridge, but that the attack would continue shortly, he told me to hold where I was, because German forces were attacking in the southeast portion of the perimeter, and that the 1st Battalion might be needed there."[40]

Lieutenant Woodrow W. Millsaps, commanding Company B, was deployed with his men in buildings on the southern and eastern sides of the Keizer Karelplein traffic circle southwest of the Nijmegen highway bridge. "At daylight, Company A started to move back through my position and [Lieutenant] Colonel Warren told me to stay in position until he returned. I did not see Colonel Warren the rest of the morning.[41]

"The city hall of Nijmegen was in our defensive position and I was using the basement of the building for the company command post. From the top of the building I could see the Nijmegen bridge and the gun emplacements on our side of the bridge. By this time, 8:00 or 9:00 a.m., we had lost radio contact with the battalion and things on our side didn't look too good."[42]

At about 10:00 a.m., Lieutenant Colonel Warren received a message from regimental headquarters. "Regiment ordered the 1st Battalion to break off the action in the town, countermarch to the vicinity of the drop zone of the previous day (some seven miles distant). [Then, we were to] counterattack two plus German companies there who were forcing D Company back, so that the landing zone would be clear for the glider landing scheduled at 13:00 hours for the three glider-borne battalions of the division artillery. The battalion S-3, Captain James Dietrich, was dispatched to have B Company break off the action; A Company, not in contact, was ordered to immediately move to an assembly area; and I started for the regimental CP on the double to get the details of the plan. Upon arrival, I found out that C Company was released to my control, with the remainder of the machine gun platoon. C Company, commanded by Captain [Frank] Schofield had been dispatched to secure a line of departure for the battalion by the regimental commander."[43]

Corporal Darrell Glass, a replacement who had joined the regiment after Normandy, moved out from De Ploeg with the rest of Company C. "We rushed to get back to the drop zone as quickly as possible. We dropped all of our gear— our knapsacks, bedrolls—everything was left behind to go back and take that drop zone."[44]

Meanwhile, Lieutenant Millsaps received the word to withdraw Company B from Nijmegen. "Contact was reestablished with the battalion when Captain Dietrich, Battalion S-3, arrived in the company area about 11:00 a.m. with orders for me to break contact with the enemy and move to the rear and rejoin the battalion. I found out from Captain Dietrich that the enemy had overrun the battalion drop zone that we dropped on the day before, and which we were to secure and hold for a glider unit that was supposed to land there at 3:00 p.m. The enemy had moved in antiaircraft guns and was defending the area.

"Company B broke contact with the enemy and moved to the rear. One of the saddest, most touching experiences for me up to that time was that pull back from Nijmegen. The natives of the town, undoubtedly thinking the town was being liberated from German rule, came out in the streets shouting and dancing, kissing soldiers, and giving us fruit and handfuls of flowers. We dared not tell them, even if we could have spoken their language, that we were giving the city back to the Germans and moving back to start all over again.

"On our withdrawal, I received oral orders from Colonel Warren for me to move back to a position about five hundred yards northwest of the drop zone, to move up on the Company C left flank and be ready to attack the drop zone on his orders. The gliders were to land on the drop zone at 3:00 p.m. and here my company was marching on the road toward the drop area with a long way to go.

"I was guided into position on the Company C left flank and I reported to Colonel Warren my position and in turn received orders from him to attack the drop zone without delay. By hand signal and orders over the walkie-talkie radio which we had in the company, we were able to deploy in the attack formation. The Germans had moved antiaircraft personnel on the field with very few infantry for protection. It was now approximately 2:30 p.m. when we jumped off in the attack to regain the drop zone. Time was of the essence at this point."[45]

Company B moved out on the left of Company C, followed by Headquarters Company about two hundred yards behind, and Company A another two hundred yards behind Headquarters Company. The battalion swept forward from the line of departure, a wooded area on the northwest side of Landing Zone "T", across open fields toward the German infantry facing south toward the 3rd Platoon of Company D. German 20mm antiaircraft guns and mortars were positioned in gun pits dug in around the landing zone. As Companies B and C came over the gentle slope, the Germans at Voxhil and around Vossendaal unleashed an absolute storm of 20mm, machine gun, and small arms fire.

Corporal Darrell Glass was an assistant squad leader with Company C and this was his first taste of ground combat. "We were under a lot of fire. The drop zone was virtually surrounded by 20mm antiaircraft guns."[46]

Company B and C were quickly pinned down, taking what little shelter a slightly sunken road and the furrows of the fields offered them to avoid the terrific volume of fire coming at them. Private First Class Jim Allardyce, an assistant light machine gunner with Company B, took refuge in one of the ruts of the farm road. "The Jerries had small arms and flak guns and they really peppered us. I remember hearing the bullets whistle by and kick up the dust. Once a machine gun peppered the ground just in front of my face as I tried to squeeze into an obviously too small wagon rut to get cover."[47]

Technician Fifth Grade Walter Barrett and two other B Company troopers seemed to be the specific target of one of the 20mm antiaircraft gun crews. "One of my best friends, [Corporal] Frank Hernandez, another trooper I didn't know by name [Private Cecil G. Hines], and I were unable to move without the German 20mm gunner opening fire on us. When the 20mm shells hit a sugar beet beside us, the juice sprayed everywhere. The trooper whose name I didn't know [Private Hines] was immediately hit. The wound was a gushing hole in his neck. He was lying in a furrow to my left and forward of me by a few feet. I could see him and his wound. I felt I should get to him and at least prop his body into a better position so as to prevent a greater loss of blood. It would have been in vain, because he died while Frank and I remained in the furrows, unable to get to him."[48]

From his position at the line of departure, Captain Ben Delamater, the 1st Battalion executive officer, observed the battalion begin to recover from the shock of the intense enemy fire. "Prodded by the leaders' shouts, small groups of both companies started forward rapidly."[49]

Company B squad leader, Sergeant Jim Kurz, followed by his two scouts— Private Chester Standley, who was armed with a BAR, and Private Anthony J. Mrozinski—stood up and started across the field. Sergeant Kurz was surprised when no one else followed them. "We had gone about one hundred yards when I looked around and we were the only three people up in our company area. I yelled back and cursed the men for not coming. They said the lieutenant said it was too hot to advance. I told them to get up with me or I would be shooting at them along with the Germans. The men then came on up. You will never know how it feels to be one of three standing with 20mm, machine gun bullets, and rifle fire going by you. You think, 'How can they keep missing?'"[50]

At the same time, similar actions were taking place with Company C. Private John Hardie, a platoon sergeant with Company C, who had been busted prior to the Holland jump, was pinned down and lying in the ruts of the dirt road.[51] "[Staff] Sergeant William Traband and Private First Class James [A.] Childs were close to where 1st Sergeant Leonard A. Funk was [lying]. In the midst of a conversation between Childs (bitching about NCOs) and Traband, Childs ('Bones' as we called him—one of the older men in the company) got hit by rifle fire in the shoulder and head and died instantly. At this time, there was heavy rifle, machine gun, and 20mm fire toward our position.

"Funk, adjacent to [Technician Fifth Grade] Robert [W.] Hupp and [Private First Class] Richard J. Smith jumped up and said, 'Let's Go!' and crossed the road attacking towards the German positions. Hupp and Smith went right with him."[52]

Staff Sergeant Bill Traband admired both Funk and Hardie. "If Funk hadn't of been what he was, Hardie would have taken over. He had more guts than I'll ever have."[53]

Private Hardie quickly joined the other three troopers. "This group of four rapidly moved forward—Funk in front all the way. Hupp, perhaps fifteen to twenty yards behind Funk and off to the side; Smith, ten yards or so behind Hupp; I was about twenty yards back farther. Action was fast and this group moved forward—not running—but speedily and maintaining a steady stream of fire. Funk carried a Tommy gun as was his habit. The others had M1s. There was no stopping, getting down, taking aim, for rifle fire was from weapons held at waist level and pointed in the direction of fire—roughly.

"Behind me, two other men moved out in front of the company—[Private Thomas M.] Tom Grey and [Private First Class] Rafael [A.] Mendoza—providing cover fire for us and ensuring that any Germans we had passed were either out of action through wounds or gave up. The company and battalion moved out in assault [formation]."[54]

Still pinned down in the road with his two rifle squads, Lieutenant Robert Sickler, the platoon leader of the 3rd Platoon of Company D, now saw "an estimated two companies of troops approaching in attack formation from the north, in the rear of the pinned Germans. They appeared to stretch from the woods on the left front to beyond Voxhil on the right front. They were deployed in width and depth and looked like doomsday to the 3rd Platoon, for it was assumed that they were enemy. I immediately ordered long range fire on this new threat, but the fire seemed to have no effect on their determined advance except to draw return fire, which increased in intensity as they advanced.

"I suddenly realized that the fire from Voxhil had ceased entirely, and observed that the advancing troops were receiving extremely heavy 20mm fire from their left flank and from Voxhil.

"I ordered firing ceased immediately after studying the troops through field glasses finally recognized the familiar sight of a BAR tripod swinging crazily around the muzzle of a rifle, as one of the men made a quick dash forward.

"They were unmistakably American troops, and a cheer went up from every throat. The jubilance was short lived however, as the 1st Battalion continued its relentless attack, sweeping over Voxhil on the right, over the surprised and helpless Germans to the front of the 3rd Platoon, and [then] concentrated its fire on the road occupied by the 3rd Platoon. Having received fire initially from the road, the 1st Battalion was convinced that it was occupied by the enemy.

"Everyone was shouting, 'Cease fire, its Dog Company.' One man attempted to jump to his feet to affect recognition, but was shot down before he could get off his knees. Orange smoke had been designated in the SOI [signal operation instructions] as identification for friendly troops, but there was not a smoke grenade in the entire group. There was no possible way to affect recognition without committing suicide due to the intensity of their concentrated fire. Each man in the 3rd Platoon was forced to hug the ground flat on his face in the 'gutter' defilade until the assaulting force came plunging out onto the road, and recognized us for friendly troops—much to the surprise and disappointment of the 1st Battalion."[55]

Captain Ben Delamater, the 1st Battalion executive officer, accompanied Colonel Lindquist, Lieutenant Colonel Warren, and a few headquarters troopers to the road where Companies B and C had first received fire, to observe the attack. Delamater and the others with him were forced to hit the ground as 20mm fire raked the group, wounding four. "Enough progress of action was observed from the prone position to recommend deployment of A Company around the left flank to exploit the seemingly assured success of B Company."[56]

Advancing behind the assaulting companies, Corporal Jim Blue, with Company A, could observe them attacking across the landing zone. "They moved across the fields firing at every possible target. Company A moved to the left and took care of a few snipers along a fence line."[57]

Meanwhile, the lead element of Company C—1st Sergeant Leonard Funk, Technician Fifth Grade Robert W. Hupp, Private First Class Richard J. Smith, and Private John Hardie were far to the front of the rest of the company. To the front of the group were three 20mm antiaircraft guns firing at gliders that were now beginning to land. With Sergeant Funk leading the way, they overran and shot the infantry protecting the guns. Private Hardie and the lead group now approached the 20mm gun positions. "The group was spread both in lateral and in vertical position, providing cover for one another and especially for Funk, who steadily moved towards, overcame, and moved beyond those positions."[58]

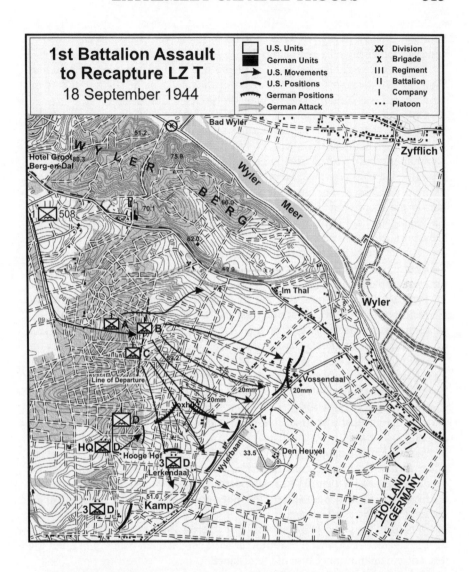

1st Battalion Assault to Recapture LZ T
18 September 1944

First Sergeant Funk single-handedly assaulted the 20mm antiaircraft gun positions, killing about twenty and wounding the remainder of the gun crews. After overrunning these positions, Private Hardie and the other three troopers "got as far out as four to six hundred yards [from the line of departure] and there held up to begin to consolidate, and as others came up, ensured that the German positions were nonfunctioning."[59]

Private Frank Longiotti advanced with his machine gun slung over his shoulder as Company C moved forward. "My ammo bearer and I went past farm buildings down a ditch. We were called back. I picked up my gun and stood up and got shot through the right lung."[60]

Longiotti's squad leader saw him get hit and immediately went to help him. "When [Staff Sergeant] John [W. Auger] picked me up he helped me walk to the farmhouse. I was bleeding and sucking air through the bullet hole."[61]

Corporal Darrell Glass was advancing with one of the troopers in his Company C squad who was also carrying a machine gun and had belts of machine gun ammunition slung over his shoulders. "We had passed a little pump house and I looked around and this guy was coming at my damn buddy [Private First Class Ivan W. Terry] with a rifle with a bayonet. I shouted at him, 'Behind you Terry.' He turned around and smashed the guy's face and killed him—right there—barehanded...His face was gone...He hit him with his fist. He had big hands. He was a real tough guy. He had been raised in a steel town in New York. He was as strong as a bull."[62]

On the left, Lieutenant Millsaps moved forward with his Company B troopers across the open ground under intense German fire. "We broke through the line of infantry and had a field day with the antiaircraft personnel."[63]

Sergeant Jim Kurz was still out in front of Company B as it overran the German positions. "We continued on across the field, killing twenty and capturing twelve Germans and two machine guns. Just as we reached the far side of the field, the first gliders started coming in."[64]

As his light machine gun team moved forward with Company B, Private First Class Jim Allardyce looked up as the gliders came in to land among the troopers. "Some landed off in the distance where the Germans were. Some were shot down. Some cartwheeled in. One in particular just overhead took a flak burst in the tail that just lifted it and set it into a steep but safe glide into the ground.

"I saw some men and guns way off, but couldn't tell whether they were glider men with antitank guns or Jerries with flak guns. When finally I could make Lieutenant [William H.] Cross understand that I wanted his [field] glasses, the firing was so loud we couldn't hear one another. He tossed them to me and I spotted the gunners as German.

"I noticed then that [Private William] Askren with the machine gun and I were separated—and what a beautiful target! I shot at them with my M1, but the results were unknown because of the distance.

"I dropped the lieutenant's [field] glasses in the action, thinking that he was behind me to pick them up, but he wasn't. He was quite put out later about them. As the firing sputtered down, I dashed to the crest of a hill of sugar beet [fields], and just as I slowed down, I got it in the right upper arm by a sniper. I thought it was a chance shot, so I rose to get out of there and the bugger shot at me again. I then emptied my clip into a church steeple in the distance and rolled back down the hill to safety. I found a medic who dressed the wound while some shooting was still going on nearby."[65]

Staff Sergeant Bill Knapp took command of the 1st Platoon of Company B when the platoon leader, Lieutenant Cross, and his assistant platoon leader, Lieutenant Duane Morris, were both wounded during the attack.

The 1st Battalion attack approached the Wylerbaan, the road running from Wyler to Groesbeek, on the southern edge of the landing zone as the first gliders began to land. German machine guns and 20mm antiaircraft guns fired at the gliders in the air and mortar shells exploded on the landing zone. Corporal Darrell Glass saw one of those gliders land a short distance to the front of Company C. "The glider men got out and ran toward us to get cover in the trees behind us. Sergeant Funk asked one of the guys; 'Is there a jeep in that glider?'

"He said, 'Yes.'

"Sergeant Funk ran toward the glider and went inside and we heard a rumble and he got that damn jeep out of the glider. He drove the jeep up to one of the other guys in C Company, [Technician Fifth Grade] Bob Hupp, and told him to get in the jeep and drive and take him where he wanted to go. He stood up in the jeep and directed Bob Hupp to go here and there and he cleaned up the rest of the 20mm installations. They were all around the perimeter of the drop zone. He would go up to the rim of an installation that was like a big foxhole with the gun placed down in it. He would drive up to the edge of it and he would fire directly into the foxhole [the gun pit] and kill these Germans who were firing these cannons. Sergeant Funk must have cleared up at least a dozen installations—not only 20mm, but artillery and mortars."[66]

Lieutenant Woodrow Millsaps also observed Funk's actions. "He passed the line of attack, but continued to pursue the enemy. The battalion watched him and his jeep driver shoot up the place out in front of our lines. We all thought he and the driver would get killed any moment, but he finally returned to our lines without getting a scratch."[67]

As Captain John W. Connelly, the S-4 of the 319th Glider Field Artillery Battalion, approached the landing zone, the glider in which he was riding came under heavy antiaircraft fire. "Mortar, machine gun, and incendiary fire were getting heavy as we were coming down. I did point out to our pilot the exact field we were scheduled to land in, but he kept waiting for orders to cut loose from the tow plane. The tow plane was slow with their signal, causing us to overshoot our landing area. Five gliders in our group overshot their mark, landing in Germany near the town of Wyler. The pilot of my glider was killed as we were coming in for a landing. I took the controls from about fifteen to twenty feet up and brought it down. I received a small fragment wound in the right leg. One man received a serious leg wound—the other, a head wound. These two men and I escaped from the glider just as it caught fire and burned. I saw two Germans coming along the ditch in our direction. I emptied my carbine at them, only to find I had filled the cartridge clip only half full. Fortunately for me, this was all I needed for this occasion. I treated the wounds of the two men before taking off down a dry ditch. German troops were combing the area for the rest of the afternoon, but didn't find my hiding place."[68]

Major Fred J. Silvey, the executive officer of the 319th, was a passenger in Chalk 1, the lead glider of the battalion's serial. "I was riding in the front seat of a jeep with the driver, Private [Clavis W.] Thompson. Sergeant [Technician Fourth Grade Vernon B.] Main was in the rear seat. Passing directly over the LZ, the pilot missed his checkpoints and we flew straight into Germany, landing between Zyfflich and Wyler in the heaviest flak we had encountered.

"Sergeant Main was hit in the face, but no one was injured on landing. After giving Sergeant Main first aid, we realized the firing was increasing, so we started crawling down a ditch to try and make contact with the personnel from three other gliders which had landed about four hundred yards from ours. I soon saw this was impossible and led the party to a dike, where we hid in the tall grass until dark. One time, the Germans were within seventy-five yards of us, but failed to see us. At a distance, we could see SS troops unloading the gliders and then burning them. We could see several people with their hands up, so we figured the personnel in the other gliders had been captured."[69]

Technician Fourth Grade Ed Ryan, with Battery C, was in a glider farther back in the serial transporting the 319th. "I saw the LZ with the chutes on the ground, signaled the pilot and he cut us loose, the gliders in front of us went into German territory. Upon landing, there was small arms fire. None were wounded or injured. This landing was on level ground with CG4-A gliders. Fence posts came through the floor but avoided everyone. Some of the gliders were trying to run over the German soldiers running out of the landing area."[70]

In the haste to knock out the guns firing on the LZ, the 1st Battalion had bypassed the farm buildings at Voxhil. The Germans occupying these buildings were now to the rear of Companies B and C and preparing to open fire when Captain Frank Schofield, the Company C commander, spotted several German machine gun crews setting up their weapons, about to unleash enfilade fire into the rear of his troopers. Captain Schofield immediately got his 60mm mortars in action, and at a range of two to three hundred yards, knocked out one German crew. Schofield then directed his men to attack the farm buildings while the mortars forced the Germans to cover.

Lieutenant Millsaps heard the firing behind him and took some of his Company B troopers with him to help clean out the buildings. "I remember seeing a [German] soldier looking out a window of one of the houses that I had landed nearby on my jump the day before. I motioned for him to come out of the house. But he disappeared, and I tossed a grenade in the window and awaited results."[71] Other troopers surrounding the house did the same.

The grenades exploded, knocking Millsaps down. As he got up, Millsaps was shocked by what he saw. "Sixty German soldiers marched out of this building single file with hands overhead, which was by now a familiar sight. I went in this house to see how so many soldiers had escaped injury from the grenade and found they had been down in the basement to await capture."[72]

Private William Windom was one of the Company B troopers who cleaned out the group of farm buildings. "[Sergeant Joseph G.] Endress told me to search a rambling farmhouse. I went in with a rifle butt smash like John Wayne. 'Hande Hoche!' Very slowly a door opened and two old people looked at me in fear.

"'Sind sie Dutch?'

"'Nein, nichts Deutsch—Holland!'

"'Haben sie Deutsche soldaten hierin?'

"'Nein, nur vater und mutter.'

"I pushed through to the kitchen and sure enough there was another couple too old to get out of chairs. I felt awful. Nothing for it, but I must come into the parlor and see their son's picture in the Dutch Navy in Java."[73]

Private Windom then left the house and went back outside. "Everybody was gone. Then a Kraut in coat and pants only, popped out and stared at me arms akimbo [hands on hips with elbows bowed outward]. He wouldn't surrender and he didn't move. He watched me wrestle with my grenade launcher. Endress came around another corner and cut him in half."[74]

After the assault, Captain Delamater was given the casualty figures for the fight to clear the landing zone as the 1st Battalion counted noses. "The battalion killed about 50 enemy and captured 149. Our losses were amazingly light— about five killed and ten wounded."[75] In addition, the 1st Battalion had knocked out sixteen 20mm antiaircraft guns.

For his outstanding heroism and leadership that day, Sergeant Leonard Funk, with Company C, would later be awarded the Distinguished Service Cross. Technician Fifth Grade Robert Hupp would be awarded the Silver Star, and Private First Class Richard J. Smith and Private John Hardie were awarded the Bronze Star for their heroism in leading the attack. Sergeant Jim Kurz was awarded the Silver Star for his courageous leadership of Company B during the assault.

The casualties among Lieutenant Sickler's platoon of Company D were also surprisingly light. "The 3rd Platoon had suffered five killed in action and six wounded in action, not counting the company commander, who had been stunned by a bullet, which grazed his head.

"The 1st Platoon was later reported in Groesbeek, where it had joined the 505th Parachute Infantry Regiment. The platoon leader's radio had apparently been damaged in the jump and failed to function. Believing his platoon to be cut off by the attack which overran the 2nd Platoon, and finding himself without communications, he decided to attach his platoon to the nearest known friendly troop unit."[76]

Most of the 2nd Platoon of Company D been killed or captured, including its platoon leader, Lieutenant Temple Tutwiler, who spent the remainder of the war in a German POW camp.

General Gavin would later praise the 508th for its outstanding performance on September 18. "This particular maneuver, I believe, has few parallels and could have been executed only by extremely capable troops and unusual combat leadership on the part of the regimental, battalion, and company commanders involved. The regiment was being attacked by superior numbers from several directions, but it had managed to disengage in Nijmegen and attack and drive the Germans from the landing zone area. At the same time, it was attacking and seizing the northern bridge over the Maas-Waal canal, as well as providing contact with other units and security of its entire perimeter, which was now approximately eight miles long."[77]

The 1st Battalion pulled back from the Wylerbaan and dug in along the high ground running northeast to southwest through Voxhil, with an open left flank, tying in with Company D on its right, and establishing outposts two hundred to six hundred yards in front of the main line of resistance to prevent a repeat of the German infiltration attack.

Staff Sergeant Bill Knapp reorganized the 1st Platoon of Company B, after both the platoon leader and the assistant platoon leader were wounded during the attack. Knapp was later recommended for a battlefield commission as a result of his leadership.

After Company B finished digging in, Lieutenant Millsaps watched his troopers bring some additional firepower up to their line. "We pulled a couple of these [20mm] guns into position and fired them at the Germans just for the hell of it. I had fun passing out P-38 German pistols to all who wanted one until they ran out, which at first count were eighty or more pistols."[78]

After the fighting died down, Lieutenant Kenneth Johnson, the regiment's assistant S-4 and munitions officer, and the supply section began moving the supply dump to a safer location. "The S-4 personnel immediately set out in the direction of regimental CP with our wagon and all we could carry. This actually amounted to about one thousand pounds of supplies. About three-quarters of a mile from the drop zone, our small group was strafed by an enemy fighter, but miraculously came through unscathed. Our group was traveling across country, and as the soil was soft, the going was pitifully slow. About halfway to the regimental CP, the 1st Battalion S-4 [Lieutenant Peter E. Kelley] happened across the supply group as he was searching for some lost equipment bundles. He had a group of about ten men with him and as his unit was the most heavily committed at the time, I turned over to him the bulk of supplies, including the nearly worn out horse and cart. Our supply group continued on, now carrying only the regimental supply of batteries and some signal equipment.

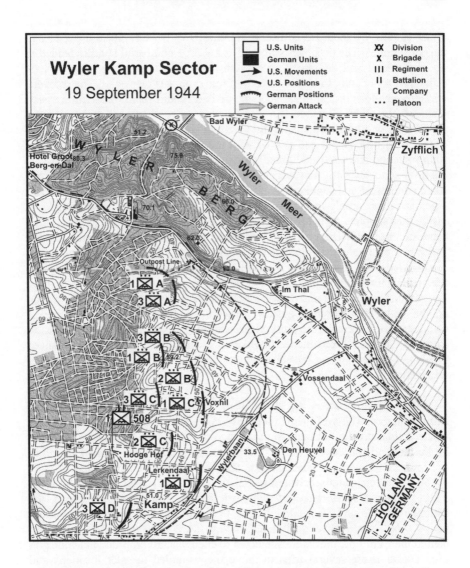

"When our group reached the 3rd Battalion area, a message was sent to the 3rd Battalion S-4 notifying him that the 1st Battalion had what extra ammunition was presently available. Without further incident, our group reached the regimental CP, and after notifying the regimental CO [Colonel Lindquist] and S-4 [Major James Casteel] of its actions, established a supply point, without supplies, a short distance from the CP."[79]

Much to his relief, Lieutenant Johnson, all four of the jeeps scheduled for delivery to the regiment with the glider landings arrived safely. "Following the glider landing by about ten to twenty minutes, 135 B-24 bombers dropped 261 tons of supplies. The drop was scattered and a large number of bundles landed in no man's land and had to be recovered after dark. Depending upon various estimates, about sixty to eighty percent of this drop was recovered. The recovery was a tremendous task and everyone the division could spare was used to assist, including the glider pilots...

"By the end of the 18th, shortages were developing in certain supplies. One of the ¼-ton trucks that had arrived with the gliders was made available to the supply section and some additional supplies were recovered from the vicinity of the drop zone. By now, however, the drop zone had been fought over twice and some equipment and supplies not previously recovered had been damaged. The other battalion supply officers were notified to make similar searches and to insure that supplies on hand were carefully conserved. A battle loss report was submitted to the division to be forwarded to the United Kingdom and included in the first available resupply. A trip was made to the division supply points and some rations and ammunition from the resupply were drawn at that time. The regimental ammunition sergeant and five men remained at division to help secure bundles. The rations drawn from division were distributed to the troops on the 18th, but sufficient quantity was not available to issue each man a complete ration. Perhaps the most critical shortage of supplies at this time was in batteries. The use of communication wire was limited because of the distances involved between units. Consequently, the drain on the small stock of batteries was heavy."[80]

The gliders of Battery A, 319th Glider Field Artillery Battalion had been badly scattered. Thirty of them landed five miles south of LZ "T", near Gennep, where antiaircraft fire hit them in the air and upon landing. One glider had been hit by flak and cut loose over DZ "O" in the 504 sector. Only six had landed in or near LZ "T" and several came down near Wyler behind German lines.

Shortly after landing, Private First Class Harold G. Tucker, a medic with the 319th, gathered fourteen badly wounded troopers who were hit during the battalion's landing. Tucker administered first aid to the wounded men, without which most would have died. Even though they were three hundred yards behind the front line, they were subjected to enemy small arms and machine gun fire. Tucker made several trips to move the wounded to safer locations and stayed with them for fifty hours until it was possible to evacuate them. Private First Class Tucker was awarded the Silver Star for his life savings actions.

The glider carrying Sergeants Milton E. Chadwick and Frank Vujevic, with the 319th, landed behind German lines near Wyler under enemy small arms and mortar fire. Vujevic and Chadwick led their section through German lines to the safety of the 508th sector, then obtained a ¼-ton truck and drove back through the lines to their glider and unloaded the 75mm howitzer and other equipment from the glider and drove the truck with the howitzer and the equipment back through the lines. Throughout the entire trip, Vujevic and Chadwick were under heavy enemy small arms and mortar fire. Sergeants Vujevic and Chadwick were both awarded the Bronze Star for their heroic actions.

After treating two of his troopers for wounds suffered during the landing, Captain John Connelly, the S-4 of the 319th Glider Field Artillery Battalion, hid from German troops searching for survivors among several gliders that had landed earlier northeast of Wyler. Connelly waited for darkness before making his move. "After darkness came, I tried to wade across the Wyler-Meer—a long narrow body of water. It was too deep and I was too heavily loaded with combat equipment, so I came back and tried to get around it to the south. I was wet and chilled, walking all night, sometimes in circles. Coming to a road and a bridge, I started across, only to meet a German soldier on a bicycle. Being alone, and not wanting to attract much attention, I decided against shooting, unless necessary. Fortunately, he failed to recognize my uniform and went on his way.

"I still couldn't spot any friendly troops. At daybreak, I concealed myself in a wooded hill, overlooking a dirt road. By midmorning I heard several troops moving on the road below, but couldn't see them.

"I heard one remark to another, 'You lousy S.O.B.!' It was music to my ears. So I came down, identified myself to them, and found them to be 82nd Airborne troopers. They directed me to my battalion headquarters. Of about forty men in these gliders, one other person and I were the only ones getting back to our outfits. About eight were killed, the others captured."[81]

Major Fred Silvey, the 319th executive officer, and the others from his glider also hid out until nightfall. "After dark, we made our way to the bridge at Wyler, crossed it and passed the town to the north. We saw no one, although shooting ahead of us changed our course several times. We crossed the fence on the German-Holland border about midnight and three hours later, stopped to rest. At first light, we moved to a concealed spot in a hedgerow, where we stayed until we ascertained where we were and knew something about the situation. We then made our way into Groesbeek and from there, to our OP."[82]

IN NIJMEGEN LATE ON THE NIGHT OF SEPTEMBER 18-19, the 2nd Platoon of Company A, which had been cut off in the city for the last twenty-four hours by German troops, attempted to break out and make its way back to friendly forces. Captain Jonathan Adams, the commanding officer of Company A, had been with the platoon when it had been isolated during its patrol to destroy the demolition controls for the Nijmgen highway bridge. "We tried a couple of breaks, however that section of town was lit by flames and all the streets were covered by killing lanes of fire."[83] Captain Adams and the 2nd Platoon were forced to return to their hiding place at a warehouse to await either the advance of friendly forces or another opportunity to break out the following night.

CHAPTER 12

"I LOST HALF OF MY COMPANY"

On the morning of September 19, the British Guards Armoured Division linked up with elements of the 504th Parachute Infantry Regiment holding the Grave bridge. The huge armored column then crossed the Maas-Waal Canal at Heumen and made contact with the 82nd Airborne Division headquarters. After briefing the British commanders and informing them that the bridges at Nijmegen were still in German hands, a combined British–American task force was quickly formed to capture the bridges. The task force was divided into three elements: one to seize the highway bridge, another to grab the railroad bridge, and a third to take the city post office, where the Dutch Underground had indicated the demolition controls for the highway bridge were housed. It was believed that the combat patrol led by Captain Adams and Lieutenant George Lamm had assaulted the post office and were likely trapped there. The force assigned to the post office was ordered to either liberate Captain Adams and his troopers if they held the post office, and if not, destroy it and the controls. It consisted of one troop of Sherman tanks of Number 1 Squadron, 2nd Grenadier Guards Battalion and two armored infantry platoons of Number 3 Company, 1st Grenadier Guards Battalion; both units of the elite Guards Armoured Division.

At about 1:30 p.m. that day, General Gavin ordered Major Otho Holmes, the commanding officer of the 2nd Battalion, to send a platoon to meet him for a special mission. Lieutenant Adolph "Bud" Warnecke and his 3rd Platoon of Company E were selected for the mission and attached to the force assigned to capture the post office. "My platoon was in battalion reserve when the British linked up with us. My platoon received an order to join a British tank platoon with the mission of going into Nijmegen. We were to capture a German headquarters and post office where intelligence thought switchboxes to blow the main bridge over the Waal River were located."[1]

British Guards Major George Thorne commanded the group and Dutchman Piet Gerrits volunteered to guide the column to the post office. The post office column followed the main column attacking the highway bridge as far as the Krayenhoff barracks, then separated from it and drove to the post office via Coehoornstraat to Van Gentstraat, then to Prins Bernhardstraat, encountering only one 50mm antitank gun, which was destroyed. The column seized the post office late that afternoon, but found it occupied by only the Dutch Underground. Captain Jonathan Adams, Lieutenant George Lamm, and the 2nd Platoon of Company A, which were thought to be holding the building, were not found. Lieutenant Warnecke looked for the purported demolition controls for the highway bridge. "A search found no switchbox and we returned to our unit that night. This had been the first time I had worked with British troops. They were good soldiers, but compared to us I thought they had a nonchalant attitude about the war."[2]

BY THE MORNING OF SEPTEMBER 19, hunger was gnawing at the stomachs of most of the regiment's paratroopers. Corporal Jim Blue, with the 1st Platoon of Company A, and his buddies decided to see if the local inhabitants could help them obtain something to eat. "We made arrangements with a Dutch farmer to use some of a beef that had been killed in clearing the DZ. He provided us with a large iron wash pot for the cooking. On our own initiative, we rounded up potatoes, carrots, and onions for the big stew. This was when we learned that [Staff] Sergeant [Sherman] Van Enwyck wasn't such a good cook. Everyone ate at least a canteen cup; after all, we had not eaten a full meal since the morning of the 17th."[3]

At 8:00 a.m. on September 19, one platoon of Company H moved into Beek and established a roadblock on Highway K at the main intersection in the town. Highway K, the international highway, ran from Wyler northwest along the Dutch–German border through Beek to Nijmegen and provided the best route for German forces to relieve the defenders of Nijmegen bridges.

At about 10:15 a.m., Company F left the roadblock positions it was manning around De Ploeg and was sent to assist the 3rd Battalion, where enemy forces were infiltrating into the battalion's wide sector.

By 10:50 a.m., the 3rd Battalion command post received a report that part of the Company H platoon manning the roadblock on Highway K at Beek was surrounded. An hour later the command post received reports of four light German tanks along with an estimated platoon of infantry dug in on the high ground overlooking the highway to Nijmegen between Berg-en-Dal and Stollenberg, and another enemy force of four light tanks armed with 37mm guns supported by infantry located between Beek and Berg-en-Dal.

With the remainder of Company I holding Hill 64.6, west of Ubbergen, Lieutenant Colonel Mendez ordered an attack to break through to the Company H platoon cutoff in Beek, secure the town, and reestablish the roadblock. "G Company, minus one platoon [which was] attached to A Company, and F Company joined the I Company platoon [the 2nd Platoon] in attacking Beek to clear the town of enemy reported there."[4]

Lieutenant Colonel Mendez ordered Company F to attack the enemy force of four light tanks and a platoon of infantry dug in on the high ground near the intersection of the highway to Nijmegen and the Stollenberg–Beek road, then capture the high ground southeast of Beek that overlooked Highway K. The 2nd Platoon of Company I was ordered to attack along the road running northeast from Berg-en-Dal to Beek. Company G, less the 2nd Platoon, was ordered to attack and clear the high ground overlooking Highway K northwest of Beek.

Corporal Bob Chisolm and the 2nd Platoon of Company I moved down the road from Berg-en-Dal to Beek, which had thick woods bordering its right side. "We had orders to establish a roadblock in Beek. We initially went down and we ran into some opposition at the hospital, which going down [the hill] was on the left side of the road. There were two halftracks and someone had dropped a bazooka and ammunition. It looked like it had been deserted by one of the other units that had gone down earlier. [Private First Class] Joe Petry and I picked up the bazooka and I fired the bazooka and knocked out both halftracks. There were four or five Germans [in the halftracks] and we got them."[5]

The 1st Platoon of Company D, 307th Airborne Engineer Battalion under the command of Lieutenant Ralph W. Hendrix, arrived about 1:15 p.m., to support the 2nd Platoon of Company I just as the attack began. "When we arrived [near Beek], we were fired upon and pinned down for about two hours. Casualties were two [Company I] BAR men wounded and one enlisted man killed. By the order of the infantry CO we retreated, formed defensive positions, reorganized, and with the engineers leading, attacked Beek the second time."[6]

Intense automatic weapons fire once again pinned down the attackers when suddenly one of the engineers, Private Ludwig Kubish, rushed fifty yards across open ground and single-handedly destroyed a German strongpoint in a building located at the edge of the village, killing four with his Thompson submachine gun and a Gammon grenade, and causing the remaining five enemy soldiers to surrender.

With the enemy strongpoint neutralized, the engineers charged toward the buildings on the edge of town. Staff Sergeant Roland C. Ziegler noticed one of his men, Private Julius A. Silverman out in front as the platoon approached the first buildings. "He went into the town first and was throwing hand grenades into buildings and firing his bazooka."[7]

During the final assault, Lieutenant Hendrix observed heroism by one of his engineers, "Private [Lewis F.] Hoskins, 1st Platoon BAR man. When both BAR men of the infantry became casualties, he continued to charge and is believed to have started the enemy on their retreat.

"The enemy was completely, as we believe, driven from the town. A search of the houses was made by our men. Immediately thereafter, the platoon carried out their mission of establishing roadblocks and covering the same. The rest of the night the men stood guard. There was no enemy action."[8]

Privates Kubish and Silverman were each awarded the Silver Star for their heroism during the assault.

The 2nd Platoon of Company I and the 1st Platoon, Company D, 307th Airborne Engineer Battalion relieved the Company H platoon in Beek, then set up a perimeter around the town and established two roadblocks on Highway K.

After driving the enemy from the high ground around the Stollenberg-Beek road, Company F attacked to capture high ground southeast of Beek. Lieutenant Wayne Smith was the platoon leader of the 2nd Platoon of Company F. "We were assigned the mission of going through a wood to our front and cleaning the enemy out of the wood. We were then to bear left into a pear orchard, situated on high ground about two hundred yards south of Beek. Along the main international highway between Holland and Germany, we met our first heavy resistance going through the woods. Our objective after we passed through the woods was the high ground to our left front. To our right front were two small hills with a valley between. Both of these hills were enemy occupied. The near one was a house that was occupied by some of the enemy. The 1st Platoon laid down a base of fire. The 3rd Platoon was held in reserve and the 2nd worked around to the right in a flanking movement. The 2nd Platoon reached the vicinity of the house and started a palaver with the enemy. They were seriously contemplating surrendering to us when the 1st Platoon, not knowing about the pending negotiations, opened fire on the Germans in the house. The Huns returned the fire at both us and the 1st Platoon. I lost two men here and withdrew toward the company, remaining on the right flank. Meanwhile, the rest of the company jumped off in an attack on the two enemy positions. I followed suit, but the company was out of sight and it was getting dark."[9]

Technician Fourth Grade Dwayne Burns was the communications NCO for the Company F headquarters. "Late in the afternoon, F Company had worked its way to the top of a hill southeast of Beek. Looking down, we could see the main road running northwest toward Nijmegen. Off to the northwest, we could see the prize we were after—the Nijmegen bridge. It was a magnificent looking structure of concrete and steel, but not worth all of the lives it would cost before it was taken. Looking northeast across the road, we could see across the flats for one thousand yards or better.

"As we stood there, taking it all in, we were concealed by trees and bushes. Up the road, going toward Beek, came what looked like the entire German army. I had never seen so many at one time. They were walking along in three columns at route step and they didn't even know we were there. It must have been at least a battalion and there was a staff car with the top down and a high ranking officer sitting in the back, acting like he was number one. It looked like something you would see in the movies. As we watched, they came right on up on the road just like they had never heard of the American army.

"I stood there, afraid to breathe, afraid they might hear me. 'My God, what are we going to do,' I said. 'There are so many of them!' I thought that maybe if we stayed hidden they would just pass on by and go into town. I was standing

with Lieutenant Polette [the platoon leader of the 1st Platoon], who was a real
soldier's soldier.

"He reached up, took his Thompson submachine gun off his shoulder,
looked at me and without a moment's hesitation, said, 'Let's get 'em!' He said it
so casually that you would have thought we were going to try to pick up a
couple of girls. I wanted to tell him how many Germans there were down there.
Maybe we should talk it over! But while I was trying to think of all the good
reasons to stay where we were, he started firing. He took off down the hill on a
dead run. The troopers of F Company would have followed Lieutenant Polette to
hell and back if he said we were going and would lead the way. So, down the
hill went F Company in what must have been one of the great classic charges of
the war. We slammed down the hill firing from the hip and screaming like a
bunch of wild Indians. It must have sounded like the entire American army was
coming down the hill. We had caught the Germans so much by surprise that they
broke and ran. We ran after them until we got to the road. Lieutenant Polette
called a halt and said, 'This is as far as we go!' He dropped down on one knee
for better aim and I could see that Thompson jump every time he cut loose.
Down on the flats, the Germans were running for their lives. There was no cover
and all they could do was try to get out of our range. There were so many of
them it was hard to concentrate on one target at a time. The staff car turned off
the road and gunned ahead. The officer in the back was madder than hell. He
was standing up, shouting and waving his arms, trying vainly to get his men to
stop and reorganize. But they had the bit in their teeth and there was no stopping
them. We stood there taking shots to help them on their way. We finally stopped
firing and sat down to rest while watching the last of the Germans make their
way across the flats. We could see scattered pieces of equipment and dead
Krauts for one thousand yards. After resting from our wild run down the hill, we
withdrew back to the top and sat up a defensive position in a pear orchard."[10]

Meanwhile, Company G, less the 2nd Platoon, attacked on the left flank of
Company I and cleared the high ground northwest of Beek and dug in on it,
overlooking the highway. Late that day, Lieutenant Colonel Mendez received
reports from the units involved in securing Beek. "By dark, the town was
cleared, G and F Companies were set up on the high ground to the left and right
of the roadblock, and the roadblock was established on the national highway. At
this time, with the addition of two 57mm antitank guns from the 80th AA
Battalion and one platoon [the 1st Platoon] from D Company of the 307th
engineers, the roadblock numbered eighty-three men."[11]

Early on the morning of September 19, the 2nd Platoon of Company G was
ordered to seize Hill 75.9, which the Dutch named Teufelberg, or Devil's Hill.
The steeply sloped hill dominated Highway K to the north. In addition, the 2nd
Platoon of Company G was ordered to establish a roadblock on Highway K at
Bad Wyler, at the foot of Devil's Hill. The 2nd Platoon of Company G sent a

reconnaissance patrol to Devil's Hill prior to an assault by the entire platoon. The assistant platoon leader, Lieutenant Bill Call, who had been a squad leader with Company B in Normandy and received a battlefield commission as a result of the courage and leadership he had exhibited during the assault of la Poterie Ridge, led the patrol.

On the way to the objective, the patrol was pinned down by an enemy machine gun firing from a well camouflaged position. When Private First Class Daniel E. Kuszmaul spotted the position, he worked his way toward the machine gun, crawling to within a few yards of it. He threw two fragmentation grenades and then rushed it firing his Thompson submachine gun. Kuszmaul killed and wounded the crew, but was himself killed in the close range gun battle. Private First Class Kuszmaul was posthumously awarded the Silver Star for his heroism.

Lieutenant Call and his men then resumed the reconnaissance patrol. "When they sent me out on the patrol to the hill, there was a farmhouse, and I stopped in it. There was an old man and a young boy; he was maybe fifteen, who spoke broken English. I showed him the map and said, 'Where is this?' I wanted to make sure I was leading this patrol in the right direction. He took us right to the back of that hill. There was a knoll in back there that was higher than the hill itself. We were looking right down on them. They didn't know we were there. That's when I decided that our fifteen to twenty guys in this patrol could not take this company alone.

"A lot of them were sitting on the edge of their holes, combing their hair. It was a sunny day. So I had the men each pick out one of them and said, 'We're going to shoot them and get the hell out of here.' So we opened fire and we got the hell out of there."[12]

Lieutenant Call reported to his platoon leader, Lieutenant Kenneth A. Covey, that the hill was held by a company of German paratroopers and this information was relayed to the 3rd Battalion headquarters. The enemy paratroopers were part of Kampfgruppe Becker, newly arrived from the Köln (Cologne), Germany area, under the command of Oberstleutnant Karl-Heinz Becker.

Company A, still without the 2nd Platoon, which was cut off in Nijmegen, was given the mission to seize the hill. Lieutenant John Foley, the company's executive officer, had been in command of Company A since withdrawing from Nijmegen the previous morning. "Shields Warren sent for me shortly after we had withdrawn from town [Nijmegen] and presented me with the following gem. He wanted me to take the remainder of A Company with additional fire support from Headquarters Company and go to the relief of a platoon from the 3rd Battalion which had been given the mission of securing the right flank of the 3rd Battalion. This unit had attempted to secure Devil's Hill earlier in the morning, but could not overcome the German resistance, and as the only recourse Colonel Mendez had requested regiment to assist in this problem.

"As a direct result of the request, we were the lucky ones of A Company [who] had been designated to secure the relief of the platoon from the 3rd

Battalion and secure at any cost Devil's Hill. I was assured that this would not be as difficult as it appeared and Colonel Warren wanted to be able to pass on to regiment that we would have it secured by nightfall."[13]

Company A at that point consisted of just two officers and forty-two men. Out of the eight officers who had jumped with the company on September 17, two were with the 2nd Platoon still cutoff in Nijmegen, Captain Jonathan Adams, the company commander, and Lieutenant George Lamm, the platoon leader of the 2nd Platoon. Two more, Lieutenant Schlesinger, the assistant platoon leader of the 2nd Platoon, and Lieutenant Rex Combs, the platoon leader of the 3rd Platoon, had been wounded during the jump. Two others, Lieutenant Fred Layman, the platoon leader of the 1st Platoon, had been wounded, and Lieutenant Boyd Alexander, the assistant platoon leader of the 3rd Platoon, had been killed in Nijmgen during the fighting on the first night. Lieutenant John Foley, the executive officer, and Lieutenant Robert Havens, the assistant platoon leader of the 1st Platoon, were the two remaining officers.

The 2nd Platoon of Company G, consisting of two officers and thirty-four men and led by Lieutenant Kenneth Covey, was attached to Company A. Lieutenant Call, the assistant platoon leader, acted as the guide, because he knew the way to the hill that the Dutch boy had shown him. The route offered concealment and would allow them to approach the hill from the rear of the German positions. "I showed them how to get back there, because I knew the route."[14]

Corporal Jim Blue, with the 1st Platoon of Company A, was told that the hill was to be taken at all cost. "We moved out through the wooded area and crossed the Wyler [to Berg-en-Dal] road, which was the Holland–Germany border. An enemy force was sighted in the direction of Wyler. Lieutenant Foley dropped off one squad of the 1st Platoon, under the command of the assistant platoon leader, Lieutenant Robert N. Havens, to protect [the rear of] his attacking force. I was with this group. We rushed up the road to a position in the woods which had a good field of fire and dug in positions. This enemy force held up and was reluctant to attack. We stayed at this position while the Foley force made the attack on Devil's Hill."[15]

As Company A and the attached platoon of Company G and Headquarters Company, 1st Battalion machine gun section approached Hill 75.9 from the southwest, the attention of the German paratroopers dug in on it was directed at the 2nd Platoon, Company D, 307th Airborne Engineer Battalion to the north as it moved southeast along Highway K. The engineer platoon had orders to establish a roadblock on the highway at a "T" intersection with the Bad Wyler dyke road, which ran north-south across the western end of the Wyler Meer. As Lieutenant Alfred R. Conrad, the platoon leader, led his troopers toward the objective, the German paratroopers on the northern slope opened fire on the platoon pinning it down.

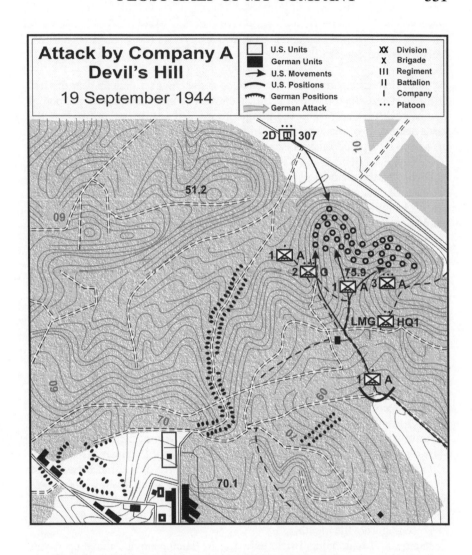

Attack by Company A
Devil's Hill

19 September 1944

	U.S. Units	XX	Division
	German Units	X	Brigade
→	U.S. Movements	III	Regiment
	U.S. Positions	II	Battalion
	German Positions	I	Company
	German Attack	•••	Platoon

Staff Sergeant James H. Sweet was the platoon sergeant of the 2nd Platoon of Company D, 307th Airborne Engineer Battalion. "Lieutenant Conrad, with Private [Anthony G.] Torres, came upon a machine gun nest. They tried to put it out of action, but Lieutenant Conrad was killed in action at 17:20. Private Torres came to his aid, but Lieutenant Conrad was already dead—shot in the stomach, chest, and left wrist. Private Torres, with a BAR tried to advance, but the opposing fire was too heavy and he withdrew. The other known casualty was Sergeant [James M.] Grove, who received a scalp wound—a bullet entering the left side of his helmet and coming out on top. Private [First Class Richard P.] Martin reported that he killed a woman sniper."[16]

With German attention and fire directed at the engineer platoon near the foot of the northern slope of Devil's Hill, Company A and the attached platoon of Company G were able to move through the wooded area to within two hundred yards southwest of the crest of the hill. There, Lieutenant John Foley deployed his troopers into a skirmish line and they charged up the hill at a run.

When he heard no firing, Technician Fifth Grade John E. Brickley knew they had achieved the element of surprise. "They apparently had no perimeter guard because our first contact was with one of their two machine guns [defending that side of the hill]. Lieutenant Foley called for a bazooka up front. He sent [a squad led by Sergeant Vince] V. G. Pierce to the left of the hill with the bazooka man. They (twelve) were cut down with one sweep of the [enemy machine] gun."[17]

Lieutenant Foley then sent a second bazooka team to try to get a shot at the German machine gun. "When we attempted to approach Devil's Hill from the left flank, we lost a few men on a poor move by me. It wasn't until they had picked off two bazooka teams that I decided we had to go at them from the front. With headquarters [company] personnel to our right rear and giving us close supporting fire we rushed the objective."[18]

Lieutenant Jones N. Epps, the platoon leader of the Light Machine Gun Platoon, Headquarters Company, 1st Battalion, set up a couple of the machine guns to the right rear of Lieutenant Foley's troopers to provide suppressive fire on the crest of the hill.

After seeing what had happened to Sergeant Pierce's squad and the two bazooka teams, Technician Fifth Grade Brickley was hesitant when he received the order to make a frontal assault on the machine gun at the crest of the hill. "The rest of us were scared and confused. Staff Sergeant [Herman W.] Jahnigen told us to yell like Indians and charge up the hill. We did—I ran between 1st Sergeant [Frank] Taylor and a new replacement. Halfway up the hill, a burst was fired into us. Taylor and the new man went down. I thought I'd better do the same. I turned to the man on my left to see how he was; he couldn't answer, he was bleeding from the mouth.

"Sergeant Taylor said, 'Brick, take my sub-Thompson and move up if you can—I'm hit in the shoulder.' I reached the top of the hill with the others."[19]

Despite the enemy machine gun fire from the crest of the hill, they quickly overran it. Several of the troopers carrying .30-caliber light machine guns advanced firing them from the hip as they moved. One of them, Corporal Lawrence Fitzpatrick, a squad leader with the Light Machine Gun Platoon, Headquarters Company, 1st Battalion, was at the point of the attack and killed approximately fifteen of the enemy during the initial assault on the hill.

After reaching the crest, Lieutenant Bill Call and the other troopers kept moving forward, overrunning the German paratroopers holding the other three sides of the hill. "When we charged from the back of the hill, down this little incline onto the face of the hill, with a little company of guys shooting and yelling and screaming; the Germans of course were taken by surprise."[20]

Most of the German paratroopers stayed in their holes and fought back, using a large number of automatic weapons and repeatedly counterattacking. Foley's Red Devils overran one hole after another until the surviving German paratroopers broke. Lieutenant Call watched the surviving German paratroopers stampede down the steep slopes of the hill. "They got the hell out of their holes, ran down the front part of the hill, across the highway, across the dike, and into the flatlands."[21] As they fled north across the flat ground and southeast along Highway K toward Wyler, Corporal Fitzpatrick killed about twenty more with his machine gun. Dead German paratroopers littered the slopes of the hill. The Germans left two staff cars, two trucks, two 20mm antiaircraft guns with over three hundred 20mm shells, approximately thirty rifles, and lots of personal equipment at the bottom of the hill.

As the attack by Foley's troopers occurred, the engineers of the 2nd Platoon of Company D, 307th Airborne Engineer Battalion, who had been pinned down by the Germans, joined in to assault the Germans on the northern slope of the hill. Staff Sergeant James H. Sweet was now in charge of the platoon after the platoon leader had been killed earlier during the initial fighting. "With part of Company G, 508th, the 2nd Platoon attacked enemy positions and drove them away in full retreat, approximately forty being killed, two taken prisoner. The 2nd Platoon then set up defensive positions near the roadblock five hundred yards southwest of Bad Wyler. At 20:00, the platoon was relieved by Company G, 508th, and withdrew as 1st Battalion reserve."[22]

After the attack, Lieutenant Call got his troopers reorganized. "Foley told me, 'You'll take the left side of the hill.' He and Lieutenant Covey were going down to look at the front part, just off the nose of the hill. There were holes there, where the Germans had been, and they were down there, and I was getting the guys settled into the German foxholes. We heard small arms fire. There was a farmhouse across the road from the front of the hill and there was a sniper there. Foley came back up and said, 'Well, you're a platoon leader now.' Covey got it right between the eyes—it blew the back of his head out."[23]

The Company A first sergeant, Frank Taylor, did what little he could to take care of the wounded troopers. "I had five men with stomach wounds that sat propped up against trees that took twelve to fifteen hours to die and didn't hear a whimper or a sound out of any of them."[24]

Ten troopers had been killed or mortally wounded and another seven wounded who survived. Lieutenant Foley organized the two platoons and headquarters of Company A, the attached 2nd Platoon of Company G, and the Headquarters Company, 1st Battalion machine gun section to defend the hill.

For his heroism in attacking the German machine gun nest, Lieutenant Alfred Conrad, the platoon leader of the 2nd Platoon of Company D, 307th

Airborne Engineer Battalion, was posthumously awarded the Silver Star. Corporal Lawrence Fitzpatrick was also awarded the Silver Star for his herosim during the capture of Devil's Hill.

During the night, the 1st Battalion S-4, Lieutenant Peter Kelley, and a group of twelve troopers reached Lieutenant Foley's position on Devil's Hill with a critical replenishment of ammunition. After the ammunition was resupplied, Lieutenant Foley sent several of his troopers that night on a "trip to the bottom of the hill to the burned out tavern for food. The only thing I remember we ever got [from the tavern] was a supply of black bread and cherry jam. [Staff Sergeant Sherman] Van Enwyck's butcher shop was set up farther back of our position."[25] Several farm animals found in the area were slaughtered and prepared by Staff Sergeant Van Enwyck to feed the troopers.

During the night of September 19, the remainder of the 2nd Battalion, less Company F (which was attached to the 3rd Battalion) and the 3rd Platoon of Company E (which was attached to the combined British–American task force in Nijmegen), moved from De Ploeg to bolster the regiment's eastern perimeter. Two platoons of Company E took over positions between the left flank of the two platoons of Company D already holding the sector around Kamp and the right flank of the 1st Battalion.

In the predawn hours of September 19, Lieutenant Woodrow Millsaps, the Company B commander, received orders to send a platoon to seize Wyler, Germany and establish blocking positions on the two highways to Nijmgen. "I gave this mission to 2nd Lieutenant [Edward] Gleim, who was commanding the 3rd Platoon. Under cover of darkness, he moved to the outskirts of Wyler and was stopped there. Later in the morning of the 19th, which was still before daybreak, I took a small party and went to Lieutenant Gleim's position and found that it would be impossible for him to remain in this position when it got light, for there was very little cover for the men and they would be sitting ducks for the enemy. I reported this to the battalion commander and received orders for me to pull the platoon back to another small farm village [Im Thal] about three hundred yards from Wyler, which I did. Several times on the 19th, Lieutenant Gleim tried to take the town of Wyler, but each time he was stopped on the outskirts of the town. On the 19th, all along the regimental front, enemy activities increased, and long range artillery became intense. All units were suffering casualties.

"The regimental commander, Colonel Roy E. Lindquist, received orders from the division commander to move a unit to Wyler, Germany, seize and hold the town at all cost. Since Lieutenant Gleim had fought in the outskirts of Wyler on the night of the 18th and his platoon was in position only a few hundred yards from Wyler at that time, I was given this mission. I received orders from the battalion commanding officer to take one of the platoons that were on line in the battalion's main line of defense and go to Lieutenant Gleim's position, pick up his platoon and make a night attack on Wyler with two platoons.

"Knowing the enemy situation in Wyler, and what I could expect from him, I argued this point with the battalion CO, for I knew it would take a lot of men to dislodge and drive the enemy out of Wyler. Colonel Warren told me he would like for me to take all of my men, but to do so would leave a gap in the battalion defense line that he wouldn't be able to close.

"At dusk on the 19th, I moved out of the battalion's line with the 2nd Platoon, 1st Lieutenant [Roy K.] Skipton commanding, accompanied by the battalion executive officer, [Captain Ben] Delamater. I was very happy to have Delamater along, but I still wondered why the battalion CO sent him along. Undoubtedly he too, realizing the seriousness of this operation, had sent the battalion XO along for moral support.

"I moved to Lieutenant Gleim's position, and from there launched the attack on Wyler. We completely caught the enemy by surprise and were in the main part of town, firing like mad and throwing grenades before he knew what was coming off. This was an old trick I learned in the Normandy campaign. This stampeded the Krauts and they were unable to bring effective fire on my men at this critical time and I was able to take the town without suffering very many casualties.

"It was dark now and I gave orders to reorganize and dig in for the defense of the town. There was very little rest or sleep in Wyler that night, for many German soldiers were in the houses when we captured the town and they were now trying to slip out of Wyler any possible way. Enemy patrols, unaware that Wyler was now in American hands, were moving about the town. Houses were on fire, which gave us aid in recognizing the Krauts, for we were dug in and low to the ground, while they were up above ground and moving around.

When light came the next day, September 20, we discovered how effective our fire was, for there were dead soldiers all over the place."[26]

Early that morning, Company B established roadblocks at the southern and eastern edges of Wyler, which were strengthened by two 57mm antitank guns from Battery B, 80th Airborne Antiaircraft (Antitank) Battalion.

ON THE EVENING OF SEPTEMBER 19, as planning was underway for elements of the 82nd Airborne and Guards Armoured Divisions to assault and capture the Nijmegen bridges the following day, five German kampfgruppen were moving into position to carry out concentric attacks against the eastern and southern portions of the 82nd Airborne perimeter. The Germans had been building their forces over the previous two days as paratroopers from the 3rd and 5th Fallschirmjäger Divisions arrived from the Köln (Cologne), Germany area to form the main striking power of the attacks.

Kampfgruppe Becker, under the command of Oberstleutnant Karl-Heinz Becker, consisting of approximately seven hundred paratroopers organized into three battalion sized groups which were formed from Fallschirmjäger Regiments 5, 8, and 9, Abteilung Isphording, and service and supply troops, all from the 3rd Fallschirmjäger Division; and supported by five StuG self-propelled guns from Fallschirm Sturmgeschütz Brigade 12; would attack west through Wyler, then push on through Beek to relieve the defenders in Nijmegen.

Kampfgruppe von Fürstenberg, under the command of Hauptmann Freiherr von Fürstenberg, composed of five hundred men of Panzer Aufklärungs Ersatz und Ausbildungs Abteilung 6 (panzer reconnaissance reserve training battalion) from Wehrkreis VI (military district VI) with halftracks and armored cars, and supported by light towed antitank guns, would strike at Beek and then drive west to Nijmegen.

Kampfgruppe Jenkel, which consisted of a Kriegsmarine cadet company previously quartered at Nijmegen, supported by remnants of Fallschirm Artilleric Regiments 2 and 4 with seven howitzers—some six hundred men in total, would attack west along the highway through Berg-en-Dal, pushing on to the Maas-Waal Canal.

Kampfgruppe Greschick would attack west out of the Reichswald to capture Groesbeek and the high ground overlooking the Maas-Waal Canal in the 505th Parachute Infantry Regiment's sector. Kampfgruppe Greschick was made up of about nine hundred men from Luftwaffe Festung Bataillon XVII (a fortress battalion) and an "ear" battalion composed of old men with hearing problems from the 406th Landesschützen Division, reinforced by several batteries of 88mm, 37mm, and 20mm antiaircraft guns from the 4th Flak Division to provide ground fire support.

And finally, Kampfgruppe Hermann, a battalion sized unit of paratroopers under the command of Oberstleutnant Harry Hermann, would strike from the south through Riethorst and Mook, also in the 505th Parachute Infantry Regiment's sector with some seven hundred troops. Kampfgruppe Hermann consisted of remnants of Bataillon 1 of his Fallschirmjäger Lehr Regiment 21 of the 6th Fallschirmjäger Division, plus remnants of the 5th Fallschirmjäger Division; as well as a company of Flemish Waffen SS, under the command of Oberleutnant Omer Van Hyfte; plus Abteilung 1, Fallschirm Artillerie Regiment 6, under the command of Major Franke; and one 88mm and three 20mm antiaircraft guns from the 4th Flak Division to be used in a ground support role. Kampfgruppe Hermann's objective was to seize the Heumen lock bridge, the lone bridge carrying heavy traffic over the Maas-Waal Canal, thereby severing the main supply line for the British Second Army and the 82nd Airborne Division. The five kampfgruppen had a total of approximately 3,400 men, with some 130 machine guns and 24 mortars.

BEFORE DAWN ON SEPTEMBER 20, the two platoons of Company A and the attached 2nd Platoon of Company G and the section of Headquarters Company, 1st Battalion machine guns defending Devil's Hill were heavily shelled by artillery and mortars. Shortly after dawn, the artillery and mortar fire subsided and a short time later, a company of paratroopers from the 3rd Fallschirmjäger Division made a fanatical assault, emanating from the dikes and flat open ground to the north.

As the German attack got under way, Lieutenant Foley spent much of his time on the company radio with "the constant requesting of artillery support, relayed through 3rd Battalion, as we did not have radio communication with [1st] Battalion."[27]

Lieutenant Foley called for Concentration 31, which was a prearranged saturation barrage by the 319th Glider Field Artillery Battalion that caught the enemy paratroopers as they crossed the open ground north of the hill, inflicting numerous casualties. Nevertheless, German paratroopers reached the hill and began attacking up the slope.

Sergeant Robert White was a squad leader with the 3rd Platoon of Company A and was armed with a Model 1928 (M1928) Thompson submachine gun. "I had the end hole; the squad was back to my left. You couldn't see too well through the woods of that hill. One of the Germans had gotten by me. I just caught him out of the corner of my eye. When I turned around he was still going up the hill, so I just opened up on him."[28]

Enemy paratroopers came to within fifteen feet of some of the light machine guns positioned on the hill. In the thick of the fighting, the Germans ceased fire and an impeccably dressed German officer stepped forward and told Lieutenant Foley that their situation was hopeless, and that he should surrender his men and assemble them on the highway below the hill. Foley's replied, "If you want me, come and get me!"[29] Foley's men then opened fire and the fighting continued for over an hour before the Germans were finally thrown back.

Lieutenant Bill Call, leading the attached 2nd Platoon of Company G, was confident they could hold the hill. "Unless they came in the backdoor like we did, there was no way if we had ammunition that they could take that hill."[30]

After the German assault was repulsed, Sergeant White realized that ammunition was running low and needed to be replenished. "I volunteered to try to get back to battalion. As I moved out, I saw this group of guys and I thought they were some of our guys, over there all bunched up. I look at them and saw the cut of their helmets. They were in range of my Thompson and they were all in a group, so I just emptied a clip into them."[31]

Technician Fifth Grade John Brickley, the company's radio operator, heard the long burst from White's submachine gun. "[First Sergeant Frank] Taylor and I ran toward the shooting and found White, who announced, 'I just killed seven Germans.' Sure enough, in the nearest clearing was a German patrol. They were apparently taking a break when White surprised them. We realized that we were cut off. Headquarters confirmed this by radio."[32]

As dawn broke on September 20, the two Company B platoons occupying Wyler were about to be hit by the main force of Kampfgruppe Becker. The company commander, Lieutenant Woodrow Millsaps, checked the roadblocks at the edge of the town covering the approaches from the east and south. "I knew there would be sniper fire all over the place at first light, so I had given orders previously that all houses would be cleared as soon as possible come daybreak. We started the day off by sampling the beer in one of the town's pubs, and tearing down one of the Führer's flags that was displayed in the pub. I kept this flag as a souvenir. The search began to pay off, for we were flushing the Krauts out of concealment and either capturing or killing them. At approximately 08:00 hours, a German truck approached one of our roadblocks from the southwest. I by chance was standing by one of the antitank weapons [a 57mm antitank gun manned by Battery B, 80th Airborne Antiaircraft (Antitank) Battalion] that was assigned to my company for the defense of Wyler, and gave the order to fire when the truck stopped before running into the roadblock. The first round went through the canvas cover and exploded in a field several feet away. No one needed the command, 'unload truck,' for they piled out headfirst and ran back down the road; two or three escaped out of ten or twelve. By now the truck was on fire and everything was quiet again.

"The only thing to do now was to continue the search for snipers and to wait for the enemy's next move. We didn't have long to wait, for shortly after we knocked out the truck, the enemy was observed moving toward our position along the shoulder of the road where the truck was burning. We held our fire until the Krauts opened fire, after which we returned the fire and the war was on in earnest. The enemy stopped about two hundred yards from our position. Fifteen or twenty minutes later, the Krauts were observed moving in position about five hundred yards to the south. We did not understand this move at first, but we realized this was a machine gun company they were moving into position when they opened up on us with so many machine guns we were unable to count them. Now [there] appeared a company firing from the first position along the road. I was in radio communication with an artillery officer somewhere in the rear of the battalion defense position. Lieutenant [Roy] Skipton stated he could see a lot of movement in the first position and he believed the enemy was planning an attack from there. I was very much excited now, and could not remember the proper sequence in calling for and directing artillery. But I told the artillery officer to look on his map and he would see a small green spot on the map about two hundred yards from Wyler and to his right. He told me he found the spot I referred to and would fire a round of smoke. We all held our breath, or at least I did, while this round was on its way. When the round landed, it was right on target, and I told the artillery officer to fire for effect, but to move his fire right and left of the round a hundred yards or so.

"He understood what I was trying to say, and said, 'OK.' Next, I heard him say, 'Artillery on its way,' and could hear its deathly sound as it passed overhead and landed on target. I asked him to fire again, but was informed that he had only a few more rounds left and would hold fire until I really needed it. This quieted the enemy temporarily, but soon afterward [StuG self-propelled guns] were observed moving in position in the vicinity of the German machine gun company and they started shelling our position from there. The two antitank guns that were attached to my position were unable to move in position due to machine gun fire to [in order to] fire on the [StuG self-propelled guns]."[33]

Company B trooper, Private First Class Ed "Bogie" Boccafogli, armed with an M1 rifle with a rifle grenade launcher, could see the enemy in the distance advancing toward the town. "They started coming across the open ground, but there were a lot of culverts. You could see them come through the ditches and then they'd jump the culverts where the little farm roads were. We were picking them off left and right. And me, I've got the M1, and I couldn't fire. It jammed on me. When I fired that rifle grenade, the thing [the blank cartridge used to launch the grenade] ruptured inside. I couldn't open it up. I had cut my hand all open trying to get it unjammed."[34]

With the flat terrain and a good field of fire to the front, Sergeant Jim Kurz could see plenty of targets as the German paratroopers closed in on the town. "It was like a shooting gallery. We started shooting when they were about six hundred yards away and kept shooting until they hit the ground. When they were about one hundred yards from us, men from the 2nd Platoon started to fall back. Some of my men started to get up. I told them to keep shooting and I would find out what the lieutenant wanted to do."[35]

Private First Class Nathan Silverlieb and the 3rd Platoon's 60mm mortar squad went to work on one German platoon advancing up the road toward the 2nd Platoon positions. "Sergeant [Paul B.] Atwood, [Corporal John E.] Payet and I went through all six rounds. That was all we had, one bag of ammo. Atwood was an excellent gunner. Payet would drop one in and as it came out I would drop one in and as it came out Atwood would drop one in. They landed all around on top of that platoon of Germans—we wiped out that platoon."[36]

That morning, the attack by Kampfgruppe Jenkel succeeded in penetrating about four hundred yards along the Wyler to Berg-en-Dal highway, between the 1st Platoon of Company B defending the main line of resistance and Company A to its left on Devil's Hill. Lieutenant Colonel Warren didn't have a reserve force to counterattack. "C Company on the right was not under attack, so not having any other reserve I used elements of the headquarters to screen C Company's position, pulled the company out of the line, and counterattacked with it. The counterattack was successful, capturing about thirty-five prisoners, killing a similar number, and erasing the penetration. C Company was then placed back in the line."[37]

The 2nd Platoon of Company D, 307th Airborne Engineer Battalion, now under the command of Lieutenant James C. Pegram, was released from division reserve and ordered to occupy Hills 62 and 62.9 overlooking the north side of the Wyler to Berg-en-Dal highway to fill the gap between the 1st Platoon of Company B and Company A on Devil's Hill. The 2nd Platoon's 3rd squad dug in on Hill 62 and the 1st and 2nd squads dug in on Hill 62.9.

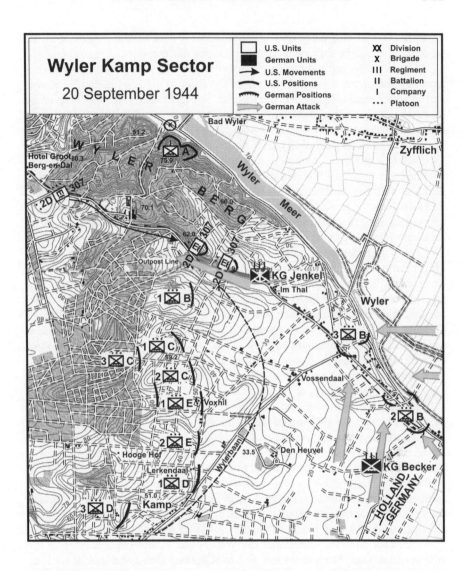

Wyler Kamp Sector
20 September 1944

U.S. Units
German Units
U.S. Movements
U.S. Positions
German Positions
German Attack

XX Division
X Brigade
III Regiment
II Battalion
I Company
... Platoon

In Wyler, Lieutenant Woodrow Millsaps and his two platoons of Company B were facing annihilation, with ammunition running critically low, as the enemy continued to move toward their positions in the town. "I noticed a company of enemy moving in attack formation toward my position from the east. The two jeep loads of ammunition that had followed me to Wyler the night before were now gone, and we had reported an ammunition shortage several hours before. I radioed battalion for ammo. Lieutenant [Peter] Kelley, battalion S-4, told me he had tried to deliver ammo by jeep, but enemy fire had turned the jeep back. He organized a carrying party and had sent them forward some hours ago, and [said] they should be there with ammunition any minute.

"I reported by radio the enemy's activities and deployment as I could see it from my position and wanted to know if the order to hold Wyler at all cost was still in effect, and he informed me that we had to hold Wyler. We were being shelled by [StuG self-propelled guns] and long range artillery was now zeroing in on our position. Somehow, or for some reason, the company moving from the east was stopped approximately three hundred yards from my position.

"Defending Wyler was now out of the question; it was a fight for survival. Ammunition was very low and men were dividing it among themselves. I was pleading with the battalion CO [Lieutenant Colonel Warren] to give me orders to move back to Lieutenant [Edward] Gleim's original position. I remember telling him if he wanted to save any part of the company he had better pull us back, and if he gave the order now, I was afraid it was too late.

"Thirty minutes or so later, [Captain Ben] Delamater, battalion executive officer, who had gone back to the battalion after I had taken Wyler on the 19th, came in on the radio and wanted to speak to me. He told me battalion had received orders from division for me to pull back to Lieutenant Gleim's original position and report to him when this was accomplished. This was about 3:00 or 4:00 p.m. The wounded were moved out first, and it appeared all my men were wounded. Some of the wounded were killed on the way back, for when we got up to move, the enemy's fire was so intense that we had to drop to the ground to keep from being hit. It took several hours to move the men back, but finally we were back on the outskirts of Wyler."[38]

Sergeant Jim Kurz was near the tail of the Company B column during the withdrawal. "We had gone about one half mile when everybody stopped. I went up front to see what the trouble was. A private was standing and just looking between two buildings. I asked what the trouble was. He said there was a German with a burp gun firing. I told him if he wasn't going to move to get out of the way. I said, 'There are a thousand Germans following us and you are going to let one German stop us?' I ran between the buildings and into the opening. The German cut loose, but missed. There was a three foot fence ahead and I just cleared it on the run. All the rest followed me and nobody got hit."[39]

Lieutenant Millsaps completed the withdrawal of his two platoons to the village of Im Thal. "I reported this fact to [Captain] Delamater and he told me that British tanks had arrived to assist the battalion and would fire on Wyler and when the fire lifted for me to move back into the town. I told him the company was shot to pieces and it would do no good to move back to Wyler. He told me the tanks would move forward to my position and on into Wyler, and to be ready to move when the tanks arrived on my left flank. The tanks opened fire, but rather than fire on Wyler, they fired into my position, and it was very effective and just about finished my company off."[40]

As the British tanks were shelling Company B, Sergeant Jim Kurz heard one of his troopers in distress. "A private, who was a Canadian, got hit and called for me. He was hit in the mouth by a piece of shell from the tanks. He said he wanted to be an American citizen before he died. I picked him up and carried him to the aid station. I told him he wouldn't die. (He made it.)

"I went back to see Staff Sergeant [Shufford C.] Rowe. He was in a house. I closed the door behind me. He said they were British tanks firing at us and we were getting word to them. I opened the door to leave and a shell from a tank sailed over my shoulder through the door. It made the loudest noise I had ever heard when it exploded in the room. That was the last thing I remembered until late that night. Staff Sergeant Rowe had over one hundred pieces of shrapnel in him and the other two men in the room were evacuated with concussions. I went to the hospital in Nijmegen with a broken shoulder blade and a piece of shrapnel about one quarter of an inch above my heart."[41]

Lieutenant Millsaps knew he had to act quickly to stop this devastating fire. "I tried to stop this fire by radio to the battalion, but the tanks kept on firing. I knew if this fire was not stopped at once, we would all be killed. I picked up a bed sheet from one of the houses and ran out to the side of our position and started waving like mad. Surprising enough, the tanks stopped firing, but not before they had killed and wounded several of my men.

"I again received a message from [Captain] Delamater stating for me to prepare to move back, but not to do so until he joined my company. He was on the way to my company to guide us back to the battalion defense line. We would have to go another route from the one we took going into Wyler, for the enemy now was deployed on Voxhil. Sometime later, [Captain] Delamater arrived at my command post and we started our withdrawal without wasting any time. There were not enough able-bodied men left to take care of the wounded. We had no stretchers, so we used doors, planks, and any other thing we could find to carry the men on. We had to carry them a short distance and return for others."[42]

During the withdrawal, Private First Class Ed Boccafogli he saw Private Herbert W. Ellerbusch get hit. Private Ellerbusch had saved his squad during the previous withdrawal to Im Thal when he had fired his bazooka into a barn that was occupied by a number of Germans, setting it on fire. Private First Class Boccafogli checked on Ellerbusch before he withdrew. "He was stone cold, and we had to leave his body there. But if he didn't hit that barn, the Germans would have crossed that road and gotten behind us. As it started to get dark, we got the German prisoners to carry the wounded. The walking wounded walked, and other guys we'd put on doors, ladders, and anything we could get.

"This one kid, a good sergeant up until that point, left his whole squad. And they found him underneath the crawl space [of a building], because there are no cellars over there. He was down there shaking like a dog with the tail between his legs. He was broken down, and we transferred him out to supplies later on. At the time I had nothing but contempt for him. But then later on, I thought [about] how many men used every method not to be there. At least this guy went his full measure. He went through Normandy all the way to there, and then all of a sudden something just went 'Poom!' That's it. Battle fatigue, whatever you call it. Later on, I had compassion for him. But he left his squad, and most of them were either killed or taken prisoner. But anyway, that guy left his squad, and as darkness set in, we started setting all the haystacks on fire with phosphorous shells. We went back with these ladders, and the Germans carried them, too. The prisoners carried the ladders with our wounded. We went in a long file, up the hill, until we finally got to the high ground."[43]

Private Nathan Silverlieb had been wounded twice earlier that day, but had stayed with the company. "It was now night time and the Germans had set fire to the many haystacks we had to pass to evacuate. Each time we passed a burning stack we would hear a mortar round leave the tube and would have to hit the deck."[44]

Lieutenant Millsaps remained at the rear of his badly decimated company's column to insure none of his wounded troopers were left behind. "This withdrawal took all night, but finally we arrived back at Company B's sector of defense on the battalion line just before daybreak."[45]

Lieutenant Millsaps was later awarded the Silver Star for his leadership and courage during the attack in Nijmegen, the attack to clear the landing zone the following day, and for the defense of Wyler on September 20.

AT NIJMEGEN ON THE MORNING OF SEPTEMBER 20, a combined task force of troops from the Grenadier Guards Regiment of the British Guards Armoured Division troops and Lieutenant Bud Warnecke's 3rd Platoon of Company E, which the previous afternoon had liberated the post office, cleared the area of Germans where Captain Jonathan Adams and the 2nd Platoon of Company A were hiding in a warehouse. Adams and his troopers immediately left to rejoin the company. Captain Adams was later awarded the Silver Star for his courage and leadership during the combat patrol in Nijmegen.

Captain Adams and the 2nd Platoon of Company A arrived at the 1st Battalion command post on the afternoon of September 20, where he was directed to take the platoon and join his company on Devil's Hill. "By dusk we had just reached the position of the engineer platoon. The platoon leader [Lieutenant James Pegram] told me they were being attacked at that particular moment. From what we could see and hear, nobody was firing a shot. (As infantrymen, this engineer platoon was not too good *early* in the campaign.)"[46]

South of Devil's Hill, Corporal Jim Blue, an assistant squad leader with the 1st Platoon of Company A, decided around dusk to clean his Thompson submachine gun. "Standing in my foxhole, I began to disassemble it. The driving rod that is compressed by a spring slipped by my thumb and flew away.

This was the first time in combat that I panicked. I went crazy feeling in the foxhole and around the outside. I knew my life and others depended on that weapon. I got myself together and formed a search plan. My plan was to start around the foxhole patting the ground one hand span, second time around another hand span and so on. About the time I was arm's length out I felt the driving rod. I reassembled the weapon in the darkness and was a pleased soldier under those circumstances."[47]

Later that night, Captain Adams and the 2nd Platoon of Company A, "started out to contact Foley. We just missed him in the dark."[48]

Private Norbert C. "Norb" Studelska was dug in with the rest of the 3rd Platoon of Company D just west of the Wylerbaan near Kamp. "I was a member of [Sergeant Robert C.] Bob Lenell's 60mm mortar squad. My foxhole was a model of comfort and protection. Because we had abundant time to make front line life as civilized as possible, I took great pride in making my house the best on the block. It was chest deep, long enough to lie flat when I slept, and narrow at the top. I recall angling it into the roots of the hedge. To keep things neat and clean, as my good mother taught me, I completely lined it with the canopy of a main chute. I had a built-in shelf for my personal gear and a picture of my childhood sweetheart, Elaine Olson, whom I married after the war.

"Early on September 20th, the platoon suffered its first KIA casualties when a Kraut 88mm zeroed in on our bazooka team. Our platoon's two bazooka men [Private Bennie S. Upton and Private Charles B. Tuttle] foolishly fired their bazooka at an enemy sniper. The flash from the bazooka drew 88mm fire and the two were literally pulverized."[49]

NORTHWEST OF WYLER, Kampfgruppe von Fürstenberg's five hundred troops struck the eighty-three troopers holding Beek and two roadblocks on Highway K with a heavy artillery and mortar barrage, followed by a massive infantry assault, supported by armor.

Corporal Bob Chisolm, with the 2nd Platoon of Company I, was one of the troopers defending Beek that morning. "We had 57mm antitank guns [one each from Battery A and Battery B, 80th Airborne Antiaircraft (Antitank) Battalion] set up on each road coming in [to Beek]. We had engineers and machine gun positions covering the flats. We had two .30-caliber machine guns with a line of defense just out of town in that flat area. They laid the artillery on us and I mean they put a [fifteen minute] barrage on us. They were attacking right across the open [ground] with their armor and infantry. The artillery was coming right in— they had everything pretty well zeroed in. The [enemy] troops were coming in with the armor, it wasn't just halftracks; they had some [armored cars], too. The 57s were in position at each end of the town and were set up to fire down the roads. I don't think we had a bazooka in the group.

"[Sergeant] Buck Hutto, our 60mm mortar squad leader, flat laid some rounds on them until he ran out of ammunition. The machine guns fired all of their ammunition. We were really short of ammunition."[50]

Sergeant James N. Sidley's Headquarters Company, 3rd Battalion machine gun section was attached to Company I. When two of the gunners manning one of his machine guns were wounded, Sergeant Sidley ran across open ground under extremely heavy enemy machine gun and mortar fire and took over the gun, stopping one of the German assaults and allowing his wounded troopers to be evacuated. When another enemy assault began from an area not covered by his machine guns, Sidley and his section displaced and moved to meet the attack, but were pinned down. Sidley set up and manned one of the machine guns alone, directing devastating fire on the Germans and drawing fire away from the point of attack. This allowed his section to withdraw, but in the course of covering their withdrawal, Sergeant Sidley was wounded and died on September 23. He was posthumously awarded the Silver Star for his valor.

Meanwhile, the situation turned critical when one lieutenant was killed after another had left before the battle began. Corporal Chisolm, an assistant squad leader with Company I, took charge of the defenders. "We had a 2nd Lieutenant [John D.] Simmons—the last we saw of him he was leaving without a weapon, heading back up the hill toward Berg-en-Dal. The lieutenant [John S. Tinker, Jr.] and [Technician Fourth Grade Emmanuel M.] Foster, our radio operator, were killed in a foxhole. A tree burst killed them.

"We saw they were coming in with a superior force and we were short of ammunition. They were still about five hundred yards away when I made the decision to pull back to the high ground. I first personally went out to where my first line of defense was [dug in] and contacted my people and saw what the situation was and I said, 'We're going to have to pull back.' We pulled them all back at one time. I said, 'You guys come on back first, pass through, and get up on the high ground. Once you're up there, then we'll pull the rest of the people back [who were] down in the town.' We got them back and we got them back without any casualties. The gunners disabled the 57s [by taking the breach blocks] because we weren't able to get them out of there. The engineers were a little farther back than we were. They were actually occupying the high ground. When the first line of defense pulled back, they came right back [with them]. Then we pulled the rest of the group back. My little command was the last group [to withdraw]. That's when I contacted Colonel Mendez.

"Colonel Mendez said, Come on back in, bring everybody back in [to Berg-en-Dal]."[51]

Through his extraordinary courage and cool leadership under an extremely critical situation, Corporal Chisolm conducted an orderly retreat to the forested high ground at Berg-en-Dal. He was later awarded the Legion of Merit, the only such award the regiment made to an enlisted man or noncommissioned officer during the war.

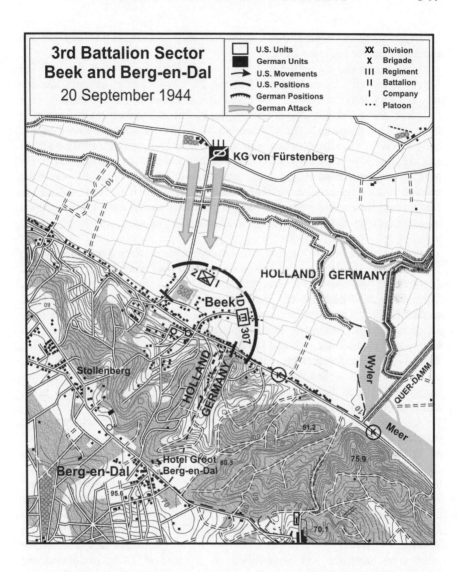

The 3rd Platoon of Company G was ordered to counterattack and retake Beek. Sergeant Stanley Stevens, the squad leader of the 1st Squad; Sergeant Maryld D. Price, the squad leader of the 2nd Squad; and Private First Class Henry H. Wade, also with the 2nd Squad; moved out as the point, and as they came around a curve in the road, a German machine gun fired from very close range, cutting down all three and killing them. The 3rd Platoon was stopped by intense enemy fire and forced to withdraw up the hill. The loss of a courageous combat leader in Sergeant Stevens was a blow not only to Company G and the 3rd Battalion, but the regiment as well.

That afternoon, General Gavin set out for Beek, but found that the 3rd Battalion had withdrawn up the hill above the town. "There, Colonel Mendez was in a very shaky condition. There was only one road up into his position on a ridgeline, and a German 20mm flak wagon had been knocked out at a curve in the road, thus blocking it for German armor. I crawled across the road on my belly and joined the infantrymen who were anxiously digging in. I assured them that the situation was under control and that they had nothing to worry about. By then, it was beginning to get dark, and as so often happened, the Germans stopped their attack when darkness set in. If they had been willing to reconnoiter, they could have overrun our positions easily, but in a methodical way they stayed right to the main roads and thus we were able to cope with them."[52]

Sergeant Don Jakeway and his Company H platoon were dug in around the Hotel de Groot, in Berg-en-Dal. "While assembled near our slit trenches near the Groot Hotel, we once again heard the distant boom from the German artillery. We made a mad dash for our trenches and the artillery came crashing down around us. When the shelling stopped, we had five men killed, including an officer, and many wounded, including myself. [Private] John [V.] Giacomelli had jumped into a slit trench and I had landed on top of him. He had been killed instantly, while underneath me. I have no explanation of how he had been killed and I was only wounded. [Privates First Class] John Delury and John Downes carried me back to the aid station. I had received shrapnel in my leg, my back, and in my face and arms. I was indeed lucky to be alive."[53]

At 7:00 p.m., Company H received orders to conduct a counterattack to extricate the Germans from Beek. The company assembled thirty minutes later at the Hotel de Groot. The plan of attack was for the 1st and 2nd Platoons to conduct the assault, with the 3rd Platoon in reserve. The company was briefed that about forty Germans were holding the town. But, Headquarters Company, 3rd Battalion troopers arrived who had been at Beek, indicated that there were approximately four hundred Germans holding the town. Two crewmen of a 57mm antitank gun crew, Privates First Class Gordon A. Walberg and Ernest Sedden, with Battery A, 80th Airborne Antiaircraft (Antitank) Battalion, whose other crew members had been killed or captured in Beek, confirmed the estimate. Those two troopers volunteered and went back to Beek with Company H, fighting as infantrymen.

The 1st Platoon, led by Lieutenant Frederick G. Humphrey and assistant platoon leader Lieutenant Vernon Thomas; was followed by Lieutenant Louis Toth, the company commander, and company headquarters; then 2nd Platoon, led by Lieutenant Bruce B. Van; and then the 3rd Platoon, under the command of Lieutenant John F. Leatherwood. Two 1st Platoon troopers armed with BARs and two bazooka teams acted as scouts in front of the 1st Platoon.

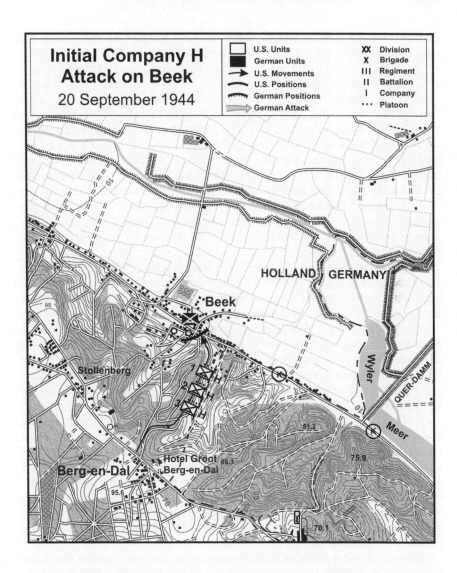

Initial Company H
Attack on Beek
20 September 1944

U.S. Units
German Units
U.S. Movements
U.S. Positions
German Positions
German Attack

XX   Division
X   Brigade
III Regiment
II   Battalion
I   Company
··· Platoon

No flank security was used because the terrain was wooded and it was now dark. The company encountered no opposition and arrived at the southeast outskirts of Beek about 8:30 p.m.

The point element of the 1st Platoon, consisting of Private Frederick H. Griffin, Jr., armed with a BAR; Private Martin P. Eltringham, with an M1; and a bazooka team of Privates Robert L. Smith and Raymond H. Wilson, on the left side of the road. BAR gunner Private Bascom M. Brown and a second bazooka team of Privates Edwin E. Hamilton and John Cook were on the right side of the road. Lieutenant Humphrey was up front with the point.

As the point came to the crossroad with Highway K, just south of the center of town, a burning British Sherman tank lit up the area. There, three MG-34 machine guns, together with another automatic weapon located in a house in the churchyard, opened fire from different directions. Lieutenant Humphrey was killed in the opening volley and the rest of the point element was pinned down.

Privates Cook and Hamilton crawled forward to fire at one of the machine guns which was located near the burning tank. However, the bazooka was unable to fire because a bullet had penetrated the front section of the tube and another bullet had cut the wires which triggered the firing mechanism.

Private First Class Joseph Nedza then made his way toward the machine gun as tracers from that machine gun and others passed just inches from him. Nedza destroyed the machine gun and killed the crew. This opened the way for the 1st Platoon to continue forward.

At 8:45 p.m., Lieutenant Vernon Thomas, the assistant platoon leader of the 1st Platoon, sent Sergeant Arthur R. Riedel to ask the Germans to surrender. The Germans refused. Thomas then led the forty or so troopers of the 1st Platoon into the churchyard, where they began digging in.

As the 1st Platoon was fighting its way into the town, another MG-34 covering the bend in the road where troopers were descending the hill, opened fire pinning down elements of the company behind the 1st Platoon. Private First Class Donald Veach, a new Company H replacement, hit the ground as machine gun bullets ripped into the ground all around him. "A burst of machine gun fire hit the ammunition box three times that I was carrying."[54]

Private First Class Harry A. Roll was also a new replacement with the 2nd Platoon. "Just as we came into view of the village, we came upon very heavy machine gun fire coming from a cupola on the corner of a large house. I ducked into a ditch and was grazed on the flesh of my shoulder. [Lieutenant Louis] Toth called for Moon and [Private First Class William P.] Tucker to get the bazooka up front as he stood in the roadway just above me."[55]

Staff Sergeant Lyle K. Kumler, the platoon sergeant of the 2nd Platoon, moved forward in the open in order to draw fire from the machine gun, allowing the platoon's bazooka team to get close enough for a shot.

Roll watched the two man bazooka team move into position and fire. "The bazooka team knocked out the machine gun nest that was hidden behind shutters in the cupola. We then proceeded into Beek, passing a cemetery where some of our company [the 1st Platoon] were digging in. That was [Staff Sergeant] Ralph Busson's platoon."[56]

Lieutenant Bruce Van and the 2nd Platoon advanced to the intersection with Highway K, where it set up machine guns on the southwest and southeast corners. A German in a nearby house with a Very pistol fired parachute flares into the sky, illuminating the area, causing the platoon to fire wildly at the suspected locations. Lieutenant Van, the platoon leader, ordered his platoon to cease fire. Then, an enemy machine gun opened fire, wounding the crew of Van's machine gun on the southeast corner of the intersection. The location of the enemy machine gun was identified and the bazooka team fired four rounds into the house and a Gammon grenade was thrown into it as well, knocking out the machine gun. The 2nd Platoon then continued north across the highway for about two hundred yards.

The darkness, punctuated by flares that lit up the area and bursts of machine gun fire using tracers, created an eerie scene as Private First Class Roll and the rest of the 2nd Platoon moved through the town. "We came upon a concertina of coiled wire, and no one had a wire cutter. It was here, as we struggled to get through, the Germans on the second floor of several houses, started throwing potato-masher grenades at us. My friend, [Private First Class] Marvin [V.] Storey was hit, so we backed out of the wire and crawled between two houses. It was at that same time up beyond the barbed wire, much machine gun fire was going off and that's where my friend Tommy Horne was hit."[57]

Private First Class Horne had broken the third lumbar in his back on the jump and was already in quite a bit of pain, when he was wounded. "I was trying to get in close enough to get a grenade in [to a house] when something hit me in the throat, I thought. This numbed my left arm, but feeling my throat with my right hand, I could find no blood. I started firing again and this guy in the back of me said, 'My God, you have a hole through your back!' The bullet had hit me in the left shoulder, close to my neck, and cut a ligament. This is what had given me the sensation I was hit in the throat."[58]

Meanwhile at about 10:15 p.m., Private Henry McLean, one of the Company H runners, delivered a message to the 1st Platoon's assistant platoon leader, Lieutenant Vernon Thomas, to move his platoon from the churchyard north through the town to the flats. A second runner delivered the message to Lieutenant Van for the 2nd Platoon to move out to the flats outside of the town.

The 1st Platoon left in column formation, using alleyways to reach the highway. There, Lieutenant Thomas heard Germans talking and the sound of armored vehicles about one hundred yards to the northwest and decided that the Germans were preparing a counterattack. He deployed the 1st Platoon in a circular defense about seventy-five yards in diameter. Lieutenant Thomas, without a radio, sent his runner, Private Bernard L. Kline, to report the situation to Lieutenant Louis Toth, the commander of Company H. Upon receiving the report, Lieutenant Toth sent Kline back with a message for the 1st Platoon to withdraw back to the company command post area on the high ground south of the town. Toth also sent a runner with the same message to Lieutenant Van and the 2nd Platoon.

During this time, Private First Class Harry Roll, one of the 2nd Platoon troopers, had worked his way between two houses to escape German grenades being thrown from the upper floors and an enemy machine gun raking the street.

"While between the houses, [Staff Sergeant] Lyle Kumler, our platoon [sergeant], came upon us and said to follow him back up the hill to regroup."[59]

As the 1st and 2nd Platoons of Company H withdrew, Privates Sherman E. Axline and Robert Z. Sherwood, a machine gun team with the 3rd Platoon, set up their machine gun and delivered effective fire into German troops attempting to overrun the withdrawing troopers, stopping a counterattack. Even though the Germans concentrated heavy automatic weapons fire on his position, Axline and Sherwood remained at the machine gun. When three Germans attempted to assault his position with grenades, Sherwood mowed them down. Other attempts to knock out his gun failed and the Germans withdrew, then brought down mortar fire on Axline and Sherwood's position.

From intelliegence gathered during the attack, Lieutenant Louis Toth learned that Beek was held by "the German Blue Dragon, 6th Parachute Division, with about 200-300 men."[60]

Throughout September 20, the 319th Glider Field Artillery Battalion fired 1,495 rounds in support of the 508th defense of Wyler, Devil's Hill, and later the counterattack on Beek. It broke up German infantry attacks at critical times throughout the day. It would be called on the next day to provide more critically needed support of the 3rd Battalion.

On the evening of September 20-21, Technician Fifth Grade Joseph Kissane, a spare communications NCO with Company G, was assigned to take a patrol to contact the company's 3rd Platoon, which was dug in on the high ground west of Beek. Kissane rounded up three volunteers and moved out. "As we approached the main road, [Private First Class Bernard] Levin and another replacement [Private First Class Walter S.] Bayne, wanted to accompany us. Six men were far too many for a reconnaissance patrol. I told Levin, 'You go behind the houses on the left side of the road and we will meet at the end of the street.'

"As we proceeded through backyards on the right side, the Germans could be heard digging holes in front of the houses. Reaching the far end, we waited for Levin. When no contact was made we returned to the CP to find him hysterical. He had accosted two men, queried them, and was fired upon. Bayne fell.

"The four of us left and resumed the patrol past the backyards. Farther on, as we ascended a small hill, a machine gun opened up on us. The tracers seemed to part my hair. [Private First Class James A.] Belcher, the lead man, miraculously was not hit. I rolled down the hill dropping my rifle. Unarmed, I realized that to return through this enemy infested area I'd need a weapon. Scrambling out into the open under a shining moon, I grabbed my rifle and scurried back to a path. With all the commotion, the Germans aware of the layout and disposition of their troops realized we must be Americans. They proceeded to barrage the area with mortar fire. With no helmet, I dug my head into the roadbed.

"When things quieted, I slithered back to the company. The next morning I went down the road and found Bayne's body in a hole. I took one of his dog tags and put the other in his mouth. There was a small hole in the back of his neck but his face was blown off."[61]

Also during the night of September 20-21, several Able Company NCOs left 75.9, known as Devil's Hill, to get ammunition from the 1st Battalion supply dump. After successfully making their way there, each of them took four bandoliers of M1 and BAR clips, a bag of Thompson submachine gun clips containing a total of two hundred rounds of .45-caliber bullets, and a can of .30-caliber machine gun ammunition. They moved out but were unable to reach the hill before dawn.

Shortly after dawn on September 21, Captain Jonathan Adams and the 2nd Platoon of Company A made contact with Lieutenant John Foley's troopers on Devil's Hill. "When dawn broke we were not more than one hundred yards away (very thick brush)."[62]

To the south of Devil's Hill, a squad of the 1st Platoon of Company A occupied a defensive position covering the approach to the hill from the rear. One of those troopers, Corporal Jim Blue, saw a couple of shadowy figures advancing toward their position in the predawn darkness of September 21. "Two German soldiers came forward with arms raised as if to surrender. At a distance of about fifty yards, we could see that one of them had something on his back. Shortly, he fell forward, and the second soldier attempted to fire the machine gun that was attached to his comrade's back. We had our sights set on them; they were riddled with gunfire.

"Later in the morning, we received an order to join the Foley force. As we moved from this position, a barrage of mortar fire came in; we were in luck to have moved just in time. We left the position on the double and were fired on by a machine gun. A bullet struck the heel of Private First Class [Donald M.] Don Johnston's boot, partially removing it.

"We were greeted by Lieutenant Foley as we arrived on the hill, and were given a sector of the hill to defend. From the foxhole I was occupying, I could see the bodies of several of my comrades. Under the situation, our troops had not had time to collect and bury them. These had been victims of the initial attack...On the north and east side, several German bodies lay sprawled."[63]

After arriving on the hill, Captain Adams reassumed command of Company A. "We had no sooner gotten things reorganized on Devil's Hill when the Germans attacked. It was a foolish move, as they came straight up the sides of the hill. Still, it was surprising just how far up they did get. This was their last attack and the remainder of our time on Devil's Hill was spent on patrols and maintaining contact with other units and killing cows and chickens."[64]

The attack that morning by German paratroopers, marines, and flak troops was the fourth such company sized assault since the hill had been seized by

Lieutenant Foley's troopers. It was repulsed after bitter fighting, with heavy German casualties.

When the NCOs arrived on Devil's Hill with the supply of ammunition, they found that all of the ammunition for the automatic weapons had been expended and the riflemen were down to an average of less than one clip apiece after repelling the attack that morning.

That night, the Germans attempted an infiltration attack against the defenders on Devil's Hill, but it was stopped before it materialized. Private First Class Theodore H. Gienger, with the 2nd Platoon of Company G, hearing noise in front of his position, crawled down the hill to within a few yards of a German force of unknown size. Gienger spoke German fluently and shouted several orders in German, confusing the enemy and causing them to reveal their exact location. Gienger opened fire with his Thompson submachine gun, killing six and disorganizing the attack. The enemy force withdrew and Gienger returned to his foxhole. Private First Class Gienger was later awarded the Silver Star for his daring action in single-handedly breaking up the enemy attack before it began.

At 4:00 a.m. on September 21, Lieutenant Toth issued orders for the 1st and 3rd Platoons of Company H to attack at 6:00 a.m. But before the attack could be launched, the Germans launched a predawn counterattack from Beek to drive the 3rd Battalion from the high ground that dominated the highway from Wyler to Nijmegen. This counterattack was broken up largely by effective fire from the 319th Glider Field Artillery Battalion. Technician Fourth Grade Ed Ryan was a member of Battery C of the 319th. "Our guns were firing at a quick rate, faster than anytime. Our forward observers and our [Piper Cub spotter] airplane was up, all directing fire into the draw."[65]

The planned attack at 6:00 a.m. was rescheduled for 6:30 a.m. At 6:20 a.m., the 319th and the Company H 60mm mortar squads fired a barrage at Beek. The battalion's 81mm mortars were unable to support the attack because the Germans had strafed the regimental supply dump the previous day and had blown up the 81mm mortar ammunition.

The attack jumped off with Company G, less the 2nd Platoon, on the left flank, the 1st Platoon of Company H on the west side of the road from Berg-en-Dal to Beek, the 3rd Platoon east of the road, and the 3rd Platoon of Company F on the right flank.

As the attack commenced, Private First Class Lewis Milkovics supported it with his Company H squad's 60mm mortar, which was dug in near the Hotel de Groot. "H Company had just moved when some of our guys yelled that an enemy patrol was in the draw. I'm not sure, but I believe it was my buddy [Private First Class James J.] Murphy, who had his .30-caliber LMG [light machine gun] facing down the draw. He started firing and called back for mortar supporting fire to land in the draw.

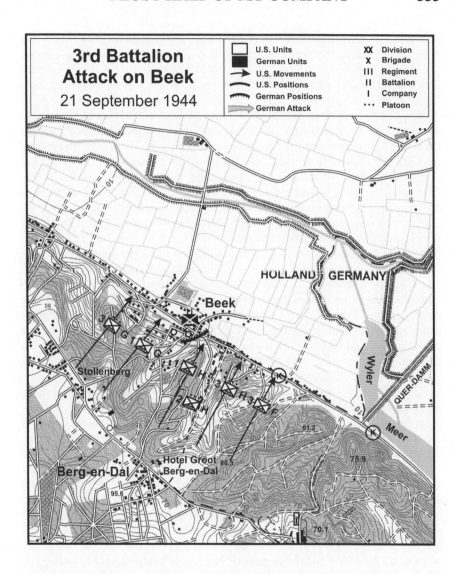

**3rd Battalion
Attack on Beek**

21 September 1944

☐ U.S. Units	**XX**	Division
■ German Units	**X**	Brigade
➡ U.S. Movements	**III**	Regiment
➤ U.S. Positions	**II**	Battalion
German Positions	**I**	Company
German Attack	**···**	Platoon

"The problem was I couldn't see where my rounds were landing. I believe it was my other friend [Sergeant Frank] Bagdonas, who went part of the way downhill so he could shout instructions to me. He started yelling and I started firing! After several rounds, the tube got really hot, so hot that the powder increments would explode before the 60mm round reached the tube bottom. The round got where it would go part way down the tube where the increments ignited causing the round to go out at reduced velocity. It would go only a short distance before landing. A noncom came running up chewing me out; I was accused of shooting up the battalion's quota of 60mm mortar rounds! The only thing I remember is that someone kept yelling and I kept firing. I guess Murphy had already run the German patrol out of the draw with his machine gun, but I didn't know this. I learned one thing that day; you can't fire a mortar too fast, for it can get 'hot' and dangerous."[66]

The 75mm pack howitzers of the 319th pounded Beek throughout the day in support of the 3rd Battalion attacks. Captain Charles Sartain, the commander of Battery A, which was the battery assigned to support the 3rd Battalion, had worked with Lieutenant Colonel Mendez since Normandy and had a great deal of respect for him, which only increased as he witnessed how Mendez led the 3rd Battalion during the attacks on Beek. "He was not a rear echelon battalion commander. I thought he was a first class battalion commander and a first class soldier. I became very close to Colonel Mendez and his staff. The same should be said about our forward observers and the officers of the 508th's 3rd Battalion. A strong bond existed between them and A Battery's forward observers."[67]

Sergeant Ted Covais was a member of the Battery A forward observer team. "As a forward observer you have to be with the battalion commander all the time. Every time he wanted direct fire, Mendez would say, 'I want fire on that point and that point.' You've got to call it in, get on the phone, radio, or whatever we had. We called it in. But Colonel Mendez, hey, hey, what a fighter! He was a great guy. Man, I'll tell you, this guy, there could be artillery bursting here, machine guns—he didn't care, he'd stand there like he was untouchable! Untouchable! He was a great, great man."[68]

Corporal Louis Sosa, also with the Able Battery forward observer team, observed Mendez during the fighting for Beek. "Mendez, he wasn't scared of a fight, he wasn't afraid of nothing! When we were in Holland, bullets flying all around us and he was walking straight up and down! He didn't even hit the dirt. He was a hell of a man I'll tell you, he was one tough little guy."[69]

Even though Captain Sartain was the commanding officer of Battery A, he was typically up front with Mendez at his forward command post. "Most of the time, he had a back CP and a forward CP. His forward CP was right behind the companies. The back CP would be, you know, a quarter of a mile back. You always had an advance CP and a rear CP. That was routine; that was routine infantry tactics. Generally, his forward CP was out in the line, or out in the woods, and he'd have his radio operator and one or two people at his advanced CP, that's all. Very seldom was there a command post in any kind of structure. Now in Holland, a couple of times he had his command post in the cellar of a residence. But the advanced CP was wherever the colonel decided to squat. It could be on the back of a little hill, or if they had time they'd dig a pretty good sized hole and put timbering over it and all of that business. It all depended. But the advanced CP would be very, very close to the company that he'd keep in reserve—that way he would be closer to the companies that were in the line, because Mendez and the others liked to stay pretty close to where the action was.

"The rear CP was where Major [Alton] Bell would be. He was the XO, 3rd Battalion, under Mendez. His code name was Dingdong and he had this great big handlebar mustache. I'll never forget it. He and Bell made a good pair, good combination. The rear CP would have communication with regiment and division. Generally, nine times out of ten they would have a telephone. There'd be eight or nine people at the absolute most, in the rear CP. Major Bell, his communication people, linemen—people that would run and find a break in the wire—a runner or two, and a liaison officer from our battalion if they had one. A lot of times, I acted as the liaison officer because we only had two in the battalion. In three battalions, we had only two liaison officers. So, I generally stayed with the 3rd Battalion and the two liaison officers would stay with the 1st or 2nd Battalions."[70]

Approaching the edge of Beek, the 1st Platoon of Company H was pinned down by a crossfire from rifles and automatic weapons. Lieutenant Vernon Thomas, the assistant platoon leader now leading the 1st Platoon, sent a twelve man squad led by Sergeants Hiram C. Stevens and Kenneth O. Benson to feel out enemy strength in the houses lining the road down to the highway. The patrol made it into the churchyard and yelled back to Lieutenant Thomas that the enemy resistance was strong. Lieutenant Thomas then shouted for the patrol to return, but only Sergeant Arthur Riedel and Private First Class Clyde Nestor made it back. Four more members of the squad were later found wounded, Sergeant Stevens was captured, and the remaining five, including Sergeant Benson, were found killed in action.

The enemy fire eventually subsided and Lieutenant Thomas led his 1st Platoon into the town. Private First Class Oliver Griffin was a member of Sergeant Curtis B. Sides' squad. The previous night, when they had entered the town, the 1st Platoon troopers had dug slit trenches in the churchyard on the southwestern side of the town square, which was at the road junction with Highway K. Now on the morning of the 21st, as Private First Class Griffin moved with the squad back into the churchyard, he had an uneasy feeling, because they weren't receiving any fire from Germans who he knew had to be in buildings around the square. "I guess the Germans suckered us, because they held their fire until we got next to the slit trenches. When they opened up, not thinking, we each jumped into the holes we dug the night before. There must have been several snipers looking right down at us. Sergeant Sides was in a hole about ten feet from mine. [Private William J.] Kurzawski was in another one about ten feet in front of Sides. The first shot hit Kurzawski in the head, killing him. The next shot hit Sides' rifle, ruining it. He turned to me and said he couldn't use his rifle. I said to get down, but I should have said let's move. Almost immediately, the next shot hit Sides in the head, killing him. At that moment I knew to move—but where?

"I took off heading for the house where I thought the shots were coming from. I figured I would be better off going in shooting than I would be staying outside. As I was running, I saw an open gate in the brick wall next to a house. I cut to go through the opening just as they sprayed the wall where I had cut. I got there okay and worked my way into the woods, where I could look right into Beek.

"After a few minutes came [Sergeant] Frank Bagdonas. We found a place a little up the hill with a good view. We were observing the closest house, when out the door walked a tall German soldier. He acted like no one was within a hundred miles. I guess he thought we all took off for Berg-en-Dal. We decided to aim, count to three, and both shoot. We did and he went down. I pulled my rifle, so I know Bagdonas got him. When we went back in we passed the German. Lieutenant [John] Leatherwood was leading the way. After he was about ten steps past the German, he must have thought that he might still be alive, so he walked back and shot him through the head with his .45."[71]

Lieutenant Vernon Thomas sent a runner to Lieutenant Leatherwood requesting that the 3rd Platoon cross to the west side of the Berg-en-Dal to Beek road and attack on his right flank.

However, the 3rd Platoon became pinned down by machine gun fire coming from a house at the bend in the road before reaching the road junction with the Highway K. Sergeants Jay Daugherty and Henning Olson, Private First Class Joseph Nedza, and Privates Sherman Axline and Robert Sherwood attacked the house where the machine gun nest was located. Sergeant Olson sent Private First Class Nedza and Privates Axline and Sherwood around the right side of the house to go after the machine gun, but they were all killed as they rounded the corner of the house. Lieutenant Leatherwood joined Sergeant Olson, and the two of them could hear Germans talking inside the house. Leatherwood directed Private First Class Thurlow W. Matteson to fire his .30-caliber machine gun into the house and another trooper fired two rifle grenades into it, silencing the Germans. Lieutenant Leatherwood and Sergeants Daugherty and Olson then returned to the platoon.

At noon, both Company H platoons were ordered to withdraw to reorganize and prepare for an attack at 2:00 p.m. The plan was for the 1st and 2nd Platoons of Company H to advance west of the road from Berg-en-Dal to Beek and the 3rd Platoon of Company F to advance east of the road.

The attack jumped off at 2:00 p.m. as ordered. The two Company H platoons and the 3rd Platoon of Company F became pinned down by flat trajectory artillery and machine gun fire before reaching the town. Lieutenant Edward M. King, the platoon leader of the 3rd Platoon of Company F, was killed and the platoon became disorganized and did not continue into the town.

Staff Sergeant Lyle Kumler, the platoon sergeant of the 2nd Platoon of Company H, got his platoon's machine guns and mortars into position where suppressive fire was delivered on the German positions in buildings on the edge of Beek. The two Company H platoons resumed the advance toward the village, but a machine gun once again pinned them down. Staff Sergeant Kumler took a couple of men and worked his way into a position to attack the machine gun. Telling the two men to cover him, Kumler assaulted the machine gun single-handedly and killed the crew, allowing his platoon to continue into Beek. For his extraordinary heroism during this and the previous day's assault, Staff Sergeant Lyle Kumler would later be awarded the Distinguished Service Cross.

As the Company H platoons entered Beek, Sergeant Kumler observed one of the 1st Platoon troopers use deception to eliminate one enemy position. "Private [First Class Clyde] Nestor was pinned down by a German machine gun in the cemetery in Beek. He tied a handkerchief on his Tommy gun and the Germans stopped firing. He raised his gun and walked up to the machine gun, then pulled his gun down and shot the Germans, turned and ran back to us."[72]

The assault, however, was again stopped by the numerically superior force of German paratroopers and at 3:00 p.m., was called off and another withdrawal conducted back up the hill.

From his position on the high ground above Beek, Lieutenant Louis Toth observed German ambulances in Beek at around 5:00 p.m. He sent a combat patrol, led by Lieutenant William J. Garry, the Company H executive officer, to investigate enemy strength in the town. The patrol encountered strong resistance as it fought its way into the town. Having determined that strong enemy forces still held the town, Lieutenant Garry ordered the patrol to withdraw. However, German troops attempted to block the withdrawal of the patrol, eventually surrounding it. Lieutenant Garry led the breakout of the encirclement, then moved to the rear of the patrol and covered its withdrawal. He engaged pursuing enemy troops each time they attempted to close on the patrol, until both he and the patrol members escaped and returned to the Company H positions on the hill below Berg-en-Dal.

Later that afternoon, Company H made a final assault to capture the town. When two German machine guns pinned down the 3rd Platoon, Corporal Roger L. Atherton, a bazooka section leader, directed his bazooka teams to move to positions not covered by the two enemy machine guns, so that they could fire bazooka rounds at the enemy positions. While his teams maneuvered into position, Corporal Atherton covered them by firing his rifle as he moved toward the machine guns. Atherton drew machine gun fire as well as rifle fire from German soldiers who were providing security for the two machine guns. Just as Atherton's bazooka teams fired at the German positions, knocking out the machine guns, Atherton was killed by enemy fire. The bazooka fire broke the enemy line, allowing Company H to penetrate it and drive into the town.

By 6:15 p.m., after a great deal of fighting house-to-house to dig out the Germans, the 3rd Battalion cleaned out the town of Beek, capturing a significant number of prisoners. Company H was reduced to little more than half strength after nearly two full days and nights of almost continuous fighting.

For the Company H commander, Lieutenant Louis Toth, Beek had been a very costly piece of the real estate. "I lost half of my company through casualties and deaths (seventeen killed and thirty-two wounded)."[73]

One of the survivors, Private First Class Oliver Griffin, felt fortunate to have survived the brutal fighting to capture the town. "I believe the rest of us would have been KIAs if the Germans had not pulled out and left."[74]

Corporal Atherton, Private First Class Joseph Nedza, and Privates Sherman Axline and Robert Sherwood were posthumously awarded Silver Stars for their valorous actions.

That evening, Lieutenant Neal Beaver, with Headquarters Company, 3rd Battalion, heard the ominous sound of incoming large caliber artillery shells. "Long range heavy German artillery landed in front of Hotel de Groot in Berg-en-Dal. It took all of the meat from the back of one of [Lieutenant] Bill Garry's legs, from the buttocks to the knee.

"Doc [Captain James] Klein amputated the leg in the Nijmegen hospital. After the operation, Garry seemed to be fine. He was talking and having a cigarette at 11:00 p.m. He died before morning."[75]

Lieutenant Garry was posthumously awarded the Silver Star for his heroism while leading the combat patrol into Beek.

During those first days, Lieutenant Toth and his troopers had received vital help from the local citizens and he was very grateful for their assistance. "The Dutch Underground gave us food, shelter, lent us carts and horses, carried ammunition for us and gave us hot stimulants. We used them as scouts and they located positions for us. We kept some of these men in our own company and gave them dead men's uniforms. They stayed with us and said they wanted to join the U.S.A. paratroops!"[76]

Lieutenant Woodrow Millsaps completed the withdrawal of the 2nd and 3rd Platoons of Company B from Wyler, Germany to the main line of resistance just before daybreak on September 21. "I was informed by 1st Lieutenant [William] Cross, platoon commander of the 1st Platoon, who was left behind to defend the company's sector of the battalion's defense, that there were gaps in the line, and some of our strongpoints of defense had been knocked out the previous day by artillery. First Lieutenant [Herbert] Hoffman, company executive officer, was checking these positions when I ran into the battalion's 81mm mortar platoon leader [Lieutenant George I. Stoeckert]. We were discussing the defense of our position when suddenly he remarked that he didn't think we had troops in front of our defense line. I looked in the direction he was looking and there the Krauts were, coming out of the fog thirty or forty yards away in attack formation and coming straight toward us. I said, 'Man, that isn't friendly troops, that's the enemy,' and gave the order to fire. Hell broke loose all along the line. The 81mm officer opened up with his 81mm platoon and the shells landed in front, all around us, which was OK with me, for our rifle fire and the mortar fire stopped the Krauts.

"I remember hearing the machine gunner [Corporal Cecil W. Cassity] that I had just left call, 'Millsaps!' I made a couple of bounds and landed in his position and found all of the machine gun team [Cassity and Privates First Class Raymond C. Kurtz and William L. Peterson] dead.

"I found out later this was part of a coordinated attack on the regimental defense line. This also was the reason the enemy wanted so badly to take Wyler, Germany, for Wyler was the ideal point for the enemy to mass his forces and jump off in the attack. The attack all along the regimental front was stopped and when the fog lifted, several dead Germans were in our line of defense.

"By 10:00 hours, all was quiet again and I remember asking Sergeant [Jim] Smith, my first sergeant, what was wrong with me, for I was shaking all over like I was frozen to death and my teeth were chattering. He told me that I needed rest and something to eat. It was then that I discovered that all the canned food [rations that] I had jumped with was still in my pack and I didn't recall eating anything since the jump. I asked him what date it was, and he told me it was the 21st of September. I couldn't believe it, for it seemed so long ago since we made the jump on Voxhil."[77]

As part of the attack, an estimated battalion of Germans struck Lieutenant Robert Sickler's 3rd Platoon of Company D, which was defending the village of Kamp, on the regiment's right flank. The German battalion attacked at dawn, supported by heavy artillery and 20mm antiaircraft guns being used in a ground attack role. It penetrated the Company D line twice, but accurate fire from Private Harry M. Rhodus stopped both assaults. When the platoon withdrew to a finger of high ground to the west, Private Rhodus stayed behind as the rear guard and covered them. The Germans, seeing the withdrawal, attempted to close in, but Rhodus stopped several enemy advances, until the platoon was safely in position. Private Rhodus was killed in action on October 15, and posthumously awarded the Silver Star for his heroic actions.

The same German attack also hit the 2nd Platoon of Company D, 307th Airborne Engineer Battalion to the north on Hills 62 and 62.9. As he had done the previous day, Captain Ben Delamater, the 1st Battalion executive officer, coordinated a Company C counterattack to assist the engineer company. "When C Company did go to help the engineers, the situation there was about the worst they too had encountered. In skillfully maneuvering to this position, C Company encircled a group of careless Germans and killed twenty-five. A few got away. There were no prisoners. By this time the constant close struggle was telling on nerves and tempers. I doubt that many prisoners would have been taken by either side. However, the late afternoon marked the ebb of activity."[78]

Later on the morning of September 21, 1st Lieutenant Charles Chaplinski, the commanding officer of Company D, 307th Airborne Engineer Battalion, received orders to form a defensive line with his company astride the road from

Wyler to Berg-en-Dal. The 1st Platoon was withdrawn from the fighting at Beek and assembled with the 3rd Platoon and instructed regarding the mission by Lieutenant Chaplinski. "Marching down the road to our positions we contacted the enemy in a house named Holdeurn. I instructed the 3rd Platoon to attack around the right of the house and Lieutenant [Joseph J.] Jammaer with the 1st Platoon to attack around the left. We got close to the house and requested the occupants to withdraw from inside, but no one came out. We shot some BAR fire into the house and two Germans came out with a white cloth. They stepped out about ten feet and went back into the house."[79]

The Germans opened fire, wounding Private Julius Silverman, a bazooka gunner, in the buttocks, which infuriated him. Staff Sergeant Roland Ziegler then observed Silverman as he "ran through heavy fire about two hundred yards, stuck the bazooka in the window and blew a hole through the second floor and out the roof. The whole house shook; windows smashed out and even shingles fell off the roof. Out of every opening came tumbling Germans. In front of this house was a duck pond—six inches of water, four feet of mud—into which dove two Germans and started to swim across. Two troopers merely walked around and captured them as they came out."[80]

Lieutenant Chaplinski and his two platoons of engineers killed two, wounded four, and rounded up twenty-eight German prisoners. The 3rd Platoon dug in around several farm buildings across the Wyler to Berg-en-Dal road from Hill 62.9, about one thousand yards west of the village of Im Thal.

Lieutenant Chaplinski's 2nd Platoon which already held positions on two hills that overlooked the Wyler to Berg-en-Dal road had been receiving long range German fire. "One squad on Hill 62 and two squads on Hill 62.9 were pinned down during daylight and unable to move around at night."[81]

On the morning of September 21, Private Thomas J. Broderick, a new replacement with Headquarters Company, 1st Battalion, in only his fifth day in combat, was in his foxhole observing a German soldier in the distance. "I was lining up my aim on a German. I got a little high in the foxhole and I got shot clean through the head—through the left temple."[82]

Despite being grievously wounded, Broderick somehow beat the long odds and survived. He would be blinded for life, but was one of many of the regiment's troopers who were badly wounded and who went on to live full and productive lives.

Private First Class Jim Allardyce returned to Company B after being wounded on September 18, during the attack to secure the landing zone. "The fellows were all glad to see me, but they were all hungry and cold. They had very few British rations, which they were stretching out for everyone. I was given a spot to cover and dug my hole—in soft sand, fortunately. Then they started talking food. I discovered that I was lucky having had some sandwiches at the farmhouse aid station and Dutch hospital, and the stolen Limey rations, but even so, my stomach was eating itself. The rest of the fellows had had nothing, until the British gave them so little [in the way of rations] to divvy up. I gave [Private First Class Michael S.] Mickey Niklauski the last half of a D-bar I had. Then we tried eating raw turnips or sugar beets from the field, but that just gave us cramps.

"When I had arrived, they had asked for water, because the well just down the hill from us was covered by a Jerry machine gun. They were getting their water by the canteen full from the company by the path I had taken. We were on the defense on the high ground, but it apparently was a strongpoint defense. We had a hillock. Some hundreds of yards over, the engineers had a hill and so on. No one ventured between the hills in daylight unless they circled back.

"[Private Arthur] Wolfe, a fellow platoon member, crawled out in broad daylight to a farm. He found a chicken and under machine gun fire, brought it back. He was that hungry; but when he got back he didn't know how to clean it! He was determined to cook it in his helmet once it was cleaned, but he or no one else knew what to do. Fortunately, I had farmer relatives, so I pulled feathers and drew blood, the first with my father's gift knife, and sectioned the bird. Everyone was very grateful; and after boiling, the unseasoned bird did taste good. I even pointed out that the liquid broth could be considered chicken soup and that also disappeared. That day was one of life's little pleasures." [83]

CHAPTER 13

"MY BOYS ARE PINNED DOWN"

On the morning of September 22, Corporal Jim Blue, with Company A, was sitting in his foxhole on Devil's Hill, after another sleepless night. "At daybreak a BAR opened up full blast. Lieutenant Foley shouted, 'Who in the hell is wasting that ammo?'

"Sergeant Joe [H.] Boone answered from a position on the east side, 'If you think we've wasted ammo, come have a look!' He had knocked off the lead element of an attack force. About an hour later the hill came under mortar fire. All during this day and night, Germans probed around the hill."[1]

Later that morning, Corporal Blue was assigned a heartbreaking task that would become a painful memory. "Lieutenant Foley issued an order to the 1st Platoon to bury our dead. [Staff] Sergeant [Sherman] Van Enwyck gave me this detail. I took several men with entrenching tools and started digging a massive grave for our eleven KIAs. Sergeant Van Enwyck and I recovered the bodies and laid them out for burial...These bodies were laid in the grave with faces uncovered. I told Sergeant Van Enwyck that we must cover the faces of these comrades before covering them with dirt. Van Enwyck detailed four men; he and these four made a dash for the guest house (tavern) and secured tablecloths. They returned without being fired upon. We covered our deceased comrades and buried them with respect. A cross was made from a tree we chopped down and placed at the center of the grave. A dog tag from each body was draped over the cross, leaving the identity of our comrades."[2]

In all, thirteen troopers were killed in action on Devil's Hill. The Company A troopers killed were Sergeant Vince G. Pierce; Technician Fifth Grade Paul B. Singer; Privates First Class George E. Barron, Clyde Deaver; Privates Manuel L. Alvarez, Eugene B. Anderson, Richard R. Davis, Willard H. Davis, Julius P. Musmeci, and Donald C. Weaver. The 2nd Platoon, Company G lost Lieutenant Kenneth Covey, the platoon leader, and Private First Class Fay J. Crandell. Headquarters Company, 1st Battalion lost Sergeant Rudolph E. Bolin.

That night, Lieutenant Foley asked for a volunteer to infiltrate through German lines to bring ammunition to Devil's Hill. One of the men in Corporal Blue's platoon wanted to volunteer, but he had one overriding concern. Blue discussed it with the young trooper. "Private First Class [Donald W.] Bonge told me he could make it to regiment through the Germans. His only sweat and fear is getting back on Devil's Hill without being shot by our troops. I [assured him that I would] stand guard and await his return. Our signal was when he approached the hill to call, 'Blue.' Bonge was briefed and he was on his way. Sometime before morning, I heard his voice, loud and clear, 'Blue.'

"I answered, 'Come on up, Bonge.' Private First Class Bonge had contacted regiment and led an ammo carrying detail back to Devil's Hill. Bonge is one of the many heroes that are not on record for valor."[3]

In Beek on the morning of September 22, Lieutenant Neal Beaver helped to collect the 3rd Battalion dead; killed during the assaults to capture the town the previous day. "By dawn we still held Beek, but we laid thirty-one or thirty-two bodies on the sidewalk from H Company, G Company, the bazooka section, and our attached engineer team."[4]

Staff Sergeant Ralph Busson, the platoon sergeant of the 1st Platoon of Company H, also helped with the collection of the bodies. "Picking them up and putting them in a GI truck was my saddest [experience of the campaign]."[5]

Private First Class Oliver Griffin had been a 60mm mortar gunner with Company H prior to the fighting at Beek. "By the process of elimination I was made a buck sergeant after Beek. After a few more days, I was made a staff sergeant under the same method."[6]

Corporal Edward N. "Toby" Bailey, with Headquarters Company, 3rd Battalion, was impressed by the fact that "when someone got killed or wounded there was always someone capable of taking over. Although I shouldn't have been, I was amazed at the bravery of my buddies."[7]

On the morning of September 22, Company H conducted a platoon sized attack southeast from Beek along Highway K toward Smorenhook, which was found to be well defended. When a machine gun pinned down at least half of the platoon on the left flank with grazing fire, Private First Class Walter L. Coltrin, an assistant squad leader, maneuvered close to the enemy position and attacked the machine gun nest with grenades and his rifle, killing two of the crew and momentarily neutralizing the machine gun. This diverted fire away from his platoon and onto him, mortally wounding him, but allowing his platoon to open fire on the machine gun position. Private First Class Coltrin died on September 25, and was posthumously awarded the Silver Star for his courageous sacrifice.

That same day, Company I, supported by a troop of four tanks from the British 8th Armoured Brigade's Sherwood Rangers Yeomanry, moved north from Beek and attacked east toward Wercheren Lake and Erlekom to clear the flatland on the southern side of the Waal River east of Nijmegen. The attack ran into two companies of Germans, dug in and backed up by antitank guns and artillery at the south end of the lake. The company was forced to withdraw back to the high ground around Beek.

That night, the entire 3rd Battalion moved into Beek, then at 4:30 a.m. on September 23, it conducted a night march from Beek to the vicinity of Polder, moving through the front line of the 2nd Battalion, 504th Parachute Infantry Regiment. Corporal Frank Ruppe was a medic assigned to the 3rd Battalion. "It was a night maneuver, a tricky one at that. The entire battalion moved into the town [of Beek] under cover of darkness without a shot being fired. We had to secure all objects dangling from our harness. Under no circumstances were we to engage the enemy until we reached our objective, as it was to be our jumping off point for the next day's mission, that objective being the flat area on the other side of Beek."[8]

The 3rd Battalion then moved from Polder to a dike road which was the line of departure, to attack southeastward to clear the flat ground south of the Waal River. The plan called for Company G to attack on the right toward a few farm buildings and a windmill known as Thorensche Molen; in echelon to its left rear, Company H would capture for Hill 9.2 in the center; and in echelon to its left rear, Company I would seize Erlekom and brick kilns located near the river.

Twelve British tanks of the Sherwood Rangers were attached for the attack. However, one was a command tank and two others were knocked out on the way to join the 3rd Battalion prior to the attack. Four tanks were attached to Company G, three attached to Company H, and two tanks to Company I.

Lieutenant Bill Call was the platoon leader of the 2nd Platoon, Company G, which had been released from attachment to Company A on Devil's Hill the previous night and had rejoined Company G. Looking through his binoculars, Lieutenant Call could see the company's objective, the Thorensche windmill, in the distance. "It was like a three story silo with a windmill on it. The rest of the land was so flat that if you had that as an observation post, you could call in artillery anywhere and that's why they wanted Thorensche mill taken."[9]

The assault began at 7:10 a.m. The plan of attack for Lieutenant Russell Wilde's Company G was to guide on a dike road which ran roughly northwest to southeast toward the mill. The 1st Platoon, led by Lieutenant Ralph DeWeese, would advance to the right of the dike road. The 2nd Platoon, led by Lieutenant Bill Call, would attack on the left side of the dike road. The 3rd Platoon, led by Lieutenant Howard Greenawalt, would follow in reserve. Lieutenant Wilde and his headquarters group would accompany the 2nd Platoon. The four British tanks advanced along the dike road, slightly ahead of the two attacking platoons.

As Company G moved forward, it encountered almost no resistance for the first one thousand yards. As the company drew abreast of Hill 9.2, the Company H objective, it ran into intense fire from an enemy outpost line. Company G quickly overran the outposts, capturing three prisoners, while the other surviving Germans withdrew to the main line of resistance. The British tanks continued to move forward just ahead of the company and soon opened fire on targets of opprtunity, while company's 60mm mortars were set up and went to work on the enemy positions.

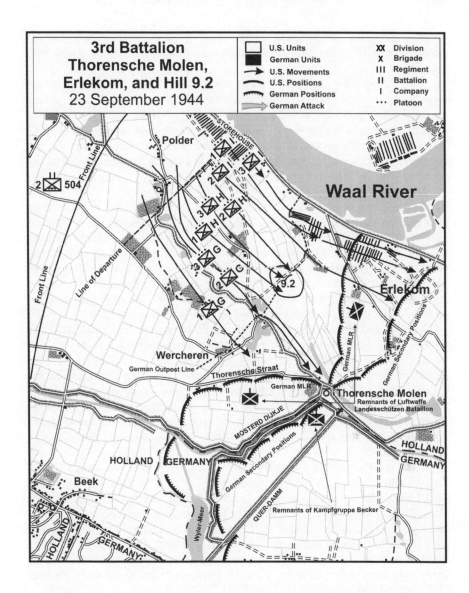

3rd Battalion
Thorensche Molen,
Erlekom, and Hill 9.2
23 September 1944

☐ U.S. Units
■ German Units
→ U.S. Movements
↶ U.S. Positions
⁀⁀⁀ German Positions
⇨ German Attack

XX Division
X   Brigade
III Regiment
II Battalion
I   Company
••• Platoon

Technician Fifth Grade Joseph Kissane was glad to have armor with Company G for the attack. "For a spectator, it must have been an impressive sight—the tanks spurting lead, tracers firing up the stacked corn stalks, [and] wild animals fleeing across the fields. A Dutch farmer and his wife walking along the approach to the dike, tried to appear unconcerned. At the dike, the tankers machine gunned the dug in Germans, burying them in their holes. On the point, [Private First Class Warren C.] Jeffers was busy shooting and bayoneting.

"A grenade was dropped into a hole. The German jumped out seemingly in good shape. The enemy put the old men out front and counterattacked with paratroopers."[10]

The 3rd Battalion captured sixteen enemy troops who indicated that they were members of a Luftwaffe Landesschützen battalion, part of Kampfgruppe Becker. They told the battalion's S-2 interrogator that the battalion was composed of approximately 250 men divided into two companies of four platoons each. All sixteen captured were thirty-five to forty years old and members of the same platoon. Kampfgruppe Becker's partroopers were in fact being used as the reserve force to conduct counterattacks to restore the main line of resistance if it was penetrated.

On the right side of the dike road, Lieutenant DeWeese's 1st Platoon became pinned down by automatic weapons and rifle fire. On the other side, Lieutenant Call and his 2nd Platoon were able to get close to the mill. "We weren't getting that much fire, getting up near the mill. The land came down to like a bottleneck [where a small narrow body of water on the left converged near the dike road], right by the side of the mill. The Jerries were soon, from the other side [of the dike], throwing hand grenades over—the potato-mashers. We were picking them up and throwing them back and throwing some of our own over there."[11]

Then the 2nd Platoon also became pinned down and the 3rd Platoon attacked through it and penetrated the enemy MLR, but was unable to exploit it.

At about 10:00 a.m., the enemy brought down heavy artillery and 50mm mortar fire on Company G. Two of the four British tanks were knocked out by antitank fire. When Sergeant Marvin Risnes saw a squad of Germans maneuvering on the exposed left flank, he launched a one man attack on them. Using his rifle and grenades, he killed six and forced the remainder to withdraw. Sergeant Risnes was later awarded the Silver Star for his quick, decisive, and heroic action.

When the German artillery fire began, Lieutenant Call saw some of his troopers take cover in foxholes the Germans had dug along the sides of the dike road. "Those dikes were about eight or ten feet high and they came down at a slant. The dirt from the dike down to the fields was kind of soft. Artillery was coming right in on us and one of them [an explosion of an artillery shell] buried a kid by the name of [Private First Class Ernest P.] Beck. [Staff Sergeant Frank] Sirovica wasn't in a hole, but he ran up there and dug him out by hand. The shells were coming in, you know. He pulled him out of there—he saved his life. He [Sirovica] was quite a guy.

"There was a lot of noise. [Lieutenant] DeWeese showed up on our side.

"There was a field of cornstalks stacked up on the other side [of the dike]. Sergeant Risnes, [Private First Class Joseph] Joe Metar, and I saw this GI standing out there, maybe about fifty yards in front of us—an American soldier.

"I said, 'Hey, what the hell are you doing out there?' At that, he turned around and took off. We knew then he was dressed in an American uniform. I said, 'Hey Metar. Get that machine gun going.' He racked it back. It was so muddy—you wouldn't believe the mud. He couldn't get it going—it was clogged up, not with mud, but it just wouldn't fire. I brought my M1 down and I was going to shoot him and something was wrong with my M1. Risnes fired, but the guy was long gone by then. He was a good hundred or hundred fifty yards away.

"We moved back one dike, which was maybe about fifty yards from this little bottleneck. Colonel Mendez and our regimental commander, Lindquist, were standing on a dike. I didn't see them. But Russ [Lieutenant Russell Wilde, who was talking to Lieutenant Colonel Mendez on a field telephone] motioned to me that they were back there. And they were telling us how we could take the damn thing. We were firing and [the Germans] were sending artillery in.

"DeWeese was there and Russ said, 'Jimmy, what the hell are you doing?'

"He said, 'Well, my boys are pinned down and I thought I would come over here and see what we could do.'

"Russ said, 'I'm on the phone.'

"DeWeese said, 'Boy, I've got to take a leak.'

"[Lieutenant Wilde replied,] 'Well, you can't do it here.' We were in mud almost up to our knees.

"I said, 'You'll have to go up there [on the dike] by the mill.'

"So he went up there on his hands and knees. He was maybe ten yards in front of us. He whipped it out and he was going. All at once I heard this shot and plunk—his head bent down.

"I yelled at Russ, 'Hey, DeWeese got hit.' I crawled out there and grabbed him by the collar from behind and pulled him back. His mouth was opening and shutting and his eyes were in the back of his head. Russ was still talking to Mendez, getting instructions on how we could take that damn mill. I said, 'Lieutenant, Jimmy DeWeese got hit.'

"He took that phone and shoved it in the mud, I think about a foot and a half. He and I got our jump knives out and we were trying to locate the wound. He examined his head and he ripped open his jacket with his jump knife. We felt around his armpits. We couldn't find a bullet hole. To this day, I don't know what happened. He was dead.

"What a handsome guy he was—you could have used him for a poster of a paratrooper. He was about six feet two. I think he was about thirty inches around the waist and about forty through the chest. I didn't know him that long, but he and Russ Wilde, I guess were together a long time prior to me coming into that outfit. Russ and he had a close relationship. We pulled back farther. Russ got instructions to pull back farther. I carried one of the wounded."[12]

After pulling back, Technician Fifth Grade Joseph Kissane and most of the Company G headquarters troopers found what little cover that was available behind a dike. "[Staff Sergeant and acting first sergeant] Edward Trybulowski, [Technician Fourth Grade] Reynold Como, [Technician Fourth Grade] Francis

Lamoureux, and myself were sitting in a depression taking a breather when some mortar rounds started to come close. I crawled down the dike and climbed a tree. I saw that the Germans were trying to hit an English weapons carrier and were overshooting the mark."[13]

Technician Fourth Grade Bob Kolterman was also among those in the group. "Company headquarters section, minus Lieutenant Wilde and radio operator [Private First Class John] Hargrave, was rather foolishly huddled in a shallow gully to escape small arms fire.

"An 88 shell exploded in our midst, immediately killing the acting first sergeant, communications sergeant, and a company runner. Two others were injured, but the remaining three of us were not injured. We evacuated the wounded to the battalion aid station and returned to our position."[14]

Technician Fourth Grade Lamoureux was one of the troopers wounded by the explosion. "I was facing away from the dike testing the field telephone when shells started coming in. Trybulowski and Como were next to the bank. One shell landed very near me. The concussion sent me into the air and flat down in the mud. When I hit the ground, I felt numb. I looked around. I saw Trybulowski and Como. I could tell from the ashen color of their faces that they were dead. I tried to push myself up. I couldn't.

"Robert Kolterman of headquarters ran over to me. 'Let me take care of you.' He gave me an injection of morphine.

"I asked him, 'Do I have any legs?'

"'You're kind of messed up,' he said, 'but you've still got 'em. Lamoureux, lie still.'

"There were pigs in the mud, ten feet from us. Before I knew it, there was a litter there. The next thing I knew, I was on a jeep, the litter horizontally across the back of the jeep, tied on.

"'So long Lamoureux.' You could read their thoughts: 'We're not going to see that guy again.'"[15]

Technician Fifth Grade Kissane crawled back along the dike, where he found the headquarters personnel. "I found Como and Trib dead. Lamoureux was wounded, but had left."[16] Kissane would later learn that the shell that had killed and wounded his buddies was a possible friendly fire mistake by one of the 3rd Battalion's 81mm mortars, firing with improper increments.

In the center, the plan of attack for Lieutenant Louis Toth's Company H was three platoons on line, with the 1st Platoon on the right, the 3rd Platoon in the center, and the 2nd Platoon on the left.

In the distance, Company H trooper Private First Class Harry Roll could see the chimneys of the brick kilns on the left flank. "Some British tanks pulled up and one of our officers told us to climb on and ride over to the dike. Fearing I'd be a sitting duck riding over, I elected to run over and I beat the tanks. As soon as we reached the top of the dike, the Germans opened fire from the kilns. This went on for a time. Looking back over the field we traversed, a lanky soldier came striding over. As he neared, we then noticed it was General Jim Gavin—the division commander—right on the frontline. We cautioned him to stay low, but he insisted we lay a few rounds into the kilns."[17]

During the attack, Staff Sergeant Lyle Kumler, the platoon sergeant of the 2nd Platoon, knocked out an enemy machine gun position in the Company I sector, using a Gammon grenade. Company H reached its objective, Hill 9.2 by about 8:30 a.m., with no casualties. The size of the hill could not accommodate the entire company, so the 2nd Platoon dug in there, while the 1st Platoon was withdrawn and placed in reserve. The 3rd Platoon was attached to Company G.

The plan of attack for Company I, now under the command of Lieutenant Francis Mahan, was for Lieutenant Delbert C. Roper's 3rd Platoon to advance on the left, guiding on a dike road to its left. The 2nd Platoon, led by Lieutenant Robert Wickes, would attack on the right, guiding on the 3rd Platoon. The 1st Platoon, led by Lieutenant William Bush, would follow in reserve behind the 3rd Platoon.

Company I moved out in squad columns, but at a drainage ditch about a hundred yards from the line of departure, heavy small arms fire forced the two leading platoons to deploy in a skirmish line. Lieutenant Foy Rice was the company executive officer. "Early in the attack to capture Erlekom, Lieutenant Mahan was shot through the chest and I became company commander."[18]

Two British tanks advanced along a dike road to the left of the 3rd Platoon, firing on possible enemy strongpoints. The 3rd Platoon became pinned down just beyond the drainage ditch by enemy machine guns firing from the brick kilns, and it put its own machine guns into action to establish a base of fire. As the 3rd Platoon crawled forward under this cover fire, the 2nd Platoon on its right rushed forward to outflank the brick kilns, which drew the fire of the machine guns and allowed the 3rd Platoon to rush into the brick yard and kilns. Taking the initiative, Lieutenant Bush quickly brought his 1st Platoon up behind the 3rd Platoon into the brick kilns. There, the two platoons assaulted several well placed enemy machine gun positions.

Corporal Frank Ruppe, a medic assigned to the 3rd Battalion, and Private Edwin C. Flintz, an ambulance driver with the 307th Airborne Medical Company, had already shown extreme bravery in evacuating wounded troopers during the earlier fighting around Beek. Now, Ruppe watched Company I in the distance, advance into the brick yard and assault the kilns. "They came close, but could not capture [the brick kilns]. Colonel Mendez, Captain [Briand] Beaudin, and myself were leaning against a dirt embankment overlooking the action. I suppose the report must have come over the walkie-talkie that I Company had sustained moderate casualties and had no way to remove them. They were also ordered to make a tactical withdrawal. At this time, I do believe I did pass a sarcastic remark or a remark uncalled for at such a time. I also did not think anyone else but the man next to me should have heard it (this was our jeep driver [Private Flintz]). To this day, I don't know if Colonel Mendez or Captain Beaudin did hear the remark, 'There goes another company.'

"But I had no sooner spoken those words, when Colonel Mendez turned in my direction and with a sharp command said, 'Go get them.' Having served almost eighteen months under Colonel Mendez prior to this time, I knew he expected each man to obey a command to the letter. Not only to obey, but to think for himself. His command, 'Go get them' probably never sank quite fully, but my reaction was instantaneous. I told the jeep driver [Private Flintz] to get the jeep and that we were to get over that flat area as fast as that jeep would move. I also ordered the jeep driver not to stop for any reason, no matter if anyone got hit on the way, but to reach the nearest building for cover. We were a very easy target due to the fact that the roads were five to eight feet higher than the fields and were used as dikes during the rainy season.

"Credit goes to that driver; he never stopped until we reached the first barn for cover. We collected all wounded in a hurry, as we were under heavy small arms fire. It was good to know that every man down to the last wounded made it out of there that afternoon."[19]

For their heroism while saving a number of lives that day, Corporal Ruppe and Private Flintz were awarded Silver Stars.

The 1st and 3rd Platoons of Company I, in tough fighting finally cleared the brick kilns of enemy troops. As this was occurring, the 2nd Platoon kept moving forward, clearing the ground as far as a thousand yards east of the kilns. The company suffered one killed and twelve wounded.

Meanwhile, Lieutenant Colonel Mendez ordered Company G to conduct a second attack that morning. The 1st Platoon made a frontal assault along the south side of the dike road. North of the dike road, the 2nd Platoon moved to within fifty yards of the enemy main line of resistance and established a base of fire. The 3rd Platoon in the center just north of the the dike road attack toward the mill, then turned right, crossing the dike road, and attempted to roll up the enemy's right flank. However, the attack was broken up by concentrated artillery fire on the relatively short front.

That afternoon, Company G received a resupply of ammunition and the 3rd Platoon of Company H was attached for a third attack. This time, a section of Headquarters Company, 3rd Battalion machine guns established a base of fire just north of the dike road, while the 1st Platoon advanced south of the road and set up a base of fire within fifty yards of the enemy's main line of resistance. Under cover of this fire, the 2nd and 3rd Platoons of Company G on the left of the Headquarters Company machine guns overran the German MLR positions on the left or north side of the dike road.. Sergeant Risnes was in the lead, ahead of the two assaulting platoons. "The town was located on a dike along a canal and there was a small wooden bridge across the canal. I went across the bridge for recon purposes and took another guy with me. When we reached the other side, he went to the left and I turned right. I walked right into the middle of a

German platoon before I even knew it. They were dug in and I didn't see them. I got right in the middle of them when this German got up and threw one of those potato-masher grenades at me. I dove into a clump of corn shocks growing at the side of the road. We were at a standoff. He would throw a grenade and I would duck. I started moving around the corn shocks to get a better shot at him when I felt a rifle brush against my back and shoulder. I whipped around and fired by reflex and hit this young German soldier in the arm. Evidently, he had gotten scared and hid in the corn, standing straight up, and I brushed up against him when I started moving. He couldn't have been more than seventeen or eighteen years old. As soon as I fired, I ran across the road and dove into the canal close to the bank. And the kid followed me! He had dropped his rifle when I hit him and evidently got excited and started running. It just happened that he ran the same way I did. When he came over the bank, I grabbed him and held his head under water until I saw he wasn't going to put up a fight. Then, I let him up and took a couple of grenades off him."[20]

After penetrating the enemy's main line of resistance, the two platoons of Company G were pinned down by artillery, mortar, and automatic weapons fire. The 3rd Platoon of Company H, attacked through the 3rd Platoon of Company G, and the assault carried over the dike, where the Company H platoon seized positions south of the house directly in front of the enemy's secondary positions. Wilde then ordered all three Company G platoons to assault the junction of the two dike roads. The 2nd and 3rd Platoon assault reached the dike road fronting them. The Company H platoon, thinking they were being fired upon by their own men, withdrew back across the road. The 3rd Platoon of Company G was able to advance beyond the road, while the 2nd Platoon was pinned down on it. At this point, ammunition was again running low, so Lieutenant Russell Wilde, the company commander, ordered a withdrawal to an orchard a thousand yards back, where it dug in and set up a defense for the night.

During the withdrawal, Technician Fifth Grade Joseph Kissane carried Private First Class James Belcher, who had been shot in the back. "When I couldn't carry him any farther, I laid him down. The Germans, coming up to him, covered him with a coat. He wasn't captured and returned to our company for the Bulge."[21]

That night, the Germans reoccupied the main line of resistance near the mill, its outpost line around the dike road, and infiltrated to within a hundred yards of the Company G positions and set up automatic weapons.

At 6:00 a.m., the Germans fired a ten minute artillery barrage, followed by a counterattack. Fire from four British tanks broke up the counterattack. Lieutenant Colonel Mendez ordered another attack at 9:00 a.m. The plan was to use two tanks on the north side of the dike road and two on the south side. The 1st and 2nd Platoons of Company G would attack on the left, north of the road, while the 3rd Platoon of G Company and the 3rd Platoon of Company H would attack on the right, south of the road.

The attack began at 9:45 a.m. with the tanks leading slightly, the platoons leapfrogged each other about every hundred yards. The two tanks on the left focused their fire on the narrow passage between the dike road and the water to the left, which had proven so difficult the previous day. The four platoons broke through the German MLR and reached an orchard south of the objective. German artillery heavily saturated the area once again, pinning down the troopers and forcing another withdrawal at 11:30 a.m. to the start line. Company G was relieved at 5:00 p.m., having lost ten killed, one missing, and twenty-four wounded during the two day attack.

On September 24, the 504th Parachute Infantry Regiment relieved the 1st and 2nd Battalions beginning at 4:00 p.m. The 3rd Battalion was relieved after dark the following night and the 508th was placed in division reserve.

Company A left Devil's Hill during the night of September 24, after being cut off since September 19. For his extraordinary heroism and leadership during the capture and defense of Devil's Hill, Lieutenant John Foley, the company's executive officer, was awarded the Distinguished Service Cross.

On Sunday morning, September 24, 1st Sergeant Wilbur J. Scanlon and two of his Company F troopers received permission to attend a church service in Beek. "We were fully equipped and I believe I've never felt as close to our Lord as I did that day. Someone had to be looking over us. After mass, a few people who could speak English came up to us, shaking our hands and thanking us."[22]

Because of the casualties suffered by Company H during the fighting for Beek, Oliver Griffin had been promoted from private first class with the 1st Platoon to staff sergeant with the 3rd Platoon. "We had been assigned a new platoon leader, his first experience being in Holland. It had been quiet that day, so [Sergeant Frank] Bagdonas caught a chicken and we cooked it in a big Limey cookie can. We sat down to enjoy the chicken and drink the broth. While eating, we noticed the new lieutenant watching us. He was a stranger, so I guess he felt he shouldn't ask us for a share. After a minute, courtesy got the best of us, so we asked him to have some. Four of us enjoyed the feast. That was the beginning of a close comradeship between a platoon leader and the men under him.

"That was 2nd Lieutenant John Leatherwood. I believe I had as much respect for him as any officer I served under."[23]

While the regiment was in division reserve, Corporal Thomas M. Dobbs, with Company A, volunteered for a patrol behind the German front line on the night of September 27, to lay antitank mines on a road that was being used as a supply route. Corporal Dobbs, using great caution in moving his patrol, penetrated the enemy front line and was laying the mines when the patrol was discovered. The Germans brought a heavy artillery concentration down on them, killing two and wounding several others. Corporal Dobbs moved from one man to another during the barrage, gained control of the men, and quieted them down. The patrol finished laying the mines from a prone position and those who were able, returned to the friendly main line of resistance. Corporal Dobbs was unable to contact medics to retrieve the wounded members of his patrol who were still behind German lines. However, he quickly gathered volunteers and returned to the wounded men and successfully evacuated them. Corporal Dobbs would be killed on December 29, 1944 during the Ardennes campaign. He was awarded the Silver Star posthumously for his actions during the patrol.

On September 29, the 1st and 2nd Battalions relieved the 3rd Battalion, 504th Parachute Infantry, and reoccupied the same positions on the high ground west of the Wylerbaan. That night, the 2nd Battalion sent two combat patrols to clear the Den Heuvel woods east of the Wylerbaan, the scene of brutal fighting by the 3rd Battalion, 504th earlier. The patrol moving into the southern portion met some resistance, but reached its objective. The other patrol fought its way into the woods a couple of hundred yards and was hit by fire from at least eight machine guns and a 20mm flak wagon. The patrol advanced by assaulting the Germans in their holes; killing the occupants of one hole then attacking the next one. The patrol returned with four prisoners.

The 2nd Battalion's main line of resistance was extremely strong. Lieutenant Wayne Smith, the platoon leader of the 2nd Platoon of Company F, was impressed by the firepower in his platoon sector and on call to stop an enemy attack, even though Company F was in reserve. "We had 57mm antitank guns, British 17-pounders, both British and U.S. artillery OPs [observation posts], a bazooka, two light machine guns, four BARs, about five riflemen and the rest Tommy guns. D Company was on the right, E Company on the left, and F Company was in reserve. There was plenty of concealment in the area and wonderful observation. From our positions we could see miles into Germany. We organized strong defensive positions here with machine gun emplacements like pillboxes and escape trenches that resembled World War I fortifications. We had five thousand rounds of ammunition for each machine gun, about fifty rounds of bazooka ammunition, two hundred rounds of 60mm mortar ammunition, and twelve magazines per BAR, plus plenty of reload ammunition. There were quantities of hand grenades available for those who wanted them."[24]

On the afternoon of October 1, Staff Sergeant Paul Sands, with Headquarters Company, 2nd Battalion's 81mm mortar platoon, heard an incoming artillery round "from our deep right flank, killing [Private Joseph L.] Joe Laky [Jr.] and wounding [Private Augustine V.] Gus Wolosechek. Lieutenant James Gidding and I were on a ridge at our observation post (OP) to the left of our mortar positions. Sergeants [Robert W.] Bob Speers and George Fairman were also on the ridge at their OP directly above our mortar positions. We all saw smoke from a German gun, but did not recognize the fact that the shot was a zeroing in round. Around 11:30 p.m. that night, we found out the significance of that afternoon shot. The Germans started out with mortar fire, threw in some artillery rounds, and then started throwing big stuff. An eyeball measurement figured the big stuff was from a railroad gun (274mm). The bombardment lasted some five hours. The phone wires connecting both observation posts with our mortar positions were knocked out in minutes of the first salvo. Lieutenant Gidding and I ran a new wire line to our OP, but it didn't last very long under the heavy German barrage. We also ran another wire line to Speers and Fairman and it too was knocked out."[25]

That same afternoon, Private Fred Infanger was in his foxhole when enemy artillery began zeroing in on the Company E positions. "A smoke shell landed right behind my squad of the 2nd Platoon, E Company. I tried to smother it with sand, but it was too late. We knew they were zeroed in on us. About 10 o'clock that night, we got hit with everything but the kitchen sink."[26]

After a long barrage on the 2nd Battalion sector a large German force struck Companies D and E from Voxhil to Kamp, at five minutes past midnight on the night of October 1-2, with the objective of penetrating the 508th line and turning south to capture Groesbeek. The primary striking power of the assault consisted of elements of Panzer Brigade 108—infantry of Panzer Grenadier Bataillon 2108, supported by its halftracks, nine Mark V Panther tanks and Jagdpanzer IV assault guns of Panzer Abteilung 2108, and Panzer Pioniere Kompanie 2108. Two or more companies of Bataillon 2, Grenadier Regiment 1051, 84th Infantrie Division and paratroopers of Kampfgruppe Becker also took part in the assault.

Private Norb Studelska, with Company D's 3rd Platoon 60mm mortar squad, waited in his carefully constructed foxhole near a Dutch farmhouse as waves of German infantry approached. "All hell seemed to engulf us. A combination of artillery bursts, Kraut flares, machine gun tracers, [and] our own and enemy mortar shelling created a nightmare of insane fireworks. Forms of the enemy to our front were clearly visible during the many flare and shell bursts. Squads of determined enemy seemed to swarm the field like spectators coming to a sporting event. The price of admission would be their lives. One of their targets in our immediate area was the relentless machine gun posted to the right of the house. From my vantage point, I could see the enemy alternately running and hitting the ground. Some were so close that it was impossible to miss our shots. Some were tossing potato-mashers, some had rifles, and some were firing burp guns. For a moment, I felt guilty because I thought I hit a medic attending to a downed comrade. Although I had a full belt of M1 ammunition, plus an extra bandoleer, I recall fearing the consequences of what would happen if we ran out of ammo. With the intensity of the attack, that seemed within the realm of reason. The prospects of our position being overrun seemed imminent. I recall the thumping sounds of our mortar blasting at unknown targets that happened to be in its field of fire. Well into the action, Lieutenant [Robert] Sickler called out to tell two of us to join him behind the farmhouse, because the Krauts broke through and were now behind us. I reluctantly left the safety of my deluxe foxhole to join Lieutenant Sickler and another trooper by the name of [Private First Class William S.] Perkins, a member of our mortar squad. About that time, [German] tanks were clunking up the road to our left."[27]

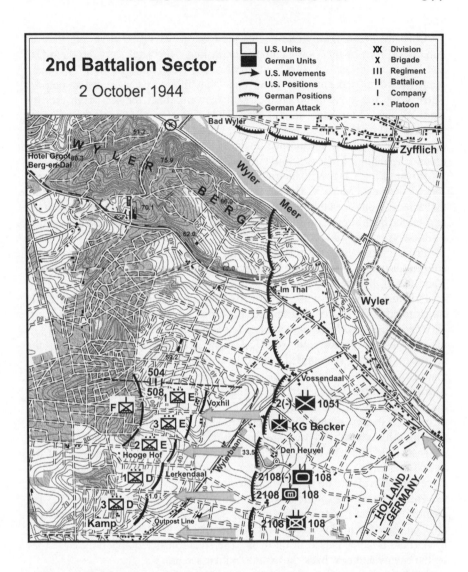

Private First Class Billy McClure was a machine gunner with Company D. "[Private First Class Charles F.] Hayden and I had a pretty good crossfire with our .30-caliber machine guns. The Germans broke through on both sides of our company. They needed a little help on the left side, so five or six of us grabbed our M1 rifles and started that way. This German Mark V tank, about 150 yards away on a little hill, turned on a spotlight and lit up our whole line. I raised my M1 and fired. Lights went out immediately."[28]

Corporal Frank Haddy and one of the men in his squad were dug in at an outpost in front of the Dog Company main line. "[Private] Luis Arellano [Jr.] and I were in the same foxhole—in front of the trees, close to the [Wylerbaan] road. They didn't take much time with us—they figured we were just an outpost. Then, when the tanks came up the road we were about ten feet from the first tank. We loaded the bazooka and fired. Then, Luis forgot to hook the wires [to the bazooka] on the second [rocket], then I fired the third round, under its tracks and it blew up. Then we jumped up in the road and the second [tank] turned around. We shot it in the rear and crippled it, so it was out of action."[29]

Private First Class McClure suddenly saw the sky light up as an explosion rocked the huge Mark V Panther tank. "The trooper [Corporal Frank Haddy] that knocked out the tank jumped up on the hedgerow, put his foot on the tank and started beating his chest like Tarzan. The tank was burning and tracer bullets were going in every direction."[30]

Private Norb Studelska also saw the tank explode. "We were treated to another display of spectacular fireworks from the turret of the lead tank. Frank Haddy and Luis Arellano scored with the bazooka.

"Lieutenant Sickler, Perkins, and I were on the ground observing the Kraut forms to our rear. A grouping of three or four [Germans] were huddled less than fifty yards from us. I had one grenade left and suggested that I let them have it, but Lieutenant Sickler told us to let them get closer. In the midst of the confusion of being surrounded, a lone form staggered toward us calling out the names of troopers in our platoon. He fell about twenty yards from Lieutenant Sickler's position. We dashed out to help him. It was [Private] George Thorne, our platoon runner, who made it from the company CP, several hundred yards through the enemy, which had broken through. The ordeal cost him a bullet hole through the stomach. His message from the company commander was, 'Hold at all costs.' George had done his duty. We carried him to the basement of the farmhouse, where he was cared for by our medic. Since we were surrounded, there was little else to do but continue to hold out."[31]

The darkness was punctuated by white flashes of exploding mortar and artillery shells and crisscrossing tracers. Staff Sergeant Carroll B. Calvert told the Company D squad where he was positioned to hold at all costs as a company of German infantry closed in on them. The squad inflicted appalling casualties on the enemy and beat back the assault in their sector.

In the Company E sector on the left flank of Company D, Private Fred Infanger, a rifle grenadier with the 2nd Platoon, was dug in on the main line of resistance. "The German poured out of the Den Heuvel Woods like Indians, whooping and hollering. I had a box of rifle grenades, and I thought, 'This will be good.' After firing three grenades, a shell hit my foxhole and it caved in.

"When I dug myself out, I discovered my rifle had a ruptured cartridge. I used the extractor from the butt of the rifle, but just couldn't remove the shell. I saw the Krauts were about fifty to seventy-five yards from us, and I started firing my .45 pistol. Upon looking around, I realized a new officer and I were the only ones left. We both had lost our communications—he to the company CP, and I to the outpost one hundred yards to the front.

"I asked the officer, 'What's the story?'

"He answered, 'We had better get our asses out of here!' We then started shooting at five or six Krauts coming along a ditch where our position was [located]. The officer said, 'Let's go!' We crawled back some distance, and then got up and ran like hell to the edge of the woods where the platoon was setting up a new line…I lost my hearing for a few days due to a near miss.

"Sergeant Dale [R.] Roudebush's squad was at the outpost, having relieved me there the night before. He withdrew his men along the tree lined dirt road in good order. [Private] Frank Tafoya received the Bronze Star for his actions on the outpost. He put down quite a few Germans with his machine gun."[32]

Company F, the 2nd Battalion reserve, was dug in behind the main line of resistance. Lieutenant Wayne Smith, the platoon leader of the 2nd Platoon, had been slightly wounded in the back earlier when a German mortar shell exploded behind him as he watched the assault from a shallow trench. "E Company withdrew into my platoon area under cover of fire from our machine guns, BARs, and primary and secondary mortar concentrations. We fired these mortars, five rounds on each target then changed targets. At this time, an enemy machine gun moved into a house in front of us and opened fire. I directed about six rounds of mortar ammunition on this house, silencing the Jerries and moved back to the platoon CP to give instructions to the signal corporal, and to get an aid man up to the platoon. A mortar shell landed close by, wounding me in the arm, and I was sent back to the aid station. I have not ceased to regret my lack of curiosity on my way back to the aid station. I stepped over a dead paratrooper, whom I feel convinced was my best friend. I would not have gained anything by stopping, but I would like to know for sure."[33]

From his observation post, Lieutenant John Gutshall, a forward observer with Battery A, 319th Glider Field Artillery Battalion, assigned to support the 2nd Battalion, directed 75mm artillery fire on the assault, destroying two armored halftracks, killing or wounding all of the occupants, and disorganizing the attack. German artillery and mortar fire struck his forward observation post, wounding Lieutenant Gutshall in the head, but he stayed at his post. Intense shelling eventually destroyed his communication gear. Gutshall crossed the fire swept ground and obtained replacement equipment. There, he received first aid treatment for his head wound and promptly returned to the observation post to continue directing deadly accurate artillery fire on enemy troops and vehicles.

During the German assault, Private First Class Charles F. Andrews, one of the Company F runners, moved through artillery and mortar fire to deliver instructions to Headquarters Company, 2nd Battalion's light machine platoon. After the Germans penetrated the Company E sector, Andrews killed two Germans who had infiltrated into the Company F positions during one of his trips to deliver messages. Upon his return to the company command post, he assisted in the care of wounded troopers. When one of the Company F machine gunners was killed, Andrews manned the weapon and delivered effective fire into the oncoming Germans until the gunner could be replaced.

Throughout the German artillery barrage and assault, Major Otho Holmes, the commanding officer of the 2nd Battalion, moved along the front lines of Companies D and E, checking on the troopers and the situation while under heavy artillery, mortar, and then tank, machine gun, and small arms fire. Holmes conferred with the two company commanders and then decided to commit the battalion reserve, Company F.

Technician Fourth Grade Dwayne Burns was at the Company F command post when the German assault broke through. "Major [Otho] Holmes and his runner showed up at F Company headquarters. They said that E Company had been hit by a German battalion and been forced to withdraw five hundred yards. As we talked, a mortar round almost landed on top of us, just a swish and boom! Before we were halfway to the ground, dirt and bushes flew in all directions. My left arm and leg felt numb. I thought, 'Oh, Lord, I'm hit.' But I crawled back to my feet and started feeling around. I still was in one piece and no holes in my body. Captain [Harold] Martin and Major Holmes both were okay, but their runners were hit in the back and had to be evacuated.

"It was after midnight and F Company was ordered to counterattack and restore the line. The word was passed down to get ready to move out. We hated to leave our nice safe foxholes. Attacking in the daylight was bad enough, but at night it really can get nasty. It didn't take long to find the Germans. The trooper next to me went down and I called, 'Medic!' I went to see if I could help, but no one would be able to help him. He had been hit in the left side of his face with more than one round. He had died instantly.

"I jumped up, running on as I slipped a new clip in my M1. In the dark I could see muzzle blasts through the foliage. It reminded me of fireflies on a summer night. We ran toward the trees firing from the hip, not even knowing if we are doing any good. Smoke was hanging close to the ground. The smell of gunpowder and death all mixed together made it hard to get my breath. Or maybe, it was the taste of fear in the back of my throat."[34]

Private Steve A. Mauro, an acting squad leader with Headquarters Company, 2nd Battalion, led his machine gun squad forward with Company F during the counterattack. When automatic weapons fire from Den Heuvel pinned down Company F, Mauro led his squad under heavy fire to a position from where it delivered suppressive fire on the German positions there, knocking out one machine gun, along with its crew and several supporting riflemen. An artillery shell landed close by and knocked out one of his machine guns, killing the two man crew. With German artillery and mortar fire falling all around him, Mauro retrieved the gun and replaced the damaged parts, then put the gun back into action.

With German fire from Den Heuvel suppressed, Company F resumed the assault, overwhelming the German infantry and forcing the survivors to break and run. Technician Fourth Grade Burns and Company F pursued the retreating Germans until the troopers reached the Company E front line positions. "The firing became sporadic as the Germans withdrew. It became quiet. We stopped to lick our wounds and count our dead. They said it was a brilliant attack; that's because we were still alive. They should have asked the twelve troopers who were killed and the thirty-six who were wounded what they thought about it. But then, dead troopers don't get a vote."[35]

In the Company D sector, Private Norb Studelska was exhausted after an intense, two-hour firefight. "The Kraut attack waned to a few intermittent shots. The Krauts to our rear seemed to disappear into the night. Lieutenant Sickler told Perkins and me to go back to our holes while he checked out the rest of the platoon."[36]

Studelska returned to his deep foxhole just as a massive German artillery barrage struck the 2nd Battalion. "The barrage that followed the failed attack was one of the most terrifying that I experienced in Holland or the Bulge. The earth literally trembled and the sound of the incoming artillery and Screaming Meemies humbled all on the receiving end. The pounding lasted for an eternity and every shell sounded as if would hit my hole. An absurdity of battle would be to live through an all-out attack and then die from a force which the soldier has no defense, other than lie in a hole and sweat it out. To me the barrage was the most frightening part of my entire night. My rosary was well used that night."[37]

One of Staff Sergeant Carroll Calvert's Company D troopers counted sixty-five enemy dead and wounded in front of the squad's positions the following morning. The squad had also captured eight additional Germans.

At dawn, Private Studelska peered out of his covered foxhole to survey the battlefield. "The early morning light revealed the heinous carnage of battle—the smell of a still smoldering tank, the dead and dying enemy, the moans of the wounded. One wounded enemy stood up and staggered away into the misty morning, ignoring our offers to help. Through the early morning fog, we could detect three or four German halftracks moving around to our front, probably picking up wounded or dead. Dead enemy were to our rear. Some that had broken through were victims of their own artillery barrage. A few unguarded prisoners milled about the farmyard, probably grateful, because for them the war was over. One of the troopers asked an English speaking prisoner about the outcome of the war. He replied that the Allies had the most airplanes, guns, and soldiers, but Germany still had Hitler."[38]

At sunrise, Staff Sergeant Paul Sands, with the 2nd Battalion's 81mm mortar platoon, left the observation post he had shared with the assistant platoon leader. "We met with [Sergeants Bob] Speers and [George] Fairman at their OP and we saw three unexploded 274mm rounds within a thirty foot radius of the OP, any one of which, had they blown up, would have been the end of all four of us.

"About three hundred yards below where [Lieutenant James] Gidding and I were positioned originally, [Corporal] Sherwood [H.] Bollier and [Private First Class] Frank [T.] Smith had a machine gun emplacement. They had an artillery round hit a treetop close by. Bollier was killed and Smith had his thumb blown off. Smith was also wounded in other parts of his body."[39]

Major Otho Holmes and Lieutenant Robert Sickler were awarded the Silver Star for their valor and courageous leadership in stemming the German assault. Lieutenant John Gutshall was awarded the Silver Star for his heroism in directing devastating artillery fire on the enemy. Staff Sergeant Carroll Calvert, Corporal Frank Haddy, Private First Class Charles Andrews, and Private Steve Mauro also received Silver Stars for their courage in the face of the huge German assault. The regiment reported to division headquarters that it captured twenty enemy soldiers and destroyed one Mark V Panther tank, three halftracks, and two self-propelled guns.

During the night of October 3-4, Lieutenant Donald W. Hardwick and several other troopers with Headquarters Company's demolition platoon set fire to the damaged and abandoned German armored vehicles to insure that they couldn't be salvaged or weapons in them turned on the regiment's defensive positions.

The 508th continued to hold the line until the night of October 5-6. That night, before the regiment was relieved by the newly arrived 325th Glider Infantry Regiment, Lieutenant Rex Combs, the platoon leader of the 3rd Platoon of Company A, called Sergeant Joe Boone to his command post. "Sergeant Boone's squad was assigned the mission of finding and reducing the positions of the enemy who had partially infiltrated our positions and were thought to be hidden in gliders and a nearby patch of woods. Spreading his squad out and creeping forward with them for some distance, Sergeant Boone would then stand erect and advance noisily forward for approximately two hundred yards, wait until his squad came up, then repeat this action. Of the four suspected enemy positions, Sergeant Boone drew fire from three. Those positions were reduced completely. Sergeant Boone personally accounted for two of the enemy."[40]

On October 6, the 508th Regimental Combat Team was attached to the British 50th Infantry Division and moved north of the Waal River to defend a sector of the bridgehead north and east of the town of Bemmel. At 10:45 a.m. that morning, the regimental combat team crossed the Nijmegen highway bridge enroute to its new positions, where it relieved elements of the British 50th Infantry Division's 231st Infantry Brigade that evening. The regimental command post was established west and slightly north of Bemmel, about halfway between the town and the railroad tracks that ran between Nijmegen and Arnhem.

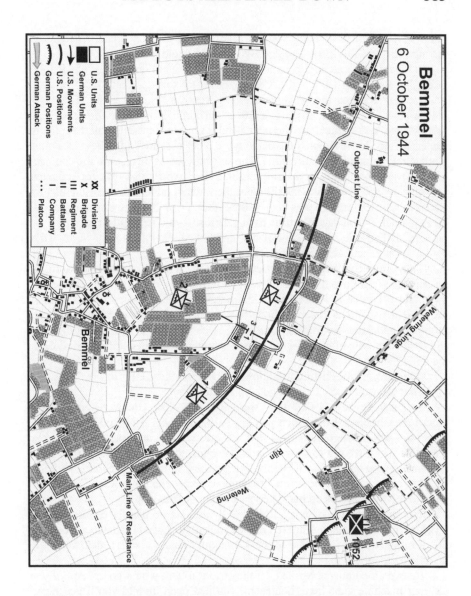

North of Bemmel the 3rd Battalion tied in with the 4th Battalion, Welsh Regiment, 160th Brigade of the British 53rd Infantry Division on its left flank and its line extended southeasterly paralleling a canal named the Wetering Linge, where it tied in with the 1st Battalion. The 1st Battalion relieved the 1st Battalion, Dorsetshire Regiment northeast of Bemmel, occupying a line that extended southeasterly parallel to the canal. The 1st Battalion tied in on its right flank with the 9th Battalion, Durham Light Infantry, 151st Infantry Brigade of the 50th Infantry Division. The 2nd Battalion was held in regimental reserve.

The German force dug in opposite of the regiment consisted of elements of Grenadier Regiment 1052 of the 84th Infantrie Division.

The area between the Waal and Rhine Rivers was known as the "Island" by the paratroopers of the 508th and 101st Airborne Divisions who spent time there. When the regiment arrived near Bemmel, Lieutenant Bill Call, the platoon leader of the 2nd Platoon of Company G, was assigned to relieve a British platoon dug in at an apple orchard. "The sergeant led us through to the company headquarters and it was in a farm building. The two British officers, a captain and a lieutenant, were in there sitting at the kitchen table. I thought the platoon we were going to relieve was right around there. Our officers stayed right with their platoons. This wasn't true in the British—the sergeants really ran the battlefield. They gave me a shot of rum and talked about how they were glad to get out of there and get a little rest.

"They gave the sergeant instructions, 'Take them up and put them in the positions.' We followed him and we came to this one dike and there was about three feet of water in [between] it [the parallel dike] and maybe two or three dead Germans who had been in there [in the water] maybe a week and they were all bloated and flat. So this sergeant said, 'This way,' and went down the bank and hopped on one of these Germans and sprang to the other side and walked up the other incline.

"I thought, 'Holy shit! I don't know whether I could do this or not.'

"This sergeant said, 'Come along, come along.'

"So I got down and God they were squeaky—like you were on a rubber inner tube—bobbed down when you got on top of them. I looked back and my guys were still on the other side. I said, 'Come on. Get your asses over here.' So they did. When we got to the orchard, the sergeant took [Staff Sergeant Frank] Sirovica around and replaced people, getting them in the holes. Sirovica and the sergeant came back and he wanted to show us where the gully was. There was a gully to the front of this orchard, maybe five or six feet deep.

"The British had gone out into this gully and set up trip flares, because the sergeant had ascertained that the only way at night those Germans could get at this position was through that gully. I thought, 'That's a smart idea. I wish to hell I had thought of that.'

"He explained how it worked, 'If they trip it a flare would go up. And if you set your machine guns here, lieutenant, you just open up and you'll get them.' So Sirovica got the machine guns set up there."[41]

At midnight October 6-7, a seven man 3rd Battalion S-2 patrol left the outpost line and reconnoitered northeast to the Wetering Linge canal dike and returned at 2:00 a.m. without contacting the enemy. The 1st Battalion conducted a similar patrol at about the same time and also didn't find the enemy on the south side of the canal, but was fired upon from the other side of the canal dike.

At noon on October 7, the regiment remained in its sector and was attached to the British 53rd Infantry Division, which was relieving the remainder of the 50th Infantry Division.

That night, a German patrol probed Lieutenant Call's platoon area. "Those damn flares went off and our guys opened up with machine gun fire and got no return of fire. It became real quiet and all at once, we heard this guy saying, 'Help me, help me, comrade.' It was dark and eerie as hell in that apple orchard. We didn't do anything about it. We thought it might be a trap.

"Finally, Sirovica said, 'Damn it lieutenant, I can't stand it anymore. We've got to get that guy.

"I said, 'Sergeant, you know it may be a trap.'

"'I don't give a damn,' he said, 'I'm going to take a couple of guys and see what I can do.' So he did and went out and dragged this guy in. This German officer was relieved—the rest of his patrol had taken off and he was wounded badly in the gut and I don't know where else. But we propped him by a tree we called the CP. I had a foxhole there and so did Sirovica.

"The British brought us breakfast every morning. We usually had pancakes and syrup—*hot*. After K-rations, these Tommies knew how to live.

"The guy was talking—he was a professor in Germany and spoke very good English. He tried to convert us. He said, 'What we should be doing comrades, is fighting the Bolsheviks. We should not be fighting one other. We are comrades, they are Bolsheviks.' He hated the Russians.

"The British, when they brought the breakfast up, they'd bring it up at four in the morning, in the dark. They took him back, but I heard that afternoon or the following morning that he had died on the way back."[42]

Upon arriving near Bemmel, Private First Class Harry Roll and the 2nd Platoon of Company H also took over British positions in an apple orchard. "We stayed eleven days in a holding position. We took many tree bursts from German mortars. During that time, my friend [Private First Class] Don Veach killed a large cow. [Staff Sergeant] Ralph Busson skinned it.

"[Lieutenant] Colonel Shanley came upon this butchery and said, 'Where did you get the beef?'

"Veach answered, 'Its pork.'

"Around the apple orchard were irrigation canals, one going due east away toward the enemy. I did go on a night patrol up that canal. Our greatest fear was tin cans hanging across the small canals that would tingle to warn the Germans [that] someone was approaching. We avoided them and reported back that they also were in a holding position."[43]

There were mortar and artillery barrages fired by both sides and numerous night patrols, but the enemy made no major attack on the 508th during its time near Bemmel. Lieutenant Louis Toth was at his company command post on October 13, when a German artillery barrage struck Company H. "I was hit (high explosive shell) and almost knocked out of my company CP and also four men of the CP [were wounded]."[44]

On October 14, the rifle company where Lieutenant Joseph W. Mullen, a forward observer with the 319th Glider Field Artillery Battalion, had his observation post was subjected to intense enemy machine gun fire. Because the ground was so flat, Lieutenant Mullen crept forward under enemy fire to the farthest outpost, so as to observe and adjust artillery fire on the German machine guns, silencing them and preventing possible friendly casualties. Lieutenant Mullen was awarded the Silver Star for his actions.

A number of reconnaissance patrols conducted by the 508th during the first week failed to penetrate enemy lines. On October 15 and 16, Technician Fifth Grade Norman Smith and Private First Class Mayo S. Heath, both members of the regimental S-2 section, conducted a daring two man reconnaissance. The patrol left the outpost line east of the town of Elst around 11:30 p.m. and penetrated north deep into enemy territory. The two troopers made observations of enemy dispositions, returning the following night. As the patrol passed back through the German front line on their return, they quietly took a prisoner and marched him back to the regimental command post. Technician Fifth Grade Smith and Private First Class Heath were both awarded a Silver Star for the execution of this bold and dangerous patrol.

On October 28, Private First Class Bill Windom, with Company B, was a member of a daylight patrol, along with Lieutenant William Cross, Private First Class Mickey Niklauski, and Private First Class John Aronis. The patrol's mission was to determine whether or not the Germans had withdrawn from the Wetering Linge. Windom and the other troopers carefully approached the dike on the near side of the canal when they found one German asleep in his hole. They were about to take him prisoner when four others showed themselves, apparently ready to surrender, just as a German machine gun to the left opened fire on the patrol. For Windom and the other three troopers it was "eight hundred daylight yards of ripping, zipping, tracer machine gun and Schmeisser fire. I lost my radio, rifle, and helmet. We got back across with one hole in a calf [Lieutenant Cross was wounded]."[45]

Lieutenant Millsaps, the company commander, was informed of the results of the Company B patrol that day, including the loss of Private First Class Windom's equipment and weapon. That night, an inspection of the company was held. Private First Class Windom was present, without his gear. "'Where's your equipment, Windom?'

"'I lost it on patrol, sir.

"'You're no good to me without a rifle."[46]

That same day, Lieutenant Rex Combs, the platoon leader of the 3rd Platoon of Company A, led another daylight reconnaissance patrol. Sergeants Robert White and Marion Kinman volunteered, even though Kinman had been awake the entire night before, while on outpost duty. After penetrating the enemy front line, the the three troopers gathered intelligence, noting on a map the locations of enemy positions, the numbers of enemy manning them, and the types of troops (SS, Wehrmacht, infantry, artillerymen, etc.). After gathering the information, the patrol started its return and looked for an enemy soldier to capture to take back for interrogation. Lieutenant Combs was watching Sergeant White attempt to take an SS soldier prisoner when the patrol was discovered and attacked. "In the ensuing attack on the patrol, Sergeant White prevented the enemy from using their machine gun by firing three rounds into the piece, damaging it to such an extent that it would not function and killing one of the gunners."[47]

Lieutenant Combs then observed Sergeant Kinman "personally kill two of the enemy who were blocking the patrol's withdrawal."[48]

A short time afterward, Lieutenant Combs was wounded. "I was near the verge of unconsciousness and bleeding from the mouth and nose due to enemy concussion grenades"[49]

Both sergeants refused to leave him, even though Combs ordered them to do so. As they carried him back to the 508th lines, Combs saw both of them "fighting off the enemy, who was laying concentrated mortar, rifle, and machine pistol fire."[50] Combs had no doubt that the actions by White and Kinman saved his life. Combs and his patrol gathered a "vast amount of information concerning the number and kind of enemy troops and their positions."[51]

That same evening, Private Norb Studelska started back from his Company D mortar squad's dug in position to the company command post to get supplies. "After walking away from our area about fifty yards, one of the heaviest barrages that I ever experienced came down on the entire area and lasted for what seemed like about a half hour. I was away from my foxhole and had no protection from shrapnel whizzing past my ears and ground bursts a few yards away, except the flatness of my body lying face down on the ground. I think prayers alone saved me. The barrage lasted until dark and then lifted.

"I skipped the supplies and hurried back to my area where I found my squad leader, [Sergeant Bob] Lenell, and his foxhole buddy, [Private Jodie L.] Parsons, the victims of a tree burst above their hole. Lenell had bad knee wounds and Parsons' legs were dangling from his upper thighs. Bob was clawing the sides of the hole and was in semi-shock. I pulled him out and soon Sergeant [Charles] Bray was taking roll, trying to figure out who got hit. By then, it was pitch-dark. We put Bob on an old shed door and the medic, [Technician Fifth Grade Robert L.] Bob Ebert, hauled him away. We did the same for Parsons, who was unconscious and was dead by the time he got to the medics at the aid station."[52]

At 11:00 p.m. that night, the 508th was relieved and trucked to a rest area at Nijmegen, where the troopers were able to take showers and get much needed sleep. On November 2, the regiment returned to the same positions it had defended north of Bemmel, where it again relieved elements of the 231st Brigade of the 50th Infantry Division.

On November 10, Canadian Army forces relieved the 82nd Airborne Division, which was trucked to the Rheims, France area for rest and refitting. The regiment had suffered far fewer casualties during the Holland campaign as compared to Normandy. It reported the following casualties at the end of the campaign: 131 killed in action, 15 died of wounds, 0 died of injuries, 389 wounded in action, 80 injured in action, and 66 missing in action. Most of those reported as missing in action were later reported to be prisoners of war.

When the regiment pulled out, Major Dave Thomas, the regimental surgeon, took along a barrel of wine that had been liberated while at Bemmel. "When we rotated back to Nijmegen on the way to France, we put the wine in a trailer, hitched to the ambulance. The ambulance was driven by a corporal who had been relieved as a squad leader because he had gotten just a little too goosey. On our way to Nijmegen, we had to cross the Nijmegen highway bridge. Well, as would be expected, the Germans were shelling the bridge. When the bridge was hit, the engineers would run out, put up a Bailey bridge to cover the damage, and effect repairs. You had to cross over these repairs slowly to go on about your business. Well, this goosey ambulance driver hit the bridge repairs a little too rapidly and disconnected the trailer. I had him stop, backed him up, and re-hitched the trailer. I then carefully eased him over the Bailey bridge repaired section, and proceeded on to Nijmegen. The wine was valuable stuff. It was good for swapping. With it, you could obtain anything you wanted, or needed, or thought you needed."[53]

Private Norb Studelska, with Company D, was very happy when he was told the division was being relieved. "The entire regiment pulled back to the city of Nijmegen and the next day walked twenty-two miles back to the village of Oss, Holland to get transport to our next training and reorganization area, Camp Sissonne. During the march, we passed English troops moving in the opposite direction toward the front. One smart alec English soldier made a remark about our reason for leaving by asking, 'Is it too rough up there for you Yanks?'

"Our machine gunner, [Private First Class Charles] Hayden, replied that we were moving back 'to set up roadblocks to keep you damn Limeys from retreating.'

"After that, we finished the trip to Sissonne in the back of top-heavy English lorries. As we were moving across the French countryside gazing out the backs of the canvas enclosed trucks, the lorry directly behind us flipped over on its side while making a sharp curve. We didn't think much about it until after we learned that our buddy, [Private First Class Henry H.] Chan [a platoon medic], received a broken neck and died during the accident."[54]

The 508th was quartered in French army barracks at Sissonne. To Private Norb Studelska and others, it was like heaven compared to the conditions in combat. "I viewed this as a very nice spot, where we received replacements (our squad got [Privates George E.] Goodgion and [Earnest L.] Semrad to replace Lenell and Parsons), did a lot of heavy training for the next mission, and had some fun hiking around the area on weekends and during time off. The village of Sissonne didn't offer much in the way of recreation, although some of the guys would go there and get drunk on the local booze and wine. I preferred the quiet outdoor life. Some troopers were given week long passes to Paris and back to England. The best I got was German prison guard duty to Rheims (site of a great cathedral), France for a day. The French barracks were fine and still had Germans murals on the hall walls. The food was OK. Most of all, we enjoyed the respite from combat, with showers and a bed to sleep in—no foxholes—for a home away from home."[55]

When the regiment left Holland, several courageous young Dutchmen accompanied it to Camp Sissonne. One of them, twenty year old Agardus M. "Gas" Leegsma, had stayed with Company G from the morning of September 18 and had fought as a member of the company, using weapons, ammunition, and equipment of wounded and dead troopers. After arriving at Camp Sissonne, Lieutenant Bill Call, the platoon leader of the 2nd Platoon of Company G, tried to get proper clothing and equipment for Leegsma. "'Gas' Leegsma was a giant, about six feet eleven, and he weighed about 240-245 pounds. He came with our company and he went with us to Sissonne and he became a part of G Company. So I was down there helping the supply sergeant issue stuff. He came down there and he said, 'Sergeant, have you got my [jump] boots yet?' He was wearing his own shoes, they didn't have boots big enough. Evidently they had told him they had ordered his boots a long time ago.

"The sergeant said, 'You know, Gas, they haven't come in yet.'

"He said, 'What the hell kind of an outfit are you running here?'"[56]

After arriving at Camp Sissonne, passes were issued to the troopers to visit Rheims and Paris. When he received his pass, Private First Class Jim Allardyce, with Company B, decided to visit Rheims. "The city of Rheims was interesting. It was the first large French city I had seen and it had the famous Rheims cathedral. It still had abandoned German artillery and knocked out trucks and tanks in the streets. The second or third night of the leaves to Rheims, the 82nd and 101st men got into a big fight. They smashed up some bars and burned some houses of ill repute. That ended our passes to Rheims for awhile.

"The first Thanksgiving after Holland was memorable. We had the usual lavish U.S. Army turkey with all the trimmings, but also a British rum ration—a treat. The problem was that the rum was served at the head of the chow line. The half canteen cup of rum had to be downed if you wanted a full cup of coffee at the end of the line. Some took only rum, some dumped theirs into a buddy's, and some chug-a-lugged the rum to make room for coffee. It ended up a mad house in the mess hall—fights, thrown food, and tipsy drunks all over the place."[57]

Major Dave Thomas, the regimental surgeon, even had one of his medics get into trouble. "I had a soldier by the name of [Edward L.] Ed Montgomery, staff sergeant. He was the leader of the 2nd Battalion medics and he was an excellent man. Well, Ed went into the town of Rheims, got into a fight with an Army Air Corps lieutenant in a bistro, and decked the lieutenant. This was not a good thing for an enlisted man to do.

"I heard about the fight the first thing the following morning, so I called Sergeant Ed Montgomery into my office and quizzed him about the fight.

"He said, 'Yes sir, that's what happened.' He also said that he was sorry, but that 'the lieutenant had it coming.'

"I said, 'Well, sit down, sergeant.' He sat. I then said, 'Get up, private. I want you to know that I just saved you from a general court martial. Am I going to expect any further troubles out of you?'

"He said, 'Oh, no sir, no sir.' As fast as I could, I promoted Ed back up the ranks, because he was a good man.

"Also while at Camp Sissonne, the 508th had a practice jump. Included in the jump manifest were seven soldiers who had gotten into the outfit by being thrown out of an airplane a couple of times in England. They had done well in Holland, but when the practice jump came along, these seven 'shake and bake' paratroopers refused to jump. A jump refusal mandated a general court martial.

"I happened to be sitting on the court martial board. These seven guys, by dictum of General Jimmy Gavin, were supposed to receive a dishonorable discharge and get thrown into the can at Fort Leavenworth Disciplinary Barracks.

"At this time however, we were having difficulty getting replacements for infantry units. So, I made the pitch about how infantry units were getting infantrymen wherever they could, to include using medics as infantry. I further indicated that there was no point in taking these seven men, all of whom had performed well in combat, and sending them off to Leavenworth—just because Jimmy Gavin said by dictum, that was what was supposed to happen. I proposed that we strip these seven men of their jump wings, take their jump boots, and put them back into the Repo-Depot. Let them go back to war as line infantry.

"The court bought my proposal, so that is what we did. The next day, old General Jimmy Gavin appointed a new general court. However, I am sure that what we did was totally the right thing to do."[58]

A U.S. Army general hospital was located near Camp Sissonne. One evening Captain James Dietrich got into a scuffle with a warrant officer over a nurse. Captain Woodrow Millsaps, who was with him, intervened to break the two men apart. "I came in to help Jimmy, and the warrant officer turned on me, hitting me in the face, and almost tore my nose off. The next blow caught me in the eyes and the third or fourth caught me in the mouth...

"The next morning I found it difficult to shave. The warrant officer had left his mark on my face. My eyes were almost swollen shut. I had bruises all over my face and my lips were bruised.

"[Lieutenant Lee] Frigo was my company executive officer. He took one look at me and said, 'Man, what have you been into?'

"I told him about Captain Dietrich and me running into the warrant officer the night before. He reminded me that I had to speak to the company at 09:00 hours, before the company took off for Paris on pass and he said he would talk to the company for me.

"I told him, 'No, I will face the company, for I will have to face up to it sometime in the near future and I would just as well do it now as later.' Then he offered to lend me his sunglasses and again I said, 'No thank you. I must take it like a soldier and face the music.' At 09:00 hours sharp, I stepped in front of the company to begin my little speech. The company was quiet, but I could tell they were ready to break out in a big laugh. I told them they were American ambassadors in uniform, representing the American people. Whatever they did, good or bad, would be a reflection on our people back home. I told them I would be most appreciative if they would conduct themselves in a favorable manner. I told them to take one look at me if they didn't believe crime didn't pay. At that, they broke out in a roar of laughter. I told them I had stepped in to break up a fight and had gotten the worst of it. About two-thirds of the company took off for Paris on a three day pass and all returned without any reported incidents.

"More trouble came later in the day when the division commander, Major General James Gavin, sent a message through the regiment commander, Colonel Lindquist, stating that he wanted to see Captain Millsaps and Captain Dietrich in his office about a delinquent report (DR) that he had just received on us. We went straight to the division headquarters to see General Gavin. I met Captain Dietrich at the office before going in. Captain Dietrich didn't have a scratch on him. I was the one showing signs of battle. Dietrich was the first one to see the general, and when he came out of the office, I asked Dietrich what the verdict was.

"He only pointed toward the door and said, 'The general is waiting to see you.' That didn't help matters much as far as I was concerned, but I went on in to see the general. He was straightening out some papers on his desk when I made my appearance before him. He looked up when I entered and a big grin came across his face. He immediately returned to his paperwork until he thought he had control of himself. When he looked at me again, he couldn't hold it any longer. He broke out in a big laugh, got up from his desk, and came around to where I was standing.

"He said, 'Let me look at you, for I haven't seen anything like this in a long time.' After the big laugh, the general gained control of himself and asked me what had happened. I told him the truth about the encounter we had with the warrant officer and that I had come out the loser in the struggle. He said he would dismiss the incident if I would promise that I would behave myself and stay out of trouble in the future. From my looks, he thought that I had received punishment enough already."[59]

On Friday morning December 15, Captain Millsaps was placed in charge of a truck convoy transporting about 350 troopers from the regiment to Paris. "We arrived in Paris on a Friday and after assigning rooms and beds to the soldiers, I turned them loose on the town. We were supposed to truck out of Paris on a Sunday night. We were to assemble at a motor pool that was operated by MPs in the city."[60]

ON SATURDAY, DECEMBER 16, the German Fifth Panzer and Sixth SS Panzer Armies, supported by the Seventh Army on the left flank, some twenty-five divisions in all, attacked four U.S. Army divisions along the thinly held American front in the Ardennes forest of eastern Belgium and Luxembourg. The objectives of the offensive were the capture of the port at Antwerp, Belgium to deny its use to the Allies, which were constrained by supply problems, and the encirclement and subsequent destruction of the 21st Army Group north of the breakthrough. Hitler hoped that this would either force the western Allies to negotiate peace with Germany on favorable terms, or disrupt them long enough to allow him to transfer the bulk of his combat power from the western front to deal with the Soviet Red Army closing in on the German border to the east.

The massive German offensive struck with almost total surprise, breaking through the American lines in several places along a forty-seven mile front. The only strategic reserves on the continent of Europe available to SHAEF were the 82nd and 101st Airborne Divisions, both having been relieved from fighting in Holland in November. Both divisions were being brought up to the authorized strength by newly arrived replacements.

By the early afternoon of December 16, the decision was made at Allied headquarters to alert both divisions for movement to Belgium to counter the German thrust. Since many of the troopers of both divisions were away at Paris, Rheims, and other cities, efforts were begun to recall them and return them to their respective encampments.

IN PARIS ON THE AFTERNOON OF DECEMBER 16, Captain Millsaps and the troopers he had brought with him to the city began to assemble for the early return to Camp Sissonne. "Saturday afternoon, MPs drove through the city with loudspeakers (bullhorns) announcing for all soldiers to report back to their units. I will never forget the scene at the motor pool when the soldiers began to assemble. Some arrived at the motor pool in taxis. Some came on two passenger bicycles with their girlfriend doing the pedaling and soldiers riding behind waving bottles of champagne. Some of the French girls were drunker than the soldiers and wanted to come along. I was only short five or six soldiers when we pulled out to return to our unit about 8:00 p.m. We arrived back at the unit early the next morning (Sunday)."[61]

CHAPTER 14

"A BEAUTIFUL DEFENSIVE POSITION"

On the evening of December 17, Major General Jim Gavin, the commanding officer of the 82nd Airborne Division, was also the acting commander of the XVIII Airborne Corps while Major General Matthew Ridgway was in England. "At about 19:30 hours, while at dinner with the staff, I received a phone call from Colonel [Ralph P.] Eaton, chief of staff, XVIII Corps (Airborne). He stated that he had just received a call from SHAEF to the effect that the situation on the front to the east appeared to be critical; that the airborne divisions were to be prepared to move twenty-four hours after daylight the following day; that the corps commander, General Ridgway, was in England and could not be contacted immediately. I instructed Colonel Eaton to issue orders to the commanding general of the 101st Airborne Division, Brigadier General [Anthony C. "Tony"] McAuliffe, to prepare immediately for movement in accordance with the SHAEF estimate, twenty-four hours after daylight. I assembled my staff in the division war room at 20:00 hours. I had listened to a radio news broadcast at 18:00 hours and was aware of the fact that a German penetration was being made in the direction of St.-Vith.

"The division was ready for a quick move, since, because of our past and usual quick commitments, we have maintained a high degree of readiness as a standard operating procedure. A basic load of ammunition was in the hands of each regiment, complete in all aspects. Two K-rations and two D-rations for the division were at hand and could be distributed in a matter of hours. All weapons, uniforms, and equipment were up to an operating standard. The staff assembled at 20:00 hours when the initial directive was issued that started their planning.

"I called General [Francis A.] March [82nd Airborne Division artillery commander] at Camp Suippes at about 19:45 hours, giving him the situation and alerting him for the move. Unit commanders at Camp Sissonne were assembled with the staff in the war room at 21:00 hours, when the situation was outlined to them, and a tentative plan for the movement to Bastogne issued. At about 21:30 hours, I received a call from the chief of staff, XVIII Corps (Airborne), who said that corps had orders to move without delay in the direction of Bastogne where further orders would be received. He also said that corps was to be attached to the First United States Army. After further discussion I decided that the 82nd

Airborne Division would move approximately one hour after daylight and move in the direction of Bastogne. The 101st Airborne Division was to move at 14:00 hours, 18 December, also in the direction of Bastogne. At that time, Oise Base Section was devoting all its efforts to pulling in all transportation off the roads to provide the necessary lift for both divisions.

"At 23:30, I left with my G-1, Lieutenant Colonel Alfred Ireland, and my aide, Captain Hugo V. Olson, for the command post of the First United States Army at Spa. The drive was very difficult due to the general conditions of the roads, rain, and fog, and the absence of bridges on a number of important highways."[1]

At 10:00 p.m. on December 17, Major John Medusky, the regimental S-3 (plans and operations staff officer), received the alert for movement of the 508th the next morning. Despite having received replacements and troopers returning from hospitals, Medusky knew the regiment was still below its authorized strength. "The regimental strength at the start of the move was only 141 officers and 1,944 enlisted men, as compared with the normal T/O strength of 2,375. The three battalions were at approximately equal strength, since it is regimental policy to redistribute personnel after an operation and when reinforcements arrive."[2]

Sergeant Jim Kurz, a squad leader with Company B, had been wounded in Holland, evacuated to England for treatment, and had departed Nottingham, England on December 10 to rejoin his unit, arriving at Sissonne at 4:30 a.m. on December 18. "At 5:00 a.m., I arrived at Company B headquarters and reported to 1st Sergeant James Smith. I told him that the doctor had said I would need to rest for two more weeks. Smith said the Germans had broken through our front line in the Ardennes and we were headed for Belgium. He said I could get my rest on the front line. The company was going to pull out in one hour, so I would have to draw a rifle and a blanket. Smith told me to get a move on. This was my welcome back from the hospital. I found my old squad. Sergeant [Robert J.] Savage had taken my place as squad leader, so I would be a spare sergeant."[3]

With troopers coming back from passes, wounded coming back from hospitals, and many new replacements, 1st Sergeant Robert Kolterman took a final headcount as G Company's troopers climbed aboard three of the eleven 10-ton, semi truck-trailers transporting the 3rd Battalion. "Company G loaded 146 troopers as we moved out."[4]

Lieutenant Bill Call was the platoon leader of the 2nd Platoon of Company G. "I think you could put about sixty or seventy guys in those trucks. It was snowing to beat hell. We had a canvas [tarp] over the top of us."[5]

At 11:00 a.m. on December 18, the 508th departed Camp Sissonne. Private First Class Allan H. Stein, a bazooka gunner with Company F, had recently received a package from home containing four cartons of cigarettes. "Where the hell do you put four cartons of cigarettes with the other stuff we had? Naturally, I somehow lost my gas mask. The container was a very nice place for all those little oddities one takes with one.

"We loaded up in open bodied trucks and with full speed ahead, headed for a place called the Ardennes. It was a miserable, cold trip. We passed through towns where already the people were on the move."[6]

Lieutenant Colonel Louis Mendez rode in a jeep at the head of the 3rd Battalion convoy as it drove toward Belgium. "The battalion, in convoy crossed the Meuse River at Sedan, France and moved northeast towards Bastogne,

Belgium. Seven miles west of Bastogne, the convoy was flagged at a crossroad by Captain [Chet] C. R. Graham of the 508th Parachute Infantry. He directed the convoy up the road north of Bastogne to Houffalize where an 82nd Airborne Division MP informed me that I was to proceed to Werbomont, Belgium."[7] The 508th began arriving at Werbomont at 4:45 a.m. on December 19, and closed in its assembly area by 6:00 a.m. in a wooded area astride the highway south of the town, where it dug in.

Private First Class Bill Windom, with Company B, stretched out on the ground and went to sleep near his newly dug slit trench. "In the morning a seven year old boy came out of his farmhouse with two buckets of hot coffee, which he proceeded to pour into our willing canteen cups."[8]

The regiment dug defensive positions in the southeast quadrant of the intersection at Werbomont of the north–south road from Houffalize and the east–west road to Trois Ponts. The 3rd Battalion established a roadblock to the south on the road from Houffalize, north of the hamlet of Champ-de-Harre, consisting of a rifle squad with a light machine gun, plus three bazooka teams. Three antitank guns were positioned on the high ground to the east, covering the highway.

Prior to leaving Camp Sissonne, the regiment had not had an opportunity to take an inventory of its crew served weapons. After arriving at Werbomont, the units within the regiment reported those numbers and they were totaled. There were three water cooled .30-caliber heavy machine guns, ninety-four air cooled .30-caliber light machine guns, fifteen 81mm mortars, and twenty-seven 60mm mortars, which gave the regiment almost its full complement of crew served weapons.

At 10:00 a.m. that morning, Lieutenant Colonel Mendez received an order from regimental headquarters "to send H Company to Bra to support a platoon of tank destroyers in holding the crossroads. Upon receipt of this order from Colonel Roy E. Lindquist, commanding officer of the 508th Parachute Infantry, I immediately sent a patrol to reconnoiter the road to H Company's position. At 13:30, H Company moved out on foot cross country, moving by compass toward their new position. H Company was in position on the high ground overlooking the crossroads at 14:40. H Company commander, Lieutenant Louis Toth, placed his platoons in the following defensive positions: one platoon on the high ground at (584941) [west of, and overlooking the north–south highway from Lierneux to Hâbièmont], one platoon at (587936) [the bridge over the Lienne River on the road running east from Bra], and one platoon in reserve at (580936) [just east of Bra]. The company CP was at (578934) [east end of the town of Bra]. The defensive position was set up facing east and southeast to control a bridge over the Lienne River and the north-south and east–west highway crossing at (587938). Four tank destroyers were set up to support H Company in its defensive position. The battalion kept in contact by radio and by a motorized patrol, which used the roads south from Werbomont to the crossroads."[9]

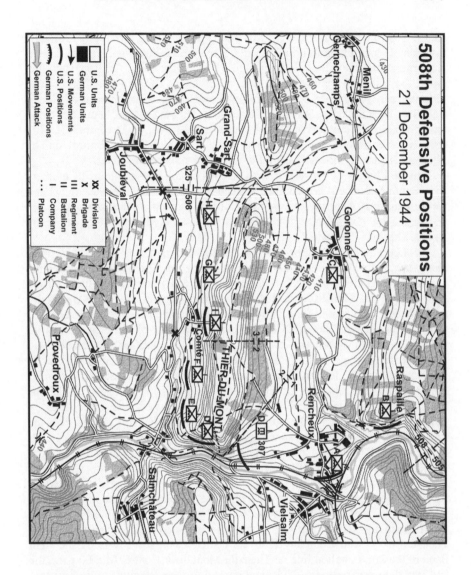

508th Defensive Positions
21 December 1944

At 6:00 p.m. on December 19, the 508th, less Company H, received orders to move east to establish defensive positions in the hills near Chevron, east of Werbomont. The 3rd Battalion, less Company H, was positioned in the vicinity of Oufny in division reserve.

At 4:30 p.m. the following day, the regiment was alerted for a move by truck southeast to occupy a sector along with west bank of the Salm River across from Vielsalm and extending west along the Thier-du-Mont ridge, located south of the village of Goronne. At 6:30 p.m., Company H began a ten mile march to secure Goronne prior to the arrival of the regiment. Upon arriving at Goronne, Company H found it unoccupied. At 8:00 p.m., the 1st Battalion; Battery B, 80th Airborne Antiaircraft Battalion; and the 319th Glider Field Artillery Battalion moved by truck, arriving at 11:50 p.m. at Goronne. The 2nd Battalion convoy followed, arriving at 5:28 a.m. the following morning. The remainder of the 3rd Battalion, because of a shortage of transport, departed at 3:50 a.m., marching through the night and arriving at Goronne at 9:30 a.m. on December 21. The regiment then moved south and east to establish defensive positions on the Their-du-Mont ridgeline and along the west bank of the Salm River.

Private Charles A. Powell, Jr. was a replacement who had joined Company D at Camp Sissonne. "We climbed a steep mile long hill [Their-du-Mont] and we were hurting. After waiting, we went halfway down the other side and dug in and slept. The next morning, we moved down a hundred yards more and really dug in. That was the front."[10]

By 8:00 a.m. on December 21, the 1st and 2nd Battalions were in position along the Salm River and the southern slope of Their-du-Mont ridgeline respectively. The 508th's defensive sector extended from the left flank on the west bank of the Salm River at Raspaille, where it tied in with the 505th, south to Rencheux, then south to the Thier-du-Mont ridgeline and west to Grand-Sart, where it tied in with the 325th Glider Infantry, a front of some five thousand yards. The 508th sector was the farthest south and east of the entire 82nd Airborne Division, protruding into the northern shoulder of the bulge created by the penetration of German forces. East of Vielsalm, the U.S. 7th Armored Division and the remnants of the U.S. 28th and 106th Infantry Divisions, occupying a salient around St.-Vith, were being attacked from three sides by powerful German forces. The only supply routes and lines of retreat were the roads through Vielsalm and Salmchâteau across the Salm River.

Company B defended the regiment's left flank on the Salm River from Raspaille to just north of Rencheux. Company C constituted the regimental reserve and was positioned at Goronne. Company A was assigned the sector at Rencheux across the Salm River from the town of Vielsalm. The area south of Rencheux was defended by Company D, 307th Airborne Engineer Battalion, where it tied in with Company D, which was positioned on the eastern end of the Their-du-Mont, with Company E in the center. Company F was on the right flank of the 2nd Battalion line on Their-du-Mont, near Comté. At 6:00 p.m., the 2nd Battalion was passed to divisional control to form the division reserve, but remained in its positions on the eastern half of Their-du-Mont. Company I was positioned to the west of Comté, tying in with Company G on its right. Company H held the regiment's right flank east of Grand-Sart, which was defended by the 325th Glider Infantry Regiment. The 2nd and 3rd Battalion's 81mm mortars were set up near the top of the northern slope of the ridge. To the south of Thier-du-Mont, an outpost line was established two thousand yards south of the main line of resistance.

Company H established a roadblock consisting of a platoon and a 57mm antitank gun on the highway that ran west from Salmchâteau to Baraque-de-Fraiture at the intersection with a road that ran north to Grand-Sart. Company I set up a roadblock to the east at the intersection of the highway and a road that ran north to Comté. Two antitank guns were positioned at Comté to fire to the southeast to cover the roadblock. Minefields were laid on the roads leading to Salmchâteau and Comté, and around the roadblocks. Patrols were dispatched south to the villages of Bodigny, Petit Langlir, Joubieval, and Ottré.

In the 1st Battalion sector on the left flank, Captain Woodrow Millsaps deployed Company B in positions that afforded good fields of fire. "Company B set up a defense position on the west bank of the Salm River, fifty yards or so behind a steep bluff, overlooking the river. To reach our lines, the Germans would have to wade the river, climb the bluff, and expose themselves out in the open for fifty yards before they made contact with my company. We dug in and waited."[11]

As the company commander's radio operator, Technician Fifth Grade Walter Barrett accompanied him during the inspection of the Company B positions. "Our defense positions had been selected in order to be able to fire from our foxholes down to the riverbank. We found that if we set machine guns to fire tracer ammunition four or five feet above the ground, we could set another machine gun to fire regular ammunition at grazing height. The Germans would see the tracer bullets and think they could crawl underneath. Of course, then our grazing fire would kill them."[12]

After Company B dug in, Sergeant Jim Kurz learned about a supply dump that had been discovered nearby. "The 106th Infantry Division had had its headquarters on the hill right behind our positions. When they pulled out, they had left most of their food supply. We took over the food and were eating like kings. We knew it wouldn't last, but we were going to enjoy it while it did."[13]

Company A's position along the Salm River at Rencheux was the most exposed position of the division's perimeter. It was subject to attack from both the east and south. Captain Adams made a careful study of the terrain before deploying his company. "The Salm River is actually a small stream about ten feet wide, running from south to north. Under ordinary circumstances this would not be considered much of a barrier. However, at this point of the country, the current was very swift and had cut a gorge about eight feet deep, thus being unfordable to both vehicles and foot soldiers.

"Two railroad bridges and a wooden road bridge were the only means of crossing. On the eastern side of the river and immediately to the north of the road crossing, the terrain was heavily wooded. The ground rose very gradually for about two hundred yards, and then very sharply. In Vielsalm, there were buildings on a cliff overlooking the river. These were about fifty to seventy-five feet above the streambed. On the west side of the river a railroad ran parallel to the stream. Beyond it, the ground rose sharply to a height of one hundred feet, for a stretch of about four hundred yards.

"The platoons were assigned their defensive positions—the 1st Platoon on the right, the 3rd Platoon on the left, and the 2nd Platoon in reserve. In assigning these positions, I kept two things in mind. First, there would be no withdrawal. Consequently, I disregarded any consideration as to routes for this. I reasoned that resupply and the feeding of the platoons could be accomplished at night under cover of darkness. Secondly, my mission was to keep the enemy from crossing the Salm River. It was therefore necessary in some instances to sacrifice fields of fire for observation of the opposite bank of the Salm.

"The 3rd Platoon was to maintain contact with B Company. There was a gap of about three hundred yards between the two companies. However, it was open ground, and could easily be covered by fire in the daytime and patrols at night. Two squads of the 3rd Platoon were placed on the slight knoll located in the triangle formed by the railroads. Once contact had been made with the Germans, it would be impossible to move to or from this knoll in the daytime. However, it was the only site which could command the banks of the river immediately to the north of the road bridge.

"The 1st Platoon on the right was in somewhat the same plight as the 3rd [Platoon]. They were located on the forward slopes of a hill, completely devoid of any cover or concealment.

"The 2nd Platoon in reserve was astride the road. Because of the numerous houses, it was necessary to have them well forward. At the most, they were only fifty yards behind the two front platoons."[14]

Captain Adams immediately put his men to work organizing and improving the company's defensive positions. "Individual foxholes were dug, and overhead cover was constructed, so that each one was virtually a fortress. Wire was laid to all positions. Each platoon was equipped with German field telephones, which had been secured in previous campaigns. Officers and noncommissioned officers became acquainted with the replacements they had received four days previously.

"Some of the more serious shortages in equipment, such as overcoats, shoes, and machine gun tripods, were made up from the meager supplies that the division had managed to secure. Shortages of supply were also supplemented by equipment thrown away by retreating American forces. Footwear more and more became an item of importance. Snow followed by rain had created a slush, which soon penetrated the parachute boots everyone was wearing.

"It did not take the men long to locate a supply dump of the 106th Division containing overshoes. Requests were made to have these issued, but were refused. By various means, the men of A Company managed to secure overshoes nevertheless."[15]

The 508th began patrolling to its front as far as three thousand yards to detect the approach of enemy forces and maintained contact patrols with the

505th Parachute Infantry and the 325th Glider Infantry on the regiment's flanks. On December 21, Corporal Robert G. Mangers, with the 3rd Battalion S-2 section, led a motorized patrol to reconnoiter south of the regiment's line. His patrol consisted of Corporal Marshall A. Goldstein, who spoke fluent French; Private Karl Behringer, who spoke German; Private John L. Bandelin; and Private Robert C. Dooley, the jeep driver. The patrol, equipped with an SCR 300 radio, left at 10:00 a.m., and at 1:30 p.m., reported there were no enemy troops in the village of Provedroux. However, the jeep became stuck in the mud, so Corporal Mangers proceed to Petit Langlir on foot, while Dooley and the others worked on getting it extricated. At 6:00 p.m., Corporal Mangers reported that the hamlets of Petit Langlir and Ottré, which were south of Grand-Sart on the regiment's right flank, were clear of enemy. It was dark by this time and Mangers returned to the site of the stuck jeep and radioed that he would try to pull it out the next morning, using a horse from a nearby farm.

The following day, December 22, Captain Adams was informed that the 7th Armored Division, plus elements of the 28th and 106th Infantry Divisions, and Combat Command B of the 9th Armored Division defending the St.-Vith pocket would begin withdrawing to the west side of the Salm River passing through the 508th sector. "A platoon from Company D, 307th Engineers, prepared the three bridges in front of A Company for demolition. A small detachment was left to supervise their destruction. A Company was given the responsibility of seeing that this was accomplished. I instructed the 2nd Platoon leader [Lieutenant George Lamm] to place a squad of men as outposts at the approaches to the bridges. During daylight, these were to be well forward, but at night the platoon leader was to pull them in, so that they would not be cut off.

"During the 22nd and 23rd of December, there was a constant flow of traffic from the front. I was greatly concerned about the effect it would have on the morale of the men to see everyone taking off to the rear, knowing that they themselves were to stay. I was especially concerned that the men might become infected with the state of terror of the majority of these retreating forces. It was no uncommon occurrence to see groups of ten and twenty men, who had thrown all their arms away in order that they might travel faster. I put out the order that none of my men would be allowed to speak to any of these troops, and they would not be allowed to stop in the A Company area. My fear, however, was unfounded."[16]

Corporal Robert Mangers, with the 3rd Battalion S-2 section, reported on December 22, that despite working all morning, they had been unable to free the jeep that had been stuck in deep mud. Mangers indicated that their effort had been interrupted by an enemy patrol from an SS panzer division moving north into the village of Ottré. Mangers directed artillery fire on the enemy patrol and then decided to leave the jeep and report on the enemy movements and strength.

By 3:00 p.m., Mangers reported a large German column moving north through Petit Langlir toward Ottré. He also observed German engineers reinforcing a bridge between Langlir and Provedroux to support the weight of armored vehicles and directed artillery fire on the bridge, temporarily halting the German advance. At 4:45 p.m., Mangers sent the other members of the patrol back to the 508th lines and he kept the radio and stayed to continue to observe and report enemy activity.

By the morning of December 23, Corporal Mangers was alone five miles in front of the 508th lines, lying hidden with an SCR 300 radio, less than ten yards from a road being used by German troops moving north. Corporal Mangers was so close that he was able to identify the troops by their uniforms as panzer grenadiers of the 2nd SS Panzer Division and reported that the Germans were using American halftracks and jeeps. Mangers then directed an artillery barrage on German armored vehicles and a command post located in a house along the road. The 319th Glider Field Artillery Battalion fired forty-six rounds of 75mm high explosive ammunition at the targets. The battalion fired for the first time, the new secret POZIT artillery shells, which used a variable fuse and a small radar transmitter in the nose of the shell to detect when the shell was within the proximity of the target and detonate the shell, delivering a far more accurate and deadly airburst than any ordnance previously used.

With his radio batteries almost drained of power, Mangers was ordered to destroy the radio and return to the 508th line. He waited until that night, then destroyed the radio, and wearing a German snow cape, fell in with the enemy column moving north. That night, he was discovered and taken prisoner. Corporal Mangers was later awarded the Silver Star for his courageous actions to disrupt the advance of the 2nd SS Panzer Division on December 22 and 23.

At Rencheux, Captain Jonathan Adams, commanding Company A, received a warning to prepare for contact with German forces. "On the morning of the 23rd, I was told that the 7th Armored Division was withdrawing its screening forces. The northern railway bridge would be blown at 15:00 hours, and the other two bridges would be destroyed at 22:00 hours, or immediately after all of the troops of the 7th had been withdrawn—whichever was earlier. The company was alerted; especially the outposts of the 2nd Platoon, whose leader [Lieutenant George Lamm] made a special point of checking the demolition charges."[17]

On the morning of December 23, Sergeant Jim Kurz, with Company B, sat in his foxhole watching Allied and German fighter aircraft engage in dogfights overhead. "My lieutenant came up and told me to get twelve men together. I was to relieve the roadblock at the bridge over the Salm River, where the 7th Armored Division and the 106th Infantry Division were pulling back from the east. I took my men to the roadblock at the bridge that crossed the Salm River near Vielsalm.

"The 7th Armored Division was coming through the roadblock with tanks. While stationed in the States, the 508th and the 7th Armored had had many fights while on leave in Georgia. However, here things were different. The 7th Armored had done a great job holding up the Germans at St.-Vith. As some of the tanks were passing by, one of the tankers yelled over to me, 'You will never stop the Germans with that roadblock.'

"We had two bazookas, two machine guns, and eight riflemen. I yelled back, 'If we don't stop the Germans, you'd better take off to Paris. Then, both of us smiled."[18]

That afternoon, Lieutenant Colonel Louis Mendez learned that the screening force holding open the east-west highway through Salmchâteau would withdraw through his 3rd Battalion sector that night. "At 17:00 on the 23rd, the battalion CP was informed that one hundred vehicles of the 106th Infantry Division and the 7th Armored Division were pulling through our lines. The roadblocks were warned and the mines were removed to the sides of the roads."[19]

That night at Salmchâteau, Private Ralph Gilson, with Company D, 307th Airborne Engineer Battalion, watched the last of the exhausted survivors of the fighting around St.-Vith pulling back through the 82nd Airborne Division's lines. "Seeing the troops of the 28th and 106th Divisions coming out of there was a very moving scene. This was one of the eeriest and scariest nights I can remember. Our company blew bridges and set up roadblocks as the troops in our section withdrew."[20]

Late that night, Lieutenant Colonel Mendez oversaw the withdrawal through the 3rd Battalion positions. "At 01:00 on the 24th, the movement of the vehicles through our lines began. Over forty vehicles and three hundred men pulled back through our main line of resistance. Elements of five American units were identified in this group."[21]

Later that night, after the engineers blew the bridge at Salmchâteau, the 2nd SS Panzer Division's Kampfgruppe Krag, which was advancing north, captured the town. This powerful force consisted of SS Panzer Aufklärungs Abteilung 2 (armored reconnaissance battalion); SS Sturmgeschutz Abteilung 2 (assault gun battalion); Kompanie 1, SS Panzer Pioniere Bataillon 2 (engineer battalion); and Batterie 1, SS Panzer Artillerie Regiment 2 (armored artillery battery).

Salmchâteau lay on the west side of the Salm River, south of Rencheux and Vielsalm. The capture of this town opened the way for an enemy attack north along the west bank of the river to seize Rencheux and open the way for the 9th SS Panzer Division driving west toward the river. Company A was in danger of attacks from the south and east by elements of those two elite divisions. If the 2nd and the 9th SS Panzer Divisions broke through Company A at Rencheux, the two divisions could attack north and roll up the 82nd Airborne Division's Salm River defensive line and its southern flank.

This could potentially result in the destruction of the division and a possible breakthrough to the 1st SS Panzer Division's Kampfgruppe Peiper, which was trapped to the north at La Gleize.

At Rencheux on the afternoon of December 23, as the last of the St.-Vith defenders were crossing the Salm River bridges at Vielsalm, Captain Adams supervised the demolition of the first of the three bridges. "At 15:00 hours the railroad bridge was blown as planned. Information was received at about the same time that the 3rd Battalion had made contact with the enemy at Salmchâteau, while the withdrawal of the 7th Armored Division was progressing effectively in the A Company sector. At 18:00 hours in the evening, I met General [Robert W.] Hasbrouck, commander of the 7th Armored Division, near the two remaining bridges. The general said he believed all of his troops had withdrawn, but that he was not sure. He told me to withhold blowing the bridges until midnight in order to take care of any isolated groups which might still be on the other side. Since this conflicted with my orders, I contacted the battalion and got permission to have the time changed to 24:00 hours.

"Almost simultaneously, I received a call from the 1st Platoon leader that the battalion [the battered 3rd Battalion, 112th Infantry, 28th Infantry Division, which had been overrun during the first days of the Ardennes campaign] on his right had withdrawn from the positions they had been occupying. I went over to contact this battalion and found it in position a good five hundred yards behind the river line. The battalion commander explained that he wanted grazing fire for his weapons, and that this position furnished him the best possible. It is true, that he did have approximately four hundred yards of grazing fire, but about one hundred yards of the western bank were in complete defilade, thus leaving A Company with an exposed flank.

"A Company's mission was to keep the enemy from crossing the Salm, not to get grazing fire. After a short and futile argument, I saw a higher authority was needed to get any changes made. I went back to my battalion command post, and notified the battalion commander [Lieutenant Colonel Shields Warren] of the situation. Regiment was immediately notified, and the 3rd Battalion, 112th Infantry was ordered to move back into their original positions. Just at this time, firing was heard from the 2nd Platoon's outpost across the river. Consequently, the 3rd Battalion, 112th Infantry never did move forward again, and for the next forty-eight hours, A Company was operating with an exposed flank. While I had been trying to straighten out this problem, the outposts had been on alert."[22]

That evening, at one of the Company A outposts on the east side of the Salm River in Vielsalm, Sergeant Charles H. Koons heard the sound of hobnail boots approaching in the still, clear night air. "Around 9:30 p.m., we were hit by a German patrol of approximately platoon strength. We fired on them, but were forced to withdraw across the river."[23]

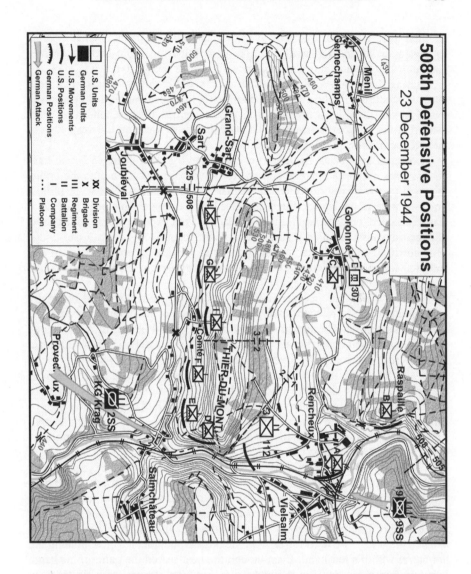

Captain Adams returned to his command post just as firing on the other side of the river erupted. "The platoon leader [of the 2nd Platoon, Lieutenant George Lamm] immediately gave the predetermined signal for the other outposts to withdraw, and started checking them back across the bridges. Some of the outposts were a little slow returning. By the time the first man was crossing the bridge the Germans had recovered from their confusion, and were almost to the edge of the river, firing across it. As Lieutenant Lamm crossed the bridge, he gave another blast on his whistle, the arranged signal for the demolition men to do their job. He then took cover behind the railroad bank. When nothing happened, he looked for, and found the demolition men who had not been in position when the action began, and were afterwards unable to reach it.

"It was then realized that a foolish and probably costly mistake had been made in preparing the bridges for demolition. No consideration had been given to the possibility of blowing them from cover. Instead, thirty second fuses were located at the bridges themselves. The Germans now were on the very edge of the river, and some had even crossed it.

"I ordered Lieutenant Lamm to get the bridges blown somehow. He, in turn, got his eight outposts together, and ordered them to rush back across the bridge followed by the demolition men. On signal the fuse lighters were to be pulled. The men were to get back to the railroad bank under cover. This plan, hasty as it was, succeeded, chiefly because the Germans did not expect such a sudden show of aggressiveness; or rather it succeeded in part, because only the railroad bridge was blown. The fuse lighter for the road bridge failed to work. Regiment and battalion called down demanding a reason for the delay, as emphatic orders had been given to blow the bridges at all costs.

"All the while, the German strength was building up. What had originally been estimated as a platoon, assumed the strength of a company; probably a reconnaissance unit. The fire of six machine guns could be heard. A tank came up, and almost approached to the abutments of the now defunct railroad bridge, from where it systematically fired at the houses just across the river.

"It was apparent that it would now take more than the fire of eight men from the 2nd Platoon to drive the Germans back. The 1st and 2nd Platoons were ordered to fire at the maximum rate, if possible at the flash of the enemy's guns. This concentrated burst caused the Germans to take cover, so enabling a small force from the 2nd Platoon to again cross the bridge, while the demolition personnel attached another fuse light."[24]

Corporal Walter Firestine, an assistant squad leader, directed his squad's machine gun to cover Lieutenant Lamm and his men as they ran across the road bridge once again. When Firestine moved the machine gun closer to the bridge to better cover the advance, his crew became casualties and the tripod of the gun was lost. Firestine picked up the machine gun and fired it from hip. When he reached the bridge, he fired it from a prone position without a tripod, holding the hot barrel with his left hand. Even though the heat seared the palm of his hand, Firestine continued providing suppressive fire until Lamm and his troopers withdrew across the bridge once again.

Watching from his command post, Captain Adams heard Lamm's whistle, then saw the covering force withdraw across the bridge. "This time the fuse exploded, but the demolition again failed to do so. Meanwhile, the 3rd Platoon was having trouble with a few Germans who had crossed the bridge on the initial assault, and were now entrenched behind some of the houses on the western bank of the stream."[25]

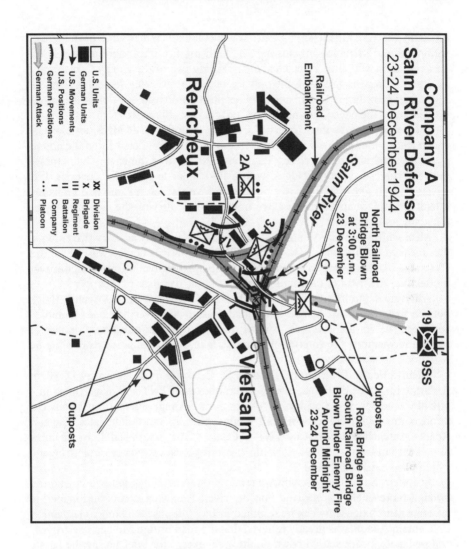

When the firing began, Lieutenant Rex Combs, the platoon leader of the 3rd Platoon, noticed one of his squad leaders who was out of his foxhole. "Sergeant [Robert] White, seeing that the enemy was preparing to attack his position under mortar and intense automatic weapons fire, moved from foxhole to foxhole, alerting the men who were down in their holes. While doing this the enemy attacked, but due to Sergeant White's alertness and disregard for himself, the enemy was driven back."[26]

It was during this enemy assault in the 3rd Platoon sector that Lieutenant Combs observed Private George P. Moskalski, an assistant gunner, take over the machine gun when his team's gunner was wounded. "When some of the enemy infiltrated and grenaded his position, he held his fire until the enemy was ten yards or less away, then dispatched them, killing two of the enemy. Mortars and automatic weapons fire were then placed on his position by the enemy, but all night long he returned all fire and held his position. Private Moskalski definitely killed nine of the enemy during this period and probably more."[27]

Lieutenant Combs then observed Corporal Murphy B. Bridges, an assistant squad leader, eliminate a threat from infiltrating SS grenadiers behind the houses along the west side of the river. "Realizing that some of the enemy had crossed the footbridge, Corporal Bridges, with a BAR man to give him covering fire, advanced well ahead of his covering fire, and with a Tommy gun and grenades, killed one and wounded at least two of the enemy, driving the rest back to the other side of the river."[28]

Meanwhile, Captain Adams heard the sound of friendly artillery fire firing in the distance behind him. "The field artillery forward observer was in the 3rd Platoon area, attempting to call for fire on the opposite bank. However, this was ineffective, and most of the rounds were lost in the darkness of the night."[29]

After the demolition again failed to blow, Private First Class Joseph J. Balek noticed that two of the troopers who had crossed the river had been wounded and were still on the east side. Without hesitation, Balek ran through a hail of automatic weapons fire to cross the bridge, then covered their retreat, while he remaining on the east side.

Meanwhile, Staff Sergeant Theodore H. Cerwood, with Company D, 307th Airborne Engineer Battalion, carried several boxes of TNT and placed them in a pile at the center of the bridge, as tracers from German automatic weapons cut through the night, crisscrossing all around him. A short time later, Captain Adams watched the boxes of TNT detonate. "They exploded it by firing a bazooka round into it. This blew up the bridge except for several stringers, which were easily destroyed."[30]

Just after the bridge was blown, Private First Class Balek jumped up and ran through more enemy fire, dived into the river. He swam across and made his way to a nearby house, where he resumed firing, killing several more Germans.

Captain Adams was greatly relieved that the road bridge had been destroyed. "Immediately, peace settled down on the area; except for brief spasmodic bursts of rifle fire, the enemy made no further moves. All during the night though, vehicles and tanks could be heard coming up into position. Early the next morning, the Germans could be heard moving wood in a lumberyard along the river, three to four hundred yards to the north of Vielsalm. There was no doubt in the minds of the A Company men that the Germans were securing this in preparation for a river crossing."[31]

Lieutenant Lamm was later awarded the Distinguished Service Cross for his extraordinary heroism and leadership during the action to demolish the bridges. Staff Sergeant Theodore Cerwood, Private First Class Joseph Balek, and Private

George Moskalski were awarded Silver Star medals for their heroic actions. Corporal Walter Firestine was killed on December 31, and never knew about the Silver Star which was posthumously awarded to him for his gallantry.

The successful withdrawal of the gallant defenders of the St.-Vith pocket— the 7th Armored Division, Combat Command B of the 9th Armored Division, the 112th Infantry Regiment of the 28th Infantry Division, and remnants of the 106th Infantry Division and 14th Cavalry Group, brought approximately fifteen thousand men and a hundred tanks into the 82nd Airborne Division's perimeter for use by General Ridgway, the commander of the XVIII Airborne Corps, to which these units were now subordinated. These forces had been in constant combat for a week and had suffered significant casualties, but would prove vital in defending a dangerous gap that existed between the right flank of the 82nd Airborne Division at Baraque de Fraiture and the left flank of the 3rd Armored Division as the 2nd SS Panzer Division drove north in an attempt to roll up the flanks of those two American divisions.

By the morning of December 23, the 82nd Airborne Division was facing elements of the 1st and 9th SS Panzer Divisions farther north along the Salm and Amblève Rivers and the 2nd SS Panzer Division and 62nd Volksgrenadier Division to the south. British Field Marshal Bernard Montgomery, in tenporary command of all Allied forces on the northern shoulder of the bulge, arrived at the XVIII Airborne Corps command post at Werbomont on December 23. Montgomery felt the 82nd Airborne Division was overextended, and there were too many gaps in the division's perimeter. Montgomery told General Ridgway that the XVIII Airborne Corps "could now withdraw with honor to itself and its units."[32] He then ordered Ridgway to withdraw the XVIII Airborne Corps to straighten the line.

Ridgway had already informed General Gavin that a withdrawal might be ordered. Accordingly, Gavin informed his staff. "Similar warning orders were given to unit commanders to be prepared to withdraw if necessary to the Trois Ponts–Erria–Manhay line. Early on December 24, therefore, they were directed to make small unit reconnaissance of the defensive positions, and sectors were allotted and missions assigned. A conference was held at Headquarters, XVIII Corps (Airborne) at 13:30 hours, December 24th, at which time orders were issued for the voluntary withdrawal to the corps defensive position. Division plans were completed and orders issued during the afternoon to effect the withdrawal starting after darkness."[33]

On the morning of December 24, Captain Henry "Hank" Le Febvre, the 2nd Battalion S-3, visited the area that was to become the battalion's new defensive position. "The battalion commander, executive officer, company commanders and I were taken to the new location and shown our positions so that we could move to them immediately upon arrival.

"After this party returned to the battalion command post, the battalion plan of withdrawal was issued. Each rifle company was to leave one platoon to occupy the present company position. This covering force was to be under the command of the company executive officer, who was to have the company's SCR 300 radio. The three platoons to be left behind, which would constitute the battalion covering force, would be under the command of Major Royal Taylor, the battalion executive officer. He would have with him the S-2, 1st Lieutenant Walter [L.] Wakefield, a radio operator, and a messenger at the covering force command post, which would be the old battalion command post. From this position he could observe the 1st Battalion positions in Rencheux and the regimental command post area in Goronne. His orders were to hold until called on the radio to withdraw. When [the covering force] did withdraw, it was to assemble at Goronne, where it would establish a delaying position. From there it was to fall back to other delaying positions in order to give the main body the maximum amount of time before being hit by the Germans. The only means of communication was to be SCR 300 radios. Each battalion left an identical covering force, and the entire force was to command of the regimental executive officer. The covering force was to withdraw at 04:00, 25 December, while the remainder of the battalion would assemble on the north slope of Thier-du-Mont ridge at 23:00, 24 December. This assembly area was near the present battalion command post. From there, the battalion would move under its commander to the new defensive area and would be in position by the time the covering force had returned through the lines.

"One of the hardest jobs of all was that of explaining to the men the necessity for the withdrawal. The Thier-du-Mont ridgeline offered a beautiful defensive position overlooking all the towns and terrain in the area. However, when the men realized that all this would mean nothing if the division should be cut off in the rear, they got in and pitched as always."[34]

Sergeant Zane Schlemmer, a forward observer with the 2nd Battalion's 81mm mortar platoon, resented the withdrawal order. "We had been the tip of an eight mile long thumb extended into the throat of the German onslaught. We had paid in blood to hold open the escape corridor [for the U.S. forces in the St.-Vith pocket] and we would surely again pay in blood to eventually regain this ridge. To a man, we were certain that by the next day, Christmas Day, there would come an assault from any of the four German divisions identified to our front."[35]

On December 24, four troopers with the 1st Battalion's light machine gun platoon were seriously wounded by enemy fire. Private Dallas L. Wall, a medic attached to Headquarters Company, 1st Battalion, crossed open terrain under enemy observation and small arms fire to render first aid. When he reached the four troopers, he discovered that he would be unable to treat their severe wounds and began evacuating them. While carrying Private Henry L. Wardenski to safety, he and Wardenski were killed by artillery fire. Private Wall was posthumously awarded the Silver Star for his actions.

On Christmas Eve morning, the Company C platoon to which, Private First Class Gordon Cullings was attached as a medic, received an order to conduct a reconnaissance patrol. "[First] Sergeant Funk said I did not have to go, but I said I was going. We finally came to a little town. Only one [person, a] woman was left in town. She had a farm at the edge of town. She was told she should leave. She told us we could each have an egg and piece of bread. This we ate, then we went into the barn with the cows to get warm. While in the barn, the Germans—a patrol I guess—hit us. The sergeant yelled for us to get the hell out of there. When I was running through the meadow behind the barn, I saw a flash of fire and smoke ahead and one of the guys falling out of it. He had a white phosphorous grenade in his pants pocket. A bullet must have hit it and set it off. I grabbed my blanket and told one of the guys to help me roll him in the blanket to smother out the burning phosphorous. Then, I fixed him up the best I could and we proceeded back to the company."[36]

At 3:00 p.m., the 1st Battalion received a firm order for the withdrawal. Lieutenant Colonel Shields Warren, his staff, and the company commanders traveled by jeep to the new defensive positions, made a quick reconnaissance, and then headed back at around 5:00 p.m. Also around 5:00 p.m., the command post and communications personnel left on foot for the new positions.

After dark, the troopers busied themselves with packing their gear. Captain Ben Delamater, the 1st Battalion executive officer, commanding the battalion's covering force, set up a command post on the western end of Rencheux. He had with him two radio operators and an SCR 300 radio, along with a runner from each of the covering force platoons. The withdrawal of the main force was scheduled to commence at 10:45 p.m.

Lieutenant George Lamm's 2nd Platoon would be the Company A covering force platoon. "I had one officer with me and thirty-nine men. Our orders were to hold the line and not leave the line until 3:00 a.m., December 25, 1944."[37]

Lieutenant Maurice E. "Ed" Wheelock, Jr.'s 3rd Platoon would be the Company B covering force platoon. Lieutenant Wheelock was a new platoon leader who had just assumed command of the platoon at about 4:00 p.m. that afternoon.

Lieutenant Arthur Stevens' 2nd Platoon would the Company C covering force platoon. It moved from its reserve location at Goronne up to the left flank of the Company B sector along the west side of the river to fill the gap with the 1st Battalion of the 505th Parachute Infantry on its left.

Late that afternoon, Technician Fifth Grade Walter Barrett returned to the Company B area after a visit to Company A. "Officers and noncommissioned officers were busy checking with the squads and keeping them informed of any news pertaining to the expected attack. A new lieutenant [Thomas L. Rockwell] had arrived at B Company only a few days prior to our commitment. About dusk, orders were given to remain in our foxholes and for no reason to go out past the front line of defense. However, for some reason, the lieutenant went down to the river without telling anyone where he was going."[38]

Captain Woodrow Millsaps, the commander of Company B, was at his command post near the hamlet of Raspaille when at about 5:00 p.m., he received a report that enemy troops were crossing the river in front of the company's positions. "I alerted the troops and told them to wait until the enemy exposed himself in the opening in front of our lines and then to give him hell. He wasn't long in coming. We had had time to dig in and the defense was strong along this line. We had plenty of ammunition for the machine guns stored at the gun site and plenty of ammunition for the troopers.

"The enemy charged our positions and we opened fire. There were intervals between the enemy attacks because it took time to cross the river and climb the cliff in preparation for the next attack. That gave us time to clear the dead soldiers from in front of our position and get ready for the next charge. This went on for some time before the enemy decided he couldn't penetrate and capture our position."[39]

At 10:45 p.m., the 1st Battalion troopers began slipping out of their positions to platoon assembly areas, then made their way to the company assembly areas, and then to the battalion assembly area. By 11:15 p.m. the battalion was ready to move out except for two platoons, which had difficulty sneaking out of their positions because of the bright moonlight. The two platoons arrived by 11:35 p.m., and the 1st Battalion moved west on the road through Goronne and then north to the new defense line. Because the 1st Battalion had the longest distance to travel, its covering forces were supposed to withdraw at 3:00 a.m. to the new defense line.

In the 2nd Battalion sector, Captain Hank Le Febvre, the battalion S-3, was hoping the Germans hadn't found out about the withdrawal and wouldn't attack as the battalion pulled out. "At 23:00 the first company began to wind down from the ridge and took its place at the head of the column. It was at this time, while waiting for all the companies to arrive that the tension was the greatest.

"A German document captured on this day indicated an enemy attack, and this would be a most inopportune moment for it to be launched. It was a bright, moonlit night, and about 23:00, just as the battalion assembled and started to move, some Nebelwerfer 41 rockets were launched. Fortunately, they landed farther north in the vicinity of Goronne."[40]

Sergeant Zane Schlemmer and the troopers of the 81mm Mortar Platoon, Headquarters Company, 2nd Battalion, carried the heaviest loads, the mortar tubes, base plates, and ammunition. "We struggled on our route march to a ridgeline seven miles to our rear, where our 'not one step farther' line would be established. Precisely at midnight on Christmas Eve came the unmistakable distant sound of artillery batteries. Each trooper immediately became elated with the thought that American artillery was providing cover for this withdrawal. It was only when the shells descended and burst among us that the reality of incoming German artillery fire became evident.

"Again, to a man, the silent columns quickened their pace to a running gait despite their equipment loads. As the march continued, sounds of distant engines could be heard, indicating the movement of enemy armored vehicles following our path. Thus, again prodded, the rapid pace continued to the new positions."[41]

Sergeant Jim Kurz, with Company B, was also heavily laden. "I carried two extra boxes of .30-caliber machine gun ammunition. I just attached them to my harness. I also had a pistol, M1 rifle, ammunition and grenades. I had filled the pockets of my jumpsuit with food [from the supply dump found earlier on the hill behind the Company B positions]. [Private First Class] George [E.] Banks and I had been in Holland and we ran low on food because our supply planes couldn't get off the ground in England because of fog. George Banks and I were never short of food during the Bulge."[42]

That night at Rencheux, it seemed like time was standing still for Lieutenant George Lamm and the troopers of the 2nd Platoon, who were covering the withdrawal of Company A. "Lieutenant [Tom] Rockwell [the new assistant platoon leader of the 3rd Platoon of Company B] came to see me and told me that he had found some German champagne and he was going to bring some over right after midnight and we would celebrate Christmas by opening a bottle. He wanted me to take him out in front, to my outpost, so that he could 'get himself some Jerries.' We could hear the Germans working in the valley below us. It sounded as though they were building a bridge across a small stream [the Salm River] there. We did not expect them to attack until daylight. I thought it very foolish for Lieutenant Rockwell to desire to go out to the outpost and do some shooting. But he said he had a new Tommy gun and wanted to try it out. I took him out to my outpost and told my men out there to point out to him where the Germans were so that he could do some shooting. It was foggy out in front and not much of anything could be seen but we could hear the Germans plainly. After we returned to my company headquarters, Lieutenant Rockwell left me and went back to his company on my left."[43]

Lieutenant Lamm's command post was in a house in Rencheux, where an observation post was set up in the attic, in order to observe the movements of the Germans across the Salm River in Vielsalm. "The enemy laid down smoke for concealment and lined up their tanks and halftracks and relentlessly blasted directly into our positions as they attempted to repair the crossing sites.

"The Germans angrily tore the roofs off the houses searching for OPs [observation posts] with their beloved 88s. Finally, they got around to us, and down the attic stairs we tumbled amid flying debris, radios, telephones, field glasses and several bottles of the best champagne. We relocated the CP in the cellar and the OP was moved to the railroad bed."[44]

At 11:45 p.m. on December 24, SS Panzer Grenadier Regiment 19 of the 9th SS Panzer Division began a full scale assault crossing of the Salm River, while supporting tanks and halftracks kept up a heavy fire to cover the river crossing by the panzer grenadiers. In the Company B sector, as Technician Fifth Grade Walter Barrett waited in his foxhole for the approach of the enemy, he suddenly heard firing and saw Lieutenant Rockwell struck by several bullets. "As he was returning up the hill to our defensive positions, the paratroopers in their foxholes at the top of the hill, thinking that the attack had begun, opened fire and killed the lieutenant."[45] Tragically, Lieutenant Rockwell's ill fated return coincided with the commencement of the enemy infantry crossing of the river.

In the Company A sector, the main enemy attack fell on Sergeant Joe Boone's squad, which pinned down the SS panzer grenadiers for more than an hour. Private First Class Edward "Woody" Wodowski, armed with a BAR, fired burst after burst into the German grenadiers as they emerged from the defilade afforded by the river. "A shell came in where [Private First Class Roland B.] Hicks and I were standing. It knocked him out; that's when I carried him up to the wall [on a high embankment above the road]. When I got Hicks back up to the wall, he was OK. The Germans had already crossed the river and were coming up the middle of town. They were firing their rifles and burp guns as they came. Sergeant [Joe] Boone and I fired our weapons down on the street. We were above them; it must have been a ten foot wall there. We were firing over the wall down on to the road."[46]

From his observation post, Lieutenant Lamm could see vicious fighting going on in the Company B sector, where its 3rd Platoon was being heavily attacked. "At one time I saw a man [Private First Class Joseph Palkiewicz] crawl out from the BAR gun position and pull German bodies out from in front of the BAR. German bodies were piled up so that they could not fire the gun anymore. They had to clear the bodies away. If anything, the fighting in front of B Company was more severe than it was in front of my company, A Company.

"Shortly after 12:00 o'clock it became apparent to me that we were going to be wiped out unless we could get some help. The Germans had filtered through and had gotten around behind us."[47]

Lieutenant Lamm sent his assistant platoon leader, Lieutenant William H. Gyami and his runner to contact Captain Delamater at his command post on the western end of Rencheux to report the situation. Meanwhile, Captain Delamater received word from regimental headquarters at 1:15 a.m. to withdraw at will. He sent out the platoon runners to give the covering force the word to withdraw and then went out to the road that ran west to Goronne to await the arrival of the three platoons. At about 2:00 a.m., a German artillery barrage shook the ground around him. The Germans, realizing that the regiment was withdrawing, hoped the barrage would catch the paratroopers withdrawing in the open.

When neither his runner nor his assistant platoon leader returned with orders to withdraw early, and with SS panzer grenadiers overrunning his platoon,

Lieutenant Lamm waited until 3:00 a.m. and then moved across the fire swept ground to give his squad leaders instructions to conduct a fighting withdrawal and a new rendezvous location for the platoon to assemble, since assembly on the road, now thick with panzer grenadiers, was no longer an option.

By that time, Private First Class Ed "Woody" Wodowski was using a second BAR, having burned up the barrel on his first one. He used up all of his ammunition, plus that of his ammo bearer. Then, he and Sergeant Joe Boone threw all of their hand grenades into the midst of the Germans flowing past them on the road below, causing heavy casualties and temporarily halting their movement. After expending their grenades, Wodowski was told to withdraw. "[Sergeant] Boone got the word and we moved back, right out of town about 4:00 in the morning. There were eight of us walking back. [Private First Class Rumaldo S.] Robledo and [Private First Class John J.] DeMario were still firing when we started to move back. Lamm sent someone to get them."[48]

Sergeant Bruno S. "Gadget" Prezto and his squad joined Sergeant Boone's squad, plus those of the other rifle and mortar squads, and platoon headquarters personnel at the revised rendezvous location. Lieutenant Lamm then led the platoon west on the north side of Rencheux, paralleling the road to Goronne to a point overlooking the planned 1st Battalion rendezvous point at the western edge of the village. "When we reached the rendezvous point, it was held by the Germans and we could not rendezvous at that point. Germans were marching through the little village which was our rendezvous point, in a column of squads, and we could throw hand grenades from a high point right down into the road and we killed a lot of them, right at the rendezvous point."[49]

Lieutenant Lamm reorganized the 2nd Platoon and led it cross country to join Company A by just after daylight on Christmas morning. Lieutenant Lamm and Sergeant Joe Boone were awarded Silver Stars for their courageous leadership during the rear guard action and withdrawal.

Some of the 9th SS Panzer Division grenadiers who had crossed the river in the Company A sector, got in behind the Company B covering force, its 3rd Platoon. Private Marino M. Michetti was an ammo bearer with the 3rd Platoon mortar squad. "About midnight, I heard shouting and noise; a group of Americans and Germans were in an open area behind us on the ridge. They had come up on the ridge behind us. The Germans were all around us. I was seeing flashes of my childhood, when I saw the white lights from the tracers in the burp gun firing at me! I asked the trooper in the foxhole to my left, 'What should we do?'

"I remember us getting out of the foxholes with our hands behind our heads! The Germans huddled us in with a small group of other prisoners, prodding us with their rifles. My whole world seemed to have crumbled around me. What would my friends think of me now? I really felt ashamed!"[50]

As SS panzer grenadiers attacked frontally from the river and from behind, they ran into a hail of fire from the 3rd Platoon troopers. Private First Class

Joseph Palkiewicz, a BAR gunner allowed them to approach to within twenty yards of his foxhole before opening fire. So many enemy dead were piled up in front of his foxhole that he had to get out of his hole and drag the enemy bodies out of the way in order to continue to have a clear field of fire. When the panzer grenadiers overran and knocked out the light machine gun position to his right, Palkiewicz left his hole and manned the position, firing his BAR into the enemy. With his ammunition expended, Palkiewicz withdrew, taking along a wounded comrade.

Two other 3rd Platoon troopers, Private First Class Raymond G. Wilson, a machine gunner, and his assistant gunner, Private John Payet, waited until the approaching Germans were within fifty yards of their position before opening fire, inflicting heavy casualties and knocking out an MG-42. Wilson moved their machine gun from position to position to meet each new attempt to rush his platoon's positions. During the fighting, when everyone else in Wilson's gun crew had been killed or wounded, he continued to move the gun from position to position without aid. Wilson continued this until every trooper who could withdraw had done so.

Private Alexander "Alex" Sopka, a replacement with the 3rd Platoon, was experiencing his first combat. "[Private] Emmett [L.] Boyce and I were together in a foxhole where we could see to the front and to our right. The men to our left could not see to our right. There were two foxholes from B Company to our right. On our immediate right were [Private Albert J.] Al Patchell and an unknown fellow. Farther right was a fellow named [Private First Class Robert W.] Hart and another fellow, whose name I didn't know.

"The battle with small arms fire and grenades was intense. Hart took off up the hill and was taken prisoner. [Private Patchell was hit in the face and badly wounded.] Patchell and his buddy went down the hill [behind the platoon] where the Germans came from and found an ambulance for Patchell.

"From our position Boyce and I could see the Germans were getting through on our right. Sergeants Ed Boccafogli and [Donald L.] Don King could not see the Germans coming up the hill toward us. They were very loud, but we had difficulty seeing them in the shadows of the trees. There was some clearance between our foxholes and the trees. Their bullets were hitting the dirt piled up around our foxhole. Boyce and I would duck down in the hole then lob a grenade out toward the Germans. Eventually, we ran out of grenades. I was raising up to a position behind my rifle—at that very instant I saw this German running toward us. I fired three rounds from my M1 rifle as fast as I could. The German fell about ten feet away, he moved slightly, then was very still. It was a close call. Boyce and I had a good view of the breakthrough to our right. We were firing to our right and running low on M1 ammo. Boyce's rifle was equipped to fire rifle grenades, but when we tried to assemble the launcher on to his rifle we could not do it. During this fighting one of the German bullets had hit the plug in his M1, to which the launcher assembled.

"Then there was an explosion at our hole that killed Boyce and wounded me. I crawled out of the foxhole and informed Sergeant King that Boyce was dead and the Germans were through our line on the right side and in back of us. We went down the hill from where the Germans came from and made our way to our forces and [found] an ambulance for me."[51]

The 3rd Platoon runner reached Lieutenant Ed Wheelock with word that he could withdraw at will. Lieutenant Wheelock, who had been wounded during the German artillery barrage, gathered those members of the 3rd Platoon who were still able to do so, and filtered out of the area making their way to Goronne, the regimental assembly area for the battalion covering forces. Privates First Class Raymond Wilson and Joseph Palkiewicz were later awarded the Silver Star for their gallantry.

After those 3rd Platoon troopers who had been able to do so, had withdrawn, the Germans rounded up the survivors as prisoners. Private Marino Michetti was taken to the house that had been used for the Company B command post and was interrogated. "I had to take everything out of my jump pants pockets. I had quite a collection, because we had just received some Christmas mail before we left Sissonne, France. I remember some nice white handkerchiefs someone had sent me. Pocket knife, fountain pen, three packs of cigarettes, five packs of razor blades, wallet with some English money (four one-pound notes) and two one-dollar bills. I remember having bread and coffee with the Germans at daylight, Christmas morning—'Merry Christmas.'"[52]

The other covering force platoon, the 2nd Platoon of Company C, on the left flank was subjected to artillery fire, but no direct attack. When they received the message from Captain Delamater to withdraw, Lieutenant Arthur Stevens and his assistant platoon leader, Lieutenant Raymond L. Kampe, assembled the platoon and moved cross country until reaching the road to Goronne and the regimental assembly area.

Meanwhile, Captain Delamater, on the high ground just south of the planned rendezvous point for the 1st Battalion covering force, saw three separate signal lights a few hundred yards away, apparently for assembly by SS Panzer Grenadier Regiment 19. Delamater used the SCR 300 radio to attempt to contact the platoons, but was unsuccessful. A German picked up his radio calls and shouted, "Baker Company, assemble here," in a thick German accent.

Captain Delamater eventually made contact with the covering force platoons. Lieutenant Lamm's Company A platoon had seven troopers missing in action, while Lieutenant Wheelock's Company B platoon had thirteen, and Lieutenant Stevens' Company C platoon suffered no casualties. Most of those missing in action had been captured.

As Captain Hank Le Febvre, the 2nd Battalion S-3, moved north with the battalion, he was unaware of the danger facing his close friend, Major Royal Taylor, the battalion's executive officer, who was commanding the battalion's covering force. Le Febvre would later learn that "at about 01:30, the SCR 300 went out and Major Taylor was unable to contact either his own troops or the regimental executive officer in Goronne. At this time, he could see German tracers in the vicinity of Goronne, and he dispatched his S-2 and the messenger to contact the platoons of the 2nd Battalion covering force, and gather them on top of Thier-du-Mont ridge. The original plan called for him to go to Goronne, but he could see that it would be useless now. He was actually worried about getting through the battalion lines ahead of the Germans, who were already past his position and were heading west on the road through the valley. Major Taylor organized his force on top of the ridge, and by making his way west along a narrow trail, he was able to lead his men to a position west of Goronne before turning north to reach the road the main part of the battalion had traveled. By skillful leadership, Major Taylor was able to bring this force through the lines about 07:00, 25 December, without loss of a man."[53]

In the 3rd Battalion sector to the west, the main force withdrawal was made without interference. However, as the battalion's covering force withdrew, Lieutenant Vernon Thomas, the platoon leader of the 1st Platoon of Company H, was killed.

The 508th, except for the covering force, reached the new line from about 3:30 to 4:30 a.m. and immediately began preparing to meet a German attack that would likely come later that day. The 82nd Airborne Division's new line ran from Trois Ponts on the left flank, extending southwest where it tied in with the 7th Armored Division, east of Tri-le-Cheslaing. The 505th Parachute Infantry Regiment held the left sector from Trois Ponts to Basse-Bodeux. The 508th Parachute Infantry Regiment held the sector from just west of Basse-Bodeux to just east of Bergifaz. The 504th Parachute Infantry Regiment's sector extended from Bergifaz to Vaux Chavanne. The 325th Glider Infantry Regiment held the area between Vaux Chavanne and Tri-le-Cheslaing. The 7th Armored Division, attached to the XVIII Airborne Corps, was on the division's right flank from Tri-le-Cheslaing to Manhay, where it tied in with the 3rd Armored Division.

In the 508th sector, the 1st Battalion line ran from west of Basse-Bodeux to the La Vaux road junction south of Haute-Bodeux on the regiment's left flank.

Upon reaching the location for the new defensive line, Captain Woodrow Millsaps and his exhausted Company B troopers immediately began digging in. "Digging a hole in the frozen soil of this hill was almost impossible, but everyone managed to get down deep. The demolition platoon from regimental Headquarters Company, in conjunction with Company D, 307th engineers, laid extensive minefields, both antitank and antipersonnel, across the front. Bands of concertina wire further strengthened the defense and every platoon was given extra automatic weapons. Heavy .30 and .50-caliber machine guns were added to the armament of the regiment. Ten boxes of ammunition were pilled by each gun site and plenty more were in reserve. Mortars, the artillery of the infantry, were zeroed in on every draw and clump of woods to the front. In addition to the usual artillery support supplied by the 319th Glider Field Artillery, a battalion of 155mm howitzers from the 106th Infantry Division was attached to the 82nd. The troopers did not have much time to prepare for the coming of the enemy. At 13:00 hours, an observation post in the regimental sector reported the presence of the enemy in a small town a couple of miles to the southeast."[54]

Sergeant Jim Kurz, a Baker Company veteran of Normandy and Holland, had learned the importance of a good foxhole. "[Private First Class] George [Banks] and I dug a fine foxhole. Where we slept was seven feet long and four feet wide and six and one half feet [deep]. We had a foot of straw on the bottom. We then had a lookout compartment seven feet [deep] with steps at the front and back. We had a slot to see out of in front and an entrance in the back. We had logs over the top and eighteen inches of dirt on top of the logs."[55]

At daybreak, a very tired Sergeant Zane Schlemmer, with the 81mm Mortar Platoon of Headquarters Company, 2nd Battalion, was still working on his new foxhole. "Dawn came gray, and with low hanging clouds over the trees at the new positions, the task of digging in was well under way. The rocky, frozen, root-bound soil was feverishly grubbed. Weary and worn, alternately sweating and freezing, we continued to dig and camouflage our holes, set up our weapons, stash backup supplies of ammunition, and place antitank mines, before the anticipated attack which would surely come. Snow began to fall, masking our line, and our canteens of water froze solid."[56]

Lieutenant Colonel Otho Holmes and his 2nd Battalion held the center. "Company D was on the left, F on the right, and E in reserve. The companies held the line from the road junction south of Haute-Bodeux to the village of Erria, a distance of about three thousand yards...The covering force under Major Taylor came in about 05:00, 25 December. During the day of the 25th, positions were secured, mines were laid, wires put in, mortars zeroed in, patrols sent out and outposts placed about four hundred yards in front of the main lines."[57]

Lieutenant Colonel Mendez and his staff had developed a fire plan for the 3rd Battalion, which held the right flank of the regimental sector. "The mission was to defend the high ground north of the east–west road between Erria and Villettes. I placed Company G on the left flank at (610945) [at Erria] running along the forward slope to the west. H Company on the right sector, facing south had its right flank at (593942) [astride the east–west highway just south of Villettes]. I Company was in reserve in a defensive position in the woods up the slope behind H Company.

"The [81mm] mortars were on top of the hill at (601951) [northwest of Erria]. The reason for placing the mortars on top of the hill was because the potential areas and avenues of approach for an enemy attack against the MLR [main line of resistance] were at extreme range and the woods on top of the hill were the only available concealment in range of the targets. Two 57mm antitank guns were placed in H Company's area covering the road leading south of the

Heid de Heirlot—the hill mass south of the MLR. One 57mm antitank gun was in G Company's area covering the road running northeast to Erria. The battalion CP was two thousand yards behind the MLR at (589961) [behind the crest of the hill due north of Bergifaz]. An OPL [outpost line] was seven hundred yards to the south."[58]

After a long march, Private First Class Lane Lewis, a new replacement with Company G, arrived at the village of Erria. "I remember as we were marching into town, seeing the displaced civilians that were leaving Erria in wagons and by foot. I felt compassion for these poor people dislocated by the war and leaving their homes with what few possessions they could carry. Being raised on a farm, I noticed that the farm stock stayed in covered barns, which were underneath the houses. This struck me as odd, as at home our livestock stayed in barns that were built separate from our house. Since it was Christmas Eve, some of the civilians of Erria who had stayed behind invited us into their homes to warm up by the fire and drink a glass of cognac in Christmas celebration. We gladly accepted their generous offer. It was a good feeling to stand by the fire and get warm again. As I sipped on my glass of cognac (my first), I began to think of Christmas at home. Christmas time was always so special at our house. Mother would always prepare a delicious Christmas dinner. We would have turkey and dressing, pork roast, potatoes, corn, green beans and corn bread, plus all kinds of cakes and pies. As a child, I couldn't wait until Christmas morning, when I could open up the Christmas presents. Usually it would be a pair of socks or a shirt, or a pair of pants, but sometimes I would receive a toy. Christmas time was the only time we would have oranges, which I loved. I wondered how my father, Steve, and Lee were doing now, and I thought of mother, alone with my two younger brothers. I wished them all well. That [morning] we set up defensive positions and waited for the German attack we knew would come. We were ordered to hold this town at all hazards. This meant that no matter how many casualties we suffered, we could not retreat from here. Christmas Day found us cold and hungry in Erria. We did receive a cold turkey dinner, but no presents or even mail, but one thing was certain; the Germans would *not* pass this line, and there would be no more withdrawals!"[59]

For their protection, the division ordered Belgian civilians to evacuate towns and farms which were located near or on the front line. It was heartbreaking for Sergeant Marvin Risnes, with Company G, who had to deliver the news to one of the families who lived near Erria. "I really hated to force that Belgian family out of their home near Erria on Christmas night. They couldn't speak English and we couldn't speak French, but they got the idea. The middle aged couple, with two kids about seven and eight years old, hitched their horses to a sleigh and loaded up a few belongings. We added some GI rations to their meager load to replace the food they left behind. It was a good thing the family moved out, because an 88 crashed through the roof a few hours after the family drove away in their two horse open sleigh."[60]

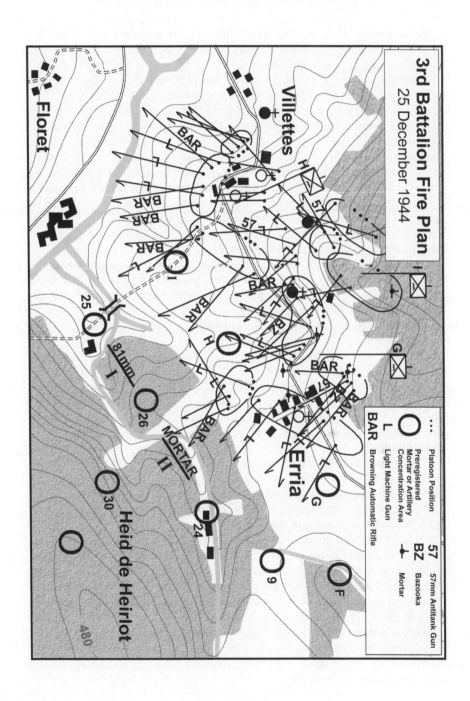

3rd Battalion Fire Plan
25 December 1944

Floret

Villettes

Erria

Heid de Heirlot

BAR

MORTAR

81mm

••• Platoon Position
━━ Preregistered
     Mortar or Artillery
◯   Concentration Area
L   Light Machine Gun
BAR Browning Automatic Rifle

57 57mm Antitank Gun
BZ Bazooka
Mortar

After arriving at Erria, Lieutenant Bill Call, the platoon leader of the 2nd Platoon of Company G, got his troopers dug in on their assigned sector. "[Staff Sergeant Frank] Sirovica and I took over this farmhouse as our CP and they had a cow in the kitchen. It shocked the hell out of us. We didn't want to kill the damn thing, because those poor people, that was probably all they had.

"[Lieutenant Howard] Greenawalt [and his 3rd Platoon] was on my left flank in a home, maybe about 250-300 yards from me. [Captain] Russ Wilde was across a little dirt road with company headquarters in a little home there. The 1st Platoon was in reserve in back of that. We had outposts out in front of my platoon. I always wanted to keep in contact [with the Germans] and find out what was going on. We had three guys out there, spread in front of the platoon.

"It wasn't long before we had to send out patrols. There was a guy, Corporal [General L.] Sexton. In Holland, he was invaluable as a patrol leader. All you had to do was give him your requirements and he'd take a patrol and get it done. He got wounded [during a patrol in Holland].

"The patrols were to go beyond the outposts and see if they could contact the Germans and find out what the hell they were doing. I told Sirovica, 'You better get Sexton.' He went and did his job and he came back and shortly after that Sexton walked into this little farmhouse.

"He said, 'Lieutenant Call, can I talk to you?'

"I said, 'Sure'

'He said, 'Can I talk to you privately?'

'Sure,' so we went outside.

"He started to cry and he said, 'Lieutenant, take me off this patrol. I can't go—I've had it. I've gone on so many—I've been wounded. I have to be honest with you. I'm not your good patrol leader anymore.'

"I said, 'OK, go on back to your hole.' I went in and told Sirovica, 'Find another leader.'

"'What the hell is the matter with Sexton?'

"I said, 'He's had it...He's had it, Frank.'

"'OK, I'll find somebody else.' So he went out and got somebody else.

"The poor guy didn't leave [in Holland] when he had combat fatigue and he had it. He didn't want to leave the outfit."[61]

During Christmas afternoon, Private Ralph Gilson, with Company D, 307th Airborne Engineer Battalion, and the battalion's engineers were establishing roadblocks on the approaches to the front line. "Our squad was sent to the rear to get more antitank mines. When we got to the rear area we stumbled across the 508th field kitchen. The mess sergeant asked who we were and we told him 307th engineers. He asked if we had eaten our turkey Christmas dinner. We told him we had eaten nothing but cold 'K' rations since we got to Belgium. He said he had enough to feed our squad. The squad leader said, 'Take ten,' so we could eat. We were traveling light, so we didn't have our mess kits with us. All we had was a spoon, canteen, and cup.

"We tore cardboard off our ration boxes for plates and ate turkey, mashed potatoes, cranberries, and bread with our spoons and fingers. The hot coffee was great. To this day, every Christmas I remember that lonely Christmas and what a wonderful dinner it was for a squad of tired engineers."[62]

Corporal Murphy Bridges, an assistant squad leader with Company A, established an outpost in front of the new 508th front line, then took another trooper on patrol to locate the enemy. After the patrol left, a German combat patrol overran the outpost and cut the field telephone lines running back to the front line.

Bridges and his companion heard the noise of the fighting and returned to the outpost, where they engaged a numerically superior force of enemy troops in an intense firefight. Bridges and the other trooper drove off the enemy combat patrol and took back the outpost. Bridges then reestablished communications and directed artillery and mortar fire on enemy troops moving north toward the 508th lines. Bridges remained at the outpost all night, relaying warnings of the approach of large numbers of enemy troops. Corporal Bridges was later awarded the Silver Star for his courageous actions.

Sergeant John J. Mullen, Jr. and two other troopers with the 3rd Platoon established another Company A outpost. To make less of a target to enemy mortar and artillery fire, Sergeant Mullen positioned his men in separate foxholes to form a "V" shaped defensive position, with his hole at its point. As enemy forces approached, Sergeant Mullen fought off numerous attempts to establish their own outposts. While engaging these enemy forces, he moved to each flank as his troopers provided cover fire. Sergeant Mullen personally engaged and repelled several attempts to infiltrate his outpost position, killing five Germans. Mullen was wounded during this action, and after receiving treatment, insisted on returning to his outpost, even though he could hardly walk. Sergeant Mullen was later awarded the Bronze Star for his leadership and courage.

Around dusk, Sergeant Zane Schlemmer with Headquarters Company, 2nd Battalion, received the word that German forces were approaching. "Each of us, when finished, sought the shelter of our foxholes for the warmth and protection afforded. There had been little time until now to think of past Christmases, of families or loved ones, of gifts or mail, for there had been none since we had been in battle. Darkness came early that Christmas Day in the Ardennes and the outposts reported in that a large concentration of German panzer grenadiers, supported by halftracks was approaching our line. Thus alerted, each trooper silently readied for the onslaught.

"Out of the night, through the falling snow, came the German columns trudging in their heavy coats, rifles slung over their shoulder, along the road fronting our positions; some talking, some smoking, all completely oblivious to the paratroopers dug in mere yards away. The wait for the signal to fire seemed endless; when it came, the firefight was both intense and devastating."[63]

Captain Woodrow Millsaps alerted his Company B troopers of the approach of the same German force on the road that ran from Rencheux through Goronne, Ordimont, and Amcômont. "Later that night, December 25, Germans moved in force down the road separating the 1st and 2nd Battalions. Two companies of infantry, acting as advance guards for two battalions attacking abreast and four halftracks, were met by the fire of A and D Companies."[64]

Captain Hank Le Febvre, the 2nd Battalion S-3, watched the battle between the Company D troopers and grenadiers of the 9th SS Panzer Division. "A small bridge in front of D Company's position which had been set for demolition failed to go off and the bazooka man's rocket launcher failed to fire, so there was some fierce close quarters fighting."[65]

Company F, defending the right flank of the 2nd Battalion sector gave Company D an assist. The Fox Company commander, Lieutenant Hoyt Goodale, proceeded to the point of attack and despite intense fire from enemy halftracks and infantry, set up a machine gun on a commanding position on high ground. The machine gun delivered devastating fire on the enemy and was instrumental in breaking up the assault.

Le Febvre continued to watch as the fighting reached a crescendo. "The advantage of good fields of fire for the Americans, an apparently unplanned night attack by the attackers, and a lot of small arms fire proved too much for the Germans, and they withdrew after about three hours of fighting."[66]

The 319th Glider Field Artillery Battalion fired over two thousand rounds of 75mm artillery shells that night, most of which targeted the German attack, helping to break it up.

After the enemy withdrew, Lieutenant Goodale led a few of his Company F troopers in clearing the area of enemy troops, and then oversaw the demolition of the bridge. For inspirational and courageous leadership during the attack, Lieutenant Goodale was awarded the Silver Star.

After the firing died away, Sergeant Schlemmer could see the equipment, weapons, and dead bodies of SS troopers strewn about in front of the 508th defensive positions. "The falling snow mercifully covered the remains of the two German battalions that in that short time ceased to exist. As we retrieved the usable enemy weapons, ammunition, and equipment from the fallen ambushed column, we discovered a large wicker basket, which had been carried on a pole between two German soldiers. To our amazement, we found that it contained butter. Then, as if on cue, an American supply patrol from the rear found us and dropped off two food containers, one full of ice cold coffee; the other full of sliced turkey, solidly frozen. Our Christmas feast had arrived! Using the captured German butter to heat the turkey and the coffee over small fires at the bottom of our individual foxholes, we savored that feast. No finer Christmas dinner has ever been relished more than that simple meal, for then we knew we had not been forgotten, there on a snowbound ridge in the Belgian forests."[67]

Shortly after sunrise on December 26, Sergeant Robert White, a squad leader with the 3rd Platoon of Company A, was in his foxhole when his platoon leader, Lieutenant Rex Combs, approached. "The CP was up on the side of the hill behind us. He came part of the way down the hill and hollered for us to come up and get some turkey, because we—the two squads—were out there Christmas Day and didn't get any turkey.

"Three of us got out of our hole and we had no more than got out of our hole and started to move up the hill when they laid a mortar [shell] right on us. I got wounded through the leg and [Corporal Lawrence H.] Larson had one [piece of shrapnel] through the chest and [it] came out and was in the back of his shirt. He died shortly afterwards. My friend, my comrade, [Sergeant Richard L.] Hunt, had an oil can in his pocket and shrapnel went through the oil can. He thought he was hit because the oil ran down his leg."[68] Sergeant White, a member of Company A since Camp Blanding, was evacuated by jeep to a hospital at Liège, Belgium.

Shortly after dark on December 26, Staff Sergeant John T. "Jack" Elliott, with Company I, was on his way to establish an outpost in the 3rd Battalion sector, when he spotted enemy troops. Elliott evaded them and reached the point where the planned outpost was to be located. Realizing that he was getting cutoff, he fought his way back to the 508th front line, eliminating the element of surprise the approaching SS troops hoped to achieve.

On the evening of December 26, Private First Class Lane Lewis, with Company G, sat in his foxhole, prepared for an inevitable German assault, which would be his first real taste of combat. "We built up our defenses while the Germans probed our lines trying to find a weakness. The Germans would shell our positions with artillery and mortar fire. This artillery fire would come without warning. The veterans of our unit could always tell when these shells would hit our position and they would yell, 'Incoming!' Anyone who happened to be outside of their foxhole would make a fast dive into the nearest foxhole to escape the flying bits of shrapnel, as the shells would explode. My buddy and I had dug a large and deep foxhole and covered it with logs and dirt. Even while protected in our foxhole we would feel the ground shake as each shell would explode. The noise was deafening! One morning when we got up out of our foxhole we were shocked to see that we had received a direct hit from a mortar shell fired during last night's artillery attack, but we didn't even hear it! Thank God it was a dud and did not explode."[69]

CHAPTER 15

"HIS EXAMPLE OF COURAGE"

Sergeant Marvin Risnes and three troopers from his Company G squad manned an outpost about 125 yards into the forest south of an open field in front of the company's main line of resistance. The outpost had a field telephone line that ran to the company command post. At about 9:00 p.m. on December 26, Risnes discovered German troops infiltrating through the woods between his outpost and the 508th front line. "We could see shadowy figures and hear the noncoms giving orders in German. I phoned and requested mortar and machine gun fire on the area. The resulting fire was very effective against the attacking Jerries. When some mortar shells fell dangerously close to us, I tried to call to correct the mortar fire. The line was dead. I pulled in the line and found it was cut by the mortars about ten feet out.

"The CP tried to call me—with no results. They had pulled the line in from their end and learned the line had been cut. Captain [Russell] Wilde sent Lieutenant James [F.] Russell and Sergeant Harry [R.] Waltman with a patrol to contact us. The patrol shot their way through the Germans and contacted our outpost, and reestablished communications with the CP. Russell's patrol returned to the CP with a wounded German prisoner whose soldier's [pay] book revealed that he was a member of the 19th SS Panzer Grenadiers.

"Two men from an I Company outpost [Staff Sergeant Jack Elliott's] came to our position and reported that a platoon sized force of Germans was moving through the woods toward the open field. I immediately called the company CP and Captain Wilde ordered us to withdraw to the company. We secured our equipment and departed by the most direct route toward the company area. At the edge of the woods, we saw two people standing about one hundred yards in front of 3rd Platoon of G Company. I couldn't recognize them as Germans, so I challenged them. They answered in German as if we were one of them. We opened fire, and to our surprise about a dozen men, lying between us and the two men, jumped up and took flight. None of them returned our fire. These men were the extreme left flank of the German attacking force. Yelling at the top of our voices to identify ourselves, we dashed toward the 3rd Platoon position. We made it to the defense line just minutes before the German attacking force opened fire all along the wood line for several hundred yards."[1]

When the Germans opened fire from the edge of the woods, there were still twelve troopers forward of the Company G line on outpost duty. Sergeant Lawrence E. McFadden, the squad leader of the 3rd Squad, 2nd Platoon of Company G, grabbed a BAR and advanced through this heavy fire to bring them back, destroying an enemy machine gun and its crew with a Gammon grenade and inflicting a number of casualties with his BAR. McFadden found the twelve troopers and then led them safely to the Company G line.

Shortly after midnight, as suppressive fire from the woods to the south raked their positions, Private First Class Lane Lewis could see shadowy figures moving toward the Company G foxholes. "Two German SS panzer grenadier battalions came out of the woods and advanced towards our lines that night with full force and determination. The attack came out of the woods across the open fields in front of our positions in Erria. Our artillery observers called in fire missions as soon as the attacking Germans entered the open fields. Soon, 105mm and 155mm artillery shells were bursting among the advancing SS soldiers. From my foxhole, I could see the shells exploding, lighting up the night sky. The artillery fire was really something to see! The noise was deafening and the whole ground shook with each blast. This artillery fire caused very heavy causalities upon the Germans, but these soldiers were very brave and well trained troops who did as they were ordered and continued their assault."[2]

SS Panzer Grenadier Regiment 19 of the 9th SS Panzer Division attacked on a narrow front in a column of battalions, each in a column of companies at the point where the positions of Company F and Company G joined.

Sergeant Leroy F. Thierolf, with Headquarters Company, 3rd Battalion, and four of his men were digging machine gun positions to cover a roadblock when the German attack commenced. Since Thierolf had orders to dig the positions and await the arrival of the machine guns, he was determined to remain in those positions as ordered. Armed only with rifles and a few grenades, Thierolf and his men were attacked from the front and both flanks. Some of the panzer grenadiers were killed within fifteen feet of their holes. Even though their ammunition ran low, Thierolf and his troopers refused to withdraw.

As wave upon wave of SS grenadiers crossed the snow covered field, Sergeant James E. Green's section of five Headquarters Company, 3rd Battalion machine guns attached to Company G, poured devastating fire into the onrushing enemy. When Sergeant Green received word that the left flank of Company G needed support, he grabbed a machine gun and called for two volunteers to follow him. The three troopers ran a hundred yards across the brightly moonlit ground under heavy fire to the new position. As Green approached it, he suddenly came almost face to face with a group of Germans. Green acted quickly, shoving the machine gun into one of the German's hands, shouting, "Here—this is for you," then fell flat on the ground and yelled to his two men behind him, "Kill them—they're Germans." The two troopers opened fire, killing two Germans and forcing the others to flee. Sergeant Green and his two troopers then set up the machine gun and opened fire on the enemy.

Corporal Lawrence Salva, a squad leader with the Headquarters Company, 3rd Battalion light machine gun section attached to Company G, allowed the oncoming grenadiers to approach to within twenty-five yards of his position before opening fire with such devastating effect that seven SS troopers were killed and the others were forced to fall back. Salva then moved his machine gun while under heavy fire to an alternate position, and repeated the same tactic of letting the enemy get close before opening fire. He continued moving the gun, delivering such effective fire and inflicting numerous casualties that the attack in front of his machine gun squad was brought to a stop.

Staff Sergeant Jack Elliott, with Company I, who had earlier returned from his outpost to give warning of the attack, joined the Company G troopers in the fight. When ammunition ran low, Elliott loaded a cart and dragged it up under heavy fire to resupply the troopers.

Company G trooper, Private John H. Hodge, Jr., an ammo bearer with the 3rd Platoon's 60mm mortar squad, was in a house in Erria when the assault began. "After being relieved of my guard duty by [Private First Class] Robert [T.] Lindsay, I went into a room where Sergeant Alfred [L.] Hess and [Private First Class William D.] Swint, our gunner, were. Being unable to sleep in my jump boots, I was in the process of taking them off when all hell began happening just outside our room. I quickly put my boots on, and Lindsay came in to inform us that the Germans were attacking. Sergeant Hess went to take up his post in front, where he could direct the mortar fire. Swint, Lindsay, and I went to our mortar emplacement. We had earlier established a field of fire, so when we got to the mortar, we began firing. It didn't take Swint long to run out of 60mm shells, and Lindsay and I were constantly going to our supply hole for more ammunition."[3]

In the Company F sector, the weight of the assault struck its 1st Platoon, dug in on the company's right flank, next to Company G. Unlike Company G, Company F didn't get a warning of the impending attack from an outpost and the Germans achieved the element of surprise. Technician Fourth Grade Dwayne Burns, assigned to the 3rd Platoon, was in a three man foxhole with two other troopers when the assault began. "[Sergeant] Ralph Burrus, who had been wounded at Hill 131 and then earned a second Purple Heart in Holland, had our machine gun crew plot out a haystack in the field close to the forest's edge. When the first shots started he requested they send a string of tracers into it. The hay flared up to provide a huge bonfire light. In the field, all we could see were Germans. There were hundreds of them down on their bellies crawling toward us. 'Good Lord almighty!' I exclaimed. 'How did they get there so fast? Another minute and they would have been in our foxholes, crawling down our shirts.' It was a shock to everyone, but the emotion was cut short as our small arms opened fire. F Company radioed back for artillery and mortar fire."[4]

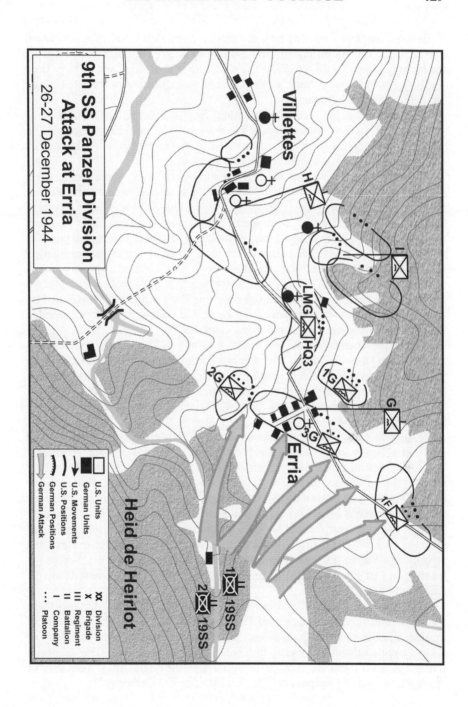

9th SS Panzer Division
Attack at Erria
26-27 December 1944

Villettes

Erria

Heid de Heirlot

Legend:
U.S. Units
German Units
U.S. Movements
U.S. Positions
German Positions
German Attack

XX   Division
X   Brigade
III   Regiment
II   Battalion
I   Company
...   Platoon

When Company F opened fire, the panzer grenadiers stood up and charged toward them. Technician Fourth Grade Burns could see them silhouetted against the burning haystack. "We radioed again and had the artillery and mortars drop shells closer to the front lines. Germans, dead and dying, were scattered across the field, but still others came on.

"One had to admire their determination, for there was no cover for them to get behind. They just kept coming right into our fire until they were able to reach the ditch on the other side of the road. It looked like they would overrun our company CP by the sheer strength of their numbers."[5]

When Company F opened fire, Private First Class Allan Stein, looked for a target to engage with his bazooka. "Our entire line opened up a continuous fire until we were down to a few clips. At that time I thought it was the proper time to try my bazooka. I aimed it at where our outpost had been. The guys had already come in. I fired it and 'bam,' it hit a tree. I was reloading the bazooka when I thought someone had hit me in the face. When my ear started bleeding, I realized that I had been hit by shrapnel.

"The next day it was discovered that my tree burst had broken up a platoon of Germans getting ready to attack our position. Their bodies were punctured by wood and shrapnel—the bazooka had worked. The field in front of us was filled with the frozen bodies of dead and dying Germans."[6]

One of the Company F NCOs, Sergeant Joseph P. Guzzy, took over firing a machine gun single-handedly after the crew was wounded and carried it from position to position, where he fired burst after burst at the onrushing enemy troops. Guzzy inflicted significant casualties, despite being subjected to small arms, mortar, and Panzerfaust fire. Sergeant Guzzy was later awarded the Silver Star for his gallantry.

In the Company F sector, the range on the friendly artillery was dropped and the shells began impacting almost on top of the 1st Platoon positions. Technician Fourth Grade Burns then observed the enemy breaking through in the 1st Platoon area on his right. "F Company machine gunner, [Private First Class] Warren [H.] Zuelke of the 1st Platoon was set up next to G Company where the Germans broke through. Upon hearing the burping of enemy guns to his right and right rear, he and his crew pulled their gun out of the foxhole and set it up where it could fire both forward and to their right. After making this adjustment, Warren said the Germans came so close, some of them died in the foxhole he had just vacated. His ammo bearer [Private First Class Robert F. Clegg] was killed."[7]

Together with his three troopers from the outpost, Sergeant Marvin Risnes had reached the positions of the 3rd Platoon of Company G on the main line of resistance just in time. Sergeant Risnes kept firing as company after company of enemy troops advanced toward the 3rd Platoon's foxholes. "The Germans charged in waves and we kept on firing all along the line. They were able to penetrate between F Company and the 3rd Platoon of G Company."[8]

As panzer grenadiers overran Lieutenant Howard Greenawalt's 3rd Platoon, Private First Class Lane Lewis, experiencing his first combat, took off for the rear with several other 3rd Platoon troopers. "Running as fast as I could, we left the Germans behind holding the town, but we weren't defeated."[9]

However, Private First Class Victor G. Walsh, a machine gunner with the 3rd Platoon of Company G, remained at his position after most of his squad withdrew. When the Germans overran his position, he attempted to rejoin his squad, but was unable to contact them. He returned to his foxhole and continued fighting, although surrounded. Walsh inflicted heavy casualties until he ran out of machine gun ammunition. He then grabbed his rifle and attempted to fight his way back to G Company, but was severely wounded before he could do so.

With the German overruning the 3rd Platoon positions, Sergeant Marvin Risnes decided to lead several troopers to the 2nd Platoon sector. "I realized the Jerries had penetrated our left flank and that we were low on ammo. I gathered our men and moved into a draw near the 2nd Platoon position. I then approached the 2nd Platoon and was able to identify myself to [Private First Class] George McGrath, who passed the word to hold fire, while we made a dash to the safety of the 2nd Platoon defense line.

"[Staff] Sergeant [Frank] Sirovica could not spare ammo for my men. They needed all they had for their own platoon. He sent us back to battalion supply. Returning with fresh ammo, we joined in the fighting from the 2nd Platoon position."[10]

Realizing that the 3rd Platoon had been overrun, the 2nd Platoon troopers poured fire into the enemy troops as they advanced through and beyond the 3rd Platoon positions.

The 1st Platoon was the Company G reserve platoon. Lieutenant James E. Fowler, the assistant platoon leader, was dug in with his troopers along a sunken road about one hundred yards to the rear of the front line. "Automatic fire was heard from across the Erria road, indicating a German attack on the 3rd Platoon. Within minutes, figures appeared in the field in front of our line. The troopers were ordered to hold their fire for fear that the people were members of our 3rd Platoon withdrawing from the MLR.

"When many cried out that the helmets were German, the order to fire was given. By holding their fire, thinking our own men may have been in the field, the platoon allowed the aggressive SS troopers to fill the field and come within close range of our rifles and machine guns."[11]

The 1st Platoon troopers opened up, cutting down the onrushing Germans, as tracers crisscrossed and exploding hand grenades burst among the SS panzer grenadiers caught in the open.

Some of the Germans turned toward the village after overrunning the 3rd Platoon line, where they overran the 3rd Platoon and company command posts, located in homes in the village. The next morning, Lieutenant Bill Call, the 2nd Platoon leader, found out from Lieutenant Greenawalt what happened when the

Germans overran the 3rd Platoon's command post. "In this cellar, they had a potato bin in this house. The Germans overran his position and he and a couple [of troopers] in his platoon headquarters hid in the potato bin."[12]

Staff Sergeant Joseph Kissane, the Company G operations sergeant, was able to make his escape from the company command post at the last moment. "The CP was ablaze. One trooper kept looking for more clips for his Tommy gun. I told him, 'Forget the damned clips—let's get the hell out of here. I joined the 1st Platoon in a ditch facing the main road...

"The infiltrating enemy was in the trees to our left. Groping past our 3rd Platoon and F Company, they could be heard calling out names, trying to get coordinated. We kept firing indiscriminately into their whereabouts. Running low on ammunition, I went to a dump about one hundred feet behind us...

"I brought back some machine gun ammo. It was so cold the cartridges taken from the belts couldn't be inserted into clips. Just loaded each round into the M1 chamber—no tracers—and fired away.

"Lieutenant [William] Bush [the platoon leader of the 1st Platoon], also in the ditch, was desperately trying to get off some 60mm mortar shells. However, the pin [on the mortar shell] was encased in ice."[13]

By the time the Germans overran the Company G command post, First Sergeant Robert Kolterman had made sure everyone had left the building. "We had evacuated the company CP with three wounded troops (two on stretchers) and three runners. We moved to H Company."[14]

Private John Hodge, an ammo bearer with the 60mm mortar squad of the 3rd Platoon of Company G was returning with an armload of mortar shells when he saw a figure coming toward him from the corner of the building in Erria where he slept. "It was hard to identify the enemy from your own men, because it was so dark. If you could get a look at the profile, the helmets and long overcoats gave them away. I dropped my mortar shells and raised my rifle. The soldier said, 'Me hande hoch,' meaning, I surrender. There was too much going on for me to take him back to the company command post. I took his rifle and threw it on the ground and illustrated for him to put his hands behind his head. Then I pointed to our company command post. He began moving in the direction I had pointed. Before he could get out of the yard, another German I had not seen, got up about twenty yards from us and threw his rifle down and followed the other German toward our command post. I continued on my way back to our gun emplacement with my mortar shells. Since we were out of mortar shells, I suggested to [Private First Class William] Swint that we try to get back to our main line of resistance. He told [Private First Class Robert] Lindsay and me to go ahead and as soon as Sergeant [Alfred] Hess got back, the rest of them would come. Lindsay and I began our trip back over an open field leading to a house at an intersection that had been established as our main line of resistance. As we approached the house, we were both running pretty fast, and as we came around the corner, we saw the silhouettes of soldiers lined up at a tall hedge running from the front corner of the house to a fence beside the road.

"We could not make out whether they were our troopers or Jerries. I was on the roadside and Lindsay was next to the building. We had gone too far to retreat to the corner when I heard a German accent say, 'They are Americans.'

"Something told me from within to hit the ground and play dead. I did. My helmet came off and rolled in front of me. My forehead was resting on my left arm that was crooked in front of me. As I was falling, I glanced to my left and saw what appeared to be sparks coming from Lindsay's chest. He always wore something like a leather vest. As I lay on that frozen ground, I could see the Germans in the doorway of the combination house and stable where we were.

"What happened next I did not understand, nor do I to this day know what caused me to do what I did. I saw this German take dead aim at my head with his rifle and pull the trigger. I could not move. Something within me kept telling me, 'Don't move.' When the bullet struck me, to the left of my nose, it came down knocking out three of my upper teeth, before going through my lower lip and opening a wide gash to the bottom of my chin. The impact partially knocked me unconscious. I lay there, waiting for the next bullet to blow my brains out.

"I was not a professing Christian at that time, but I recall making peace with God in that moment; and I believe had that second bullet come, I would be with Him even today. My whole life flashed before me within seconds. Yet, in obedience to that voice that told me not to move, I didn't.

"One of the Germans began calling his roll and each name drew a response with a 'hier.' I then realized Germans were all around me. I was slowly freezing to death, worrying all the while the Jerries would see the vapor coming from my breathing.It is not possible to guess how long I lay there, but finally a German came out, grabbed my left arm to pull my body over against the house (where they had put Lindsay). When I rolled over on my back, my eyes must have been wide open and the wound on my face horrifying, because the sight caused the German to jump back as if he had seen a ghost. He grabbed my rifle, took it by the barrel and broke it against the ground. I was hoping it wouldn't go off and kill him, because that would probably have sealed my fate. He helped me into the door of the house where a German officer was. Several Germans came in and by their action, wanted to kill me. I do not understand German, but whatever he told them was sufficient to save my life, because no one else approached him. This officer took a large bandage and placed it over my mouth after sprinkling a powdery substance on the wound. After giving my name, rank, and serial number, I was then put in a separate room and told to sit down. The German officer had one of his men get me an overcoat off one of my dead comrades."[15]

After making his way back to the 1st Platoon area, Private First Class Lane Lewis found his squad leader and others from the 3rd Platoon of Company G who had also made the withdrawal. "Several hours later, while it was still dark we regrouped and launched a counterattack to recapture Erria."[16]

The 3rd Battalion commander, Lieutenant Colonel Louis Mendez requested that the regimental reserve, Company E, be released to counterattack Erria. At 4:30 a.m., Company E, less one platoon, and the reserve Company F platoon counterattacked from the northeast, Company I counterattacked from the northwest, and Company G attacked from the north.

During the counterattack, Staff Sergeant Joseph Kissane, the Company G operations sergeant, was firing his rifle from a ditch along a sunken road that was the 1st Platoon line when he witnessed an unforgettable sight: "Lieutenant [Lloyd] Polette, leading Company E in the counterattack. He climbed over a fence shouting, 'Follow me!' running through the field towards the crossroad."[17]

Company I was in reserve in the woods behind Company H, which was on the right flank of Company G. Company I had only thirty-eight effectives due to casualties inflicted by German artillery fire while assembling, As the Company I troopers closed in on Erria, Sergeant Buck Hutto could see muzzle flashes from German automatic weapons. "The Germans were firing a machine gun from a second floor window. Someone fired a bazooka [shell] into the window, which knocked out the machine gun. I went around the back of the house and there, in the small paved courtyard, was the body of Corporal Brassie S. Cascio. He lay in a pool of blood, his head almost severed by a Schmeisser machine pistol. There was his blood all over the stones, still steaming in the cold. They had already taken his boots.

"Cascio had had a premonition that he would not survive another campaign, and before leaving Camp Sissonne, he distributed his personal belongings to friends, and sent some mementos back to his mother in Chicago."[18]

Company G trooper, Private John Hodge who had been badly wounded in the face, was lying in one of the houses in Erria when the counterattack hit the Germans. "One soldier had thrown a white phosphate grenade and it hit the metal window frame and dropped to the ground outside before exploding. Some of the shrapnel came into the building and landed on the back of one of the German's hand, causing a painful burn. The soldier who threw the grenade was wounded in the heel and was captured and put in the room with me. From where I was, I could see through the door of the room and out the side door I was brought in through by the frightened German. You could tell something was beginning to happen, because gunfire began picking up. Finally, I saw a trooper from I Company place his machine gun in the intersection and began firing down into the area where we were.

"The Germans began leaving the building and I recall the last fellow to leave looked over at us and kind of smiled and gave a salute as he left. I do recall our troopers had fixed bayonets and we could hear the Germans screaming from the area where our mortar was.

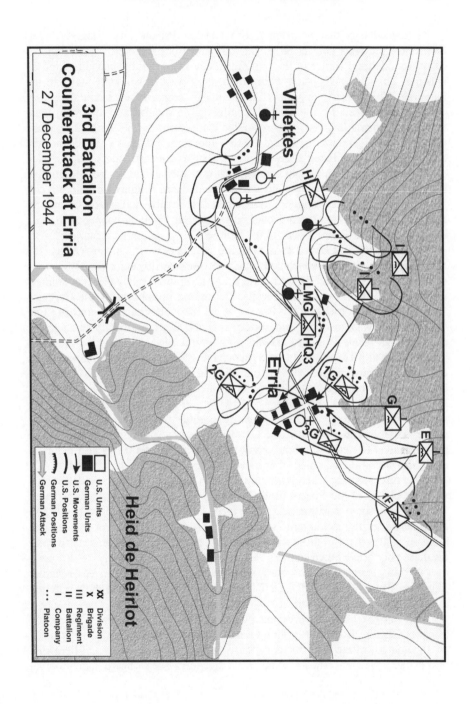

3rd Battalion
Counterattack at Erria
27 December 1944

Villettes

Erria

Heid de Heirlot

LMG HQ3

2G

1G

G

3G

1F

U.S. Units
German Units
U.S. Positions
U.S. Movements
German Positions
German Attack

XX Division
X Brigade
III Regiment
II Battalion
I Company
... Platoon

"I learned later that Sergeant [Alfred] Hess, [Private First Class William] Swint, and the other two in our squad were about one hundred yards behind us as we rounded the corner of the building. They saw what happened to Lindsay and me. Thinking both of us were killed, they went down some stairs to the basement. This is where they stayed until after I Company had cleared the area.

"As our comrades came up to the building, we shouted and told them there were no Germans left, only two wounded troopers in the building. One of the men helped us get back to our aid station, about one hundred yards behind the main intersection of Erria. We were a bunch of wounded troopers helping each other as best we could. To our immediate front, was a field where fighting had taken place earlier. Some Germans were wounded and begging for help. I recall thinking, if some were wounded, some could still be alive and armed. Therefore, I found a rifle and stood guard over our wounded. Nothing happened though, and at daybreak we were moved to the regimental aid station for treatment."[19]

Private First Class Lane Lewis, with the 3rd Platoon of Company G, realized that the predawn counterattack had caught the Germans by surprise. "They were so confident that we would not return, that we captured many German soldiers asleep in our own abandoned bedrolls. During the initial assault, the Germans had captured my friend John Hodge as he was attempting to retreat. Our counterattack was so quick and sudden that the Germans left in great haste, forgetting all about John and leaving him behind. He was sure glad to see us again. We had all heard the stories about the SS killing their prisoners. This counterattack pushed the Germans out of Erria and they were forced to retreat back across the open fields to their original starting positions.

"As they retreated, our artillery batteries began firing and caught them in the open again. Their losses were very heavy. I could hear the Germans screaming as they lay dying in the snow. The German sergeants would call out roll call to their platoons to determine how many men were lost and to try and maintain order and discipline. Not many Germans were able to answer this roll call.

"The next morning when it became light, I could see the open fields covered with the bodies of the frozen, dead Germans. The dead were frozen stiff in all kinds of gruesome positions. One German soldier was frozen with his arm outstretched as if reaching for someone. There must have been at least one hundred bodies there in those snow covered fields. I felt a strange sense of pity for these poor brave fallen soldiers.

"We later learned that this attack was made by the 19th SS Panzer Grenadier Regiment from the 9th SS Panzer Division, and they had earned the reputation as the elite regiment of the division."[20]

After the Germans were driven out of Erria, it became quiet. Company I trooper, Sergeant Buck Hutto, found a mattress lying on the side of the road. "I cut the end out of the mattress, and [Staff] Sergeant [Jack] Elliott and I crawled into it like a sleeping bag for some warm sleeping. Then I heard some hobnail boots walking up the road toward us. I didn't want to get out of the mattress, so when he got close, I yelled, 'Halt!'

"That Kraut dropped something and took off running back the other way like a scared rat. Next morning, when it was light, we found the machine gun ammo which the Kraut had dropped. During the darkness, a wounded German kept saying, 'Save us, Amerikanisch! Save us!' I could hear the German noncoms yelling orders as they pulled back and regrouped. We weren't about to risk getting shot helping the wounded Krauts."[21]

As dawn broke, Private First Class Lewis returned to his foxhole in the 3rd Platoon area. "That morning we strengthened our positions and captured a few more German soldiers who had been left behind and were hiding following our attack that had recaptured Erria.

"I remember seeing the graves registration unit as it gathered all the dead and stacked them up like firewood in one of the streets of Erria. Several of the dead had their fingers cut off by the graves registration people, who had stolen their rings. This was my first real combat experience and I was scared to death the whole time! I had never fired a weapon in anger before. Death was new to me, I had never seen so many dead people before, and I hoped that I never would again. I thought back to the time that I was so anxious to get into action. How naive I had been. Little did I know that this was just the beginning of a time filled with blood and gore, and death."[22]

At dawn, Company G troopers began policing the battlefield, which included removing weapons left behind by the enemy. Staff Sergeant Joseph Kissane came across a trooper inflicting payback for the Malmedy massacre. "The coming of dawn revealed the company area littered with dead and dying SS troops and varieties of equipment. Meandering around collecting German weapons, I started to pass by a trooper carrying a Tommy gun. He was assuaging the agonies of the ill fated Germans. The medics were preoccupied caring for our casualties. As I started by, he lowered his gun. Then suddenly, he raised it and fired, missing my leg by an inch. I called him something. While stacking rifles, one of them discharged, narrowly missing my head. Exhausted, I reckoned that's it, I have had it, and went into the barn to sleep."[23]

First Sergeant Bob Kolterman's Company G morning report included the casualty count from the fighting. "One hundred enemy dead were counted in the company area. G Company suffered seven KIA, thirteen WIA, and two MIA."[24]

Private John Hodge, with the 3rd Platoon of Company G, was among those wounded, having been wounded in the mouth. "Our regimental surgeon [Major Dave Thomas], while examining me, kept looking at my head for a wound. Finally, he asked me if I was wounded anywhere other than my mouth. My reply was, 'No,' and he began helping me take the overcoat off that was given to me earlier. My comrade's brains were still on the collar and back of the coat.

"Later that morning, an ambulance loaded up a group of us to take us back to the hospital. Since I was not a stretcher case, I was placed in the front with the driver. As we began our journey back, it was clearly evident a major battle had taken place. We then began passing mile after mile of our armored vehicles, which were getting ready to launch a counteroffensive on the Germans. Boy, did I feel great when I saw these men and tanks. About this time, the morphine I had received at the regimental aid station plus the warm sunshine coming in the cab of the ambulance began to make me sleepy. But before I drifted off, I remembered wondering why was I spared and so many others died. Why?"[25]

Staff Sergeant Jack Elliott, Sergeants James Green, Lawrence McFadden, and Leroy Thierolf, as well as Corporal Lawrence Salva were awarded Silver Stars for their actions in repulsing the attack. Private First Class Victor Walsh died from his wound on December 29 and was posthumously awarded the Silver Star for his heroism during the attack.

Lieutenant Colonel Mendez was justifiably proud of the victory his 3rd Battalion troopers had achieved. "One hundrerd twenty-seven dead Germans were found in G Company's area alone. The artillery, in its vital role of saturating the German assembly area for the attack, fired 1,700 rounds of artillery in one hour. The 81mm mortars fired 660 rounds of ammunition in the same period of time. Trucks had run ammunition directly into the town during the firefight. Patrols were sent to maintain contact with the retreating enemy units immediately after the enemy had withdrawn. The battalion reestablished its OPL [outpost line]...The 9th SS Panzer Division had attacked through a Volksgrenadier outfit, so there was still a German MLR to the south after the withdrawal of the 9th SS Panzer Division."[26]

In addition to the casualties counted by the 3rd Battalion, thirty-two dead and five wounded enemy were found that morning in front of the Company F line. Company F lost one trooper killed during the assault.

That morning, Lieutenant Bill Call, the platoon leader of the 2nd Platoon of Company G, was called to the company command post. "After things settled down, Captain Wilde said, 'Lieutenant Call, you're my new exec. Leave [Staff Sergeant Frank] Sirovica in charge of the platoon.'

"He was in charge of it anyway. It was just a matter of form.

"He said, 'You'll be my exec officer. [Lieutenant Brewster] Sunday isn't here and he won't be back for awhile.'

"So, I didn't know what the hell happened and I told Frank, 'You're in charge, Frank.'

"'What the hell is going on, lieutenant?'

"'I don't know. Sunday isn't here anymore.'

"'Well good, you'll make a hell of an exec officer and I'll make a hell of a platoon leader. But I don't want [lieutenant's] bars.' He respected officers, but he made good decisions. Sometimes us officers didn't make good decisions. But I don't know that Frank ever made a bad one."[27]

Later, Lieutenant Call learned what had happened to Lieutenant Sunday during the German attack the previous night. "He broke and walked back to battalion and kept right on going to the rear to regiment."[28]

In the Company D sector on the morning of December 27, Sergeant Warren F. Albrecht led a daylight patrol to clear snipers in front of the main line of resistance. Albrecht maneuvered his patrol to ambush a group of Germans, killing four. A short time later, Albrecht and his patrol observed a column of infantry, supported by two self-propelled guns. He sent back a runner with the information, which brought down an artillery barrage on the column. Albrecht and his troopers took advantage of the barrage to also fire on the enemy troops, further demoralizing them and causing their withdrawal. Sergeant Albrecht was awarded the Silver Star for his gallant and aggressive leadership of the patrol.

The next day, Lieutenant Joseph Hall led five of his Company D troopers on another patrol, taking with them a 60mm mortar and twenty shells. He found a vantage point on a hill overlooking the village of Reharmont. From that position, he observed a group of Germans standing around outside of one of the buildings. The patrol fired all twenty mortar shells into the group, causing severe casualties among them.

On December 31, Lieutenant Hall led another daylight combat patrol into the enemy rear area. Advancing through the forested hills, Hall found a trail that led along a firebreak. When Hall and his troopers sighted a group of enemy troops, he immediately deployed his men and they opened fire as they advanced, killing one German. Despite enemy automatic weapons fire, the sight of Hall and his troopers closing in, unnerved several Germans, who abandoned their machine guns and fled into the woods. Lieutenant Hall and his patrol then attacked the main body of enemy troops who had taken refuge in a ditch, killing another twelve and driving off the remainder. Hall then assembled his patrol and returned to the 508th lines without having suffered a casualty. Lieutenant Hall was awarded a Silver Star and an oak leaf cluster (second award) for his heroic leadership during the two patrols.

That same day, a single German mortar shell landed in the area where the 2nd Platoon of Company A was dug in, killing Staff Sergeant George Clement, Corporal Walter Firestine, Technician Fifth Grade Jean LeBoeuf, and Private First Class Hugh Van Winkle. Private First Class Woody Wodowski was in his foxhole just yards from the explosion. "They were having a little meeting. That was the first time I ever saw Lieutenant [George] Lamm shook up."[29]

For Private First Class Jim Allardyce, with Company B, the time spent in those defensive positions was miserable, mostly because of the weather and the food. "What we lived on during the Bulge were C and K-rations. The C-rations were cans of cheese and ham, beans and franks, and I think a stew. These cans had to be heated to be palatable. Since we had a minimum of heating capability, we usually got these rations heated in a field kitchen when we were relieved as a unit for rest. That happened only three times while I was in the line.

"Once, at Basse Bodeux, we were given the new 10 in 1 ration—enough in a box for ten men. I forgot the main part, but I remember enjoying a can of peas, one of peaches, and one of green beans all by myself. Our main ration was the K. It was for one man. There was a can of Spam, or cheese and ham, and I can't remember the rest. This was supplemented by crackers, hard candy, dry coffee or lemonade, cigarettes, and toilet tissue (camouflaged). This food had to be heated, too. The guys would use the waxed cardboard box for heat (about Crackerjack size) or tear off a piece of Composition C from their Gammon grenade and light it. I did well with a German pocket folding stove I had found in Holland. It had heat tablets, and one was enough for heating the K cans or water for coffee or lemonade. Yes, hot lemonade—anything for a little heat. We lived out in it like animals in the ground. If we could find a candle in a home, it provided a little warmth in our hole. The snow eventually got almost [up] to our knees. We were cold all the time and often wet from the snow melting on our clothing."[30]

On New Year's Day, Private First Class Norb Studelska, was sitting in his foxhole on the Company D main line of resistance, when troopers manning an outpost returned after being relieved. "[Sergeant Robert J.] White was on outpost duty and came back to the line with a smiling face and a bullet wound through his upper thigh, taking him back to a warm and comfortable hospital stay—no glory."[31]

ON JANUARY 1, 1945, LIEUTENANT COLONEL SHIELDS WARREN, commanding officer of the 1st Battalion, and other key officers of the regiment attended a meeting at division headquarters near Hâbièmont, a small village southeast of Werbomont, to receive the attack order for the First Army counteroffensive. "As I entered the division CP, I noticed General [Matthew] Ridgway [commander of the XVIII Airborne Corps] talking to Major General [Jim] Gavin, the division commander. Since I was not about to interrupt that conversation, I moved over next to my regimental commander and kept my mouth shut. After a few more minutes of conversation with General Gavin, General Ridgway came over to me with a puzzled look on his face, extending his hand and said, 'You remember me don't you, Shields?'

"I was more than startled, but managed to stammer, 'I could never forget you, General Ridgway, but didn't want to interrupt your talk with the division commander.' In any event, my remark seems to have made him feel better and he then went on to greet other newly arriving regimental and battalion commanders. This incident, to me, reaffirmed the personal warmth and concern that General Ridgway had for all who were subordinate to him in the chain of command."[32]

At dawn on January 3, 1945, the U.S. First Army counteroffensive began in the midst of one to two feet deep snow, fog, and an overcast sky. The 82nd Airborne Division's orders were to capture the ground relinquished during the withdrawal on Christmas Eve. The 62nd Volksgrenadier Division, with a full regiment of four battalions of artillery and reinforced by two attached infantry regiments, was dug in opposite of the division. It was very bloody as the division pushed forward against tough resistance. The volksgrenadiers fought from deeply dug in and camouflaged positions, taking advantage of hilltops and stone buildings. The densely forested hilly terrain was ideal for the defenders.

The 508th, in division reserve, advanced behind the 505th Parachute Infantry as it pushed southeast. On January 6, the regiment was brought out of reserve and committed for an attack t the following morning. The objective would be the Thier-du-Mont ridgeline, which the 508th had occupied prior to the Christmas Eve withdrawal.

Thier-du-Mont was defended by remnants of Grenadier Regiment 164 of the 62nd Volksgrenadier Division as well as remnants of two other Volksgrendier regiments attached to the division—Grenadier Regiments 295 and 753. The defense was further bolstered by the 62nd Volksgrenadier Division's artillery, engineer, and antitank units. For veterans of Normandy, thoughts of Hill 95 and the la Poterie ridgeline passed through their consciousness. For replacements like Private First Class Lane Lewis, a Company G bazooka gunner, thoughts of the slaughter of the attacking German troops at Erria just days before, passed through their minds. "We all tried to look like we weren't scared. We would joke and carry on, anything to take our minds off what we would have to face in the next day's attack. Although we were all scared, we were good soldiers and we were ready to do our duty and finish this war, so we could all go home. No one wanted to let his buddies down, this was unthinkable."[33]

On the evening of January 6, the 3rd Battalion bivouacked in a wooded area near Arbrefontaine. Lieutenant Bill Call was the new executive officer of G Company. "That night, [Captain] Russ [Wilde] and I took over a German CP in these woods. It was like a palace. You could stand up in it, they had logs over it all covered with dirt and everything, and an entryway. It was wonderful."[34]

At 3:30 a.m. on January 7, the battalion commanders and their respective staffs reported to the regimental command post to receive the attack order for a dawn assault to seize Thier-du-Mont. At that time, Lieutenant Colonel Louis Mendez learned that his 3rd Battalion would lead the attack. "A platoon of tanks and a platoon of TDs [tank destroyers] were to be attached to the battalion. The battalion was to wait until the 325th Glider Infantry captured Thier-del-Preux (hill mass to the west of the battalion objective) and then it was to hit from this hill mass into the left flank of the enemy position because the frontal approach to the enemy position was open and up hill. The route of approach from the assembly area to the LD [line of departure] south of Menil was to be along the road from Arbrefontaine to Menil."[35]

When Lieutenant Colonel Mendez returned to his command post, he issued his attack order for the 3rd Battalion. "G Company was to lead the attack in a column of platoons with the leading platoon as skirmishers. I Company was to follow G and H Company was to follow I. The leading elements were to cross the LD [line of departure] as the left flank company of the 325th Glider Infantry reached the base of Thier-del-Preux. There was to be no [preliminary] artillery fire support, only the battalion's 81mm mortars."[36]

Captain Hank Le Febvre, the 2nd Battalion S-3, was also present at the regimental command post when the attack order was issued. "The regiment was to move out at 06:00 the following morning, 7 January 1945, in the attack. The formation was to be a column of battalions up to the line of departure, which was to be the road which ran from Goronne, southwest to Grand-Sart. From this position, the 3rd Battalion would move east on the south side of Thier-du-Mont ridge and down a small trail that led to the town of Comté. The 1st Battalion would attack east on the north side of Thier-du-Mont ridge, clear it of enemy, and advance to the eastern edge of the ridge. They would then tie in with the 505th Regiment near the town of Rencheux on the left and the 2nd Battalion on the right, near the crown of the ridge. The 2nd Battalion was to follow the 3rd Battalion as it began to go down on the south side of the ridge and pass through the gap that would be created in its area of responsibility, and advance to the eastern edge of the ridge. This meant that the 2nd Battalion was to return to the same area it had previously occupied, however, the left flank would not be extended so far this time. The tie-in on the left flank was to be with the 1st Battalion in the vicinity of the peak of the ridge and on the right with the 3rd Battalion in the vicinity of Comté.

"After coordinating with the commanders of the 3rd and 1st Battalions, the 2nd Battalion commander returned to issue his attack order. The battalion was again fortunate in that it knew the terrain over which it would operate, including the location of trails leading to its objective. The plan was to move behind the 3rd Battalion in column until it crossed the line of departure, then to move up the ridge toward Thier-du-Mont with two companies abreast, E on the left, D on the right, and F following D by two hundred yards. This would put the companies in the same relative location they had formerly occupied when they returned to the position. The two forward companies each had a section of light machine guns attached. The four 81mm mortars were to be emplaced as far forward as possible to give maximum coverage for the attacking companies, with a minimum number of displacements. In addition, the two leading companies were to have a forward observer from the mortars with them. The enemy's strength in the area was unknown, but it could be assumed he would defend, at least in some places, along Thier-du-Mont ridge, as positions there could cover the whole valley, in which the towns of Vielsalm, Rencheux, Goronne, and Abrefontaine were located. After the battalion order was issued, the light machine gun crews and mortar forward observers joined the units to which they had been attached. The company commanders then briefed their companies for the following day's mission."[37]

Upon returning to Company G, Captain Russell Wilde briefed his platoon leaders and noncommissioned officers on the plan of attack. It was at that time that 1st Sergeant Bob Kolterman learned that Company G, already depleted by the losses incurred at Erria, would lead the assault. "We had six officers, eighty-two men, three medics, and twenty-three replacements."[38]

In the predawn hours of January 7, at the 3rd Battalion assembly area north of Arbrefontaine, Private First Class Lane Lewis, was asleep in his shallow two man slit trench with another Company G trooper. "Sergeant [Alfred] Hess, our platoon NCO, woke us up while it was still dark; we held our weapons tight as we nervously waited for first light and the order to advance. Our attack would start out by moving through fifty yards of wooded area, then having to cross about eight hundred yards of open fields until we reached our objective of the wooded ridge of Thier-du-Mont. I couldn't help but think of the SS soldiers who had been slaughtered as they had crossed the open fields during their attack on Erria. I tried to put these thoughts out of my mind. The ground was still covered with a heavy snowfall and it was very cold."[39]

Just before the company moved out, Private First Class Lewis noticed that the trooper who had occupied the slit trench with him was still lying in it. "A soldier that had been in the foxhole with me did not come out as I was leaving. He was still asleep! I tried to wake him, but he wouldn't wake up, so I left him behind. He had been so frightened that he had gone into a state of deep sleep and nothing could wake him up."[40]

As Sergeant Fred Gladstone, with Company I, waited for the order to move out, his buddy Private William J. "Bill" Sobolewski began "asking me questions about God, and what would happen to our souls if we died. Later, I was to learn the answers to his questions, but that morning I was ignorant of such matters and do not recall what I said to him. Our conversation did not last too long."[41]

As the regiment moved south along the road from Arbrefontaine to Menil, Company A passed several American Sherman tanks parked in a column on the road. As they did, Private First Class Woody Wodowski heard the sudden blast of a machine gun from one of those tanks. "An American tanker, I guess it was the driver, got in the tank and hit the .30-caliber machine gun button and shot and killed Private [Claborn A.] Steele."[42]

As usual, Lieutenant Colonel Mendez was up front with Company G as the regiment moved south to the line of departure. "German artillery hit Menil, the north slope of Thier-del-Preux and the saddle between the hills. It was a very heavy shelling. G Company moved along its prescribed route at the base of Thier-del-Preux and met 325th infantrymen who were being driven off the hill."[43]

Colonel Roy Lindquist, the regimental commander, could see that the 325th Glider Infantry Regiment ahead of them had not yet secured the Thier-del-Preux hill mass. "Captain Wilde received permission from the 325th Glider Infantry to pass through them and proceed to his objective (elements of the 325th were blocking his approach). Company G started the attack by deploying to the left of the 325th Glider Infantry and moving toward its objective. At the same time, Company A of the 325th Glider Infantry was attacking along a road to the right. Almost immediately after the company started, German 88s, tanks, and SPs opened up with pointblank fire."[44]

Company G left the road and crossed a field, using shallow slate pits and the fog to conceal its approach to a wooded area which was the line of departure. Just as he left the road, crossing a wire fence bordering it, Private First Class Angel Romero, with 1st Squad of the 2nd Platoon, saw a shell explode nearby. "Our machine gunner, [Private First Class William A.] Kovensky, got hit trying to cross a wire fence. He flew through the air about five feet, even though he weighed about two hundred pounds, but he was not killed."[45]

Company G moved into the fifty yard deep wooded area just before the line of departure, where 1st Sergeant Bob Kolterman assisted in getting the company deployed into attack formation: "1st Platoon on the left, 2nd Platoon on the right, and 3rd Platoon behind in the middle. Snow, fog, and smoke hampered the advance. The company was already suffering casualties from German rifle, machine gun, mortar, and artillery fire, and even tanks from Grand-Sart to the south."[46]

The platoon of Sherman tanks attached to the 3rd Battalion failed to arrive due to a logistics problem. The only armored support for the attack would be an attached platoon of four M10 tank destroyers.

Meanwhile, the 325th Glider Infantry captured the Thier-del-Preux hill, west of the objective. As Company G moved through the wooded area, Lieutenant Colonel Mendez made sure that fire support was available for the assault. "A battalion machine gun section set up at (655885) on the [eastern slope of Thier-del-Preux] hill to give fire support for G Company in its drive across the saddle. The battalion OP [observation post] was placed at (654891) [near the road running south to Grand-Sart]."[47]

As he made his way through the woods, Company G trooper, Private First Class Lane Lewis's peripheral vision saw movement nearby. "I caught a glimpse of someone standing behind me. I turned around rapidly, ready to fire, and there was standing a sizeable German soldier with his hands raised up in the air. He wanted to surrender. He could have very easily killed me, but he didn't.

"'Hande hoch!' I said to him as I led him to [the slate pits] where we were keeping all the Germans prisoners that we had captured. He was happy to go there. For him the war was now over. Maybe this attack wouldn't be so difficult after all."[48]

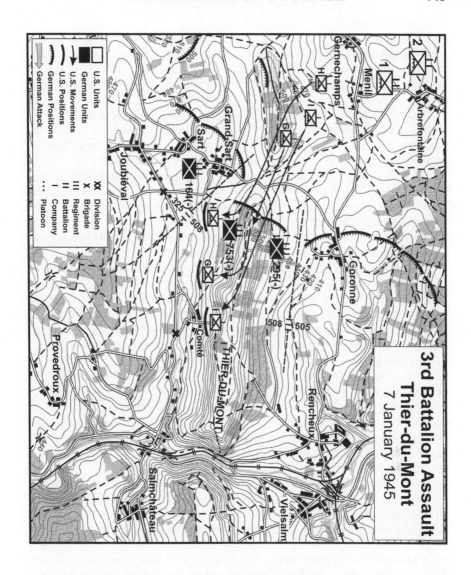

3rd Battalion Assault
Thier-du-Mont
7 January 1945

Captain Russell Wilde, the commander of Company G, was advancing with his radio man as the company emerged from the woods. "The company came under heavy artillery fire as it came within a thousand yards of the objective and the intensity of the fire increased as we drew closer. Between the last cover and the heavily wooded ridge that was our objective, lay six hundred yards of entirely open ground and as the company started across, it came under direct fire from eight field pieces emplaced on the objective."[49]

As Company G moved into the flat open ground west of the ridge, German 88mm antiaircraft guns, 75mm antitank guns, mortars, machine guns, and rifle fire rained down from the ridge, while enfilade fire from the Grand-Sart area on the right rear and the vicinity of Goronne to the left front crisscrossed the open pasture.

Captain Russell Wilde saw his Company G troopers being cut down all around him. "The company suffered numerous casualties and fell back to the woods to regroup. The 2nd Platoon, commanded by Staff Sergeant Frank L. Sirovica was ordered to resume the advance as the leading platoon."[50]

From the 3rd Battalion observation post, the regimental commander, Colonel Lindquist, watched the assault through binoculars. "Captain Wilde, showing superb leadership under very trying circumstances, reorganized the company under heavy artillery fire."[51]

First Sergeant Bob Kolterman again helped G Company get reorganized and moving forward again. "A quick regrouping put the 2nd Platoon in front, followed by company headquarters, 1st Platoon, and 3rd Platoon."[52]

As the company reached the edge of the woods to resume the attack, Captain Wilde noticed that the the 2nd Platoon troopers hesitated to move into the open. "Staff Sergeant Sirovica moved out alone ahead of his platoon and by his example of courage, inspired his platoon and the rest of the company to move rapidly and aggressively across the open ground to close with the enemy."[53]

Sergeant Merl A. Beach, one of Sirovica's squad leaders, moved out behind him. "The whole company, inspired by his example, moved across the long stretch of open ground despite the direct and murderous fire of the artillery."[54]

Following just behind Staff Sergeant Sirovica and forming the point of the Company G attack were Private First Class George "Mick" McGrath, the 2nd Platoon's scout and BAR gunner; Corporal Thomas Beno, the assistant squad leader of the 1st Squad of the 2nd Platoon; Private First Class Loren W. Carter, with the 3rd Squad of the 2nd Platoon; and Captain Wilde.

As he crossed the open ground, Sergeant Marvin Risnes was a witness to a horrible sight. "I saw one machine gunner whose head was blown off by a direct hit from an 88 as he moved forward. With his head gone, he took three or four more steps with the gun still on his shoulder before dropping in the snow."[55]

Lieutenant Colonel Mendez and his small command group moved forward behind Company G as it advanced toward the ridge. A liaison team from Battery A, 319th Glider Field Artillery Battalion, which was set up to fire from the village of Fosse to the north, stayed close by Mendez during the advance. Sergeant Ted Covais was a member of that liaison team. "There was this wounded paratrooper. He was trying to crawl away when one of our [tank destroyers] ran over him. He wasn't far from me."[56]

When Private First Class McGrath spotted a machine gun delivering enfilade fire into the left flank of the company, he immediately advanced toward it. As he did so, he encountered two enemy riflemen providing security for the machine gun. McGrath fired a burst from his BAR, killing both and then charged the machine gun, firing as he ran, killing the enemy machine gun crew.

As he advanced, Staff Sergeant Joseph Kissane, the Company G operations sergeant, passed the 1st Platoon's wounded assistant platoon leader. "Lieutenant [James] Fowler, who had lost a leg, was being attended by two medics."[57]

After leaving his prisoner at the collection point, Private First Class Lane Lewis caught up with the 3rd Platoon as it started across the open ground behind the 1st Platoon. "'Bazookas up front!' Captain Wilde ordered. At that same moment the German 88s opened fire. Blam! Blam! Just like that, four of the M10s [tank destroyers] were hit and destroyed. One of the M10s caught fire and the ammunition it had stored exploded with a huge, fiery blast. Along with another bazooka man, Private [First Class] Gerald G. Jones, I ran forward. We both could see a German 88 hidden in the woods located along a fence row. The gun crew was working feverishly to load and fire their gun as fast as they could. We both took aim at the 88 gun as our loaders worked fanatically to load our weapons. The Germans could see us preparing to fire at them and they began to concentrate their fire at us."[58]

As the two bazooka teams loaded, Staff Sergeant Kissane and the company headquarters troopers following behind the 3rd Platoon suddenly saw the well camouflaged 88mm antiaircraft gun. "While pointing at the 88, Wilde shouted, 'Hit it! Hit it!' Private First Class [William T.] Kenny, directly in front of me, flipped his machine gun off his shoulder and fired."[59]

Private First Class Lewis tried to focus on aiming and firing his bazooka as enemy shells burst around him and machine bullets zipped by his head. "It was a miracle that neither one of us was hit! Our loaders placed high-explosive rounds into our bazookas as we waited for the signals from our loaders that we were loaded and ready to fire. The noise was deafening as artillery shells exploded all around us; several German infantrymen were firing their weapons at us. How could we survive this?

"My weapon was loaded first as my loader tapped me on the helmet as a signal to me that he had loaded the bazooka and I was ready to fire. I got off the first round, as Private Jones was not loaded yet. After I pulled the trigger I could see my round as it left the tube and went about thirty yards before it spiraled out of control to the ground. It was a dud round!"[60]

Private First Class Gerald Jones also fired a bazooka round at the 88 from a standing position, which didn't explode. The gun then fired two rounds back at Jones, who was getting another round loaded into his bazooka, while Private First Class Kenny fired his machine gun at the enemy crew, forcing some of them to seek cover.

Private First Class Lewis was still getting his bazooka reloaded when he heard the whooshing sound of a bazooka rocket leaving the tube. "Private Jones fired his round next and it was a direct hit on the protective shield of the 88, killing or wounding most of the gun crew. The few survivors who were left abandoned their gun and ran away. The two remaining German 88s fired on us with a renewed determination. Shells were bursting all around us. We were being slaughtered! Realizing that to remain where we were would be certain death, Captain Wilde ordered us to charge the ridge ahead of us."[61]

Private First Class Angel Romero, with the 2nd Platoon, was rushing forward just behind the point when he was wounded by two large pieces of shrapnel that hit him in the back, knocking him unconscious.

Private First Class Lewis, carrying his bazooka, along with a "grease gun" submachine gun, in addition to his other gear, struggled to keep up with the 3rd Platoon. "We did not hesitate or even think about the chances of our survival. We all ran forward; I could see my fellow soldiers falling on both sides of me as I ran towards the defending Germans. I saw one soldier after another get hit and fall to the ground, his red blood staining the white snow. The noise was deafening, bullets were throwing up the snow all around me, and artillery shells were bursting everywhere.

"As I was running forward, a German artillery shell from an 88 landed between me and another soldier. The blast from this shell picked us both up and threw us into the air. I landed very hard on my back upon the frozen ground. I lay there dazed for a few moments, I don't know for how long. I was afraid to look at myself. I just knew that I had been badly wounded. I ran my hands over my body to make sure everything was where it was supposed to be. I reluctantly looked at my hands expecting to see blood. I hadn't been hit! It was a miracle! The thought never even occurred to me to just lie there and let the others continue the attack. I got back up and continued to move forward, because of the excitement of battle and the adrenaline that was flowing in my body; I didn't even notice the pain in my lower back."[62]

The Company G commander, Captain Russell Wilde ran forward just a short distance behind the 2nd Platoon point. "As the company moved up the slope of the objective, Sergeant Sirovica, from his position ahead of his platoon, sighted an 88mm gun that the crew was attempting to bring to bear on the company. Sergeant Sirovica signaled his platoon to take cover and without regard for his own safety, moved forward alone to engage the enemy crew. He moved in close without being seen, wounded the two man crew of a machine gun that was providing security for the field piece and forced the other six artillerymen to surrender. By his skillful and courageous action, Sergeant Sirovica succeeded in capturing the gun and ammo intact and undoubtedly prevented numerous casualties."[63]

As Company I followed Company G into the open ground, it was subjected to the same intense enemy fire. As he moved forward, Sergeant Fred Gladstone heard his buddy, Private Bill Sobolewski, cry for help. "When I got to Bill, he was lying on his back in the snow, already turning red from his blood. I could not see the extent of his injury, but I could see one leg broken and twisted. His face was deathly white and was marked with intense pain as he pleaded for help.

The shells were coming in fast and furious. They didn't stop the war because someone was wounded and suffering. I recalled how annoying the shellfire was when I was wounded in Normandy, but Bill was in such agony that he didn't seem to notice. He continued to ask me to help him, but all I could do was to try to stop some of the bleeding. I had never felt such pity for anyone in my life, nor at the same time felt so helpless."[64]

Colonel Lindquist watched Company G as it charged up the slope. "Nearing the objective, an extremely well camouflaged 88, hitherto unobserved, opened up at less than 150 yards range, killing two and wounding eight. Captain Wilde, without the slightest hesitation, again moved to a forward observation point and there, directed on this target the fire of a light machine gun whose gunner did not have clear observation from his position."[65]

Meanwhile, Staff Sergeant Sirovica was still out front, leading the attack. "As the company got closer to its objective, the artillery fire increased and at times was almost at pointblank range, the company again became disorganized and sought cover. Captain Wilde moved forward to an observation point from which he directed artillery fire. As a result of this artillery fire, the tanks, a self-propelled gun, and a German high-velocity gun which was well camouflaged and dug in, were knocked out. A machine gun position was also neutralized by the artillery fire which Captain Wilde directed upon it."[66]

Corporal Wallace C. Judd, a squad leader with Headquarters Company, 3rd Battalion, whose machine guns had provided overhead fire for the attack, now displaced the guns and moved forward as Company G advanced up the slope. When he spotted an enemy emplacement on the flank, Judd exposed himself to its fire to knock it out. Corporal Judd, carrying one of his squad's machine guns up the hill behind Company G, also turned it on a German mortar position on Their-du-Mont and neutralized it. Later, when two German self-propelled guns threatened the attack, Judd moved his machine gun forward to a position where it could engage the two armored vehicles. He successfully killed some of the crew of one of the self-propelled guns, causing the survivors to scatter. Judd also assisted in knocking out the other self-propelled gun.

Staff Sergeant Sirovica reached the dug in German positions and raked them with his Tommy gun, shooting Germans in their holes, as his 2nd Platoon closed in on the German positions. Despite his injured back, Private First Class Lewis kept moving up the ridge with the 3rd Platoon. "[Almost] half of my company had been killed or wounded in making this attack, but those of us who were left were determined to take that ridge.

"Seeing that we would not be denied no matter what our losses were, the Germans lost their nerve and began to run away. One by one the Germans would climb out of their foxholes and dash towards the rear. Soon this turned into a rout and the remaining Germans left in full retreat! Strange things happen in combat and this was one of them. The defending Germans had us outnumbered, and they were entrenched upon the ridge, protected from our fire. There was no logical reason for them to run away. If they had kept their nerve, they could have shot down every one of us before we reached the ridge. Fear is a powerful emotion. The Germans were not cowards, but at this moment in time we were just more determined than they were.

"I couldn't believe it, but somehow I made it to the top of the ridge alive. All the Germans who could do so, were in full retreat. I came upon one of the German 88mm guns, which had been hit by our artillery fire. There lay scattered around the gun the dead and wounded German gun crew. I saw one young German soldier sitting on the ground in a pool of blood, wounded. His friends had wrapped a tourniquet around his bloody leg before fleeing. I looked down at him, and he looked up at me with fear in his eyes. He was crying. I raised my weapon with the intention of killing him. He closed his eyes and lowered his head as he expected to be shot, but I changed my mind and continued to move forward. I couldn't kill an unarmed man, even if he was the enemy. I can still see the look of fear in his eyes as I stood over him with my weapon pointed at his head. His tears were running down his face as he lay dying in the snow. I suppose that he died of his wounds during the coming cold night. Would his family ever know what happened to him? I suppose his family received a letter saying that he died in defense of the Fatherland and what a good soldier he was, but what I will always remember is a young boy who should have been in school, wounded, crying for his mother. What a tragic waste!

"The Germans were moving back down the [southern side of] ridge as fast as they could run. Some of them would fall to the ground and roll down the hill trying to throw off our aim as we fired at them. One German jumped into an abandoned foxhole to hide. We saw where he was hiding and he was quickly captured. Captain Wilde ordered us to take that 'son of a bitch' back to the battalion headquarters and be back in ten minutes! Of course we all knew what the captain wanted. Battalion headquarters was at least a mile to the rear. No way could we take him back there and return back here in ten minutes, so he was taken into the woods and shot. Now you have to remember and understand that we had just charged across this field, and these were the men who had been firing on us. We left a lot of our friends behind as either killed or wounded, and these were the guys who did it! Our blood lust was all charged up. I couldn't justify killing a prisoner, but I understood why it had happened. From on top of the ridge, I could look down below and see the German tanks and other vehicles retreating along the road back towards Germany."[67]

Lieutenant Bill Call, the new G Company executive officer, was moving through the woods up the slope of the Thier-du-Mont ridge with some of the company headquarters personnel following behind the 3rd Platoon. "Maybe we got halfway up the ridge and the column stopped and the word passed down that we were stopping. When we stopped, I told the guys in company headquarters, 'You might as well eat.' We grabbed a K-ration and they all plopped down in the snow. I was leaning against a tree and that's when the shelling started.

"I told the guys, 'Take cover! Incoming!' The next thing I knew, it felt like somebody had driven a long spike down in through my shoulder into the chest area. It burned like a blow torch. I lost my breath; I couldn't get any breaths. They kept shelling and it let up a little bit. I yelled out, 'Medic! Medic!'

"I called for [Lieutenant Howard] Greenawalt, because he was right in front of me. No one but this medic came. I tried to sit up and I passed out. The medic cut my air flight jacket open with his jump knife, he took snow and he packed it in my back where I had been wounded. My lung was collapsed and that's why I couldn't breathe.

"He said, 'Lieutenant, here,' and he pulled the jacket apart and shoved me down in the snow.

"God, it froze. I could breathe fairly well. I was very lightheaded. I was just going into shock.

"The next I knew, the guys were retreating and any paratrooper hates that thought. They were carrying me—they had my legs and arms. Lindquist came by and said, 'Put the lieutenant down.' He said, 'Lieutenant, we can't take you any farther. But I promise this, we'll be back to get you.'

"I said, 'OK, OK, colonel.' They laid me in the snow."[68]

After regrouping, Company G moved forward and secured the western slope of the Thier-du-Mont ridgeline. First Sergeant Bob Kolterman, despite being wounded, stayed with the company until it reached its objective on the ridge. "The Company objective was secured at 2:00 p.m., with sixty-two men and three officers present. Company G lost fourteen KIA, forty-four WIA, and two MIA. I was wounded and evacuated to the first aid station during this action.

"After the rest of the 3rd Battalion moved onto the ridge, General Gavin said to Major [Alton] Bell, 'Tell Lou Mendez and those men that this is the best job I've ever had done for me.'"[69]

Back on the open ground below the ridge, Sergeant Fred Gladstone, with Company I, stayed as long as he could with his wounded buddy, Private Bill Sobolweski. "As soon as the 88s let up, our platoon sergeant Jack Elliott, came over to tell me that Company I had orders to move through Company G and that I was wanted up front right away. I had to leave Bill, much as I hated to. Speaking a few words of encouragement, I covered him with my overcoat and stuck his rifle up in the snow so the medics would find him."[70]

After securing the western side of the Thier-du-Mont ridgeline, Private First Class Lewis became aware for the first time of an excruciating pain in his back, caused by the concussion from the explosion of an 88mm shell earlier in the attack. But, Lewis decided to stay with his platoon instead of being evacuated. Later that day, Lewis was present when General Gavin visited the Company G troopers who were still on their feet. "This was the first time I had ever seen a real live general up close. He had an M1 strapped across his shoulder. He talked with us, asked where we were from, and told us about the good job we had done. He was a natural leader and we all loved him.

"A lot of my friends were left dead and dying in the snow. It was so cold that night that many of the wounded died from exposure. As for myself, I was just glad to be alive. I still don't know how I was able to make that charge and not be killed."[71]

Sergeant Fred Gladstone caught up with Company I on the ridge just as it moved through Company G to push the attack eastward along the southern slope of the ridge. "I Company was to lead the way as we moved out towards our company's specific objective, Comté, a small village on the southern side of the ridge.

"I do not recall following the trail of any retreating Germans in the snow, but Comté was over a mile away, and we would run into more German defensive action at any time. I felt more like a snowplow than a scout as we made our way in an easterly direction along the ridge. As we neared Comté, I was able to get the drop on a German outpost, a soldier who looked so old and cold. He quickly obeyed my command to drop his weapon and raise his hands, and others who were behind him did the same. Company I deployed and we soon had a 'bag' of prisoners. With the approaching darkness came bitter cold, the temperature reaching subzero. I wondered if the medics had found Bill."[72]

The 1st Battalion moved up behind the 3rd Battalion and into the wooded area just west of the line of departure. The 1st Battalion's mission was to attack eastward along northern side of the Thier-du-Mont ridgeline. As Company C medic, Private First Class Gordon Cullings and his platoon "were moving through the woods, a shell hit in a tree that one of the guys was under. It just blew him to pieces. I almost lost it."[73]

As Company C continued through the woods, Cullings "heard someone yelling, 'Doc! Doc!' Everyone called me Doc. I don't know what happened, but I was no longer cold, scared, or any tears running down my checks. I headed as fast as I could to the sound of 'Doc!' Bullets were hitting the trees everywhere. I got to one of my buddies who had been shot through the ankle. I told him to put his arm around my neck and hang on. I got him out to the edge of the woods, where I thought it was safer to work on him, until we could get him out of there.

"I had just gotten his boot cut to get it off when something hit me in the back and shoulder, knocking me forward on my face. I had been shot by a German sniper. I guess the guy I was working on yelled, 'Doc's been shot.'

"Sergeant [Harry J.] Street and the lieutenant came up. I told Sergeant Street to give me a shot of morphine out of my bag, then help me up, which he did. Then we both took the buddy I was working on—Sergeant Street on one side and I on the other and we walked a long way down a logging trail to a jeep that took us to the regimental aid station."[74]

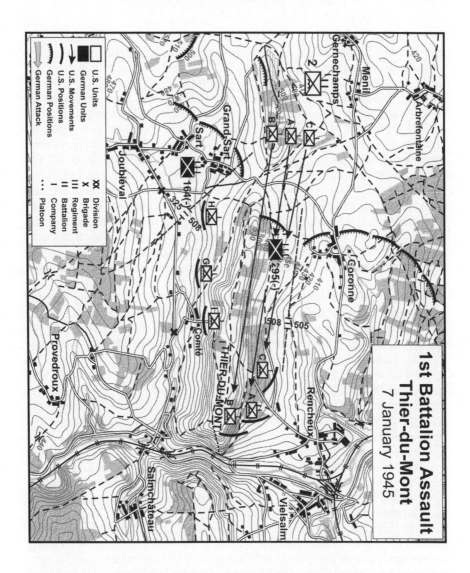

1st Battalion Assault
Thier-du-Mont
7 January 1945

Private First Class Cullings' courage under fire was indicative of that of all of the medics who went to the aid of wounded troopers, despite the danger.

As he advanced across the same open ground the 3rd Battalion had crossed earlier, Private First Class Cipriano Gamez, a Normandy pathfinder and Company C trooper, saw dead and wounded troopers, mostly of G Company, lying everywhere. "I have never known so much fear. It was a terrible slaughter for us."[75]

Technician Fourth Grade Ed Ryan was a radio operator with the liaison team from Battery C, 319th Glider Field Artillery Battalion, which was supporting the 1st Battalion attack. Two German Mark VI Tiger tanks, positioned in the 505th sector near Goronne, engaged the three M10 tank destroyers attached to the 1st Battalion. Ryan and his assistant, Sergeant Henry Broski, were caught on the open ground between them as the 88mm main guns from the German tanks and the tank destroyers' 90mm main guns sent shells screeching past their heads. As this was occurring, Lieutenant John Eskoff, the team's liaison officer, radioed Ryan and told him that he wanted him and Sergeant Broski to move up the hill to join the 1st Battalion troopers advancing along the northern slope of the ridge. Ryan had an SCR 300 radio, weighing almost forty pounds, strapped to his back in addition to his other gear. "He wanted us to come out there where he was with the infantry. So I carried that radio equipment up a hill in a wide open space. The country there was an upward slope, wide open. I was carrying all this stuff through that snow with Kraut tanks shooting at me and the tank destroyer was behind me, shooting back at that Kraut tank. You could hear those shells going right past us."[76]

Sergeant Jim Kurz was up front with the lead element of Company B as the 1st Battalion attacked the northern slope of the Thier-du-Mont ridgeline. "We had easy going until we got abreast of the 3rd Battalion, then we turned left. We got hit with rifle, machine gun, 20mm and 88mm fire. During this heavy fighting, Sergeant [Robert] Savage got killed.

"It was starting to get dark. We then hit a group of white caped men who opened fire. We were in a firefight again. I then heard a voice I recognized. I yelled, 'Walker' and he answered. We were fighting I Company. They had come too far over and bumped into B Company. Five men were killed because of this mistake. Since we had a short way to go to get to our objective, I said so long to [Private Milton A.] Walker.

"We continued forward with [Private First Class] George Banks and myself leading the way. We hit another group of Germans, but they withdrew after a short fight. I heard a cry behind me. [Corporal] Jesse Womble had been hit in the stomach. I ran back and got a medic for him."[77]

After getting a medic for his wounded assistant squad leader, Sergeant Jim Kurz reluctantly left him to continue the attack with B Company eastward along the northern slope of Thier-du-Mont. "We reached our objective and we set up a defense. I told [Private First Class] George [Banks] that I was going back and make sure Jesse got to an aid station. The temperature was now below zero and the snow in the hills was two and a half to three feet deep.

"It was dark when I found Jesse. There were two aid men putting him on a stretcher. I told them that I would make sure Jesse got to the aid station and for them to hunt for other wounded men. I got three other men to help carry Jesse. The four of us had a rough time carrying Jesse, who weighed over two hundred pounds.

"It was a mile up and down hills through three feet of snow to the aid station. We were ready to drop when we got to the aid station. We left Jesse in good hands. As I walked back to the squad, I thanked the men for helping out. I told them I would never let Jesse freeze to death. Many men who were wounded in this attack on January 7, 1945 couldn't be found, because of the snow and darkness, so they froze to death.

"Jesse had been with George Banks and me when we jumped in Normandy. When I hurt my foot on the Holland jump, Jesse had helped me up the hills on the attack from the drop zone. When I got back to the front line, I told George that I figured Jesse would die. I had left word at the aid station for them to let me know how Jesse did. We both prayed for Jesse. When George and I finished digging the foxhole, it was after midnight. We then took turns sleeping (two hours on guard and two hours of sleep)."[78]

When Company B reached the east end of the ridge on the northern slope overlooking Rencheux, it halted. Private First Class Jim Allardyce and the other troopers dug shallow slit trenches in the rocky frozen ground. "It was in these positions that Lieutenant [Raymond] Kampe got his comeuppance. He was a noisy, self-satisfied showoff. He came over on the boat with me and used to do handstands, etcetera, to showoff to the nurses on the boat. When we dug in on the Thier-du-Mont ridge, we were exhausted, cold, understrength—just worn out. One of the fellows dozed off in his hole while on guard in the night. We always had one man asleep and another awake alternating even though it was one man holes widely separated. Anyway, Kampe caught him and proceeded to read him the riot act. 'You're asleep on guard, I'll court martial you, you'll be shot,' etcetera.

"All of a sudden Kampe had a rifle in his back and the platoon sergeant said, 'Shut up lieutenant and get back in your hole.'

"The sergeants had more understanding of the men's physical condition and exhaustion than did the self important lieutenant. The next day, Kampe was gone. The platoon and squad sergeants had gone to Captain Millsaps with the story, and Millsaps sent the misfit lieutenant to the rear. Millsaps understood his men and the conditions. Nothing was done to the guy who couldn't keep his eyes open."[79]

Captain Hank Le Febvre, the S-3, moved forward with the 2nd Battalion as it pushed east along the spine of the ridge. "As the 3rd Battalion began moving toward the town of Comté, the 2nd Battalion passed through the gap, and became involved immediately in a firefight, and both E and D Companies were engaged with enemy riflemen and automatic weapons. The area was extremely wooded and mountainous, so it was a matter of fighting from tree to tree. Visual contact was hard to maintain between the two forward companies, but the radios were working well, and by reference to old positions and checkpoints, the companies were able to tell where they were in relation to each other. The enemy firing was now dying down a bit, but there was still the problem of getting to the eastern edge, the objective by darkness. The attack thus far had lasted all day and it was now approximately 16:00 hours and there was still 1,500 yards to go. The men pushed forward, firing from the hip and spraying all likely hiding places with fire. The Germans were using Panzerfausts in addition to small arms fire, and although none of these hit the men, many hit large trees and the resulting explosions were terrific. The men became accustomed to this however, and pushed rapidly on. After one more hot exchange of fire, a group a Germans surrendered. A brief interrogation revealed that they were trying to hold, while the remainder of the unit withdrew. With this information, the battalion continued moving forward, and just as it was getting dark, secured the final objective, the eastern edge of Thier-du-Mont ridge. Patrols were sent out, contact was established with the 1st and 3rd Battalions, and so ended a bitter struggle for this high, wooded, cold, rocky piece of ground."[80]

As darkness approached, Sergeant Fred Gladstone took one of the troopers in his squad and established an outpost in front of the Company I positions on the southern slope of the ridge, about eighty yards above the village of Comté. "The Germans were apparently set up in the shelter of the houses in the village. Our bedrolls had never reached us, but [Private First Class Chadford C.] Conway had a raincoat. We lay down in the snow and huddled together under that raincoat for warmth. Conway and I were supposed to be awake and watching, but because of our exhausted condition, we fell asleep."[81]

That afternoon, search parties were organized to look for the wounded, both American and German, who were in danger of dying from exposure in the bitter cold and deepening snow. It was close to dark when Private First Class Angel Romero, with the 2nd Platoon of Company G, regained consciousness after being hit by shrapnel during the earlier assault. Romero got up and started down the slope of the hill, where he found two other wounded troopers. "We were close to the base of the hill when some medics caught up with us. They were pushing and pulling a 'Weasel' ambulance. They asked if we had seen other wounded. These medics were exhausted to the point that I thought they needed to be tended to more than we did. The bottom parts of their legs were covered with ice and they were half frozen themselves; but they let us ride while they pushed and pulled."[82]

Despite a hand wound, Technician Fourth Grade Rinaldo R. "Zeke" Zuccala, with the medical detachment, worked to evacuate the Company G wounded from the western slope of Thier-du-Mont. "We formed a daisy chain and passed the wounded from man to man down the hill to the ambulances."[83]

Zuccala and a captured German medic worked that night to save about twenty troopers who had been wounded farther up the ridge, using a hunting lodge cabin on the southern slope as an aid station. However, Private John A. Tomaseski, with Company G, who had been wounded during the assault, died that night despite heroic efforts to save him.

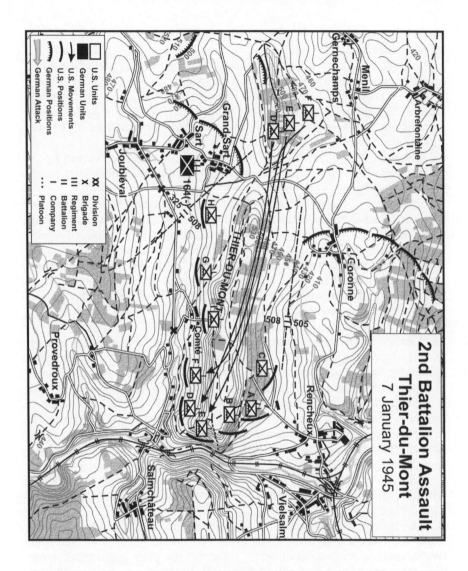

**2nd Battalion Assault
Thier-du-Mont
7 January 1945**

When darkness descended, Private First Class Lane Lewis and the 3rd Platoon of Company G were occupying their old positions on the southern slope of Thier-du-Mont. "My friend Sergeant Al Hess and I slept in the same foxhole we had dug in December. It was so very cold that night, but I fell right off to sleep."[84]

By the end of the day on January 7, the regiment had secured the Thier-du-Mont ridgeline. The 508th had captured 119 prisoners, killed an estimated 95 Germans, and captured or destroyed a 75mm infantry howitzer, a halftrack, three

88mm antiaircraft guns, two self-propelled guns, five 75mm antitank guns, and six other vehicles.

Sergeant Frank Sirovica was later awarded the Distinguished Service Cross for his extraordinary heroism and leadership during the attack. Captain Russell Wilde, Corporal Wallace Judd, and Privates First Class Gerald Jones and George McGrath were awarded Silver Stars for their heroism during the assault. Private First Class Gordon Cullings was awarded the Silver Star for his bravery and devotion to saving the lives of his fellow troopers.

As he lied at the battalion aid station that night awaiting evacuation, 1st Sergeant Bob Kolterman, with Company G, could only think about "no supply that night and the men had nothing but what they wore and carried."[85]

Somewhere in the woods on Thier-du-Mont, Lieutenant Bill Call, the new Company G executive officer, lied wounded with a partially collapsed lung, where he had been left earlier. "The Germans took over the position and at least they were human. There must have been other wounded around there. They moved us into a depression. There was a depression in this hillside and it was maybe ten or twelve feet deep. The wind and the snow were blowing so damn hard. They put this soldier with us. He had great big thick horn rimmed glasses and he was very accommodating. They left him with us. It was his job to guard us, I don't know why.

"I didn't die and it was because of him. Every so often, I was throwing up [blood] in great big clots. That cold weather stopped a lot of the bleeding and inflated the lung to some extent. We were there all that night. And God it was like a blizzard. Thank God they put us down in that little depression.

"When one of the guys would die...I think he laid three overcoats on top of me. He gave me part of that dark [German] bread and put that in my mouth. He gave me a sip of water and a drag on a cigarette. I threw everything up again. After the third overcoat, he said, 'Comrade gone,' [then] put it over me. I don't know where he got it. I don't know whether it was my group or not.

"The next thing I knew—I kept passing out and coming to—I woke up and it was quiet, deathly quiet. You could hear the whistling of the wind. I thought, 'God, I'm dead.'

"Shortly after that I heard a voice say, 'Anyone there?' I tried to make a sound and I made one, thank God. These two medics came down and said, 'We're going to get you out of here.' There was one other guy, I think it was [Sergeant Louis] Calcagno [with Company G]. We had no communication; we never talked to one another. But I think it was him. They must have picked up some other wounded and had him on the jeep. You could carry two litters on the jeep. They said, 'We'll take this guy first.' So they took Calcagno. But he said, 'I'll be back.' God, I never sweated anything in all of my life as bad. They came and got me and I was the only one on the stretcher [on the jeep]."[86]

Before dawn the next morning, Sergeant Fred Gladstone and one of his Company I troopers awoke at their outpost position above the village of Comté, on the southern slope of Thier-du-Mont. "When we awoke, a light snow had fallen and covered us.

"At dawn, a German patrol came up the ridge in our direction. They were wearing white capes and helmets. We too were camouflaged by the fallen snow and five of them got to within feet of us and were about to stumble over us, when suddenly a shot rang out. Corporal [James A.] Jim Campbell, from his position farther up the ridge, had fired at some other Germans he saw coming up from the village. At the sound of that shot, the German patrol stopped dead in their tracks, and at the same time, [Private First Class Chadford] Conway and I popped right up from under the raincoat and snow. For a split second we found ourselves staring at five startled Germans. Suddenly, they turned and started running and sliding down the slope. We brushed the snow off our weapons and fired some shots, but by this time they were ducking back into the houses they had come from. Forty years later, I had the opportunity to thank Jim Campbell for firing that shot. Not long afterwards, the German patrol and the rest of the Germans in the village, about forty in all, came out of the houses with a white flag and their hands up. They surrendered. Some of the fellows thought Conway and I were heroes of a sort for breaking up an attack, but actually we were sleeping on the job."[87]

Sergeant Gladstone later received news about his buddy, who had been wounded on the open ground in front of the ridgeline, who he had reluctantly been forced to leave behind during the attack. "The medics found Bill Sobolewski and he was evacuated. However, I was saddened to learn several weeks later that he died of his wound. I trust he found an answer to his questions [about God] before he died."[88]

On the morning of January 8, the 1st Battalion moved down the eastern slope of Thier-du-Mont and occupied Rencheux. Captain Woodrow Millsaps established the Company B command post in a building there. "We were able to hold our lines without any further trouble, except for the German artillery. They kept shelling our position day and night. Lieutenant [Roy] Skipton, one of my platoon leaders, and I were near one of the buildings when an artillery barrage came in on the town. Shells hit the building and destroyed it, covering us with debris. I managed to work myself loose and went to help Skipton. When I got him out from under the debris, his eye was missing. He was unable to stand. A couple of my soldiers and I placed him against a building and made him as comfortable as possible. He was conscious and knew I was there.

"He said, 'Don't leave me here, Millsaps.' I told him I would make sure that he was moved out of the area. We moved him back to the aid station, and that was the last time I saw Skipton until after the war."[89]

Upon returning to Rencheux, Lieutenant George Lamm looked for the bodies of his Company A troopers who had been missing since the Christmas Eve night of the German assault crossing of the Salm River. "The Germans had occupied this territory and had buried some of our dead. I even opened graves and found men in graves, in parachute infantry uniforms of the 508th Parachute Infantry, the uniforms apparently new, men who were not on the regimental roster and who were unknown at regimental headquarters. It was a very strange thing and the only thing I know is that the Germans had some of their own men dressed up in our uniforms.

"When we were searching for the bodies, I tried, with Captain Woodrow Wilson Millsaps, to find Lieutenant [Thomas] Rockwell's body. We did not find any trace of him. Later however, I heard that Captain Millsaps or someone had found Lieutenant Rockwell's body in a building in the town of Rencheux."[90]

CHAPTER 16

"They Are The Heroes"

During January 8 and 9, the 508th Parachute Infantry occupied the same positions it had held prior to the Christmas Eve withdrawal. The 7th Armored Division pushed across the area south of the Thier-du-Mont ridgeline on January 9, eliminating German forces in front of the 2nd and 3rd Battalion positions. Having fought their way through heavy snow and difficult terrain, troopers like Private First Class Lane Lewis, with Company G, were worn out. "On January 10, we learned that we were going to be relieved and pulled back into a rest camp. The next morning, we left our positions at Thier-du-Mont to begin our march back to Chevron, Belgium. The 75th Infantry Division was marching up to take over our old defensive positions. As we passed by them, the soldiers of the 75th would tell us what a great job we had done. They had heard about the battle we had just fought to take back Thier-du-Mont ridge. We wished them good luck. This made us all feel proud and gave us a good feeling for what we had just accomplished, but we were also filled with sadness. We were leaving a lot of good men behind who had given the last full measure for us and for their country. We marched into Chevron that night. For the next ten days this would be our home. Here, we received a new issue of clothes; some of the men received white colored camouflaged winter clothing. The engineers set up huge tents and heated water for us to take hot showers. After being in the field for twenty-four days, I'm sure we all needed a shower! I can't tell you how good this felt to be clean again. I had rejoined the human race again. My back continued to improve and I finally got thawed out."[1]

For troopers such as Private Charles Powell, with Company D, Chevron was heaven. "Hot chow twice a day and the Red Cross Club Mobile had coffee and doughnuts one evening; saw movies and stage shows...

"We had a good time and we got some ski-paratrooper replacements [from the recently disbanded 1st Special Service Force]. They'd seen lots of combat."[2]

On January 11, Sergeant Jim Kurz received word that his Company B buddy, Corporal Jesse Womble, had finally succumbed to the stomach wound he had received on January 7, during the assault on the Thier-du-Mont ridgeline. "It really hurt. I wrote to my mother and to Jesse's mother about his death. [Private First Class] George [Banks] and I had lost a real friend."[3]

Since leaving Camp Sissonne, the 508th had killed an estimated 445 German soldiers and captured 285 more. It had lost two officers and sixty-three enlisted men killed in action. Another 21 officers and 356 of its enlisted men had been wounded. Two officers and fifty-seven enlisted men were missing in action, mostly taken prisoner by the enemy. Another 17 officers and 368 enlisted men had been evacuated due to sickness, frostbite, trench foot, and other debilitating conditions.

While at Chevron, replacements began to increase the ranks of the pitifully thin rifle companies. Training began to integrate them in preparation for the next operation. Some of the wounded and trench foot cases began returning from hospitals. There were many promotions, some transfers among units, and a few, such as Private First Class Lane Lewis with Company G, who wanted a change in responsibility. "Tired of hearing, 'Bazookas up front! Bazookas up front!' I asked Sergeant [Alfred] Hess if I could be transferred to the 60mm mortar [squad] our company had, and he agreed. My job would now be to carry the mortar tube. 'Let one of the new guys carry the bazooka,' I thought. A 60mm mortar team was made up of three men: one to carry the base plate, one to carry the tube, and one to carry the mortar shells. Our unit received new replacements who were anxious to find out what combat was really like. I remembered when I once was young and anxious to get into action. I had listened with excitement to stories told to me by the returning veterans of the battle for Holland. That seemed like it was a hundred years ago. These new guys would soon find out for themselves what combat was all about, and they wouldn't like it, but how could I explain that to them? There were rumors every day about us going back into the line."[4]

While receiving replacements and being reequipped and reorganized, the division concentrated on training in combined tank–infantry tactics and the use of the German Panzerfaust, many of which had been captured in Holland and Belgium. Gavin felt the Panzerfaust was the only effective antitank weapon against the new German main battle tanks, the Mark V Panther and Mark VI Tiger I and II models.

Private First Class Jim Allardyce, with Company B, attended some of the classes conducted to teach troopers among other things, how to adjust mortar and artillery fire, and the prevention of trench foot and frostbite. "We had tanks come in and we spent a day learning how to work closely with them. They showed us their marksmanship by blasting a couple of haystacks—one shot a piece! General Gavin came around and the whole battalion gathered in a large barn, manure and all, to sit and hear him tell us what we had done and what our next step was.

I was impressed again with his common touch, utmost confidence, and obvious caring for the troops. He said, 'You fellows often think we are screwed up and don't know what we are doing. The Germans have even worse problems. In the attack on Thier-du-Mont ridge, we captured a battalion commander and some of his staff in a car. They were out looking for their battalion. Hell, we had eliminated that battalion three days ago!'"[5]

All too quickly, the men of the 82nd Airborne Division would be called upon to spearhead a drive through eastern Belgium and into Germany.

WHILE THE 82ND AIRBORNE DIVISION rested and reorganized, the First Army pushed the northern shoulder of the German salient south, meeting Lieutenant General George S. Patton's Third Army coming up from the south at Houffalize on January 16.

On January 21, the 508th Parachute Infantry Regiment, supported by the units of the regimental combat team—the 319th Glider Field Artillery Battalion; Company D, 307th Airborne Engineer Battalion; and Battery B, 80th Airborne Antiaircraft (Antitank) Battalion moved by truck to Deidenberg, north of St.-Vith. Upon arrival, the combat team was attached to Combat Command A of the 7th Armored Division, which was preparing to attack southward to seize St.-Vith.

Private First Class Jim Allardyce was riding in the back of a two and a half ton truck with the rest of the 1st Platoon of Company B as the convoy drove toward Deidenberg. "[Sergeant] Frank Hernandez had the GIs (diarrhea). He was trapped in the truck. At the first stop, he jumped out and did his business. I remember this because the truck started to move without him, and he was our squad leader. We all yelled to stop the truck and he got back on. The next day he was OK. The trucks dropped us off at dusk, and we moved out on foot at a very fast pace on ice covered roads. We practically ran as we were all soon huffing and puffing. I remember the officers and guides at points on the road and trails pointing us to our positions. We ended up in a small pine woods with a dirt road through it. The trees were cleared well away on both sides of the road. We split up what was left of the platoon. Enemy action and frozen feet had us down to about fourteen men. Hernandez had about six men on my side of the road and [Sergeant] Ed Suits had about eight men on the other side. The platoon usually had thirty to thirty-five men, never a full organizational strength of about forty-five.

"We dug in on the edge of the woods in the dark. [Private First Class Joseph G.] Joe Wise and I buddied up for this. We had to dig in a good six to ten feet back from the edge to find ground that wasn't frozen. It was a bad field of fire, but a hole was more important to protect us from the artillery fire we had been receiving as we moved up. It wasn't long before they found us in the woods and we literally dug in under fire. Every time they hit close, we'd hit the dirt. We laughed at each other and dug deep. The shelling wrecked a lot of trees, so we dragged the limbs and branches over to cover our hole and piled dirt on top. That shelling was persistent and came from three directions...

"We had been told to dig in good, as there would be a heavy artillery preparation the next day, prior to the 7th Armored [Division] attacking through us.

"That was the way it was too. We just ducked in our holes when it started and waited. We heard tanks go through our positions and of course the Germans shot at them. We got the German artillery [fire] on us, trying to hit the tanks and armored infantry and our artillery firing back. It was some noisy, earth-shaking experience..."[6]

Company B squad leader, Sergeant Jim Kurz, suspected that the particularly accurate German artillery fire was being adjusted by an observer. "Since we were having some pretty accurate artillery fire by the Germans, we decided to clear the town of all German civilians. We also picked up all radios in civilian hands. A German sergeant, who was on leave, was found during the search of the town. He had been directing the artillery fire for the Germans.

"The snow was the deepest of any that we had encountered so far. It was waist deep. This made it difficult to get any man who was wounded by artillery fire to the aid station. Our outposts could hear German tank movement to the south, but no German tanks or infantry were encountered."[7]

That day, Corporal Millard A. Newman, a medic on duty at the 1st Battalion aid station, was in the process of removing the harness of a casualty, when he cut the tape on a fragmentation grenade, from which the pin had been removed. Everyone except Corporal Newman attempted to leave the room before the grenade exploded. Newman grabbed some blankets to smother the grenade in an effort to protect three litter cases and others still in the room. The grenade exploded before Newman could cover it, causing penetrating wounds in his face and leg. Corporal Newman was awarded the Silver Star for his heroic efforts in protecting those in the aid station.

Company E, commanded by Lieutenant Lloyd Polette, was positioned on the 2nd Battalion's left, northwest of Amel, Belgium. Lieutenant George Miles was the executive officer of Company E and his best friend. "Polette left to inspect defensive positions. Word came that he had been hit by shell fragments. I ran to see him loaded on a jeep. We exchanged greetings, he looked green. I took over as CO of E Company. I never saw him again."[8]

Tragically, Lieutenant Polette, a recipient of the Distinguished Service Cross for extraordinary heroism during the capture of Bridge Number 10 in Holland, one of the regiment's most courageous officers, and a superb combat leader, succumbed to his wounds later that day. It was a blow to everyone who knew him.

At 6:00 p.m. on January 24, the 424th Infantry Regiment, 106th Infantry Division relieved the 508th, which moved to Basse Bodeux and was placed in XVIII Airborne Corps reserve.

LIEUTENANT GENERAL OMAR BRADLEY, the commanding officer of the 12th Army Group, planned a powerful drive over a relatively small front by the U.S. First and Third Armies commencing on January 28, which had the objective of driving east, piercing the Siegfried Line, and pushing on to the Rhine River. General Matthew Ridgway's XVIII Airborne Corps, which was subordinated to the First Army, would spearhead the offensive. The First Army's V Corps would be employed on the left flank and the Third Army's VIII Corps would advance on the right flank of Ridgway's corps. The plan called for Ridgway to drive from a point northeast of St.-Vith towards Schleiden, Germany, some forty miles away, and on to Euskirchen, Germany.

The XVIII Airborne Corps would attack through terrain that was heavily forested, with few roads. The snow was knee deep, with drifts approaching waist high, and continuing terrible weather conditions made the area unsuited for the employment of large armored formations. Ridgway, therefore, decided on a plan that would have been somewhat unorthodox under normal circumstances, but made good sense under these conditions. Two infantry divisions would attack abreast with two more following close behind. Resupply would be accomplished by the extensive use of "Weasels," a lightly armored, open topped, tracked vehicle, and jeeps. Ridgway reasoned that infantry could move through the deep snow and heavy forests, where armor could not venture. The normal armored vehicle complement for an infantry division would be utilized where feasible, along roads and firebreaks in the forests.

The two divisions spearheading the attack would push forward until they lost momentum; then the two divisions following them would pass through and take over the drive, maintaining the impetus and keeping the enemy under constant pressure. The two divisions spearheading the initial attack would resupply, then follow behind, ready to leapfrog and continue the drive.

Arguably the two best combat divisions in the entire European Theater of Operations, the 82nd Airborne Division and the 1st Infantry Division, the "Big Red One," were selected to spearhead the attack. The 30th Infantry Division and the 84th Infantry Division would advance behind them, ready to continue the drive when called upon. The attack would be made against remnants of the once elite German 3rd Fallschirmjäger Division, which had fought against the 508th during the campaign in Holland, just months earlier. Despite the infusion of replacements and the return of others from hospitals, the 82nd Airborne Division was woefully under its authorized strength, especially in the rifle companies.

For security reasons, the 82nd Airborne Division boarded trucks and left its billets during the middle of the night of January 26–27. The people of the towns in which they stayed were sad to see the troopers leave, and the men didn't relish the thought of going back into action in the terrible weather conditions. The division was trucked on January 27, to areas around St.-Vith behind the 7th Armored Division lines, with the 508th moving on foot to Sart-lez-St.-Vith.

General James Gavin's plan for the 82nd Airborne Division attack was for two regiments abreast to make the initial attack, with the 325th Glider Infantry Regiment on the left and the 504th Parachute Infantry Regiment on the right. The 505th would move behind the 325th, and the 508th would follow the 504th.

That night, the men left behind musette bags, overcoats, blankets, bedrolls, and sleeping bags before moving out, hopefully to be brought up later. The men were now better clothed for winter weather than when they left France. Most now had white snow capes, pullovers, bed sheets, or mattress covers. They had been issued long-john underwear, wool sweaters, gloves, and shoe-pacs, but they were going into weather and snow depths much worse than before.

On the morning of January 28, the attack commenced, with both the 325th and the 504th breaking through the initial resistance and penetrating deep into the German rear area, despite moving through deep snow and heavily forested terrain, almost devoid of roads.

The 505th and 508th moved up behind the attacking regiments to take over the advance the next morning. As Private First Class Lane Lewis, with Company G, made the long, grueling march from Sart-lez-St.-Vith eastward through St.-Vith to the regimental assembly area west of Herresbach, he saw the evidence of the heavy fighting that had occurred earlier around St.-Vith. "It was snowing hard and a high wind was blowing, chilling us to the bone, as we moved our way forward. While advancing toward St.-Vith, I came across an abandoned foxhole. In it were three U.S. soldiers still manning their .30-caliber machine gun. They had been killed by a direct artillery hit; their frozen bodies still staring forward, waiting. I can still see this scene so clearly today.

"We could hear gunfire to our front; sometimes a stray artillery shell would land nearby. As long as we kept moving we could stay warm, but the minute we stopped moving the cold would set in. It was the same old routine, run fifty steps, pause, run fifty steps, then stop. I thought I would freeze to death! As we were moving forward toward St.-Vith, I remember seeing forty or fifty bloated dead horses scattered along the roadside. These horses had been caught in an artillery barrage. The Germans used horses to move their artillery. Being from a farm, it troubled me to see these poor dead horses. Late that afternoon we arrived in Wallerode, and settled down for a rest. My back continued to bother me; it was becoming a real struggle to walk and carry my gear.

"We heard about an incident that happened at the 2nd Battalion area. A group of bypassed Germans mistakenly wandered into the battalion area. [The 2nd Battalion] immediately opened fire on the surprised Germans. All the Germans were either killed or captured. About 8:00 that night we moved into the forward assembly area. Our regiment would lead the attack tomorrow. By midnight we had reached our area and were issued ammunition and rations for the next day's assault."[9]

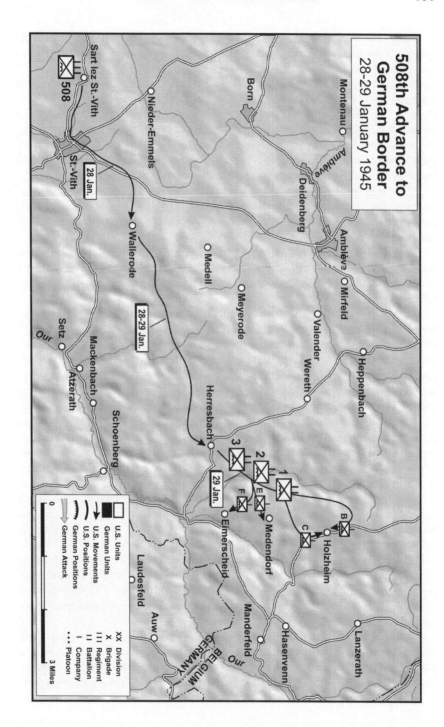

508th Advance to
German Border
28-29 January 1945

Sadly, the incident of the bypassed group of Germans wandering into the 2nd Battalion area resulted in another devastating loss of one of the regiment's finest combat leaders.

Private First Class Norb Studelska, with Company D, was an acting squad leader in his platoon. "My squad was way up front, ahead of the rest of the 2nd Platoon. We didn't know where, we were except that we were in middle of a forest, alone. We stopped to wait for others to get up to us. While waiting in the snow covered dense forest, two figures approached the area. I didn't see them, but heard one say, 'Cap-i-tan' in a foreign accent. [A new replacement, Private Earnest] Semrad spotted them close up, and let them both have it with his M1.

"This was among the saddest days in the entire war for me. We lost (killed) our very fine company commander [Lieutenant Hoyt Goodale] and his Hispanic runner (by not so friendly fire). He was the best company commander a company could have."[10]

That evening, attack orders were issued for the following morning. The 1st Battalion's objective would be the village of Holzheim and the 2nd Battalion's objectives would be Medendorf and Eimerscheid. The 3rd Battalion would follow in reserve.

At 9:00 p.m., the regiment began marching northeast from Wallerode to the line of departure. For Technician Fifth Grade Harry Hudec, with the regiment's Headquarters Company, the advance was particularly frustrating. "We had one tank bulldozer with us, plowing the way and a jeep with a blackout tent. I tell you, that was a time I would have gladly killed [Lieutenant] Colonel Shanley, the way he screamed at us. That damn jeep would get stuck every fifty feet or so and he'd scream at us to hoist the jeep and the trailer out of the snow."[11]

At 4:00 a.m. on the 29th, the 508th moved up to the positions of the 504th Parachute Infantry around Herresbach. Lieutenant Colonel Otho Holmes issued orders to his 2nd Battalion commanders and staff for the impending attack. "Company E was to seize Medendorf, Company F Eimerscheid, while Company D was in reserve."[12]

The 1st Battalion would attack northeast and seize Holzheim. The attack commenced at 7:45 a.m. Sergeant Jim Kurz, with Company B, felt that the weather and deep snow was even more miserable than that of early January. "It was snowing and the snow was waist deep to five feet deep. Our scouts would tire out breaking a trail, so I broke the trail over half the time. We struggled up the snow covered hills and slid down the hills on the snow. We had to wade creeks, some were frozen and some were not. Temperatures were near zero. B Company arrived at Holzheim in the afternoon and after a short firefight, we controlled the north half of town."[13]

Meanwhile, Company C attacked Holzheim from the south. Sergeant Bill Traband, a squad leader with Company C, could see activity in and around the town as they approached it. "We were on the high ground going into Holzheim. We first started to attack this town, but they were all looking like American soldiers, they had American jeeps they had taken. So when we did attack they were already down [below us] and we got right to the town."[14]

As Company C entered the town, several automatic weapons and a 75mm antitank gun opened fire on Traband's platoon. "They were hitting us from the right flank; that's when we saw Lieutenant [Joseph A.] Shirley. I went up to him and said, 'They're murdering us on the flank here.'

"He said, 'What do you think you're getting paid for Traband?' So I got two guys and we went around. There was a breezeway and this courtyard back there, where all of the backdoors were; we were going from house to house. One guy took this one house, which we always did—we threw a grenade in before we went into a house. I was getting the other guy started, when here came this lady screaming at me, begging me. I told the guys, 'No more grenades—just break down the doors and get in there.' The lady had two little kids about two or three years old. I took the last house, and that's when we got the prisoners."[15]

The last house was a strongpoint defended by several automatic weapons. While his two men laid down a base of fire, Sergeant Traband single-handedly assaulted the house with grenades as the Germans concentrated automatic weapons fire on him as he approached. Traband threw several grenades through the windows of the house, causing the Germans inside to surrender. Traband took forty-one prisoners, allowing Company C to continue the advance through Holzheim. Sergeant Traband was later awarded the Silver Star for his heroic assault on the German strongpoint.

Private Merrel Arthur and a couple of other Company C troopers saw Traband approach with the prisoners he had captured. "Here came Sergeant Traband with about eighty prisoners he captured in one house and gave them to me to guard. We proceeded to march the prisoners out of town for about three hundred yards or so, when we came upon [1st] Sergeant [Leonard] Funk and the headquarters group of about three or four men. Here we stopped and made the prisoners sit on the ground out of observation of the Germans, who were shelling us at the time. We did have some hedgerow coverage protection."[16]

The line of prisoners ran along the side of a house near the road, then along the side of the road, forming an L shape. A wall that extended parallel to the road from the rear of the house prevented an escape in that direction. First Sergeant Funk and the headquarters group were at the rear corner of the house by the wall.

As the 1st Battalion was securing the town, a three-man contact patrol sent by the 2nd Battalion to Holzheim was captured. A German officer and three men marched their prisoners to Holzheim, apparently believing the town was still in German hands. Many Germans and Americans were now wearing white snow capes, pullovers, and bed sheets that covered most of their uniforms and helmets, making identification of friendly or enemy troops difficult. As the Germans marched their prisoners into Holzheim, the officer saw the German prisoners who Private Merrel Arthur and two other troopers were guarding, and realized the town must now be in American hands. The German officer decided to liberate the prisoners, rearm them, attack Company C from the rear, and retake the town. The officer and his men, along with their three American prisoners, approached the end of the *L*-shaped line that ran along the side of the road, where two of the guards were positioned. The Germans quickly jumped and disarmed them, then began to rearm the German prisoners.

Arthur was standing outside of the elbow of the *L*-shaped line of prisoners when he noticed a commotion at the end of the line down the road. "There was a lot of confusion and milling around when the prisoners jumped up. I stepped around the column and looked down the row to see what the commotion was all about. I saw men dressed in snow capes and yelling to our guards there. The impression I had was that it was some Belgian Resistance fighters giving us a hard time on what to do with the prisoners."[17]

Arthur saw four men in snow capes approach. "That's when Funk came over to where I was and said, 'What's going on down there?' In the meantime, some of the prisoners were taking off to a vacant house about fifty yards away."[18]

As the three men approached, Arthur noticed one of the men suddenly point his weapon at Funk. "The German officer was waving his Schmeisser at Funk and jabbering and wanted us to drop our weapons. Funk looked a little bewildered at what was going on until the captured patrol man told us they were captured and now we are to become their prisoners, 'He wants us to surrender.'

"Funk started mumbling to himself softly like, 'Surrender hell,' as in not knowing what to do, sort of pondering it. He was standing there with his Tommy gun slung arms, and the German was standing there waving his Schmeisser in Funk's belly. In a flash, that gun was in the German's belly and he ripped off a burst. The German started to sink slowly down. When he was on his knees, he tried to raise his gun at Funk, but didn't have the strength to pull the trigger.

"That's when Funk said to me, 'Get help.'"[19]

Technician Foruth Grade Erwin E. Stark was one of those who had been guarding the prisoners and had been disarmed. "At first, we couldn't believe that Sergeant Funk had decided to fight. all those Germans. Then I grabbed up a gun and shot the German who was nearest me. We had quite a fight."[20]

Meanwhile Private Arthur started back to the village to get help. "The first trooper I saw was my buddy [Corporal George D.] Askew, the one that wanted to get into the action. Sure enough, he did and got shot in the leg. I dragged him to the aid station, and on the way saw no help. I left the aid station and raced back to where Funk was. As I neared the end of the street, I could see that Funk, with some help that had arrived when they heard shots, [had] rounded up what was alive of the German prisoners, which was about half of the original group. The other half were dead, due to Funk's quick action."[21]

The official count was twenty-one Germans killed and many others wounded. However, in the melee, one of Funk's closest friends, the company's operations sergeant and clerk, Staff Sergeant Edward W. Wild, was killed, possibly accidently by 1st Sergeant Funk's fire. Wild's death hit Funk hard.

For his intrepid courage, First Sergeant Leonard Funk was later awarded the Medal of Honor, making him the most decorated soldier in the 82nd Airborne Division. Funk had already been awarded the Silver Star for his actions in Normandy and the Distinguished Service Cross for his extraordinary heroism while clearing the landing zone in Holland. With the award of the Medal of Honor, Funk also became the most decorated paratrooper of World War II.

Like almost every trooper with Company C, the regiment, and indeed the division, Sergeant John Hardie had great admiration for Funk. "At a time when courage was commonplace and prevalent, he had a brand of unique courage beyond that of the rest of the men. He had a sense of modesty about those actions for which he was cited—always maintaining things would not have been so, were it not for the actions of the rest of the troops with him. Yet, his modesty did not interfere with his intense self confidence and capacity for instantaneous decision making, which led to the eruptive actions resulting in those incidents for which he was awarded those accolades."[22]

Even years later with the perspective of a lifetime, Dr. Hardie said, "Leonard is certainly the most outstanding human I have known in my life."[23]

As the 1st Battalion was clearing Holzheim, the 2nd Battalion advanced toward Medendorf and Eimerscheid. As Company E moved in to capture three buildings on the edge of Medendorf, Lieutenant George Miles, the commanding officer, along with his executive officer were taken under fire by a sniper. "I had to discard my Tommy gun and a pistol that I borrowed from a trooper. It froze and I asked [Lieutenant] Dave Liebmann [the executive officer] for his .45 pistol. He handed it to me, then swore as his helmet was knocked off his head. He finally killed the young sniper and proceeded to a barn to rest.

"I thanked him for the .45 and he replied, 'Good you didn't have to use it—there were no bullets in it.'

"We examined his helmet, which had a small hole—front and center. The back was blown out. We had a long laugh at this episode."[24]

Meanwhile, Company F moved south toward Eimerscheid. Corporal Frank McKee was an assistant squad leader with the 3rd Platoon. "I was advancing across an open field with a few of my men when a sniper opened up on us. He got the man next to me through the eye at an angle which just seemed to take out his eye, but didn't drop or kill him. The next shot went through my harness and overcoat collar right next to my neck. We hightailed out of there fast and hit some brush at the edge of the field. The Germans were in the houses and I guess they didn't want to leave the warmth of the fires, as they fought hard for this group of houses. There was nothing but woods around the village and the weather was fierce. I don't blame them."[25]

Technician Fourth Grade Dwayne Burns, with the 3rd Platoon of Company F, decided to check on the trooper who had been shot in the head by the sniper. "[Private Glenn H.] Billy ['the Kid' Ward] and I went back through the woods to see about the trooper who had gone down beside us. He had taken a head shot and was bound to be dead, but Billy knew him from jump training and wanted to make sure. If he was only wounded, we couldn't let him freeze to death.

"When we returned to the spot, we saw a medic had moved him under a tree and was still with him. The man was sitting up with his back against the trunk. His head had bandages in both the front and back. He was smoking a cigarette and smiled as we approached. Billy kneeled down and spoke to him.

"I asked the medic, 'How bad is it?'

"'Looks like he'll make it, the medic replied. 'But he should be dead; the bullet hit him below his right eye, passed through his head and came out below his left ear. He's doing okay. I don't know why, but he's doing okay.'

"'Nothing in his head to hurt,' Billy laughed."[26]

Company F was unable to capture Eimerscheid and before another attack was launched, the 504th Parachute Infantry moved up to relieve the company.

At 4:00 a.m. the following morning, the regiment attacked from Holzheim toward Lanzerath and high ground to its north. The 3rd Battalion's objective was the town and the 2nd Battalion objective was the high ground to the north. The 1st Battalion followed behind and mopped up bypassed enemy troops.

The 2nd Battalion, under the command of Lieutenant Colonel Otho Holmes, advanced in a column of companies, with Company D leading, followed by Company F, and then Company E in reserve. "The enemy was contacted at the LD [line of departure], and it was necessary to deploy two platoons abreast, attacking up a fifty percent slope for a distance of three hundred yards, and breaking trails over snow three to four feet deep."[27]

The 2nd Battalion encountered little opposition after overwhelming the enemy's initial defenses. It reached the high ground that was its objective and found it occupied by a German artillery unit. The battalion quickly overran the unit, capturing three 105mm howitzers and ammunition for the guns.

As one Company F platoon cleared a wooded area at the objective, German machine guns opened fire, killing Sergeant Lawrence V. Nelson, who was Private John Dobransky's squad leader. Enraged, Dobransky seized a BAR and charged one of the machine guns as it was firing at him, and killed the crew. The platoon leader, Lieutenant David B. Owen, grabbed another BAR and crawled to within twenty yards of another machine gun position, then stood up and fired burst after burst as the machine gun fired back at him, until he killed the crew and silenced the gun. Private Dobransky reorganized his squad and led it until the area was cleared of the enemy. Lieutenant Owen and Private Dobransky were awarded the Silver Star for their courageous actions.

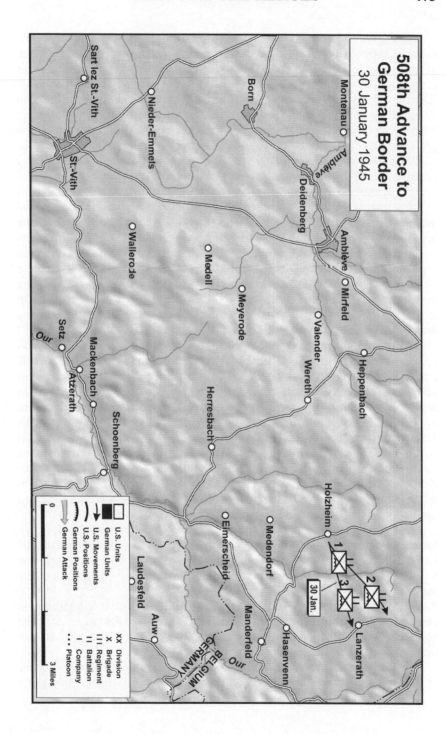

508th Advance to German Border
30 January 1945

During the 3rd Battalion's three mile march through deep snow that day, Private Charles R. Martin was the point man for his Company H squad for much of it. "We were ordered to cross this wide open area, about six hundred yards from one forest to the next. Before we started, my squad leader, Staff Sergeant [Don] Jakeway and I captured three prisoners. Then we set out to cross this open space. Being the BAR man, I led the way. The snow was waist deep. Sergeant Jakeway was maybe fifty feet behind me when shots rang out. I dropped in the snow. Sergeant Jakeway called out he had been shot through the left lung. The medics started working on him and one wanted to cut off his boots. Jakeway raised holy hell, saying he wanted to die with his boots on.

"I again started across the opening and more shots rang out. I recognized it as firing from an M1 rifle, so I called out, 'Who's there?' It was E Company and they had encircled the hill and did not know we were attacking from the opposite side. We still didn't know who shot Sergeant Jakeway."[28]

When the 3rd Battalion reached the edge of the woods outside of Lanzerath, Lieutenant Colonel Louis Mendez and his company commanders conducted a visual reconnaissance of the town. They could see German infantry withdrawing from the town. Mendez immediately ordered the two leading companies to attack the town. "H and I Companies attacked abreast from the edge of the woods southwest of the village."[29]

As the 3rd Battalion advanced on the town, Technician Fourth Grade Francis Lamoureux, with Company G, had a bad feeling about the situation. "There was a wide field between us and the town. It was covered with snow halfway up to our knees. You could see the buildings in the town. If there were Germans in there, they could just mow us down. There was no place to take cover. We were just waiting to be cut in two. When are they going to start shooting? We got all the way into the town. The buildings seemed empty. We had to check each building with guns and grenades ready. We were inside one house not more than five minutes when the Germans started opening up on us with everything. Artillery...bullets were going right through the house, coming in one window, going out the window on the other side. All we could do was hit the floor and just lie there for what seemed like forever. What were we going to do next?

"Our mortars finally pushed them out—the 81mm mortar platoon from battalion headquarters. Things became quiet. We set up defensive positions. The Germans had known we were coming, but did not know in what strength. It was a favorite trick to lull you into a false sense of security until you got out in the open."[30]

On January 31, the 1st Battalion attacked eastward to capture high ground east of the Manderfeld–Lanzerath road. The 2nd and 3rd Battalions attacked northeast astride the highway from Lanzerath to capture high ground overlooking Losheim, Germany.

The 1st Battalion moved to its objective by 7:30 a.m., under the concealment of a heavy fog. When it lifted later in the morning, two German Tiger tanks suddenly appeared out of the mist at close range in front of Company C. Moving north along the road were six additional tanks and at least a hundred German infantrymen. Lacking any antitank weapons other than bazookas, and with no American tanks or tank destroyers nearby, the 319th Glider Field Artillery Battalion came to the rescue, delivering a barrage of 135 rounds of 75mm high explosive shells that knocked out one of the Tiger tanks and two enemy halftracks. As this was occurring, Company C unleashed a torrent of fire to stop the German infantry in its tracks. Meanwhile, Company B, armed with captured Panzerfausts counterattacked on the right of Company C, but the Germans had already pulled back. When Captain John Manning, the 319th liaison officer with the 1st Battalion, spotted German armor and infantry massing for another attack, he quickly called down another barrage of 183 rounds, which forced a complete withdrawal. A prisoner taken during the fighting was identified as a member of the 9th Panzer Division.

Lieutenant Colonel Otho Holmes' 2nd Battalion attack jumped off on time. "Company D ran into a reinforced company, which had orders to retake Lanzerath, but who were resting in a railroad defile, without flank guards or any kind of guards. D Company put them out of action without much organized resistance. They seemed to be disorganized to begin with."[31] It was a short fight, as the 2nd Battalion killed or captured the entire enemy unit, taking some forty odd prisoners.

As was his usual practice, Technical Sergeant Zane Schlemmer, now the platoon sergeant for the 81mm Mortar Platoon, Headquarters Company, 2nd Battalion, moved with the rifle companies during any advance or attack. "The weather there was intensely cold. To keep reasonably warm, in addition to my usual uniform, I had a turtleneck wool knit sweater (an American Red Cross donation), an American army officer short overcoat (which I had taken from a frozen dead 106th Infantry Division major's body that I discovered in the forest); at times, I also wore my army issue 'mummy' type sleeping bag, by cutting arm holes and cutting the bottom out of it. I had also acquired a long-haired white German dog from a company of German soldiers [Company D] had ambushed in a railroad cut. We called the dog 'Adolph' and he was my sleeping companion, curling up against each other, wherever we could find a place to sleep. We modified our wool gloves by slitting the fingers and sewing them together, except for the thumb and trigger finger, thus making them modified mittens. Even with all of this damn clothing, I never was warm! The only nice thing about this winter war was that the snow had covered all of the battlefield debris, the dead were frozen, and none of the smell of the battlefield permeated as usual. The flip side of that was the probability of freezing before evacuation should you become wounded under these circumstances.

"The only vehicle which we could use, due to the lack of roads, the snow drifts, and the terrain, was a small tracked Weasel. It brought up ammunition, K-rations, and took back the wounded and those with frozen feet or fingers. The weather was nearly as much an enemy as were the Germans.

"We used the element of surprise, for the Germans were confident that no one could advance under these conditions, and they didn't want to give up any shelter that they were in. One night, I filled my canteen completely full of water, not knowing when I could get more. During the night, the water froze so solidly that the ice expanded and split the seams of my canteen. When the rations couldn't reach us, we existed on captured German black bread and canned horse meat rations, along with canned vegetables and fruit that we found in the cellars of most of the farmhouses there.

"Existing under such conditions, coupled with our experiences in Normandy, Holland, and during the Bulge, we developed an intense hatred of anything and everything German. Thus, we blamed them for every discomfort, vowed to make each and every one of them pay dearly for our plight and losses...they did!

"We were particularly unhappy about sending them, as prisoners, to our rear. We had to stay up there and resented anyone going back to shelter and warmth. So, we always cut their belts and, with our jump knives, cut the buttons off their pants, so they had to hold up their pants in order to keep them. It was humiliating for them, particularly the officers, but we took some of our frustrations out on them in that way.

"Whenever and wherever the terrain permitted, we were supported by several tanks assigned to the forward advancing companies. Both the tankers and we paratroopers had a mutual admiration for each other—the paratroop/tank combination was a terrific marriage! Besides, the tankers generally always had hot coffee, clinging to the hull of a tank certainly beat walking, and it was like having our own private artillery!

"After advancing and clearing a huge snow-flocked forest, I spotted a hunting lookout tower (which deer and boar hunters [must] have used in the peaceful past). The tower was taller than the surrounding fir forest. So, being a forward observer, I climbed it for a look around. While up there, fog or low-hanging clouds suddenly lifted, so that I could then see rows and rows of 'dragons teeth' (antitank obstacles) extending as far as I could see, there in the fields on the side of this forest. It was only then that we were certain that we were in the middle of the Siegfried Line—Germany's West Wall."[32]

The 2nd and 3rd Battalions captured the high ground overlooking Losheim and the Siegfried Line just as the fog lifted. The Germans had withdrawn to those fortifications to await the inevitable assault from the protection of pillboxes, with minefields, barbed wire, and tank obstacles in front of them.

Early on the morning of January 31, Sergeant Jack L. Johnson, with Service Company, was asleep at the regimental command post at Lanzerath. "It was well below zero when [Captain] Bill [Nation] awakened me and asked if I knew where his driver was sleeping. I did not know, but volunteered to drive him. Bill informed me that he was going to the F Company CP. Enroute, Bill stated that a short time ago, F Company had received some shellfire and that the regiment had lost radio contact with them. It was only about two miles to F Company, and everything seemed to be quiet when we arrived, so Bill said to drive on up to the CP. I stopped the jeep next to the CP, and as I shut off the motor, a shell hit the right front portion of the jeep. I broke the steering wheel as I was thrown out, landing on my shoulder and back. I returned to the jeep and found Bill still in it. He had not suffered, as he died instantly from shrapnel wounds in the chest and stomach areas, either from the shell or pieces of the jeep. I made my report to a lieutenant in F Company and left Bill in their care. I walked back to regimental headquarters and made my sad report to Colonel Mendez. From there, I was transported to a field hospital where metal was removed from my right arm, shoulder, and right hand."[33] Captain Nation had been a member of the regiment since Camp Blanding and was one of its most beloved officers.

The 508th remained in the positions that it captured on January 31 until February 4. During that time, Technical Sergeant Zane Schlemmer and most of the men in the regiment were rotated back to the rear area for a brief time. "One of my fondest memories was being pulled off the line for a rear twenty-four hour break. During the relief, we hiked to a road, where trucks took us back quite some distance to a farmhouse, which had a portable rubber shower station set up beside it. The rubber exterior was frost covered, but inside, it was warm and steamy! In the farm building, we undressed and separated our underwear and socks, which we had worn well over a month. In groups of twenty-five, we were given soap and five luxurious minutes under the hot showers. Then, we were given clean underwear and two pairs each of clean socks…truly heavenly! No five minutes in my entire life gave me more pleasure! Then clothed, we were 'puffed' with DDT. God knows how any bugs could have survived that cold, freezing weather…then it was back to the line."[34]

Corporal Frank McKee, with Company F, like so many troopers who were afflicted by serious health problems caused by the terrible conditions, would not leave his buddies and seek medical attention, even though it would get him out of combat. "We were now suffering badly from the weather and began to lose men with frostbite and frozen feet. During a lull one afternoon the medics came into the area of our platoon and had all men take off their boots and socks and examined their feet. I had been stumbling a lot lately as my feet were numb. With my socks off, my feet were a sick gray.

"The medics took one look and said to me, 'You are out.' I was evacuated with a lot of guys. We had what was called trench foot. I called it frostbitten and almost, frozen feet. I ended up in a hospital in Paris. What a luxury after the frozen, hungry days in the forests of Belgium and Germany I was sure now I was going to be a survivor."[35]

Despite the fact that the regiment was maintaining defensive positions, the dying continued. Private First Class Norb Studelska, with Company D, was on patrol on February 1, when his buddy, Private First Class William Vacca was wounded in the stomach. "He died because we couldn't get him out to good medical attention. He begged for someone to put him out of his misery before he died." [36]

On February 4, the 508th was relieved and trucked to Rencheux, where it was quartered in the old Belgian army barracks located there. Just three days later on February 7, the regiment moved by truck to Hahn, Germany, southeast of Aachen. The following day, the 508th relieved the 517th Parachute Infantry Regiment in the Hürtgenwald, near the town of Bergstein, about three miles west of the Roer River.

The objective of the bloody campaign the previous fall for control of the Hürtgen forest was control of the Schwammenauel and the Urft dams, along the Roer River. As long as the Germans controlled the water flow from those dams, offensive operations in the Roer River valley to the north, was restricted because of the threat of massive flooding washing out bridges and isolating any forces that crossed the valley moving east. Several belts of well camouflaged German concrete and steel pillboxes that were part of Germany's Siegfried Line were hidden from aerial view by the Hürtgenwald's thick pine forest at the beginning of the campaign. The previous fall, it had been a meat grinder, drawing in U.S. Army divisions one after another, where heavy casualties were suffered. The 82nd Airborne Division was now tasked with finishing the job.

The last dominate terrain feature west of the Roer River was Hill 400, east of Bergstein, which rose sharply from the flat open ground around it. It afforded the Germans with excellent observation for its artillery positioned on the east side of the river. It had changed hands a number of times during the vicious fighting the previous fall and was again in German hands. Hill 400 and the high ground to the south were defended by elements of Fallschirmjäger Regiment 6, which had so tenaciously defended Carentan against the 101st Airborne Division during the Normandy campaign.

The 2nd Battalion established a line running northeast to southwest about one thousand yards south of Brandenburg, just north of Bergstein. Early the following morning, Lieutenant Colonel Otho Holmes, the commanding officer of the 2nd Battalion received an attack order from regimental headquarters. "The battalion, on regimental orders, was ordered to move from its present positions and seize and hold the high ground, 084325 [Hill 400], proceeding down the Kall River valley and attacking the high ground from the south. Company E, followed by Company D, while Company F remained in position south of Brandenburg, but this was changed so that Company F caught up with Company D and thus made a column of companies. The column moved down the Kall River valley where Company E came under heavy small arms fire from the high ground. Besides, the mines were so thick that advance was very slow, and their presence prevented any flanking movement." [37]

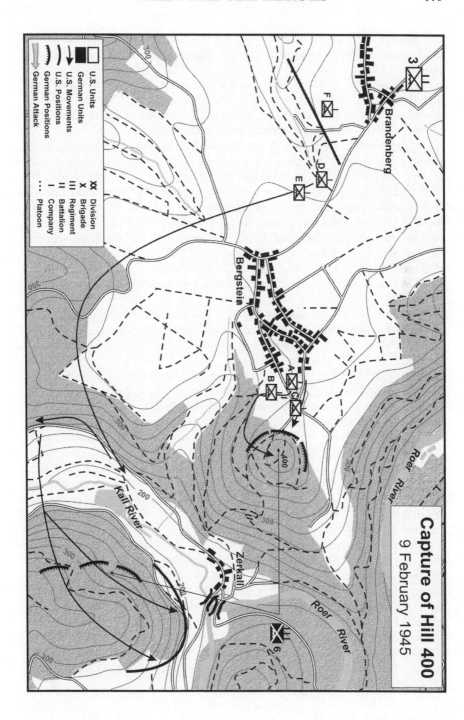

Capture of Hill 400
9 February 1945

Lieutenant Colonel Holmes reported the situation to regimental headquarters and received orders to withdraw and establish positions along the trail on the valley floor. "Regiment then ordered after the withdrawal had been made, that the battalion attack to the south across the Kall River, then turn east and clean out the slopes of the south side of the Kall River, [and] seize and hold the ground overlooking the Roer River. This was done and the battalion remained in position until relieved on 10 February with the regiment."[38]

On the evening of February 9, the 1st Battalion was ordered to make a night attack eastward out of Bergstein to assault Hill 400 across open ground sewn thickly with mines. The attack would commence at 2:00 a.m. on February 10. During daylight hours prior to the attack, the Company B commander, Captain Woodrow Millsaps, could see the ghastly results of previous attempts to capture Hill 400. "As you looked out over the area to the front, you could see dead soldiers lying all over the place. It was obvious they were American soldiers. The 1st Battalion's immediate objective was Hill 400, right across the minefield where the soldiers were lying. The engineer company furnished each [rifle] company four men with mine detectors to assist the companies in removing mines.

"Company C moved out leading the attack, followed by Company B. Immediately after Company C moved out, they ran into machine gun fire and were forced to call for artillery fire. However, the enemy's fire was not silenced."[39]

Sergeant Bill Traband was a squad leader with Company C. "We were there all night going down this path. They would open up on the path and we'd jump into the mines, knowing there were mines. We thought all along they were mortars, because mortars when they come down you don't hear them until the last second. We were caught in the middle of a minefield. That's when Lieutenant [Joe] Shirley took off.

"I lost three men there. And this one, [Corporal] Roy Henderson, had been through everything. I crawled over to him and I laid his head on my lap. He was telling me his confession—he was a Mormon. I'm a Catholic and I said, 'Gee, you're going to tell me your confession? Never a Catholic, they know better.' That was funny. He died in my lap."[40]

During the assault, Lieutenant Rodney A. Renfrew, leading a forward observer party for the 319th Glider Field Artillery Battalion, that was supporting the 1st Battalion attack, stepped on a mine, mortally wounding him. Despite being paralyzed, Lieutenant Renfrew refused to allow his men to stop and treat him. He gave them complete instructions and sent them forward with the infantry. For his courage and determination in putting the mission before his own well being, Lieutenant Renfrew was posthumously awarded the Silver Star.

A short time after Company C was stopped, Captain Millsaps was contacted by radio. "Company B was ordered to go around the hill from the right [south] and attack the enemy from that position."[41]

As Company B moved forward, Sergeant Jim Kurz "could hear and see the great amount of fire that C Company was laying down. It was dark, but as we advanced we could make out bodies of men lying beside the path. When we looked, we found that they were American paratroopers. Then our scout hit a mine. We were in the middle of a minefield."[42]

Technician Fifth Grade Bill Windom was just a short distance behind the scout when the mine was tripped. "[Private First Class] Joe Wise, ten yards in front of me, stepped on the first Schu [mine], jumped, hit another, fell, and rolled screaming into more. There was silence—we waited."[43]

Sergeant Kurz halted his squad behind him when he saw the mines explode. "Captain Millsaps told everybody to stay right where they were. He would get the engineers to make us a path through the minefield. The Germans would fire mortar shells at any spot where a mine was set off. When we set off the mines, we had a few casualties from the mortars. But since we stopped when we hit the first mine, the Germans returned their fire towards C Company."[44]

Captain Millsaps saw the flash and explosion when the mines were tripped. "Rather than have my men move around on foot, I had them get down and crawl forward, using the mine detectors to search for mines. I found this was working very well and we were making progress, so I kept at it.

"[Lieutenant] Colonel [Shields] Warren was shouting over the radio, wanting to know what was coming off, since everything was quiet in my area. We were getting close to the enemy's position and couldn't talk over the radio. I had the operator turn the radio down and not answer the call, but he kept the radio operative, in case I needed to call for artillery. This went on all night with Warren screaming over the radio, wanting to know what was coming off."[45]

As Sergeant Jim Kurz laid on the trail with other Company B troopers, waiting for the engineers to clear a path through the minefield, "a new lieutenant [William C. Jones], just out of West Point, asked me if I would go with him to try to get around the minefield. I told him that the captain had told us to stay in place, so we wouldn't set off anymore mines. The Germans had this minefield laid down for at least three months and had all points zeroed in. The lieutenant kept asking me to go around the minefield so we could hit the Germans from the far side. I told the lieutenant to stay where he was, because the captain said we would be through the minefield in another hour. However, he wanted to be a hero. He got a couple of privates from another squad to go with him. The three of them started around to our right. In a few minutes I heard some mines go off.

"The engineers got through the minefield in a couple of hours. They laid white tape for us to follow. It was still dark, but everybody going through the minefield kept their feet on the white tape. It was over one hundred yards through the minefield."[46]

Captain Millsaps was successful in getting Company B through the extensive minefield. "We got as close as we could to the enemy's line without being seen before I called for the artillery to bring everything they had on the enemy's lines. As you looked toward the east you could see that it was getting light and I didn't have much time left before closing with the enemy. A decision had to be made; either expose my men to the mines when they rushed forward to close with the enemy, or be caught out in the open field exposed to the enemy's machine gun and mortar fire when daylight came. I decided to take the chance on the mines and rush the German lines. We were ready when I called for the artillery to cease firing, and we made a mad dash for the German lines. We were on the Germans before they knew what had hit them. We moved through the lines and Company A followed. We were on our objective on Hill 400 when I contacted Colonel Warren and told him that he could send his bulldogs forward, for Company B and Company A were sitting on Hill 400.

"It was almost daylight by now when the regiment started through the gap that Company B and Company A had made in the German lines. When Colonel Warren arrived in the area with his command group, he said to me, "Damned you Millsaps, you had me frightened to death. I didn't know what you were doing, and I thought I had lost contact with you.'

"I told him why I had closed out the radio and he understood. As the regiment passed through the area, the officers shook my hand and told me when they found out I was leading the attack, they knew if anyone could break through the German lines, it would be Millsaps—that made me feel good. Most of the snow had melted the day before, which made it much easier to find the mines, but made it more dangerous to the men walking over them. It was several hours before a search could be made of the area."[47]

When it got light enough, a search was conducted to look for the lieutenant and the troopers who had followed him into the minefield. Sergeant Jim Kurz was disgusted by the completely preventable casualties caused by this officer. "We found the lieutenant with a foot blown off. One of the privates lost his eyesight and the other one broke his arm and back. This was caused because the lieutenant didn't follow orders. He spent four years in West Point and lasted two days in combat."[48]

After securing the hill, Captain Millsaps had an opportunity to inspect the German defensive positions on Hill 400. "I found that they had machine guns pointing straight at us with ammunition belts in the guns, with only a few rounds fired. Apparently they had broken and run when we opened fire."[49]

The 1st Battalion secured Hill 400 by around 8:50 a.m. The 2nd Battalion moved through enemy minefields along the Kall River valley, but otherwise met no opposition, and occupied the ridge south of the Kall River before dawn.

Outpost lines were established along the low ground on the west bank to prevent enemy infiltration across the river. The outposts were relieved during darkness every night. The division remained in these positions, with individual units being rotated to allow men to get a hot meal and clean up.

ON FEBRUARY 18, THE 82ND AIRBORNE DIVISION was notified that it was being relieved by the 9th Infantry Division, which occurred over the next three days. Except for organic transportation units, the division was put on trains and moved mostly in 40 and 8 boxcars, first to Aachen, Germany and then to its base camps in the Rheims, France area. The Camp Sissonne and Camp Suippes barracks had been taken over by army hospitals, so the 325th, 505th, and 508th were billeted in tents around the main posts, while the 504th was moved to accommodations at nearby Laon.

The skeleton force that was the 82nd Airborne Division, arrived in France in terrible need of rest, new equipment, and replacements. At the end of the Ardennes campaign, the 508th reported 101 killed in action, 33 died of wounds, 0 died of injuries, 398 wounded in action, 273 injured in action, and 23 missing in action. Most of those reported as missing in action were later confirmed to be prisoners of war.

The 508th once again settled in at Camp Sissonne. The officers and men were given a few days to rest and passes were issued, while replacements were brought in, many directly from the United States after graduation from jump school. Men and officers wounded in Holland and Belgium and those few fortunate enough to have been in the Unites States on thirty-day furloughs when the division was fighting in Belgium and Germany returned and helped bring unit cohesion back to their respective outfits.

However, the personnel makeup of most of the rifle companies was almost unrecognizable from those that had jumped in Holland less than six months earlier. Most companies had new officers; many had enlisted men who were now noncoms, having assumed those responsibilities during the fighting over the last two months. During the next several weeks, numerous promotions and changes in command took place.

Parades and reviews were held, where the decorations for individual and unit valor were awarded. General Gavin spoke to the assembled division and told them that they would be getting in on the fighting to finish the war in Europe.

The division began more training, working to rebuild teamwork in the units decimated in the earlier campaign. The veterans were tired of the repetitious training they knew by heart. But the young replacements had to learn the tricks and techniques that would not only keep them alive, but insure the success of the unit in combat.

Rumors swirled that the division would jump across the Rhine River to open the way into the heart of Germany and that the division would jump into Berlin to grab it before the Russians. The first rumor was dispelled when on March 7, the U.S. First Army seized the Remagen Bridge over the Rhine River.

During the next month there were several alerts for possible missions, and a couple of practice jumps were held. On March 14, the 1st and 2nd Battalions made a practice jump to maintain jump status. As the 1st Battalion troopers began jumping, a C-47 lost a propeller and began to lose altitude, flying down through the helpless paratroopers, catching the chutes of some of the troopers on its wings and tail. Lieutenant Charles A. Yates, with Headquarters Company, 1st Battalion, was the jumpmaster on the stricken plane. "The C-47 was bucking over the jump field and guys were falling down as they headed for the door. We helped them back up. When I got to the door, two of our men were stuck in the door, both trying to get out at the same time...Anyway, I jammed my boot against the two in the door and literally fell out of the plane myself. I was immediately knocked unconscious and came to when my chute opened. Someone's boot was hanging upside down in front of my face—hanging from my suspension lines. Before releasing the boot, I looked to see if the two of us would have to go down together, but there was no one there. It was my own boot. I released it and it swung back and forth in the air.

"Looking up, I saw my chute was open only about six feet in diameter, and I was going down faster than the jumpers around me. I pulled my reserve, but it just laid out there. It didn't go up and open. Looking at the ground which seemed to be coming up very fast, I could see it was going to be a rough landing. I pulled my leg up as high as I could, and prepared to take it all on my right leg. It was a rough landing. Guys who came to see me in the hospital said my reserve snapped open just before I hit the ground.

"Whether I got hit by the plane or got tangled up in my own suspension lines, I'll never know because I was knocked out so fast. I think the plane went into a slip slide as I went out the door and the stabilizer clipped me. My left leg had four breaks between the knee and the ankle and one between the knee and the hip. Results—after one and a half years in various hospitals, my left leg is one and a half inches shorter than my right one."[50]

The crippled plane crashed, bursting into flames upon impact. Seven paratroopers were killed, Lieutenant Nick C. Emanuel, Privates First Class Luther M. Tillery, Charles "Chief" Underbaggage, Jr., and Alfred J. Vaughan, George W. Wall, and Private Charles L. Clemons, all with Headquarters Company, 1st Battalion. Private First Class Bernard Levin, with Company G, was on the plane without a parachute making sketches of the jump and died along with four members of the plane's crew when the plane crashed.

Technician Fourth Grade Dwayne Burns, with Company F, made the 2nd Battalion jump later that day and when his chute popped open, he looked up to check the canopy to make sure it deployed properly. "I looked down to check the drop zone. What I saw caused me to suddenly cry out, 'Oh my God!'

"There was a wreck of a C-47 sprawled out in the middle of our landing field. Its burned out shell, still smoking, and the fresh plowed dirt surrounding the ship told me the crash had occurred earlier in the day. Riding the trucks back to camp, it was all anybody could talk about. Later, we were told the accident happened that morning while dropping the 1st Battalion. Command thought it best not to let us know much about it. However, we later learned even more details. The movie actress Marlene Dietrich, a fan of the American airborne, just happened to be visiting the regiment during this time. The training jump was already scheduled, but the officers started calling it a parade jump for Miss Dietrich and she believed them. When the plane crashed, she was hysterical and afterwards quite distraught."[51]

The following day, when the 3rd Battalion made its practice jump, Private First Class Lane Lewis, with Company G, like most of the troopers was nervous. "Everyone in our battalion had heard about what had happened yesterday. As I jumped out, I looked back at the planes that were in the rear of the formation. I was not anxious to have a repeat performance from yesterday's jump. We all made it to the ground safely."[52] It was particularly haunting for those who had made it through all of the combat, and wondered if they might die in a training accident.

ON APRIL 4, 1945, THE 508TH PARACHUTE INFANTRY REGIMENT was detached from the 82nd Airborne Division when the division strength was reduced to the TO&E (Table of Organization and Equipment) level, which authorized one glider regiment (the 325th) and two parachute regiments (the 504th and 505th). The 508th had been a valuable part of the 82nd Airborne Division and it would be missed. After everything the regiment had done as part of the division, the troopers of the 508th considered themselves to be an integral part of the 82nd and hated ending their association with the All Americans.

However, the 508th was alerted for a potentially critical mission. Captain Woodrow Millsaps, the commanding officer of Company B, was briefed along with the other company commanders and battalion staffs. "The rumor went around that Hitler might have the POWs killed before the prisons were overrun by Allied troops. The 508th Regiment became detached from the 82nd Division and was alerted for a possible jump to liberate the POWs, if needed. The 508th moved to an airfield near Chartres, France, to await further orders."[53]

After arriving at the airfield on April 5, Private First Class Lane Lewis and the rest of the troopers of the regiment were briefed about the possible mission. "We were prepared to jump on as little as forty-eight hours' notice to liberate any prisoner of war camps, should the Germans resort to atrocities."[54]

Captain Millsaps and the rest of the regiment remained at the airfield through the remainder of April and into May. "The fly boys would arrive at the field daily to piddle around and waste time. We had the planes loaded with equipment and sat around waiting for orders."[55]

Fortunately, the jump to rescue POWs was not required and war in Europe ended on May 8, 1945. It was a time of celebration and for reflection on the loss of so many who had done so much to make that day possible. Most of the troops in Europe were earmarked for the planned invasion of Japan.

Fighting in three campaigns during the war, the 508th had lost 539 killed in action, 74 died of wounds, 3 died of injuries, 1,274 wounded in action, 526 injured in action, and 254 missing in action. Most of those who had been reported as missing in action were later confirmed to be prisoners of war.

Captain Millsaps, like others with the 508, knew little about who and when any of the troopers might be sent home and discharged. "The one question in every trooper's mind was, 'When do I go home?' Immediately after VE Day, a point system was announced to determine eligibility for discharge. The regiment began to send a few soldiers to the States every week or so. It was then that I discovered that there were only eleven soldiers left in the company who were originally assigned prior to our departure from Camp Mackall, North Carolina. There had been no transfers; all the others had either been killed or wounded.[56]

"About the first of June 1945, we received orders that the 508th Regiment would return to Camp Sissonne to await further orders. We then received orders to move to Frankfurt-am-Main, Germany, where we were assigned to General Eisenhower's headquarters as headquarters guard. The 29th Infantry, my old regiment that I had been assigned to after completing training in the Provisional Test Company at Fort Benning, Georgia, had been General Eisenhower's guard and had been following Eisenhower all across Europe. Now they were preparing to return to the States.

"Company B was designated as the first company to relieve the 29th. I had several days to prepare for this changeover. Meanwhile, the regimental commander had ordered a new uniform for all troops in the regiment. I took my officers and made a tour of installations and of the [29th Infantry Regiment] troops on guard. I found the men dressed in old boots with canvas tops sewn on and old uniforms that had never been dry cleaned or pressed. We were all surprised to see men on guard dressed in such a manner. They had no written special orders or instructions pertaining to the installations they were guarding. Everything seemed to be done in a haphazard manner. We figured perhaps they had been pulling guard so long that dress or instructions didn't matter.

"I reported our findings to the battalion commander, [Lieutenant] Colonel Warren, and we got busy writing up special orders for each guard post. Without being conspicuous, I had my troopers who were assigned to certain installations go by the posts and observe what was taking place. Written orders were given to each sentry and he was required to memorize them verbatim.

"General Eisenhower's headquarters, known as Comm-Z (communications zone) moved into the huge I.G. Farben building. It was five or six stories tall and was enclosed by a steel fence with a small building at the entrance to the area. A smaller building in the area was used as an officers' mess for all Allied officers attached to the headquarters. The Comm-Z area we were to guard had over sixty installations, including General Eisenhower's office, offices for other officers, and the officers' mess.

"The day that we relieved the 29th Infantry, Company B was dressed out in the company area. The dress consisted of a highly polished dark green helmet liner, white scarf, a new uniform, highly polished black [jump] boots, white boot laces, white gloves, a dark green pistol belt, a black pistol holder, and a .45-caliber pistol. We were ready. We loaded on trucks and at 13:00 hours we relieved the 29th. This only took about ten minutes.

"This caught several officers out of the office. When they returned to go into the office, the sentry asked to see their pass. We had written orders signed by General [Walter Bedell] Smith, Eisenhower's chief of staff, stating that no one without a special pass would be allowed to enter the office. Some of the officers checked their wallets and clothing, but could not come up with a pass, so they were not allowed to go in. The sentry explained that they would not be able to go into the office without proper identification. They wanted to know who in the hell was the 'officer of the day,' and the sentry told them Captain Millsaps was. They explained that I could be reached at number such and such.

"My post was a little building at the entrance to the compound. The phone began to ring. When I answered, the caller would say, 'This is colonel so and so, and the sentry at my office won't let me in. I would ask why not, and the officer would reply that he needed some kind of pass that he had never heard of. I was polite and courteous, but firmly unyielding, and told him that he would not be permitted to enter the office unless he was properly identified. Some of the officers had friends identify them and they were admitted. Others took off for the rest of the day. This was taking place all over the building.

"I had two sentries posted at the officers' mess, and about 4:00 p.m. the same thing happened. They had to have a pass and be in proper uniform to get in the mess hall. The calls began to come in and I told them that if they didn't have a pass to the mess hall and they weren't properly dressed, they wouldn't be allowed in. Some of the officers were outraged and came to see me, wanting to know who put out such crazy orders. By now, I was getting a kick out of the excitement that was taking place. Everything that I had anticipated before we took over the guard was taking place. That was the reason that I went to the trouble of having written orders for each post authenticated by having General Smith sign them. At the bottom of each order were the words, 'By order of Chief of Staff, General Smith.'

"I politely handed the order to the officer and waited for him to return it to me and to see what he would say after reading it and finding the general's signature at the bottom. Most of them didn't say a word. They just scratched their heads and walked away. I knew I would prevail in sticking by my sentries on guard and not giving in to the pressure that was being applied.

"About 09:00 p.m. that evening, I received a call from Colonel Lindquist, the regimental commander. He wanted to know if it would be possible for me to continue on guard for another twenty-four hours. He told me that ever since I had gone on guard he had done nothing but answer the phone, and he had received nothing but favorable comments on how the guard was performing. He wanted it to continue to function the way it had begun. He said he wanted to contact [Captain] Jimmie Dietrich, commander of Company C, who was to relieve my company, and see if he was prepared to take over from me and perform as we had. I told him that we could continue without difficulty. I told him that several men had been assigned to the same post and knew the orders pertaining to the post. They would be able to relieve the old guard without any trouble.

"He said, 'Are you sure?' I told him he could count on it and to go to bed and get a good night's sleep.

"Company B remained on guard for the next twenty-four hours, and when Company C relieved us, they were ready to perform in similar fashion. That was the way the regiment performed from that time on: Company B alternating with Company C, while Headquarters Company and Company A were guarding such installations as ammunition dumps, motor pools, etc."[57]

Technician Fourth Grade Dwayne Burns, who had served with Company F in combat through Normandy, Holland, Belgium, and Germany, was pleased with the regiment's new accommodations. "We were billeted in Heddernheim, a suburb of Frankfurt, in four story apartment buildings. There were four men to an apartment, each completely furnished and with hot and cold running water. I was now with company headquarters, so [Technician Fifth Grade] John [S.] Hurst, [Private First Class Woodrow W.] Woody Phelps, [Corporal] Tom Clevenger, and myself had one apartment. This seemed like a great deal of luxury, but suddenly nothing was too good for Eisenhower's Red Devils. We were destined to become a spit and polish unit. Getting cleaned up for honor guard duty felt really good for a change. Each trooper was issued a set of white gloves and scarf, white utility belt and even white bootlaces. The big worry was not if we were being shot at, but how good was the crease in our pants and how we could get a better shine on our boots."[58]

One battalion of the 508th provided security for General Eisenhower's headquarters, while a second battalion provided security for the nearby towns of Bad Homberg, Königstein, and Oberursel, where 192 general officers assigned to the headquarters were housed. The remaining battalion was kept in reserve at Heddernheim. The battalions rotated among responsibilities every two months.

The regiment formed and maintained an honor guard for ceremonial purposes such as the arrival of visiting dignitaries, which included President Harry S. Truman, U.S. cabinet secretaries, Prince Bernhard of the Netherlands, and Allied military leaders such as Soviet Field Marshal Georgy K. Zhukov.

When the war in the Pacific ended with the surrender of Japan, the U.S. military began a massive demobilization. Troopers with enough points to be sent home to the United States for discharge from the army were transferred to the 507th Parachute Infantry Regiment, a unit of the 17th Airborne Division. The 13th and 17th Airborne Divisions were being deactivated and the low point troopers from those divisions were transferred to the 82nd Airborne Division and the 508th Parachute Infantry Regiment. The flow of troopers being sent home continued and the ranks of the regiment were filled by troopers from other units. When the 101st Airborne Division was deactivated on November 30, 1945, low point troopers from that legendary division were sent to the 82nd Airborne and the 508th. It was a very unhappy group of troopers from the 101st who arrived at Frankfurt-am-Main—transferred to the 508th. Corporal Jerry F. Graf was among that group. "Turned down for the trip home and shuffled off to a new outfit was a really low point. So, I decided the hell-with-it-all and once again became a screw up. We had the Germans doing all the dirty jobs, so there wasn't a lot they could do to punish us."[59]

Sergeant Ed "Bogie" Boccafogli had been with Company B through combat in Normandy, Holland, and the Ardennes. He had plenty of reason to despise the German people. But, Boccafogli observed some of the replacements treating the civilians with cruelty. "We were in Germany as occupation troops, and the young punks had never even seen an enemy would say, 'Hey, ya damn Kraut' to an old man. This old man could be his grandfather. 'Get out of here, ya damn Kraut.' They acted nasty to people. We'd go to the mess hall. We had the three garbage cans where we'd put the edible and non-edible. You'd see an old lady there with gray hair, a little kid over there with a bucket waiting to get something. You were not supposed to fraternize or give them anything. What, are you kidding? All of us would say, 'Hey Hans, come over here, Fritz.' We'd call the woman over and give her whatever we saved—a potato or something. Then you thought, 'It could be my mother.' The suffering these people went through..."[60]

Private First Class Jim Allardyce, with Company B, found the policy of non-fraternization to be "unnatural and unenforceable. Our politicians said it was to make them feel as outcasts of the human race. There was no theatre, restaurants, bars, etcetera. The city was devastated and starving—bombed flat or bomb damaged. Exploring the city was fruitless, as nothing beautiful remained.

"Two other fellows and I met a family named Wurzer—mother, father, daughter, grandma, and a son [who had been] killed in Russia. They showed us how they were living. They had a chicken or two in a cage and the day we met them unexpectedly and unannounced, the meal on the table was cooked grass. At that time, the Germans could not even mail a letter. When I found out they had relatives in Oregon, I wrote them and explained the need for food and clothing. Before we went to Bad Homberg, they had food from Oregon."[61]

In late 1945, the 82nd Airborne Division departed for the United States, leaving the 508th as the only parachute regiment in the European Theater of Operations, where it was designated as strategic reserve on January 1, 1946. The regiment returned as a unit to the United States in November of 1946, and was disbanded at Camp Kilmer, New Jersey on November 24.

Thus, the 508th Parachute Infantry Regiment passed into history. It had been one of the great parachute infantry regiments of World War II and its combat record was outstanding. Most of its veterans returned to civilian life, where many excelled in their chosen fields of endeavor. Others chose the military as their vocation. Roy Lindquist retired from the U.S. Army in 1960 at the rank of major general. Thomas J. B. Shanley studied physics at Princeton University's graduate school after the war and eventually became the head of the Nuclear and Chemical Weapons Branch, Office of the Army Chief of Staff. He retired at the rank of colonel in 1961. Louis Mendez served as a regimental commander during the Korean War and in a wide variety of roles with the army until his retirement at the rank of colonel in 1970.

THE EXPERIENCE OF SERVING WITH THE 508TH PARACHUTE INFANTRY in combat during World War II affected all of its veterans in some way. Bill Windom became an actor in Hollywood, starring in the popular television series *Murder She Wrote*. "It must have affected my whole life. I don't hunt, camp, or ski. I hang out with women and young children. I avoid groups. Acting is suitably lightweight for me. I still enjoy sailing, chess, tennis, and astronomy. Life teems with quiet fun. I do what I can as a husband, father, and grandpa."[62]

Thanks to great effort on the part of O. B. Hill, a regimental association was formed and reunions were held on an annual basis until the association was retired in October 2004 at an emotional ceremony at Camp Blanding, Florida.

The reunions helped maintain the bonds of brotherhood that only veterans who have held each other's lives in their hands can understand. One year, at an upcoming reunion, two troopers who had been buddies in Company I and had been involved in an accidental shooting just prior to the Normandy jump were both planning to attend and would be seeing each other for the first time since the incident. Bob Chisolm was helping to organize the reunion and was calling the veterans to confirm their attendance. "We were collecting the names of the people who were coming to the reunion. I was talking to Joe Petry and I said, 'We've got a guy out in Arizona by the name of John Henscheid who is coming to the reunion. Do you remember him?'

"Joe Petry said, 'Know him, hell—I shot him!'

"When these two guys saw each other for the first time, they just hugged each other. John said, 'Joe, you probably saved my life.' They just loved one another and had spent a lot of time together [while serving with the 508th]."[63]

Louis Mendez, one of the regiment's greatest combat commanders, felt that the credit for the 508's outstanding combat record lay with the young troopers he had so courageously led. "They are the heroes; they are the men who deserve the accolades; they are the men worthy of emulation by our children and all Americans everywhere. They are role models for our country and for the world; they put their lives on the line for you, for me, and for freedom. They are the ones 'who taught me what men can do in war' as a team."[64]

NOTES

Chapter 1 "See You On The Ground"

1. William J. Call, interview with author.
2. Woodrow W. Millsaps, "This is My Story," April 22, 1986, courtesy of the Camp Blanding Museum, p. 10.
3. Lynn C. Tomlinson, oral history transcript, courtesy of the Eisenhower Center.
4. Call, interview.
5. Ibid.
6. Ibid.
7. Ibid.
8. Adolph F. Warnecke, as quoted in, Gerald Astor, *June 6, 1944*, St. Martin's Press, 1994, p. 57.
9. Ibid
10. Robert B. White, interview with author.
11. Broughton L. Hand, "The War Story of Broughton Lynn Hand, 508 Parachute Infantry, 82nd Airborne," courtesy of Broughton L. Hand, pp. 3–4.
12. Dr. John Hardie, transcript of speech at the dedication of the Leonard Funk Memorial, Camp Blanding, Florida, courtesy of Richard O'Donnell.
13. Richard C. Reardon, as quoted in, "Lieutenant Robert Mason Mathias," edited by Richard C. Reardon, courtesy of the Camp Blanding Museum, pp. 1–4.
14. Joseph E. Watson, as quoted in, "Lieutenant Robert Mason Mathias," edited by Richard C. Reardon, courtesy of the Camp Blanding Museum, pp. 1–4.
15. Chester E. Graham, "My Memories of World War II," courtesy of the Camp Blanding Museum, pp. 2–4.
16. Frank E. McKee, as quoted in, Gerald Astor, *June 6, 1944*, St. Martin's Press, 1994, p. 60.
17. William G. Lord, as quoted in, Gerald Astor, *June 6, 1944*, St. Martin's Press, 1994, p. 59.
18. Ibid., pp. 59–60.
19. Woodrow W. Millsaps, "This is My Story," pp. 10–11.
20. Frank E. McKee, oral history transcript, courtesy of the Eisenhower Center.
21. White, interview.
22. Call, interview.
23. McKee, oral history transcript.
24. Call, interview.
25. White, interview.
26. Ibid.

27. Ibid.
28. Call, interview.
29. Ibid.
30. Graham, "My Memories of World War II," p. 2.
31. Call, interview.
32. David E. Thomas, as quoted in, Gerald Astor, *June 6, 1944*, St. Martin's Press, 1994, p. 55.
33. Call, interview.
34. Graham, "My Memories of World War II," pp. 2 and 9.
35. Frederick J. Infanger, as quoted in, "Lieutenant Robert Mason Mathias," edited by Richard C. Reardon, courtesy of the Camp Blanding Museum, p. 14.
36. Colonel Roy E. Lindquist, Headquarters 508th Parachute Infantry, Office of the Regimental Commander, "History of the 508th Parachute Infantry," National Archives, p. 3.
37. Millsaps, "This is My Story," pp. 11–12.
38. Briand N. Beaudin, M.D., oral history transcript, courtesy of the Eisenhower Center.
39. Call, interview.
40. Beaudin, oral history transcript.
41. Ralph E. DeWeese, diary, courtesy of the 82nd Airborne Division War Memorial Museum.
42. Beaudin, oral history transcript.
43. Shields Warren, Jr., letter to Clay Blair, October 24, 1983, the Clay and Joan Blair Collection, U.S. Army Heritage and Education Center.
44. Worster M. Morgan, "My Paratroop Activities," courtesy of www.508pir.org.
45. Ibid.
46. Captain Neal L. McRoberts, "Report of Pathfinder Employment for Operation Neptune," 11 June 1944, National Archives.
47. Paul R. Sands, "A Walk Down Memory Lane," courtesy of the Camp Blanding Museum, pp. 1–2.
48. HQ 508th Parachute Infantry, APO 514, "Field Order No. 6 (Revised)," 27 May 1944, National Archives.
49. Captain Barry E. Albright, "Operations of the 2d Battalion, 508th Parachute Infantry Regiment (82d Airborne Division) in the Invasion of Normandy, June 5 – 13 1944 (Normandy Campaign) (Personal Experience and Observation of a Rifle Platoon Leader)," courtesy of the Donovan Research Library, Fort Benning, Georgia, pp. 9–10.
50. Robert C. Moss, Jr., written account, courtesy of www.6juin1944.com.
51. George D. Lamm, oral history transcript, courtesy of the Eisenhower Center.

52. David E. Thomas, "Military Career Memoirs of Brigadier General David Edward Thomas, M.C.," courtesy of Normand E. Thomas.

53. David M. Jones, oral history transcript, courtesy of the Eisenhower Center.

54. Charles L. Sartain, Jr., as quoted in, Joseph S. Covais, *Battery! – C. Lenton Sartain and the Airborne G.I.s of the 319th Glider Field Artillery*, Andy Red Enterprises, 2011, p. 198.

55. Edward C. Boccafogli, oral history transcript, courtesy of the Eisenhower Center.

56. Lamm, oral history transcript.

57. David M. Jones, oral history transcript.

58. Tomlinson, oral history transcript.

59. Boccafogli, oral history transcript.

60. Carlos W. Ross, "Things That I Remember," courtesy of www.508pir.org.

61. Donald I. Jakeway, *Paratroopers Do or Die*, Privately Published, p. 53.

62. Robert E. Chisolm, interview with author.

63. Jakeway, *Paratroopers Do or Die*, p. 53.

64. Ralph H. Mann, as quoted in, "We were afraid the cows would give us away," *Lehigh Valley Morning Call*, June 6, 2011.

65. Malcolm D. Brannen, written account, courtesy of the 82nd Airborne War Memorial Museum.

66. John D. Boone, oral history transcript, courtesy of the Eisenhower Center.

67. Wesley T. Leeper, written account, courtesy of the Eisenhower Center.

68. William H. Nation, letter to parents, June 22, 1944, courtesy of William C. Nation.

69. Warnecke, as quoted in, *June 6, 1944*, p. 147.

70. Frederick J. Infanger, written account, courtesy of the Camp Blanding Museum.

71. Leeper, written account.

72. Warnecke, as quoted in, *June 6, 1944*, pp. 147–148.

73. Millsaps, "This is My Story," p. 13.

74. Brannen, written account.

75. Call, interview.

76. McKee, oral history transcript.

77. Warnecke, as quoted in, *June 6, 1944*, p. 148.

78. George E. Christ, "D-Day, June 6, 1944, One Soldier's Experience," courtesy of D. Zane Schlemmer.

79. Infanger, written account.

80. A Final Protective Line is a series of predetermined interlocking bands of grazing fire established to stop enemy assaults. The elevation and direction of the fire are fixed and capable of being delivered under any condition of visibility.

81. Robert J. Weaver, "Invasion," courtesy of David Berry and Richard O'Donnell.
82. Francis M. Lamoureux, as quoted in "In Their Own Words," audio collection, Topics Entertainment, Cassette Number 1, Side B.
83. Ibid.
84. D. Zane Schlemmer, oral history transcript, courtesy of the Eisenhower Center.
85. Brannen, written account.

Chapter 2 "No Idea Where The Hell I Was"

1. D. Zane Schlemmer, oral history transcript, courtesy of the Eisenhower Center.
2. Harold O. I. Kulju, "Harold Oliver Isaac Kulju," U.S. Army Heritage and Education Center, p. 1.
3. Lieutenant Colonel Thomas J. B. Shanley, as quoted in "Debriefing Conference—Operation Neptune," 13 August 1944, courtesy of the 82nd Airborne Division War Memorial Museum.
4. Kulju, "Harold Oliver Isaac Kulju," pp. 1–2.
5. Ibid., p. 2.
6. "Narrative statement of the crew of A/C #42-93002, 62nd TC Sq., 314th TC Gp., in connection with the events of BIGOT – Neptune #1," 14 June 1944, courtesy of www.6juin1944.com.
7. Edward V. Ott, "1st Lieutenant Edward V. Ott, 508 P.I.R. 82nd Airborne Headquarters, Company, 2nd Battalion," U.S. Army Heritage and Education Center, p. 1.
8. Paul R. Sands, "A Walk Down Memory Lane," U.S. Army Heritage and Education Center, p. 2.
9. Schlemmer, oral history transcript.
10. Frank L. Staples, V-Mail June 25, 1944, courtesy of Kristine Nymoen.
11. Lynn C. Tomlinson, oral history transcript, courtesy of the Eisenhower Center.
12. William M. Sawyer, oral history transcript, courtesy of the Eisenhower Center.
13. Billy B. McClure, written account, courtesy of the Camp Blanding Museum, p. 2.
14. Frank Haddy, written account, courtesy of the Camp Blanding Museum, p. 4.
15. Frederick J. Carden, response to questionnaire, courtesy of the Cornelius Ryan Collection, Alden Library, Ohio University.
16. Trino F. Maldonado, as quoted in, Ralph H. Thomas, "Trino, A Short History," courtesy of the Camp Blanding Museum.

17. Ibid.

18. Louis W. Yourkovich, as quoted in, "Bellaire Man's apple tree wish granted," *The Times Leader*, Belmont County, Ohio, June 6, 2004, courtesy of Robert B. Newhart, pp. 3 and 11.

19. Captain Barry E. Albright, Operations of the 2d Battalion, 508th Parachute Infantry Regiment (82d Airborne Division) in the Invasion of Normandy June 5 – 13 1944 (Normandy Campaign) (Personal Experience and Observation of a Rifle Platoon Leader)," courtesy of the Donovan Research Library, Fort Benning, Georgia, p. 13.

20. Richard R. Hill written account, courtesy of www.6juin1944.com.

21. Ralph H. Thomas, "D-Day, 6 June 1944," courtesy of www.508pir.org.

22. Ralph E. Cook, oral history transcript, courtesy of the Eisenhower Center.

23. Robert B. Newhart, response to author's questionnaire.

24. Dwyane T. Burns, unpublished manuscript, courtesy of Dwayne T. Burns, pp. 73–75.

25. Ibid, pp. 75–76.

26. Frank E. McKee, as quoted in, Gerald Astor, *June 6, 1944*, St. Martin's Press, 1994, p. 150.

27. Ralph Burrus, Jr., interview, courtesy of www.geschiedenisgroesbeek.nl.

28. Statement of the crew of A/C #42-93002.

29. James M. Gavin, written account, courtesy of the Ryan Collection, Alden Library, Ohio University, pp. 2–3.

30. Colonel Roy E. Lindquist, as quoted in, "Debriefing Conference—Operation Neptune," 13 August 1944, courtesy of the 82nd Airborne Division War Memorial Museum.

31. Ralph H. Mann, as quoted in, "We were afraid the cows would give us away," *Lehigh Valley Morning Call*, June 6, 2011.

32. William H. Nation, letter to parents, June 22, 1944, courtesy of William C. Nation.

33. Colonel Roy E. Lindquist, as quoted in, "Debriefing Conference—Operation Neptune," 13 August 1944, courtesy of the 82nd Airborne Division War Memorial Museum.

34. Worster M. Morgan, "My Paratroop Activities," courtesy of www.508pir.org.

35. David E. Thomas, "Military Career Memoirs of Brigadier General David Edward Thomas," courtesy of Normand E. Thomas.

36. Paul E. Bouchereau, oral history transcript, courtesy of the Eisenhower Center.

37. Marcel Bollag, "Escape in Normandy," courtesy of Aaron Elson, www.tankbooks.com.

38. Carl H. Porter, "Men at War: Chow Call," courtesy of www.508pir.org.

39. Captain William H. Johnson, as quoted in, Headquarters, 307th Airborne Engineer Battalion, APO 469, U.S. Army, "Unit History," Normandy After-Action Report, 10 August 1944, courtesy of Brian Siddall.

40. Lieutenant Alfred A. Cappa, as quoted in, Headquarters, 307th Airborne Engineer Battalion, APO 469, U.S. Army, "Unit History," Normandy After-Action Report, 10 August 1944, courtesy of Brian Siddall.

41. James A. Rightley, response to author's questionnaire.

42. Thomas C. Goins, response to author's questionnaire.

43. Lieutenant Edward P. Whalen, as quoted in, Headquarters, 307th Airborne Engineer Battalion, APO 469, U.S. Army, "Unit History," Normandy After-Action Report, 10 August 1944, courtesy of Brian Siddall.

44. Shields Warren, Jr., letter to Clay Blair, January 5, 1984, the Clay and Joan Blair Collection, U.S. Army Heritage and Education Center.

45. David M. Jones, oral history transcript, courtesy of the Eisenhower Center.

46. Otis E. "Gene" Hull, as quoted in "We Served Proudly—The Men of Hq1," George I. Stoeckert (album collator), courtesy of www.508pir.org, pp. 16–17.

47. Owen B. Hill, "My Normandy Invasion Experience," courtesy of Owen B. Hill.

48. Ibid.

49. Ibid.

50. Thomas J. Gintjee, oral history transcript, courtesy of the Eisenhower Center.

51. Kenneth J. Merritt, oral history transcript, courtesy of the Eisenhower Center.

52. Gintjee, oral history transcript.

53. John D. Boone, oral history transcript, courtesy of the Eisenhower Center.

54. Jonathan E. Adams, Jr., response to questionnaire, courtesy of the Cornelius Ryan Collection, Alden Library, Ohio University.

55. Herman W. Jahnigan, *Herman Jahnigan Interview, D-Day Jump at Normandy*, courtesy of www.youtube.com.

56. George D. Lamm, written account, courtesy of www.508pir.org.

57. Henry E. Le Febvre, letter to Zig Boroughs, September 15, 1989, courtesy of Henry E. Le Febvre.

58. Robert B. White, interview with author.

59. Adolph F. Warnecke, oral history transcript, courtesy of the Eisenhower Center.

60. Ibid.

61. Adolph F. Warnecke, as quoted in, Gerald Astor, *June 6, 1944*, St. Martin's Press, 1994, p. 148.

62. John R. Taylor, oral history transcript, courtesy of the Eisenhower Center.

63. James Q. Kurz, as quoted in, Gerald Astor, *June 6, 1944*, St. Martin's Press, 1994, pp. 146–147.
64. William J. Call, interview with author.
65. Harry L. Reisenleiter, as quoted in, Ronald Drez, *Voices of D-Day*, Louisiana State University Press, 1994, p. 138.
66. Edward C. Boccafogli, oral history transcript, courtesy of the Eisenhower Center.
67. William F. Knapp, response to author's questionnaire.
68. Woodrow W. Millsaps, "This is My Story," April 22, 1986, courtesy of the Camp Blanding Museum, pp. 13–14.
69. William H. Traband, interview with author.
70. William R. Tumlin, response to author's questionnaire.
71. Carlos W. Ross, "Things That I Remember," courtesy of www.508pir.org.
72. Robert E. Nobles, as quoted in, Lewis Milkovics, *The Devils Have Landed*, Creative Printing and Publishing, 1993, p. 97.
73. Broughton L. Hand, "The War Story of Broughton Lynn Hand, 508 Parachute Infantry, 82nd Airborne," courtesy of Broughton L. Hand, pp. 19–20.
74. Ibid.
75. Ibid.
76. Louis G. Mendez, Jr., as quoted in, Zig Boroughs, *The 508th Connection*, Privately Published, 2004, p. 121.
77. R. B. Lewellen, "Jump into Gourbesville," courtesy of www.508pir.org.
78. Kelso C. Horne, as quoted in, "Conversations with Kelso," Perry Knight, editor, courtesy of Kelso C. Horne, Jr., p. 11.
79. Ibid., p. 12.
80. Robert E. Chisolm, interview with author.
81. Denver D. Albrecht, interview transcript with Cornelius Ryan, courtesy of the Cornelius Ryan Collection, Alden Library, Ohio University.
82. Fred Gladstone, as quoted in, Donald I. Jakeway, *Paratroopers Do or Die*, Privately Published, p. 71.
83. Donald M. Biles, response to author's questionnaire.
84. James C. Hutto, "World War II Memoirs – Staff Sergeant James C. 'Buck' Hutto, January 31, 1923 – December 6, 1993," courtesy of Sharon Hutto Marks.
85. John W. Richards, oral history transcript, courtesy of the Eisenhower Center.
86. James A. Campbell, letter to John W. Richards, courtesy of the Eisenhower Center.
87. Herbert M. James, oral history transcript, courtesy of the Eisenhower Center.
88. William G. Lord, as quoted in, Gerald Astor, *June 6, 1944*, St. Martin's Press, 1994, p. 151.
89. Ibid.

90. Neal W. Beaver, response to questionnaire, courtesy of the Cornelius Ryan Collection, Alden Library, Ohio University.

91. Lord, as quoted in, *June 6, 1944*, pp. 151–152.

92. Paul E. Lehman, letter to mother, June 28, 1944, courtesy of the 82nd Airborne Division War Memorial Museum.

93. Lawrence F. Salva, oral history transcript, courtesy of the Eisenhower Center.

94. Curtis L. Johnson, written account, courtesy of www.508pir.org.

95. Malcolm D. Brannen, written account, courtesy of the 82nd Airborne War Memorial Museum.

96. Ibid.

97. Robert J. Kolterman, "World War II as Remembered by Robert J. Kolterman – 1st Sergeant, Company G," courtesy of Robert J. Kolterman.

98. Joseph M. Kissane, "WW2 Memoirs," courtesy of Robert J. Kolterman.

99. Ralph E. DeWeese, diary, courtesy of the 82nd Airborne Division War Memorial Museum.

100. John P. Delury, "D-Day Plus 40 Odd Years – Normandy Thoughts," courtesy of the Eisenhower Center.

101. Tomaso W. Porcella, oral history transcript, courtesy of the Eisenhower Center.

102. Dan Furlong, oral history transcript, courtesy of the Eisenhower Center.

103. Robert C. Moss, Jr., written account, courtesy of www.6juin1944.com.

Chapter 3 "Move To Hill 30"

1. Lieutenant Colonel Thomas J. B. Shanley, as quoted in, "Debriefing Conference—Operation Neptune," 13 August 1944, courtesy of the 82nd Airborne Division War Memorial Museum.

2. Ralph Burrus, Jr., interview, courtesy of www.geschiedenisgroesbeek.nl.

3. Ibid.

4. Ibid.

5. Edward V. Ott, written account, courtesy of the Camp Blanding Museum, p. 2.

6. Shanley, as quoted in, "Debriefing Conference—Operation Neptune."

7. Lynn C. Tomlinson, oral history transcript, courtesy of the Eisenhower Center.

8. Lieutenant Norman MacVicar, recommendation, 3 July 1944, awards file, Corporal Ernest T. Roberts, National Archives, Record Group 338, Stack 290, First Army awards, Box 27, Roberts DSC file.

9. Lieutenant Colonel Shields Warren, Jr., as quoted in, "Debriefing Conference—Operation Neptune," 13 August 1944, courtesy of the 82nd Airborne Division War Memorial Museum.

10. Woodrow W. Millsaps, "This is My Story," April 22, 1986, courtesy of the Camp Blanding Museum, p. 14.

11. Ibid., pp. 14–15.

12. Ibid., p. 15.

13. Shanley, as quoted in, "Debriefing Conference—Operation Neptune."

14. Millsaps, "This is My Story," p. 15.

15. Warren, as quoted in, "Debriefing Conference—Operation Neptune."

16. Ralph E. DeWeese diary, courtesy of the 82nd Airborne Division War Memorial Museum.

17. D. Zane Schlemmer, oral history transcript, courtesy of the Eisenhower Center.

18. Thomas A. Horne, oral history transcript, courtesy of the Eisenhower Center.

19. Tomaso W. Porcella, oral history transcript, courtesy of the Eisenhower Center.

20. Ibid.

21. DeWeese, diary.

22. Ibid.

23. Shanley, as quoted in, "Debriefing Conference—Operation Neptune."

24. Ibid.

25. Paul E. Bouchereau, oral history transcript, courtesy of the Eisenhower Center.

26. David E. Thomas, "Military Career Memoirs of Brigadier General David Edward Thomas, MC," courtesy of Normand E. Thomas.

27. Lieutenant John H. Wisner, as quoted in, "Operation of the 507th Regiment Following Drop," Combat Interviews, Army Historical Section, courtesy of the Cornelius Ryan Collection, Alden Library, Ohio University, p. 4.

28. George D. Lamm, oral history transcript, courtesy of the Eisenhower Center.

29. William A. Dean, oral history transcript, courtesy of the Eisenhower Center.

30. Adolph F. Warnecke, oral history transcript, courtesy of the Eisenhower Center.

31. John W. Marr, oral history transcript, courtesy of the Eisenhower Center.

32. Homer H. Jones, interview with author.

33. Dean, oral history transcript.

34. Homer H. Jones, interview.

35. Ralph H. Thomas, "D-Day, 6 June 1944," courtesy of www.508pir.org.

36. Homer H. Jones, interview.

37. George D. Lamm, as quoted in, Zig Boroughs, *The Devil's Tale*, Privately Published, 1992, p. 42.

38. Homer H. Jones, interview.

39. Dean, oral history transcript.

40. "Levy's Group, (A Statement by Lt. Joseph Kormylo, of D Company who was with Levy)," Combat Interviews, Army Historical Section, courtesy of the Cornelius Ryan Collection, Alden Library, Ohio University.

41. Homer H. Jones, interview.

42. Ibid.

43. Dean, oral history transcript.

44. Warnecke, oral history transcript.

45. John R. Taylor, oral history transcript, courtesy of the Eisenhower Center.

46. Dean, oral history transcript.

47. Homer H. Jones, interview.

48. Robert J. Kolterman, "World War II as Remembered by Robert J. Kolterman—1st Sgt., Company G," courtesy of Robert J. Kolterman.

49. Owen B. Hill, "My Normandy Invasion Experience," courtesy Owen B. Hill.

50. David M. Jones, oral history transcript, courtesy of the Eisenhower Center.

51. Hill, "My Normandy Invasion Experience."

52. David M. Jones, oral history transcript.

53. Hill, "My Normandy Invasion Experience."

54. David M. Jones, oral history transcript.

55. Kenneth J. Merritt, oral history transcript, courtesy of the Eisenhower Center.

56. John D. Boone, oral history transcript, courtesy of the Eisenhower Center.

57. Robert B. White, interview with author.

58. Boone, oral history transcript.

59. White, interview.

60. Boone, oral history transcript.

61. Merritt, oral history transcript.

62. Boone, oral history transcript.

63. White, interview.

64. Joseph C. Bressler, as quoted in, "We Served Proudly—The Men of Hq1," George I. Stoeckert (album collator), courtesy of www.508pir.org, p. 22.

65. George E. Miles, oral history transcript, courtesy of the Eisenhower Center.

66. Bressler, as quoted in, "We Served Proudly," p. 22.

67. George E. Christ, "D-Day, June 6, 1944, One Soldier's Experience," courtesy of D. Zane Schlemmer.

68. Tomaso W. Porcella, oral history transcript, courtesy of the Eisenhower Center.

69. D. Zane Schlemmer, oral history transcript, courtesy of the Eisenhower Center.

70. Walter H. Barrett, *My Story: Every Soldier Has A Story*, Privately Published, 2004, pp. 37–38.

71. Frank L. Staples written account, courtesy of Kristine Nymoen.

72. Ibid.

73. Edward C. Boccafogli, oral history transcript, courtesy of the Eisenhower Center.

74. Lieutenant Colonel James C. Todd, "Historical Record of the 319th Glider Field Artillery Battalion, for June, 1944," National Archives.

75. Salvatore J. Covais, as quoted in, Joseph S. Covais, *Battery! – C. Lenton Sartain and the Airborne G.I.s of the 319th Glider Field Artillery*, Andy Red Enterprises, 2011, p. 205.

76. Edward R. Ryan, response to author's questionnaire.

77. John R. Manning, as quoted in, Joseph S. Covais, *Battery! – C. Lenton Sartain and the Airborne G.I.s of the 319th Glider Field Artillery*, Andy Red Enterprises, 2011, p. 206.

78. Salvatore J. Covais, as quoted in, Joseph S. Covais, *Battery!*, p. 208.

79. Laurence F. Cook, as quoted in, Joseph S. Covais, *Battery! – C. Lenton Sartain and the Airborne G.I.s of the 319th Glider Field Artillery*, Andy Red Enterprises, 2011, p. 209.

80. Silas Hogg, as quoted in, Joseph S. Covais, *Battery! – C. Lenton Sartain and the Airborne G.I.s of the 319th Glider Field Artillery*, Andy Red Enterprises, 2011, p. 209.

81. Todd, "Historical Record of the 319th Glider Field Artillery Battalion."

82. Harry L. Reisenleiter, oral history transcript, courtesy of the Eisenhower Center.

83. Ibid.

Chapter 4 "The Germans Hunted Us"

1. Paul E. Lehman, letter to mother, June 28, 1944, courtesy of the 82nd Airborne War Memorial Museum.

2. Briand N. Beaudin, M. D., oral history transcript, courtesy of the Eisenhower Center.

3. Lehman to mother, June 28, 1944.

4. Beaudin, oral history transcript.

5. Lehman to mother, June 28, 1944.

6. Ibid.

7. Beaudin, oral history trascript.

8. R. B. Lewellen, "Jump into Gourbesville," courtesy of www.508pir.org.

9. "Report on James R. Hattrick," Headquarters 82d Airborne Division, Office of the Assistant Chief of Staff, G-2, July 7, 1944, National Archives.

10. John W. Richards, oral history transcript, courtesy of the Eisenhower Center.

11. Private Frank M. Ramirez, statement, Escape and Evasion Report, G-2, 82nd Airborne Division, 21 August 1944, courtesy of www.508pir.org.

12. Private First Class Roland E. Archambault, statement, Escape and Evasion
    Report, G-2, 82nd Airborne Division, 21 August 1944, courtesy of
    www.508pir.org.
13. Thomas J. Gintjee, oral history transcript, courtesy of the Eisenhower
    Center.
14. William M. Sawyer, oral history transcript, courtesy of the Eisenhower
    Center.
15. Carl H. Porter, "Men at War: Chow Call," courtesy of www.508pir.org.
16. John D. Kersh, as quoted in, Zig Boroughs, *The 508th Connection*, Privately
    Published, 2004, pp. 135–136.
17. Marcel Bollag, "Escape in Normandy," courtesy of Aaron Elson,
    www.tankbooks.com.
18. Elmer E. Martell, interview transcript, courtesy of www.508pir.org.
19. Frederick J. Infanger, written account, courtesy of the Camp Blanding
    Museum.
20. Otis E. "Gene" Hull, as quoted in, "We Served Proudly—The Men of Hq1,"
    George I. Stoeckert (album collator), courtesy of www.508pir.org, p. 17.
21. Henry E. LeFebvre, letter to Zig Boroughs, September 15, 1989, courtesy of
    Henry E. LeFebvre.
22. Trino F. Maldonaldo, as quoted in, "Lieutenant Robert Mason Mathias,"
    edited by Richard C. Reardon, courtesy of the Camp Blanding Museum, p.
    16.
23. Leonard A. Funk, Jr., as quoted in, Zig Boroughs, *The 508th Connection*,
    Privately Published, 2004, p. 64.
24. William H. Traband, interview with author.
25. Ibid.
26. Ibid.
27. Francis E. Williamson, written account, courtesy of Kristine Nymoen.
28. Lee Roy Wood, written account, courtesy of Kristine Nymoen.
29. Brannen, written account.
30. Ibid.
31. Lieutenant Harold V. Richard survived and was taken prisoner. The German
    prisoner, Gefreiter Baumann, remained a prisoner and was subsequently
    turned over to the 325th Glider Infantry Regiment, along with the valuable
    information in the two briefcases.
32. Brannen, written account.
33. Lieutenant Colonel Louis G. Mendez, Jr., as quoted in, "Debriefing
    Conference—Operation Neptune," 13 August 1944, courtesy of the 82nd
    Airborne War Memorial Museum.
34. John P. Delury, "D-Day Plus 40 Odd Years – Normandy Thoughts,"
    courtesy of the Eisenhower Center.

Chapter 5 "The Best Soldier In The 508th"

1. Malcolm D. Brannen, written account, courtesy of the 82nd Airborne War Memorial Museum.
2. Joseph C. Bressler, as quoted in, "We Served Proudly—The Men of Hq1," George I. Stoeckert (album collator), courtesy of www.508pir.org, p. 23.
3. Trino F. Maldonado, as quoted in, Ralph H. Thomas, "Trino, A Short History," courtesy of the Camp Blanding Museum.
4. Commanded by Oberst Robert Reiter, commanding officer of Artillerie Regiment 1709.
5. Harold O. Kulju, oral history transcript, courtesy of the Eisenhower Center.
6. Private First Class Deem died of his wounds later that day.
7. Tomaso W. Porcella, oral history transcript, courtesy of the Eisenhower Center.
8. George E. Miles, oral history transcript, courtesy of the Eisenhower Center.
9. D. Zane Schlemmer, oral history transcript, courtesy of the Eisenhower Center.
10. Paul E. Bouchereau, oral history transcript, courtesy of the Eisenhower Center.
11. William M. Sawyer, oral history transcript, courtesy of the Eisenhower Center.
12. Jack W. Schlegel, as quoted in, Dominique Francois, *Les Diables Rouges, The 508th Parachute Infantry Regiment*, Privately Published, 2001, p. 39.
13. John Z. Posadas was captured and spent the rest of the war in Europe as a POW.
14. John P. Delury, "D-Day Plus 40 Odd Years – Normandy Thoughts," courtesy of the Eisenhower Center.
15. Delury, "D-Day Plus 40 Odd Years."
16. Robert G. Rappi, as quoted in, Joseph S. Covais, *Battery! – C. Lenton Sartain and the Airborne G.I.s of the 319th Glider Field Artillery*, Andy Red Enterprises, 2011, p. 216.
17. Lieutenant Colonel James C. Todd, "Historical Record of the 319th Glider Field Artillery Battalion, for June, 1944," National Archives.
18. Edward C. Boccafogli, oral history transcript, courtesy of the Eisenhower Center.
19. Schlemmer, oral history transcript.
20. Billy B. McClure, written account, courtesy of the Camp Blanding Museum, pp. 4–5.
21. Ralph E. DeWeese, diary, courtesy of the 82nd Airborne Division War Memorial Museum.
22. William J. Call, interview with author.
23. DeWeese, diary.
24. Call, interview.

25. David E. Thomas, "Military Career Memoirs of Brigadier General David Edward Thomas, MC," courtesy of Normand E. Thomas.
26. Brannen, written account.
27. Kenneth J. Merritt, oral history transcript, courtesy of the Eisenhower Center.
28. DeWeese, diary.
29. Kulju, oral history transcript.
30. Todd, "Historical Record of the 319th Glider Field Artillery Battalion."
31. Kulju, oral history transcript.
32. Schlemmer, oral history transcript.
33. Woodrow W. Millsaps, "This is My Story," April 22, 1986, courtesy of the Camp Blanding Museum, pp. 15–16.
34. Ibid, p. 16–17.
35. Ibid, pp. 17–18.
36. Ibid, p. 18.
37. Frank Haddy, written account, courtesy of the Camp Blanding Museum, p. 5.
38. Privates First Class John F. Quigg and Russell S. Nocera both survived and were taken prisoner.
39. Brannen, written account.
40. William R. Tumlin, response to author's questionnaire.
41. William H. Traband, interview with author.
42. Thomas, "Military Career Memoirs."
43. Bouchereau, oral history transcript.
44. James T. Wynne, as quoted in, Zig Boroughs, *The 508th Connection,* Privately Published, 2004, pp. 123–124.
45. Delury, "D-Day Plus 40 Odd Years."

Chapter 6 "The Finest Man I Had Ever Met"
1. Captain Barry E. Albright, "Operations of the 2d Battalion, 508th Parachute Infantry Regiment (82d Airborne Division) in the Invasion of Normandy, June 5 – 13 1944 (Normandy Campaign) (Personal Experience and Observation of a Rifle Platoon Leader)," courtesy of the Donovan Research Library, Fort Benning, Georgia, p. 17.
2. Ralph E. DeWeese, diary, courtesy of the 82nd Airborne Division War Memorial Museum.
3. Albright, "Operations of t-he 2d Battalion," pp. 17–18.
4. Shields Warren, Jr., letter to Clay Blair, January 5, 1984, the Clay and Joan Blair Collection, U.S. Army Heritage and Education Center.
5. Malcolm D. Brannen, written account, courtesy of the 82nd Airborne War Memorial Museum.

6. Owen B. Hill, "My Normandy Invasion Experience," courtesy of Owen B. Hill.
7. Kenneth J. Merritt, oral history transcript, courtesy of the Eisenhower Center.
8. Ibid.
9. Harold L. Parris, as quoted in, Lewis Milkovics, *The Devils Have Landed*, Creative Printing and Publishing, 1993, p. 98.
10. Ibid, p. 99.
11. Ibid.
12. Carlos W. Ross, "Things That I Remember," www.508pir.org.
13. Broughton L. Hand, "The War Story of Broughton Lynn Hand, 508 Parachute Infantry, 82nd Airborne," courtesy of Broughton L. Hand, pp. 23–24.
14. Parris, *The Devils Have Landed*, pp. 99–101.
15. Dwayne T. Burns, unpublished manuscript, courtesy of Dwayne T. Burns, pp. 83–84.
16. Edward B. Chatoian, as quoted in, Zig Boroughs, *The 508th Connection*, Privately Published, 2004, p. 186.
17. Burns, unpublished manuscript, p. 84.
18. Ibid.
19. Robert B. White, interview with author.
20. Edward C. Boccafogli, interview with Aaron Elson, *A Mile in Their Shoes*, 2003, courtesy of www.tankbooks.com.
21. Lieutenant Rex G. Combs, award recommendation for 1st Sergeant Frank C. Taylor, courtesy of www.508pir.org.
22. Shields Warren, Jr., letter to Clay Blair, October 24, 1983, the Clay and Joan Blair Collection, U.S. Army Heritage and Education Center.
23. Robert E. Chisolm, interview with author.
24. Albright, "Operations of the 2d Battalion," p. 19.
25. Robert B. Newhart, response to author's questionnaire.
26. Herbert Sellers, as quoted in, Zig Boroughs, *The 508th Connection*, Privately Published, 2004, pp. 189–190.
27. Burns, unpublished manuscript, p. 84.
28. Robert Broderick, interview transcript, October 14, 2002, courtesy of Andrew Reed.
29. Ralph Burrus, Jr., interview, courtesy of www.geschiedenisgroesbeek.nl.
30. Burns, unpublished manuscript, pp. 84–85.
31. Newhart, questionnaire.
32. Frank Haddy, written account, courtesy of the Camp Blanding Museum, p. 6.
33. Burns, unpublished manuscript, pp. 85–86.
34. Robert J. Weaver, "Invasion," courtesy of David Berry and Richard O'Donnell.

35. Joseph E. Bullard, letter to Leslie Baldwin, in "508th's C. K. Baldwin killed June 14, 1944," *The News Reporter*, Whiteville, North Carolina, May 26, 1994, p. 5B.
36. Paul E. Lehman, letter to mother, June 28, 1944, courtesy of the 82nd Airborne War Memorial Museum.
37. David E. Thomas, "Military Career Memoirs of Brigadier General David Edward Thomas, MC," courtesy of Normand E. Thomas.
38. General James M. Gavin, as quoted in, Mark J. Alexander and John Sparry, *Jump Commander*, Casemate, 2010, p. 220.
39. Major General Matthew B. Ridgway, letter to General G. H. Weems, August 13, 1944, the Clay and Joan Blair Collection, U.S. Army Heritage and Education Center.
40. Mark J. Alexander and John Sparry, *Jump Commander*, Casemate, 2010, p. 219.
41. Leonard A. Funk, Jr., as quoted in, Zig Boroughs, *The 508th Connection*, Privately Published, 2004, p. 64.
42. Tomaso W. Porcella, oral history transcript, courtesy of the Eisenhower Center.

Chapter 7 "A Time To Be Bold"

1. Ralph E. DeWeese, diary, courtesy of the 82nd Airborne Division War Memorial Museum.
2. Tomaso W. Porcella, oral history transcript, courtesy of the Eisenhower Center.
3. DeWeese, diary.
4. Ibid.
5. William W. Farris, "The Attack on Pretot," courtesy of www.508pir.org.
6. Francis M. Lamoureux, as quoted in, Patrick K. O'Donnell, *Beyond Valor*, The Free Press, 2001, pp. 169.
7. Farris, "The Attack on Pretot."
8. DeWeese, diary.
9. Porcella, oral history transcript.
10. Ibid.
11. Ibid.
12. John P. Delury, "D-Day Plus 40 Odd Years – Normandy Thoughts," courtesy of the Eisenhower Center.
13. Farris, "The Attack on Pretot."
14. Marvin L. Risnes, as quoted in, Zig Boroughs, *The 508th Connection*, Privately Published, 2004, p. 199.
15. Farris, "The Attack on Pretot."
16. Porcella, oral history transcript.

17. Ibid.
18. DeWeese, diary.
19. Delury, "D-Day Plus 40 Odd Years."
20. Fayette O. Richardson, as quoted in, Donald I. Jakeway, *Paratroopers Do or Die*, Privately Published, p. 56.
21. Woodrow C. Plunkett, as quoted in, Zig Boroughs, *The 508th Connection*, Privately Published, 2004, p. 199.
22. Lamoureux, as quoted in *Beyond Valor*, pp. 169–170.
23. Delury, "D-Day Plus 40 Odd Years."
24. Fayette O. "Rich" Richardson, "Straight Talk – Back to Normandy," *The Brooklyn Paper*, 1987, courtesy of Thomas McArdle.
25. Lamoureux, as quoted in *Beyond Valor*, pp. 170–171.
26. Ibid., pp. 171–172.
27. DeWeese, diary.
28. Lamoureux, as quoted in *Beyond Valor*, p. 172.
29. Paul E. Lehman, letter to mother, June 28, 1944, courtesy of the 82nd Airborne Division War Memorial Museum.
30. Lieutenant Rex G. Combs, award recommendation for Private Charles E. Schmalz, courtesy of www.508pir.org.
31. Robert E. Chisolm, interview with author.
32. Ibid.
33. Mark J. Alexander, as quoted in, Mark J. Alexander and John Sparry, *Jump Commander*, Casemate, 2010, p. 221.
34. Ibid.
35. Ibid., p. 222.
36. Porcella, oral history transcript.
37. Lieutenant Elbert F. Hamilton, "Patrol Report for Night 26/27 June," National Archives.
38. Edward R. Ryan, as quoted in, Joseph S. Covais, *Battery! – C. Lenton Sartain and the Airborne G.I.s of the 319th Glider Field Artillery*, Andy Red Enterprises, 2011, p. 235.
39. Malcolm D. Brannen, "Two Weeks of Celebrating the Fourth of July 1944," courtesy of the Camp Blanding Museum.
40. James M. Gavin, oral history transcript, the Clay and Joan Blair Collection, U.S. Army Heritage and Education Center.
41. Edward V. Ott, written account, courtesy of the Camp Blanding Museum, pp. 2–3.
42. Alexander, as quoted in *Jump Commander*, p. 224.
43. Brannen, "Two Weeks of Celebrating the Fourth of July 1944."
44. Robert B. White, interview with author.
45. D. Zane Schlemmer, "Bois de Limors to Hill 131," courtesy of D. Zane Schlemmer, p. 1.

46. Brannen, "Two Weeks of Celebrating the Fourth of July 1944."
47. Thomas A. Horne, oral history transcript, courtesy of the Eisenhower Center.
48. Ibid.
49. Donald M. Biles, response to author's questionnaire.
50. Dwayne T. Burns, unpublished manuscript, courtesy of Dwayne T. Burns, pp. 87–88.
51. Schlemmer, "Bois de Limors to Hill 131," p. 1.
52. Ibid.
53. Ibid., p. 2.
54. Thomas J. B. Shanley, as quoted in, Clay Blair, *Ridgway's Paratroopers*, The Dial Press, 1985, p. 346.
55. Frank L. Staples written account, courtesy of Kristine Nymoen.
56. Mark J. Alexander, "Thirty Four Days in Normandy in 1944," courtesy of Mark J. Alexander, p. 8.
57. Alexander, as quoted in, *Jump Commander*, p. 225.
58. Lieutenant Rex G. Combs, award recommendation for Private Wayne F. Campbell, courtesy of www.508pir.org.
59. Lieutenant Rex G. Combs, award recommendation for Lieutenant John P. Foley, courtesy of www.508pir.org.
60. Alexander, as quoted in, *Jump Commander*, p. 225.
61. Schlemmer, "Bois de Limors to Hill 131," p. 2.
62. Brannen, "Two Weeks of Celebrating the Fourth of July 1944."
63. Fayette O. Richardson, as quoted in, Donald I. Jakeway, *Paratroopers Do or Die*, Privately Published, p. 56.
64. Alexander, "Thirty Four Days in Normandy," p. 8.
65. Ibid., pp. 8–9.
66. Virgil M. McGuire, as quoted in Zig Boroughs, *The 508th Connection*, Privately Published, 2004, p. 182.

Chapter 8 "We Practically Got Annihilated"

1. Chester E. Graham, as quoted in, Dominique Francois, *The 508th Parachute Infantry Regiment*, Heimdal, Bayeux, France, 2003.
2. Mark J. Alexander, as quoted in, Mark J. Alexander and John Sparry, *Jump Commander*, Casemate, 2010, p. 230.
3. Graham, as quoted in, *The 508th Parachute Infantry Regiment*.
4. Kelso C. Horne, as quoted in, "Conversations with Kelso," Perry Knight, editor, courtesy of Kelso C. Horne, Jr., p. 32.
5. Graham, as quoted in, *The 508th Parachute Infantry Regiment*.
6. Albert W. Giegold, letter to Mrs. Henry and Philip Vasselin, April 3, 1987.
7. Dwayne T. Burns, unpublished manuscript, courtesy of Dwayne T. Burns, pp. 89–90.

8. Frank E. McKee, as quoted in, Gerald Astor, *June 6, 1944*, St. Martin's Press, 1994, p. 326.
9. Ibid.
10. Burns, unpublished manuscript, pp. 88–89.
11. Robert B. Newhart, response to author's questionnaire.
12. Burns, unpublished manuscript, p. 90.
13. Malcolm D. Brannen, "Two Weeks of Celebrating the Fourth of July 1944," courtesy of the Camp Blanding Museum.
14. Ralph E. DeWeese, diary, courtesy of the 82nd Airborne Division War Memorial Museum.
15. Donald I. Jakeway, *Paratroopers Do or Die*, Privately Published, p. 68.
16. DeWeese, diary.
17. John P. Delury, "D-Day Plus 40 Odd Years – Normandy Thoughts," courtesy of the Eisenhower Center.
18. Jakeway, *Paratroopers Do or Die*, p. 68.
19. Delury, "D-Day Plus 40 Odd Years."
20. Kelso C. Horne, as quoted in, "Conversations with Kelso," Perry Knight, editor, courtesy of Kelso C. Horne, Jr., pp. 32–33.
21. Fred Gladstone, as quoted in, Zig Boroughs, *The 508th Connection*, Privately Published, 2004, pp. 210–211.
22. Tomaso W. Porcella, oral history transcript, courtesy of the Eisenhower Center.
23. Oliver W. Griffin, written account, courtesy of Oliver W. Griffin.
24. Fayette O. Richardson, as quoted in, Donald I. Jakeway, *Paratroopers Do or Die*, Privately Published, p. 56.
25. Louis G. Mendez, Jr., as quoted, in Patrick K. O'Donnell, *Beyond Valor*, The Free Press, 2001, p. 173.
26. Marvin Ragland, as quoted in, Joseph S. Covais, *Battery! – C. Lenton Sartain and the Airborne G.I.s of the 319th Glider Field Artillery*, Andy Red Enterprises, 2011, p. 240.
27. Ibid.
28. DeWeese, diary.
29. Jakeway, *Paratroopers Do or Die*, pp. 68–69.
30. Porcella, oral history transcript.
31. Ibid.
32. Delury, "D-Day Plus 40 Odd Years."
33. DeWeese, diary.
34. Richardson, as quoted in *Paratroopers Do or Die*, p. 56.
35. William J. Call, interview with author.
36. Adolph F. Warnecke, oral history transcript, courtesy of the Eisenhower Center.

37. Staff Sergeant Sherman Van Enwyck, statement, March 29, 1945, David Axelrod award file, courtesy of www.508pir.org.
38. Lieutenant Homer H. Jones, statement, March 26, 1945, David Axelrod award file, courtesy of www.508pir.org.
39. Lieutenant Rex G. Combs, statement, March 28, 1945, David Axelrod award file, courtesy of www.508pir.org.
40. Call, interview.
41. Ibid.
42. Ibid.
43. Porcella, oral history transcript.
44. Alexander, as quoted in, *Jump Commander*, p. 232.
45. D. Zane Schlemmer, "Bois de Limors to Hill 131," courtesy of D. Zane Schlemmer, p. 3.
46. DeWeese, diary.

Chapter 9 "Put Us Down in Hell"

1. George D. Glass, interview with author.
2. Ibid.
3. Eugene C. Metcalfe, interview with author.
4. Ralph E. DeWeese, diary, courtesy of the 82nd Airborne Division War Memorial Museum.
5. Ibid.
6. Robert E. Chisolm, interview with author.
7. Ibid.
8. Worster M. Morgan, "My Paratroop Activities," courtesy of www.508pir.org.
9. Robert B. White, interview with author.
10. The James M. Gavin Papers, Personal Diaries, Box 8, Folder – Diary Passages, courtesy of the U.S. Army Military History Institute.
11. Captain Kenneth L. Johnson, "Supply Operations of the 508th Parachute Infantry Regiment (82nd Airborne Division) in the Invasion of Holland, 15 – 19 September 1944, (Rhineland Campaign) (Personal Experience of the Regimental S-4)," courtesy of the Donovan Research Library, Fort Benning, Georgia, pp. 16–18.
12. Francis L. Mahan, letter to Jan Bos, "Tragedy at Fullbeck," 2001, courtesy of Jan Bos.
13. Eugene G. Walton, III, as quoted in Donald I. Jakeway, *Paratroopers Do or Die*, Privately Published, p. 89.
14. Gavin Papers, Personal Diaries, Box 8, Folder – Diary Passages.
15. Ibid.
16. Chester E. Graham, "My Memories of World War II," courtesy of the Camp Blanding Museum, p. 6.

17. HQ 508th Parachute Infantry, APO 514, U.S. Army, "Field Order No. 1," 13 September 1944, National Archives.

18. Thomas A. Horne, response to questionnaire, courtesy of the Cornelius Ryan Collection, Alden Library, Ohio University.

19. Johnson, "Supply Operations of the 508th," p. 12.

20. Ibid., p. 18.

21. Robert B. White, interview with author.

22. James R. Blue, written account, courtesy of the 82nd Airborne Division War Memorial Museum, p. 1.

23. Ibid., p. 3.

24. Ibid., pp. 1–2.

25. Major Jonathan E. Adams, Jr., letter to Major Benjamin F. Delamater, III, April 7, 1947, in Major B. F. Delamater, III, "The Action of the 1st Battalion, 508th Parachute Infantry (82nd Airborne Division) in the Holland Invasion, 15 – 24 September 1944 (Rhineland Campaign, European Theater of Operations) (Personal Experience of the Battalion Executive Officer)," courtesy of the Donovan Research Library, Fort Benning, Georgia.

26. William H. Nation, letter to parents, October 20, 1944, courtesy of William C. Nation.

27. Wilbur J. Scanlon, response to questionnaire, courtesy of the Cornelius Ryan Collection, Alden Library, Ohio University.

28. Johnson, "Supply Operations of the 508th," pp. 19–20.

29. Neal W. Beaver, response to questionnaire, courtesy of the Cornelius Ryan Collection, Alden Library, Ohio University.

30. Major Benjamin F. Delamater, III, "The Action of the 1st Battalion, 508th Parachute Infantry (82nd Airborne Division) in the Holland Invasion, 15 – 24 September 1944 (Rhineland Campaign, European Theater of Operations) (Personal Experience of the Battalion Executive Officer)," courtesy of the Donovan Research Library, Fort Benning, Georgia, p. 6.

31. Blue, written account, p. 2.

32. Eugene C. Metcalfe, interview with author.

33. Blue, written account, pp. 2–3.

34. Metcalfe, interview.

35. Joseph M. Kissane, "WW2 Memoirs," courtesy of Robert J. Kolterman.

36. Francis M. Lamoureux, as quoted in, "From Normandy to Nijmegen, Holland," *The Ludlow Register*, April 11, 2001, courtesy of Thomas McArdle, p. 9.

37. James R. Allardyce, letter to Heather Chapman, November 20, 1967, courtesy of the Cornelius Ryan Collection, Alden Library, Ohio University.

38. John P. Foley, response to questionnaire, courtesy of the Cornelius Ryan Collection, Alden Library, Ohio University.

39. Nation to parents, October 20, 1944.
40. First Lieutenant Wayne H. Smith, interview, 97th General Hospital, National Archives.
41. Woodrow W. Millsaps, letter to Heather Chapman, July 27, 1967, courtesy of the Cornelius Ryan Collection, Alden Library, Ohio University.
42. Blue, written account, p. 4.
43. Adams to Delamater.
44. Roland C. Ziegler, response to questionnaire, courtesy of the Cornelius Ryan Collection, Alden Library, Ohio University.
45. Metcalfe, interview.
46. Millsaps to Chapman, July 27, 1967.
47. Lieutenant Colonel Shields Warren, Jr., "Narrative of Events of the 1st Battalion 508th Parachute Infantry for Period 17 – 21 September 1944, in the Vicinity of Nijmegen, Holland," courtesy of the 82nd Airborne War Memorial Museum, p. 1.
48. James Q. Kurz, "Holland Jump, September 17, 1944, Through the Eyes of a Squad Leader," courtesy of the Camp Blanding Museum, p. 3.
49. Corporal Jesse J. Womble, statement, Missing Air Crew Report, Aircraft Number 42-15102, courtesy of http://www.Fold3.com.
50. Allardyce to Chapman, November 20, 1967.
51. Millsaps to Heather Chapman, July 27, 1967.
52. When Private Beaver was hit, he also suffered a penetrating chest wound and as a result was evacuated to the United States.
53. Blue, written account, p. 4.
54. Ibid., p. 5.
55. Adams to Delamater.
56. Sergeant Walter Firestine and Private Edward J. Wodowski, statement, 12 December 1944, Missing Air Crew Report, courtessy of www.Fold3.com, p. 11.
57. Edward J. Wodowski, interview with author.
58. Firestine and Wodowski, statement, p. 11.
59. Lieutenant John P. Foley, statement, 15 December 1944, Missing Air Crew Report, courtesy of www.Fold3.com, p. 9.
60. Sergeant Joseph B. McCann, statement, 16 December 1944, Missing Air Crew Report, courtesy of www.Fold3.com, p. 12.
61. White, interview.
62. Gordon H. Cullings, response to author's questionnaire.
63. Dwayne T. Burns, unpublished manuscript, courtesy of Dwayne T. Burns, pp. 105–108.

64. Captain Robert L. Sickler, "The Operations of Company D, 2nd Battalion, 508th Parachute Infantry Regiment (82nd Airborne Division) at Nijmegen, Holland, 17 – 19 September 1944 (Rhineland Campaign, European Theater of Operations) (Personal Experience of a Platoon Leader)," courtesy of the Donovan Research Library, Fort Benning, Georgia, p. 11.

65. Frank Haddy, written account, courtesy of the Camp Blanding Museum, p. 8.

66. Frank L. Staples written account, courtesy of Kristine Nymoen.

67. Ibid.

68. Adolph F. Warnecke, as quoted in, Gerald Astor, *The Greatest War*, Presidio Press, 1999, p. 681.

69. First Lieutenant James D. Tibbetts, interview, 160th General Hospital, National Archives.

70. Lamoureux, as quoted in, "From Normandy to Nijmegen, Holland," p. 9.

71. Lyle K. Kumler, response to questionnaire, courtesy of the Cornelius Ryan Collection, Alden Library, Ohio University.

72. Donald I. Jakeway, *Paratroopers Do or Die*, Privately Published, p. 108.

73. George T. Sheppard, response to author's questionnaire.

74. Robert E. Chisolm, interview with author.

75. Okey A. Mills, as quoted in, Zig Boroughs, *The 508th Connection*, Privately Published, 2004, p. 243–244.

76. Richard G. Wolch, "From the Sky We Lead," courtesy of http://marketgarden.secondworldwar.nl.

Chapter 10 "Use Trench Knives and Bayonets"

1. Major Benjamin F. Delamater, III, "The Action of the 1st Battalion, 508th Parachute Infantry (82nd Airborne Division) in the Holland Invasion, 15 – 24 September 1944 (Rhineland Campaign, European Theater of Operations) (Personal Experience of the Battalion Executive Officer)," courtesy of the Donovan Research Library, Fort Benning, Georgia, pp. 7–9.

2. Major Jonathan E. Adams, Jr., letter to Major Benjamin F. Delamater, III, April 7, 1947, in Major B. F. Delamater, III, "The Action of the 1st Battalion, 508th Parachute Infantry (82nd Airborne Division) in the Holland Invasion, 15 – 24 September 1944," courtesy of the Donovan Research Library, Fort Benning, Georgia.

3. Lieutenant Colonel Shields Warren, Jr., "Narrative of Events of the 1st Battalion 508th Parachute Infantry for Period 17 – 21 September 1944, in the Vicinity of Nijmegen, Holland," courtesy of the 82nd Airborne War Memorial Museum, p. 2.

4. Adams to Delamater.

5. Delamater, "The Action of the 1st Battalion," pp. 9–10.

6. Warren, "Narrative of Events of the 1st Battalion," pp. 2–3.
7. Gordon H. Cullings, response to author's questionnaire.
8. Eugene C. Metcalfe, interview with author.
9. Cullings, questionnaire.
10. Captain Robert L. Sickler, "The Operations of Company D, 2nd Battalion, 508th Parachute Infantry Regiment (82nd Airborne Division) at Nijmegen, Holland, 17 – 19 September 1944 (Rhineland Campaign, European Theater of Operations) (Personal Experience of a Platoon Leader)," courtesy of the Donovan Research Library, Fort Benning, Georgia, pp. 12–13.
11. Richard G. Wolch, "First Contact with the Enemy," courtesy of http://marketgarden.secondworldwar.nl.
12. Dwyane T. Burns, unpublished manuscript, courtesy of Dwayne T. Burns, pp. 108–109.
13. First Lieutenant Wayne H. Smith, interview, 97th General Hospital, National Archives.
14. First Lieutenant Louis L. Toth, interview, 97th General Hospital, National Archives.
15. Lieutenant Colonel Louis G. Mendez, Jr., letter to Major General James M. Gavin, November 8, 1945, courtesy of the Cornelius Ryan Collection, Alden Library, Ohio University.
16. Robert E. Chisolm, interview with author.
17. Ibid.
18. Toth, interview.
19. Donald I. Jakeway, *Paratroopers Do or Die*, Privately Published, p. 109.
20. Henry McLean, as quoted in, Tim Saunders, *Nijmegen*, Pen and Sword Books Limited, 2001, p. 109.
21. Richard G. Wolch, "First Contact with the Enemy," and "Bringing Supplies to Berg-en-Dal," courtesy of http://marketgarden.secondworldwar.nl.
22. Mendez to Gavin, November 8, 1945.
23. Lieutenant Howard A. Greenwalt, "Statement of Lt. Greenwalt on the Nijmegen Attack by Co. G," courtesy of the Cornelius Ryan Collection, Alden Library, Ohio University.
24. Mendez to Gavin, November 8, 1945.
25. Chisolm, interview.
26. Chester E. Graham, "My Memories of World War II," courtesy of the Camp Blanding Museum, p. 6.
27. Michael Reynolds, *Sons of the Reich – II SS Panzer Corps*, Casemate, 2002, p. 122.
28. Warren, "Narrative of Events of the 1st Battalion," pp. 3–4.
29. James R. Blue, written account, courtesy of the 82nd Airborne War Memorial Museum, p. 6.

30. Captain Jonathan E. Adams, Jr., Headquarters First Battalion 508th Parachute Infantry APO 757, U.S. Army, "Holland Operation," November 2, 1945," courtesy of the Cornelius Ryan Collection, Alden Library, Ohio University.
31. Blue, written account, pp. 6–7.
32. Warren, "Narrative of Events of the 1st Battalion," p. 4.
33. Adams, "Holland Operation."
34. Blue, written account, p. 7.
35. George D. Lamm, as quoted in, Zig Boroughs, *The 508th Connection*, Privately Published, 2004, p. 253.
36. Blue, written account, pp. 7–8.
37. Warren, "Narrative of Events of the 1st Battalion," p. 4.
38. Lamm, as quoted in, *The 508th Connection*, pp. 253–254.
39. Edward J. Wodowski, interview with author.
40. Blue, written account, p. 8.
41. Ibid., pp. 9–10.
42. Warren, "Narrative of Events of the 1st Battalion," pp. 4–5.
43. Walter H. Barrett, *My Story: Every Soldier Has A Story*, Privately Published, 2004, p. 58.
44. Nathan Silverlieb, interview with author.
45. James Q. Kurz, "Holland Jump, September 17, 1944, Through the Eyes of a Squad Leader," courtesy of the Camp Blanding Museum, p. 1.
46. James R. Allardyce, letter to Heather Chapman, November 20, 1967, courtesy of the Cornelius Ryan Collection, Alden Library, Ohio University.
47. Adams, "Holland Operation."
48. Adams to Delamater.
49. Ibid.

Chapter 11 "Extremely Capable Troops"

1. Lieutenant Lloyd L. Polette, Jr., statement, October 23, 1944, Headquarters, 508 Parachute Infantry, APO 230, U.S. Army, "Capture of Bridge Number 10," courtesy of the Cornelius Ryan Collection, Alden Library, Ohio University.
2. Lieutenant Jean H. Trahin, statement, October 23, 1944, Headquarters, 508 Parachute Infantry, APO 230, U.S. Army, "Capture of Bridge Number 10," courtesy of the Cornelius Ryan Collection, Alden Library, Ohio University.
3. Polette, statement.
4. Redmond L. Daggett, as quoted in, William G. Lord, II, *History of the 508th Parachute Infantry Regiment*, Infantry Journal Press, 1948, p. 47.
5. Polette, statement.

6. First Lieutenant Edward V. Ott, interview, 160th General Hospital, National Archives.
7. Sergeant George D. Fairman, Jr., statement, Headquarters, 508 Parachute Infantry, APO 230, U.S. Army, "Capture of Bridge Number 10," courtesy of the Cornelius Ryan Collection, Alden Library, Ohio University.
8. Polette, statement.
9. Lieutenant Colonel Louis G. Mendez, Jr., letter to Major General James M. Gavin, November 8, 1945, courtesy of the Cornelius Ryan Collection, Alden Library, Ohio University.
10. Captain Jonathan E. Adams, Jr., Headquarters First Battalion 508th Parachute Infantry APO 757, U.S. Army, "Holland Operation," November 2, 1945," courtesy of the Cornelius Ryan Collection, Alden Library, Ohio University.
11. Major General James M. Gavin, letter to Captain John G. Westover, July 25, 1945, U.S. Army Heritage and Education Center.
12. Agardus M. Leegsma, letter to James R. Blue, April 27, 1963, courtesy of the Cornelius Ryan Collection, Alden Library, Ohio University.
13. Lieutenant Howard A. Greenawalt, "Statement of Lt. Greenawalt on the Nijmegen Attack by Co. G," courtesy of the Cornelius Ryan Collection, Alden Library, Ohio University.
14. Ibid.
15. Glen W. Vantrease, response to questionnaire, courtesy of the Cornelius Ryan Collection, Alden Library, Ohio University.
16. Angel Romero, as quoted in, Zig Boroughs, *The 508th Connection*, Privately Published, 2004, p. 262.
17. Greenawalt, "Nijmegen Attack by Co. G."
18. John P. Dube, as quoted in, Lewis Milkovics, *The Devils Have Landed*, Creative Printing and Publishing, 1993, p. 17.
19. Greenawalt, "Nijmegen Attack by Co. G."
20. Mendez to Gavin, November 8, 1945.
21. Romero, as quoted in *The 508th Connection*, p. 262.
22. Leegsma to Blue, April 27, 1963.
23. Vantrease, questionnaire.
24. Captain Robert L. Sickler, "The Operations of Company D, 2nd Battalion, 508th Parachute Infantry Regiment (82nd Airborne Division) at Nijmegen, Holland, 17 – 19 September 1944 (Rhineland Campaign, European Theater of Operations) (Personal Experience of a Platoon Leader)," courtesy of the Donovan Research Library, Fort Benning, pp. 13–14.
25. Ibid., pp. 14–15.
26. John M. Greene, response to author's questionnaire.
27. Cornelius M. Cahill, response to author's questionnaire.

28. Joseph E. Bullard, as quoted in, "Paratrooper recalls Normandy jump," *The News Reporter*, Whiteville, North Carolina, May 26, 1994, p. 5B.
29. Greene, questionnaire.
30. Cahill, questionnaire.
31. Bullard, as quoted in, "Paratrooper recalls Normandy jump."
32. Sickler, "Operations of Company D," pp. 15–18.
33. Captain Kenneth L. Johnson, "Supply Operations of the 508th Parachute Infantry Regiment (82nd Airborne Division) in the Invasion of Holland, 15 – 19 September 1944, (Rhineland Campaign) (Personal Experience of the Regimental S-4)," courtesy of the Donovan Research Library, Fort Benning, Georgia, p. 27.
34. Lieutenant John Eskoff, statement, "The History of the 319th Glider Field Artillery Battalion, Wednesday September 13, 1944 to Monday October 16, 1944," Enclosure Number 1, National Archives.
35. Sickler, "Operations of Company D," p. 18.
36. Johnson, "Supply Operations of the 508th," p. 28.
37. Ibid., pp. 28–29.
38. Ibid., p. 29.
39. Sickler, "Operations of Company D," p. 18.
40. Lieutenant Colonel Shields Warren, Jr., "Narrative of Events of the 1st Battalion 508th Parachute Infantry for Period 17 – 21 September 1944, in the Vicinity of Nijmegen, Holland," courtesy of the 82nd Airborne War Memorial Museum, p. 6.
41. Lieutenant Woodrow W. Millsaps, APO 757, U.S. Army, "Headquarters, Company B, 508th Parachute Infantry," November 2, 1945," courtesy of the Cornelius Ryan Collection, Alden Library, Ohio University.
42. Woodrow W. Millsaps, letter to Heather Chapman, July 27, 1967, courtesy of the Cornelius Ryan Collection, Alden Library, Ohio University.
43. Warren, "Narrative of Events of the 1st Battalion," pp. 6–7.
44. George D. Glass, interview with author.
45. Millsaps to Chapman, July 27, 1967.
46. Glass, interview.
47. James R. Allardyce, letter to Heather Chapman, November 20, 1967, courtesy of the Cornelius Ryan Collection, Alden Library, Ohio University.
48. Walter H. Barrett, *My Story: Every Soldier Has A Story*, Privately Published, 2004, p. 67.
49. Major Benjamin F. Delamater, III, "The Action of the 1st Battalion, 508th Parachute Infantry (82nd Airborne Division) in the Holland Invasion, 15 – 24 September 1944 (Rhineland Campaign, European Theater of Operations) (Personal Experience of the Battalion Executive Officer)," courtesy of the Donovan Research Library, Fort Benning, Georgia, p. 13.

50. James Q. Kurz, "Holland Jump, September 17, 1944, Through the Eyes of a Squad Leader," courtesy of the Camp Blanding Museum, p. 4.
51. Hardie had been temporarily reduced in rank to private for improper protest of the heavy training schedule to rebuild the company after Normandy.
52. Dr. John Hardie, written account, May 20, 1999, courtesy of Starlyn R. Jorgensen.
53. William H. Traband, interview with author.
54. Hardie, written account.
55. Sickler, "Operations of Company D," pp. 18–19.
56. Delamater, "Action Of The 1st Battalion," p. 13.
57. James R. Blue, written account, courtesy of the 82nd Airborne Division War Memorial Museum, p. 11.
58. Hardie, account.
59. Ibid.
60. Frank Longiotti, email to author, January 14, 2004.
61. Longiotti, email.
62. Glass, interview.
63. Millsaps to Chapman, July 27, 1967.
64. James Q. Kurz, "Holland Jump, September 17, 1944," p. 4.
65. Allardyce to Chapman, November 20, 1967.
66. Glass, interview.
67. Woodrow W. Millsaps, "This is My Story," April 22, 1986, courtesy of the Camp Blanding Museum, pp. 20–21.
68. John W. Connelly, response to questionnaire, courtesy of the Cornelius Ryan Collection, Alden Library, Ohio University.
69. Major Fred J. Silvey, statement, "The History of the 319th Glider Field Artillery Battalion, Wednesday September 13, 1944 to Monday October 16, 1944," Enclosure Number 3, National Archives.
70. Edward R. Ryan, response to author's questionnaire.
71. Millsaps to Chapman, July 27, 1967.
72. Ibid.
73. William Windom, response to author's questionnaire.
74. Ibid.
75. Delamater, "Action of the 1st Battalion," p. 14.
76. Sickler, "Operations of Company D," pp. 20–21.
77. Gavin to Westover.
78. Millsaps to Chapman, July 27, 1967.
79. Johnson, "Supply Operations of the 508th," pp. 29–30.
80. Ibid., pp. 31–32.
81. Connelly, questionnaire.
82. Silvey, statement.
83. Adams, "Holland Operation."

Chapter 12 "I Lost Half Of My Company"
1. Adolph F. Warnecke, as quoted in, Gerald Astor, *The Greatest War*, Presidio Press, 1999, p. 681.
2. Ibid.
3. James R. Blue, written account, courtesy of the 82nd Airborne Division War Memorial Museum, p. 11.
4. Lieutenant Colonel Louis G. Mendez, Jr., letter to Major General James M. Gavin, November 8, 1945, courtesy of the Cornelius Ryan Collection, Alden Library, Ohio University.
5. Robert E. Chisolm, interview with author.
6. Lieutenant Ralph W. Hendrix, as quoted in, Headquarters, 307th Airborne Engineer Battalion, APO 469, U.S. Army, "Record of Action," Holland, National Archives.
7. Sergeant Roland C. Ziegler, as quoted in, Headquarters, 307th Airborne Engineer Battalion, APO 469, U.S. Army, "Record of Action," Holland, National Archives.
8. Hendrix, as quoted in, "Company D, Record of Action."
9. First Lieutenant Wayne H. Smith, interview, 97th General Hospital, National Archives.
10. Dwyane T. Burns, unpublished manuscript, courtesy of Dwayne T. Burns, pp. 111–113.
11. Mendez to Gavin, November 8, 1945.
12. William J. Call, interview with author.
13. John P. Foley, letter to James R. Blue, January 31, 1963, courtesy of the Cornelius Ryan Collection, Alden Library, Ohio University.
14. Call, interview.
15. Blue, written account, pp. 11–12.
16. Staff Sergeant James H. Sweet, as quoted in, Headquarters, 307th Airborne Engineer Battalion, APO 469, U.S. Army, "Record of Action," Holland, National Archives.
17. Dr. John E. Brickley, letter to James R. Blue, December 6, 1962.
18. Foley to Blue, January 31, 1963.
19. Brickley to Blue, December 6, 1962.
20. Call, interview.
21. Call, interview.
22. Sweet, as quoted in, "Record of Action."
23. Call, interview.
24. Frank C. Taylor, response to questionnaire, courtesy of the Cornelius Ryan Collection, Alden Library, Ohio University.
25. Foley to Blue, January 31, 1963.
26. Woodrow W. Millsaps, letter to Heather Chapman, July 27, 1967, courtesy of the Cornelius Ryan Collection, Alden Library, Ohio University.

27. Foley to Blue, January 31, 1963.

28. Robert B. White, interview with author.

29. Lieutenant John P. Foley, as quoted in, Headquarters, 508th Parachute Infantry APO 230, "57 Days in Holland and Germany with the 508th Parachute Infantry," National Archives, p. 5.

30. Call, interview.

31. White, interview.

32. Dr. John E. Brickley, as quoted in, Zig Boroughs, *The Devil's Tale*, Privately Published, 1992, p. 194.

33. Millsaps to Chapman, July 27, 1967.

34. Edward C. Boccafogli, interview with Aaron Elson, *A Mile in Their Shoes*, 2003, www.tankbooks.com.

35. James Q. Kurz, "Holland Jump, September 17, 1944, Through the Eyes of a Squad Leader," courtesy of the Camp Blanding Museum, p. 5.

36. Nathan Silverlieb, interview with author.

37. Lieutenant Colonel Shields Warren, Jr., "Narrative of Events of the 1st Battalion 508th Parachute Infantry for Period 17 – 21 September 1944, in the Vicinity of Nijmegen, Holland," courtesy of the 82nd Airborne War Memorial Museum, pp. 8–9.

38. Millsaps to Chapman, July 27, 1967.

39. Kurz, "Holland Jump," p. 6.

40. Millsaps to Chapman, July 27, 1967.

41. Kurz, "Holland Jump," pp. 6–7.

42. Millsaps to Chapman, July 27, 1967.

43. Boccafogli, interview, *A Mile in Their Shoes*.

44. Nathan Silverlieb, written account, courtesy of the Camp Blanding Museum.

45. Millsaps to Chapman, July 27, 1967.

46. Major Jonathan E. Adams, Jr., letter to Major Benjamin F. Delamater, III, April 7, 1947, in Major B. F. Delamater, III, "The Action of the 1st Battalion, 508th Parachute Infantry (82nd Airborne Division) in the Holland Invasion, 15 – 24 September 1944," courtesy of the Donovan Research Library, Fort Benning, Georgia.

47. Blue, written account, p. 13.

48. Adams to Delamater.

49. Norbert C. Studelska, written account, courtesy of Norbert C. Studelska.

50. Chisolm, interview.

51. Ibid.

52. James M. Gavin, letter to Matthew B. Ridgway, June 27, 1973, U.S. Army Heritage and Education Center.

53. Donald I. Jakeway, *Paratroopers Do or Die*, Privately Published, p. 109.

54. Donald Veach, response to questionnaire, courtesy of the Cornelius Ryan Collection, Alden Library, Ohio University.

55. Harry A. Roll, response to author's questionnaire.

56. Ibid

57. Ibid.

58. Thomas A. Horne, response to questionnaire, courtesy of the Cornelius Ryan Collection, Alden Library, Ohio University.

59. Roll, questionnaire.

60. First Lieutenant Louis L. Toth interview, 97th General Hospital, National Archives.

61. Joseph M. Kissane, "WW2 Memoirs," courtesy of Robert J. Kolterman.

62. Adams to Delamater.

63. Blue, written account, p. 12.

64. Adams to Delamater.

65. Edward R. Ryan, response to author's questionnaire.

66. Lewis Milkovics, written account, courtesy of http://strictly-gi.com.

67. Charles L. Sartain, as quoted in, Joseph S. Covais, *Battery! – C. Lenton Sartain and the Airborne G.I.s of the 319th Glider Field Artillery*, Andy Red Enterprises, 2011, p. 275.

68. Salvatore J. Covais, as quoted in, Joseph S. Covais, *Battery! – C. Lenton Sartain and the Airborne G.I.s of the 319th Glider Field Artillery*, Andy Red Enterprises, 2011, p. 285.

69. Louis Sosa, as quoted in, Joseph S. Covais, *Battery! – C. Lenton Sartain and the Airborne G.I.s of the 319th Glider Field Artillery*, Andy Red Enterprises, 2011, p. 284.

70. Sartain, as quoted in, *Battery!*, pp. 286–287.

71. Oliver W. Griffin, written account, courtesy of Oliver W. Griffin.

72. Lyle K. Kumler, response to questionnaire, courtesy of the Cornelius Ryan Collection, Alden Library, Ohio University.

73. Toth interview.

74. Griffin, written account.

75. Neal L. Beaver, response to questionnaire, courtesy of the Cornelius Ryan Collection, Alden Library, Ohio University.

76. Toth interview.

77. Woodrow W. Millsaps, letter to Heather Chapman, July 27, 1967, courtesy of the Cornelius Ryan Collection, Alden Library, Ohio University.

78. Major Benjamin F. Delamater, III, "The Action of the 1st Battalion, 508th Parachute Infantry (82nd Airborne Division) in the Holland Invasion, 15 – 24 September 1944 (Rhineland Campaign, European Theater of Operations) (Personal Experience of the Battalion Executive Officer)," courtesy of the Donovan Research Library, Fort Benning, Georgia, p. 21.

79. Lieutenant Charles W. Chaplinski, as quoted in, Headquarters, 307th Airborne Engineer Battalion, APO 469, U.S. Army, "Record of Action," Holland, National Archives.

80. Roland C. Ziegler, response to questionnaire and interview, courtesy of the Cornelius Ryan Collection, Alden Library, Ohio University.
81. Chaplinski, as quoted in, "Record of Action."
82. Thomas J. Broderick, as quoted in, Tom Brokaw, *The Greatest Generation*, Random House, 1998, p. 19.
83. James R. Allardyce, letter to Heather Chapman, November 20, 1967, courtesy of the Cornelius Ryan Collection, Alden Library, Ohio University.

Chapter 13 "My Boys Are Pinned Down"
1. James R. Blue, written account, courtesy of the 82nd Airborne Division War Memorial Museum, pp. 13–14.
2. Ibid., p. 14.
3. Ibid.
4. Neal L. Beaver, response to questionnaire, courtesy of the Cornelius Ryan Collection, Alden Library, Ohio University.
5. Ralph J. Busson, response to questionnaire, courtesy of the Cornelius Ryan Collection, Alden Library, Ohio University.
6. Oliver W. Griffin, written account, courtesy of Oliver W. Griffin.
7. Edward N. Bailey, response to questionnaire, courtesy of the Cornelius Ryan Collection, Alden Library, Ohio University.
8. Frank Ruppe, response to questionnaire, courtesy of the Cornelius Ryan Collection, Alden Library, Ohio University.
9. William J. Call, interview with author.
10. Joseph M. Kissane, "WW2 Memoirs," courtesy of Robert J. Kolterman.
11. Call, interview.
12. Ibid.
13. Joseph Kissane, response to questionnaire, courtesy of the Cornelius Ryan Collection, Alden Library, Ohio University.
14. Robert J. Kolterman, "World War II as Remembered by Robert J. Kolterman—1st Sgt., Company G," courtesy of Robert J. Kolterman.
15. Francis M. Lamoureux, as quoted in, "From Normandy to Nijmegen, Holland," *The Ludlow Register*, April 11, 2001, p. 9.
16. Kissane, questionnaire.
17. Harry A. Roll, response to author's questionnaire.
18. Foy Rice, letter to Jan Bos, August 23, 1984, courtesy of Jan Bos.
19. Wilbur J. Scanlon, response to questionnaire, courtesy of the Cornelius Ryan Collection, Alden Library, Ohio University.
20. Marvin L. Risnes, as quoted in, "Holland Veteran Still with 82nd Div.; Looks Back 26 Years to Campaign," *The Paraglide*, Winter 1970, courtesy of Robert J. Kolterman, p. 23–24.
21. Kissane, questionnaire.

22. Ruppe, questionnaire.

23. Griffin, written account.

24. First Lieutenant Wayne H. Smith, interview, 97th General Hospital, National Archives.

25. Paul R. Sands, "A Walk Down Memory Lane," courtesy of the Camp Blanding Museum, p. 3.

26. Frederick J. Infanger, as quoted in Zig Boroughs, *The 508th Connection*, Privately Published, 2004, p. 294.

27. Norbert C. Studelska, written account, courtesy of Norbert C. Studelska.

28. Billy B. McClure, written account, courtesy of the Camp Blanding Museum, p. 6.

29. Frank Haddy, written account, courtesy of the Camp Blanding Museum, p. 9.

30. McClure, written account, pp. 6–7.

31. Studelska, written account.

32. Infanger, as quoted in *The 508th Connection*, pp. 294–295.

33. Smith, interview.

34. Dwayne T. Burns, unpublished manuscript, courtesy of Dwayne T. Burns, pp. 116–117.

35. Ibid., p. 118.

36. Studelska, written account.

37. Ibid.

38. Ibid.

39. Sands, "A Walk Down Memory Lane," p. 3.

40. Lieutenant Rex G. Combs, award recommendation for Sergeant Joe H. Boone, courtesy of www.508pir.org.

41. Call, interview.

42. Ibid.

43. Roll, questionnaire.

44. First Lieutenant Louis L. Toth interview, 97th General Hospital, National Archives.

45. William Windom, response to author's questionnaire.

46. Ibid.

47. Lieutenant Rex G. Combs, award recommendation for Sergeant Robert B. White, courtesy of www.508pir.org.

48. Lieutenant Rex G. Combs, award recommendation for Sergeant Marion E. Kinman, courtesy of www.508pir.org.

49. Combs, award recommendation for White.

50. Combs, award recommendation for Kinman.

51. Combs, award recommendation for White.

52. Studelska, written account, and Norbert C. Studelska, letter to Nelson S. Bryant, February 5, 2002, courtesy of the Camp Blanding Museum.

53. David E. Thomas, "Military Career Memoirs of Brigadier General David Edward Thomas, MC," courtesy of Normand E. Thomas.
54. Studelska, written account.
55. Ibid.
56. Call, interview.
57. James R. Allardyce, "Out of Holland, The Bulge, Frankfurt, and Berlin," courtesy of the Camp Blanding Museum, p. 3.
58. Thomas, "Military Career Memoirs."
59. Woodrow W. Millsaps, "This is My Story," April 22, 1986, courtesy of the Camp Blanding Museum, pp. 26–28.
60. Ibid., p. 28.
61. Ibid.

Chapter 14 "A Beautiful Defensive Position"
1. Major General James M. Gavin, "The Story of the 82nd Airborne Division in the Battle of the Belgian Bulge, in the Siegfried Line, and of the Roer River, Section II—Division Commander's Report," 82nd Airborne War Memorial Museum, p. 1.
2. Major John W. Medusky, interview with Captain Kenneth W. Hechler, February 15, 1945, Combat Interviews, Army Historical Section, National Archives.
3. James Q. Kurz, "A Sergeant's View of the Battle of the Bulge," courtesy of the Camp Blanding Museum, p. 1.
4. Robert J. Kolterman, "World War II as Remembered by Robert J. Kolterman—1st Sgt., Company G," courtesy of Robert J. Kolterman.
5. William J. Call, interview with author.
6. Allan H. Stein, response to author's questionnaire.
7. Lieutenant Colonel Louis G. Mendez, Jr., CO, 3rd Battalion, 508th Parachute Infantry and Lieutenant John T. Little, S-2, 3rd Battalion, 508th Parachute Infantry, interview with Lieutenant Francis P. Halas, March 28, 1945, Combat Interviews, Army Historical Section, National Archives.
8. William Windom, response to author's questionnaire.
9. Mendez and Little, interview, March 28, 1945.
10. Charles A. Powell, Jr., "All I Say is True," courtesy of the Camp Blanding Museum.
11. Woodrow W. Millsaps, "This is My Story," April 22, 1986, courtesy of the Camp Blanding Museum, p. 29.
12. Walter H. Barrett, *My Story: Every Soldier Has A Story*, Privately Published, 2004, p. 90.
13. Kurz, "A Sergeant's View of the Battle of the Bulge," pp. 2–3.

14. Major Jonathan E. Adams, Jr., "The Operations of A Company, 508th Parachute Infantry, (82nd Airborne Division) Near Rencheux, Belgium, (Ardennes Campaign) 22-25 December, 1944, (Personal Experience of a Company Commander)," courtesy of the Donovan Research Library, Fort Benning, Georgia, pp. 8–9.
15. Ibid., p. 9.
16. Ibid., pp. 9–10.
17. Ibid., p. 10.
18. Kurz, "A Sergeant's View of the Battle of the Bulge," pp. 3–4.
19. Mendez and Little, interview, March 28, 1945.
20. Ralph Gilson, written account, courtesy of Ralph Gilson.
21. Mendez and Little, interview, March 28, 1945.
22. Adams, "The Operations of A Company," pp. 10–12.
23. Sergeant Charles H. Koons, sworn statement, 16 March 1945, awards file, Lieutenant George D. Lamm, National Archives, Record Group 338, Stack 290, Ninth Army awards, Box 6, Lamm DSC file.
24. Adams, "The Operations of A Company," pp. 12–13.
25. Ibid., p. 13.
26. Lieutenant Rex G. Combs, award recommendation for Sergeant Robert B. White, courtesy of www.508pir.org.
27. Lieutenant Rex G. Combs, award recommendation for Private George P. Moskalski, courtesy of www.508pir.org.
28. Lieutenant Rex G. Combs, award recommandation for Corporal Murphy B. Bridges, courtesy of www.508pir.org.
29. Adams, "The Operations of A Company," p. 13.
30. Ibid.
31. Ibid., p. 14.
32. Field Marshal Bernard Law Montgomery, as quoted in, Clay Blair, *Ridgway's Paratroopers*, The Dial Press, 1985, p. 468.
33. Gavin, "The Story of the 82nd Airborne Division," p. 7.
34. Captain Henry E. Le Febvre, "The Operations of the 2nd Battalion 508th Parachute Infantry (82nd Airborne Division) in the Withdrawal from and Recapture of Thier-du-Mont Ridge, Belgium, 22 December – 7 January 1945 (Ardennes – Alsace Campaign) (Personal Experience of a Battalion Operations Officer)," courtesy of Henry E. Le Febvre, pp. 7–8.
35. D. Zane Schlemmer, "Christmas Memories," courtesy of D. Zane Schlemmer, p. 1.
36. Gordon H. Cullings, response to author's questionnaire.
37. George D. Lamm, "Memorandum of Statements made by Lieutenant George Lamm at the Hotel Commodore, New York City on Sunday, March 11, 1945," courtesy of www.508pir.org.
38. Barrett, *My Story: Every Soldier Has a Story*, p. 92.

39. Millsaps, "This is My Story," p. 30.
40. Le Febvre, "Operations of the 2nd Battalion 508th," p. 8–10.
41. Schlemmer, "Christmas Memories," p. 1–2.
42. Kurz, "A Sergeant's View of the Battle of the Bulge," p. 5.
43. Lamm, "Memorandum of Statements."
44. George D. Lamm, as quoted in, Zig Boroughs, *The Devil's Tale*, 1992, Zig Boroughs, pp. 229–230.
45. Barrett, *My Story: Every Soldier Has a Story*, p. 92.
46. Edward J. Wodowski, interview with author.
47. Lamm, "Memorandum of Statements."
48. Wodowski, interview.
49. Lamm, "Memorandum of Statements."
50. Marino M. Michetti, written account, courtesy of www.battleofthebulgememories.be.
51. Alex Sopka, response to author's questionnaire.
52. Michetti, written account.
53. Le Febvre, "Operations of the 2nd Battalion," pp. 10–11.
54. Millsaps, "This is My Story," p. 32.
55. Kurz, "A Sergeant's View of the Battle of the Bulge," p. 6.
56. Schlemmer, "Christmas Memories," p. 2.
57. Lieutenant Colonel Otho E. Holmes, interview with Major J. F. Sullivan, March 28, 1945, Combat Interviews, Army Historical Section, National Archives.
58. Mendez and Little, interview, March 28, 1945.
59. Lane Lewis, written account, courtesy of Lane Lewis.
60. Marvin L. Risnes, as quoted in, "Erria," courtesy of Robert J. Kolterman.
61. William J. Call, interview with author.
62. Gilson, written account.
63. Schlemmer, "Christmas Memories," pp. 2–3.
64. Millsaps, "This is My Story," pp. 32–33.
65. Le Febvre, "Operations of the 2nd Battalion," p. 11
66. Ibid.
67. Schlemmer, "Christmas Memories," p. 3.
68. Robert B. White, interview with author.
69. Lewis, written account.

Chapter 15 "His Example Of Courage"

1. Marvin L. Risnes, as quoted in, "Erria," courtesy of Robert J. Kolterman.
2. Lane Lewis, written account, courtesy of Lane Lewis.
3. John H. Hodge, Jr., "Why Was I Spared," courtesy of www.508pir.org.

4. Dwayne T. Burns, as quoted in, Dwayne T. Burns and Leland Burns, *Jump Into the Valley of the Shadow*, Casemate, 2006, p. 171.

5. Ibid., pp. 171–172.

6. Allan H. Stein, response to author's questionnaire.

7. Burns, as quoted in, *Jump Into the Valley of the Shadow*, p. 175.

8. Risnes, as quoted in, "Erria."

9. Lewis, written account.

10. Risnes, as quoted in, "Erria."

11. James E. Fowler, as quoted in, "Erria," courtesy of Robert J. Kolterman.

12. William J. Call, interview with author.

13. Joseph M. Kissane, "WW2 Memoirs," courtesy of Robert J. Kolterman.

14. Robert J. Kolterman, response to author's questionnaire.

15. Hodge, "Why Was I Spared."

16. Lewis, written account.

17. Kissane, "WW2 Memoirs."

18. James C. Hutto, "World War II Memoirs – Staff Sergeant James C. 'Buck' Hutto, January 31, 1923 – December 6, 1993," courtesy of Sharon Hutto Marks.

19. Hodge, "Why Was I Spared."

20. Lewis, written account.

21. Hutto, "World War II Memoirs."

22. Lewis, written account.

23. Kissane, "WW2 Memoirs."

24. Robert J. Kolterman, "World War II as Remembered by Robert J. Kolterman—1st Sgt., Company G," courtesy of Robert J. Kolterman.

25. Hodge, "Why Was I Spared."

26. Lieutenant Colonel Louis G. Mendez, Jr., CO, 3rd Battalion, 508th Parachute Infantry and Lieutenant John T. Little, S-2, 3rd Battalion, 508th Parachute Infantry, interview with Lieutenant Francis P. Halas, March 28, 1945, Combat Interviews, Army Historical Section, National Archives.

27. Call, interview.

28. Ibid.

29. Edward J. Wodowski, interview with author.

30. James R. Allardyce, "Out of Holland, the Bulge, Frankfurt, and Berlin," courtesy of the Camp Blanding Museum, p. 9.

31. Norbert C. Studelska, written account, courtesy of Norbert C. Studelska.

32. Shields Warren, Jr., letter to Clay Blair, October 24, 1983, the Clay and Joan Blair Collection, U.S. Army Heritage and Education Center.

33. Lewis, written account.

34. Call, interview.

35. Mendez and Little, interview, March 28, 1945.

36. Ibid.

37. Captain Henry Le Febvre, "Operations of the 2nd Battalion 508th Parachute Infantry (82nd Airborne Division) in the Withdrawal from and Recapture of Thier-du-Mont Ridge, Belgium, 22 December – 7 January 1945 (Ardennes – Alsace Campaign) (Personal Experience of a Battalion Operations Officer)," courtesy of Henry Le Febvre, pp. 14–15.
38. Kolterman, "World War II as Remembered by Robert J. Kolterman."
39. Lewis, written account.
40. Ibid.
41. Fred Gladstone, as quoted in, Donald I. Jakeway, *Paratroopers Do or Die*, Privately Published, p. 152.
42. Wodowski, interview.
43. Mendez and Little, interview, March 28, 1945.
44. Colonel Roy E. Lindquist, recommendation, 14 March 1945, awards file, Captain Russell C. Wilde, National Archives, Record Group 338, Stack 290, First Army awards, Box 36, Wilde DSC file.
45. Angel Romero, as quoted in, "Thier-du-Mont, 7 January 1945," courtesy of Robert J. Kolterman.
46. Kolterman, "World War II as Remembered by Robert J. Kolterman."
47. Mendez and Little, interview, March 28, 1945.
48. Lewis, written account.
49. Captain Russell C. Wilde, statement, 24 March 1945, awards file, Staff Sergeant Frank L. Sirovica, National Archives, Record Group 338, Stack 290, First Army awards, Box 30, Sirovica DSC file.
50. Ibid.
51. Lindquist, recommendation.
52. Kolterman, "World War II as Remembered by Robert J. Kolterman."
53. Wilde, statement.
54. Sergeant Merl A. Beach, sworn statement, 24 March 1945, awards file, Staff Sergeant Frank L. Sirovica, National Archives, Record Group 338, Stack 290, First Army awards, Box 30, Sirovica DSC file.
55. Marvin L. Risnes, as quoted in, "Thier-du-Mont, 7 January 1945," courtesy of Robert J. Kolterman.
56. Salvatore J. Covais, as quoted in, Joseph S. Covais, *Battery! – C. Lenton Sartain and the Airborne G.I.s of the 319th Glider Field Artillery*, Andy Red Enterprises, 2011, p. 392.
57. Kissane, "WW2 Memoirs."
58. Lewis, written account.
59. Kissane, "WW2 Memoirs."
60. Lewis, written account.
61. Ibid.
62. Ibid.
63. Wilde, statement.

64. Gladstone, as quoted in *Paratroopers Do or Die*, p. 152.

65. Lindquist, recommendation.

66. Staff Sergeant Frank L. Sirovica, sworn statement, 24 March 1945, awards file, Captain Russell C. Wilde, National Archives, Record Group 338, Stack 290, First Army awards, Box 36, Wilde DSC file.

67. Lewis, written account.

68. Call, interview.

69. Kolterman, "World War II as Remembered by Robert J. Kolterman."

70. Gladstone, as quoted in, *Paratroopers Do or Die*, p. 152.

71. Lewis, written account.

72. Gladstone, as quoted in, *Paratroopers Do or Die*, p. 152.

73. Gordon H. Cullings, response to author's questionnaire.

74. Ibid.

75. Cipriano Gamez, interview transcript, courtesy of the the U.S. Latino and Latina WWII Oral History Project, Nettie Lee Benson Latin American Collection, University of Texas at Austin.

76. Edward R. Ryan, as quoted in, Joseph S. Covais, *Battery! – C. Lenton Sartain and the Airborne G.I.s of the 319th Glider Field Artillery*, Andy Red Enterprises, 2011, p. 393.

77. James Q. Kurz, A Sergeant's View of the Battle of the Bulge," courtesy of the Camp Blanding Museum, pp. 9–10.

78. Ibid., pp. 10–11.

79. Allardyce, "Out of Holland, the Bulge, Frankfurt, and Berlin," p. 12.

80. Le Febvre, "Operations of the 2nd Battalion," p. 17.

81. Gladstone, as quoted in, *Paratroopers Do or Die*, p. 153.

82. Romero, as quoted in, "Thier-du-Mont, 7 January 1945."

83. Rinaldo R. Zuccala, as quoted in, "Thier-du-Mont, 7 January 1945," courtesy of Robert J. Kolterman.

84. Lewis, written account.

85. Kolterman, "World War II as Remembered by Robert J. Kolterman."

86. Call, interview.

87. Gladstone, as quoted in, *Paratroopers Do or Die*, p. 153.

88. Ibid.

89. Woodrow W. Millsaps, "This is My Story," April 22, 1986, courtesy of the Camp Blanding Museum, pp. 34–35.

90. George D. Lamm, "Memorandum of Statements made by Lieutenant George Lamm at the Hotel Commodore, New York City on Sunday, March 11, 1945," courtesy of www.508pir.org.

Chapter 16 "They Are The Heroes"

1. Lane Lewis, written account, courtesy of Lane Lewis.

2. Charles A. Powell, Jr., "All I Say is True," courtesy of the Camp Blanding Museum.
3. James Q. Kurz, A Sergeant's View of the Battle of the Bulge," courtesy of the Camp Blanding Museum, p. 11.
4. Lewis, written account.
5. James R. Allardyce, "Out of Holland, the Bulge, Frankfurt, and Berlin," courtesy of the Camp Blanding Museum, p. 13.
6. Ibid., p. 14.
7. Kurz, A Sergeant's View of the Battle of the Bulge," pp. 13–14.
8. George E. Miles, response to author's questionnaire.
9. Lewis, written account.
10. Norbert C. Studelska, written account, courtesy of Norbert C. Studelska and letter to Charles Powell, January 1, 1993, courtesy of the Camp Blanding Museum.
11. Harry Hudec, interview transcript, courtesy of Kristine Nymoen.
12. Lieutenant Colonel Otho E. Holmes, interview with Major J. F. Sullivan, March 28, 1945, Combat Interviews, Army Historical Section, National Archives.
13. Kurz, A Sergeant's View of the Battle of the Bulge," pp. 14–15.
14. William H. Traband, interview with author.
15. Ibid.
16. Merrel Arthur, written account, courtesy of Merrel Arthur.
17. Ibid.
18. Ibid.
19. Ibid.
20. Technician Fourth Grade Erwin E. Stark, witness statement, National Archives.
21. Arthur, written account.
22. John Hardie, transcript of speech at the dedication of the Leonard Funk Memorial, Camp Blanding, Florida.
23. Ibid.
24. Miles, questionnaire.
25. Frank E. McKee, written account, courtesy of Frank E. McKee.
26. Dwayne T. Burns, as quoted in, Dwayne T. Burns and Leland Burns, *Jump Into the Valley of the Shadow*, Casemate, 2006, pp. 181–182.
27. Holmes, interview, March 28, 1945.
28. Charles R. Martin, response to author's questionnaire.
29. Lieutenant Colonel Louis G. Mendez, Jr., CO, 3rd Battalion, 508th Parachute Infantry and Lieutenant John T. Little, S-2, 3rd Battalion, 508th Parachute Infantry, interview with Lieutenant Francis P. Halas, March 28, 1945, Combat Interviews, Army Historical Section, National Archives.

30. Francis M. Lamoureux, as quoted in, "Back in Action with the 508th," *The Ludlow Register*, April 18, 2001, p. 9.

31. Holmes, interview, March 28, 1945.

32. D. Zane Schlemmer, "Germany 1945 Recollections," courtesy of D. Zane Schlemmer, pp. 1–2.

33. Jack L. Johnson, letter to William C. Nation, September 25, 1996, courtesy of William C. Nation, p. 1.

34. Schlemmer, "Germany 1945 Recollections," p. 2.

35. McKee, written account.

36. Studelska, written account, and Studelska to Powell, January 1, 1993.

37. Holmes, interview, March 28, 1945.

38. Ibid.

39. Woodrow W. Millsaps, "This is My Story," April 22, 1986, courtesy of the Camp Blanding Museum, p. 36.

40. Traband, interview.

41. Millsaps, "This is My Story," p. 36.

42. Kurz, "A Sergeant's View of the Battle of the Bulge," pp. 7–8.

43. William Windom, response to author's questionnaire.

44. Kurz, "A Sergeant's View of the Battle of the Bulge," p. 8.

45. Millsaps, "This is My Story," p. 36.

46. Kurz, "A Sergeant's View of the Battle of the Bulge," pp. 8–9.

47. Millsaps, "This is My Story," pp. 36–37.

48. Kurz, A Sergeant's View of the Battle of the Bulge," p. 8.

49. Millsaps, "This is My Story," p. 37.

50. Charles A. Yates, as quoted in, Lewis Milkovics, *The Devils Have Landed*, Creative Printing and Publishing, 1993, pp. 122–123.

51. Burns, as quoted in, *Jump Into the Valley of the Shadow*, p. 202.

52. Lewis, written account.

53. Millsaps, "This is My Story," p. 40.

54. Lewis, written account.

55. Millsaps, "This is My Story," p. 40.

56. Ibid., p. 52.

57. Ibid., pp. 42–44.

58. Burns, as quoted in, *Jump Into the Valley of the Shadow*, p. 204.

59. Jerry F. Graf, written account, courtesy of Robert J. Kolterman.

60. Edward C. Boccafogli, interview with Aaron Elson, *A Mile in Their Shoes*, 2003, courtesy of www.tankbooks.com.

61. Allardyce, "Out of Holland, the Bulge, Frankfurt, and Berlin," p. 25.

62. Windom, questionnaire.

63. Robert E. Chisolm, interview with author.

64. Louis G. Mendez, Jr., as quoted in, Zig Boroughs, *The Devil's Tale*, Privately Published, 1992, Inside Rear Cover.

BIBLIOGRAPHY

Published Sources

Alexander, Mark J., and Sparry, John, *Jump Commander*, Casemate, 2010.

Astor, Gerald, *June 6, 1944*, St. Martin's Press, 1994.

Astor, Gerald, *The Greatest War*, Presidio Press, 1999.

Barrett, Walter H., *My Story: Every Soldier Has A Story*, Privately Published, 2004.

Blair, Clay, *Ridgway's Paratroopers*, The Dial Press, 1985.

Boroughs, Zig, *The 508th Connection*, Privately Published, 2004.

Boroughs, Zig, *The Devil's Tale*, Privately Published, 1992.

Brokaw, Tom, *The Greatest Generation*, Random House, 1998.

Burns, Dwayne T., and Burns, Leland, *Jump Into the Valley of the Shadow*, Casemate, 2006.

Cole, Hugh M., *The Ardennes: Battle of the Bulge*, Office of the Chief of Military History, Department of the Army, 1965.

Covais, Joseph S., *Battery! – C. Lenton Sartain and the Airborne G.I.s of the 319th Glider Field Artillery*, Andy Red Enterprises, 2011.

Dougdale, J., *Panzer Divisions, Panzergrenadier Divisions, Panzer Brigades of the Army and Waffen SS in the West, Autumn 1944-Februray 1945, Ardennes and Nordwind*, Galago Publishing, 2000.

Drez, Ronald, *Voices of D-Day*, Louisiana State University Press, 1994.

Francois, Dominique, *Les Diables Rouges, The 508th Parachute Infantry Regiment*, Privately Published, 2001.

532

Francois, Dominique, *The 508th Parachute Infantry Regiment*, Heimdal, Bayeux, France, 2003.

Harrison, Gordon A., *Cross Channel Attack*, Center of Military History, United States Army, 1951.

Jakeway, Donald I., *Paratroopers Do or Die*, Privately Published, n.d.

Kershaw, Robert J., *It Never Snows in September*, Ian Allan Publishing, 1990.

Lord, William G., II, *History of the 508th Parachute Infantry Regiment*, Infantry Journal Press, 1948.

MacDonald, Charles B., *The Siegfried Line Campaign*, Center of Military History, United States Army, 1963.

Margry, Karel, Editor, *Operation Market-Garden Then and Now*, Battle of Britain International Limited, 2002.

Milkovics, Lewis, *The Devils Have Landed*, Creative Printing and Publishing, 1993.

Nordyke, Phil, *All American All The Way*, The Combat History of the 82nd Airborne Division in World War II, Zenith Press, 2005.

O'Donnell, Patrick K., *Beyond Valor*, The Free Press, 2001.

Reynolds, Michael, *Sons of the Reich – II SS Panzer Corps*, Casemate, 2002.

Ruppenthal, Major Roland G., *Utah Beach to Cherbourg*, Department of the Army Historical Division, 1948.

Ryan, Cornelius, *A Bridge Too Far*, Simon and Schuster, 1974.

Saunders, Tim, *Nijmegen*, Pen and Sword Books Limited, 2001.

Thuring, G., *Roll of Honor 82nd Airborne Division World War Two*, Nijmegen University Press, 1997.

Warren, Dr. John C., *Airborne Operations in World War II, European Theater – USAF Historical Studies: No. 97*, MA/AH Publishing, 1956.

Zetterling, Niklas, *Normandy 1944*, J.J. Fedorowicz Publishing, Inc., 2000.

Articles

Bullard, Joseph E., in, "508th's C. K. Baldwin killed June 14, 1944," *The News Reporter*, Whiteville, North Carolina, May 26, 1994, p. 5B.

Bullard, Joseph E., in "Paratrooper recalls Normandy jump," *The News Reporter*, Whiteville, North Carolina, May 26, 1994, p. 5B.

Lamoureux, Francis M., in, "Back in Action with the 508th," *The Ludlow Register*, April 18, 2001.

Lamoureux, Francis M., in, "From Normandy to Nijmegen, Holland," *The Ludlow Register*, April 11, 2001.

Mann, Ralph H., in, "We were afraid the cows would give us away," *Lehigh Valley Morning Call*, June 6, 2011.

Richardson, Fayette O., in, "Straight Talk – Back to Normandy," *The Brooklyn Paper*, 1987.

Risnes, Marvin L., in, "Holland Veteran Still with 82nd Div.; Looks Back 26 Years to Campaign," *The Paraglide*, Winter 1970, Robert J. Kolterman.

Yourkovich, Louis W., in, "Bellaire Man's apple tree wish granted," *The Times Leader*, Belmont County, Ohio, June 6, 2004.

Unpublished Diaries, Sworn Statements, Letters, Emails, Written Accounts, Memoirs, and Manuscripts

Alexander, Mark J., "Thirty Four Days in Normandy in 1944," Mark J. Alexander.

Allardyce, James R., letter to Heather Chapman, November 20, 1967, Cornelius Ryan Collection, Alden Library, Ohio University.

Allardyce, James R., "Out of Holland, the Bulge, Frankfurt, and Berlin," Camp Blanding Museum.

Arthur, Merrel, written account, Merrel Arthur.

Blue, James R., written account, 82nd Airborne Division War Memorial Museum.

Bollag, Marcel, "Escape in Normandy," Aaron Elson, www.tankbooks.com.

Brannen, Malcolm D., "Two Weeks of Celebrating the Fourth of July 1944," Camp Blanding Museum.

Brannen, Malcolm D., written account, 82nd Airborne Division War Memorial Museum.

Bressler, Joseph C., "We Served Proudly—The Men of Hq1," George I. Stoeckert (album collator), www.508pir.org.

Brickley, Dr. John E., letter to James R. Blue, December 6, 1962, Cornelius Ryan Collection, Alden Library, Ohio University.

Burns, Dwyane T., unpublished manuscript, Dwayne T. Burns.

Campbell, James A., letter to John W. Richards, Eisenhower Center.

Christ, George E., "D-Day, June 6, 1944, One Soldier's Experience," D. Zane Schlemmer.

Delury, John P., "D-Day Plus 40 Odd Years – Normandy Thoughts," Eisenhower Center.

DeWeese, Ralph E. diary, 82nd Airborne Division War Memorial Museum.

Farris, William W., "The Attack on Pretot," www.508pir.org.

Foley, John P., letter to James R. Blue, January 31, 1963, Cornelius Ryan Collection, Alden Library, Ohio University.

Gavin, James M., letter to Matthew B. Ridgway, June 27, 1973, U.S. Army Heritage and Education Center.

Gavin, James M., written accounts, Cornelius Ryan Collection, Alden Library, Ohio University.

Giegold, Albert W., letter to Mrs. Henry and Philip Vasselin, April 3, 1987.

Gilson, Ralph, written account, Ralph Gilson.

Graf, Jerry F., written account, Robert J. Kolterman.

Graham, Chester E., "My Memories of World War II," Camp Blanding Museum.

Griffin, Oliver W., written account, Oliver W. Griffin.

Frank Haddy, written account, Camp Blanding Museum.

Hand, Broughton L., "The War Story of Broughton Lynn Hand, 508 Parachute Infantry, 82nd Airborne," Broughton L. Hand.

Hardie, Dr. John, written account, May 20, 1999, Starlyn R. Jorgensen.

Hill, Owen B., "My Normandy Invasion Experience," Owen B. Hill.

Hill, Richard R., written account, www.6juin1944.com.

Hodge, John H. Jr., "Why Was I Spared," www.508pir.org.

Hull, Otis E., "We Served Proudly—The Men of Hq1," George I. Stoeckert (album collator), www.508pir.org.

Hutto, James C., "World War II Memoirs – Staff Sergeant James C. 'Buck' Hutto, January 31, 1923 – December 6, 1993," Sharon Hutto Marks.

Infanger, Frederick J., "Lieutenant Robert Mason Mathias," edited by Richard C. Reardon, Camp Blanding Museum.

Infanger, Frederick J., written account, Camp Blanding Museum.

Johnson, Curtis L., written account, www.508pir.org.

Johnson, Jack L., letter to William C. Nation, September 25, 1996, William C. Nation.

Jones, Lieutenant Homer H., statement, March 26, 1945, David Axelrod award file, www.508pir.org.

Kissane, Joseph M., "WW2 Memoirs," Robert J. Kolterman.

Kolterman, Robert J., "Erria," courtesy of Robert J. Kolterman.

Kolterman, Robert J., "Thier-du-Mont, 7 January 1945," Robert J. Kolterman.

Kolterman, Robert J., "World War II as Remembered by Robert J. Kolterman – 1st Sergeant, Company G," Robert J. Kolterman.

Kulju, Harold O. I., "Harold Oliver Isaac Kulju," U.S. Army Heritage and Education Center.

Kurz, James Q., "A Sergeant's View of the Battle of the Bulge," Camp Blanding Museum.

Kurz, James Q., "Holland Jump, September 17, 1944, Through the Eyes of a Squad Leader," Camp Blanding Museum.

Lamm, George D., "Memorandum of Statements made by Lieutenant George Lamm at the Hotel Commodore, New York City on Sunday, March 11, 1945," www.508pir.org.

Lamm, George D., written account, www.508pir.org.

Le Febvre, Henry E., letter to Zig Boroughs, September 15, 1989, Henry E. Le Febvre.

Leegsma, Agardus M., letter to James R. Blue, April 27, 1963, Cornelius Ryan Collection, Alden Library, Ohio University.

Leeper, Wesley T., written account, Eisenhower Center.

Lehman, Paul E., letter to mother, June 28, 1944, 82nd Airborne Division War Memorial Museum.

Lewellen, R. B., "Jump into Gourbesville," www.508pir.org.

Lewis, Lane, written account, Lane Lewis.

Longiotti, Frank, email to author, January 14, 2004.

Maldonaldo, Trino F., "Lieutenant Robert Mason Mathias," edited by Richard C. Reardon, Camp Blanding Museum.

McClure, Billy B., written account, Camp Blanding Museum.

McKee, Frank E., written account, Frank E. McKee.

Michetti, Marino M., written account, www.battleofthebulgememories.be.

Milkovics, Lewis, written account, http://strictly-gi.com.

Millsaps, Woodrow W., letter to Heather Chapman, July 27, 1967, Cornelius Ryan Collection, Alden Library, Ohio University.

Millsaps, Woodrow W., "This is My Story," April 22, 1986, Camp Blanding Museum.

Morgan, Worster M., "My Paratroop Activities," www.508pir.org.

Moss, Robert C. Jr., written account, www.6juin1944.com.

Nation, William H., letters to parents, William C. Nation.

Ott, Edward V., "1st Lieutenant Edward V. Ott, 508 P.I.R. 82nd Airborne Headquarters, Company, 2nd Battalion," U.S. Army Heritage and Education Center.

Ott, Edward V., written account, Camp Blanding Museum.

Porter, Carl H., "Men at War: Chow Call," www.508pir.org.

Powell, Charles A. Jr., "All I Say is True," Camp Blanding Museum.

Reardon, Richard C., "Lieutenant Robert Mason Mathias," edited by Richard C. Reardon, Camp Blanding Museum.

Rice, Foy, letter to Jan Bos, August 23, 1984, Jan Bos.

Ridgway, Major General Matthew B., letter to General G. H. Weems, August 13, 1944, the Clay and Joan Blair Collection, U.S. Army Heritage and Education Center.

Ross, Carlos W., "Things That I Remember," www.508pir.org.

Sands, Paul R., "A Walk Down Memory Lane," Camp Blanding Museum.

Schlemmer, D. Zane, "Bois de Limors to Hill 131," D. Zane Schlemmer.

Schlemmer, D. Zane, "Christmas Memories," D. Zane Schlemmer.

Schlemmer, D. Zane, "Germany 1945 Recollections," D. Zane Schlemmer.

Staples, Frank L., V-Mail June 25, 1944, Kristine Nymoen.

Staples Frank L., written account, Kristine Nymoen.

Studelska, Norbert C., letter to Nelson S. Bryant, February 5, 2002, Camp Blanding Museum.

Studelska, Norbert C., letter to Charles Powell, January 1, 1993, Camp Blanding Museum.

Studelska, Norbert C., written account, Norbert C. Studelska.

The James M. Gavin, Papers, Personal Diaries, Box 8, Folder – Diary Passages, courtesy of the U.S. Army Military History Institute.

Thomas, David E., "Military Career Memoirs of Brigadier General David Edward Thomas, M.C.," Normand E. Thomas.

Thomas, Ralph H., "D-Day, 6 June 1944," www.508pir.org.

Thomas, Ralph H., "Trino, A Short History," Camp Blanding Museum.

Warren, Shields Jr., letters to Clay Blair, the Clay and Joan Blair Collection, U.S. Army Heritage and Education Center.

Watson, Joseph E., "Lieutenant Robert Mason Mathias," edited by Richard C. Reardon, Camp Blanding Museum.

Weaver, Robert J. "Invasion," David Berry and Richard O'Donnell.

Williamson, Francis E., written account, Kristine Nymoen.

Wolch, Richard G., "Bringing Supplies to Berg-en-Dal," http://marketgarden.secondworldwar.nl.

Wolch, Richard G., "First Contact with the Enemy," http://marketgarden.secondworldwar.nl.

Wolch, Richard G., "From the Sky We Lead,"
http://marketgarden.secondworldwar.nl.

Wood, Lee Roy, written account, Kristine Nymoen.

Responses by Veterans to Questionnaires

Cornelius Ryan Collection, Alden Library, Ohio University, questionniares with
the following veterans:

Jonathan E. Adams, Jr.	John P. Foley	Frank C. Taylor
Edward N. Bailey	Thomas A. Horne	Glen W. Vantrease
Neal W. Beaver	Joseph Kissane	Donald Veach
Ralph J. Busson	Lyle K. Kumler	Roland C. Ziegler
Frederick J. Carden	Frank Ruppe	
John W. Connelly	Wilbur J. Scanlon	

Author's questionnaires with the following veterans:

Donald M. Biles	Robert J. Kolterman	George T. Sheppard
Cornelius M. Cahill	Charles R. Martin	Alexander Sopka
Gordon H. Cullings	Robert B. Newhart	Allan H. Stein
Thomas C. Goins	James A. Rightley	William R. Tumlin
John M. Greene	Harry A. Roll	William Windom
William F. Knapp	Edward R. Ryan	

U.S. Military Documents, After-Action Reports, Studies, Monographs, Statements, and Combat Interviews

Adams, Captain Jonathan E. Jr., Headquarters First Battalion 508th Parachute
Infantry APO 757, U.S. Army, "Holland Operation," November 2, 1945,"
Cornelius Ryan Collection, Alden Library, Ohio University.

Adams, Major Jonathan E. Jr., letter to Major Benjamin F. Delamater, III, April
7, 1947, in Major B. F. Delamater, III, "The Action of the 1st Battalion, 508th
Parachute Infantry (82nd Airborne Division) in the Holland Invasion, 15 – 24

September 1944 (Rhineland Campaign, European Theater of Operations) (Personal Experience of the Battalion Executive Officer)," Donovan Research Library, Fort Benning, Georgia.

Adams, Major Jonathan E. Jr., "The Operations of A Company, 508th Parachute Infantry, (82nd Airborne Division) Near Rencheux, Belgium, (Ardennes Campaign) 22-25 December, 1944, (Personal Experience of a Company Commander)," Donovan Research Library, Fort Benning, Georgia.

Albright, Captain Barry E., "Operations of the 2d Battalion, 508th Parachute Infantry Regiment (82d Airborne Division) in the Invasion of Normandy, June 5 – 13 1944 (Normandy Campaign) (Personal Experience and Observation of a Rifle Platoon Leader)," Donovan Research Library, Fort Benning, Georgia.

Archambault, Private First Class Roland E., statement, Escape and Evasion Report, G-2, 82nd Airborne Division, 21 August 1944, www.508pir.org.

Awards file, Lieutenant George D. Lamm, National Archives, Record Group 338, Stack 290, Ninth Army awards, Box 6, Lamm DSC file.

Awards file, Corporal Ernest T. Roberts, National Archives, Record Group 338, Stack 290, First Army awards, Box 27, Roberts DSC file.

Awards file, Staff Sergeant Frank L. Sirovica, National Archives, Record Group 338, Stack 290, First Army awards, Box 30, Sirovica DSC file.

Awards file, Captain Russell C. Wilde, National Archives, Record Group 338, Stack 290, First Army awards, Box 36, Wilde DSC file.

Combs, Lieutenant Rex G., award recommendations for, www.508pir.org:

Sergeant Joe H. Boone
Corporal Murphy B. Bridges
Private Wayne F. Campbell
Lieutenant John P. Foley
Sergeant Marion E. Kinman

Private George P. Moskalski
Private Charles E. Schmalz
1st Sergeant Frank C. Taylor
Sergeant Robert B. White

Combs, Lieutenant Rex G., statement, March 28, 1945, David Axelrod award file, www.508pir.org.

"Debriefing Conference—Operation Neptune," 13 August 1944, 82nd Airborne Division War Memorial Museum.

Delamater, Major Benjamin F. III, "The Action of the 1st Battalion, 508th Parachute Infantry (82nd Airborne Division) in the Holland Invasion, 15 – 24 September 1944 (Rhineland Campaign, European Theater of Operations) (Personal Experience of the Battalion Executive Officer)," Donovan Research Library, Fort Benning, Georgia.

G-2 Reports, 82nd Airborne Division, Normandy and Holland, 82nd Airborne Division War Memorial Museum.

Gavin, Major General James M., letter to Captain John G. Westover, July 25, 1945, U.S. Army Heritage and Education Center.

General Orders, various units, for copies of award citations and verification of names, National Archives.

Greenwalt, Lieutenant Howard A., "Statement of Lt. Greenwalt on the Nijmegen Attack by Co. G," Cornelius Ryan Collection, Alden Library, Ohio University.

Hamilton, Lieutenant Elbert F., "Patrol Report for Night 26/27 June," National Archives.

Headquarters, IX Troop Carrier Command, "Operation Market, Air Invasion of Holland," Cornelius Ryan Collection, Alden Library, Ohio University.

Headquarters, 82nd Airborne Division, "Loading Table 82d Airborne Division," 10 July 1944.

Headquarters, 307th Airborne Engineer Battalion, APO 469, U.S. Army, "Historical Narrative," Belgium After-Action Report, 1 January 1945, National Archives.

Headquarters, 307th Airborne Engineer Battalion, APO 469, U.S. Army, "Historical Narrative," Holland After-Action Report, 16 October 1944, National Archives.

Headquarters, 307th Airborne Engineer Battalion, APO 469, U.S. Army, "Record of Action," Holland, National Archives.

Headquarters, 307th Airborne Engineer Battalion, APO 469, U.S. Army, "Report of Action, Company B," Normandy, Brian Siddall.

Headquarters, 307th Airborne Engineer Battalion, APO 469, U.S. Army, "Unit History," Normandy After-Action Report, 10 August 1944, Brian Siddall.

Headquarters, 508th Parachute Infantry, APO 230, "57 Days in Holland and Germany with the 508th Parachute Infantry," 82nd Airborne Division War Memorial Museum.

Headquarters, 508th Parachute Infantry, APO 230, U.S. Army, "Capture of Bridge Number 10," Cornelius Ryan Collection, Alden Library, Ohio University.

Headquarters, 508th Parachute Infantry, APO 230, U.S. Army, "Unit Journal," Holland, National Archives.

Headquarters, United States Army Europe, Foreign Military Studies 1945-1954, National Archives:

A-983 "353d Infantry Division (Nov 1943-24 Jul 1944)."
B-010 "91st Airborne Division (10 Jul-Aug 1944)."
B-028 "62d Volks Grenadier Division (16 Dec 1944-27 Jan 1945)."
B-051 "II Parachute Corps (15 Sep 1944-21 Mar 1945)."
B-092 "326th Volks Grenadier Division (16 Dec 1944-25 Jan 1945)."
B-093 "II Parachute Corps (15 Sep 1944-21 Mar 1945). (Revision of B-051)."
B-260 "Cotentin Artillery (6-18 Jun 1944)."
B-262 "II Parachute Corps (19 Sep 1944-10 Mar 1945)."
B-339 "Comments on Manuscript #B-010."
B-469 "91st Airborne Division Artillery (18 Jun-31 Jul 1944)."
B-688 "18th Volks Grenadier Division (1 Sep 1944-25 Jan 1945)."
B-763 "Seventh Army (6 Jun-29 Jul 1944)."
B-784 "LXXXIV Corps (Jan-17 Jun 1944)."
B-843 "84th Infantry Division (19 Jan-25 Mar 1945)."
C-085 "406th Division (Sep 1944)."

Holmes, Lieutenant Colonel Otho E., interview with Major J. F. Sullivan, March 28, 1945, Combat Interviews, Army Historical Section, National Archives.

HQ 82nd Airborne Division, APO 469, U.S. Army, "Field Order No. 6," 14 May 1944, National Archives.

HQ 82nd Airborne Division, APO 469, U.S. Army, "Field Order No. 6 (Revised)," 28 May 1944, National Archives.

HQ 82nd Airborne Division, APO 469, U.S. Army, "Field Order No. 11," 13 September 1944, Cornelius Ryan Collection, Alden Library, Ohio University.

HQ 82nd Airborne Division, APO 469, US Army, "Order of Battle Summary," 11 September 1944, Cornelius Ryan Collection, Alden Library, Ohio University.

HQ 508th Parachute Infantry, APO 514, U.S. Army, "Field Order No. 1 (Revised)," 27 May 1944, National Archives.

HQ 508th Parachute Infantry, APO 514, U.S. Army, "Field Order No. 1," 13 September 1944, National Archives.

HQ 508th Parachute Infantry, APO 230, U.S. Army, "The Belgium Campaign,"13 January 1945, National Archives.

Johnson, Captain Kenneth L., "Supply Operations of the 508th Parachute Infantry Regiment (82nd Airborne Division) in the Invasion of Holland, 15 – 19 September 1944, (Rhineland Campaign) (Personal Experience of the Regimental S-4)," Donovan Research Library, Fort Benning, Georgia.

Le Febvre, Captain Henry E., "The Operations of the 2nd Battalion 508th Parachute Infantry (82nd Airborne Division) in the Withdrawal from and Recapture of Thier-du-Mont Ridge, Belgium, 22 December – 7 January 1945 (Ardennes – Alsace Campaign) (Personal Experience of a Battalion Operations Officer)," Henry E. Le Febvre.

"Levy's Group, (A Statement by Lt. Joseph Kormylo, of D Company who was with Levy)," Combat Interviews, Army Historical Section, Cornelius Ryan Collection, Alden Library, Ohio University.

Lindquist, Colonel Roy E., Headquarters 508th Parachute Infantry, Office of the Regimental Commander, "History of the 508th Parachute Infantry," National Archives.

McRoberts, Captain Neal L., "Report of Pathfinder Employment for Operation Neptune," 11 June 1944, National Archives.

Medusky, Major John W., interview with Captain Kenneth W. Hechler, February 15, 1945, Combat Interviews, Army Historical Section, National Archives.

Mendez, Lieutenant Colonel Louis G. Jr., CO, 3rd Battalion, 508th Parachute Infantry and Little, Lieutenant John T., S-2, 3rd Battalion, 508th Parachute Infantry, interview with Lieutenant Francis P. Halas, March 28, 1945, Combat Interviews, Army Historical Section, National Archives.

Mendez, Lieutenant Colonel Louis G. Jr., letter to Major General James M. Gavin, November 8, 1945, Cornelius Ryan Collection, Alden Library, Ohio University.

Millsaps, Lieutenant Woodrow W. APO 757, U.S. Army, "Headquarters Company B, 508th Parachute Infantry," November 2, 1945, Cornelius Ryan Collection, Alden Library, Ohio University.

"Narrative statement of the crew of A/C #42-93002, 62nd TC Sq., 314th TC Gp., in connection with the events of BIGOT – Neptune #1," 14 June 1944, www.6juin1944.com.

"Operation of the 507th Regiment Following Drop," Combat Interviews, Army Historical Section, Cornelius Ryan Collection, Alden Library, Ohio University.

"Operation Market, A Graphic History of the 82nd Airborne Division," 82nd Airborne Division War Memorial Museum.

"Operation Market," Combat Interviews, Cornelius Ryan Collection, Alden Library, Ohio University.

"Operation Neptune, 82nd Airborne Division Action in Normandy, France," 82nd Airborne Division War Memorial Museum.

Ramirez, Private Frank M., statement, Escape and Evasion Report, G-2, 82nd Airborne Division, 21 August 1944, www.508pir.org.

"Report on James R. Hattrick," Headquarters 82d Airborne Division, Office of the Assistant Chief of Staff, G-2, July 7, 1944, National Archives.

"Record of Participation of 508th Parachute Infantry in Normandy Operations, From 6 June to 15 July 1944," 82nd Airborne Division War Memorial Museum.

Sickler, Captain Robert L., "The Operations of Company D, 2nd Battalion, 508th Parachute Infantry Regiment (82nd Airborne Division) at Nijmegen, Holland, 17 – 19 September 1944 (Rhineland Campaign, European Theater of

Operations) (Personal Experience of a Platoon Leader)," courtesy of the Donovan Research Library, Fort Benning, Georgia.

Supreme Headquarters Allied Expeditionary Force, Office of Assistant Chief of Staff, G-2, "Weekly Intelligence Summary, For Week Ending 16 September 1944," Cornelius Ryan Collection, Alden Library, Ohio University.

"The History of the 319th Glider Field Artillery Battalion, Wednesday September 13, 1944 to Monday October 16, 1944," National Archives.

"The Story of the 82nd Airborne Division in the Battle of the Belgian Bulge, in the Siegfried Line, and of the Roer River," 82nd Airborne Division War Memorial Museum.

Todd, Lieutenant Colonel James C., "Historical Record of the 319th Glider Field Artillery Battalion, for June, 1944," National Archives.

"Unit Journal, 508th Parachute Infantry," Belgium, National Archives.

"Unit Journal, 508th Parachute Infantry," Holland, National Archives.

"Unit Journal, 508th Parachute Infantry, Operation Neptune, Normandy, France, 28 May to 8 July 1944," National Archives.

Van Enwyck, Staff Sergeant Sherman, statement, March 29, 1945, David Axelrod award file, www.508pir.org.

Warren, Lieutenant Colonel Shields Jr., "Narrative of Events of the 1st Battalion 508th Parachute Infantry for Period 17 – 21 September 1944, in the Vicinity of Nijmegen, Holland," 82nd Airborne War Memorial Museum.

Womble, Corporal Jesse J., statement, Missing Air Crew Report, Aircraft Number 42-15102, www.Fold3.com.

Taped Interviews and Oral Histories, Interview and Oral History Transcripts

Albrecht, Denver D., interview transcript, Cornelius Ryan Collection, Alden Library, Ohio University.

Boccafogli, Edward C., interview with Aaron Elson, *A Mile in Their Shoes*, 2003, www.tankbooks.com.

Broderick, Robert, interview transcript, October 14, 2002, Andrew Reed.

Burrus, Ralph Jr., interview, www.geschiedenisgroesbeek.nl.

Eisenhower Center, oral history transcripts of the following veterans:

Briand N. Beaudin	Herbert M. James	John W. Richards
Edward C. Boccafogli	David M. Jones	Lawrence F. Salva
John D. Boone	George D. Lamm	William M. Sawyer
Paul E. Bouchereau	John W. Marr	D. Zane Schlemmer
Ralph E. Cook	Frank E. McKee	John R. Taylor
William A. Dean	Kenneth J. Merritt	Lynn C. Tomlinson
Dan Furlong	George E. Miles	Adolph F. Warnecke
Thomas J. Gintjee	Tomaso W. Porcella	
Thomas A. Horne	Harry L. Reisenleiter	

Cipriano Gamez, interview transcript, U.S. Latino and Latina World War II Oral History Project.

Gavin, James M., oral history transcript, the Clay and Joan Blair Collection, U.S. Army Heritage and Education Center.

Hardie, Dr. John, transcript of speech at the dedication of the Leonard Funk Memorial, Camp Blanding, Florida, Richard O'Donnell.

Horne, Kelso C., "Conversations with Kelso," Perry Knight, editor, Kelso C. Horne, Jr.

Hudec, Harry, interview transcript, Kristine Nymoen.

Interviews with author with the following veterans:

William J. Call	Nathan Silverlieb
Robert E. Chisolm	William H. Traband
George D. Glass	Robert B. White
Homer H. Jones	Edward J. Wodowski
Eugene C. Metcalfe	

Jahnigan, Herman W., *Herman Jahnigan Interview, D-Day Jump at Normandy*, www.youtube.com.

Lamoureux, Francis M., "In Their Own Words," Topics Entertainment.

Martell, Elmer E., interview transcript, www.508pir.org.

Ott, First Lieutenant Edward V., interview, 160th General Hospital, National Archives.

Smith, First Lieutenant Wayne H., interview, 97th General Hospital, National Archives.

Tibbetts, First Lieutenant James D., interview, 160th General Hospital, National Archives.

Toth, First Lieutenant Louis L., interview, 97th General Hospital, National Archives.

Internet Web Pages

Combined Arms Research Library, Digital Library, The Nafziger Collection of Orders of Battle, http://usacac.army.mil/cac2/cgsc/carl/nafziger.htm.

Foreign Military Studies, www.fold3.com.

Foreign Military Studies, www.sturmpanzer.com.

General research of 508th Parachute Infantry Regiment, www.508pir.org.

Missing Air Crew Reports, www.fold3.com.

Photographs, www.histomil.com.

Research of German army orders of battle and unit histories, www.axishistory.com.

Research of German army orders of battle and unit histories, www.feldgrau.net.

Research of German army orders of battle and unit histories, www.wehrmacht-awards.com.

U.S. Latino & Latina WWII Oral History Project, Nettie Lee Benson Latin American Collection, University of Texas at Austin, www.lib.utexas.edu.

INDEX TO MAPS

INDEX

Printed in Great Britain
by Amazon.co.uk, Ltd.,
Marston Gate.